PRINCIPLES OF INTERNATIONAL LITIGATION AND ARBITRATION

Second Edition

Ralph H. Folsom
Professor of Law
University of San Diego
A.B. Princeton University, J.D. Yale Law School
LLM London School of Economics

CONCISE HORNBOOK SERIES™

WEST ACADEMIC PUBLISHING

444 Cedar Street, Suite 700
St. Paul, MN 55101
1-877-888-1330

Printed in the United States of America

ISBN: 978-1-68467-176-2

Preface

Principles of International Litigation and Arbitration 2d is part of West Academic Publishing's Concise Hornbook series. It is intended to provide law students and professionals considerably more depth, analysis, citations and related documents than found in the West Nutshell Series.

Principles' updated coverage commences in Chapter 1 with the Fundamentals of International Business Dispute Settlement. Chapters 2 focuses on Choice of Law and Choice of Forum options of the parties. Chapter 3 concerns International Commercial Arbitration, while Chapter 4 examines Foreign Investment Arbitration.

International Business Litigation is detailed in Chapters 5 through 9 covering jurisdiction, procedure, sovereign defenses, enforcement of judgments and the EU litigation system. Finally, Intergovernmental Dispute Settlement of Trade Disputes is reviewed in Chapter 10.

Principles of International Business Litigation and Arbitration 2d can be used in connection with **any** international dispute settlement text. It can also serve as an inexpensive course book on its own, notably in conjunction with the legal documents appended at the end of its chapters.

Your feedback is welcomed.

Ralph H. Folsom

rfolsom@sandiego.edu

July 2019

About the Author

Ralph H. Folsom has been a Professor at the University of San Diego School of Law since 1975. A graduate of Princeton University, Yale Law School and the London School of Economics (LLM), Professor Folsom teaches, writes and consults extensively in the field of international business law.

Folsom has been a Senior Fulbright resident scholar in Singapore and a Visiting Professor at the University of Hong Kong, University of Aix-Marseille, University of Brest, University of Paris, University of Toulouse, University of Puerto Rico, Monash University in Australia and Tecnológico de Monterrey in México.

Professor Folsom has authored or co-authored a range of books with West Academic Publishing. These include co-authoring the 13th Edition of the popular, problem-oriented course book on *International Business Transactions*.

He is the author in the Concise Hornbook series of:

Principles of European Union Law including BREXIT;

Principles of International Business Transactions (co-authored);

Principles of International Trade Law; and

Principles of Free Trade Agreements, From GATT 1947 through NAFTA Re-Negotiated 2018.

Summary of Contents

Table of Contents

PRINCIPLES OF INTERNATIONAL LITIGATION AND ARBITRATION

Second Edition

Chapter 1

FUNDAMENTALS OF INTERNATIONAL BUSINESS DISPUTE SETTLEMENT

Table of Sections

Three distinct types of international business transactions (IBT) dominate global commerce: International Sales, Technology Transfers and Foreign Investment. There many variations of these transactions, and they often overlap. Foreign investment transactions, for example, often have technology transfer components, e.g. licensing of intellectual property and proprietary knowledge. Foreign investment transactions also often contain international sales commitments, say for components of goods that will be produced abroad.

These three types of IBT can generate disputes that are best understood in their distinct transactional contexts. This book will examine international business dispute settlement law and procedure in each context. It is primarily focused on U.S. law and practice.

Litigation may not be the method selected or preferred to resolve an international dispute arising from international trade, licensing or investment. Litigation has some distinct disadvantages: It can occur in multiple venues (known as "parallel proceedings"), will be conducted in the languages of the forum states, may be tried before generalist judges lacking international expertise, often is slow, public and costly, and may not be enforceable in jurisdictions where there are assets to recover.

There are numerous other methods to resolve cross-border business disputes. Which method is chosen by the parties is critical. See Chapter 2. Mediation and conciliation, pervasive in Asia, are discussed below. Arbitration is commonly used for commercial contracts. See Chapter 3. Trade and foreign investment agreements, such as those of the World Trade Organization and NAFTA 1994, have developed unique processes for dispute resolution, notably dispute panels and appeals, often combining elements of litigation and arbitration. See Chapters 4 and 10.

But many international business disputes remain handled by traditional courtroom litigation, covered in Chapters 5 through 8. I am indebted to Professor Michael Gordon of Florida for his original work on Sections 1.3 and 1.4 below.

§ 1.1 Planning for International Business Dispute Settlement

Planning for potential international business disputes is an essential, undervalued role for attorneys. Whereas the economics and mutual benefit of international business transactions are of great concern for the parties to transaction, their lawyers get to worry about what will happen if the deal goes sour. Negotiating and drafting IBT dispute settlement clauses is a challenge, particularly when the lawyers involved have different legal training and traditions, and come from different legal systems. Naturally, each side seeks a "home court" advantage, which tends to drive the negotiations toward neutral judicial venues, mediation, conciliation and arbitration.

The Importance of Culture, Friendly Consultations and Mediation in Asia

Culture also matters. In Asia, especially China, South Korea, Vietnam and Japan, there is a great aversion to confrontational, adversarial dispute settlement. In Japan, international business litigation or arbitration may be perceived as a failure of management. In China, longstanding Confucian values, including harmony and the saving of face in particular, influence business disputes. In both countries, friendly consultations and mediation frequently resolve international business disputes without need for arbitration or litigation. Chinese contracts sometimes provide for "joint mediation": Each side chooses a mediator and the two work together to resolve the dispute. The majority of China business disputes are settled using friendly consultations and mediation.

Understanding and planning for Asian dispute settlement preferences is critical to negotiating and drafting business dispute settlement provisions in that part of the world. In doing so, it helps to remember that United States attorneys, like it or not, typically carry cultural legal baggage with them. Foreign attorneys may expect them to be aggressive representatives from a litigation-happy legal culture.

Fundamental cultural differences regarding contracts should also be considered when engaged in crafting international business dispute settlement rules. United States and European attorneys tend to view the contract as defining the full expectations, limits and details of business relationships. The contract spells out the "law of the relationship." Asian parties, in contrast, may perceive that the signing of a contract represents the creation of a friendly relationship, with each party expected to adapt flexibly at the request of the other, even when to do so differs from the contract's terms. Indeed, relationships and connections (guanxi in China) dominate the business environment in Asia. Planning for renegotiation of international business contracts can help smooth over difficulties of this kind.

Corruption Issues

It is no secret that a significant number of judicial systems around the world may lack integrity. In some, justice can literally be bought. In others, corruption is more subtle, such as the substantial erosion or absence of judicial independence. Information on the level of judicial corruption in various countries can be researched through Transparency International or more formally in World Bank and other assessments of a nation's "rule of law".

When your client is involved with a suspect jurisdiction, the desire to avoid international business litigation increases. Arbitration proceedings become more attractive, particularly so if undertaken in well-regarded arbitral institutions. That said, arbitrators are not necessarily immune to corruption, and judicial intervention in arbitration proceedings and judicial review of arbitral awards may not come to the rescue. See Chapter 3.

Questionable Judicial Systems

In general, U.S. courts are reluctant to pass judgment on foreign judicial systems and require more than conclusory allegations of corruption.[1]

---

1 *See, e.g.*, Base Metal Trading v. Russian Aluminum, 253 F.Supp.2d 681 (S.D.N.Y. 2003).

In *forum non conveniens* (*fnc*) proceedings before U.S. courts (see Section 2.4), and when enforcement of foreign judgments is sought in U.S. states (see Section 8.1), the integrity and efficacy of various foreign court systems have been challenged from time to time. Some, at least in the opinion of U.S. judges, have not measured up. These have included the courts of: Morocco,[2] Liberia,[3] Nicaragua,[4] India,[5] Ecuador,[6] Bolivia,[7] Chile under a military junta,[8] and Iran.[9]

It is almost never advisable to raise corruption issues when negotiating international business dispute settlement clauses. Far better to emphasize the positive attributes and traditions of courts and arbitration bodies of good repute, and hopefully reach agreement on their utilization.

The Role of States and Organizations

International business dispute settlement is not necessarily a purely private matter. State-owned or controlled enterprises, such as national oil and gas companies like PEMEX of Mexico, are common throughout the developing world and often a source of great cultural pride. Though less prominent, state enterprises are not scarce in Europe or Japan. Whether through ownership or control rights, or simply local law, governments are often involved in dispute settlement. Regulatory disputes between government agencies and international business parties permeate the globe. See at length R. Folsom, *Principles of International Trade Law*.

Regional and international legal regimes may be involved, notably for example "investor-state" arbitrations such as are found in bilateral investment treaties (BITs) and NAFTA 1994. See Chapter 4. Purely intergovernmental settlement of trade disputes, such as that of the World Trade Organization (WTO), typically concern business interests of the member countries. One WTO dispute

---

2 *See* DeJoria v. Maghreb Petroleum Exploration S.A., 2014 WL 4065614 (W.D. Tex. 2014).

3 *See* Bridgeway Corp. v. Citibank, 45 F.Supp.2d 276 (S.D.N.Y. 1999).

4 *See* Nicaragua Osorio v. Dole Food Co., 665 F.Supp.2d 1307 *aff'd*, 635 F.3d 1277 (11th Cir. 2011).

5 *See* Bhatnagar v. Surrendra Overseas Ltd., 52 F.3d 1220 (3d Cir. 1995) (*fnc* dismissal denied for reasons of litigation delays) . . . compare In re Union Carbide Corp. Gas Plant Disaster, 809 F.2d 195 (2d Cir. 1987) (*fnc* granted) and USHA (India) v. Honeywell Int'l, 421 F.3d 129 (2d Cir. 2005) (*fnc* suspended for two years pending results in India).

6 *See* Chevron Corp. v. Donziger, 833 F.3d 74 (2d Cir. 2016).

7 *See* Eastman Kodak Co. v. Kavlin, 978 F.Supp. 1078 (S.D.Fla. 1997).

8 *See* Canadian Overseas Ores v. Compania de Acero del Pacifico, 528 F.Supp. 1337 (S.D.N.Y. 1982).

9 *See* McDonnell Douglas Corp. v. Iran, 758 F.2d 341 (8th Cir. 1985).

labeled United States v. Japan, for example, was *de facto* Kodak v. Fuji. See Chapter 10.

§ 1.2 Dispute Settlement Alternatives

The range of international business dispute settlement alternatives is rich. In subsequent chapters, these alternatives will be explored in depth. Here is a basic listing for students and attorneys to consider:

Friendly Consultations

Mediation and Conciliation

"Mini-Trials"

Ad Hoc or Institutional Commercial Arbitration

Ad Hoc or Institutional Foreign Investment Arbitration

Arbitration via the International Centre for the Settlement of Investment Disputes (ICSID), the World Bank's center for arbitration of investment disputes, or the Permanent Court of Arbitration at The Hague.

Free trade agreement intergovernmental or arbitral tribunals (e.g., those of NAFTA 1994)

Litigation in the courts of one of the nations of the parties

Litigation in a third nation forum that favors selection of its forum even with minimum links

Litigation before the European Court of Justice and EU General Court—for interpretation of the consistency of business agreements with EU obligations

WTO intergovernmental dispute settlement

There are many variations on theme of international business dispute settlement alternatives. This author prefers, in escalating sequence, three phases: Friendly consultations, then mediation, and then arbitration or litigation before designated entities. Each phase needs a relatively short time limit (trigger clause) allowing either party to move the dispute along the sequence.

The imaginations of the attorneys and the willingness of the parties to agree are the only real limits to international business dispute settlement alternatives.

§ 1.3 Introduction to International Business Dispute Settlement Issues

Negotiating and drafting "choice of law" and "choice of forum" clauses in international business agreements is an art form. Most attorneys have their favorite versions of these critical clauses, but will the other side agree? The pros and cons of friendly consultations, mediation, arbitration and litigation as dispute settlement alternatives must be weighed and evaluated from both sides of the transaction. Chapter 2 is devoted to Choice of Law and Choice of Forum issues.

Not only is there a question raised regarding *how* a dispute ought to be resolved, such as arbitration versus litigation, but there are further questions such as *where* the dispute should be resolved, and under *what* rules and in *which* language. These questions are best addressed well before any dispute arises through provisions in the initial contract or agreement. For example, the parties may stipulate that a contract for the cross-border sale of goods is to be governed by the ICC INCOTERMS, or the provisions of the applicable U.S. state version of the Uniform Commercial Code (UCC). For substantive contract terms, the parties may choose to opt out of the otherwise applicable Convention on the International Sale of Goods (CISG), instead preferring the UNIDROIT Principles of International Commercial Contracts, or a particular nation's sales law such as the Spanish Codigo Comercio.

The parties may choose the applicable forum for dispute resolution, although they may not thrust upon a court otherwise inapplicable subject matter jurisdiction. The chosen forum might be the courts of one of the party's nations, or a third nation, or perhaps an international tribunal. There may not be an applicable international or regional court with jurisdiction, but the agreement might provide for international arbitration and further determine how the panel should be selected, or defer that to the procedures of a recognized organization such as the Paris-based International Chamber of Commerce (ICC), or the American Arbitration Association. See Chapter 3. Investors and the host nation may agree to use the World Bank's International Centre for the Settlement of Investment Disputes (ICSID) for investment dispute resolution. See Chapter 4.

While the contracts and agreements concluded may not have any provisions regarding how, where or under what rules and in which language any dispute shall be resolved, that may be because the matter was not discussed, or because it was discussed but no agreement was reached. Hopefully most contracts and agreements will be fulfilled, and not lead to any dispute. If they do result in a dispute, however, the parties may view the appropriate method of dispute resolution very differently than at the negotiation stage, when neither party could foresee the nature of the forthcoming dispute. For example, one of the parties may regret having agreed to arbitrate all matters relating to the contract or agreement, and later discover arbitration is demanded by the other party over a matter that does not seem among those areas contemplated to be arbitrable.

If one party feels especially strong about their position, they may be disinclined to consider mediation or arbitration, and wish to move directly to litigation. But that view may change when they realize that the litigation may take place in the other party's courts, where the judiciary is inclined to apply its own national law and may be biased. Each form of dispute resolution has advantages and disadvantages to the parties from their perspectives at the time of drafting the contract or agreement, or at a later time when a dispute has arisen. A client will expect to be advised as to the most favorable form of dispute resolution for its interests, not some form of resolution based upon some philosophical value judgment of the "fairest" method of dispute resolution or the "best" legal system.

Every form of dispute resolution may not be available to the parties. For example, mandatory laws in some nations may prohibit arbitration outside the country. Or one form of resolution may be mandatory, such as where the appropriate jurisdiction for litigation has a rule requiring some attempt at mediation before a suit may proceed to trial. This is true in China for example. One form of dispute resolution may be available, but there may be obstacles to its effective use, such as where civil dockets are not addressing many cases in order to deal with crowded criminal prosecutions. The latter is a problem in some U.S. federal courts, where drug related criminal cases have overwhelmed the courts and effectively forced business parties to turn to the arbitration of civil disputes.

The capacity to make decisions and the inclination (or perception of such inclination) to resolve matters on non-legal grounds will influence parties' choice of dispute resolution. Mediation is usually by definition a process where the mediator has relatively little power to force conclusions on the parties—rather, the mediator is expected to keep the parties negotiating so they reach a settlement or perhaps narrow the issues. Mediators are basically facilitators. Just getting persons who have the power to resolve the dispute in the same room is a major achievement.

But the dispute may require more, it may require someone to step in and make decisions. Arbitration may or may not be the answer. Sometimes arbitrators are perceived as persons who believe that they must find a resolution which satisfies both parties to some degree, leading to the charge of "splitting the baby" rather than awarding all to the party whose legal arguments are correct. However untrue this perception of arbitration may be, it may cause a party who strongly believes that its position is correct, to reject arbitration and turn to litigation.

§ 1.4 Varieties of International Business Litigation

The varieties of international business litigation are endless. Here are some basic varieties with their associated issues, which will be explored in Chapter 2 and Chapters 5 through 8. Always remember that civil law traditions predominate in the world community. . .common law dispute settlement traditions and perspectives are in the minority.

Foreign plaintiff/U.S. defendant—in a U.S. forum. Often arises where the foreign plaintiff has been forum shopping and could have brought the suit in its own nation. Usually easy to obtain personal jurisdiction but have to choose a proper forum within the United States. Prime cases for *forum non conveniens* motions (see Chapter 2). Service of process should present few problems.

U.S. plaintiff/Foreign defendant—in a U.S. forum. Often a U.S. individual injured by some product that was manufactured abroad, or had parts that allegedly were the cause of the accident made abroad. Service of process important. Personal jurisdiction a main issue. Discovery abroad may be very difficult.

U.S. plaintiff/Foreign state defendant—in a U.S. forum. Subject matter jurisdiction based on Foreign Sovereign Immunities Act (FSIA, see Chapter 7). Personal jurisdiction mandates still must be met. Difficult to define exceptions to the FSIA but much precedent to help.

Foreign plaintiff/Foreign defendant—in a U.S. forum. Subject matter jurisdiction—what is the link to the U.S.? Good area for *forum non conveniens* motions, especially if both foreigners from same country. This may happen when two foreign producers make a product that allegedly causes an injury to someone in the United States, and one of the two foreigners cross complains against the other foreign producer regarding their respective liability.

Foreign plaintiff/U.S. defendant—in a (the plaintiff's) foreign forum. Personal jurisdiction abroad over the U.S. party by extraordinary means not recognized in the United States? Service of process issues. Will the U.S. courts enforce a foreign judgment? Will any third nation court where there are assets of the defendant enforce the judgment? Defendant may commence parallel litigation in the United States.

U.S. plaintiff/Foreign defendant—in a foreign forum. Personal jurisdiction probably little problem. Are discovery rules adequate? Are damages adequate? Does the plaintiff face a loser pays all costs and attorneys' fee rule?

There are many more variations, especially when there are plaintiffs and/or defendants from different nations all in the same case.

Litigation Related to Arbitration

International business litigation is also more common than appreciated when arbitration is chosen to resolve disputes. Pre-arbitration litigation may be undertaken to challenge the validity of arbitration agreements, to compel arbitration or attach property. Litigation during the arbitration may raise questions of arbitrator integrity, evidence taking, or interim judicial relief. If an award is granted, litigation in the arbitral seat may seek to vacate the award. Ultimately, the award may need to be enforced in the courts where the arbitration took place or elsewhere. All of these themes are reviewed in Chapters 3 and 4.

These days, international business arbitration is less than litigation free. This raises the fundamental question of "Why arbitrate?" See Section 3.1.

§ 1.5 Mediation and Conciliation, Mini-Trials

The preference in Asia for more harmonious, non-adjudicatory international business dispute settlement has been noted above. In any part of the world, such an approach can especially benefit long-term (or wanna-be long-term) business relationships. The premise behind not turning the lawyers loose immediately by going directly to arbitration or litigation is that the business relationship might not survive, a premise that represents a serious risk in Asia particularly and to a lesser extent Germany. The ability of mediators and conciliators to bring together persons from both sides who have the power to resolve the dispute is critical to success or failure.

Traditionally, only conciliators could make settlement proposals, but this is now often done in the context of international business mediations as well. One critical issue is whether mediation is mandatory or optional prior to arbitration or litigation. How is the mediator(s) selected?

Once mediation is undertaken, how long will it last, can experts be consulted, and when can either party trigger arbitration or litigation? Will the mediation be conducted confidentially, so that (for example) offers to settle are not entered into evidence in future proceedings? Section 6 of the U.S. Uniform Mediation Act so provides.

If a mediated settlement is reached, will it be formalized in writing? How might that settlement be enforced? The answers will depend on how the dispute settlement clause is drafted and whether institutional mediation or conciliation rules apply.

The World Intellectual Property Organization (WIPO) features mediation services for IP disputes. Almost all international arbitration centers, such as the London Court of International Arbitration, the AAA International Centre for Dispute Resolution, and the China Council for the Promotion of International Trade (CCPIT), offer optional mediation and conciliation services. CCPIT has over 40 mediation centers in China and since 2004 there is a specific U.S. China Business Mediation Center. Mediation service is also available from China's premier arbitration center, CIETAC, and its regional affiliates. See Section 3.8.

Mediation and conciliation are commonplace in China, and expressly encouraged in China's Contract, Cooperative Joint Venture and Equity Joint Venture Laws. Judicial mediation is also frequently offered or even required, enabling judges to avoid the risk of reversal or remand by a higher court. Written, enforceable settlements follow successful Chinese judicial mediations.

Another variation on nonbinding international business dispute resolution is a "Mini-Trial". Typically, a neutral judge is chosen to run a confidential "trial" under procedures agreed to by the parties that include evidence and arguments, but no pre-trial discovery. At the parties' request, the judge may issue a settlement recommendation. The relative formality of a mini-trial reveals strengths and weaknesses on both sides, and promotes assessments and settlements.

The AAA International Mediation Rules, along with suggested mediation clauses, are reproduced in Section 1.7. There is also an UNCITRAL Model Law on International Commercial Conciliation (2002), reproduced in Section 1.6.

§ 1.6 Text of UNCITRAL Model Law on International Commercial Conciliation (2002)

Article 1. Scope of application and definitions

1. This Law applies to international1 commercial conciliation.

2. For the purposes of this Law, "conciliator" means a sole conciliator or two or more conciliators, as the case may be.

3. For the purposes of this Law, "conciliation" means a process, whether referred to by the expression conciliation, mediation or an expression of similar import, whereby parties request a third person or persons ("the conciliator") to assist them in their attempt to reach an amicable settlement of their dispute arising out of or relating to a contractual or other legal relationship. The conciliator does not have the authority to impose upon the parties a solution to the dispute.

4. A conciliation is international if:

(a) The parties to an agreement to conciliate have, at the time of the conclusion of that agreement, their places of business in different States; or

(b) The State in which the parties have their places of business is different from either:

(i) The State in which a substantial part of the obligations of the commercial relationship is to be performed; or

(ii) The State with which the subject matter of the dispute is most closely connected.

5. For the purposes of this article:

(a) If a party has more than one place of business, the place of business is that which has the closest relationship to the agreement to conciliate;

(b) If a party does not have a place of business, reference is to be made to the party's habitual residence.

6. This Law also applies to a commercial conciliation when the parties agree that the conciliation is international or agree to the applicability of this Law.

7. The parties are free to agree to exclude the applicability of this Law.

8. Subject to the provisions of paragraph 9 of this article, this Law applies irrespective of the basis upon which the conciliation is carried out, including agreement between the parties whether reached before or after a dispute has arisen, an obligation established by law, or a direction or suggestion of a court, arbitral tribunal or competent governmental entity.

9. This Law does not apply to:

(a) Cases where a judge or an arbitrator, in the course of judicial or arbitral proceedings, attempts to facilitate a settlement; and

(b) [. . .]

Article 2. Interpretation

1. In the interpretation of this Law, regard is to be had to its international origin and to the need to promote uniformity in its application and the observance of good faith.

2. Questions concerning matters governed by this Law which are not expressly settled in it are to be settled in conformity with the general principles on which this Law is based.

Article 3. Variation by agreement

Except for the provisions of article 2 and article 6, paragraph 3, the parties may agree to exclude or vary any of the provisions of this Law.

Article 4. Commencement of conciliation proceedings

1. Conciliation proceedings in respect of a dispute that has arisen commence on the day on which the parties to that dispute agree to engage in conciliation proceedings.

2. If a party that invited another party to conciliate does not receive an acceptance of the invitation within thirty days from the day on which the invitation was sent, or within such other period of time as specified in the invitation, the party may elect to treat this as a rejection of the invitation to conciliate.

Article 5. Number and appointment of conciliators

1. There shall be one conciliator, unless the parties agree that there shall be two or more conciliators.

2. The parties shall endeavour to reach agreement on a conciliator or conciliators, unless a different procedure for their appointment has been agreed upon.

3. Parties may seek the assistance of an institution or person in connection with the appointment of conciliators. In particular:

(a) A party may request such an institution or person to recommend suitable persons to act as conciliator; or

(b) The parties may agree that the appointment of one or more conciliators be made directly by such an institution or person.

4. In recommending or appointing individuals to act as conciliator, the institution or person shall have regard to such considerations as are likely to secure the appointment of an independent and impartial conciliator and, where appropriate, shall take into account the advisability of appointing a conciliator of a nationality other than the nationalities of the parties.

The following text is suggested for States that might wish to adopt a provision on the suspension of the limitation period:

Article X. Suspension of limitation period

1. When the conciliation proceedings commence, the running of the limitation period regarding the claim that is the subject matter of the conciliation is suspended.

2. Where the conciliation proceedings have terminated without a settlement agreement, the limitation period resumes running from the time the conciliation ended without a settlement agreement.

5. When a person is approached in connection with his or her possible appointment as conciliator, he or she shall disclose any circumstances likely to give rise to justifiable doubts as to his or her impartiality or independence. A conciliator, from the time of his or her appointment and throughout the conciliation proceedings, shall without delay disclose any such circumstances to the parties unless they have already been informed of them by him or her.

Article 6. Conduct of conciliation

1. The parties are free to agree, by reference to a set of rules or otherwise, on the manner in which the conciliation is to be conducted.

2. Failing agreement on the manner in which the conciliation is to be conducted, the conciliator may conduct the conciliation proceedings in such a manner as the conciliator considers appropriate, taking into account the circumstances of the case, any wishes that the parties may express and the need for a speedy settlement of the dispute.

3. In any case, in conducting the proceedings, the conciliator shall seek to maintain fair treatment of the parties and, in so doing, shall take into account the circumstances of the case.

4. The conciliator may, at any stage of the conciliation proceedings, make proposals for a settlement of the dispute.

Article 7. Communication between conciliator and parties

The conciliator may meet or communicate with the parties together or with each of them separately.

Article 8. Disclosure of information

When the conciliator receives information concerning the dispute from a party, the conciliator may disclose the substance of that information to any other party to the conciliation. However, when a party gives any information to the conciliator, subject to a specific condition that it be kept confidential, that information shall not be disclosed to any other party to the conciliation.

Article 9. Confidentiality

Unless otherwise agreed by the parties, all information relating to the conciliation proceedings shall be kept confidential, except where disclosure is required under the law or for the purposes of implementation or enforcement of a settlement agreement.

Article 10. Admissibility of evidence in other proceedings

1. A party to the conciliation proceedings, the conciliator and any third person, including those involved in the administration of the conciliation proceedings, shall not in arbitral, judicial or similar proceedings rely on, introduce as evidence or give testimony or evidence regarding any of the following:

(a) An invitation by a party to engage in conciliation proceedings or the fact that a party was willing to participate in conciliation proceedings;

(b) Views expressed or suggestions made by a party in the conciliation in respect of a possible settlement of the dispute;

(c) Statements or admissions made by a party in the course of the conciliation proceedings;

(d) Proposals made by the conciliator;

(e) The fact that a party had indicated its willingness to accept a proposal for settlement made by the conciliator;

(f) A document prepared solely for purposes of the conciliation proceedings.

2. Paragraph 1 of this article applies irrespective of the form of the information or evidence referred to therein.

3. The disclosure of the information referred to in paragraph 1 of this article shall not be ordered by an arbitral tribunal, court or other competent governmental authority and, if such information is offered as evidence in contravention of paragraph 1 of this article, that evidence shall be treated as inadmissible. Nevertheless, such information may be disclosed or admitted in evidence to the extent required under the law or for the purposes of implementation or enforcement of a settlement agreement.

4. The provisions of paragraphs 1, 2 and 3 of this article apply whether or not the arbitral, judicial or similar proceedings relate to the dispute that is or was the subject matter of the conciliation proceedings.

5. Subject to the limitations of paragraph 1 of this article, evidence that is otherwise admissible in arbitral or judicial or similar

proceedings does not become inadmissible as a consequence of having been used in a conciliation.

Article 11. Termination of conciliation proceedings

The conciliation proceedings are terminated:

(a) By the conclusion of a settlement agreement by the parties, on the date of the agreement;

(b) By a declaration of the conciliator, after consultation with the parties, to the effect that further efforts at conciliation are no longer justified, on the date of the declaration;

(c) By a declaration of the parties addressed to the conciliator to the effect that the conciliation proceedings are terminated, on the date of the declaration; or

(d) By a declaration of a party to the other party or parties and the conciliator, if appointed, to the effect that the conciliation proceedings are terminated, on the date of the declaration.

Article 12. Conciliator acting as arbitrator

Unless otherwise agreed by the parties, the conciliator shall not act as an arbitrator in respect of a dispute that was or is the subject of the conciliation proceedings or in respect of another dispute that has arisen from the same contract or legal relationship or any related contract or legal relationship.

Article 13. Resort to arbitral or judicial proceedings

Where the parties have agreed to conciliate and have expressly undertaken not to initiate during a specified period of time or until a specified event has occurred arbitral or judicial proceedings with respect to an existing or future dispute, such an undertaking shall be given effect by the arbitral tribunal or the court until the terms of the undertaking have been complied with, except to the extent necessary for a party, in its opinion, to preserve its rights. Initiation of such proceedings is not of itself to be regarded as a waiver of the agreement to conciliate or as a termination of the conciliation proceedings.

Article 14. Enforceability of settlement agreement

If the parties conclude an agreement settling a dispute, that settlement agreement is binding and enforceable . . . [*the enacting State may insert a description of the method of enforcing settlement agreements or refer to provisions governing such enforcement*].

When implementing the procedure for enforcement of settlement agreements, an enacting State may consider the possibility of such a procedure being mandatory.

§ 1.7 Text of American Arbitration Association (AAA) Mediation Rules and Clauses

1. Agreement of Parties

Whenever parties have agreed in writing to mediate disputes under these International Mediation Rules, or have provided for mediation or conciliation of existing or future international disputes under the auspices of the International Centre for Dispute Resolution, the international division of the American Arbitration Association, or the American Arbitration Association without designating particular Rules, they shall be deemed to have made these Rules, as amended and in effect as of the date of the submission of the dispute, a part of their agreement.

The parties by mutual agreement may vary any part of these Rules including, but not limited to, agreeing to conduct the mediation via telephone or other electronic or technical means.

2. Initiation of Mediation

Any party or parties to a dispute may initiate mediation under the ICDR's auspices by making a request for mediation to any of the ICDR's regional offices or case management centers via telephone, email, regular mail or fax. Requests for mediation may also be filed online via AAA WebFile at http://www.adr.org/.

The party initiating the mediation shall simultaneously notify the other party or parties of the request. The initiating party shall provide the following information to the ICDR and the other party or parties as applicable:

(a) A copy of the mediation provision of the parties' contract or the parties' stipulation to mediate.

(b) The names, regular mail addresses, email addresses, and telephone numbers of all parties to the dispute and representatives, if any, in the mediation.

(c) A brief statement of the nature of the dispute and the relief requested.

(d) Any specific qualifications the mediator should possess.

Where there is no preexisting stipulation or contract by which the parties have provided for mediation of existing or future disputes under the auspices of the ICDR, a party may request the ICDR to invite another party to participate in "mediation by voluntary submission". Upon receipt of such a request, the ICDR will contact the other party or parties involved in the dispute and attempt to obtain a submission to mediation.

3. Representation

Subject to any applicable law, any party may be represented by persons of the party's choice. The names and addresses of such persons shall be communicated in writing to all parties and to the ICDR.

4. Appointment of the Mediator

Parties may search the online profiles of the ICDR's Panel of Mediators . . . in an effort to agree on a mediator. If the parties have not agreed to the appointment of a mediator and have not provided any other method of appointment, the mediator shall be appointed in the following manner:

(a) Upon receipt of a request for mediation, the ICDR will send to each party a list of mediators from the ICDR's Panel of Mediators. The parties are encouraged to agree to a mediator from the submitted list and to advise the ICDR of their agreement.

(b) If the parties are unable to agree upon a mediator, each party shall strike unacceptable names from the list, number the remaining names in order of preference, and return the list to the ICDR. If a party does not return the list within the time specified, all mediators on the list shall be deemed acceptable. From among the mediators who have been mutually approved by the parties, and in accordance with the designated order of mutual preference, the ICDR shall invite a mediator to serve.

(c) If the parties fail to agree on any of the mediators listed, or if acceptable mediators are unable to serve, or if for any other reason the appointment cannot be made from the submitted list, the ICDR shall have the authority to make the appointment from among other members of the Panel of Mediators without the submission of additional lists.

5. Mediator's Impartiality and Duty to Disclose

ICDR mediators are required to abide by the Model Standards of Conduct for Mediators in effect at the time a mediator is appointed to a case. Where there is a conflict between the Model Standards and any provision of these Mediation Rules, these Mediation Rules shall govern. The Standards require mediators to (i) decline a mediation if the mediator cannot conduct it in an impartial manner, and (ii) disclose, as soon as practicable, all actual and potential conflicts of interest that are reasonably known to the mediator and could reasonably be seen as raising a question about the mediator's impartiality.

Prior to accepting an appointment, ICDR mediators are required to make a reasonable inquiry to determine whether there are any facts that a reasonable individual would consider likely to create a potential or actual conflict of interest for the mediator. ICDR mediators are required to disclose any circumstance likely to create a presumption of bias or prevent a resolution of the parties' dispute within the time frame desired by the parties.

Upon receipt of such disclosures, the ICDR shall immediately communicate the disclosures to the parties for their comments.

The parties may, upon receiving disclosure of actual or potential conflicts of interest of the mediator, waive such conflicts and proceed with the mediation. In the event that a party disagrees as to whether the mediator shall serve, or in the event that the mediator's conflict of interest might reasonably be viewed as undermining the integrity of the mediation, the mediator shall be replaced.

6. Vacancies

If any mediator shall become unwilling or unable to serve, the ICDR will appoint another mediator, unless the parties agree otherwise, in accordance with section 4.

7. Duties and Responsibilities of the Mediator

(a) The mediator shall conduct the mediation based on the principle of party self-determination. Self-determination is the act of coming to a voluntary, uncoerced decision in which each party makes free and informed choices as to process and outcome.

(b) The mediator is authorized to conduct separate or ex parte meetings and other communications with the parties and/or their representatives, before, during, and after any scheduled mediation conference. Such communications may be conducted via telephone, in writing, via email, online, in person or otherwise.

(c) The parties are encouraged to exchange all documents pertinent to the relief requested. The mediator may request the exchange of memoranda on issues, including the underlying interests and the history of the parties' negotiations. Information that a party wishes to keep confidential may be sent to the mediator, as necessary, in a separate communication with the mediator.

(d) The mediator does not have the authority to impose a settlement on the parties but will attempt to help them reach a satisfactory resolution of their dispute. Subject to the discretion of the mediator, the mediator may make oral or written recommendations for settlement to a party privately or, if the parties agree, to all parties jointly.

(e) In the event that a complete settlement of all or some issues in dispute is not achieved within the scheduled mediation conference(s), the mediator may continue to communicate with the parties, for a period of time, in an ongoing effort to facilitate a complete settlement.

(f) The mediator is not a legal representative of any party and has no fiduciary duty to any party.

8. Responsibilities of the Parties

The parties shall ensure that appropriate representatives of each party, having authority to consummate a settlement, attend the mediation conference.

Prior to and during the scheduled mediation conference(s) the parties and their representatives shall, as appropriate to each party's circumstances, exercise their best efforts to prepare for and engage in a meaningful and productive mediation.

9. Privacy

Mediation conferences and related mediation communications are private proceedings. The parties and their representatives may attend mediation conferences. Other persons may attend only with the permission of the parties and with the consent of the mediator.

10. Confidentiality

Subject to applicable law or the parties' agreement, confidential information disclosed to a mediator by the parties or by other participants (witnesses) in the course of the mediation shall not be divulged by the mediator. The mediator shall maintain the confidentiality of all information obtained in the mediation, and all records, reports, or other documents received by a mediator while serving in that capacity shall be confidential.

The mediator shall not be compelled to divulge such records or to testify in regard to the mediation in any adversary proceeding or judicial forum.

The parties shall maintain the confidentiality of the mediation and shall not rely on, or introduce as evidence in any arbitral, judicial, or other proceeding the following, unless agreed to by the parties or required by applicable law:

(a) Views expressed or suggestions made by a party or other participant with respect to a possible settlement of the dispute;

(b) Admissions made by a party or other participant in the course of the mediation proceedings;

(c) Proposals made or views expressed by the mediator; or

(d) The fact that a party had or had not indicated willingness to accept a proposal for settlement made by the mediator.

11. No Stenographic Record

There shall be no stenographic record of the mediation process.

12. Termination of Mediation

The mediation shall be terminated:

(a) By the execution of a settlement agreement by the parties; or

(b) By a written or verbal declaration of the mediator to the effect that further efforts at mediation would not contribute to a resolution of the parties' dispute; or

(c) By a written or verbal declaration of all parties to the effect that the mediation proceedings are terminated; or

(d) When there has been no communication between the mediator and any party or party's representative for 21 days following the conclusion of the mediation conference.

13. Exclusion of Liability

Neither the ICDR nor any mediator is a necessary party in judicial proceedings relating to the mediation. Neither the ICDR nor any mediator shall be liable to any party for any error, act or omission in connection with any mediation conducted under these Rules.

14. Interpretation and Application of Rules

The mediator shall interpret and apply these Rules insofar as they relate to the mediator's duties and responsibilities. All other Rules shall be interpreted and applied by the ICDR.

15. Deposits

Unless otherwise directed by the mediator, the ICDR will require the parties to deposit in advance of the mediation conference such sums of money as it, in consultation with the mediator, deems necessary to cover the costs and expenses of the mediation and shall render an accounting to the parties and return any unexpended balance at the conclusion of the mediation.

16. Expenses

All expenses of the mediation, including required traveling and other expenses or charges of the mediator, shall be borne equally by the parties unless they agree otherwise. The expenses of participants for either side shall be paid by the party requesting the attendance of such participants.

17. Cost of the Mediation

There is no filing fee to initiate a mediation or a fee to request the ICDR to invite parties to mediate.

The cost of mediation is based on the hourly mediation rate published on the mediator's ICDR profile. This rate covers both mediator compensation and an allocated portion for the ICDR's services. There is a four-hour minimum charge for a mediation conference. Expenses referenced in Section M-16 may also apply.

If a matter submitted for mediation is withdrawn or cancelled or results in a settlement after the agreement to mediate is filed but prior to the mediation conference the cost is $250 plus any mediator time and charges incurred.

The parties will be billed equally for all costs unless they agree otherwise.

18. Language

If the parties have not agreed otherwise, the language(s) of the mediation shall be that of the documents containing the mediation agreement.

AAA Mediation Clauses

If the parties want to adopt mediation as a part of their contractual dispute settlement procedure, they can insert the following mediation clause into their contract in conjunction with a standard arbitration provision:

If a dispute arises out of or relates to this contract, or the breach thereof, and if the dispute cannot be settled through negotiation, the parties agree first to try in good faith to settle the dispute by mediation in accordance with the International Mediation Rules of the International Centre for Dispute Resolution before resorting to arbitration, litigation or some other dispute resolution procedure.

If the parties want to use a mediator to resolve an existing dispute, they can enter into the following submission:

The parties hereby submit the following dispute to mediation administered by the International Centre for Dispute Resolution in accordance with its International Mediation Rules. (The clause may also provide for the qualifications of the mediator(s), method of payment, locale of meetings and any other item of concern to the parties.)

The ICDR can schedule the mediation anywhere in the world and will propose a list of specialized international mediators.

Chapter 2

CHOICE OF LAW, CHOICE OF FORUM, AND FORUM NON CONVENIENS

Table of Sections

There is an increasing trend around the globe to honor what is referred to as "party autonomy." In other words, when the parties to international transactions select a specific court, arbitral mechanism or other procedures to settle disputes that may arise in the future, this selection is increasingly upheld. So, too, when the parties choose a particular law to govern their transaction, a large number of jurisdictions will honor that choice.

Of course, this does not mean that the chosen forum (particularly courts) must accept jurisdiction, or must apply the law the parties have chosen to govern their business relationship. In the United States, for example, the doctrine of *forum non conveniens (fnc)* may be invoked to dismiss causes of action U.S. courts believe could be satisfactorily litigated elsewhere. See Section 2.4. *Forum non conveniens* is commonly disputed when foreign plaintiffs seek damages, notably punitive damages, in U.S. courts, often under contingency fee arrangements with their attorneys. What to do about such "forum shopping" by foreign plaintiffs has become a major strategic issue in international business litigation and the subject of several important U.S. Supreme Court cases.

Forum shopping issues also permeate questions of jurisdiction (see Chapter 5), procedure (Chapter 6), sovereign defenses (Chapter 7) and enforcement of judgments (Chapter 8). It is for that reason that we first focus on choice of law and choice of forum. I am indebted to Professor Michael Gordon of Florida for his original work on material appearing in this chapter and to USD Professor Herbert Lazerow for his Choice of Law insights.

§ 2.1 Choice of Law

Cross-border litigation or arbitration inherently provides for the possible applicability of the law of at least two nations. Because of the international character of a transaction, the parties often choose the applicable substantive law, frequently in conjunction with a choice of forum provision which will generally govern procedural matters. The parties should be fully aware of the substance of each possibly applicable law before stipulating the chosen law. And they should draft the clause very carefully to reflect whether it covers validity, defense and remedial issues as well as interpretational questions.

For example, a clause stating "This contract shall be construed in accordance with. . .law" is quite different in scope from one stating "This contract shall be governed by. . .law". Even more broadly worded clauses may state "All disputes arising out of or related to this contract shall be governed by. . .law." Presumably, non-contractual disputes related to the contract would be controlled by this latter clause. The parties may also choose customary *lex mercatoria* (merchant law) or *ex aequo et bono* ("justice and fairness") as controlling.

Choice of law preferences instinctively drift towards home country jurisdictions. But these instincts may not be in the client's best interests. For example, a U.S. party selling goods to a German party might discover that German law favors the seller in such a transaction. Hence the U.S. party would want to specify that German law applies, and might even gain concessions on other issues if the German party prefers German law, not because it has been researched, but because it is German and familiar.

Just as a choice of forum agreement may not thrust subject matter jurisdiction upon a court, a choice of law provision may not thrust that decision upon the court. U.S due process law, for example, requires that the chosen law bear a significant relationship to the transaction or parties at issue, such that the application of the choice of law is not arbitrary nor fundamentally unfair.[1] With subject matter jurisdiction and choice of forum, the key question usually is whether the court has the capacity to hear the case. Contrastingly, with choice of law, it is usually a question of whether the court is willing to hear the case applying the law of a foreign nation.

---

1 Home Insurance Co. v. Dick, 281 U.S. 397 (1930); Phillips Petroleum Co. v. Shutts, 427 U.S. 797 (1985).

Courts usually respect a choice of law provision, especially in a commercial contract where the choice is one of the laws of the parties' nations. UCC Section 1–301(b) specifies that a chosen law must have an appropriate relation to the state in question. In contrast, European Union Regulation 593/2008 (Rome I), allows substantial freedom to choose any law to govern civil and commercial contracts.

That said, a choice of law clause, like an arbitration clause, may not escape the application of "mandatory" public law of the forum jurisdiction, or possibly that of a third jurisdiction having a paramount interest in the litigation. See Section 3.3. And the clause may be invalidated if obtained by fraud or duress, it is unconscionable, or violates due process or public policy in the forum jurisdiction.[2] For example, the public policy of a U.S. forum may notably cause it to deny application of limitations on damages of the chosen law.[3]

At the other end of the spectrum, where the choice has absolutely no relevance to the contract, such as where German and U.S. parties choose the law of Mongolia, that choice of law may not be honored. A court is likely to reject such a choice because the chosen law has no linkage to the case, but also because the court may feel uncomfortable in applying the law of a nation without a highly developed contract law, which may be difficult to prove. In contrast, the choice of a well-developed, neutral, and easily researched body of law, such as English or German contract law, though lacking any significant contacts with the transaction, may well be honored.

Conflict of Laws

Choice of law has two sides. First is as part of a conflict of laws determination (often referred to as a private international law in Europe) when a court is using conflicts rules to determine what law applies in the absence of a choice of law clause. Second is when parties wish to argue that a chosen foreign law is applicable, and are faced with convincing the court of its merits and, if accepted, proving the foreign law.

In the United States, choice of law determinations in federal courts exercising diversity jurisdiction are governed by the U.S. state law in which that court sits,[4] whereas when federal question

---

[2] *See, e.g.*, Milanovich v. Costa Crociere, 954 F.2d 763 (D.C.Cir. 1992); Roby v. Lloyd's, 96 F.3d 216 (2d Cir. 1993) (choice of English law upheld despite absence of punitive damages and different securities law standards); Home Ins. Co. v. Dick, 281 U.S. 397 (1930) (due process bars applying Texas law to a Mexican insurance policy).

[3] *See, e.g.*, Eli Lilly Do Brasil v. Federal Express, 502 F.3d 78 (2d Cir. 2007); Marsh v. Burrell, 805 F.Supp. 1493 (N.D. Cal. 1992).

[4] Day & Zimmerman Inc. v. Challoner, 423 U.S. 3 (1975).

jurisdiction is utilized, federal common law applies.[5] Choice of law issues vary considerably among U.S. states, influenced to some degree by the First and Second Restatements of Conflict of Laws. For the conflicts determination, parties to commercial contracts are allowed under most jurisdictions to choose the applicable law in the contract. When they do not, the court will turn to its own conflicts rules in seeking to apply what may be the law that has the "most significant relationship to the transaction",[6] or that "bears an appropriate relation",[7] or of the country "with which it is most closely connected."[8]

Most international cases involve the presence of at least two different sets of substantive rules. The approaches to deciding a choice of law question may differ depending upon whether the issue is contract or tort. It is an important decision for a court because a ruling that a foreign law applies that offers very nominal damages is tantamount to a victory for the defendant. In the United States, the Supreme Court has ruled that quantification of damages is not procedural, but rather substantive, and therefore governed by the law controlling the claim.[9]

Contract

A sales contract negotiated across borders might reasonably be decided in the nation of the seller or the buyer. Fortunately, international sales of goods rules have been partly harmonized by the United Nations Convention on Contracts for the International Sale of Goods of 1980 (CISG), which has been adopted by more than 80 nations. See R. Folsom, M.Gordon, M. Van Alstine, and M.Ramsey, *Principles of International Business Transactions*. Absent an express contract disclaimer of its applicability, the CISG controls when both parties are from signatory CISG nations, for example China and the United States. But different nations may reach different interpretations of the same CISG article, just as may different U.S. states in interpreting the Uniform Commercial Code.

A choice of law provision is often included in a contract, and such choices are respected in many nations. For example, the California Supreme Court upheld a Hong Kong choice of law clause as governing even non-contractual claims.[10] But European Union law may

---

5 *See, e.g.*, Aaron Ferer & Sons v. Chase Manhattan Bank, 731 F.2d 112 (2d Cir. 1984).

6 Restatement, Conflicts of Law (Second) (1971) § 188.

7 U.C.C. § 1–105.

8 Convention on the Law Applicable to Contractual Obligations (EEC) (1980) art. 4.

9 Gasperini v. Center for Humanities Inc. 518 U.S. 415 (1996).

10 Nedlloyd Lines BV v. Seawinds Ltd., 3 Cal. 4th 459 (Sup Ct. 1992).

override choices of law that conflict with its rules for specific contracts. This was the case in *Ingmar GB Ltd v. Eaton Leonard Technologies Inc.*[11] where the European Court of Justice disallowed the choice of California law by U.S. and U.K. parties to a commercial agency agreement.

Where no choice of law is made in the contract, conflict of laws' rules determining the controlling law tend to focus on the nation most closely connected to the transaction or at least having a significant relationship to the transaction, such as the place of contracting.[12]

Tort

Torts usually occur outside of the framework of a contract that might have an applicable choice of law provision. But there are some such provisions, for example where a person signs an agreement for a stay at a resort or to take a cruise, and the contract has a choice of law (and quite possibly a choice of forum) provision in the event of any injury. But in many tort cases, such as the numerous cases brought against companies for injuries allegedly caused by the company's products or practices abroad, there is no contract and therefore no choice of law provision.

In such cases, the courts tend to use the long held theory that the law of the place where the injury occurred (*lex loci delicti*) is the proper choice. But the injury that occurs in one country may be attributable to negligence in another, such as when a product is negligently made in the United States and an injury occurs in a foreign nation after the product is exported. The consequences of the decision may be very important, because damages under U.S. law are likely to be much higher than under the foreign law.

Proving Foreign Law

Part of the analysis of what law should apply may include the problems associated with proving foreign law. While a U.S. court is deemed to know U.S. law, it is not deemed to know foreign law. Because the court does not "know" foreign law, it must be proved.[13]

That necessitates an understanding of Rule 44.1 of the Federal Rules of Civil Procedure, assuming the matter is before a federal court. Rule 44.1 requires a party who plans to request the application of foreign law to give reasonable notice or face the possibility of a

---

11 (2000 ECR I–9305).

12 *See, e.g.*, Nedlloyd Lines BV v. Superior Court, 834 P.2d 1148 (Cal. 1992).

13 *See especially*, Hay, "The Use and Determination of Foreign Law in Civil Litigation in the United States," 62 Am. J. Comp. L. 213 (2014).

waiver.[14] It also allows the court wide latitude in determining foreign law. That determination usually includes the use of experts to explain both the nature of the foreign legal system, such as how case law fits into the hierarchy of law, and the substantive characteristics of the applicable law. Experts usually provide affidavits that include translations of the applicable legal provisions.

All that said, proving foreign law is not easy. For a Seventh Circuit decision struggling with proof of controlling Spanish law, see *Twohy v. First National Bank of Chicago.*[15] For a controversial decision undertaken by Seventh Circuit Judges Frank Easterbrook and Richard Posner that relies exclusively on written English-language materials available in the USA to prove French law, dispensing with expert testimony on French law, see *Bodum v. La Cafetiere.*[16] Other notable Circuit Court decisions have concerned proof of Japanese, Indian, Tongan, Nevis, Indonesian, Egyptian and Korean law.[17]

A court asked to accept the application of a foreign law is likely to inquire about whether that law will cover the dispute. If a foreign law is chosen that provides no cause of action or inadequate remedies, the court may reject the application of such foreign law. There thus may be some process, possibly a hearing, where the court conducts an analysis of the substance of the foreign law and even whether it is likely that translations of the law can be obtained and experts can be found to explain the law to the court.

There is a relationship between choice of law and *forum non conveniens*. When a court considers a motion to dismiss for *forum non conveniens* reasons, the court may believe a foreign forum is more appropriate because the law of that foreign nation is the proper choice of law. See Section 2.4.

---

[14] *See* Laminoirs-Trefileries-Cableries de Lens, S.A. v. Southwire Co., 484 F.Supp. 1063, 1067 (N.D.Ga.1980); Whirlpool Fin Corp. v. Sevaux, 96 F.2d 216 (7th Cir. 1996).

[15] 758 F.2d 1185 (7th Cir. 1185).

[16] 621 F.3d 624 (2010). Accord, JPMorgan Chase Bank v. PT Indah Kiat Pulp and Paper, 854 F.Supp.2d 528 (N.D. Ill. 2012) (rejecting expert testimony on Indonesian law).

[17] Kaho v. Ilchert, 765 F.2d 877 (9th Cir. 1985) (Tongan family law); Lesley v. Spike TV, 241 Fed. App'x 357 (9th Cir. 2007) (Japanese contract law); Bhatnagar v. Surrendra Overseas Ltd., 52 F.3d 1220 (3d Cir. 1995) (Indian tort law); Ratonis Enterprises v. Hyundai Mipo Dockyard, 426 F.3d 580 (2d Cir. 2005); In re Condor Insurance Ltd., 601 F.3d 319 (5th Cir. 2010) (Nevis bankruptcy law); Karaha Bodas v. Perusahaan Pertambangan, 313 F.3d 70 (2d Cir. 2002) (Indonesian ownership law; U.S. v. Schultz, 333 F.3d 393 (2d Cir. 2003) (Egyptian law).

§ 2.2 Forum Selection Clauses: Courts

In negotiating an international business contract, the parties should always at least consider the appropriateness of stipulating a chosen forum. They may not be able to agree and do nothing, but at least they considered the issue. If a choice is made and they submit to a specific judicial forum exclusively or nonexclusively, it does not mean that jurisdiction may be thrust upon a court that under its rules does not have jurisdiction. Nor does it mean that a court that has not been selected, but that under its rules could have jurisdiction, will respect the choice of forum.

There is a long history of U.S. hostility to choice of court clauses. They were and to some degree still are seen as "ousting" courts of their jurisdiction. That has changed (see *Bremen* below) and while U.S. courts generally respect forum selection clauses today absent contract defects, unreasonableness, or public policy objections,[18] foreign courts may follow rules that require the court to go forward if it has jurisdiction, regardless of the party's choice of a different forum. In Europe, for example, this may be particularly the case in consumer, insurance and other standardized contract disputes that contain choice of forum clauses (compare *Carnival Cruise* below).

Negotiations for more than a dozen years to achieve a jurisdiction and recognition of foreign judgments convention were not successful. Instead of totally abandoning their efforts, the Hague Conference on Private International Law reduced its scope of aspirations considerably, and in June of 2005 adopted the Hague Convention on Choice of Court Agreements.[19] Mexico has acceded to it, but ratification to date is extremely limited. The United States signed but has not ratified the Choice of Court Convention. Though the Convention is not yet in force, its influence can be seen in EU law (see Section 8.2) and in the agreement on reciprocal enforcement of choice of court clauses between China and its Hong Kong Special Administrative Region.

Various U.S. states have specific rules on choice of court clauses. Only Idaho, Iowa and Montana refuse as a rule to honor an exclusive choice of court preference. In those states, such clauses are treated as in "derogation" of open court access principles. New York will enforce clauses choosing its courts provided New York law is also chosen by the parties, and the contract involves at $1 million.[20] No

---

[18] *See* Atlantic Marine Construction v. U.S. District Court, 134 S.Ct. 568 (2013).

[19] Convention on Jurisdiction and Enforcement of Foreign Judgments in Civil and Commercial Matters at Brussels, Sept. 27, 1968, Art. 17–1. 8 I.L.M. 229 (1969). See Art. 23.

[20] N.Y. General Obligations Code Section 5–1402.

other contacts with New York are required. In a post-*Bremen* decision, the California Supreme Court affirmed the general validity of choice of court clauses.[21] Florida is less welcoming to choice of court clauses, mandating relations with the state and at least one party with residency, incorporation or a place of business in the state.[22]

These days, most jurisdictions will accept the parties' judicial forum selection, though non-exclusivity is likely to be presumed in the United States absent clear indications to the contrary.[23] When parties choose a third nation as the forum, there should be some assurance that the courts of that chosen nation will assume jurisdiction. Within the European Union, under the Brussels Convention/Regulation (see Section 8.2), parties from EU nations may select the courts of any nation within the EU. Indeed, since 2015, EU member state courts accept jurisdiction even if none of the selecting parties are from the Union. And the EU rules specify a presumption of exclusivity.

Forum selection has become a critical battleground in international business negotiations and litigation. The controlling forum will substantially influence the judgment on the merits and damages' awards. Convenience, bias and costs will also be at issue. Choosing a nation with civil law traditions introduces a very different form of litigation. The proceedings will be controlled in depth and the decision made by an assigned judge. There is no jury trial as known in common law systems and very often no punitive or mandatory multiple damages, or contingency fee agreements. Moreover, many civil law jurisdictions will require the loser to pay the other party's legal fees, which is much less common in the United States. For parties in civil law nations, the idea of a jury trial under these conditions may be as much of a concern as the absence of one to a party from the United States.

U.S. Jurisprudence

In *The Bremen v. Zapata Off-Shore Co.,*[24] the U.S. Supreme Court upheld a clause selecting the London Court of Justice in a contract between an American corporation, the owner of an oil rig, and a German corporation, an ocean towing company, for delivery of

---

[21] Smith, Valentino & Smith v. Superior Court, 551 P.2d 1206 (Cal. 1976).

[22] Fla. Stat. ch. 685.101(2).

[23] *See, e.g.*, Docksider Ltd. v. Sea Technology Ltd., 875 F.2d 762 (9th Cir. 1987).

[24] M/S Bremen v. Zapata Off-Shore Co., 407 U.S. 1, 92 S.Ct. 1907, 32 L.Ed.2d 513 (1972) (provision choosing London courts upheld). Accord, Albemarle Corp. v. AstraZeneca UK Ltd., 628 F.3d 643 (4th Cir. 2010) (English law and English High Court upheld as mandatory); Stewart Org Inc. v. Ricoh Corp., 487 U.S. 22 (1988); Karl Koch Erecting Inc. v. New York Convention Center, 838 F.2d 656 (2d Cir. 1988); Mercury Coal & Coke Inc. v. Manesmann Pipe & Steel Corp., 696 F.2d 315 (4th Cir. 1982); Pelleport Investors v. Budco Quality Theatres, 741 F.2d 273 (9th Cir. 1984).

an oil rig from the USA to Italy. The Court determined the forum selection clause was not unreasonable, did not constitute a "grave" inconvenience, and was part of "a freely negotiated private international agreement, unaffected by fraud, undue influence, or overweening bargaining power," which should be given effect.[25]

Bremen is the foundation pronouncement by the Court on the subject of choice of forum clauses in international transactions. The dissent presents fully the arguments of the rig-owner: That use of an English forum determines this outcome of the case because English courts under English law would allow a tug by contract to disclaim its own negligence, while a U.S. court under U.S. law would not allow it to do so. Thus, the rig owner lost substantive rights that it would otherwise have had under U.S. law. Likewise, U.S.-based Lloyd's insurance syndicate "names" have been held to their choice of the London Court of Justice as a forum.[26] The choice of Mexican, German and Vatican courts have also been reviewed in U.S. judicial opinions.[27]

If there is any doubt as to the acceptability of forum selection clauses in the United States, the *Carnival Cruise Lines, Inc. v. Shute* decision is mandatory reading.[28] In *Carnival* a plaintiff from the state of Washington purchased a ticket for a cruise out of Los Angeles. The ticket contained a fine print forum selection clause designating Florida courts, the home of the cruise line. The plaintiff fell and was injured in international waters. The Supreme Court upheld the forum selection provision, which was never negotiated, unconvinced that it would be an unreasonable burden on the plaintiff to bring suit in Florida.

The Court did not believe that Florida was a "remote alien forum", language taken from the earlier *Bremen* decision. The Florida court was not "seriously inconvenient" and it was not unreasonable for Carnival Cruise Lines to want to consolidate cases brought against it in Florida. In contrast, the Supreme Court did find a "remote alien forum" stipulated rather than bargained for in a N.Y.

---

[25] On fraud, *see* Petersen v. Boeing Co., 715 F.3d 276 (9th Cir. 2013).

[26] Lipton v. Underwriters at Lloyd's, 148 F.3d 1285 (11th Cir. 1998); Richards v. Lloyd's of London, 135 F.3d 1289 (9th Cir. 1998); Bonny v. Lloyd's, 3 F.3d 156 (7th Cir. 1993); Roby v. Lloyd's, 996 F.3d 1353 (2d Cir. 1993).

[27] *See*, Adams v. Raintree Vacation Exchange LLC, 702 F.3d 436 (7th Cir. 2012) (choice of Mexican court upheld), Copperweld Steel v. Demag-Mannesman-Boehler, 578 F.2d 953 (3rd Cir. 1978) (choice of German court rejected), Magi XXI Inc. v. Stato della Citta del Vaticano, 714 F.3d 714 (2d Cir. 2013) (choice of Vatican courts upheld).

[28] 499 U.S. 585, 111 S.Ct. 1522, 113 L.Ed.2d 622 (1991). Compare Sun Trust Bank v. Sun Int'l Hotels, Ltd., 184 F.Supp.2d 1246 (S.D. Fla. 2001) (hotel front desk form mandating use of Bahamian courts and law unreasonable).

wrongful death action against an Italian cruise line under a contract calling for dispute settlement in Italian courts.[29]

In an international shipping case, *Fireman's Fund Ins. Co. v. M.V. DSR Atlantic,*[30] the court stated that *Vimar Seguros y Reaseguros, S.A. v. M/V Sky Reefer,*[31] allows the parties to choose any forum (foreign court as well as arbitral tribunal) for any issue. If "mandatory law" governing international contracts can now be determined by arbitration tribunals under an arbitration clause, it can also be determined by foreign courts under a forum selection clause. In other words, the traditional statutory rule requiring Carriage of Goods by Sea Act (COGSA) issues to be decided by U.S. courts, and not foreign courts, is no longer valid.[32]

One of the most difficult issues for a court is to determine whether a forum selection clause was freely negotiated and accepted by the parties, or whether it was the consequence of the use of a standard contract with a forum selection clause chosen by one party and imposed upon the other. In such situation it may be more likely that a court will uphold a forum selection clause that requires a Texas party (for example) to submit to a clause selecting another state's courts, such as California, than for that same court to uphold a forum selection clause that requires the Texas party to submit to a foreign court, such as Argentina. The international characteristics of the facts leading to the dispute may be the only difference in the court's decision.

In 2005, a Florida appellate court upheld a non-neutral forum selection clause in a franchising agreement between a Florida franchisor and Spanish franchisee choosing the courts of Madrid.[33] The court concluded that: "It should be incumbent on the party seeking to escape his contract to show that trial in the contractual forum will be so gravely difficult and inconvenient that he will for all practical purposes be deprived of his day in court. Absent that, there is no basis for concluding that it would be unfair, unjust, or unreasonable to hold that party to his bargain." But if a choice of court clause is perceived to be permissive (not mandatory), it may not

---

29 *See* Lauro Lines SRL v. Chasser, 490 U.S. 495, 497, 109 S.Ct. 1976, 104 L.Ed.2d 548 (1989). *But see* Spradlin v. Lear Siegler Management Services Co., 926 F.2d 865 (9th Cir. 1991) (Saudi Arabia forum selection upheld in contract for services to be performed in Saudi Arabia). *See generally*, Liles v. Ginn-La West End Ltd., 631 F.3d 1242 (11th Cir. 2011).

30 131 F.3d 1336 (9th Cir. 1997).

31 515 U.S. 528, 115 S.Ct. 2322, 132 L.Ed.2d 462 (1995).

32 *But see* Central National-Gottesman Inc. v. M.V. "Gertrude Oldendorff", 204 F.Supp.2d 675 (S.D.N.Y. 2002) rejecting a bill of lading selection clause that chose English courts and law completely eliminating the applicability of COGSA.

33 Corsec, S.L. v. VMC Int'l Franchising, LLC, 909 So.2d 945 (Fla.App. 3d DCA 2005).

be enforced.[34] The doctrine of *forum non conveniens* (see Section 2.4) does not provide a basis for rejecting a choice of court clause.[35]

Which Court Forum?

In many commercial sales agreements, the parties do not include a forum selection provision, or if they do it is buried in fine print on a standardized Invoice or other document. Indeed, in an international "battle of the forms", both parties may have buried their forum choices in fine print, resulting not in agreement but confusion. It may also be that they did not discuss the matter, or they did discuss it at arm's length, but could not agree on a forum. Many international business parties do not expect issues of the proper dispute resolution forum to arise, and in fact relatively few disputes emerge from the enormous volume of international sales transactions. There are far fewer cross-border licensing and foreign investment transactions, but a higher percentage of them will end up in dispute, suggesting the need for particular attention to choice of forum and law clauses in such agreements.

Where no forum has been chosen by the parties, a U.S. plaintiff will usually assume that a U.S. forum is the best choice. That may not be true. A foreign forum may be the only place where the defendant may be subject to jurisdiction, or where the law is most favorable, or where the defendant has most or all of its assets. If the defendant is a foreign party, the U.S. plaintiff nevertheless may wish to litigate in the United States, but may have to address complex issues of personal jurisdiction over the foreign defendant in the U.S. court. See Section 5.2.

If the defendant is also a U.S. party, the dispute is likely to constitute domestic rather than international litigation. But the issue could be the liability of a U.S. hotel operating in a foreign country to a U.S. guest injured while staying in the foreign located hotel. The injured U.S. party has come home to recover and sues the owner of the hotel at home, regardless whether the defendant is only the parent of the foreign subsidiary that operated the hotel abroad. The U.S. plaintiff may assume that the U.S. court will apply U.S. law, but the U.S. defendant may argue successfully in the U.S. court that the law of the place of the injury applies, which would be foreign law.

Foreign plaintiffs increasingly seek a favorable U.S. forum to decide matters that often have far more links to their home nation.

---

[34] *See, e.g.*, Albemarle Corp. v. AstraZeneca UK Ltd., 628 F.3d 643 (4th Cir. 2010) (construing clause stating that "this contract shall be subject to English law and the jurisdiction of the English High Court" to be mandatory under English law though permissive under U.S. federal law).

[35] AAR Int'l v. Nimelias Enterprises SA, 250 F.3d 510 (7th Cir. 2001).

The reason for such forum shopping, especially where the issue is a tort, is usually the prospect of damages not available in the foreign plaintiff's nation, such as for pain and suffering and punitive damages. See Sections 5.2 and 5.3. But even for commercial litigation, the U.S. system may appear the better choice to a foreign plaintiff, with its more extensive discovery, jury system and possible contingent fee arrangement.

It may be that it is inappropriate to proceed because there is parallel litigation elsewhere. If the defendant has simultaneously sued the plaintiff in the plaintiff's foreign forum on the same facts, comity may suggest that one of the forums should dismiss or stay the matter in respect of the other. The U.S. court may consider both forums to be proper forums, but the foreign forum to be a more convenient, and dismiss the matter under the doctrine known as *forum non conveniens*. See Section 2.4. That is a doctrine generally limited to common law nations. Civil law legal systems usually reject *forum non conveniens* in favor of the position that a court vested of jurisdiction must go forward with the case. A court alternatively may believe it is the *only* appropriate forum, and issue an anti-suit injunction (see Section 6.2) against the defendant, ordering withdrawal from the suit it filed abroad.

§ 2.3 Forum Selection Clauses: Arbitration

Given the absence, discussed above, of an international agreement on enforcement of court judgments, the selection of arbitration versus litigation for dispute settlement is greatly incentivized by the 1958 New York Convention on the Recognition and Enforcement of Arbitral Awards. Widely adopted, the New York Convention provides judicial pathways for enforcement of foreign commercial arbitration agreements and awards. In the United States, federal courts have exclusive jurisdiction for these purposes. See Section 3.8.

Forum selection clauses are used to designate arbitration in lieu of judicial resolution. In many jurisdictions, these clauses may conflict with provisions alleged to give exclusive jurisdiction to courts over "mandatory law." See Section 3.3. But two U.S. Supreme Court 5–4 decisions involving arbitration selection clauses in antitrust and securities cases upheld arbitration despite such arguments.[36] These cases involved international agreements, commonly resolved by arbitration. The need for predictability in international commerce

---

[36] Scherk v. Alberto-Culver Co., 417 U.S. 506, 94 S.Ct. 2449, 41 L.Ed.2d 270 (1974) (securities law issues), Mitsubishi Motors Corp. v. Soler Chrysler-Plymouth, 473 U.S. 614, 105 S.Ct. 3346, 87 L.Ed.2d 444 (1985) (antitrust issues).

may be persuasive in overriding notions that the U.S. Congress meant to restrict application of the law to U.S. courts.

Litigation versus arbitration may be viewed by different institutions dealing with specific legal issues. Banks dealing with letters of credit use arbitration as a longstanding preference, as does generally the securities industry. It is important for U.S. lawyers representing clients engaged in a dispute with a foreign party to be able to understand not only the characteristics of the various choices of dispute resolution, but how opposing foreign counsel may view the alternatives.

Choosing arbitration to settle international business disputes avoids litigation pitfalls. Personal and subject matter jurisdiction (see Chapter 5) are not an issue, service of process is not an issue (see Section 6.1), *forum non conveniens* (see Section 2.4 below) is not an issue, foreign sovereign immunity (see Chapter 7) is not an issue, and often contentious litigation discovery rules (see Chapter 6) are not an issue.

What's not to like about international business arbitration? For an extended answer to that question by some leading academics, see Section 3.1 titled "Why Arbitrate?" One major problem with arbitration is that the limited discovery permitted may hinder fact development. Thus, an important criterion for choosing litigation or arbitration will be the relative need for this type of fact development in your client's case, and in your opponent's case.

Much of the analysis of the utility of arbitration goes back to the original drafting of choice of forum clauses. It is at that time that each attorney should consider whether to choose a tribunal located in a New York Convention Contracting State, where the assets of the other party are most likely to be found, and whether that location is in a Contracting State—as well as the competence, impartiality, cost, language, procedural rules, method of selection etc., of the proposed arbitral tribunal. See Sections 3.1 and 3.2.

Remember that both parties must agree if litigation is not to be used and arbitration substituted. The reception of a suggestion to use arbitration will depend upon what the parties believe the most likely judicial forum will be if no agreement is reached. See Chapter 5. A determination as to what court or courts have jurisdiction in the absence of agreement will allow the parties to make a comparison between arbitration and courts as a choice of forum.

§ 2.4 Forum Non Conveniens

The *forum non conveniens* doctrine is a creature of equity and focused on venue. It is rooted in international comity, an abstention doctrine deferring to foreign state law and sovereignty, including judicial sovereignty.[37] Forum non conveniens and international comity doctrines allow a U.S. court to dismiss a case that it believes is better brought in another forum, but not apparently if the parties have by contract selected a U.S. court forum and chosen a U.S. state law to govern that contract.[38]

Many cases are brought in the United States for no reason other than that appears to be where the rainbow ends in a pot of gold—called punitive damages. U.S. lawyers are notorious for going abroad to sign-up foreign plaintiffs for a suit in the United States. Shopping in the United States is a major pastime. It has more recently included foreigners shopping not for goods, but for a favorite forum. To quote Lord Denning of Britain: "As a moth is drawn to light, so is a litigant drawn to the United States. If he can only get his case into their courts, he stands to win a fortune."[39]

Forum non conveniens is a doctrine of common law, commenced and developed in cases rather than legislation. The U.S. doctrine has origins in *Gulf Oil Corp. v. Gilbert*,[40] a case involving two U.S. forum choices. Even so it has had immense impact on the use of the theory in international litigation—when the alternate forums are from two different countries. In *Gilbert*, the Supreme Court allowed courts to decline to exercise jurisdiction where public and private factors favored another forum.

This theory was adopted in two important international cases. First, in *Piper Aircraft Co. v. Reyno*,[41] a court granted a *forum non conveniens* motion to dismiss a suit in the United States in favor of Scotland, where the plaintiffs represented Scottish decedents for a crash of a U.S. made aircraft flown by a Scottish pilot that crashed in Scotland. Scots law was clearly less favorable, but the Court significantly negated the consideration of relative favorableness of the law. Piper also indicated that a foreign plaintiff's choice of a U.S. forum was entitled to less deference (because presumptively more inconvenient) than the same choice by a U.S. plaintiff.

---

[37] Hilton v. Guyot, 159 U.S. 113 (1895). *See* Ungaro-Benages v. Dresdner Bank AG, 379 F.3d 1227 (11th Cir. 2004) and Finanz AG Zurich v. Banco Eonomico, 192 F.3d 240 (2d Cir. 1999).

[38] GDG Acquisitions LLC v. Belize, 749 F.3d 1024 (11th Cir. 2014). *See* Atlantic Marine Construction Co. v. U.S. Dist. Ct. for W. Dist. of Texas, 134 S.Ct. 568 (2013).

[39] Smith Kline & French Labs. v. Block (1983) 2 All E.R. 72, 74.

[40] 330 U.S. 501, 67 S.Ct. 839, 91 L.Ed. 1055 (1947).

[41] 454 U.S. 235, 102 S.Ct. 252, 70 L.Ed.2d 419 (1981). Accord, Myers v. The Boeing Company, 115 Wn.2d 123 (1990) (Boeing plane crash over Pacific, liability to be determined in Japan); U.S.O. Corp. v. Mizuho Holding Co., 547 F.3d 749 (7th Cir. 2008) (dismissal to Japanese forum upheld).

Second, in *In re Union Carbide Corp. Gas Plant Disaster,*[42] the trial court dismissed a case brought in *parens patriae* by the Government of India on behalf of numerous Indian nationals injured in an explosion in the Union Carbide subsidiary plant in Bhopal, India. The court accepted as conditions for the dismissal of the $6 billion suit Union Carbide's agreement to submit to personal and subject matter jurisdiction in India, waiver of any Indian statute of limitations, submission in full to U.S. style discovery, and mandatory payment of any resulting Indian judgment. Conditions of these kinds have become common in *forum non conveniens* dismissals. On appeal, the Second Circuit declared the discovery and mandatory payment conditions unduly burdensome. Litigation in India generated a settlement of about $500 million. It is estimated that less than $5 million actually reached the injured persons.

The *forum non conveniens* test has evolved to include several considerations. There must be an available and adequate alternative forum. The plaintiff's choice is weighed against all private interests. When private interests are generally equal, public interests are considered. Each of these has been subject to development in the case law, particularly as the granting of *forum non conveniens* is treated as a final, immediately appealable judgment, but a denial is not an immediately appealable order.[43] Some U.S. states have more demanding criterion, such as Delaware's requirement that the defendant demonstrate "overwhelming hardship."[44] Such states become magnets for foreign plaintiffs injured abroad, with their lawyers pursuing strategies that avoid removal from state to federal courts.

Available and Adequate Alternative Forum

The law of any alternate forum, whether common or civil law based, will be different from that where the suit was filed. That is not sufficient in itself to find the alternative forum inadequate. *Gilbert* held that dismissal is allowed only when holding the trial in the forum poses a heavy burden on the defendant or the court, and the plaintiff is unable to note sufficiently convincing reasons for his choice. Often the choice is made to obtain punitive damages and obtain representation on a contingent fee basis. Neither is sufficient justification for retaining the suit in a U.S. forum chosen by a foreign plaintiff.

---

[42] 809 F.2d 195 (2d Cir. 1987), *cert. denied,* 484 U.S. 871, 108 S.Ct. 199, 98 L.Ed.2d 150 (1987).

[43] Van Cauwenberghe v. Baird, 486 U.S. 517 (1988).

[44] *See* Ison v. E.I. Dupont de Nemours, 729 A.2d 832 (Del. 1999).

Availability has traditionally been limited to whether the law of the foreign nation provides jurisdiction over the issue and parties, with some consideration also of procedural differences. But it is currently also addressing whether any alleged lack of availability is due to the plaintiff's actions. See the coverage of Latin America below.

Adequacy, the second related issue, usually considers whether the foreign forum recognizes theories of action that the United States recognizes, such as strict liability, antitrust, class actions or consumer protection. But adequacy also has become enmeshed with considering whether the foreign forum is so corrupt, inefficient, inadequate and/or intimidating, that it would be unjust to transfer the matter abroad only to meet a certain doom.[45] Note the irony that in *forum non conveniens* disputes it is the U.S. defendants who sing praises of foreign judicial systems, which the foreign plaintiffs seek to trash. Courts do not like to classify other nations' courts as incapable of providing justice, but the reality is that there are such courts. See the coverage of *Suspect Judicial Systems* in Section 1.1. In 2013, largely because of security issues in Pakistan, the Fourth Circuit ruled Pakistan did not provide an adequate alternative forum.[46]

Private and Public Interest Factors

In evaluating *forum non conveniens* motions, U.S. courts consider both private and public interest factors.[47] Such factors may overcome the strong presumption favoring the plaintiff's initial choice of forum, though less so if the plaintiff is foreign.[48] Private factors include where evidence is located and getting it to the forum; the movement, inconvenience and emotional impact of bringing parties, witnesses and experts to the forum; issues of language, including the need to translate documents, depositions and testimony; the ability to implead third-party defendants; whether the defendant can be sued abroad; the plaintiff's motives in suing in U.S. courts; the location of assets should plaintiff prevail; and implications from fragmenting the suit if it were dismissed in favor of different nations of different plaintiffs, and non-U.S. defendants.[49]

---

[45] *See, e.g.*, Loya v. Starwood Hotels & Resorts Worldwide, 583 F.3d 656 (9th Cir. 2009) (U.S. plaintiff's case for injury in Mexico dismissed).

[46] DiFederico v. Marriot Inc., 714 F.3d 796 (4th Cir. 2013).

[47] *See* Piper Aircraft Co v. Reyno, 454 U.S. 235, 102 S.Ct. 252, 70 L.Ed.2d 419 (1981); Gilbert v. Gulf Oil Co., 330 U.S. 501 (1947).

[48] *See* Piper Aircraft Co v. Reyno, 454 U.S. 235, 102 S.Ct. 252, 70 L.Ed.2d 419 (1981).

[49] *See* Carijano v. Occidental Petroleum Corp., 643 F.3d 1216 (9th Cir. 2011) (*fnc* dismissal reversed, stressing questions of enforceability of foreign forum judgment).

Public interest factors, on the other hand, usually involve matters of public policy or legal certainty. Public factors considered include each nation's interest in being the location of the litigation, the burden on the court system and interest of jurors in serving, the need to apply foreign law, and sometimes deterring U.S. companies from producing defective products for export. In a surprising contrast, U.S. antitrust law claims are not subject to *forum non conveniens* dismissals,[50] but U.S. securities law claims are.[51] Foreign sovereigns may raise *forum non conveniens* motions under the FSIA.[52]

Foreign Law and Litigation, FNC Conditions

Often a court will inquire extensively about the substance of the foreign law applicable to the case. If the motion to dismiss is denied, the court may have to apply that foreign law. This alone may be a major factor in the court's decision to grant the *forum non conveniens* motion, especially where the foreign law is that of a nation without a highly developed sector dealing with civil litigation. Whether or not the court considers the foreign law in its *forum non conveniens* determination, it will almost assuredly have to address that issue if the matter remains in the U.S. court. Discovery and payment conditions may be struck down as unreasonable.[53]

Courts almost always condition a dismissal subject to some promises from the defendant. The most prevalent is a promise by the defendant to submit to service of process and jurisdiction of the foreign court. Added may be a waiver of any right to use the foreign statute of limitations, but that may not be subject to waiver under foreign law. The next most common condition is an agreement to pay any judgment rendered in the foreign court, a promise that may be regretted if the foreign nation renders a very large judgment.

In most *forum non conveniens* cases the litigation has been initiated only in the United States. But there are many instances where the same matter is the subject of litigation in the United States and another nation. The plaintiff and defendant in the U.S. court may be, respectively, the defendant and plaintiff in the foreign nation. This is called parallel litigation. A U.S. court could dismiss the case on *forum non conveniens* grounds, but also might stay under the doctrine of *lis pendens* for reasons of comity, allowing the other

---

Compare Altmann v. Austria, 317 F.3d 954 (9th Cir. 2002) (*fnc* dismissal upheld, U.S. plaintiffs needs, expense and age emphasized).

[50] *See* Laker Airways v. Pan American Airways, 568 F.Supp. 811 (D.D.C. 1983)

[51] *See* Howe v. Goldcorp Investments, 946 F.2d 944 (1st Cir. 1991).

[52] Verlinden BV v. Central Bank of Nigeria, 461 U.S. 480 (1983).

[53] See coverage of the *Bhopal* litigation at note 41.

court to proceed and avoiding a race for the first judgment. See Section 6.2.

Be Careful What You Ask For

Motions for *forum non conveniens* rulings are presented by defendants as part of litigation strategy. If they are successful, the case is sometimes moved to a remote forum where the case dies. The death is because the U.S. attorneys no longer have visions of large punitive damage awards. Indeed, they may have little involvement as attorneys in the foreign forum.

The defendants in both the *Piper* and *Bhopal* cases were obviously pleased with the outcome. The *Piper* case has never gone to trial in Scotland. The *Bhopal* case resulted in a settlement far less than what might have been a jury's award in the United States, and little of the settlement funds have ever reached the injured plaintiffs. Moreover, the Supreme Court has decided that *forum non conveniens* dismissals can be granted prior to consideration of personal and subject matter jurisdiction (see Chapter 5)... convenient for the court and the litigants.[54]

The law of *forum non conveniens* seems sufficiently elastic that it is hard to predict the outcome, and additionally hard to predict possible conditions that the court may impose upon the defendant in return for granting the *forum non conveniens* motion. The law is a product of equity, and is somewhat amorphous and difficult to foresee. Courts have thus increasingly asked about the nature of the proceeding in the foreign forum, especially about the nature of the process. If there is a viable legal system that provides for the resolution of disputes of the form presented, the *forum non conveniens* motion may be granted. Even so, plaintiffs may elect to file in a U.S. state court, as did a Singaporean plaintiff filing and ultimately prevailing in Texas.[55]

One problem for defendants and their attorneys in obtaining a successful *forum non conveniens* ruling is that control over the case may be diminished or lost. If the case is moved abroad, the attorneys likely will not be able to appear before the foreign court, and foreign counsel must be hired. The U.S. defendant will have to learn about the foreign law and legal system.

Chevron's successful invocation of *forum non conveniens* in an environmental pollution dispute[56] resulted in a multi-billion dollar

---

[54] Sinochem Int'l Co. v. Malaysia Int'l Shipping Corp., 127 S.Ct. 1184 (2007). Accord, GDG Acquisitions LLC v. Belize, 749 F.3d 1024 (11th Cir. 2014).

[55] *See* Chick Kam Choo v. Exxon Corp., 486 U.S. 140 (1988) (denying a federal injunction against the Texas proceedings).

[56] Aguinda v. Texaco Inc., 303 F.2d 470 (2d Cir. 2002).

2013 judgment against it in Ecuador. Chevron has spent a small fortune defending itself against collection of this judgment around the world. A federal district court opinion found the Ecuadorean judge had been bribed and his opinion fraudulently "ghost-written" by plaintiffs' U.S. attorneys.[57] Chevron successfully utilized arbitration proceedings to obtain an interim award ordering Ecuador not to seek enforcement of the judgment until a final decision is reached, but failed to persuade U.S. courts to enjoin enforcement globally in the absence of enforcement proceedings in the United States.[58]

As Chevron suggests, the better choice for a defendant may be to keep the matter in the U.S. court, but to seek application of foreign law. Many such cases merit the application of foreign law, and when a court so rules the difficulty of proving foreign law may be an impossible burden for the plaintiff. See Section 6.3.

For an analogous case also suggesting be careful what you wish for, see *Hubei Gezhouba Sanlian Industrial Ltd. v. Robinson Helicopter Inc.*[59] In *Robinson,* a U.S. helicopter firm succeeded in obtaining a *forum non conveniens* dismissal against Chinese parties alleging damages from a helicopter crash inside China. This dismissal led to a default judgment of about $650,000 against the firm in Chinese court proceedings. This judgment was held enforceable in California under the Uniform Foreign Money Judgments Recognition Act (UFMJRA, see Section 8.1).

Forum Non Conveniens and Europe

Civil law jurisdictions as a rule disallow court divestiture of jurisdiction: Their courts must proceed with the litigations properly before them. The common law theory of *forum non conveniens* has its origins in Scottish and later English law. Two cases, one in the House of Lords and the other in the European Court of Justice, cast a shadow on the future of the theory in the United Kingdom.

In *Lubbe and Others v. Cape PLC,*[60] Lord Bingham stated that "public interest considerations not related to the private interests of the parties and the ends of justice have no bearing on the decision which the Court has to make." Lord Hope added "I would decline to follow those judges in the United States who would decide issues as to where a case ought to be tried on broad grounds of public policy: see Union Carbide Corporation Gas plant Disaster at Bhopal, and Piper Aircraft Co. v. Reyno. . . [T]he Court is not equipped to conduct

[57] Chevron Corp. v. Donziger, 833 F.3d 74 (2d Cir. 2016).

[58] Chevron Corp. v. Najanjo, 667 F.3d 332 (2d Cir. 2012).

[59] 2009 WL 2190197 (C.D. Cal. 2009).

[60] [2000] 2 Lloyd's Rep. 383 (H.L.).

the kind of inquiry and assessment of the international as well as domestic implications that would be needed if it were to follow that approach."

While this case limited the scope of *forum non conveniens*, the 2005 European Court of Justice decision in *Owusu v. Jackson*,[61] affects it use much more extensively. The EU Court found the use of the theory to be inconsistent with the U.K.'s obligations under the EU Regulation on Jurisdiction and the Recognition and Enforcement of Judgments in Civil and Commercial Matters (the Brussels Regulation, see Section 8.2). The doctrine of *forum non conveniens* was held incompatible with the legal certainty provided by the Brussels Regulation that allows a defendant to foresee which courts in which he may be sued. The Regulation prohibits EU courts from declining jurisdiction on the ground that a non-member state would be the more appropriate forum.

The case involved a British national and domiciliary (Owusu) against another British domiciliary (Jackson) and other Jamaican defendants for an accident occurring at a Jamaican villa rented by Jackson to Owusu. The decision suggests that a U.K. court could not dismiss a matter brought by a U.S. plaintiff in a U.K. court on *forum non conveniens* grounds, a theory that is an important part of the law in both nations. The EU Court of Justice said that jurisdiction could not be declined "even if the jurisdiction of no other Contracting State is in issue or the proceedings have no connecting factors to any other Contracting State."

Forum Non Conveniens and Latin America

There is a movement, largely in Latin America, called Parlatino, which tries to block convenient forum litigation after a *forum non conveniens* dismissal occurs in a U.S. court. This movement arose out of a major case involving plaintiffs from twelve nations.[62] The theory is apparently that the filing in the United States terminates what would otherwise be valid jurisdiction in the home nation, and therefore the U.S. court should not dismiss the case because there is no available foreign forum. Parlatino has not been successful, as the *Bridgestone/Firestone* case study below illustrates.

Because it has had no impact on dismissals based on *forum non conveniens*, some of the nations have tried another tactic—they have changed their domestic law to allow the damages law of the dismissing country to be used in the case when refiled in their nation. That has led to some very large judgments, such as in the Chevron example above. But when attempts to enforce such judgments have

61 C–281/02 [2005] E.C.R. 0.

62 Delgado v. Shell Oil Co., 890 F.Supp. 1324 (S.D. Tex. 1995).

been made in U.S. courts, grounds for non-recognition have blocked them.

A Case Study: Bridgestone/Firestone and Ford

Accidents involving Ford Explorers equipped with Bridgestone/Firestone (B/F) tires occurred in a number of Latin American countries. Suits were filed in the United States, in both state and federal courts, and most of the latter were consolidated in Indiana.[63] Defendants sought dismissal of the 121 Venezuelan and Colombian plaintiff cases before the court on *forum non conveniens* grounds. The Venezuelan and Colombian cases were addressed separately, the Venezuelan plaintiffs arguing that Venezuelan law foreclosed the Venezuelan courts from asserting jurisdiction when a Venezuelan citizen chose to initiate the suit abroad rather than in Venezuela. Indiana federal district court judge Barker ruled that the Venezuelan courts were not available because they did not have jurisdiction, and dismissed the suit on *forum non conveniens* grounds.

What the court did not address was why Venezuela might enact a law that seemed to deprive its citizens of access to Venezuelan courts. The law in question is Venezuela's Statute on Private International Law. Plaintiffs' expert noted that Article 39 provided that "the first forum for bringing suit against a non-domiciliary defendant is the country where the defendant is domiciled." Because such a law could not create jurisdiction in the United States, the Venezuelan law includes exceptions. One, in Article 40(4), provides that "Venezuelan courts shall have jurisdiction to hear trials resulting from the actions in property when the parties should expressly or tacitly submit to their jurisdiction." That reads very much like a fairly common provision in the law of many nations that allows parties to choose a forum in a contract. It is an affirmation of the use of a forum selection clause by providing that the courts shall recognize such provisions.

But plaintiff's expert responded that 40(4) requires *both* of the parties to provide an express submission to the Venezuelan courts subsequent to a *forum non conveniens* dismissal. The defendants would of course agree to such submission. But the plaintiffs would not because refusal held out hope of returning to the land of large damages. Unfortunately, Judge Barker was unaware of any of the background that would have illustrated the recent attempts in Latin America to nullify U.S. *forum non conveniens* based motions to dismiss that were the core of the plaintiffs' arguments.

---

[63] In re Bridgestone/Firestone, Inc., Tires Products Liability Litigation, 190 F.Supp.2d 1125 (S.D.Ind. 2002).

Parlatino

Arguments regarding the lack of availability of the courts of Panama, Costa Rica, Guatemala and Ecuador, based on the absence of jurisdiction of the foreign plaintiffs' domestic forum, if a U.S. court dismissed a case brought by the foreign plaintiff on *forum non conveniens* grounds, arose in *Patrickson v. Dole Food Company, Inc.*[64] The court considered each of the four nation's laws and dismissed the case on *forum non conveniens*, finding that the plaintiffs had the right to file the action in their home courts, notwithstanding varying degrees of attempts to remove local jurisdiction following a U.S. dismissal on *forum non conveniens* grounds.

The Ecuadorian attempt also was raised in another case, *In re Ecuadorian Shrimp Litigation*,[65] in a Florida state court. The court dismissed the action on *forum non conveniens* grounds and the plaintiffs returned to Ecuador first to seek the enactment of Law 55, which stated that if an Ecuadorian chose first to initiate a suit outside Ecuador and it was dismissed, Ecuadorian jurisdiction was terminated.

With that law in place the plaintiffs took the unusual step of filing suit solely to then seek its dismissal. With the dismissals in hand, the plaintiffs were soon back in the Florida court asking for reassertion of jurisdiction. The court rejected Ecuador's attempt to "force" the Florida court "to expend scarce and valuable resources on cases that have no connection with the state's interests," suggesting that "if Ecuador refuses to provide a forum to its own citizens to litigate claims arising from acts occurring in Ecuador that is its prerogative."

Ecuador's passage of Law 55 was consistent with a movement in a few Latin American nations to assist their nationals in responding to *forum non conveniens* dismissals in U.S. courts. The Latin American Parliament (Parlatino), is little known in the United States. It is an organization of a few members of some of the Latin American legislatures apparently organized after a U.S. federal district court in Texas dismissed a case on *forum non conveniens* grounds involving plaintiffs from twelve nations, including Costa Rica, Ecuador, Guatemala, Honduras, Nicaragua and Panama[66] for injuries allegedly from use of a nemotocide on their farms. Some of the rejected plaintiffs returned to their nations not to initiate suit but to find some way back to the U.S. court.

---

[64] Civil No. 97–01516 (Haw. 1998).

[65] Case No. 94–10138–27 (1999).

[66] Delgado v. Shell Oil Co., 890 F.Supp. 1324 (S.D.Tex. 1995).

In 1998 Parlatino challenged *forum non conveniens* by drafting a brief Model Law on International Jurisdiction and Applicable Law to Tort Liability. The law reads:

> Art. 1. National and international jurisdiction. The petition that is validly filed, according to both legal systems, in the defendant's domiciliary court, extinguishes national jurisdiction. The latter is only reborn if the plaintiff desists of his foreign petition and files a new petition in the country, in a completely free and spontaneous way.
>
> Art. 2. International tort liability. Damages. In cases of international tort liability, the national court may, at the plaintiff's request, apply to damages and to the pecuniary sanctions related to such damages, the relevant standards and amounts of the pertinent foreign law.

Parlatino suggested that its proposed law would allow a plaintiff to choose a foreign forum and that the foreign "judge will not be able to close the doors of the [foreign] court on him as, for instance, has been happening with the theory of forum non conveniens." Since none of the Parlatino nations recognizes the doctrine of *forum non conveniens*, the reference of foreclosure can only refer to the United States, or other foreign courts recognizing that theory. But it is not the parliaments of other nations that open or close the doors to the U.S. courts. U.S. judges have discretion to decide *forum non conveniens* based motions to dismiss that civil law system judges do not share. But failure to possess such discretion is hardly a justifiable reason to attempt to abolish it from abroad. Parlatino has been careful not to fully extinguish jurisdiction of a plaintiff from a member state when it files abroad. Each plaintiff is presented with an escape valve.

The Parlatino Model Law allows one of its citizens who has been dismissed abroad, presumably for any reason, whether it be lack of subject matter or personal jurisdiction, statute of limitations or *forum non conveniens*, to file an action in the home court, as long as it is done in a "completely free and spontaneous way." If a suit has been dismissed in the U.S. court, the foreign plaintiff is "completely free" to decide what to do next. That may be to propose settlement negotiations with the other parties who were the defendants in the dismissed suits, to appeal the dismissal to the appropriate appellate court in the United States, to file a suit in any other country including but not necessarily that of the plaintiff, or to do absolutely nothing.

Two years after the Indiana decision in *Bridgestone/Firestone* (above) the federal district court for the South District of Texas analyzed and rejected the reasoning of the Indiana court on the issue of availability, and found Venezuela to be an available forum.[67] The Texas court viewed the Venezuelan plaintiffs' argument as being based on "unwillingness" rather than unavailability. The plaintiffs were unwilling to file suit in Venezuela, whether before or after the action filed in the United States, a motivation that the court would not find justifying characterizing Venezuela as an unavailable forum.

Perhaps the most curious feature of the movement of Parlatino is its members' apparent belief that there is no hope of reforming Latin American legal systems so that they might be able to deal effectively with complex tort litigation. Some nations have or prefer to develop that ability and have consequently rejected the Parlatino theory (e.g., Mexico, Chile), some have that ability but seem not to believe in their systems (e.g., Costa Rica), and some have very good reason to believe that their systems are currently incapable of providing due process in any such action (e.g., Guatemala, Bolivia, Nicaragua, etc.).

In some countries, the laws on the books provide a very effective system for the resolution of such disputes, but the system functions so corruptly, inefficiently, or subject to intimidation or political influence that its plaintiffs are justified in being litigation immigrants. The ongoing question facing U.S. courts is whether they are legal or illegal litigation immigrants.

§ 2.5 Hague Convention on Choice of Court Agreements (2005)

CHAPTER I—SCOPE AND DEFINITIONS

Article 1. Scope

1. This Convention shall apply in international cases to exclusive choice of court agreements concluded in civil or commercial matters.

2. For the purposes of Chapter II, a case is international unless the parties are resident in the same Contracting State and the relationship of the parties and all other elements relevant to the dispute, regardless of the location of the chosen court, are connected only with that State.

3. For the purposes of Chapter III, a case is international where recognition or enforcement of a foreign judgment is sought.

Article 2. Exclusions from scope

1. This Convention shall not apply to exclusive choice of court agreements—

[67] Morales v. Ford Motor Co., 313 F.Supp.2d 672 (S.D.Tex. 2004).

(a) to which a natural person acting primarily for personal, family or household purposes (a consumer) is a party;

(b) relating to contracts of employment, including collective agreements.

2. This Convention shall not apply to the following matters—

(a) the status and legal capacity of natural persons;

(b) maintenance obligations;

(c) other family law matters, including matrimonial property regimes and other rights or obligations arising out of marriage or similar relationships;

(d) wills and succession;

(e) insolvency, composition and analogous matters;

(f) the carriage of passengers and goods;

(g) marine pollution, limitation of liability for maritime claims, general average, and emergency towage and salvage;

(h) anti-trust (competition) matters;

(i) liability for nuclear damage;

(j) claims for personal injury brought by or on behalf of natural persons;

(k) tort or delict claims for damage to tangible property that do not arise from a contractual relationship;

(*l*) rights in rem in immovable property, and tenancies of immovable property;

(m) the validity, nullity, or dissolution of legal persons, and the validity of decisions of their organs;

(n) the validity of intellectual property rights other than copyright and related rights;

(*o*) infringement of intellectual property rights other than copyright and related rights, except where infringement proceedings are brought for breach of a contract between the parties relating to such rights, or could have been brought for breach of that contract;

(p) the validity of entries in public registers.

3. Notwithstanding paragraph 2, proceedings are not excluded from the scope of this Convention where a matter excluded under that paragraph arises merely as a preliminary question and not as an object of the proceedings. In particular, the mere fact that a matter

excluded under paragraph 2 arises by way of defence does not exclude proceedings from the Convention, if that matter is not an object of the proceedings.

4. This Convention shall not apply to arbitration and related proceedings.

5. Proceedings are not excluded from the scope of this Convention by the mere fact that a State, including a government, a governmental agency or any person acting for a State, is a party thereto.

6. Nothing in this Convention shall affect privileges and immunities of States or of international organisations, in respect of themselves and of their property.

Article 3. Exclusive choice of court agreements

For the purposes of this Convention—

(a) "exclusive choice of court agreement" means an agreement concluded by two or more parties that meets the requirements of paragraph c) and designates, for the purpose of deciding disputes which have arisen or may arise in connection with a particular legal relationship, the courts of one Contracting State or one or more specific courts of one Contracting State to the exclusion of the jurisdiction of any other courts;

(b) a choice of court agreement which designates the courts of one Contracting State or one or more specific courts of one Contracting State shall be deemed to be exclusive unless the parties have expressly provided otherwise;

(c) an exclusive choice of court agreement must be concluded or documented—

(i) in writing; or

(ii) by any other means of communication which renders information accessible so as to be usable for subsequent reference;

(d) an exclusive choice of court agreement that forms part of a contract shall be treated as an agreement independent of the other terms of the contract. The validity of the exclusive choice of court agreement cannot be contested solely on the ground that the contract is not valid.

Article 4. Other definitions

1. In this Convention, "judgment" means any decision on the merits given by a court, whatever it may be called, including a decree or order, and a determination of costs or expenses by the court

(including an officer of the court), provided that the determination relates to a decision on the merits which may be recognised or enforced under this Convention. An interim measure of protection is not a judgment.

2. For the purposes of this Convention, an entity or person other than a natural person shall be considered to be resident in the State—

(a) where it has its statutory seat;

(b) under whose law it was incorporated or formed;

(c) where it has its central administration; or

(d) where it has its principal place of business.

CHAPTER II—JURISDICTION

Article 5. Jurisdiction of the chosen court

1. The court or courts of a Contracting State designated in an exclusive choice of court agreement shall have jurisdiction to decide a dispute to which the agreement applies, unless the agreement is null and void under the law of that State.

2. A court that has jurisdiction under paragraph 1 shall not decline to exercise jurisdiction on the ground that the dispute should be decided in a court of another State.

3. The preceding paragraphs shall not affect rules—

(a) on jurisdiction related to subject matter or to the value of the claim;

(b) on the internal allocation of jurisdiction among the courts of a Contracting State. However, where the chosen court has discretion as to whether to transfer a case, due consideration should be given to the choice of the parties.

Article 6. Obligations of a court not chosen

A court of a Contracting State other than that of the chosen court shall suspend or dismiss proceedings to which an exclusive choice of court agreement applies unless—

(a) the agreement is null and void under the law of the State of the chosen court;

(b) a party lacked the capacity to conclude the agreement under the law of the State of the court seised;

(c) giving effect to the agreement would lead to a manifest injustice or would be manifestly contrary to the public policy of the State of the court seised;

(d) for exceptional reasons beyond the control of the parties, the agreement cannot reasonably be performed; or

(e) the chosen court has decided not to hear the case.

Article 7. Interim measures of protection

Interim measures of protection are not governed by this Convention. This Convention neither requires nor precludes the grant, refusal or termination of interim measures of protection by a court of a Contracting State and does not affect whether or not a party may request or a court should grant, refuse or terminate such measures.

CHAPTER III—RECOGNITION AND ENFORCEMENT

Article 8. Recognition and enforcement

1. A judgment given by a court of a Contracting State designated in an exclusive choice of court agreement shall be recognised and enforced in other Contracting States in accordance with this Chapter. Recognition or enforcement may be refused only on the grounds specified in this Convention.

2. Without prejudice to such review as is necessary for the application of the provisions of this Chapter, there shall be no review of the merits of the judgment given by the court of origin. The court addressed shall be bound by the findings of fact on which the court of origin based its jurisdiction, unless the judgment was given by default.

3. A judgment shall be recognised only if it has effect in the State of origin, and shall be enforced only if it is enforceable in the State of origin.

4. Recognition or enforcement may be postponed or refused if the judgment is the subject of review in the State of origin or if the time limit for seeking ordinary review has not expired. A refusal does not prevent a subsequent application for recognition or enforcement of the judgment.

5. This Article shall also apply to a judgment given by a court of a Contracting State pursuant to a transfer of the case from the chosen court in that Contracting State as permitted by Article 5, paragraph 3. However, where the chosen court had discretion as to whether to transfer the case to another court, recognition or enforcement of the judgment may be refused against a party who objected to the transfer in a timely manner in the State of origin.

Article 9. Refusal of recognition or enforcement

Recognition or enforcement may be refused if—

(a) the agreement was null and void under the law of the State of the chosen court, unless the chosen court has determined that the agreement is valid;

(b) a party lacked the capacity to conclude the agreement under the law of the requested State;

(c) the document which instituted the proceedings or an equivalent document, including the essential elements of the claim,

(i) was not notified to the defendant in sufficient time and in such a way as to enable him to arrange for his defence, unless the defendant entered an appearance and presented his case without contesting notification in the court of origin, provided that the law of the State of origin permitted notification to be contested; or

(ii) was notified to the defendant in the requested State in a manner that is incompatible with fundamental principles of the requested State concerning service of documents;

(d) the judgment was obtained by fraud in connection with a matter of procedure;

(e) recognition or enforcement would be manifestly incompatible with the public policy of the requested State, including situations where the specific proceedings leading to the judgment were incompatible with fundamental principles of procedural fairness of that State;

(f) the judgment is inconsistent with a judgment given in the requested State in a dispute between the same parties; or

(g) the judgment is inconsistent with an earlier judgment given in another State between the same parties on the same cause of action, provided that the earlier judgment fulfils the conditions necessary for its recognition in the requested State.

Article 10. Preliminary questions

1. Where a matter excluded under Article 2, paragraph 2, or under Article 21, arose as a preliminary question, the ruling on that question shall not be recognised or enforced under this Convention.

2. Recognition or enforcement of a judgment may be refused if, and to the extent that, the judgment was based on a ruling on a matter excluded under Article 2, paragraph 2.

3. However, in the case of a ruling on the validity of an intellectual property right other than copyright or a related right, recognition or enforcement of a judgment may be refused or postponed under the preceding paragraph only where—

(a) that ruling is inconsistent with a judgment or a decision of a competent authority on that matter given in the State under the law of which the intellectual property right arose; or

(b) proceedings concerning the validity of the intellectual property right are pending in that State.

4. Recognition or enforcement of a judgment may be refused if, and to the extent that, the judgment was based on a ruling on a matter excluded pursuant to a declaration made by the requested State under Article 21.

Article 11. Damages

1. Recognition or enforcement of a judgment may be refused if, and to the extent that, the judgment awards damages, including exemplary or punitive damages, that do not compensate a party for actual loss or harm suffered.

2. The court addressed shall take into account whether and to what extent the damages awarded by the court of origin serve to cover costs and expenses relating to the proceedings.

Article 12. Judicial settlements (transactions judiciaries)

Judicial settlements (transactions judiciaires) which a court of a Contracting State designated in an exclusive choice of court agreement has approved, or which have been concluded before that court in the course of proceedings, and which are enforceable in the same manner as a judgment in the State of origin, shall be enforced under this Convention in the same manner as a judgment.

Article 13. Documents to be produced

1. The party seeking recognition or applying for enforcement shall produce—

(a) a complete and certified copy of the judgment;

(b) the exclusive choice of court agreement, a certified copy thereof, or other evidence of its existence;

(c) if the judgment was given by default, the original or a certified copy of a document establishing that the document which instituted the proceedings or an equivalent document was notified to the defaulting party;

(d) any documents necessary to establish that the judgment has effect or, where applicable, is enforceable in the State of origin;

(e) in the case referred to in Article 12, a certificate of a court of the State of origin that the judicial settlement or a part of it is enforceable in the same manner as a judgment in the State of origin.

2. If the terms of the judgment do not permit the court addressed to verify whether the conditions of this Chapter have been complied with, that court may require any necessary documents.

3. An application for recognition or enforcement may be accompanied by a document, issued by a court (including an officer of the court) of the State of origin, in the form recommended and published by the Hague Conference on Private International Law.

4. If the documents referred to in this Article are not in an official language of the requested State, they shall be accompanied by a certified translation into an official language, unless the law of the requested State provides otherwise.

Article 14. Procedure

The procedure for recognition, declaration of enforceability or registration for enforcement, and the enforcement of the judgment, are governed by the law of the requested State unless this Convention provides otherwise. The court addressed shall act expeditiously.

Article 15. Severability

Recognition or enforcement of a severable part of a judgment shall be granted where recognition or enforcement of that part is applied for, or only part of the judgment is capable of being recognised or enforced under this Convention.

CHAPTER IV—GENERAL CLAUSES

Article 16. Transitional provisions

1. This Convention shall apply to exclusive choice of court agreements concluded after its entry into force for the State of the chosen court.

2. This Convention shall not apply to proceedings instituted before its entry into force for the State of the court seised.

Article 17. Contracts of insurance and reinsurance

1. Proceedings under a contract of insurance or reinsurance are not excluded from the scope of this Convention on the ground that the

contract of insurance or reinsurance relates to a matter to which this Convention does not apply.

2. Recognition and enforcement of a judgment in respect of liability under the terms of a contract of insurance or reinsurance may not be limited or refused on the ground that the liability under that contract includes liability to indemnify the insured or reinsured in respect of—

(a) a matter to which this Convention does not apply; or

(b) an award of damages to which Article 11 might apply.

Article 18. No legalisation

All documents forwarded or delivered under this Convention shall be exempt from legalisation or any analogous formality, including an Apostille.

Article 19. Declarations limiting jurisdiction

A State may declare that its courts may refuse to determine disputes to which an exclusive choice of court agreement applies if, except for the location of the chosen court, there is no connection between that State and the parties or the dispute.

Article 20. Declarations limiting recognition and enforcement

A State may declare that its courts may refuse to recognise or enforce a judgment given by a court of another Contracting State if the parties were resident in the requested State, and the relationship of the parties and all other elements relevant to the dispute, other than the location of the chosen court, were connected only with the requested State.

Article 21. Declarations with respect to specific matters

1. Where a State has a strong interest in not applying this Convention to a specific matter, that State may declare that it will not apply the Convention to that matter. The State making such a declaration shall ensure that the declaration is no broader than necessary and that the specific matter excluded is clearly and precisely defined.

2. With regard to that matter, the Convention shall not apply—

(a) in the Contracting State that made the declaration;

(b) in other Contracting States, where an exclusive choice of court agreement designates the courts, or one or more specific courts, of the State that made the declaration.

Article 22. Reciprocal declarations on non-exclusive choice of court agreements

1. A Contracting State may declare that its courts will recognise and enforce judgments given by courts of other Contracting States designated in a choice of court agreement concluded by two or more parties that meets the requirements of Article 3, paragraph c), and designates, for the purpose of deciding disputes which have arisen or may arise in connection with a particular legal relationship, a court or courts of one or more Contracting States (a non-exclusive choice of court agreement).

2. Where recognition or enforcement of a judgment given in a Contracting State that has made such a declaration is sought in another Contracting State that has made such a declaration, the judgment shall be recognised and enforced under this Convention, if—

(a) the court of origin was designated in a non-exclusive choice of court agreement;

(b) there exists neither a judgment given by any other court before which proceedings could be brought in accordance with the non-exclusive choice of court agreement, nor a proceeding pending between the same parties in any other such court on the same cause of action; and

(c) the court of origin was the court first seised.

Article 23. Uniform interpretation

In the interpretation of this Convention, regard shall be had to its international character and to the need to promote uniformity in its application.

Article 24. Review of operation of the Convention

The Secretary General of the Hague Conference on Private International Law shall at regular intervals make arrangements for—

(a) review of the operation of this Convention, including any declarations; and

(b) consideration of whether any amendments to this Convention are desirable.

Article 25. Non-unified legal systems

1. In relation to a Contracting State in which two or more systems of law apply in different territorial units with regard to any matter dealt with in this Convention—

(a) any reference to the law or procedure of a State shall be construed as referring, where appropriate, to the law or procedure in force in the relevant territorial unit;

(b) any reference to residence in a State shall be construed as referring, where appropriate, to residence in the relevant territorial unit;

(c) any reference to the court or courts of a State shall be construed as referring, where appropriate, to the court or courts in the relevant territorial unit;

(d) any reference to a connection with a State shall be construed as referring, where appropriate, to a connection with the relevant territorial unit.

2. Notwithstanding the preceding paragraph, a Contracting State with two or more territorial units in which different systems of law apply shall not be bound to apply this Convention to situations which involve solely such different territorial units.

3. A court in a territorial unit of a Contracting State with two or more territorial units in which different systems of law apply shall not be bound to recognise or enforce a judgment from another Contracting State solely because the judgment has been recognised or enforced in another territorial unit of the same Contracting State under this Convention.

4. This Article shall not apply to a Regional Economic Integration Organisation.

Article 26. Relationship with other international instruments

1. This Convention shall be interpreted so far as possible to be compatible with other treaties in force for Contracting States, whether concluded before or after this Convention.

2. This Convention shall not affect the application by a Contracting State of a treaty, whether concluded before or after this Convention, in cases where none of the parties is resident in a Contracting State that is not a Party to the treaty.

3. This Convention shall not affect the application by a Contracting State of a treaty that was concluded before this Convention entered into force for that Contracting State, if applying this Convention would be inconsistent with the obligations of that Contracting State to any non-Contracting State. This paragraph shall also apply to treaties that revise or replace a treaty concluded before this Convention entered into force for that Contracting State, except to

the extent that the revision or replacement creates new inconsistencies with this Convention.

4. This Convention shall not affect the application by a Contracting State of a treaty, whether concluded before or after this Convention, for the purposes of obtaining recognition or enforcement of a judgment given by a court of a Contracting State that is also a Party to that treaty. However, the judgment shall not be recognised or enforced to a lesser extent than under this Convention.

5. This Convention shall not affect the application by a Contracting State of a treaty which, in relation to a specific matter, governs jurisdiction or the recognition or enforcement of judgments, even if concluded after this Convention and even if all States concerned are Parties to this Convention. This paragraph shall apply only if the Contracting State has made a declaration in respect of the treaty under this paragraph. In the case of such a declaration, other Contracting States shall not be obliged to apply this Convention to that specific matter to the extent of any inconsistency, where an exclusive choice of court agreement designates the courts, or one or more specific courts, of the Contracting State that made the declaration.

6. This Convention shall not affect the application of the rules of a Regional Economic Integration Organisation that is a Party to this Convention, whether adopted before or after this Convention—

(a) where none of the parties is resident in a Contracting State that is not a Member State of the Regional Economic Integration Organisation;

(b) as concerns the recognition or enforcement of judgments as between Member States of the Regional Economic Integration Organisation.

CHAPTER V—FINAL CLAUSES

Article 27. Signature, ratification, acceptance, approval or accession

1. This Convention is open for signature by all States.

2. This Convention is subject to ratification, acceptance or approval by the signatory States.

3. This Convention is open for accession by all States.

4. Instruments of ratification, acceptance, approval or accession shall be deposited with the Ministry of Foreign Affairs of the Kingdom of the Netherlands, depositary of the Convention.

Article 28. Declarations with respect to non-unified legal systems

1. If a State has two or more territorial units in which different systems of law apply in relation to matters dealt with in this Convention, it may at the time of signature, ratification, acceptance, approval or accession declare that the Convention shall extend to all its territorial units or only to one or more of them and may modify this declaration by submitting another declaration at any time.

2. A declaration shall be notified to the depositary and shall state expressly the territorial units to which the Convention applies.

3. If a State makes no declaration under this Article, the Convention shall extend to all territorial units of that State.

4. This Article shall not apply to a Regional Economic Integration Organisation.

Article 29. Regional Economic Integration Organisations

1. A Regional Economic Integration Organisation which is constituted solely by sovereign States and has competence over some or all of the matters governed by this Convention may similarly sign, accept, approve or accede to this Convention. The Regional Economic Integration Organisation shall in that case have the rights and obligations of a Contracting State, to the extent that the Organisation has competence over matters governed by this Convention.

2. The Regional Economic Integration Organisation shall, at the time of signature, acceptance, approval or accession, notify the depositary in writing of the matters governed by this Convention in respect of which competence has been transferred to that Organisation by its Member States. The Organisation shall promptly notify the depositary in writing of any changes to its competence as specified in the most recent notice given under this paragraph.

3. For the purposes of the entry into force of this Convention, any instrument deposited by a Regional Economic Integration Organisation shall not be counted unless the Regional Economic Integration Organisation declares in accordance with Article 30 that its Member States will not be Parties to this Convention.

4. Any reference to a "Contracting State" or "State" in this Convention shall apply equally, where appropriate, to a Regional Economic Integration Organisation that is a Party to it.

Article 30. Accession by a Regional Economic Integration Organisation without its Member States

1. At the time of signature, acceptance, approval or accession, a Regional Economic Integration Organisation may declare that it exercises competence over all the matters governed by this Convention and that its Member States will not be Parties to this Convention but shall be bound by virtue of the signature, acceptance, approval or accession of the Organisation.

2. In the event that a declaration is made by a Regional Economic Integration Organisation in accordance with paragraph 1, any reference to a "Contracting State" or "State" in this Convention shall apply equally, where appropriate, to the Member States of the Organisation.

Article 31. Entry into force

1. This Convention shall enter into force on the first day of the month following the expiration of three months after the deposit of the second instrument of ratification, acceptance, approval or accession referred to in Article 27.

2. Thereafter this Convention shall enter into force—

(a) for each State or Regional Economic Integration Organisation subsequently ratifying, accepting, approving or acceding to it, on the first day of the month following the expiration of three months after the deposit of its instrument of ratification, acceptance, approval or accession;

(b) for a territorial unit to which this Convention has been extended in accordance with Article 28, paragraph 1, on the first day of the month following the expiration of three months after the notification of the declaration referred to in that Article.

Article 32. Declarations

1. Declarations referred to in Articles 19, 20, 21, 22 and 26 may be made upon signature, ratification, acceptance, approval or accession or at any time thereafter, and may be modified or withdrawn at any time.

2. Declarations, modifications and withdrawals shall be notified to the depositary.

3. A declaration made at the time of signature, ratification, acceptance, approval or accession shall take effect simultaneously with the entry into force of this Convention for the State concerned.

4. A declaration made at a subsequent time, and any modification or withdrawal of a declaration, shall take effect on the first day of the

month following the expiration of three months after the date on which the notification is received by the depositary.

5. A declaration under Articles 19, 20, 21 and 26 shall not apply to exclusive choice of court agreements concluded before it takes effect.

Article 33. Denunciation

1. This Convention may be denounced by notification in writing to the depositary. The denunciation may be limited to certain territorial units of a non-unified legal system to which this Convention applies.

2. The denunciation shall take effect on the first day of the month following the expiration of twelve months after the date on which the notification is received by the depositary. Where a longer period for the denunciation to take effect is specified in the notification, the denunciation shall take effect upon the expiration of such longer period after the date on which the notification is received by the depositary.

Article 34. Notifications by the depositary

The depositary shall notify the Members of the Hague Conference on Private International Law, and other States and Regional Economic Integration Organisations which have signed, ratified, accepted, approved or acceded in accordance with Articles 27, 29 and 30 of the following—

(a) the signatures, ratifications, acceptances, approvals and accessions referred to in Articles 27, 29 and 30;

(b) the date on which this Convention enters into force in accordance with Article 31;

(c) the notifications, declarations, modifications and withdrawals of declarations referred to in Articles 19, 20, 21, 22, 26, 28, 29 and 30;

(d) the denunciations referred to in Article 33.

In witness whereof the undersigned, being duly authorised thereto, have signed this Convention.

Done at The Hague, on 30 June 2005, in the English and French languages, both texts being equally authentic, in a single copy which shall be deposited in the archives of the Government of the Kingdom of the Netherlands, and of which a certified copy shall be sent, through diplomatic channels, to each of the Member States of the Hague Conference on Private International Law as of the date of its Twentieth Session and to each State which participated in that Session.

Chapter 3

INTERNATIONAL COMMERCIAL ARBITRATION

Table of Sections

---

§ 3.1 Introduction

We focus in this chapter on international commercial arbitration, which represents at least 90% of all international business arbitration. In Chapter 4, we take up foreign investment arbitrations, a small but growing subset, often with large sums involved.

One variation of a *forum* selection clause is one that chooses no court at all, but selects an alternate dispute resolution mechanism, such as an arbitration tribunal. For a long time, courts of many nations resisted validating such clauses, holding that they deprived the parties of due process of law (a reaction one might expect toward a competitor). For example, England was slow to adopt arbitration anywhere near its current use, largely due to the belief that adversaries were entitled to their day in court. Legislatures were far more sympathetic to allowing arbitration, and around the early years of the last century began to enact statutes validating arbitration clauses. The issue now is firmly settled in most jurisdictions. The volume of international commercial arbitration has grown enormously in recent decades, particularly in the Americas, Europe and the Middle East.

In the United States, major milestones overcoming judicial hostility to domestic and international arbitration of commercial disputes comprise the Federal Arbitration Act of 1925, the adoption in 1958 of the New York Convention on Recognition and Enforcement of Foreign Arbitral Awards, and adoption in 1990 of its Inter-American Convention counterpart. See Sections 3.10, 3.11 and 3.12. These milestones have been reinforced by a series of remarkably pro-arbitration rulings by the U.S. Supreme Court. See Sections 3.3 and 3.9.

Dispute resolution in international commercial transactions ranges from friendly consultations to litigation everywhere. In between, nonbinding conciliation and mediation do their best at facilitating a compromise, an approach common to Asia. See Section 1.3. In between also are commercial arbitrations of international sales and licensing disputes, a binding alternative to days in court and a professional expertise that common law juries in particular may lack. But choosing arbitration hardly removes litigation from the dispute settlement picture. Courts are frequently involved in pre-arbitration, post-arbitration and concurrent-with-arbitration judicial proceedings. The most common proceedings are in the jurisdiction where arbitral proceedings are compelled or undertaken, with secondary proceedings in jurisdictions where confirmation or enforcement of awards is sought.

The range of arbitral legal issues taken to court is considerable: Is the agreement to arbitrate valid? Should arbitration be compelled? Should pre-arbitration attachments be issued? Is the dispute arbitrable, or subject to mandatory judicial remedies? What is the scope of the arbitration clause. . .does it cover all disputes arising under, out of, relating to, or in connection with the contract? Absent designation by the parties, what procedural rules will be employed, and what is the controlling law? Is there jurisdiction (competence) to arbitrate? Will attorney-client or work-product privileges be recognized? Are non-signatories bound by the arbitration? Should an award be vacated or upheld? The law of the arbitration's seat, frequently designated by agreement, will generally govern the answers to these questions.

In addition to arbitration, there are many even less formal alternate dispute resolution mechanisms. The mini-trial, for example, comes in a variety of packages, each with a different impact on resolution of the dispute. It can be nonbinding if used with a "neutral advisor"; it can be semi-binding if its results are admissible in later judicial proceedings; or it can be binding before a court appointed master.[1]

§ 3.2 Why Arbitrate?

The growth of international commercial arbitration is in part a retreat from the vicissitudes and uncertainties of international business litigation. See Chapters 2, and 5 through 9. More positively, international commercial arbitration offers neutrality as a forum (who knows which court you otherwise may end up in) and the potential for specialized expertise (most judges have relatively little experience in applying international or foreign law). As the noted author, Attorney Gary Born, puts it: "A party typically does not agree to arbitrate because arbitration is the *most favorable* possible forum, but because it is the *least unfavorable* forum the party can obtain in arm's length negotiations."[2]

Who is selected as an arbitrator will impact neutrality, raising the delicate, ethical question of whether potential arbitrators should allow themselves to be interviewed by a party or the parties jointly in advance. . .a kind of *voir dire* for arbitrators. Arbitrator candidates should engage in full disclosure of their past relations with the parties. The U.S. Supreme Court has ruled that failure to do so can create an appearance of bias ("evident partiality") that can result in the setting aside of awards.[3] In 2004, the AAA/ABA Code of Ethics for Arbitrators in Commercial Disputes (see Section 3.16) was amended to require all arbitrators, including party-nominated

---

1 For a review of the variety of such alternative dispute resolution mechanisms, *see* Nelson, "Alternatives to Litigation of International Disputes," 23 *Int'l Lawyer* 187 (1989).

2 G. Born, *International Arbitration: Law and Practice* (2012), page 10.

3 Commonwealth Coatings Corp. v. Continental Casualty, 393 U.S. 145 (1968). *See* Sphere Drake Ins. Co. v. All Am. Life Ins. Co., 307 F.3d 617 (7th Cir. 2002); Applied Industrial Materials Corp. v. Ovalar Makine Ticaret Ve Senayi AS, 492 F.3d 132 (2d Cir. 2007); Fertilizer Corp. of India v. IDI Management, 517 F.Supp. 948 (S.D. Ohio 1981).

arbitrators, to be neutral, meaning independent and impartial, absent an agreement otherwise by the parties.

International commercial arbitration also allows the parties to select and shape the procedures and costs of dispute resolution, and in selecting the seat (place) of arbitration to ensure they are represented by their regular counsel in an arbitration friendly jurisdiction. That selection will also determine the law which generally governs the arbitration proceedings. But in relatively rare instances the parties' choice of law clause may over-ride procedural *lex arbitri*.[4] International commercial arbitration clauses generally prevail over bankruptcy stays of proceedings.[5]

All that said, international commercial arbitration procedures and awards are less subject to "the law" than litigation. To quote Judge Learned Hand:

> Arbitration may or may not be a desirable substitute for trials in courts; as to that the parties must decide in each instance. But when they have adopted it, they must be content with its informalities; they may not hedge it about with those procedural limitations which it is precisely its purpose to avoid. They must content themselves with looser approximations to the enforcement of their rights than those that the law accords them, when they resort to its machinery.[6]

One of the most attractive attributes of international commercial arbitration is the enforceability in national courts of arbitral agreements and awards under the 1958 U.N. Convention on Recognition and Enforcement of Arbitral Awards, commonly called the New York Convention.[7] Roughly 150 nations participate in the New York Convention. See Sections 3.9 and 3.11. There is no comparable convention for the enforcement of court judgments. Although lengthy negotiations took place around the end of the last century for the adoption of a Hague Convention on Jurisdiction and Enforcement of Judgments, it was not concluded. Only a less encompassing 2005 Convention on Choice of Court Agreements was concluded, but it has not been successful in attracting signatories. See Section 2.2 and 2.5.

---

4 *See, e.g.*, Volt Info Sciences v. Stanford, 489 U.S. 468 (1989).

5 *See, e.g.*, Sonatrach v. Distrigas Corp., 80 B.R. 606 (Bankr. D. Mass. 1987).

6 American Almond Products Co. v. Consolidated Pecan Sales Co., Inc., 144 F.2d 448, 451 (2d Cir. 1944). For a provocative article suggesting that arbitrators may apply "the law" in a more rigorous way than some courts, *see* Park, "The Predictability Paradox: Arbitrators and Applicable Law", ICC Publication No. 753E (2014), Ch 4.

7 U.N. Convention on Recognition and Enforcement of Arbitral Awards (1958), 21 U.S.T. 2517, 330 U.N.T.S. 38.

Other less encompassing agreements governing aspects of arbitration exist, one of the more important to the United States being the Inter-American Convention on International Commercial Arbitration of 1975, commonly called the Panama Convention, and reproduced in Section 3.12. The Inter-American Convention was implemented in 1990 as part of the federal Arbitration Act.[8] That 1975 Convention renders arbitral awards enforceable in Latin America. It has attracted about 20 members, nearly all the nations of Latin America with the exception of Cuba.

Another major advantage of international commercial arbitration is the support of legal regimes that give arbitration agreements dispositive effects. In the United States, for example, the Federal Arbitration Act provides a level of legal security unknown to international business litigation. Many countries have similar statutes, thus avoiding issues of subject matter and personal jurisdiction, *forum non conveniens,* and the like.[9] Professor Park has noted that, excepting New York, there are no statutory frameworks supporting court selection clauses at the state or federal level.[10] In worst case scenarios, parties selecting a court to resolve their disputes may end up with a court that refuses to hear the case.

One of the least attractive attributes of international commercial arbitration is the minimal availability of pre-trial discovery and provisional remedies.[11] The ICC and CIETAC Rules of Procedure, for example, provide for no prehearing disclosure, whereas the UNCITRAL Rules give the tribunal discretion to compel production of documents or other evidence.[12] To a common law attorney, the relative absence of oral argument and hearings in favor of written statements and filings of law and fact (often called "memorials"), not to mention the general power of arbitrators to mandate payment of costs and attorneys' fees by the loser, may also be unattractive.

In addition, arbitrators (whose decisions are rarely reversible for mistakes of law) sometimes focus on splitting the differences between the parties, not the vindication of legal rights which in courts might

---

[8] Inter-American Convention on International Commercial Arbitration of 1975, 14 I.L.M. 336 (1975). See Section 3.12 for the FAA provisions related thereto.

[9] *See* Park, "When and Why Arbitration Matters" in Hartwell (ed.), The Commercial Way of Justice (1997); Richards v. Lloyd's of London, 107 F.3d 1422 (9th Cir. 1997) *reversed* 135 F.3d 1289 (9th Cir. 1998).

[10] Park, "Bridging the Gap in Forum Selection: Harmonizing Arbitration and Court Selection," 8 Transnat'l Law & Contemp. Probs. 19 (Spring 1998).

[11] *See* Borden, Inc. v. Meiji Milk Products Co., 919 F.2d 822 (2d Cir. 1990), *cert. denied,* 500 U.S. 953, 111 S.Ct. 2259, 114 L.Ed.2d 712 (1991).

[12] *See* Publicis Coomunication v. True North Communications, 206 F.2d 725 (7th Cir. 2000).

result in "winner takes all." But such extreme results could permanently disrupt otherwise longstanding and mutually beneficial business relationships. Perhaps, therefore, "splitting the baby" through arbitration really is the optimal outcome, even when the split is not equal.

Clearly international commercial arbitration has its pros and cons. Regardless of which way you would like to see the balance tipped, the use of international arbitral dispute resolution methods is growing. One distinguished set of authors believes that this trend is hardly surprising. Here is their analysis of why:

> "Trade and investment across state lines is on the rise, and parties from different jurisdictions who engage in such activity frequently seek the comparative neutrality of a non-state tribunal to resolve their differences. Parties to a transaction from different states may be reluctant to submit to the jurisdiction of the courts of the other. This reluctance may arise from lack of enthusiasm about operating in another language, or according to the procedures and, insofar as it infiltrates procedure, the substantive law of another state. In some circumstances, one party may fear that the courts of the other may have a preference for their own nationals, may share a dislike of a particular foreign nationality or may, in cases involving very large amounts of money, lean toward finding in favor of their national because of the consequences for their national economy and political system. Where one of the parties is a state or state agency, a non-state party may prefer arbitration to submitting a dispute to the courts of the other contracting party. Arbitration may thus serve to "equalize" the non-state entity by transferring the dispute to a setting which may be designed to minimize or ignore the sovereign character of one of the parties rather more than would a national court.
>
> Arbitration may also be utilized because the various national laws which might be relevant have not developed enough to treat problems raised in a pioneer industry. Thus issues regarding intellectual property rights in computer software of companies from different states may be submitted to arbitration as a way of resolving a dispute by shaping new law on the matter. In some circumstances potential litigants may also seek out arbitration because it is touted as more rapid, private and cheaper than domestic adjudication, though many of these characteristics of

> international commercial arbitration may be relative and sometimes overstated.
>
> International commercial arbitration is also on the increase because many national court systems not only help international arbitration but appear anxious to externalize a larger amount of the disputes that are formally within their jurisdiction. The willingness of national courts to compel parties who have made prior commitments to engage in private arbitration and then to enforce the awards that ensue, subject only to limited judicial review, increases the likelihood that parties will resort to that mode of dispute resolution."[13]

Other distinguished authors are more critical of international commercial arbitration, suggesting its benefits may have been oversold:

> The [parties] hope that arbitration will prove speedy, cheap, informal and confidential. Such hopes are sometimes disappointed. A determined and evasive opponent can introduce a variety of delays into the process, by going to court to contest the validity of the contract clause calling for arbitration, by challenging arbitrators as biased, and by resisting enforcement of the award. States pay for judges, but the costs of arbitrators and those who administer the process must be borne by the parties. The leading arbitrators generally receive more in compensation for their services than judges get by way of salaries, and there have been complaints about the fees charged by major arbitration centers. In any case, expensive counsel must spend time away from home, usually in expensive hotels located in cities where the cost of living may be even higher than New York. Nor should one assume that arbitration will always be confidential. Generally, such confidentiality requires the agreement of both of the parties, and may be lost at the enforcement stage if resort must be had to a national court.[14]

§ 3.3 Ad Hoc and Institutional International Commercial Arbitrations

There are two distinct types of international commercial arbitrations: ad hoc and institutional. Ad hoc arbitrations involve

[13] W. Michael Reisman, W. Laurence Craig, William W. Park & Jan Paulsson, International Commercial Arbitration (Foundation Press, 1997).

[14] Detlev F. Vagts, William S. Dodge, Harold Hongju Koh, Hannah L. Buxbaum, Transnational Business Problems (Foundation Press, 2014).

selection by the parties of the arbitrators and rules governing the arbitration. The classic formula involves each side choosing one arbitrator who in turn agree upon a third arbitrator. The ad hoc arbitration panel selects its procedural rules (such as the UNCITRAL Arbitration Rules, see Section 3.6). Ad hoc arbitration can be agreed upon in advance or, quite literally, selected ad hoc as disputes arise. But some jurisdictions, such as the People's Republic of China, are hostile to ad hoc arbitrations, fearing perhaps they may operate too far beyond government influence.

Institutional arbitration involves selection of a specific arbitration center or "court," often accompanied by its own basic rules of arbitration. Such rules typically cover the selection of arbitrators, resolution of disputes about the neutrality of arbitrators, designation of the place of arbitration, and fees. Institutional arbitration is in a sense pre-packaged, and the parties need only "plug in" to the arbitration system of their choice. There are numerous competing centers of arbitration, each busy marketing its desirability to the world business community.

Some centers are longstanding and busy, such as the International Chamber of Commerce (ICC) "Court of Arbitration" headquartered in Paris, which has its own Rules of Arbitration. The ICC may assist in the formation of tribunals anywhere in the world with arbitrators from any country using any language. Other centers are more recent in time and still struggling for clientele, such as the Commercial Arbitration and Mediation Center for the Americas, the Kuala Lumpur Regional Arbitration Center, and the Cairo Regional Center for International Arbitration. The lower cost nature of arbitrations, underwritten by the World Court, of the Permanent Court of Arbitration at The Hague has made it attractive.

Proceedings conducted in "arbitration friendly" seats (jurisdictions) such as London, New York, Paris, Stockholm, Hong Kong and Singapore allow considerable freedom to choose home-country lawyers, what procedures to follow, which language to use, where to meet, whether to pursue class arbitrations, and face minimal mandatory legal provisions (see Section 3.3). Florida, competing for the substantial economic benefits of hosting international commercial arbitrations, has created an "International Commercial Arbitration Court" staffed with judges that are well-versed in arbitration law. This is particularly notable because the seat or legal *situs* of the arbitration will influence the degree to which courts interject themselves before, during or after the proceedings, and facilitate enforcement of the award under the New York or Inter-American Conventions (see Section 3.8).

Ad hoc arbitration presupposes a certain amount of goodwill and flexibility between the parties. It can be speedy and less costly than institutional arbitration. The latter, on the other hand, offers ease of incorporation in an international business agreement, supervisory services, a stable of experienced arbitrators and a fixed fee schedule. The institutional environment is professional, a quality that sometimes can get lost in ad hoc arbitrations. Awards from well-established arbitration centers (including default awards) are more likely to be favorably recognized in the courts if enforcement is needed. Many institutional arbitration centers now also offer "fast track" or "mini" services to the international business community.

Uncertainty about identity of the country and the court in which a dispute may be heard, about procedural and substantive rules to be applied, about the degree of publicity to be given the proceedings and the judgment, about the time needed to settle a dispute, and about the efficacy which may be given to a resulting judgment all have combined to make arbitration the preferred mechanism for solving international commercial disputes. Some Western European countries, notably France, Switzerland, Britain and Sweden, have been long accustomed to arbitration. The English Arbitration Act dates from 1889, for example. The London Court of International Arbitration, a private arbitration institution with its own set of procedural rules, has existed since 1892. The United States has had a Federal Arbitration Act since 1925,[15] and, since 1996, the American Arbitration Assn's International Centre for Dispute Resolution in New York readily embraces international commercial arbitration.

Arbitration of international commercial disputes is favored by the People's Republic of China, if mediation and conciliation fail (see Chapter 1), either through the Chinese International Economic and Trade Arbitration Commission (CIETAC) or the Chinese Maritime Arbitration Commission (CMAC). Most of the nations of the former Soviet Union also favor arbitration, and have organizations similar to the Chinese CIETAC and MAC. In terms of volume, CIETAC is now the world's largest arbitration center, followed by the ICC in Paris, the AAA International Centre for Dispute Resolution, the Hong Kong International Arbitration Center and the Singapore International Arbitration Center.

Headquartered in Beijing, CIETAC has regional offices in Tianjin, Shanghai, Shenzhen and Chongqing. In a change from earlier practices, CIETAC's approved list of arbitrators is now quite international and any language can be chosen for the proceedings. It

---

[15] 9 U.S.C.A. § 1 et seq. See Section 3.10 *infra*.

is not clear, however, whether foreign attorneys may serve as lead counsel in CIETAC arbitrations.

The Japan Commercial Arbitration Association has been active since 1953. Virtually all countries in Africa have arbitration statutes. Latin America, historically disadvantaged in many arbitral awards, increasingly is accepting arbitration. For example, the 1975 Inter-American Convention on International Commercial Arbitration[16] provides, in part, that "The Governments of the Member States of the Organization of American States. . .have agreed that. . .an agreement in which parties undertake to submit to arbitral decision any differences. . . with respect to a commercial transaction is valid." The 1979 Inter-American Convention on Extraterritorial Validity of Foreign Judgments and Arbitral Awards expands upon the scope of the 1975 Convention.

§ 3.4 Mandatory Law

Almost all jurisdictions have enacted law they consider "mandatory," *i.e.* public law that private parties cannot avoid by contract. Article 2060 of the French Civil Code, for example, forbids arbitration of "all matters in the realm of public policy." Chinese law applicable to the formation and approval of joint ventures involving foreign parties is mandatory, whereas the joint venture and third parties may choose any law to govern commercial contracts inside China. European Union law protecting commercial agents is mandatory and cannot be avoided by choice of law clauses in arbitration agreements.[17] Within the EU, mandatory legal rules of the forum state generally trump contract law.[18]

Articles II(1) and V(2) of the New York Convention recognize mandatory laws by creating an exception for "subject matters not capable of settlement by arbitration." Exactly where the line is drawn between mandatory and non-mandatory law is thus crucial to international commercial arbitration, and usually turns upon the law of the arbitral seat.

Many lower U.S. federal courts had held that "mandatory laws" could not be the subject matter of arbitration because of the public interest indicated by the legislative intent underlying the enactment of mandatory law and the public policy favoring judicial enforcement

---

16 See 14 Int'l Legal Mat. 336. Reproduced in section 3.12.

17 Ingmar GB v. Eaton Leonard Technologies, 2000 Eur.Comm.Rep. I—9305 (Nov. 9, 2000) (California choice of law clause rejected). *See, e.g.*, Accentuate Ltd. v. ASIGRA, 2009 WL 34441737 (UK High Court of Justice, QB Div. 2009) (arbitration choice of law clause rejected).

18 See Article 7, European Convention on Laws Applicable to Contractual Obligations (1980).

of such law. However, the Supreme Court has repeatedly rejected that doctrine. In *Scherk v. Alberto-Culver Co.*[19], the Court, reversing its own precedent, held that Securities and Exchange Commission law issues arising out of an international contract are subject to arbitration under the Federal Arbitration Act despite the public interest in protecting the United States investment climate. And an English choice of law clause combined with an English choice of court clause can eliminate entirely the right to pursue U.S. securities' law and RICO remedies.[20]

In *Mitsubishi Motors Corp. v. Soler Chrysler-Plymouth, Inc.*[21], the Supreme Court held that U.S. antitrust claims arising out of an international transaction were arbitrable, despite the public interest in a competitive national economy, and the legislative pronouncements favoring enforcement by private parties. This was the case even though the parties had chosen Swiss law to govern their contract. That choice could not waive mandatory U.S. law, but it was for the arbitrators to decide the merits the U.S. antitrust claims at issue.[22] Likewise, the European Court of Justice has held EU business competition law claims (see Chapter 9) arbitrable.[23]

In *Vimar Seguros y Reaseguros, S.A. v. M/V Sky Reefer*,[24] claims that the foreign arbitrators would not apply the United States mandatory COGSA bill of lading law were rejected on the ground that the U.S. could "review" the arbitral award at the award-enforcement stage. That power may, however, be very narrow under the 1958 United Nation's Convention on the Recognition and Enforcement of Foreign Arbitral Awards (the New York Convention). *See* Section 3.8.

In both *Mitsubishi Motors* and *M/V Sky Reefer*, the Court determined that issues arising out of international transactions involving U.S. mandatory law were arbitrable. However, in *dictum* at the end of the *Mitsubishi* opinion, the Court stated that U.S. courts

---

19 417 U.S. 506, 94 S.Ct. 2449, 41 L.Ed.2d 270 (1974). Accord, Rodriguez de Quijas v. Shearson/Amercian Express Inc., 490 U.S. 477 (1989). Compare Wilko v. Swan, 346 U.S. 427 (1953) (securities claims non-arbitrable). Section 921 of the "Dodd-Frank" Act authorizes the SEC to restrict mandatory pre-dispute arbitration clauses. See Public Act No. 111–203 (2010).

20 Roby v. Corporation of Lloyd's, 996 F.2d 1353 (2d Cir. 1993). Accord, Richards v. Lloyd's of London, 135 F.3d 1289 (9th Cir. 1998).

21 473 U.S. 614, 105 S.Ct. 3346, 87 L.Ed.2d 444 (1985). *See* Baxter Int'l v. Abbott Labs, 315 F.3d 829 (7th Cir. 2003) and American Express Co. v. Italian Colors Restaurant, 133 S.Ct. 2304 (2013).

22 *Id.* Soler subsequently filed for bankruptcy seeking a stay of the arbitration, which was denied in a ruling that the Federal Arbitration Act prevailed over the Bankruptcy Code. *See* Mitsubishi Motors v. Soler Chrysler-Plymouth, No. 85–838 (D.P.R. April 14, 1986).

23 Eco-Swiss China time Ltd. v. Benneton Int'l, 1999 Eur.Comm.Rep. I–3055.

24 515 U.S. 528, 115 S.Ct. 2322, 132 L.Ed.2d 462 (1995).

would have a second chance at the enforcement stage to examine whether the arbitral tribunal "took cognizance of the antitrust claims and actually decided them." Similar language can be found in *M/V Sky Reefer* regarding COGSA claims.

It would seem to be difficult to fit any such examination by the U.S. courts properly into the structure of the New York Convention. It is not clear whether *Mitsubishi* invites the U.S. courts merely to examine whether the arbitrators state that they considered the antitrust issues, or further invites them to examine whether the arbitrators considered these issues *correctly* (review on the merits). The former can be evaded by a mechanical phrase; the latter can harm the arbitral process, especially if the parties have chosen non-U.S. law to govern their agreement. Federal Circuit Courts of Appeal have held on the basis of *Mitsubishi* that private antitrust claims are arbitrable, with relatively little "second look" judicial review.[25]

In either case, the arbitrators' enforcement of U.S. antitrust laws may not be to the standards of U.S. courts, and the status of recognition and enforcement of arbitral awards involving antitrust issues is not yet clear. Under the New York Convention (see Section 3.8), a mere "misunderstanding," or error in interpretation, of a mandatory law by an arbitral tribunal has generally not been held to "contravene public policy." The cases are split as to whether even a "manifest disregard" of United States law constitutes such a violation of public policy. See Section 3.9. Similarly, agreements to arbitrate RICO claims have been upheld as not involving mandatory U.S. law.[26]

Thus, it is not certain, under the New York Convention, that United States courts retain the "second look" review powers assumed by the *Mitsubishi* and *M/V Sky Reefer* Courts to be available at the "award-enforcement stage" of the proceedings. Recognizing this problem, some courts have ordered periodic reports from arbitrators on mandatory law claims.[27]

§ 3.5 The Swedish Example

Major centers for international arbitration include Geneva, London, Hong Kong, Singapore, New York, Paris, and Stockholm. Arbitration associations at such places have adopted fairly settled

---

[25] *See, e.g.*, Seacoast Motors of Salisbury, Inc. v. DaimlerChrysler Motors Corp., 271 F.3d 6 (1st Cir. 2001), *cert. denied*, 535 U.S. 1054, 122 S.Ct. 1911, 152 L.Ed.2d 821 (2002); Baxter Int'l v. Abbott Laboratories, 315 F.3d 829 (7th Cir. 2003).

[26] *See* Shearson/American Express Inc. v. McMahon, 482 U.S. 220 (1987); Pacificare Health Systems v. Book, 538 U.S. 401 (2002).

[27] *See* Cole v. Burns Int'l Security Services, 105 F.3d 1465 (D.C.Cir. 1997) (Title VII dispute).

rules for conducting arbitrations. An accurate anatomy of even one country's law governing arbitration is beyond the purview of this book, but some typical considerations surrounding an arbitration may be illustrated by traditional Swedish arbitral rules. Sweden is a party to the New York Convention.

A valid arbitration in Sweden, whether or not involving foreigners, may proceed only in accordance with applicable Swedish law (including the 1929 Arbitration Act and the 1929 Act Concerning Foreign Arbitration Agreements and Awards). Swedish law has granted parties considerable leeway in deciding whether to create their own "ad hoc" rules for arbitration, whether to use the rules of the Swedish Chamber of Commerce Arbitration Institute, or whether to use some other set of pre-existing arbitral rules.

However, Swedish law has also provided that there are limitations upon the power of persons to specify what rules should govern their contractual relationship (including aspects of dispute settlement). As between two contracting parties, many provisions of Swedish law may be excluded from usual applicability to a commercial relationship (such excludable legal rules are called "*jus dispositivum*"), but the applicability of certain legal rules may not be excluded by the parties (such non-excludable legal rules are called "*jus cogens*").

The *jus cogens/jus dispositivum* dichotomy is found in the law of many European countries. It is also found in the United States Uniform Commercial Code and lies underneath the rationales of United States cases which had held that issues of antitrust liability could not be arbitrated. The dichotomy's relevance to arbitration results in a conclusion that any arbitration rules chosen by parties to govern their dispute may not be honored in Sweden if such rules contravene a non-excludable provision of Swedish law. For example, notwithstanding that parties may desire otherwise, in Sweden it has been a non-excludable rule that "when there are several arbitrators, one of them shall be chairman of the tribunal".

Swedish law has permitted an arbitration to be held in Sweden if the parties specify Sweden as the locale for arbitration even though (subject to overriding *jus cogens*) the parties have specified that some procedural rules other than those of the Stockholm Chamber of Commerce should apply or have specified that substantive law other than Swedish law should govern the resolution of a dispute. To the extent that issues of substantive law may raise further "conflict of laws" (choice of law) issues, Swedish law has usually given effect to a choice of law clause drafted by the parties. If the parties have not drafted such a clause into their contract, Swedish conflict of laws rules may determine the applicable substantive law.

A Swedish arbitration begins with a written "request for arbitration" (the demand), which must include an unequivocal statement that the party desires arbitration and which must serve clear notice of the issues upon which an arbitration decision is requested. Service of the request must be made upon the other party in accordance with law. Qualified arbitrator(s) next must be chosen. If there is an issue about the validity of the underlying contract which provides for arbitration, that issue may be addressed properly to the arbitrators although the question may be raised concurrently in an appropriate Swedish court. Other preliminary steps, such as an attachment of property in aid of execution pending outcome of the arbitration or a challenge to the competence of an arbitrator, may occur before the arbitration commences.

§ 3.6 Elements of an Agreement to Arbitrate

Some considerations should be weighed for inclusion in any agreement to arbitrate regardless of the rules or locale chosen for the arbitration. The Swedish example illustrates considerations such as:

(1) *The locale and legal situs (seat, place) of arbitration*—In Sweden visas can be obtained easily, physical facilities for arbitration are readily available, and communications facilities are good. Apart from logistical matters, the seat or place of arbitration is a critical choice, and may well differ from the location of hearings. Typically, the *situs* will determine arbitral procedural rules, the courts responsible for enforcing the agreement to arbitrate and supervising its procedural rules, and the courts and arbitration law applicable to annulment (*vacatur*) of arbitral awards.[28]

A host of other significant issues may turn on the national law of the arbitral seat. Examples include the rights of lawyers to appear, discovery, confidentiality, provisional remedies, and qualification and removal of arbitrators. Absent choice of the *situs* by the parties, this selection is usually made by the arbitrators or relevant arbitral institution's "appointing authority." The most commonly chosen seats are France and Switzerland, followed by the United Kingdom. There has been almost no application of the doctrine of *forum non conveniens* (see Section 2.4) to arbitral seat selections.

---

[28] See Section 3.9 for FAA grounds for annulment. In some jurisdictions, for example Britain, the parties may agree to waive appeals of arbitral awards. See U.K. Arbitration Act of 1996, Section 69(1).

(2) *The jus cogens (mandatory law) problem (see Section 3.3).*

(3) *Choice of governing substantive legal rules*—If no law is chosen by the parties, the arbitrators may follow the law of the forum country or may apply conflicts of law principles to select the governing substantive rules. See Section 2.1.

Other considerations include:

(4) *Scope of the arbitral clause*—The most common interpretational disputes regarding arbitral agreements involve their scope. Compare the language in Section 3.7 suggested by several prominent arbitration centers. Clauses that refer to arbitration of disputes "arising under" an agreement are generally treated as narrow in scope, versus broad clauses referring to disputes "related to" or "in connection with" the agreement.[29] The language employed in drafting arbitration clauses will be important to resolving questions of whether tort claims must be arbitrated, and whether the arbitrators get to decide their competence (jurisdiction) to arbitrate. See Section 3.9.

Some countries may not consider a clause about arbitration to apply *in futuro* unless it is made expressly applicable to existing and to future disputes. Some countries may give effect only to an arbitration clause that relates to a particular relationship, such as "all differences that may arise out of or in connection with this Agreement" between the parties. The clause should include a reference to any actions by a party that constitute a waiver of the right to invoke arbitration, and also should include, if desired, reference to conciliation efforts that must occur before arbitration becomes appropriate.

(5) *Selection of arbitrators*—A minimum number of three may be required; an odd number usually is required. Countries may require that all arbitrators be drawn from an approved list of arbitrators who are nationals of that country, while other countries may prohibit more than one arbitrator of the same nationality as a party litigant. Some countries, such as Sweden, list factors which disqualify an arbitrator from service (e.g., certain financial connections with a party litigant).

---

[29] *See, e.g.,* Mediterranean Enterprises v. Ssangyong Corp., 708 F.2d 1458 (9th Cir. 1983) (arising under); Pennzoil Exploration v. Ramco Energy, 139 F.3d 1061 (5th Cir. 1998) (relating to); J.J. Ryan & Sons v. Rhone Poulence Textile, 863 F.3d 315 (4th Cir. 1988) (in connection with).

More generally, the International Bar Assn has issued Guidelines on Conflicts of Interest in International Arbitration. Because parties often cannot agree upon procedures for choosing arbitrators, some countries, such as Sweden, provide that an "appointing authority" shall intervene, as appropriate, to effect the selection. Parties may define, in advance, the circumstances which warrant intervention. Whether "non-neutral" arbitrators can be appointed, a traditional American practice widely scorned elsewhere, should be specified.

(6) *Payment of arbitrator fees*—In some instances arbitrators are paid a flat fee or per diem fee, while in other instances arbitrators are paid a fee based upon a percentage of the value of the dispute. It should be made clear who, and under which circumstances, has an obligation to pay which arbitrator(s) and whether arbitrators are due reimbursement for costs in addition to fees.

(7) *Language to be used*—Common languages for arbitrations are English and French. If interpreters are to be used, their payment and their number should be settled. The authoritative language of documentary evidence, transcripts and of the arbitral award should be specified.

The use of interpreters substantially slows the pace of arbitration proceedings and may spawn further difficulties because the interpreter is one more fallible person taking part in the negotiations. Interpreting is exhausting work and rarely exact. For example, during an international commercial arbitration in Los Angeles, a witness testified in German alongside a skilled interpreter whose job it was to translate the testimony into English. While the arbitrators waited, it required the interpreter's efforts, the efforts of a United States lawyer fluent in German, and the efforts of a German lawyer fluent in English, to produce an oral translation which all agreed was sufficiently accurate. Even assuming the availability of an accurate literal translation, a Japanese person saying "yes" in answer to a question may not be signifying agreement but may only mean, "Yes, I understand the question."

(8) *Nature of the proceedings, judicial assistance*—In the People's Republic of China arbitration proceedings may be public, while in other countries they are private. In some countries the proceedings may not last longer than a specific time, unless extended for good reason, after which the authority to conduct the proceeding will be considered

to have lapsed. In many countries parties may be represented by counsel. The scope of judicial assistance regarding pre-award attachments and injunctions should be specified,[30] as well as whether related proceedings be consolidated or pursued as a group (class arbitrations).[31] U.S. courts mandate authorization of consolidated arbitration proceedings.[32]

(9) *Procedure to be followed*—In some places the arbitration is decided customarily upon submission of documents without a hearing. Other places permit hearings, allow oral testimony (including testimony under oath), allow cross examination, allow limited "discovery", issue subpoenas, take written submissions from counsel, permit arbitrators to make personal investigations or to introduce evidence, permit expert witnesses, and permit a written record of the proceedings to be taken. The law governing procedural issues should be specified by the parties, particularly so as to avoid application of the "procedural" conflicts of law rules of the designated substantive law jurisdiction.

If ex parte representations by counsel to the tribunal are not desired, they should be prohibited. Countries differ about whether an arbitration proceeding can take place in the absence of all of the arbitrators. Confidentiality and preliminary relief rules should be spelled out, particularly as very few arbitration statutes or Rules provide for confidentiality. Whether consolidated class arbitrations are to be permissible is an important issue, particularly in light of U.S. Supreme Court decisions denying class arbitration where the agreement is silent on the issue,[33] upholding the rejection of class arbitrations when so agreed,[34] and upholding consumer class action waivers in favor of arbitration despite contrary state law.[35]

---

[30] *See* I.T.A.D. Asstes v. Podar Bros., 636 F.2d 75 (4th Cir. 1981) (pre-award attachments cannot be ordered by a court). Compare Carolina Power & Light v. Uranex, 451 F.Supp. 1044 (N.D. Cal. 1977) (pre-award attachment allowed).

[31] *See* Stolt-Nielsen SA v. Animal Feeds Int'l Corp., 559 U.S. 662 (2010) (no implicit agreement to class arbitrations).

[32] *See* American Express v. Italian Colors, 133 S.Ct. 1740 (2013); Hall St. Assoc. LLC v. Mattel Inc., 552 U.S. 576 (2008); U.K. v. Boeing, 998 F.2d 68 (2d Cir. 1993).

[33] Stolt-Nielsen SA v. AnimalFeeds Int'l Corp., 130 S.Ct. 1758, 559 U.S. 662 (2010). *See* New England Energy v. Keystone Shipping, 855 F.2d 1 (1st Cir. 1988) (consolidated class arbitration ordered despite silence when chosen MA law so provides).

[34] American Express Co. v. Italian Colors Restaurant, 133 S.Ct. 2304 (2013).

[35] *See* AT&T Mobility v. Concepcion, 563 U.S. 321 (2011).

(10) *Ex aequo et bono*—In some countries, the arbitrators may not decide a dispute *ex aequo et bono* (according to what is just and good) unless the parties empower the arbitrators to act on that basis.

(11) *The award*—The agreement to arbitrate should specify that an arbitrator's award be in writing. Countries differ about whether an award must be accompanied by reasons, whether an award requires the unanimous consent of all arbitrators and whether the losing party pays all costs of the arbitration (including counsel fees and the costs of stenographers, "facility use" costs, and costs of expert witnesses).

The award should be made as final and binding as applicable law allows, recognizing that in some countries substantive legal questions arising during an arbitration may be reviewed subsequently by a court of law and that in other countries part or all of the procedure and merits of the dispute may be reviewed by a court.

It may be useful to agree specifically to exclude judicial review of the validity of the award or not to contest awards. Consent to jurisdiction in any New York Convention state, to personal and in rem jurisdiction there, and not to seek *forum non conveniens* (see Section 2.4) dismissals of actions to recognize and enforce awards are all worthy of inclusion in the arbitration agreement. So too are limitations on the award of "punitive damages" and the like.[36] Agreeing to the currency and interest to be paid on awards can remove contentious issues.

The agreement to arbitrate should specify that the award shall be enforceable in any competent court of law and in accordance with the 1958 New York Convention on the Recognition and Enforcement of Arbitral Awards. See Section 3.8. If a record is to be kept of the award, the place of its retention should be specified.

(12) *Severability*—It may be desirable to indicate whether invalidity of part(s) of the provisions concerning arbitration is intended to affect the validity of all provisions dealing with arbitration or other parts of the contract in which such arbitral provisions may appear. However, the consequences

[36] For cases upholding such clauses, *see* Mastrobuono v. Shearson/Lehmann Hutton, 514 U.S. 52 (1995); Pacificare Health Systems v. Book, 538 U.S. 401 (2002); Lagstein v. Certain Underwriters at Lloyd's, 607 F.3d 634 (2010).

of including a severability provision should be calculated with care.

(13) *The trigger clause*—When the agreement calls for mediation and conciliation, or even just "friendly consultations" as many Chinese contracts do prior to arbitration, a "trigger clause" is essential so that the parties will know when they have a right to go to arbitration. The Chinese, for example, prefer not to trigger arbitration whenever "there is a prospect of amicable settlement." Foreign parties to contracts with the PRC prefer a more certain, if not an absolute, right to move disputes to mediation and/or arbitration.

(14) *Controlling law*—Ideally, the parties will have designated the law controlling their business agreement and disputes arising thereunder through a "choice of law" clause. See Section 2.1. Such clauses are widely honored in the international community, including in the United States. Ideally, also, the parties will have made clear the controlling law governing their agreement to arbitrate, the arbitration proceedings and any applicable conflict of law rules. The choice of law governing the commercial contract may differ from the choice of law governing the agreement to arbitrate, which is treated as severable from the contract as a whole.

§ 3.7 Model International Arbitral Rules and Laws: UNCITRAL

The United Nations Commission on International Trade Law (UNCITRAL) has been active for decades in promoting international commercial arbitration. Its Model Arbitration Rules and Model Law on International Commercial Arbitration have been widely adopted and utilized in both civil and common law jurisdictions. In 2012, UNCITRAL published an excellent, detailed Digest of Case law on the Model Law that is global in scope. This Digest can be found on the UNCITRAL website.

Model Arbitration Rules

The elements of arbitration agreements considered above are incorporated in Model International Commercial Arbitration Rules[37] issued in 1976 by the United Nations Commission on International Trade Law (UNCITRAL) following ten years of study. They were revised in 2010 and are reproduced in Section 3.13. The UNCITRAL Rules are intended to be acceptable in all legal systems and in all

[37] *See* 15 Int'l Legal Mat. 701 (1978).

parts of the world. Rapidly developing countries favor the Rules because of the care with which they have been drafted, and because UNCITRAL was one forum for developing arbitration rules in which their concerns would be heard. Because the UNCITRAL Rules do not have a supervising authority, they tend to be less expensive and can be customized in ways not always possible with institutionalized arbitration (see Section 3.7).

The Arbitral Institute of the Stockholm Chamber of Commerce has been willing to work with the UNCITRAL Rules, as has the London Court of Arbitration and AAA's International Center for Dispute Resolution. The Iran-United States Claims Tribunal used the UNCITRAL Rules in dealing with claims arising out of the confrontation between the two countries in 1980. Unlike the Stockholm Chamber of Commerce Rules, the UNCITRAL Rules are not identified with any national or international arbitration organization such as the AAA International Center, the ICC, the LCIA, and the HKIAC, all of which have their own arbitration rules. Though intended for commercial matters, foreign investment arbitrations have also been conducted under the UNCITRAL Rules. See Chapter 4.

Among other things, UNCITRAL rules provide that an "appointing authority" shall be chosen by the parties or, if they fail to agree upon that point, shall be chosen by the Secretary-General of the Permanent Court of Arbitration at The Hague from a body of persons prepared to act as arbitrators if requested. The UNCITRAL rules cover notice requirements, representation of the parties, challenges of arbitrators, evidence, hearings, the place of arbitration, language, statements of claims and defenses, pleas to the arbitrator's jurisdiction, provisional remedies, experts, default, rule waivers, the form and effect of the award, applicable law, settlement, interpretation of the award and costs. The UNCITRAL Rules also require that an award be supported by reasons.

Model Arbitration Law

In addition to its Model Arbitration Rules, UNCITRAL also promulgated in 1985 a Model Law on International Commercial Arbitration, amended in 2006, and reproduced in Section 3.12.[38] While the Model Rules are directed to potential or actual disputing parties, the Model Law is directed to nation states. Drawing on the 1958 New York Convention (see Section 3.8), the Model Law covers arbitration communications, waivers, judicial intervention, forms of arbitration agreements, the number of arbitrators, their

---

[38] http://www.uncitral.org/. *See* Lowry, Critical Documents Sourcebook Ann. 345 (1991).

appointment and challenges thereto, substitute arbitrators, arbitrator competence to rule on its jurisdiction, interim relief, conduct of the proceedings and determination of the place or arbitration, consolidated and multi-party proceedings, default, use of experts, governing law, awards and setting aside awards, and recognition and enforcement of awards.

The Model Law, or legislation based on the Model Law, has been enacted in more than 60 nations, including Mexico and a number of Latin American nations. It has also been enacted as state law by several states of the U.S., including California, Connecticut, Florida, Illinois, Louisiana, Oregon, and Texas. Additionally, China has not adopted the law, but both Hong Kong and Macao have. Similarly, the United Kingdom has not adopted the law, but both Bermuda and Scotland have.

Under the UNCITRAL Model Law, submission to arbitration may be *ad hoc* for a particular dispute, but is accomplished most often in advance of the dispute by a general submission clause within a contract. Under Article 8 of the Model Law, an agreement to arbitrate is specifically enforceable.

Although no specific language will guarantee the success of an arbitral submission, UNCITRAL recommends the following model submission clause:

> Any dispute, controversy or claim arising out of or relating to this contract, or the breach, termination or invalidity thereof, shall be settled by arbitration in accordance with the UNCITRAL Arbitration Rules as at present in force.

§ 3.8 ICC, LCIA, AAA and CIETAC Arbitral Rules and Clauses

Institutional arbitral rules differ and careful consideration should be given to the choice. Costs, confidentiality, the number of arbitrators and their appointment, discovery, use of experts, protective measures, language, and procedure are some of the variables to consider.

International Chamber of Commerce (ICC)

Many parties use the Rules of the Court of Arbitration of the International Chamber of Commerce (ICC) at Paris. Although the ICC International Court of Arbitration is not a court in the judicial meaning of that label, its primary role is to administer arbitrations. The Court does not itself resolve disputes, such function being that of independent arbitral tribunals appointed under the ICC Rules. The ICC Rules are modern, most recently revised in 2019, and often used in international arbitration. The "2019 Note" updates the disclosure duties of arbitrators, transparency in commercial ICC arbitrations, and the publishing of case data and awards. Some 14,000 arbitrations have been administered by the ICC.

The Court of Arbitration of the ICC in Paris recommends use of the following model clause for the adoption of its rules:

> All disputes arising in connection with the present contract shall be finally settled under the Rules of Conciliation and Arbitration of the International Chamber of Commerce by one or more arbitrators appointed in accordance with the said Rules.

London Court of International Arbitration (LCIA)

The London Court of International Arbitration (LCIA), with roots to 1883, is another leading global forum for dispute resolution using arbitration, although it also is active in mediation. The London Court has its own rules and procedures. Its hourly rates are often less expensive than the ICC's percentage of the amount in controversy fees.

Parties who wish to refer any dispute to the equally prominent London Court of International Arbitration may use the following model clause:

> The validity, construction and performance of this contract (agreement) shall be governed by the laws of England and any dispute that may arise out of or in connection with this contract (agreement), including its validity, construction and performance, shall be determined by arbitration under the Rules of the London Court of International Arbitration at the date hereof, which Rules with respect to matters not regulated by them, incorporate the UNCITRAL Arbitration Rules. The parties agree that service of any notices in reference to such arbitration at their addresses as given in this contract (agreement) (or as subsequently varied in writing by them) shall be valid and sufficient.

AAA International Centre for Dispute Resolution

The American Arbitration Association's embrace of international commercial arbitration is relatively recent. In 1996 the AAA created the International Centre for Dispute Resolution, headquartered in New York but operational in a number of U.S. cities. Miami, for example, has a growing volume of arbitrations, notably $1.6 billion disputes between the Panama Canal Authority and a consortium of construction companies from Spain, Italy and

Belgium. The AAA, like the ICC and LCIA, has its own set of arbitration rules, reproduced in Section 3.15.

The AAA recommends the following clauses for adoption of its rules:

> Any controversy or claim arising out of or relating to this contract, or the breach thereof, shall be determined by arbitration administered by the International Centre for Dispute Resolution in accordance with its International Arbitration Rules.
>
> **or**
>
> Any controversy or claim arising out of or relating to this contract, or the breach thereof, shall be determined by arbitration administered by the American Arbitration Association in accordance with its International Arbitration Rules.

The parties may wish to consider adding:

(a) The number of arbitrators shall be (one or three);

(b) The place of arbitration shall be (city and/or country); or

(c) The language(s) of the arbitration shall be _______.

China International Economic and Trade Arbitration Commission (CIETAC)

China has been steadily promoting, improving and internationalizing its CIETAC international arbitration center, which has its own set of arbitration rules. CIETAC is now by good measure the most voluminous of all international commercial arbitration centers. The following example models a CIETAC arbitration clause:

Any dispute arising from or in connection with this Contract shall be submitted to the Beijing/Shanghai/Tianjin/Chongqing/Shenzhen branch of the China International Economic and Trade Arbitration Commission (CIETAC) for final and binding arbitration, which shall be conducted in accordance with the Commission's arbitration rules then in effect. Each party shall appoint one arbitrator (either from or outside the CIETAC roster) within 30 days from the filing of the arbitration proceedings. If a party fails to appoint an arbitrator within 30 days, then the CIETAC president shall appoint such arbitrator to serve. The two appointed arbitrators shall jointly select a third arbitrator from the CIETAC roster within 30 days. The third arbitrator shall serve as arbitrator-in-chief. If the two arbitrators fail to appoint the third arbitrator within 30 days, the President of CIETAC shall appoint the third.

The arbitration shall be conducted in English with translators provided by the party requiring such services. All written records of this proceeding will occur in English. All fees charged by CIETAC shall initially be the joint responsibility of the parties but the arbitrators may award fees. The parties shall bear their own costs associated with arbitration, including, but not limited to experts, translators and attorneys' fees.

§ 3.9 Compelling Arbitration, Recognition and Enforcement of Arbitral Agreements and Awards: The New York and Inter-American Conventions

Arbitration is only as useful as its agreements and awards are recognized and enforced. Perhaps no other instrument has been more important to the success of international commercial arbitration than the New York Convention. As Yale Law Professor Michael Reisman has succinctly said:

> "The genius of the [N.Y. Convention] is to be found in the way in which it mobilizes national courts as enforcement agencies while simultaneously restricting their scope of national judicial supervision over international arbitration awards."[39]

In approximately 150 countries, the enforcement of arbitral agreements and awards is greatly facilitated by the 1958 United Nations Convention on the Recognition and Enforcement of Foreign Arbitral Awards (the "New York Convention").[40] "[T]he principal purpose underlying American. . .implementation. . .was to encourage the recognition and enforcement of commercial arbitration agreements in international contracts and to unify the standards by which agreements to arbitrate are observed and arbitral awards are enforced in the signatory countries."[41] China, for example, is a N.Y. Convention signatory and U.S. courts have enforced CIETAC awards,[42] whereas effective enforcement of foreign arbitral awards

---

39 Preface to Gaillard and Di Pietro, *Enforcement of Arbitration Agreements and International Arbitration Awards* (2008).

40 21 U.S.T. 2518, T.I.A.S. No. 6997, 330 U.N.T.S. 38, implemented in the United States by 9 U.S.C.A. §§ 201–208. http://www.newyorkconvention1958.org/.

41 Scherk v. Alberto-Culver Co., 417 U.S. 506, 520 n. 15, 94 S.Ct. 2449, 41 L.Ed.2d 270 (1974).

42 *See* Polytek Engineering Ltd. v. Jacobson Cos., 984 F.Supp. 1238 (D.Minn. 1997) (defendant did not appear in Chinese arbitration proceedings).

by Chinese courts tends to encounter local protectionism and be elusive

The 1975 Inter-American Convention on Commercial Arbitration, reproduced in Section 3.12 with its Federal Arbitration Act provisions, generally tracks the New York Convention. The United States and many Latin American nations participate. If both the New York and Inter-American Conventions apply, the New York Convention governs unless a majority of the parties to the arbitration agreement are citizens of Inter-American Convention states.

Compelling Commercial Arbitration

In an abbreviated procedure, under the Federal Arbitration Act (FAA) enactment of the New York Convention, federal district courts entertain motions to compel compliance with a written foreign *commercial* arbitration agreement, or confirm or challenge a foreign or non-domestic award.[43] Subject matter jurisdiction for such suits is expressly conveyed by the FAA enactment. As needed, federal courts are also authorized to stay litigation proceedings when a valid agreement to arbitrate exists. Note that in a "battle of forms" transaction, it is possible that no written agreement to arbitrate exists.[44]

International arbitration-related litigation commenced in state courts can be removed to federal courts. Federal courts may compel arbitration at any place designated in the arbitration agreement, not just in their own judicial districts. U.S. courts can compel arbitration anywhere in the world, provided a reasonable relationship to that jurisdiction exists.[45] For these purposes, awards between U.S. citizens may be treated as foreign based upon performance or property located abroad. Awards made in the USA concerning entirely foreign parties can be enforced; they are treated as non-domestic.[46] See Section 3.11 for the text of the New York Convention and its FAA enactment.

The New York Convention commits the courts in each Contracting State to recognize and enforce arbitration clauses and written arbitration agreements for the resolution of international commercial disputes between parties having a "defined legal relationship." Agreements to arbitrate are severable from the contract as a whole, and require minimal indications from the parties

---

[43] *See* Yusef Ahmed Alghanim & Sons v. Toys "R" Us, 126 F.3d 15 (2d Cir. 1997).

[44] *See, e.g.*, Kahn Lucas Lancaster v. Lark Int'l Ltd., 186 F.3d 210 (2d Cir. 1999).

[45] *See, e.g.*, Jones v. Sea Tow Services, 30 F.3d 360 (2d Cir. 1994) (salvage operation between U.S. parties in U.S. territorial waters not reasonably related to England, arbitration not compelled). *See also* Fuller Co. v. Compagnie des Bauxites de Guinee, 421 F.Supp. 938 (W.D. Pa. 1976).

[46] Sival Bergesen v. Joseph Muller Corp., 710 F.2d 928 (1983).

of agreement in light of the strong pro-enforcement bias of the N.Y. Convention.[47]

The New York Convention, however, does not create rules for when courts may examine whether an agreement to arbitrate exists. In the United States, courts may examine questions of arbitral jurisdiction at any time,[48] including prior to review of such issues by the arbitrators. See Section 3.9. In contrast, French courts normally wait until the entire arbitral process is over and an award is issued before examining arbitral challenges.

Where the court finds an arbitral clause or agreement, it "*shall* . . . refer the parties to arbitration, unless it finds that the said agreement is null and void, inoperative, or incapable of being performed" (emphasis added).[49] Nearly identical language is repeated in the UNCITRAL Model Law on Arbitration (see Section 3.6). This amounts to a judicial duty to compel arbitration under the N.Y. Convention absent contract deficiencies or non-arbitrable subject matter (mandatory law, see Section 3.3). The duty to compel arbitration has led U.S. courts, despite opposition, to order arbitration in other countries.[50]

But which contract law guides the interpretation of "null and void, inoperative, or incapable of being performed" under the N.Y. Convention? U.S. courts have rejected application of the law of the arbitral seat, and allowed "internationally recognized" defenses such as duress, mistake, fraud, fraudulent inducement, impossibility, incapacity, or waiver, along with violations of fundamental forum policies.[51] It is less certain that "unconscionability" will be recognized as a defense against compelling arbitration under the N.Y.

---

[47] *See, e.g.*, Nicaragua v. Standard Fruit, 937 F.2d 469 (9th Cir. 1991).

[48] *See, e.g.*, Bridas SAPIC v. Turkmenistan, 345 F.3d 347 (5th Cir. 2003) (reversal of jurisdiction finding, sovereign state not bound to arbitration under agency or collateral estoppel theories).

[49] Article II(3), New York Convention. *See* Sedco v. Pemex, 767 F.2d 1140 (5th Cir. 1985) (enforcing arbitration clause).

[50] *See, e.g.*, Apple & Eve LLC v. Yanai North Andre Juice Co, 499 F.Supp.2d 245 (E.D.N.Y. 2007) (arbitration in China); Acosta v. Norwegian Cruise Lines, 303 F.Supp.2d 1327 (S.D. Fla. 2003) (arbitration in Philippines); Marchetto v. De Kalb Genetics Corp., 711 F.Supp. 936 (N.D. Ill. 1989).

[51] *See, e.g.*, Ledee v. Ceramiche Ragno, 684 F.2d 184 (1st Cir. 1982); Rhone Mediterranee . . . v. Achille Lauro, 712 F.2d 50 (3d Cir. 1983); Stone v. E.F. Hutton, 898 F.2d 1542 (11th Cir. 1990); Thomas v. Carnival Corp., 573 F.3d 1113 (11th Cir. 2009) (rejecting prospective waiver of statutory claims); SA Mineracao da Trinidade-Samitri v. Utah Int'l Inc., 745 F.2d 190 (2d Cir. 1984) (fraudulent inducement); In re Kinoshita, 287 F.2d 951 (2d Cir. 1961) (fraudulent inducement).

Convention.[52] Compelling non-signatories to arbitrate is subject to close judicial scrutiny.[53]

The Federal Arbitration Act rules on compelling domestic arbitrations differ from those of the New York Convention. For comparison, see Section 2 of the Federal Arbitration Act of 1925 providing for enforcement of domestic arbitral agreements "save upon such grounds as exist at law or in equity for the revocation of any contract."

Recognition and Enforcement of Awards

Most international commercial arbitration awards are reasoned, and some may contain dissenting opinions. The vast majority of international commercial arbitration awards are voluntarily complied with. Where voluntary compliance is absent, the first course of action by the losing party is frequently to appeal the award before the courts of the arbitral seat, asking for its annulment or modification under local law. Success in these proceedings may well deny enforcement of the award under Article V of the New York Convention (below).

The prevailing party, on the other hand, often seeks "confirmation" or "recognition" (exequatur) of the award by the national courts of the arbitral seat, leading to a judgment based upon that award. In the United States, for example, Section 9 of the FAA allows for confirmation proceedings within one year of the award. Such a judgment typically enables local enforcement of the award by attachment or similar means.

If the losing party has no readily available assets in the arbitral seat jurisdiction, and regardless of whether the award has been confirmed by courts of that seat (double exequatur is thus eliminated), the New York Convention commits the courts in each Contracting State to recognize and enforce final foreign and non-domestic commercial arbitral awards made in a Contracting State, and enunciates the limited grounds under which recognition and enforcement may be refused. Mistakes of law by the arbitrators are not grounds for denying enforcement. Award enforcement lawsuits are subject to local procedural rules, which may prove difficult, as has sometimes been the case in the People's Republic of China. Procedures for enforcement of foreign awards in the United States are generally perceived to be easy.

---

[52] *See* Brower v. Gateway, 676 N.Y.S.2d 569 (App. Div. 1998) (affirming defense); Bautista v. Star Cruises, 396 F.3d 1289 (11th Cir. 2005) (uncertain defense); Khan v. Parsons Global Services, 480 F.Supp.2d 327 (D.D.C. 2007) (rejecting defense).

[53] *See* Thompson CSF v. American Arbitration Assn., 64 F.3d 773 (2d Cir. 1995).

Under the New York Convention, grounds for refusal to enforce an arbitral award include:

(1) Incapacity of the parties, or invalidity of the arbitration agreement under the law the parties chose to govern it, or in the absence of any such choice, under the law of the country where the award was made,

(2) Lack of proper notice of the arbitration proceedings, the appointment of the arbitrator, or other reasons denying an adequate opportunity to present a defense,[54]

(3) Failure of the arbitral award to restrict itself to the terms of the submission to arbitration, or decision of matters not within the scope of that submission,[55]

(4) Composition of the arbitral tribunal or arbitral procedure was not according to the arbitration agreement or, absent agreement, the law of the country where the arbitration took place, and

(5) Non-finality or the setting aside or suspension of the arbitral award by authorities in the country where the award was rendered, or by authorities of the country under whose law the award was made.[56] [Note that criteria for setting aside (vacating) arbitral awards are not spelled out in the N.Y. Convention. These criteria are to be found in national arbitration laws, typically the law of the arbitral *situs*. Hence, for example, United States courts may as a rule only vacate awards issued in the USA. *See, e.g.*, the UNCITRAL Model Arbitration Law reproduced in Section 3.14, and the Federal Arbitration Act in Section 3.10.]

In addition to these grounds for refusal, recognition or enforcement may also be refused if it would be contrary to the public policy of the country in which enforcement is sought,[57] or if the subject matter of the dispute cannot be settled by arbitration under the law of that country.[58] Courts in the United States have taken the

---

[54] *See* Parsons & Whittemore Overseas Co., Inc. v. Societe Generale De L'Industrie Du Papier (RAKTA), 508 F.2d 969 (2d Cir. 1974) (law of the forum where recognition is sought governs notice and opportunity to be heard, due process applies). *See also* Iran Aircraft Industries v. Avco Corp., 980 F.2d 141 (2d Cir. 1992).

[55] *See* Encyclopedia Universalis v. Encyclopedia Britannica, 403 F.3d 85 (2d Cir. 2005).

[56] Article V.

[57] *See* Parsons & Whittemore Overseas Co., Inc. v. Societe Generale De L'Industrie Du Papier (RAKTA), 508 F.2d 969 (2d Cir. 1974); Telenor Mobile Comm. AS v. Storm LLC, 584 F.3d 396 (2d Cir. 2009) (violations most basic notions of morality and justice); National Oil Corp. v. Libyan Sun Oil Co., 733 F.Supp. 800 (D.Del. 1990).

[58] *Id.* See Section 3.3 on mandatory law.

position that the "public policy limitation on the New York Convention is to be construed narrowly [and] to be applied only where enforcement would violate the forum state's most basic notions of morality and justice."[59] Lastly, the United States reserved, as do many other signatories, the right to apply the N.Y. Convention on the basis of reciprocity, meaning enforcement for U.S. awards in the jurisdiction from whence the foreign award originates.[60] The U.S. and others also reserve application of the N.Y. Convention only to commercial legal relationships.

Recourse to other limitations of the Convention in order to defeat its applicability has been greeted with judicial caution in the absence of violation of basic U.S. notions of morality and justice.[61] However, the Second Circuit has held that the doctrine of *forum non conveniens* (see Section 2.4) applies in arbitral award confirmation proceedings under the New York Convention.[62] The Circuits are split as to whether, for personal jurisdiction purposes (see Section 5.2), the U.S. property sought to be enforced against under the N.Y. Convention must relate to the underlying cause of action.[63] Obtaining a judgment based upon an arbitral award, and then seeking enforcement, avoids the N.Y. Convention's limited defenses, and in the United States turns primarily on state law (see Section 8.1).[64]

Whether the N.Y. Convention applies generally turns upon where the award was or will be made, not the citizenship of the parties.[65] A growing number of courts in developing nations are issuing injunctions against arbitration proceedings before they commence. Many of these injunctions seem deliberately intended to protect local companies. Parties who proceed to arbitrate after such an injunction has been issued do so at their peril. Subsequent

---

59 Fotochrome, Inc. v. Copal Co., Ltd., 517 F.2d 512 (2d Cir. 1975). *See* Karaha Bodas Co v. Perusahaan Pertambangan, 364 F.3d 274 (5th Cir. 2004). *See generally*, Commonwealth Coatings Corp. v. Continental Casualty Co., 393 U.S. 145 (1968).

60 *See* National Iranian Oil Co. v. Ashland Oil Inc., 817 F.2d 326 (5th Cir. 1987) (Iran not a party, no reciprocity).

61 Parsons & Whittemore Overseas Co., Inc. v. Societe Generale De L'Industrie Du Papier (RAKTA), 508 F.2d 969 (2d Cir. 1974); Telenor Mobile Comm. AS v. Storm LLC, 584 F.3d 396 (2d Cir. 2009) (violations most basic notions of morality and justice); National Oil Corp. v. Libyan Sun Oil Co., 733 F.Supp. 800 (D.Del. 1990).

62 In re Monegasque de Reassurances S.A.M. v. Nak Naftogaz of Ukraine, 311 F.3d 488 (2d Cir. 2002).

63 Compare Base Metal Trading v. OJSC, 283 F.3d 208 (4th Cir. 2002) (property must relate to cause of action) with Glencore Grain v. Shivnath Rai Harnarian, 284 F.3d 1114 (9th Cir. 2002) (any property gives personal jurisdiction).

64 *See* Curacao v. Solitron Devices Inc., 489 F.2d 1313 (2d Cir. 1973).

65 *See* Ministry of Defense of the Islamic Republic of Iran v. Gould Inc., 887 F.2d 1357 (9th Cir. 1989), *cert. denied*, 494 U.S. 1016, 110 S.Ct. 1319, 108 L.Ed.2d 494 (1990); Bergesen v. Joseph Muller Corp., 710 F.2d 928 (2d Cir. 1983) (New York arbitration between foreign entities enforced).

enforcement of the award under the New York Convention in the enjoining nation will almost certainly be voided on grounds of public policy. Hence enforcement can only proceed in non-enjoining jurisdictions, assuming that their public policy permits this.

§ 3.10 Arbitration Agreements, Arbitrators and Awards Under United States Law

Arbitration agreements were unenforceable at common law in the United State and frequently encountered judicial hostility. As late as 1956, the U.S. Supreme Court expressed skepticism about the adequacy of arbitral proceedings: "Arbitration carries no right to trial by jury . . . arbitrators do not have the benefit of judicial instruction on the law [and} need not give their reasons for their results; the record of their proceedings is not as complete as it is in a court trial; and judicial review of an award is more limited than judicial review of a trial".[66]

That perspective is long gone. The Federal Arbitration Act of 1925 (FAA, see Section 3.10) and repeated U.S. Supreme Court decisions now reflect a strong pro-arbitration enthusiasm. The Supreme Court's 1984 decision in *Southland Corp. v. Keating,* holding that California's Franchise Investment Law could not invalidate arbitration agreements, represents something of a highpoint of this enthusiasm. In that case the Court stated that the purpose of the FAA was to overcome "the old hostility toward arbitration" and represents a "national policy favoring arbitration".[67]

The Federal Arbitration Act

Section 2 of the Federal Arbitration Act indicates that written arbitration agreements shall be valid, irrevocable and enforceable save for "such grounds as exist at law or in equity for the revocation of any contract." The federal Act creates a presumption of validity of arbitration agreements and preempts inconsistent state law, notably any state law that bars enforcement of arbitration agreements. For example, a California rule that consumer contract waivers of class action rights in form arbitration agreements were unconscionable, and therefore invalidated the arbitration agreements, was overturned by the U.S. Supreme Court.[68] While it does not entirely preempt state law,[69] it is the dominant substantive law in a field

---

66 Bernhardt v. Polygraphic Co, 350 U.S. 198 (1956).

67 465 U.S. 1 (1984). *See* Allied-Bruce Terminix Cos. v. Dobson, 513 U.S. 52 (1995) (Alabama statute invalidating pre-dispute arbitration agreements preempted by FAA).

68 AT&T Mobility LLC v. Concepcion, 131 S.Ct. 1740 (2011).

69 *See* Southland, *supra* and Volt Information Sciences v. Board of Trustees, 489 U.S. 468 (1989) (California stay of arbitration pending litigation upheld given choice

(contracts) normally governed by state rules.[70] California, for example, has ruled that *Concepcion* overrides state provisions establishing non-waivable labor wage and hour rights when arbitration is agreed upon.[71]

The FAA empowers arbitrators to call third-party witnesses, compel their appearance with documents, and subject them to contempt if compliance does not follow. In Section 10, the FAA establishes exclusive criteria for vacating arbitral awards: Fraud, corruption, or undue means; evident partiality or corruption in the arbitrators; arbitrator misconduct or prejudicial misbehavior; and the arbitrators exceeded their powers or imperfectly executed them, such as by addressing issues that fell outside the scope of the agreement to arbitrate. These criteria have been restrictively construed.[72] An additional ground, manifest disregard for the law, has sometimes recognized (see below). There is a split of opinions on whether the New York Convention limits the FAA grounds for vacating arbitral awards.[73] There is authority that the parties, however, may restrict the standards for review of arbitral awards.[74]

Case Law

International commercial arbitration agreements, traditionally called *compromis,* come in a variety of forms. Many arbitration centers sponsor model clauses that can be incorporated into business agreements. As noted above in Section 3.8, the New York Convention obliges courts of participating nations, upon request, to refer disputes to arbitration unless the agreement is "null and void, inoperative or incapable of being performed."[75]

---

of California law in contract). *See also* Cable Connect v. DIRECTV, 190 P.3d 586 (Cal. 2008) (state law on *vacatur* affirmed). *But see* Mastrobuono v. Shearson/Lehmann Hutton, 514 U.S. 52 (1995) (New York choice of law no bar to punitive damages award).

[70] *See, e.g.,* Rent-A-Center West Inc. v. Jackson, 130 S.Ct. 2772 (2010) (employment discrimination claims subject to arbitration as agreed).

[71] *See* Iskanian v. CLS Transportation Los Angeles LLC, 59 Cal. 4th 348 (2014) *reversing* Gentry v. Superior Court, 42 Cal. 4th 443 (2007).

[72] *See, e.g.,* Northrup Corp. v. Triad Int'l Marketing, 811 F.2d 1265 (9th Cir. 1987); I/S Stavborg v. National Metal Converters, 500 F.2d 424 (2d Cir. 1974); Yusef Ahmed Alghanim & Sons v. Toys "R" Us, 126 F.3d 15 (2d Cir. 1997); Inter-City Gas Corp. v. Boise Cascade Corp., 845 F.2d 184 (8th Cir. 1988). *See generally,* Commonwealth Coatings Corp. v. Continental Casualty Co., 393 U.S. 145 (1968).

[73] Compare Yusef Ahmed Alghanim & Sons v. Toys "R" Us, 126 F.3d 15 (2d Cir. 1997) (no limits) with Industrial Risk Insurers v. M.A.N. Gutehoffnungshutte GmbH, 141 F.3d 1434 (11th Cir. 1998) (N.Y. Convention defenses exclusively apply).

[74] *See* Roadway Package System v. Kayser, 257 F.3d 287 (3d Cir. 2001); Gateway Technologies v. MCI Telecommunications Corp., 64 F.3d 993 (5th Cir. 1995) ("errors in law" appeals agreed); Bowen v. Amoco Pipeline, 254 F.3d 925 (10th Cir. 2001). Contra, Hoeft v. MVL Group Inc., 343 F.3d 57 (2d Cir. 2003).

[75] Article II(3).

Whether a valid agreement to arbitrate exists depends on the specifics of the arbitration clause, not the entire business agreement. The arbitration clause is severable, and issues of validity (such as forgery, fraud in the inducement of the arbitration clause and unconscionability) are directed to it.[76]

The U.S. Supreme Court has repeatedly affirmed that arbitrators have jurisdiction to decide their own jurisdiction (*Kompetenz-Kompetenz*).[77] But challenges to arbitral jurisdiction (competence) are to be decided by the arbitrators only if there "clear and unmistakable evidence" that the parties so intended.[78] Silence or ambiguity should favor judicial review of arbitrability issues.[79] Arbitration clauses that adopt the UNITRAL Rules meet the requirement of clarity to arbitrate because Article 21 conveys jurisdictional issues to the tribunal.[80]

As to the scope of the arbitration clause, any doubts should be resolved in favor of arbitration.[81] Gateway questions prior to arbitration, such as waiver and time limits, are as a rule for the arbitrators to decide.[82] Challenges to contract validity as a whole must go to the arbitrators designated in the contract, not courts.[83] But challenges to the very existence of an international commercial contract go to the courts.[84] Pre-trial attachments, anti-suit and other injunctions in aid of arbitration may or may not be available.[85] An

---

[76] Prima Paint Corp. v. Flood & Conklin Mfg. Co., 388 U.S. 395, 87 S.Ct. 1801, 18 L.Ed.2d 1270 (1967). *See* Republic of Nicaragua v. Standard Fruit Co., 937 F.2d 469 (9th Cir. 1991); China Minmetals Materials Import and Export Co. v. Chi Mei Corp., 334 F.3d 274 (3d Cir. 2003); Alliance Bernstein Investment v. Schaffran, 445 F.3d 121 (2d Cir. 2006). *See also* Hunt v. Up North Plastics, Inc., 980 F.Supp. 1046 (D.Minn.1997), *cert. denied*, 503 U.S. 919, 112 S.Ct. 1294, 117 L.Ed.2d 516 (1992).

[77] *See, e.g.*, Howsam v. Dean Witter Reynolds, Inc., 537 U.S. 79, 123 S.Ct. 588, 154 L.Ed.2d 491 (2002); Pacificare Health Systems, Inc. v. Book, 538 U.S. 401, 123 S.Ct. 1531, 155 L.Ed.2d 578 (2003).

[78] First Options of Chicago v. Kaplan, 514 U.S. 938 (1995).

[79] *Id. See, e.g.*, Bridas SAPIC v. Turkmenistan, 345 F.3d 347 (5th Cir. 2003) (reversal of jurisdiction finding, sovereign state not bound to arbitration under agency or collateral estoppel theories).

[80] Wal-Mart Stores v. PT Multiploar Corp., 202 F.2d 280 (9th Cir. 1999) (unpublished).

[81] First Options, *supra.*

[82] Howsam, *supra. See* Painewebber v. Elahi, 87 F.3d 589 (1st Cir. 1996). Compare Lynch v. Cohen, 62 F.3d 381 (11th Cir. 1995).

[83] Buckeye Check Cashing Inc. v. Cardegna, 546 U.S. 440 (2006). *See* Rent-A-Center Inc. v. Jackson, 130 S.Ct. 2772 (2010).

[84] *Id. See* Three Valleys Municipal Water District v. E.F. Hutton & Co., 925 F.2d 1136 (2d Cir. 1991) (signatory power issue) and Apollo Computer v. Berg, 886 F.2d 469 (1st Cir. 1989) (no assignment clause).

[85] See generally Chapter 6. *See* Paramedics Electromedicina Comercial v. GE Medical Systems Onf. Tech., 369 F.3d 645 (2d Cir. 2004) (anti-suit injunction against Brazilian action granted to compel arbitration); PMS Dist. Co. v. Huber & Suhner, 863

arbitral award forbidding litigation becomes enforceable under the N.Y. Convention, and hence operates like an anti-suit injunction.[86]

Article II (2) of the New York Convention requires states to recognize written arbitration agreements *signed* by the parties "or contained in an exchange of letters or telegrams." In most jurisdictions exchanges of fax, email and the like embracing arbitration will also be recognized. However, arbitration clauses in unsigned purchase orders do not amount to a written agreement to arbitrate.[87] Pre-arbitration litigation often revolves around motions to compel arbitration.[88] If no such motion is made, and a court judgment is rendered (even by default), the right to arbitrate may be waived.[89] Delays in triggering arbitration or invocation of litigation rights may constitute a waiver of arbitration rights.[90]

Many courts will stretch the limits of the New York Convention in order to uphold an arbitration clause.[91] When there is a battle of forms, the same judicial bias towards arbitration is often found.[92] But, in most cases, the disputes must "arise under" the business transaction to be arbitrable,[93] and legal claims falling outside the transaction remain in court.[94] In order to enforce arbitral awards under the New York Convention, personal jurisdiction over the award debtor must be had, typically obtained by the presence of assets within the court's domain that relate to the award creditors

F.2d 639 (9th Cir. 1988); I.T.A.D. Assocs. v. Podar Bros, 636 F.2d 75 (4th Cir. 1981) (injunction denied under N.Y. Convention mandate to "refer" parties to arbitration).

86 *See* Four Seasons Hotels and Resorts v. Consorcio Barr, 377 F.3d 1164 (11th Cir. 2004).

87 Kahn Lucas Lancaster, Inc. v. Lark Int'l Ltd., 186 F.3d 210 (2d Cir. 1999).

88 *See, e.g.*, Tennessee Imports, Inc. v. P.P. Filippi & Prix Italia, S.R.L., 745 F.Supp. 1314 (M.D.Tenn.1990).

89 *See* Menorah Insurance Co. v. INX Reinsurance Corp., 72 F.3d 218 (1st Cir. 1995).

90 *See* O.J. Distributing, Inc. v. Hornell Brewing Co., 340 F.3d 345 (6th Cir. 2003); Colón v. R. K. Grace & Co., 358 F.3d 1 (1st Cir. 2003).

91 *See* Sphere Drake Insurance PLC v. Marine Towing, Inc., 16 F.3d 666 (5th Cir. 1994), *cert. denied*, 513 U.S. 871, 115 S.Ct. 195, 130 L.Ed.2d 127 (1994) (absence of signature to standard insurance policy contract no barrier to arbitration); Nicaragua v. Standard Fruit, 937 F.2d 469 (9th Cir. 1991) (lack of specificity in arbitration clause no barrier); Rhone Mediterranee v. Achille Lauro, 712 F.2d 50 (3d Cir. 1983) (strong presumption of enforceability of arbitration clauses, law of forum not contract controls).

92 *See* I.T.A.D. Associates, Inc. v. Podar Bros., 636 F.2d 75 (4th Cir. 1981).

93 *See* Mediterranean Enterprises, Inc. v. Ssangyong Corp., 708 F.2d 1458 (9th Cir. 1983).

94 *Id. See* Coors Brewing Co. v. Molson Breweries, 51 F.3d 1511 (10th Cir. 1995).

claim.[95] But there is case law supporting dismissal of award enforcement proceedings on *forum non conveniens* grounds.[96]

Closure or misdescription of an arbitration center designated in the agreement (e.g., the New York Chamber of Commerce) is no barrier to arbitration. A substitute arbitrator will be appointed by the court if the parties cannot agree.[97] The U.S. Supreme Court has held that arbitrators are subject to "requirements of impartiality" and must "disclose to the parties any dealings that might create an impression of possible bias."[98] That said, most U.S. courts loath to intrude upon or vacate an arbitration on disclosure grounds.[99]

Article V of the New York Convention, and its corresponding FAA Sections 10 and 11, do not recognize manifest disregard of the law as a basis for denial of enforcement, a doctrine developed in domestic U.S. arbitration case law. The Supreme Court, in *Hall St. Assoc., L.L.C. v. Mattel, Inc.,*[100] held that Sections 10 and 11 are exclusive, suggesting that manifest disregard of the law is inapplicable, at least in foreign award enforcement proceedings. Some Circuits have held manifest disregard of the law is no longer a valid ground for vacating a domestic award.[101]

The Supreme Court also ruled in *Hall* that the parties cannot expand upon Sections 10 and 11 by agreement. In *Hall*, the parties had agreed to allow the U.S. District Court for Oregon to review and reject awards based on the arbitrators' findings of fact and conclusions of law, a provision deemed severable so as to allow arbitration to proceed. California, and other states, have rejected the *Hall* rationale and allowed parties to expand judicial review of

---

[95] *See* Frontera Resources Azerbaijan Corp. v. State Oil Co. of Azerbaijan Republic, 582 F.3d 393 (2d Cir. 2009); Base Metal Trading Ltd v. OJSC, 283 F.3d 208 (4th Cir. 2002). Contra, Glencore Crain Rotterdam BV v. Shinath Rai Harnarain Co., 284 F.3d 1114 (9th Cir. 2002) (presence of assets not related to claim suffices for personal jurisdiction).

[96] *See* Monegasque De Reassurances SAM v. Nak Naftogaz of Ukraine, 311 F.3d 488 (2d Cir. 2002). See generally, Section 2.4.

[97] *See* Astra Footwear Industry v. Harwyn International, Inc., 442 F.Supp. 907 (S.D.N.Y.1978).

[98] Commonwealth Coatings Corp. v. Continental Casualty Co., 393 U.S. 145, 89 S.Ct. 337, 21 L.Ed.2d 301 (1968).

[99] *See* Andros Compania Maritima v. Marc Rich & Co., 579 F.2d 691 (2d Cir. 1978).

[100] 552 U.S. 576 (2008). *But see* Stolt-Nielsen SA v. Animal-Feeds Int'l, 559 U.S. 662 (2010) suggesting that "willful flouting" of the law by an arbitrator is grounds for vacating an award.

[101] See, rejecting manifest disregard of the law, Frazier v. Citifinancial Corp., 604 F.3d 1313 (11th Cir. 2010); Medicine Shoppe Int'l v. Turner Invs, 614 F.3d 485 (8th Cir. 2010); Citigroup Global Markets v. Bacon, 562 F.3d 349 (5th Cir. 2009). *But see* Comedy Club Inc. v. Improv. West Assc., 553 F.3d 1277 (9th Cir. 2009) (characterizing manifest disregard as included in the statutory ground of arbitrators exceeding their powers).

arbitral awards.[102] But in 2019, citing FAA Section 10, the U.S. Supreme Court rejected "wholly groundless" as an exception to arbitrability fashioned by the Fifth Circuit.[103]

Another issue concerning the New York Convention is whether to adjourn U.S. enforcement proceedings if parallel proceedings to vacate the award have been commenced in the country of arbitration. Despite the risks of forum shopping and delay, the Second Circuit indicated that adjournment can be appropriate, depending upon the circumstances.[104] The Second Circuit has also denied use of 28 U.S.C. § 1782 (see Section 6.6) to obtain compulsory non-party discovery in private commercial arbitrations. The issue was whether the I.C.C. in Paris constituted a "tribunal" within the scope of that statute.[105]

Cases in the United States have pointed out that parties cannot refer a dispute to a court while an arbitration is in progress,[106] or block enforcement of an award in the United States in reliance upon the fact that the award, although binding in the country where rendered, is under appeal there.[107] Interim orders of arbitrators, such as records disclosures, may be enforceable "awards" under the N.Y. Convention.[108] After the arbitration is concluded, a party may be able to block enforcement of the award in reliance upon the United States Foreign Sovereign Immunities Act,[109] but a court may not decline to enforce in reliance upon the Act of State Doctrine.[110] Collateral attacks on foreign arbitral awards have been rejected for want of subject matter jurisdiction.[111] Under Section 15 of the federal Arbitration Act, a three year statute of limitations applies to enforcement of foreign arbitral awards commencing with the date of the award.

One court granted enforcement, under the Convention, of a New York award rendered in favor of a non-citizen claimant against a non-

---

102 *See* Cable Connection v. DIRECTV, 44 Cal. 4th 1334 (2008).

103 Henry Schein Inc. v. Archer & White Sales Inc., ___ S.Ct. ___ (Jan. 8, 2019).

104 Europcar Italia, S.p.A. v. Maiellano Tours, Inc., 156 F.3d 310 (2d Cir. 1998).

105 National Broadcasting Co. v. Bear Stearns & Co., 165 F.3d 184 (2d Cir. 1999).

106 Siderius, Inc. v. Compania de Acero del Pacifico, S.A., 453 F.Supp. 22 (S.D.N.Y.1978).

107 Fertilizer Corp. of India v. IDI Management, Inc., 517 F.Supp. 948 (S.D.Ohio 1981).

108 *See* Publicis Communication v. True North Communications, Inc. 206 F.3d 725 (7th Cir. 2000).

109 See generally Chapter 7. *See* Ipitrade International, S.A. v. Federal Republic of Nigeria, 465 F.Supp. 824 (D.D.C.1978) and Creighton Ltd. v. Government of Qatar, 181 F.3d 118 (D.C.Cir. 1999).

110 See generally Chapter 7 and Section 15 of the FAA. Libyan American Oil Co. v. Socialist People's, etc., 482 F.Supp. 1175 (D.D.C.1980).

111 *See* Gulf Petro Trading Co. v. Nigerian National Petroleum Co., 512 F.3d 742 (5th Cir. 2008).

citizen defendant.[112] U.S. awards granted to foreign firms against U.S. companies may also be enforced under the New York Convention.[113] Awards entirely between U.S. citizens are not subject to the New York Convention unless they concern property located abroad, envisage performance or enforcement abroad, or have some other reasonable relation with foreign state(s).[114] Non-signatories may be bound to agreements to arbitrate under a variety of theories: Incorporation by reference; assumption; agency; veil-piercing/alter ego and estoppel.[115]

When arbitral awards are annulled at their *situs*, courts in enforcing jurisdictions have taken different positions on the enforceability of the award. French courts enforced an improperly vacated award to the detriment of the claimant who had prevailed in a second arbitration.[116] A U.S. federal district court refused to honor the clearly legitimate annulment of an arbitral award deemed mistaken in law by an Egyptian court because the parties had agreed not to appeal the award.[117] The Second Circuit, on the other hand, recognized the annulment of two arbitral awards vacated by a Nigerian court and refused enforcement,[118] and likewise the federal S.D.N.Y. court upheld a *vacatur* order of the Malaysian High Court.[119] The latter approach seems more consistent with the terms of Article V(e) of the New York Convention regarding awards that have been set aside or suspended in their source country. *See* Section 3.8.

---

112 Bergesen v. Joseph Muller Corp., 710 F.2d 928 (2d Cir. 1983).

113 *See* Industrial Risk Insurance v. M.A.N. Gutehoffnungshutte, 141 F.3d 1434 (11th Cir. 1998).

114 9 U.S.C. § 202 (1994). *See* Lander Co. v. MMP Investments, 107 F.3d 476 (7th Cir. 1996) (contract performance between two U.S. companies in Poland renders New York award "nondomestic" and enforceable).

115 Arthur Andersen v. Carlisle, 129 S.Ct. 1896 (2009). Accord, Todd v. Steamship Mutual Underwriting Assn Bermuda, 601 F.3d 329 (5th Cir. 2010).

See Thomson-CSF SA v. American Arbitration Assn, 64 F.3d 773 (2d Cir. 1995).

116 Hilmarton v. OTV, 1997 Rev. Arb. 376, note Ph. Fouchard discussed in Park, "Duty and Discretion in International Arbitration," 93 Am. J. Int'l Law 805 (1999).

117 Chromalloy Aeroservices v. Egypt, 939 F.Supp. 907 (D.D.C. 1996). Accord, In re COMMISA, (S.D.N.Y. Aug. 27, 2013) (unpublished) (award annulled in Mexico, the arbitral seat, enforced).

118 Baker Marine (Nig.) Ltd. v. Chevron (Nig.) Ltd., 191 F.3d 194 (2d Cir. 1999). *See* Spier v. Calzaturificio Technica, 71 F.Supp.2d 279 (S.D.N.Y. 1999) (Italian nullification on grounds that arbitrators exceeded their powers recognized); TermoRio v. Eltranta, 487 F.3d 928 (D.C.Cir. 2007) (Colombian nullification recognized).

119 Thai-Lao Lignite Co. v. Government of the Lao People's Democratic Republic, 997 F.Supp.2d 214 (S.D.N.Y. 2014).

§ 3.11 Text of the U.S. Federal Arbitration Act of 1925

Title 9, US Code, Section 1–14, was first enacted February 12, 1925 (43 Stat. 883), codified July 30, 1947 (61 Stat. 669), and amended September 3, 1954 (68 Stat. 1233). Chapter 2 was added July 31, 1970 (84 Stat. 692), two new Sections were passed by the Congress in October of 1988 and renumbered on December 1, 1990 (PL 669 and 702); Chapter 3 was added on August 15, 1990 (PL 101–369); and Section 10 was amended on November 15.

CHAPTER 1—GENERAL PROVISIONS

Section 1. "Maritime transactions" and "commerce" defined; exceptions to operation of title

"Maritime transaction", as herein defined, means charter parties, bills of lading of water carriers, agreements relating to wharfage, supplies furnished vessels or repairs to vessels, collisions, or any other matters in foreign commerce which, if the subject of controversy, would be embraced within admiralty jurisdiction; "commerce", as herein defined, means commerce among the several States or with foreign nations, or in any Territory of the United States or in the District of Columbia, or between any such Territory and another, or between any such Territory and any State or foreign nation, or between the District of Columbia and any State or Territory or foreign nation, but nothing herein contained shall apply to contracts of employment of seamen, railroad employees, or any other class of workers engaged in foreign or interstate commerce.

Section 2. Validity, irrevocability, and enforcement of agreements to arbitrate

A written provision in any maritime transaction or a contract evidencing a transaction involving commerce to settle by arbitration a controversy thereafter arising out of such contract or transaction, or the refusal to perform the whole or any part thereof, or an agreement in writing to submit to arbitration an existing controversy arising out of such a contract, transaction, or refusal, shall be valid, irrevocable, and enforceable, save upon such grounds as exist at law or in equity for the revocation of any contract.

Section 3. Stay of proceedings where issue therein referable to arbitration

If any suit or proceeding be brought in any of the courts of the United States upon any issue referable to arbitration under an agreement in writing for such arbitration, the court in which such suit is pending, upon being satisfied that the issue involved in such suit or proceeding is referable to arbitration under such an agreement, shall on application of one of the parties stay the trial of the action until such arbitration has been had in accordance with the terms of the agreement, providing the applicant for the stay is not in default in proceeding with such arbitration.

Section 4. Failure to arbitrate under agreement; petition to United States court having jurisdiction for order to compel arbitration; notice and service thereof; hearing and determination

A party aggrieved by the alleged failure, neglect, or refusal of another to arbitrate under a written agreement for arbitration may petition any United States district court which, save for such agreement, would have jurisdiction under Title 28, in a civil action or in admiralty of the subject matter of a suit arising out of the controversy between the parties, for an order directing that such arbitration proceed in the manner provided for in such agreement. Five days" notice in writing of such application shall be served upon the party in default. Service thereof shall be made in the manner provided by the Federal Rules of Civil Procedure.

The court shall hear the parties, and upon being satisfied that the making of the agreement for arbitration or the failure to comply therewith is not in issue, the court shall make an order directing the parties to proceed to arbitration in accordance with the terms of the agreement. The hearing and proceedings, under such agreement, shall be within the district in which the petition for an order directing such arbitration is filed. If the making of the arbitration agreement or the failure, neglect, or refusal to perform the same be in issue, the court shall proceed summarily to the trial thereof.

If no jury trial be demanded by the party alleged to be in default, or if the matter in dispute is within admiralty jurisdiction, the court shall hear and determine such issue. Where such an issue is raised, the party alleged to be in default may, except in cases of admiralty, on or before the return day of the notice of application, demand a jury trial of such issue, and upon such demand the court shall make an order referring the issue or issues to a jury in the manner provided by the Federal Rules of Civil Procedure, or may specially call a jury for that purpose.

If the jury find that no agreement in writing for arbitration was made or that there is no default in proceeding thereunder, the proceeding shall be dismissed. If the jury find that an agreement for arbitration was made in writing and that there is a default in proceeding thereunder, the court shall make an order summarily directing the parties to proceed with the arbitration in accordance with the terms thereof.

Section 5. Appointment of arbitrators or umpire

If in the agreement provision be made for a method of naming or appointing an arbitrator or arbitrators or an umpire, such method shall be followed; but if no method be provided therein, or if a method be provided and any party thereto shall fail to avail himself of such method, or if for any other reason there shall be a lapse in the naming of an arbitrator or arbitrators or umpire, or in filling a vacancy, then upon the application of either party to the controversy the court shall designate and appoint an arbitrator or arbitrators or umpire, as the case may require, who shall act under the said agreement with the same force and effect as if he or they had been specifically named therein; and unless otherwise provided in the agreement the arbitration shall be by a single arbitrator.

Section 6. Application heard as motion

Any application to the court hereunder shall be made and heard in the manner provided by law for the making and hearing of motions, except as otherwise herein expressly provided.

Section 7. Witnesses before arbitrators; fees; compelling attendance

The arbitrators selected either as prescribed in this title or otherwise, or a majority of them, may summon in writing any person to attend before them or any of them as a witness and in a proper case to bring with him or them any book, record, document, or paper which may be deemed material as evidence in the case. The fees for such attendance shall be the same as the fees of witnesses before masters of the United States courts. Said summons shall issue in the name of the arbitrator or arbitrators, or a majority of them, and shall be signed by the arbitrators, or a majority of them, and shall be directed to the said person and shall be served in the same manner as subpoenas to appear and testify before the court; if any person or persons so summoned to testify shall refuse or neglect to obey said summons, upon petition the United States district court for the district in which such arbitrators, or a majority of them, are sitting may compel the attendance of such person or persons before said arbitrator or arbitrators, or punish said person or persons for contempt in the same manner provided by law for securing the attendance of witnesses or their punishment for neglect or refusal to attend in the courts of the United States.

Section 8. Proceedings begun by libel in admiralty and seizure of vessel or property

If the basis of jurisdiction be a cause of action otherwise justiciable in admiralty, then, notwithstanding anything herein to the contrary, the party claiming to be aggrieved may begin his proceeding hereunder by seizure of the vessel or other property of the other party according to the usual course of admiralty proceedings, and the court shall then have jurisdiction to direct the parties to proceed with the arbitration and shall retain jurisdiction to enter its decree upon the award.

Section 9. Award of arbitrators; confirmation; jurisdiction; procedure

If the parties in their agreement have agreed that a judgment of the court shall be entered upon the award made pursuant to the arbitration, and shall specify the court, then at any time within one year after the award is made any party to the arbitration may apply to the court so specified for an order confirming the award, and thereupon the court must grant such an order unless the award is vacated, modified, or corrected as prescribed in sections 10 and 11 of this title. If no court is specified in the agreement of the parties, then such application may be made to the United States court in and for the district within which such award was made. Notice of the application shall be served upon the adverse party, and thereupon the court shall have jurisdiction of such party as though he had appeared generally in the proceeding. If the adverse party is a resident of the district within which the award was made, such service shall be made upon the adverse party or his attorney as prescribed by law for service of notice of motion in an action in the same court. If the adverse party shall be a nonresident, then the notice of the application shall be served by the marshal of any district within which the adverse party may be found in like manner as other process of the court.

Section 10. Same; vacation; grounds; rehearing

(a) In any of the following cases the United States court in and for the district wherein the award was made may make an order vacating the award upon the application of any party to the arbitration

(1) Where the award was procured by corruption, fraud, or undue means.

(2) Where there was evident partiality or corruption in the arbitrators, or either of them.

(3) Where the arbitrators were guilty of misconduct in refusing to postpone the hearing, upon sufficient cause shown, or in refusing to hear evidence pertinent and material to the controversy; or of any other misbehavior by which the rights of any party have been prejudiced.

(4) Where the arbitrators exceeded their powers, or so imperfectly executed them that a mutual, final, and definite award upon the subject matter submitted was not made.

(5) Where an award is vacated and the time within which the agreement required the award to be made has not expired the court may, in its discretion, direct a rehearing by the arbitrators.

(b) The United States district court for the district wherein an award was made that was issued pursuant to section 590 of title 5 may make an order vacating the award upon the application of a person, other than a party to the arbitration, who is adversely affected or aggrieved by the award, if the use of arbitration or the award is clearly inconsistent with the factors set forth in section 582 of Title 5.

Section 11. Same; modification or correction; grounds; order

In either of the following cases the United States court in and for the district wherein the award was made may make an order modifying or correcting the award upon the application of any party to the arbitration.

(a) Where there was an evident material miscalculation of figures or an evident material mistake in the description of any person, thing, or property referred to in the award.

(b) Where the arbitrators have awarded upon a matter not submitted to them, unless it is a matter not affecting the merits of the decision upon the matter submitted.

(c) Where the award is imperfect in matter of form not affecting the merits of the controversy.

The order may modify and correct the award, so as to effect the intent thereof and promote justice between the parties.

Section 12. Notice of motions to vacate or modify; service; stay of proceedings

Notice of a motion to vacate, modify, or correct an award must be served upon the adverse party or his attorney within three months after the award is filed or delivered. If the adverse party is a resident of the district within which the award was made, such service shall be made upon the adverse party or his attorney as prescribed by law for service of notice of motion in an action in the same court. If the adverse party shall be a nonresident then the notice of the application shall be served by the marshal of any district within which the adverse party may be found in like manner as other process of the court. For the purposes of the motion any judge who might make an order to stay the proceedings in an action brought in the same court may make an order, to be served with the notice of motion, staying the proceedings of the adverse party to enforce the award.

Section 13. Papers filed with order on motions; judgment; docketing; force and effect; enforcement

The party moving for an order confirming, modifying, or correcting an award shall, at the time such order is filed with the clerk for the entry of judgment thereon, also file the following papers with the clerk:

(a) The agreement; the selection or appointment, if any, of an additional arbitrator or umpire; and each written extension of the time, if any, within which to make the award.

(b) The award.

(c) Each notice, affidavit, or other paper used upon an application to confirm, modify, or correct the award, and a copy of each order of the court upon such an application.

The judgment shall be docketed as if it was rendered in an action.

The judgment so entered shall have the same force and effect, in all respects, as, and be subject to all the provisions of law relating to, a judgment in an action; and it may be enforced as if it had been rendered in an action in the court in which it is entered.

Section 14. Contracts not affected

This title shall not apply to contracts made prior to January 1, 1926.

Section 15. Inapplicability of the Act of State doctrine

Enforcement of arbitral agreements, confirmation of arbitral awards, and execution upon judgments based on orders confirming such awards shall not be refused on the basis of the Act of State doctrine.

Section 16. Appeals

(a) An appeal may be taken from

(1) an order

(A) refusing a stay of any action under section 3 of this title,

(B) denying a petition under section 4 of this title to order arbitration to proceed,

(C) denying an application under section 206 of this title to compel arbitration,

(D) confirming or denying confirmation of an award or partial award, or

(E) modifying, correcting, or vacating an award;

(2) an interlocutory order granting, continuing, or modifying an injunction against an arbitration that is subject to this title; or

(3) a final decision with respect to an arbitration that is subject to this title.

(b) Except as otherwise provided in section 1292(b) of title 28, an appeal may not be taken from an interlocutory order

(1) granting a stay of any action under section 3 of this title;

(2) directing arbitration to proceed under section 4 of this title;

(3) compelling arbitration under section 206 of this title; or

(4) refusing to enjoin an arbitration that is subject to this title.

§ 3.12 Text of the New York Convention (1958) (NYC) and U.S. Federal Arbitration Act Enactment of the NYC

CONVENTION ON THE RECOGNITION AND ENFORCEMENT OF FOREIGN ARBITRAL AWARDS

Article I

1. This Convention shall apply to the recognition and enforcement of arbitral awards made in the territory of a State other than the State where the recognition and enforcement of such awards are sought, and arising out of differences between persons, whether physical or legal. It shall also apply to arbitral awards not considered as domestic awards in the State where their recognition and enforcement are sought.

2. The term "arbitral awards" shall include not only awards made by arbitrators appointed for each case but also those made by permanent arbitral bodies to which the parties have submitted.

3. When signing, ratifying or acceding to this Convention, or notifying extension under article X hereof, any State may on the basis of reciprocity declare that it will apply the Convention to the recognition and enforcement of awards made only in the territory of another Contracting State. It may also declare that it will apply the Convention only to differences arising out of legal relationships,

whether contractual or not, which are considered as commercial under the national law of the State making such declaration.

Article II

1. Each Contracting State shall recognize an agreement in writing under which the parties undertake to submit to arbitration all or any differences which have arisen or which may arise between them in respect of a defined legal relationship, whether contractual or not, concerning a subject matter capable of settlement by arbitration.

2. The term "agreement in writing" shall include an arbitral clause in a contract or an arbitration agreement, signed by the parties or contained in an exchange of letters or telegrams.

3. The court of a Contracting State, when seized of an action in a matter in respect of which the parties have made an agreement within the meaning of this article, shall, at the request of one of the parties, refer the parties to arbitration, unless it finds that the said agreement is null and void, inoperative or incapable of being performed.

Article III

Each Contracting State shall recognize arbitral awards as binding and enforce them in accordance with the rules of procedure of the territory where the award is relied upon, under the conditions laid down in the following articles. There shall not be imposed substantially more onerous conditions or higher fees or charges on the recognition or enforcement of arbitral awards to which this Convention applies than are imposed on the recognition or enforcement of domestic arbitral awards.

Article IV

1. To obtain the recognition and enforcement mentioned in the preceding article, the party applying for recognition and enforcement shall, at the time of the application, supply:

(a) The duly authenticated original award or a duly certified copy thereof;

(b) The original agreement referred to in article II or a duly certified copy thereof.

2. If the said award or agreement is not made in an official language of the country in which the award is relied upon, the party applying for recognition and enforcement of the award shall produce a translation of these documents into such language. The translation shall be certified by an official or sworn translator or by a diplomatic or consular agent.

Article V

1. Recognition and enforcement of the award may be refused, at the request of the party against whom it is invoked, only if that party furnishes to the competent authority where the recognition and enforcement is sought, proof that:

(a) The parties to the agreement referred to in article II were, under the law applicable to them, under some incapacity, or the said agreement is not valid under the law to which the parties have subjected it or, failing any indication thereon, under the law of the country where the award was made; or

(b) The party against whom the award is invoked was not given proper notice of the appointment of the arbitrator or of the arbitration proceedings or was otherwise unable to present his case; or

(c) The award deals with a difference not contemplated by or not falling within the terms of the submission to arbitration, or it contains decisions on matters beyond the scope of the submission to arbitration, provided that, if the decisions on matters submitted to arbitration can be separated from those not so submitted, that part of the award which contain decisions on matters submitted to arbitration may be recognized and enforced; or

(d) The composition of the arbitral authority or the arbitral procedure was not in accordance with the agreement of the parties, or, failing such agreement, was not in accordance with the law of the country where the arbitration took place; or

(e) The award has not yet become binding on the parties, or has been set aside or suspended by a competent authority of the country in which, or under the law of which, that award was made.

2. Recognition and enforcement of an arbitral award may also be refused if the competent authority in the country where recognition and enforcement is sought finds that:

(a) The subject matter of the difference is not capable of settlement by arbitration under the law of that country; or

(b) The recognition or enforcement of the award would be contrary to the public policy of that country.

Article VI

If an application for the setting aside or suspension of the award has been made to a competent authority referred to in article V(1)(e), the authority before which the award is sought to be relied upon may, if it considers it proper, adjourn the decision on the enforcement of the award and may also, on the application of the party claiming enforcement of the award, order the other party to give suitable security.

* * *

Article XIV

A Contracting State shall not be entitled to avail itself of the present Convention against other Contracting States except to the extent that it is itself bound to apply the Convention.

* * *

Article XVI

1. This Convention, of which the Chinese, English, French, Russian and Spanish texts shall be equally authentic, shall be deposited in the archives of the United Nations.

2. The Secretary-General of the United Nations shall transmit a certified copy of this Convention to the States contemplated in article VIII.

Done at New York June 10, 1958: entered into force for the United States December 29, 1970, subject to declarations.[120]

Appendix

FEDERAL ARBITRATION ACT PROVISIONS ENACTING NEW YORK CONVENTION 9 U.S.C. §§ 201–208

Public Law 91–368, Approved July 31, 1970,
9 U.S.C. §§ 201–208, 84 Stat. 692

§ 201. Enforcement of Convention

The Convention on the Recognition and Enforcement of Foreign Arbitral Awards of June 10, 1958, shall be enforced in United States courts in accordance with this chapter.

---

[120] The United States of America will apply the Convention, on the basis of reciprocity, to the recognition and enforcement of only those awards made in the territory of another Contracting State.

The United States of America will apply the Convention only to differences arising out of legal relationships, whether contractual or not, which are considered as commercial under the national law of the United States.

The Convention applies to all of the territories for the international relations of which the United States of America is responsible.

§ 202. Agreement or Award Falling Under the Convention

An arbitration agreement or arbitral award arising out of a legal relationship, whether contractual or not, which is considered as commercial, including a transaction, contract, or agreement described in section 2 of this title, falls under the Convention. An agreement or award arising out of such a relationship which is entirely between citizens of the United States shall be deemed not to fall under the Convention unless that relationship involves property located abroad, envisages performance or enforcement abroad, or has some other reasonable relation with one or more foreign states. For the purpose of this section a corporation is a citizen of the United States if it is incorporated or has its principal place of business in the United States.

§ 203. Jurisdiction; Amount in Controversy

An action or proceeding falling under the Convention shall be deemed to arise under the laws and treaties of the United States. The district courts of the United States (including the courts enumerated in section 460 of title 28) shall have original jurisdiction over such an action or proceeding, regardless of the amount in controversy.

§ 204. Venue

An action or proceeding over which the district courts have jurisdiction pursuant to section 203 of this title may be brought in any such court in which save for the arbitration agreement an action or proceeding with respect to the controversy between the parties could be brought, or in such court for the district and division which embraces the place designated in the agreement as the place of arbitration if such place is within the United States.

§ 205. Removal of Cases from State Courts

Where the subject matter of an action or proceeding pending in a State court relates to an arbitration agreement or award falling under the Convention, the defendant or the defendants may, at any time before the trial thereof, remove such action or proceeding to the district court of the United States for the district and division embracing the place where the action or proceeding is pending. The procedure for removal of causes otherwise provided by law shall apply, except that the ground for removal provided in this section need not appear on the face of the complaint but may be shown in the petition for removal. For the purposes of Chapter 1 of this title any action or proceeding removed under this section shall be deemed to have been brought in the district court to which it is removed.

§ 206. Order to Compel Arbitration; Appointment of Arbitrators

A court having jurisdiction under this chapter may direct that arbitration be held in accordance with the agreement at any place therein provided for, whether that place is within or without the United States. Such court may also appoint arbitrators in accordance with the provisions of the agreement.

§ 207. Award of Arbitrators; Confirmation; Jurisdiction; Proceeding

Within three years after an arbitral award falling under the Convention is made, any party to the arbitration may apply to any court having jurisdiction under this chapter for an order confirming the award as against any other party to the arbitration. The court shall confirm the award unless it finds one of the grounds for refusal or deferral of recognition or enforcement of the award specified in the said Convention.

§ 208. Chapter 1; Residual Application

Chapter 1 applies to actions and proceedings brought under this chapter to the extent that that chapter is not in conflict with this chapter or the Convention as ratified by the United States.

§ 3.13 Text of Inter-American Convention on International Commercial Arbitration (1975) (IAC) and U.S. Federal Arbitration Act Enactment in 1990 of the IAC

The Governments of the Member States of the Organization of American States, desirous of concluding a convention on international commercial arbitration, have agreed as follows:

Article 1

An agreement in which the parties undertake to submit to arbitral decision any differences that may arise or have arisen between them with respect to a commercial transaction is valid. The agreement shall be set forth in an instrument signed by the parties, or in the form of an exchange of letters, telegrams, or telex communications.

Article 2

Arbitrators shall be appointed in the manner agreed upon by the parties. Their appointment may be delegated to a third party, whether a natural or juridical person. Arbitrators may be nationals or foreigners.

Article 3

In the absence of an express agreement between the parties, the arbitration shall be conducted in accordance with the rules of procedure of the Inter-American Commercial Arbitration Commission.

Article 4

An arbitral decision or award that is not appealable under the applicable law or procedural rules shall have the force of a final judicial judgment. Its execution or recognition may be ordered in the same manner as that of decisions handed down by national or foreign ordinary courts, in accordance with the procedural laws of the country where it is to be executed and the provisions of international treaties.

Article 5

1. The recognition and execution of the decision may be refused, at the request of the party against which it is made, only if such party is able to prove to the competent authority of the State in which recognition and execution are requested:

(a) That the parties to the agreement were subject to some incapacity under the applicable law or that the agreement is not valid under the law to which the parties have submitted it, or, if such law is not specified under the law of the State in which the decision was made; or

(b) That the party against which the arbitral decision has been made was not duly notified of the appointment of the arbitrator or of the arbitration procedure to be followed, or was unable, for any other reason, to present his defense; or

(c) That the decision concerns a dispute not envisaged in the agreement between the parties to submit to arbitration; nevertheless, if the provisions of the decision that refer to issues submitted to arbitration can be separated from those not submitted to arbitration, the former may be recognized and executed; or

(d) That the constitution of the arbitral tribunal or the arbitration procedure has not been carried out in accordance with the terms of the agreement signed by the parties or, in the absence of such agreement, that the constitution of the arbitral tribunal or the arbitration procedure has not been carried out in accordance with the law of the State where the arbitration took place; or

(e) That the decision is not yet binding on the parties or has been annulled or suspended by a competent authority of the State in which, or according to the law of which, the decision has been made.

2. The recognition and execution of an arbitral decision may also be refused if the competent authority of the State in which the recognition and execution is requested finds:

(a) That the subject of the dispute cannot be settled by arbitration under the law of that State; or

(b) That the recognition or execution of the decision would be contrary to the public policy ("order public") of that State.

Article 6

If the competent authority mentioned in Article 5.1.e has been requested to annul or suspend the arbitral decision, the authority before which such decision is invoked may, if it deems it appropriate, postpone a decision on the execution of the arbitral decision and, at the request of the party requesting execution, may also instruct the other party to provide appropriate guaranties.

Article 7

This Convention shall be open for signature by the Member States of the Organization of American States.

Article 8

This Convention is subject to ratification. The instruments of ratification shall be deposited with the General Secretariat of the Organization of American States.

Article 9

This Convention shall remain open for accession by any other 28 State. The instruments of accession shall be deposited with the General Secretariat of the Organization of American States.

Article 10

This Convention shall enter into force on the thirtieth day following the date of deposit of the second instrument of ratification.

For each State ratifying or acceding to the Convention after the deposit of the second instrument of ratification, the Convention shall enter into force on the thirtieth day after deposit by such State of its instrument of ratification or accession.

Article 11

If a State Party has two or more territorial units in which different systems of law apply in relation to the matters dealt with in this

Convention, it may, at the time of signature, ratification or accession, declare that this Convention shall extend to all its territorial units or only to one or more of them. Such declaration may be modified by subsequent declarations, which shall expressly indicate the territorial unit or units to which the Convention applies. Such subsequent declarations shall be transmitted to the General Secretariat of the Organization of American States, and shall become effective thirty days after the date of their receipt.

Article 12

This Convention shall remain in force indefinitely, but any of the States Parties may denounce it. The instrument of denunciation shall be deposited with the General Secretariat of the Organization of American States. After one year from the date of deposit of the instrument of denunciation, the Convention shall no longer be in effect for the denouncing State, but shall remain in effect for the other States Parties.

Article 13

The original instrument of this Convention, the English, French, Portuguese and Spanish texts of which are equally authentic, shall be deposited with the General Secretariat of the Organization of American States. The Secretariat shall notify the Member States of the Organization of American States and the States that have acceded to the Convention of the signatures, deposits of instruments of ratification, accession, and denunciation as well as of reservations, if any. It shall also transmit the declarations referred to in Article 11 of this Convention.

FEDERAL ARBITRATION ACT ENACTMENT OF IAC

CHAPTER 3—INTER-AMERICAN CONVENTION ON INTERNATIONAL COMMERCIAL ARBITRATION

Added Pub. L. 101–369, § 1, Aug. 15, 1990, 104 Stat. 448.

Section 3 of Pub. L. 101–369 provided that: "This Act [enacting this chapter] shall take effect upon the entry into force of the Inter-American Convention on International Commercial Arbitration of January 30, 1975, with respect to the United States." The Convention was entered into force for the United States on Oct. 27, 1990.

§ 301. Enforcement of Convention

The Inter-American Convention on International Commercial Arbitration of January 30, 1975, shall be enforced in United States courts in accordance with this chapter.

§ 302. Incorporation by reference

Sections 202, 203, 204, 205, and 207 of this title shall apply to this chapter as if specifically set forth herein, except that for the purposes of this chapter "the Convention" shall mean the Inter-American Convention.

§ 303. Order to compel arbitration; appointment of arbitrators; locale

(a) A court having jurisdiction under this chapter may direct that arbitration be held in accordance with the agreement at any place therein provided for, whether that place is within or without the United States. The court may also appoint arbitrators in accordance with the provisions of the agreement.

(b) In the event the agreement does not make provision for the place of arbitration or the appointment of arbitrators, the court shall direct that the arbitration shall be held and the arbitrators be appointed in accordance with Article 3 of the Inter-American Convention.

§ 304. Recognition and enforcement of foreign arbitral decisions and awards; reciprocity

Arbitral decisions or awards made in the territory of a foreign State shall, on the basis of reciprocity, be recognized and enforced under this chapter only if that State has ratified or acceded to the Inter-American Convention.

§ 305. Relationship between the Inter-American Convention and the Convention on the Recognition and Enforcement of Foreign Arbitral Awards of June 10, 1958

When the requirements for application of both the Inter-American Convention and the Convention on the Recognition and Enforcement of Foreign Arbitral Awards of June 10, 1958, are met, determination as to which Convention applies shall, unless otherwise expressly agreed, be made as follows:

(1) If a majority of the parties to the arbitration agreement are citizens of a State or States that have ratified or acceded to the Inter-American Convention and are member States of the Organization of American States, the Inter-American Convention shall apply.

(2) In all other cases the Convention on the Recognition and Enforcement of Foreign Arbitral Awards of June 10, 1958, shall apply.

§ 306. Applicable rules of Inter-American Commercial Arbitration Commission

(a) For the purposes of this chapter the rules of procedure of the Inter-American Commercial Arbitration Commission referred to in Article 3 of the Inter-American Convention shall, subject to subsection (b) of this section, be those rules as promulgated by the Commission on July 1, 1988.

(b) In the event the rules of procedure of the Inter-American Commercial Arbitration Commission are modified or amended in accordance with the procedures for amendment of the rules of that Commission, the Secretary of State, by regulation in accordance with section 553 of title 5, consistent with the aims and purposes of this Convention, may prescribe that such modifications or amendments shall be effective for purposes of this chapter.

§ 307. Chapter 1; residual application

Chapter 1 applies to actions and proceedings brought under this chapter to the extent chapter 1 is not in conflict with this chapter or the Inter-American Convention as ratified by the United States.

§ 3.14 Text of the UNCITRAL Model International Commercial Arbitration Rules (1976)

Section I. Introductory Rules

Article 1. Scope of application

1. Where the parties to a contract have agreed in writing that disputes in relation to that contract shall be referred to arbitration under the UNCITRAL Arbitration Rules, then such disputes shall be settled in accordance with these Rules subject to such modification as the parties may agree in writing.

2. These Rules shall govern the arbitration except that where any of these Rules is in conflict with a provision of the law applicable to the arbitration from which the parties cannot derogate, that provision shall prevail.

Article 2. Notice, calculation periods of time

1. For the purposes of these Rules, any notice, including a notification, communication or proposal, is deemed to have been received if it is physically delivered to the addressee or if it is delivered at his habitual residence, place of business or mailing address, or, if none of these can be found after making reasonable inquiry, then at the addressee's last-known residence or place of business. Notice shall be deemed to have been received on the day it is so delivered.

2. For the purposes of calculating a period of time under these Rules, such period shall begin to run on the day following the day when a notice, notification, communication or proposal is received. If the last day of such period is an official holiday or a non-business day at the residence or place of business of the addressee, the period is extended until the first business day which follows. Official holidays or non-business days occurring during the running of the period of time are included in calculating the period.

Article 3. Notice of arbitration

1. The party initiating recourse to arbitration (hereinafter called the "claimant") shall give to the other party (hereinafter called the "respondent") a notice of arbitration.

2. Arbitral proceedings shall be deemed to commence on the date on which the notice of arbitration is received by the respondent.

3. The notice of arbitration shall include the following:

(a) A demand that the dispute be referred to arbitration;

(b) The names and addresses of the parties;

(c) A reference to the arbitration clause or the separate arbitration agreement that is invoked;

(d) A reference to the contract out of or in relation to which the dispute arises;

(e) The general nature of the claim and an indication of the amount involved, if any;

(f) The relief or remedy sought;

(g) A proposal as to the number of arbitrators (ie. one or three), if parties have not previously agreed thereon.

4. The notice of arbitration may also include:

(a) The proposals for the appointments of a sole arbitrator and an appointing authority referred to in article 6, paragraph 1;

(b) The notification of the appointment of an arbitrator referred to in article 7;

(c) The statement of claim referred to in article 18.

Article 4. Representation and assistance

The parties may be represented or assisted by persons of their choice. The names and addresses of such persons must be communicated in writing to the other party; such communication must specify whether the appointment is being made for purposes of representation or assistance.

Section II. Composition of the Arbitral Tribunal

Article 5. Number of arbitrators

If the parties have not previously agreed on the number of arbitrators (ie. One or three), and if within fifteen days after the receipt by the respondent of the notice of arbitration the parties have not agreed that there shall be only one arbitrator, three arbitrators shall be appointed.

Article 6. Appointment of arbitrators

1. If a sole arbitrator is to be appointed, either party may propose to the other:

(a) The names of one or more persons, one of whom should serve as the sole arbitrator; and

(b) If no appointing authority has been agreed upon by the parties, the name or names of one or more institutions or persons, one of whom would serve as appointing authority.

2. If within thirty days after receipt by a party of a proposal made in accordance with paragraph 1 the parties have not reached agreement on the choice of a sole arbitrator, the sole arbitrator shall be appointed by the appointing authority agreed upon by the parties. If no appointing authority has been agreed upon by the parties, or if the appointing authority agreed upon refuses to act or fails to appoint the arbitrator within sixty days of the receipt of a party's request therefor, either party may request the Secretary-General of the Permanent Court of Arbitration at The Hague to designate an appointing authority.

3. The appointing authority shall, at the request of one of the parties, appoint the sole arbitrator as promptly as possible. In making the appointment the appointing authority shall use the following list-procedure, unless both parties agree that the list-procedure should not be used or unless the appointing authority determines in its discretion that the use of the list-procedure is not appropriate for the case:

(a) At the request of one of the parties the appointing authority shall communicate to both parties an identical list containing at least three names;

(b) Within fifteen days after the receipt of this list, each party may return the list to the appointing authority after having deleted the name or names to which he objects and numbered the remaining names on the list in the order of his preference;

(c) After the expiration of the above period of time the appointing authority shall appoint the sole arbitrator from among the names approved on the lists returned to it and in accordance with the order of preference indicated by the parties;

(d) If for any reason the appointment cannot be made according to this procedure, the appointing authority may exercise its discretion in appointing the sole arbitrator.

4. In making the appointment, the appointing authority shall have regard to such considerations as are likely to secure the appointment of an independent and impartial arbitrator and shall take into account as well the advisability of appointing an arbitrator of a nationality other than the nationalities of the parties.

Article 7.

1. If three arbitrators are to be appointed, each party shall appoint one arbitrator. The two arbitrators thus appointed shall choose the third arbitrator who will act as the presiding arbitrator of the tribunal.

2. If within thirty days after the receipt of a party's notification of the appointment of an arbitrator the other party has not notified the first party of the arbitrator he has appointed:

(a) The first party may request the appointing authority previously designated by the parties to appoint the second arbitrator; or

(b) If no such authority has been previously designated by the parties, or if the appointing authority previously designated refuses to act or fails to appoint the arbitrator within thirty days after receipt of a party's request therefor, the first party may request the Secretary-General of the Permanent Court of Arbitration at the Hague to designate the appointing authority. The first party may then request the appointing authority so designated to appoint the second arbitrator. In either case, the appointing authority may exercise its discretion in appointing the arbitrator.

3. If within thirty days after the appointment of the second arbitrator the two arbitrators have not agreed on the choice of the presiding arbitrator, the presiding arbitrator shall be appointed by an appointing authority in the same way as a sole arbitrator would be appointed under article 6.

Article 8.

1. When an appointing authority is requested to appoint an arbitrator pursuant to article 6 or article 7, the party which makes the request shall send to the appointing authority a copy of the notice of arbitration, a copy of the contract out of or in relation to which the

dispute has arisen and a copy of the arbitration agreement if it is not contained in the contract. The appointing authority may require from either party such information as it deems necessary to fulfil its function.

2. Where the names of one or more persons are proposed for appointment as arbitrators, their full names, addresses and nationalities shall be indicated, together with a description of their qualifications.

Article 9. Challenges of arbitrators

A prospective arbitrator shall disclose to those who approach him in connection with his possible appointment any circumstances likely to give rise to justifiable doubts as to his impartiality or independence. An arbitrator, once appointed or chosen, shall disclose such circumstances to the parties unless they have already been informed by him of these circumstances.

Article 10.

1. Any arbitrator may be challenged if circumstances exist that give rise to justifiable doubts as to the arbitrator's impartiality or independence.

2. A party may challenge the arbitrator appointed by him only for reasons of which he becomes aware after the appointment has been made.

Article 11.

1. A party who intends to challenge an arbitrator shall send notice of his challenge within fifteen days after the appointment of the challenged arbitrator has been notified to the challenging party or within fifteen days after the circumstances mentioned in articles 9 and 10 became known to that party.

2. The challenge shall be notified to the other party, to the arbitrator who is challenged and to the other members of the arbitral tribunal. The notification shall be in writing and shall state the reasons for the challenge.

3. When an arbitrator has been challenged by one party, the other party may agree to the challenge. In both cases the procedure provided in article 6 or 7 shall be used in full for the appointment of the substitute arbitrator, even if during the process of appointing the challenged arbitrator a party had failed to exercise his right to appoint or to participate in the appointment.

Article 12.

1. If the other party does not agree to the challenge and the challenged arbitrator does not withdraw, the decision on the challenge will be made:

(a) When the initial appointment was made by an appointing authority, by that authority;

(b) When the initial appointment was not made by an appointing authority, but an appointing authority has been previously designated, by that authority;

(c) In all other cases, by the appointing authority to be designated in accordance with the procedure for designating an appointing authority provided for in article 6.

2. If the appointing authority sustains the challenge, a substitute arbitrator shall be appointed or chosen pursuant to the procedure applicable to the appointment or choice of an arbitrator as provided in articles 6 to 9 except that, when this procedure would call for the designation of an appointing authority, the appointment of the arbitrator shall be made by the appointing authority which decided on the challenge.

Article 13. Replacement of an arbitrator

1. In the event of death or resignation of an arbitrator during the course of the arbitral proceedings, a substitute arbitrator shall be appointed or chosen pursuant to the procedure provided for in articles 6 to 9 that was applicable to the appointment or choice of the arbitrator being replaced.

2. In the event that an arbitrator fails to act or in the event of the de jure or de facto impossibility of his performing his functions, the procedure in respect of the challenge and replacement of an arbitrator as provided in the preceding articles shall apply.

Article 14. Repetition of hearings in the event of the replacement of an arbitrator

If under articles 11 to 13 the sole or presiding arbitrator is replaced, any hearings held previously shall be repeated; if any other arbitrator is replaced, such prior hearings may be repeated at the discretion of the arbitral tribunal.

Section III. Arbitral Proceedings

Article 15. General provisions

1. Subject to these Rules, the arbitral tribunal may conduct the arbitration in such manner as it considers appropriate, provided the parties are treated with equality and that at any stage of the

proceedings each party is given a full opportunity of presenting his case.

2. If either party so requests at any stage of the proceedings, the arbitral tribunal shall hold hearings for the presentation of evidence by witnesses, including expert witnesses, or for oral argument. In the absence of such a request, the arbitral tribunal shall decide whether to hold such hearings or whether the proceedings shall be conducted on the basis of documents and other materials.

3. All documents or information supplied to the arbitral tribunal by one party shall at the same time be communicated by that party to the other party.

Article 16. Place of arbitration

1. Unless the parties have agreed upon the place where the arbitration is to be held, such place shall be determined by the arbitral tribunal, having regard to the circumstances of the arbitration.

2. The arbitral tribunal may determine the locale of the arbitration within the country agreed by the parties. It may hear witnesses and hold meetings for consultation among its members at any place it deems appropriate, having regard to the circumstances of the arbitration.

3. The arbitral tribunal may meet at any place it deems appropriate for the inspection of goods, other property or documents. The parties shall be given sufficient notice to enable them to be present at such inspection.

4. The award shall be made at the place of arbitration.

Article 17. Language

1. Subject to an agreement by the parties, the arbitral tribunal shall, promptly after its appointment, determine the language or languages to be used in the proceedings. This determination shall apply to the statement of claim, the statement of defence, and any further written statements and, if oral hearings take place, to the language or languages to be used in such hearings.

Article 18. Statement of claim

1. Unless the statement of claim was contained in the notice of arbitration, within a period of time to be determined by the arbitral tribunal, the claimant shall communicate his statement of claim in writing to the respondent and to each of the arbitrators. A copy of the contract, and of the arbitration agreement if not contained in the contract, shall be annexed thereto.

2. The statement of claim shall include the following particulars:

(a) The names and addresses of the parties;

(b) A statement of the facts supporting the claim;

(c) The points at issue;

(d) The relief or remedy sought.

The claimant may annex to his statement of claim all documents he deems relevant or may add a reference to the documents or other evidence he will submit.

Article 19. Statement of defence

1. Within a period of time to be determined by the arbitral tribunal, the respondent shall communicate his statement of defence in writing to the claimant and to each of the arbitrators.

2. The statement of defence shall reply to the particulars (b), (c) and (d) of the statement of claim (article 18, para. 2). The respondent may annex to his statement the documents on which he relies for his defence or may add a reference to the documents or other evidence he will submit.

3. In his statement of defence, or at a later stage in the arbitral proceedings if the arbitral tribunal decides that the delay was justified under the circumstances, the respondent may make a counter-claim arising out of the same contract or rely on a claim arising out of the same contract for the purpose of a set-off.

4. The provisions of article 18, paragraph 2, shall apply to a counter-claim and a claim relied on for the purpose of a set-off.

Article 20. Amendments to the claim or defence

During the course of the arbitral proceedings either party may amend or supplement his claim or defence unless the arbitral tribunal considers it inappropriate to allow such amendment having regard to the delay in making it or prejudice to the other party or any other circumstances. However, a claim may not be amended in such a manner that the amended claim falls outside the scope of the arbitration clause or separate arbitration agreement.

Article 21. Pleas as to the jurisdiction of the arbitral tribunal

1. The arbitral tribunal shall have the power to rule on objections that it has no jurisdiction, including any objections with respect to the existence or validity of the arbitration clause or of the separate arbitration agreement.

2. The arbitral tribunal shall have the power to determine the existence or the validity of the contract of which an arbitration clause forms a part. For the purposes of article 21, an arbitration clause which forms part of a contract and which provides for arbitration under these Rules shall be treated as an agreement independent of the other terms of the contract. A decision by the arbitral tribunal that the contract is null and void shall not entail ipso jure the invalidity of the arbitration clause.

3. A plea that the arbitral tribunal does not have jurisdiction shall be raised not later than in the statement of defence or, with respect to a counter-claim, in the reply to the counter-claim.

4. In general, the arbitral tribunal should rule on a plea concerning its jurisdiction as a preliminary question. However, the arbitral tribunal may proceed with the arbitration and rule on such a plea in their final award.

Article 22. Further written statements

The arbitral tribunal shall decide which further written statements, in addition to the statement of claim and the statement of defence, shall be required from the parties or may be presented by them and shall fix the periods of time for communicating such statements.

Article 23. Periods of time

The periods of time fixed by the arbitral tribunal for the communication of written statements (including the statement of claim and statements of defence) should not exceed forty-five days. However, the arbitral tribunal may extend the time-limits if it concludes that an extension is justified.

Article 24. Evidence and hearings

1. Each party shall have the burden of proving the facts relied on to support his claim or defence.

2. The arbitral tribunal may, if it considers it appropriate, require a party to deliver to the tribunal and to the other party, within such a period of time as the arbitral tribunal shall decide, a summary of the documents and other evidence which that party intends to present in support of the facts in issue set out in his statement of claim or statement of defence.

3. At any time during the arbitral proceedings the arbitral tribunal may require the parties to produce documents, exhibits or other evidence within such a period of time as the tribunal shall determine.

Article 25.

1. In the event of an oral hearing, the arbitral tribunal shall give the parties adequate advance notice of the date, time and place thereof.

2. If witnesses are to be heard, at least fifteen days before the hearing each party shall communicate to the arbitral tribunal and to the other party the names and addresses of the witnesses he intends to present, the subject upon and the languages in which such witnesses will give their testimony.

3. The arbitral tribunal shall make arrangements for the translation of oral statements made at a hearing and for a record of the hearing if either is deemed necessary by the tribunal under the circumstances of the case, or if the parties have agreed thereto and have communicated such agreement to the tribunal at least fifteen days before the hearing.

4. Hearings shall be held in camera unless the parties agree otherwise. The arbitral tribunal may require the retirement of any witness or witnesses during the testimony of other witnesses. The arbitral tribunal is free to determine the manner in which witnesses are examined.

5. Evidence of witnesses may also be presented in the form of written statements signed by them.

6. The arbitral tribunal shall determine the admissibility, relevance, materiality and weight of the evidence offered.

Article 26. Interim measures of protection

1. At the request of either party, the arbitral tribunal may take any interim measures it deems necessary in respect of the subject-matter of the dispute, including measures for the conservation of the goods forming the subject-matter in dispute, such as ordering their deposit with a third person or the sale of perishable goods.

2. Such interim measures may be established in the form of an interim award.

The arbitral tribunal shall be entitled to require security for the costs of such measures.

3. A request for interim measures addressed by any party to a judicial authority shall not be deemed incompatible with the agreement to arbitrate, or as a waiver of that agreement.

Article 27. Experts

1. The arbitral tribunal may appoint one or more experts to report to it, in writing, on specific issues to be determined by the tribunal.

A copy of the expert's terms of reference, established by the arbitral tribunal, shall be communicated to the parties.

2. The parties shall give the expert any relevant information or produce for inspection any relevant documents or goods that he may require of them. Any dispute between a party and such expert as to the relevance of the required information or production shall be referred to the arbitral tribunal for decision.

3. Upon receipt of the expert's report, the tribunal shall communicate a copy of the report to the parties who shall be given the opportunity to express, in writing, their opinion of the report. A party shall be entitled to examine any document on which the expert has relied in his report.

4. At the request of either party the expert, after delivery of the report, may be heard at a hearing where the parties hall have the opportunity to be present and to interrogate the expert. At this hearing either party may present expert witnesses in order to testify on the points at issue. The provisions of article 25 shall be applicable to such proceedings.

Article 28. Default

1. If, within the period of time fixed by the arbitral tribunal, the claimant has failed to communicate his claim without showing sufficient cause for such failure, the arbitral tribunal shall order the proceedings to continue.

2. If one of the parties, duly notified under these Rules, fails to appear at a hearing, without showing sufficient cause for such failure, the arbitral tribunal may proceed with the arbitration.

3. If one of the parties, duly invited to produce documentary evidence, fails to do so within the established period of time, without showing sufficient cause for such failure, the arbitral tribunal may make the award on the evidence before it.

Article 29. Closure of hearings

1. The arbitral tribunal may inquire of the parties if they have any further proof to offer or witnesses to be heard or submissions to make and, if there are none, if may declare the hearings closed.

2. The arbitral tribunal may, if it considers it necessary owing to exceptional circumstances, decide, on its own motion or upon application of a party, to reopen the hearings at any time before the award is made.

Article 30.

A party who knows that any provision of, or requirement under, these Rules has not been complied with and yet proceeds with the arbitration without promptly stating his objection to such non-compliance, shall be deemed to have waived his right to object.

Section IV. The Award

Article 31. Decisions

1. When there are three arbitrators, any award or other decision of the arbitral tribunal shall be made by a majority of the arbitrators.

2. In the case of questions of procedure, when there is no majority or when the arbitral tribunal so authorises, the presiding arbitrator may decide on his own, subject to revision, if any, by the arbitral Tribunal.

Article 32. Form and effect of the award

1. In addition to making a final award, the arbitral tribunal shall be entitled to make interim, interlocutory, or partial awards.

2. The award shall be made in writing and shall be final and binding on the parties. The parties undertake to carry out the award without delay.

3. The arbitral tribunal shall state the reasons upon which the award is based, unless the parties have agreed that no reasons are to be given.

4. An award shall be signed by the arbitrators and it shall contain the date on which and the place where the award was made. Where there are three arbitrators and one of them fails to sign, the award shall state the reason for absence of the signature.

5. The award may be made public only with the consent of both parties.

6. Copies of the award signed by the arbitrators shall be communicated to the parties by the arbitral tribunal.

7. If the arbitration law of the country where the award is made requires that the award by filed or registered by the arbitral tribunal, the tribunal shall comply with this requirement within the period of time required by law.

Article 33. Applicable law, amiable compositeur

1. The arbitral tribunal shall apply the law designated by the parties as applicable to the substance of the dispute. Failing such designation by the parties, the arbitral tribunal shall apply the law determined by the conflict of laws rules which it considers applicable.

2. The arbitral tribunal shall decide as amiable compositeur or ex aequo et bono only if the parties have expressly authorised the arbitral tribunal to do so and if the law applicable to the arbitral procedure permits such arbitration.

3. In all cases, the arbitral tribunal shall decide in accordance with the terms of the contract and shall take into account the usages of the trade applicable to the transaction.

Article 34.

1. If, before the award is made, the parties agree on a settlement of the dispute, the arbitral tribunal shall either issue an order for the termination of the arbitral proceedings or, if requested by both parties and accepted by the tribunal, record the settlement in the form of an arbitral award on agreed terms. The arbitral tribunal is not obliged to give reasons for such an award.

2. If, before the award is made, the continuation of the arbitral proceedings becomes unnecessary or impossible for any reason not mentioned in paragraph 1, the arbitral tribunal shall inform the parties of its intention to issue an order for the termination of the proceedings. The arbitral tribunal shall have the power to issue such an order unless a party raises justifiable grounds for objection.

3. Copies of the order for termination of the arbitral proceedings or of the arbitral award on agreed terms, signed by the arbitrators, shall be communicated by the arbitral tribunal to the parties. Where an arbitral award on agreed terms is made, the provisions of article 32, paragraphs 2 and 4 to 7, shall apply.

Article 35. Interpretation of the award

1. Within thirty days after the receipt of the award, either party, with notice to the other party, may request that the arbitral tribunal give an interpretation of the award.

2. The interpretation shall be given in writing within forty-five days after the receipt of the request. The interpretation shall form part of the award and the provisions of article 32, paragraphs 2 to 7, shall apply.

Article 36. Correction of the award

1. Within thirty days after the receipt of the award, either party, with notice to the other party, may request the arbitral tribunal to correct in the award any errors in computation, any clerical or typographical errors, or any errors of similar nature. The arbitral tribunal may within thirty days after the communication of the award make such corrections on its own initiative.

2. Such corrections shall be in writing, and the provisions of article 32, paragraphs 2 to 7, shall apply.

Article 37. Additional award

1. Within thirty days after the receipt of the award, either party, with notice to the other party, may request the arbitral tribunal to make an additional award as to claims presented in the arbitral proceedings but omitted from the award.

2. If the arbitral tribunal considers the request for an additional award to be justified and considers that the omission can be rectified without any further hearings or evidence, it shall complete its award within sixty days after the receipt of the request.

3. When an additional award is made, the provisions of article 32 paragraphs 2 to 7, shall apply.

Article 38. Cost

The arbitral tribunal shall fix the costs of arbitration in its award. The term "costs" includes only:

(a) The fees of the arbitral tribunal to be stated separately as to each arbitrator and to be fixed by the tribunal itself in accordance with article 39;

(b) The travel and other expenses incurred by the arbitrators;

(c) The costs of expert advice and of other assistance required by the arbitral tribunal;

(d) The travel and other expenses of witnesses to the extent such expenses are approved by the arbitral tribunal;

(e) The costs for legal representation and assistance of the successful party if such costs were claimed during the arbitral proceedings, and only to the extent that the arbitral tribunal determines that the amount of such costs is reasonable;

(f) Any fees and expenses of the appointing authority as well as the expenses of the Secretary-General of the Permanent Court of Arbitration at The Hague.

Article 39.

1. The fees of the arbitral tribunal shall be reasonable in amount, taking into account the amount in dispute, the complexity of the subject-matter, the time spent by the arbitrators and any other relevant circumstances of the case.

2. If an appointing authority has been agreed upon by the parties or designated by the Secretary-General of the Permanent Court of Arbitration at The Hague, and if that authority has issued a schedule

of fees for arbitrators in international cases which it administers, the arbitral tribunal in fixing its fees shall take that schedule of fees into account to the extent that it considers appropriate in the circumstances of the case.

3. If such appointing authority has not issued a schedule of fees for arbitrators in international cases, any party may at any time request the appointing authority to furnish a statement setting forth the basis for establishing fees which is customarily followed in international cases in which the authority appoints arbitrators. If the appointing authority consents to provide such a statement, the arbitral tribunal in fixing its fees shall take such information into account to the extent that it considers appropriate in the circumstances of the case.

4. In cases referred to in paragraphs 2 and 3, when a party so requests and the appointing authority consents to perform the function, the arbitral tribunal shall fix its fees only after consultation with the appointing authority which may make any comment it deems appropriate to the arbitral tribunal concerning the fees.

Article 40.

1. Except as provided in paragraph 2, the costs of arbitration shall in principle be borne by the unsuccessful party. However, the arbitral tribunal may apportion each of such costs between the parties if it determines that apportionment is reasonable, taking into account the circumstances of the case.

2. With respect to the costs of legal representation and assistance referred to in article 38, paragraph (e), the arbitral tribunal, taking into account the circumstances of the case, shall be free to determine which party shall bear such costs or may apportion such costs between the parties if it determines that apportionment is reasonable.

3. When the arbitral tribunal issues an order for the termination of the arbitral proceedings or makes an award on agreed terms, it shall fix the costs of arbitration referred to in article 38 and article 39, paragraph 1, in the text of that order or award.

4. No additional fees may be charged by an arbitral tribunal for interpretation or correction or completion of its award under articles 35 to 37.

Article 41. Deposit of costs

1. The arbitral tribunal, on its establishment, may request each party to deposit an equal amount as an advance for the costs referred to in article 38, paragraphs (a), (b) and (c).

2. During the course of the arbitral proceedings the arbitral tribunal may request supplementary deposits from the parties.

3. If an appointing authority has been agreed upon by the parties or designated by The Hague, and when a party so requests and the appointing authority consents to perform the function, the arbitral tribunal shall fix the amounts of any deposits or supplementary deposits only after consultation with the appointing authority which may make any comments to the arbitral tribunal which it deems appropriate concerning the amount of such deposits and supplementary deposits.

4. If the required deposits are not paid in full within thirty days after the receipt of the request, the arbitral tribunal shall so inform the parties in order that one or another of them may make the required payment. If such payment is not made, the arbitral tribunal may order the suspension or termination of the arbitral proceedings.

5. After the award has been made, the arbitral tribunal shall render an accounting to the parties of the deposits received and return any unexpended balance to the parties.

MODEL UNCITRAL ARBITRATION CLAUSE OR SEPARATE ARBITRATION AGREEMENT

Any dispute, controversy or claim arising out of or relating to this contract, or the breach, termination or invalidity thereof, shall be settled by arbitration in accordance with the UNCITRAL Arbitration Rules as present in force. Parties may wish to consider adding: (a) The appointing authority shall be _______ (name of institution or person); (b) The number of arbitrators shall be _______ (one or three); (c) The place of arbitration shall be _______ (town or country); (d) The language(s) to be used in the arbitral proceedings shall be _______.

§ 3.15 Text of the UNCITRAL Model Law on International Commercial Arbitration (1985)

CHAPTER I—GENERAL PROVISIONS

Article 1. Scope of application[121]

1. This Law applies to international commercial[122] arbitration, subject to any agreement in force between this State and any other State or States.

---

121 Article headings are for reference purposes only and are not to be used for purposes of interpretation.

122 The term "commercial" should be given a wide interpretation so as to cover matters arising from all relationships of a commercial nature, whether contractual or

2. The provisions of this Law, except articles 8, 9, 35 and 36, apply only if the place of arbitration is in the territory of this State.

3. An arbitration is international if:

(a) the parties to an arbitration agreement have, at the time of the conclusion of that agreement, their places of business in different States; or

(b) one of the following places is situated outside the State in which the parties have their places of business:

(i) the place of arbitration if determined in, or pursuant to, the arbitration agreement;

(ii) any place where a substantial part of the obligations of the commercial relationship is to be performed or the place with which the subject-matter of the dispute is most closely connected; or

(c) the parties have expressly agreed that the subject-matter of the arbitration agreement relates to more than one country.

4. For the purposes of paragraph (3) of this article:

(a) if a party has more than one place of business, the place of business is that which has the closest relationship to the arbitration agreement;

(b) if a party does not have a place of business, reference is to be made to his habitual residence.

5. This Law shall not affect any other law of this State by virtue of which certain disputes may not be submitted to arbitration or may be submitted to arbitration only according to provisions other than those of this Law.

Article 2. Definitions and rules of interpretation

For the purposes of this Law:

(a) "arbitration" means any arbitration whether or not administered by a permanent arbitral institution;

(b) "arbitral tribunal" means a sole arbitrator or a panel of arbitrators;

---

not. Relationships of a commercial nature include, but are not limited to, the following transactions: any trade transaction for the supply or exchange of goods or services; distribution agreement; commercial representation or agency; factoring; leasing; construction of works; consulting; engineering; licensing; investment; financing; banking; insurance; exploitation agreement or concession; joint venture and other forms of industrial or business cooperation; carriage of goods or passengers by air, sea, rail or road.

(c) "court" means a body or organ of the judicial system of a State;

(d) where a provision of this Law, except article 28, leaves the parties free to determine a certain issue, such freedom includes the right of the parties to authorize a third party, including an institution, to make that determination;

(e) where a provision of this Law refers to the fact that the parties have agreed or that they may agree or in any other way refers to an agreement of the parties, such agreement includes any arbitration rules referred to in that agreement;

(f) where a provision of this Law, other than in articles 25(a) and 32(2)(a), refers to a claim, it also applies to a counter-claim, and where it refers to a defence, it also applies to a defence to such counter-claim.

Article 3. Receipt of written communications

1. Unless otherwise agreed by the parties:

(a) any written communication is deemed to have been received if it is delivered to the addressee personally or if it is delivered at his place of business, habitual residence or mailing address; if none of these can be found after making a reasonable inquiry, a written communication is deemed to have been received if it is sent to the addressee's last-known place of business, habitual residence or mailing address by registered letter or any other means which provides a record of the attempt to deliver it;

(b) the communication is deemed to have been received on the day it is so delivered.

2. The provisions of this article do not apply to communications in court proceedings.

Article 4. Waiver of right to object

A party who knows that any provision of this Law from which the parties may derogate or any requirement under the arbitration agreement has not been complied with and yet proceeds with the arbitration without stating his objection to such non-compliance without undue delay or, if a time-limit is provided therefor, within such period of time, shall be deemed to have waived his right to object.

Article 5. Extent of court intervention

In matters governed by this Law, no court shall intervene except where so provided in this Law.

Article 6. Court or other authority for certain functions of arbitration assistance and supervision

The functions referred to in articles 11(3), 11(4), 13(3), 14, 16(3) and 34(2) shall be performed by . . . [Each State enacting this model law specifies the court, courts or, where referred to therein, other authority competent to perform these functions.]

CHAPTER II—ARBITRATION AGREEMENT

Article 7. Definition and form of arbitration agreement

1. "Arbitration agreement" is an agreement by the parties to submit to arbitration all or certain disputes which have arisen or which may arise between them in respect of a defined legal relationship, whether contractual or not. An arbitration agreement may be in the form of an arbitration clause in a contract or in the form of a separate agreement.

2. The arbitration agreement shall be in writing. An agreement is in writing if it is contained in a document signed by the parties or in an exchange of letters, telex, telegrams or other means of telecommunication which provide a record of the agreement, or in an exchange of statements of claim and defence in which the existence of an agreement is alleged by one party and not denied by another. The reference in a contract to a document containing an arbitration clause constitutes an arbitration agreement provided that the contract is in writing and the reference is such as to make that clause part of the contract.

Article 8. Arbitration agreement and substantive claim before court

1. A court before which an action is brought in a matter which is the subject of an arbitration agreement shall, if a party so requests not later than when submitting his first statement on the substance of the dispute, refer the parties to arbitration unless it finds that the agreement is null and void, inoperative or incapable of being performed.

2. Where an action referred to in paragraph (1) of this article has been brought, arbitral proceedings may nevertheless be commenced or continued, and an award may be made, while the issue is pending before the court.

Article 9. Arbitration agreement and interim measures by court

It is not incompatible with an arbitration agreement for a party to request, before or during arbitral proceedings, from a court an interim measure of protection and for a court to grant such measure.

CHAPTER III—COMPOSITION OF ARBITRAL TRIBUNAL

Article 10. Number of arbitrators

1. The parties are free to determine the number of arbitrators.

2. Failing such determination, the number of arbitrators shall be three.

Article 11. Appointment of arbitrators

1. No person shall be precluded by reason of his nationality from acting as an arbitrator, unless otherwise agreed by the parties.

2. The parties are free to agree on a procedure of appointing the arbitrator or arbitrators, subject to the provisions of paragraphs (4) and (5) of this article.

3. Failing such agreement,

(a) in an arbitration with three arbitrators, each party shall appoint one arbitrator, and the two arbitrators thus appointed shall appoint the third arbitrator; if a party fails to appoint the arbitrator within thirty days of receipt of a request to do so from the other party, or if the two arbitrators fail to agree on the third arbitrator within thirty days of their appointment, the appointment shall be made, upon request of a party, by the court or other authority specified in article 6;

(b) in an arbitration with a sole arbitrator, if the parties are unable to agree on the arbitrator, he shall be appointed, upon request of a party, by the court or other authority specified in article 6.

4. Where, under an appointment procedure agreed upon by the parties,

(a) a party fails to act as required under such procedure, or

(b) the parties, or two arbitrators, are unable to reach an agreement expected of them under such procedure, or

(c) a third party, including an institution, fails to perform any function entrusted to it under such procedure, any party may request the court or other authority specified in article 6 to take the necessary measure, unless the agreement on the appointment procedure provides other means for securing the appointment.

5. A decision on a matter entrusted by paragraph (3) or (4) of this article to the court or other authority specified in article 6 shall be subject to no appeal. The court or other authority, in appointing an arbitrator, shall have due regard to any qualifications required of the arbitrator by the agreement of the parties and to such considerations

as are likely to secure the appointment of an independent and impartial arbitrator and, in the case of a sole or third arbitrator, shall take into account as well the advisability of appointing an arbitrator of a nationality other than those of the parties.

Article 12. Grounds for challenge

1. When a person is approached in connection with his possible appointment as an arbitrator, he shall disclose any circumstances likely to give rise to justifiable doubts as to his impartiality or independence. An arbitrator, from the time of his appointment and throughout the arbitral proceedings, shall without delay disclose any such circumstances to the parties unless they have already been informed of them by him.

2. An arbitrator may be challenged only if circumstances exist that give rise to justifiable doubts as to his impartiality or independence, or if he does not possess qualifications agreed to by the parties. A party may challenge an arbitrator appointed by him, or in whose appointment he has participated, only for reasons of which he becomes aware after the appointment has been made.

Article 13. Challenge procedure

1. The parties are free to agree on a procedure for challenging an arbitrator, subject to the provisions of paragraph (3) of this article.

2. Failing such agreement, a party who intends to challenge an arbitrator shall, within fifteen days after becoming aware of the constitution of the arbitral tribunal or after becoming aware of any circumstance referred to in article 12(2), send a written statement of the reasons for the challenge to the arbitral tribunal. Unless the challenged arbitrator withdraws from his office or the other party agrees to the challenge, the arbitral tribunal shall decide on the challenge.

3. If a challenge under any procedure agreed upon by the parties or under the procedure of paragraph (2) of this article is not successful, the challenging party may request, within thirty days after having received notice of the decision rejecting the challenge, the court or other authority specified in article 6 to decide on the challenge, which decision shall be subject to no appeal; while such a request is pending, the arbitral tribunal, including the challenged arbitrator, may continue the arbitral proceedings and make an award.

Article 14. Failure or impossibility to act

1. If an arbitrator becomes *de jure* or *de facto* unable to perform his functions or for other reasons fails to act without undue delay, his mandate terminates if he withdraws from his office or if the parties

agree on the termination. Otherwise, if a controversy remains concerning any of these grounds, any party may request the court or other authority specified in article 6 to decide on the termination of the mandate, which decision shall be subject to no appeal.

2. If, under this article or article 13(2), an arbitrator withdraws from his office or a party agrees to the termination of the mandate of an arbitrator, this does not imply acceptance of the validity of any ground referred to in this article or article 12(2).

Article 15. Appointment of substitute arbitrator

Where the mandate of an arbitrator terminates under article 13 or 14 or because of his withdrawal from office for any other reason or because of the revocation of his mandate by agreement of the parties or in any other case of termination of his mandate, a substitute arbitrator shall be appointed according to the rules that were applicable to the appointment of the arbitrator being replaced.

CHAPTER IV—JURISDICTION OF ARBITRAL TRIBUNAL

Article 16. Competence of arbitral tribunal to rule on its jurisdiction

1. The arbitral tribunal may rule on its own jurisdiction, including any objections with respect to the existence or validity of the arbitration agreement. For that purpose, an arbitration clause which forms part of a contract shall be treated as an agreement independent of the other terms of the contract. A decision by the arbitral tribunal that the contract is null and void shall not entail *ipso jure* the invalidity of the arbitration clause.

2. A plea that the arbitral tribunal does not have jurisdiction shall be raised not later than the submission of the statement of defence. A party is not precluded from raising such a plea by the fact that he has appointed, or participated in the appointment of, an arbitrator. A plea that the arbitral tribunal is exceeding the scope of its authority shall be raised as soon as the atter alleged to be beyond the scope of its authority is raised during the arbitral proceedings. The arbitral tribunal may, in either case, admit a later plea if it considers the delay justified.

3. The arbitral tribunal may rule on a plea referred to in paragraph (2) of this article either as a preliminary question or in an award on the merits. If the arbitral tribunal rules as a preliminary question that it has jurisdiction, any party may request, within thirty days after having received notice of that ruling, the court specified in article 6 to decide the matter, which decision shall be subject to no appeal; while such a request is pending, the arbitral tribunal may continue the arbitral proceedings and make an award.

Article 17. Power of arbitral tribunal to order interim measures

Unless otherwise agreed by the parties, the arbitral tribunal may, at the request of a party, order any party to take such interim measure of protection as the arbitral tribunal may consider necessary in respect of the subject matter of the dispute. The arbitral tribunal may require any party to provide appropriate security in connection with such measure.

CHAPTER V—CONDUCT OF ARBITRAL PROCEEDINGS

Article 18. Equal treatment of parties

The parties shall be treated with equality and each party shall be given a full opportunity of presenting his case.

Article 19. Determination of rules of procedure

1. Subject to the provisions of this Law, the parties are free to agree on the procedure to be followed by the arbitral tribunal in conducting the proceedings.

2. Failing such agreement, the arbitral tribunal may, subject to the provisions of this Law, conduct the arbitration in such manner as it considers appropriate. The power conferred upon the arbitral tribunal includes the power to determine the admissibility, relevance, materiality and weight of any evidence.

Article 20. Place of arbitration

1. The parties are free to agree on the place of arbitration. Failing such agreement, the place of arbitration shall be determined by the arbitral tribunal having regard to the circumstances of the case, including the convenience of the parties.

2. Notwithstanding the provisions of paragraph/ (1) of this article, the arbitral tribunal may, unless otherwise agreed by the parties, meet at any place it considers appropriate for consultation among its members, for hearing witnesses, experts or the parties, or for inspection of goods, other property or documents.

Article 21. Commencenent of arbitral proceedings

Unless otherwise agreed by the parties, the arbitral proceedings in respect of a particular dispute commence on the date on which a request for that dispute to be referred to arbitration is received by the respondent.

Article 22. Language

1. The parties are free to agree on the language or languages to be used in the arbitral proceedings. Failing such agreement, the arbitral tribunal shall determine the language or languages to be used in the

proceedings. This agreement or determination, unless otherwise specified therein, shall apply to any written statement by a party, any hearing and any award, decision or other communication by the arbitral tribunal.

2. The arbitral tribunal may order that any documentary evidence shall be accompanied by a translation into the language or languages agreed upon by the parties or determined by the arbitral tribunal.

Article 23. Statements of claim and defence

1. Within the period of time agreed by the parties or determined by the arbitral tribunal, the claimant shall state the facts supporting his claim, the points at issue and the relief or remedy sought, and the respondent shall state his defence in respect of these particulars, unless the parties have otherwise agreed as to the required elements of such statements. The parties may submit with their statements all documents they consider to be relevant or may add a reference to the documents or other evidence they will submit.

2. Unless otherwise agreed by the parties, either party may amend or supplement his claim or defence during the course of the arbitral proceedings, unless the arbitral tribunal considers it inappropriate to allow such amendment having regard to the delay in making it.

Article 24. Hearings and written proceedings

1. Subject to any contrary agreement by the parties, the arbitral tribunal shall decide whether to hold oral hearings for the presentation of evidence or for oral argument, or whether the proceedings shall be conducted on the basis of documents and other materials. However, unless the parties have agreed that no hearings shall be held, the arbitral tribunal shall hold such hearings at an appropriate stage of the proceedings, if so requested by a party.

2. The parties shall be given sufficient advance notice of any hearing and of any meeting of the arbitral tribunal for the purposes of inspection of goods, other property or documents.

3. All statements, documents or other information supplied to the arbitral tribunal by one party shall be communicated to the other party. Also any expert report or evidentiary document on which the arbitral tribunal may rely in making its decision shall be communicated to the parties.

Article 25. Default of a party

Unless otherwise agreed by the parties, if, without showing sufficient cause,

(a) the claimant fails to communicate his statement of claim in accordance with article 23(1), the arbitral tribunal shall terminate the proceedings;

(b) the respondent fails to communicate his statement of defence in accordance with article 23(1), the arbitral tribunal shall continue the proceedings without treating such failure in itself as an admission of the claimant's allegations;

(c) any party fails to appear at a hearing or to produce documentary evidence, the arbitral tribunal may continue the proceedings and make the award on the evidence before it.

Article 26. Expert appointed by arbitral tribunal

1. Unless otherwise agreed by the parties, the arbitral tribunal

(a) may appoint one or more experts to report to it on specific issues to be determined by the arbitral tribunal;

(b) may require a party to give the expert any relevant information or to produce, or to provide access to, any relevant documents, goods or other property for his inspection.

2. Unless otherwise agreed by the parties, if a party so requests or if the arbitral tribunal considers it necessary, the expert shall, after delivery of his written or oral report, participate in a hearing where the parties have the opportunity to put questions to him and to present expert witnesses in order to testify on the points at issue.

Article 27. Court assistance in taking evidence

The arbitral tribunal or a party with the approval of the arbitral tribunal may request from a competent court of this State assistance in taking evidence. The court may execute the request within its competence and according to its rules on taking evidence.

CHAPTER VI—MAKING OF AWARD AND TERMINATION OF PROCEEDINGS

Article 28. Rules applicable to substance of dispute

1. The arbitral tribunal shall decide the dispute in accordance with such rules of law as are chosen by the parties as applicable to the substance of the dispute. Any designation of the law or legal system of a given State shall be construed, unless otherwise expressed, as directly referring to the substantive law of that State and not to its conflict of laws rules.

2. Failing any designation by the parties, the arbitral tribunal shall apply the law determined by the conflict of laws rules which it considers applicable.

3. The arbitral tribunal shall decide *ex aequo et bono* or' as *amiable compositeur* only if the parties have expressly authorized it to do so.

4. In all cases, the arbitral tribunal shall decide in accordance with the terms of the contract and shall take into account the usages of the trade applicable to the transaction.

Article 29. Decision making by panel of arbitrators

In arbitral proceedings with more than one arbitrator, any decision of the arbitral tribunal shall be made, unless otherwise agreed by the parties, by a majority of all its members. However, questions of procedure may be decided by a presiding arbitrator, if so authorized by the parties or all members of the arbitral tribunal.

Article 30. Settlement

1. If, during arbitral proceedings, the parties settle the dispute, the arbitral tribunal shall terminate the proceedings and, if requested by the parties and not objected to by the arbitral tribunal, record the settlement in the form of an arbitral award on agreed terms.

2. An award on agreed terms shall be made in accordance with the provisions of article 31 and shall state that it is an award. Such an award has the same status and effect as any other award on the merits of the case.

Article 31. Form and contents of award

1. The award shall be made in writing and shall be signed by the arbitrator or arbitrators. In arbitral proceedings with more than one arbitrator, the signatures of the majority of all members of the arbitral tribunal shall suffice, provided that the reason for any omitted signature is stated.

2. The award shall state the reasons upon which it is based, unless the parties have agreed that no reasons are to be given or the award is an award on agreed terms under article 30.

3. The award shall state its date and the place of arbitration as determined in accordance with article 20(1). The award shall be deemed to have been made at that place.

4. After the award is made, a copy signed by the arbitrators in accordance with paragraph (1) of this article shall be delivered to each party.

Article 32. Termination of proceedings

1. The arbitral proceedings are terminated by the final award or by an order of the arbitral tribunal in accordance with paragraph (2) of this article.

2. The arbitral tribunal shall issue an order for the termination of the arbitral proceedings when:

(a) the claimant withdraws his claim, unless the respondent objects thereto and the arbitral tribunal recognizes a legitimate interest on his part in obtaining a final settlement of the dispute;

(b) the parties agree on the termination of the proceedings;

(c) the arbitral tribunal finds that the continuation of the proceedings has for any other reason become unnecessary or impossible.

3. The mandate of the arbitral tribunal terminates with the termination of the arbitral proceedings, subject to the provisions of articles 33 and 34(4).

Article 33. Correction and interpretation of award; additional award

1. Within thirty days of receipt of the award, unless another period of time has been agreed upon by the parties:

(a) a party, with notice to the other party, may request the arbitral tribunal to correct in the award any errors in computation, any clerical or typographical errors or any errors of similar nature;

(b) if so agreed by the parties, a party, with notice to the other party, may request the arbitral tribunal to give an interpretation of a specific point or part of the award. If the arbitral tribunal considers the request to be justified, it shall make the correction or give the interpretation within thirty days of receipt of the request. The interpretation shall form part of the award.

2. The arbitral tribunal may correct any error of the type referred to in paragraph (1)*(a)* of this article on its own initiative within thirty days of the date of the award.

3. Unless otherwise agreed by the parties, a party, with notice to the other party, may request, within thirty days of receipt of the award, the arbitral tribunal to make an additional award as to claims presented in the arbitral proceedings but omitted from the award. If the arbitral tribunal considers the request to be justified, it shall make the additional award within sixty days.

4. The arbitral tribunal may extend, if necessary, the period of time within which it shall make a correction, interpretation or an additional award under paragraph (1) or (3) of this article.

5. The provisions of article 31 shall apply to a correction or interpretation of the award or to an additional award.

CHAPTER VII—RECOURSE AGAINST AWARD

Article 34. Application for setting aside as exclusive recourse against arbitral award

1. Recourse to a court against an arbitral award may be made only by an application for setting aside in accordance with paragraphs (2) and (3) of this article.

2. An arbitral award may be set aside by the court specified in article 6 only if:

(a) the party making the application furnishes proof that:

(i) a party to the arbitration agreement referred to in article 7 was under some incapacity; or the said agreement is not valid under the law to which the parties have subjected it or, failing any indication thereon, under the law of this State; or

(ii) the party making the application was not given proper notice of the appointment of an arbitrator or of the arbitral proceedings or was otherwise unable to present his case; or

(iii) the award deals with a dispute not contemplated by or not falling within the terms of the submission to arbitration, or contains decisions on matters beyond the scope of the submission to arbitration, provided that, if the decisions on matters submitted to arbitration can be separated from those not so submitted, only that part of the award which contains decisions on matters not submitted to arbitration may be set aside; or

(iv) the composition of the arbitral tribunal or the arbitral procedure was not in accordance with the agreement of the parties, unless such agreement was in conflict with a provision of this Law from which the parties cannot derogate, or, failing such agreement, was not in accordance with this Law; or

(b) the court finds that:

(i) the subject-matter of the dispute is not capable of settlement by arbitration under the law of this State; or

(ii) the award is in conflict with the public policy of this State.

3. An application for setting aside may not be made after three months have elapsed from the date on which the party making that

application had received the award or, if a request had been made under article 33, from the date on which that request had been disposed of by the arbitral tribunal.

4. The court, when asked to set aside an award, may, where appropriate and so requested by a party, suspend the setting aside proceedings for a period of time determined by it in order to give the arbitral tribunal an opportunity to resume the arbitral proceedings or to take such other action as in the arbitral tribunal's opinion will eliminate the grounds for setting aside.

CHAPTER VIII—RECOGNITION AND ENFORCEMENT OF AWARDS

Article 35. Recognition and enforcement

1. An arbitral award, irrespective of the country in which it was made, shall be recognized as binding and, upon application in writing to the competent court, shall be enforced subject to the provisions of this article and of article 36.

2. The party relying on an award or applying for its enforcement shall supply the duly authenticated original award or a duly certified copy thereof, and the original arbitration agreement referred to in article 7 or a duly certified copy thereof. If the award or agreement is not made in an official language of this State, the party shall supply a duly certified translation thereof into such language. * * *

* * * The conditions set forth in this paragraph are intended to set maximum standards. It would, thus, not be contrary to the harmonization to be achieved by the model law if a State retained even less onerous conditions.

Article 36. Grounds for refusing recognition or enforcement

1. Recognition or enforcement of an arbitral award, irrespective of the country in which it was made, may be refused only:

(a) at the request of the party against whom it is invoked, if that party furnishes to the competent court where recognition or enforcement is sought proof that:

(i) a party to the arbitration agreement referred to in article 7 was under some incapacity; or the said agreement is not valid under the law to which the parties have subjected it or, failing any indication thereon, under the law of the country where the award was made; or

(ii) the party against whom the award is invoked was not given proper notice of the appointment of an arbitrator or of the arbitral proceedings or was otherwise unable to present his case; or

(iii) the award deals with a dispute not contemplated by or not falling within the terms of the submission to arbitration, or it contains decisions on matters beyond the scope of the submission to arbitration, provided that, if the decisions on matters submitted to arbitration can be separated from those not so submitted, that part of the award which contains decisions on matters submitted to arbitration may be recognized and enforced; or

(iv) the composition of the arbitral tribunal or the arbitral procedure was not in accordance with the agreement of the parties or, failing such agreement, was not in accordance with the law of the country where the arbitration took place; or

(v) the award has not yet become binding on the parties or has been set aside or suspended by a court of the country in which, or under the law of which, that award was made; or

(b) if the court finds that:

(i) the subject-matter of the dispute is not capable of settlement by arbitration under the law of this State; or

(ii) the recognition or enforcement of the award would be contrary to the public policy of this State.

2. If an application for setting aside or suspension of an award has been made to a court referred to in paragraph (1)(*a*)(v) of this article, the court where recognition or enforcement is sought may, if it considers it proper, adjourn its decision and may also, on the application of the party claiming recognition or enforcement of the award, order the other party to provide appropriate security.

§ 3.16 Text of the American Arbitration Association (AAA) International Commercial Arbitration Rules

Article 1.

(a) Where parties have agreed in writing to arbitrate disputes under these International Arbitration Rules or have provided for arbitration of an international dispute by the International Centre for Dispute Resolution or the American Arbitration Association without designating particular Rules, the arbitration shall take place in accordance with these Rules, as in effect at the date of commencement of the arbitration, subject to whatever modifications the parties may adopt in writing.

(b) These Rules govern the arbitration, except that, where any such rule is in conflict with any provision of the law applicable to the arbitration from which the parties cannot derogate, that provision shall prevail.

(c) These Rules specify the duties and responsibilities of the administrator, the International Centre for Dispute Resolution, a division of the American Arbitration Association. The administrator may provide services through its Centre, located in New York, or through the facilities of arbitral institutions with which it has agreements of cooperation.

COMMENCING THE ARBITRATION

Article 2. Notice of Arbitration and Statement of Claim

1. The party initiating arbitration ("claimant") shall give written notice of arbitration to the administrator and at the same time to the party against whom a claim is being made ("respondent").

2. Arbitral proceedings shall be deemed to commence on the date on which the administrator receives the notice of arbitration.

3. The notice of arbitration shall contain a statement of claim including the following:

(a) a demand that the dispute be referred to arbitration;

(b) the names, addresses and telephone numbers of the parties;

(c) a reference to the arbitration clause or agreement that is invoked;

(d) a reference to any contract out of or in relation to which the dispute arises;

(e) a description of the claim and an indication of the facts supporting it;

(f) the relief or remedy sought and the amount claimed; and

(g) may include proposals as to the means of designating and the number of arbitrators, the place of arbitration and the language(s) of the arbitration.

4. Upon receipt of the notice of arbitration, the administrator shall communicate with all parties with respect to the arbitration and shall acknowledge the commencement of the arbitration.

Article 3. Statement of Defense and Counterclaim

1. Within 30 days after the commencement of the arbitration, a respondent shall submit a written statement of defense, responding to the issues raised in the notice of arbitration, to the claimant and any other parties, and to the administrator.

2. At the time a respondent submits its statement of defense, a respondent may make counterclaims or assert setoffs as to any claim covered by the agreement to arbitrate, as to which the claimant shall within 30 days submit a written statement of defense to the respondent and any other parties and to the administrator.

3. A respondent shall respond to the administrator, the claimant and other parties within 30 days after the commencement of the arbitration as to any proposals the claimant may have made as to the number of arbitrators, the place of the arbitration or the language(s) of the arbitration, except to the extent that the parties have previously agreed as to these matters.

4. The arbitral tribunal, or the administrator if the arbitral tribunal has not yet been formed, may extend any of the time limits established in this article if it considers such an extension justified.

Article 4. Amendments to Claims

During the arbitral proceedings, any party may amend or supplement its claim, counterclaim or defense, unless the tribunal considers it inappropriate to allow such amendment or supplement because of the party's delay in making it, prejudice to the other parties or any other circumstances. A party may not amend or supplement a claim or counterclaim if the amendment or supplement would fall outside the scope of the agreement to **arbitrate.**

THE TRIBUNAL

Article 5. Number of Arbitrators

If the parties have not agreed on the number of arbitrators, one arbitrator shall be appointed unless the administrator determines in its discretion that three arbitrators are appropriate because of the large size, complexity or other circumstances of the case.

Article 6. Appointment of Arbitrators

1. The parties may mutually agree upon any procedure for appointing arbitrators and shall inform the administrator as to such procedure.

2. The parties may mutually designate arbitrators, with or without the assistance of the administrator. When such designations are made, the parties shall notify the administrator so that notice of the

appointment can be communicated to the arbitrators, together with a copy of these Rules.

3. If within 45 days after the commencement of the arbitration, all of the parties have not mutually agreed on a procedure for appointing the arbitrator(s) or have not mutually agreed on the designation of the arbitrator(s), the administrator shall, at the written request of any party, appoint the arbitrator(s) and designate the presiding arbitrator. If all of the parties have mutually agreed upon a procedure for appointing the arbitrator(s), but all appointments have not been made within the time limits provided in that procedure, the administrator shall, at the written request of any party, perform all functions provided for in that procedure that remain to be performed.

4. In making such appointments, the administrator, after inviting consultation with the parties, shall endeavor to select suitable arbitrators. At the request of any party or on its own initiative, the administrator may appoint nationals of a country other than that of any of the parties.

5. Unless the parties have agreed otherwise no later than 45 days after the commencement of the arbitration, if the notice of arbitration names two or more claimants or two or more respondents, the administrator shall appoint all the arbitrators.

Article 7. Impartiality and Independence of Arbitrators

1. Arbitrators acting under these Rules shall be impartial and independent. Prior to accepting appointment, a prospective arbitrator shall disclose to the administrator any circumstance likely to give rise to justifiable doubts as to the arbitrator's impartiality or independence. If, at any stage during the arbitration, new circumstances arise that may give rise to such doubts, an arbitrator shall promptly disclose such circumstances to the parties and to the administrator. Upon receipt of such information from an arbitrator or a party, the administrator shall communicate it to the other parties and to the tribunal.

2. No party or anyone acting on its behalf shall have any ex parte communication relating to the case with any arbitrator, or with any candidate for appointment as party-appointed arbitrator except to advise the candidate of the general nature of the controversy and of the anticipated proceedings and to discuss the candidate's qualifications, availability or independence in relation to the parties, or to discuss the suitability of candidates for selection as a third arbitrator where the parties or party designated arbitrators are to participate in that selection. No party or anyone acting on its behalf shall have any ex parte communication relating to the case with any candidate for presiding arbitrator.

Article 8. Challenge of Arbitrators

1. A party may challenge any arbitrator whenever circumstances exist that give rise to justifiable doubts as to the arbitrator's impartiality or independence. A party wishing to challenge an arbitrator shall send notice of the challenge to the administrator within 15 days after being notified of the appointment of the arbitrator or within 15 days after the circumstances giving rise to the challenge become known to that party.

2. The challenge shall state in writing the reasons for the challenge.

3. Upon receipt of such a challenge, the administrator shall notify the other parties of the challenge. When an arbitrator has been challenged by one party, the other party or parties may agree to the acceptance of the challenge and, if there is agreement, the arbitrator shall withdraw. The challenged arbitrator may also withdraw from office in the absence of such agreement. In neither case does withdrawal imply acceptance of the validity of the grounds for the challenge.

Article 9.

If the other party or parties do not agree to the challenge or the challenged arbitrator does not withdraw, the administrator in its sole discretion shall make the decision on the challenge.

Article 10. Replacement of an Arbitrator

If an arbitrator withdraws after a challenge, or the administrator sustains the challenge, or the administrator determines that there are sufficient reasons to accept the resignation of an arbitrator, or an arbitrator dies, a substitute arbitrator shall be appointed pursuant to the provisions of Article 6, unless the parties otherwise agree.

Article 11.

1. If an arbitrator on a three-person tribunal fails to participate in the arbitration for reasons other than those identified in Article 10, the two other arbitrators shall have the power in their sole discretion to continue the arbitration and to make any decision, ruling or award, notwithstanding the failure of the third arbitrator to participate. In determining whether to continue the arbitration or to render any decision, ruling or award without the participation of an arbitrator, the two other arbitrators shall take into account the stage of the arbitration, the reason, if any, expressed by the third arbitrator for such nonparticipation and such other matters as they consider appropriate in the circumstances of the case. In the event that the two other arbitrators determine not to continue the arbitration without the participation of the third arbitrator, the administrator

on proof satisfactory to it shall declare the office vacant, and a substitute arbitrator shall be appointed pursuant to the provisions of Article 6, unless the parties otherwise agree.

2. If a substitute arbitrator is appointed under either Article 10 or Article 11, the tribunal shall determine at its sole discretion whether all or part of any prior hearings shall be repeated.

GENERAL CONDITIONS

Article 12. Representation

Any party may be represented in the arbitration. The names, addresses and telephone numbers of representatives shall be communicated in writing to the other parties and to the administrator. Once the tribunal has been established, the parties or their representatives may communicate in writing directly with the tribunal.

Article 13. Place of Arbitration

1. If the parties disagree as to the place of arbitration, the administrator may initially determine the place of arbitration, subject to the power of the tribunal to determine finally the place of arbitration within 60 days after its constitution. All such determinations shall be made having regard for the contentions of the parties and the circumstances of the arbitration.

2. The tribunal may hold conferences or hear witnesses or inspect property or documents at any place it deems appropriate. The parties shall be given sufficient written notice to enable them to be present at any such proceedings.

Article 14. Language

If the parties have not agreed otherwise, the language(s) of the arbitration shall be that of the documents containing the arbitration agreement, subject to the power of the tribunal to determine otherwise based upon the contentions of the parties and the circumstances of the arbitration. The tribunal may order that any documents delivered in another language shall be accompanied by a translation into the language(s) of the arbitration.

Article 15. Pleas as to Jurisdiction

1. The tribunal shall have the power to rule on its own jurisdiction, including any objections with respect to the existence, scope or validity of the arbitration agreement.

2. The tribunal shall have the power to determine the existence or validity of a contract of which an arbitration clause forms a part. Such an arbitration clause shall be treated as an agreement

independent of the other terms of the contract. A decision by the tribunal that the contract is null and void shall not for that reason alone render invalid the arbitration clause.

3. A party must object to the jurisdiction of the tribunal or to the arbitrability of a claim or counterclaim no later than the filing of the statement of defense, as provided in Article 3, to the claim or counterclaim that gives rise to the objection. The tribunal may rule on such objections as a preliminary matter or as part of the final award.

Article 16. Conduct of the Arbitration

1. Subject to these Rules, the tribunal may conduct the arbitration in whatever manner it considers appropriate, provided that the parties are treated with equality and that each party has the right to be heard and is given a fair opportunity to present its case.

2. The tribunal, exercising its discretion, shall conduct the proceedings with a view to expediting the resolution of the dispute. It may conduct a preparatory conference with the parties for the purpose of organizing, scheduling and agreeing to procedures to expedite the subsequent proceedings.

3. The tribunal may in its discretion direct the order of proof, bifurcate proceedings, exclude cumulative or irrelevant testimony or other evidence and direct the parties to focus their presentations on issues the decision of which could dispose of all or part of the case.

4. Documents or information supplied to the tribunal by one party shall at the same time be communicated by that party to the other party or parties.

Article 17. Further Written Statements

1. The tribunal may decide whether the parties shall present any written statements in addition to statements of claims and counterclaims and statements of defense, and it shall fix the periods of time for submitting any such statements.

2. The periods of time fixed by the tribunal for the communication of such written statements should not exceed 45 days. However, the tribunal may extend such time limits if it considers such an extension justified.

Article 18. Notices

1. Unless otherwise agreed by the parties or ordered by the tribunal, all notices, statements and written communications may be served on a party by air mail, air courier, facsimile transmission, telex, telegram or other written forms of electronic communication

addressed to the party or its representative at its last known address or by personal service.

2. For the purpose of calculating a period of time under these Rules, such period shall begin to run on the day following the day when a notice, statement or written communication is received. If the last day of such period is an official holiday at the place received, the period is extended until the first business day which follows. Official holidays occurring during the running of the period of time are included in calculating the period.

Article 19. Evidence

1. Each party shall have the burden of proving the facts relied on to support its claim or defense.

2. The tribunal may order a party to deliver to the tribunal and to the other parties a summary of the documents and other evidence which that party intends to present in support of its claim, counterclaim or defense.

3. At any time during the proceedings, the tribunal may order parties to produce other documents, exhibits or other evidence it deems necessary or appropriate.

Article 20. Hearings

1. The tribunal shall give the parties at least 30 days advance notice of the date, time and place of the initial oral hearing. The tribunal shall give reasonable notice of subsequent hearings.

2. At least 15 days before the hearings, each party shall give the tribunal and the other parties the names and addresses of any witnesses it intends to present, the subject of their testimony and the languages in which such witnesses will give their testimony.

3. At the request of the tribunal or pursuant to mutual agreement of the parties, the administrator shall make arrangements for the interpretation of oral testimony or for a record of the hearing.

4. Hearings are private unless the parties agree otherwise or the law provides to the contrary. The tribunal may require any witness or witnesses to retire during the testimony of other witnesses. The tribunal may determine the manner in which witnesses are examined.

5. Evidence of witnesses may also be presented in the form of written statements signed by them.

6. The tribunal shall determine the admissibility, relevance, materiality and weight of the evidence offered by any party. The tribunal shall take into account applicable principles of legal

privilege, such as those involving the confidentiality of communications between a lawyer and client.

Article 21. Interim Measures of Protection

1. At the request of any party, the tribunal may take whatever interim measures it deems necessary, including injunctive relief and measures for the protection or conservation of property.

2. Such interim measures may take the form of an interim award, and the tribunal may require security for the costs of such measures.

3. A request for interim measures addressed by a party to a judicial authority shall not be deemed incompatible with the agreement to arbitrate or a waiver of the right to arbitrate.

4. The tribunal may in its discretion apportion costs associated with applications for interim relief in any interim award or in the final award.

Article 22. Experts

1. The tribunal may appoint one or more independent experts to report to it, in writing, on specific issues designated by the tribunal and communicated to the parties.

2. The parties shall provide such an expert with any relevant information or produce for inspection any relevant documents or goods that the expert may require. Any dispute between a party and the expert as to the relevance of the requested information or goods shall be referred to the tribunal for decision.

3. Upon receipt of an expert's report, the tribunal shall send a copy of the report to all parties and shall give the parties an opportunity to express, in writing, their opinion on the report. A party may examine any document on which the expert has relied in such a report.

4. At the request of any party, the tribunal shall give the parties an opportunity to question the expert at a hearing. At this hearing, parties may present expert witnesses to testify on the points at issue.

Article 23. Default

1. If a party fails to file a statement of defense within the time established by the tribunal without showing sufficient cause for such failure, as determined by the tribunal, the tribunal may proceed with the arbitration.

2. If a party, duly notified under these Rules, fails to appear at a hearing without showing sufficient cause for such failure, as determined by the tribunal, the tribunal may proceed with the arbitration.

3. If a party, duly invited to produce evidence or take any other steps in the proceedings, fails to do so within the time established by the tribunal without showing sufficient cause for such failure, as determined by the tribunal, the tribunal may make the award on the evidence before it.

Article 24. Closure of Hearing

1. After asking the parties if they have any further testimony or evidentiary submissions and upon receiving negative replies or if satisfied that the record is complete, the tribunal may declare the hearings closed.

2. The tribunal in its discretion, on its own motion or upon application of a party, may reopen the hearings at any time before the award is made.

Article 25. Waiver of Rules

A party who knows that any provision of the Rules or requirement under the Rules has not been complied with, but proceeds with the arbitration without promptly stating an objection in writing thereto, shall be deemed to have waived the right to object.

Article 26. Awards, Decisions and Rulings

1. When there is more than one arbitrator, any award, decision or ruling of the arbitral tribunal shall be made by a majority of the arbitrators. If any arbitrator fails to sign the award, it shall be accompanied by a statement of the reason for the absence of such signature.

2. When the parties or the tribunal so authorize, the presiding arbitrator may make decisions or rulings on questions of procedure, subject to revision by the tribunal.

Article 27. Form and Effect of the Award

1. Awards shall be made in writing, promptly by the tribunal, and shall be final and binding on the parties. The parties undertake to carry out any such award without delay.

2. The tribunal shall state the reasons upon which the award is based, unless the parties have agreed that no reasons need be given.

3. The award shall contain the date and the place where the award was made, which shall be the place designated pursuant to Article 13.

4. An award may be made public only with the consent of all parties or as required by law.

5. Copies of the award shall be communicated to the parties by the administrator.

6. If the arbitration law of the country where the award is made requires the award to be filed or registered, the tribunal shall comply with such requirement.

7. In addition to making a final award, the tribunal may make interim, interlocutory or partial orders and awards.

8. Unless otherwise agreed by the parties, the administrator may publish or otherwise make publicly available selected awards, decisions and rulings that have been edited to conceal the names of the parties and other identifying details or that have been made publicly available in the course of enforcement or otherwise.

Article 28. Applicable Laws and Remedies

1. The tribunal shall apply the substantive law(s) or rules of law designated by the parties as applicable to the dispute. Failing such a designation by the parties, the tribunal shall apply such law(s) or rules of law as it determines to be appropriate.

2. In arbitrations involving the application of contracts, the tribunal shall decide in accordance with the terms of the contract and shall take into account usages of the trade applicable to the contract.

3. The tribunal shall not decide as amiable *compositeur* or *ex aequo et bono* unless the parties have expressly authorized it to do so.

4. A monetary award shall be in the currency or currencies of the contract unless the tribunal considers another currency more appropriate, and the tribunal may award such pre-award and post-award interest, simple or compound, as it considers appropriate, taking into consideration the contract and applicable law.

5. Unless the parties agree otherwise, the parties expressly waive and forego any right to punitive, exemplary or similar damages unless a statute requires that compensatory damages be increased in a specified manner. This provision shall not apply to any award of arbitration costs to a party to compensate for dilatory or bad faith conduct in the arbitration.

Article 29. Settlement or Other Reasons for Termination

1. If the parties settle the dispute before an award is made, the tribunal shall terminate the arbitration and, if requested by all parties, may record the settlement in the form of an award on agreed terms. The tribunal is not obliged to give reasons for such an award.

2. If the continuation of the proceedings becomes unnecessary or impossible for any other reason, the tribunal shall inform the parties of its intention to terminate the proceedings. The tribunal shall thereafter issue an order terminating the arbitration, unless a party raises justifiable grounds for objection.

Article 30. Interpretation or Correction of the Award

1. Within 30 days after the receipt of an award, any party, with notice to the other parties, may request the tribunal to interpret the award or correct any clerical, typographical or computation errors or make an additional award as to claims presented but omitted from the award.

2. If the tribunal considers such a request justified, after considering the contentions of the parties, it shall comply with such a request within 30 days after the request.

Article 31. Costs

The tribunal shall fix the costs of arbitration in its award. The tribunal may apportion such costs among the parties if it determines that such apportionment is reasonable, taking into account the circumstances of the case.

Such costs may include:

(a) the fees and expenses of the arbitrators;

(b) the costs of assistance required by the tribunal, including its experts;

(c) the fees and expenses of the administrator;

(d) the reasonable costs for legal representation of a successful party; and

(e) any such costs incurred in connection with an application for interim or emergency relief pursuant to Article 21.

Article 32. Compensation of Arbitrators

Arbitrators shall be compensated based upon their amount of service, taking into account their stated rate of compensation and the size and complexity of the case. The administrator shall arrange an appropriate daily or hourly rate, based on such considerations, with the parties and with each of the arbitrators as soon as practicable after the commencement of the arbitration. If the parties fail to agree on the terms of compensation, the administrator shall establish an appropriate rate and communicate it in writing to the parties.

Article 33. Deposit of Costs

1. When a party files claims, the administrator may request the filing party to deposit appropriate amounts as an advance for the costs referred to in Article 31, paragraphs (a.), (b.) and (c.).

2. During the course of the arbitral proceedings, the tribunal may request supplementary deposits from the parties.

3. If the deposits requested are not paid in full within 30 days after the receipt of the request, the administrator shall so inform the parties, in order that one or the other of them may make the required payment. If such payments are not made, the tribunal may order the suspension or termination of the proceedings.

4. After the award has been made, the administrator shall render an accounting to the parties of the deposits received and return any unexpended balance to the parties.

Article 34. Confidentiality

Confidential information disclosed during the proceedings by the parties or by witnesses shall not be divulged by an arbitrator or by the administrator. Except as provided in Article 27, unless otherwise agreed by the parties, or required by applicable law, the members of the tribunal and the administrator shall keep confidential all matters relating to the arbitration or the award.

Article 35. Exclusion of Liability

The members of the tribunal and the administrator shall not be liable to any party for any act or omission in connection with any arbitration conducted under these Rules, except that they may be liable for the consequences of conscious and deliberate wrongdoing.

Article 36. Interpretation of Rules

The tribunal shall interpret and apply these Rules insofar as they relate to its powers and duties. The administrator shall interpret and apply all other Rules.

Article 37. Emergency Measures of Protection

1. Unless the parties agree otherwise, the provisions of this Article 37 shall apply to arbitrations conducted under arbitration clauses or agreements entered on or after May 1, 2006.

2. A party in need of emergency relief prior to the constitution of the tribunal shall notify the administrator and all other parties in writing of the nature of the relief sought and the reasons why such relief is required on an emergency basis. The application shall also set forth the reasons why the party is entitled to such relief. Such notice may be given by e-mail, facsimile transmission or other reliable means, but must include a statement certifying that all other parties have been notified or an explanation of the steps taken in good faith to notify other parties.

3. Within one business day of receipt of notice as provided in paragraph 2, the administrator shall appoint a single emergency arbitrator from a special panel of emergency arbitrators designated to rule on emergency applications. Prior to accepting appointment, a

prospective emergency arbitrator shall disclose to the administrator any circumstance likely to give rise to justifiable doubts to the arbitrator's impartiality or independence. Any challenge to the appointment of the emergency arbitrator must be made within one business day of the communication by the administrator to the parties of the appointment of the emergency arbitrator and the circumstances disclosed.

4. The emergency arbitrator shall as soon as possible, but in any event within two business days of appointment, establish a schedule for consideration of the application for emergency relief. Such schedule shall provide a reasonable opportunity to all parties to be heard, but may provide for proceedings by telephone conference or on written submissions as alternatives to a formal hearing. The emergency arbitrator shall have the authority vested in the tribunal under Article 15, including the authority to rule on her/his own jurisdiction, and shall resolve any disputes over the applicability

5. The emergency arbitrator shall have the power to order or award any interim or conservancy measure the emergency arbitrator deems necessary, including injunctive relief and measures for the protection or conservation of property. Any such measure may take the form of an interim award or of an order. The emergency arbitrator shall give reasons in either case. The emergency arbitrator may modify or vacate the interim award or order for good cause shown.

6. The emergency arbitrator shall have no further power to act after the tribunal is constituted. Once the tribunal has been constituted, the tribunal may reconsider, modify or vacate the interim award or order of emergency relief issued by the emergency arbitrator. The emergency arbitrator may not serve as a member of the tribunal unless the parties agree otherwise.

7. Any interim award or order of emergency relief may be conditioned on provision by the party seeking such relief of appropriate security.

8. A request for interim measures addressed by a party to a judicial authority shall not be deemed incompatible with this Article 37 or with the agreement to arbitrate or a waiver of the right to arbitrate. If the administrator is directed by a judicial authority to nominate a special master to consider and report on an application for emergency relief, the administrator shall proceed as in Paragraph 2 of this article and the references to the emergency arbitrator shall be read to mean the special master, except that the special master shall issue a report rather than an interim award.

9. The costs associated with applications for emergency relief shall initially be apportioned by the emergency arbitrator or special

master, subject to the power of the tribunal to determine finally the apportionment of such costs.

ADMINISTRATIVE FEES

Administrative Fee Schedules (Standard and Flexible Fee)

The ICDR has two administrative fee options for parties filing claims or counterclaims, the Standard Fee Schedule and Flexible Fee Schedule. The Standard Fee Schedule has a two payment schedule, and the Flexible Fee Schedule has a three payment schedule which offers lower initial filing fees, but potentially higher total administrative fees of approximately 12% to 19% for cases that proceed to a hearing. The administrative fees of the ICDR are based on the amount of the claim or counterclaim. Arbitrator compensation is not included in this schedule. Unless the parties agree otherwise, arbitrator compensation and administrative fees are subject to allocation by the arbitrator in the award.

Fees for incomplete or deficient filings: Where the applicable arbitration agreement does not reference the ICDR or the AAA, the ICDR will attempt to obtain the agreement of the other parties to the dispute to have the arbitration administered by the ICDR. However, where the ICDR is unable to obtain the agreement of the parties to have the ICDR administer the arbitration, the ICDR will administratively close the case and will not proceed with the administration of the arbitration. In these cases, the ICDR will return the filing fees to the filing party, less the amount specified in the fee schedule below for deficient filings.

Parties that file demands for arbitration that are incomplete or otherwise do not meet the filing requirements contained in these Rules shall also be charged the amount specified below for deficient filings if they fail or are unable to respond to the ICDR's request to correct the deficiency.

Fees for additional services: The ICDR reserves the right to assess additional administrative fees for services performed by the ICDR beyond those provided for in these Rules which may be required by the parties' agreement or stipulation.

Suspension for Nonpayment: If arbitrator compensation or administrative charges have not been paid in full, the administrator may so inform the parties in order that one of them may advance the required payment. If such payments are not made, the tribunal may order the suspension or termination of the proceedings. If no arbitrator has yet been appointed, the ICDR may suspend the proceedings.

Standard Fee Schedule

An Initial Filing Fee is payable in full by a filing party when a claim, counterclaim, or additional claim is filed. A Final Fee will be incurred for all cases that proceed to their first hearing. This fee will be payable in advance at the time that the first hearing is scheduled. This fee will be refunded at the conclusion of the case if no hearings have occurred. However, if the administrator is not notified at least 24 hours before the time of the scheduled hearing, the Final Fee will remain due and will not be refunded.

These fees will be billed in accordance with the following schedule:

Amount of Claim	Initial Filing Fee	Final Fee
Above $0 to $10,000	$775	$200
Above $10,000 to $75,000	$975	$300
Above $75,000 to $150,000	$1,850	$750
Above $150,000 to $300,000	$2,800	$1,250
Above $300,000 to $500,000	$4,350	$1,750
Above $500,000 to $1,000,000	$6,200	$2,500
Above $1,000,000 to $5,000,000	$8,200	$3,250
Above $5,000,000 to $10,000,000	$10,200	$4,000
Above $10,000,000	Base fee of $12,800 plus .01% of the amount of claim above $10,000,000 Fee Capped at $65,000	$6,000
Nonmonetary Claims[1]	$3,350	$1,250

[1] This fee is applicable when a claim or counterclaim is not for a monetary amount. Where a monetary claim amount is not known, parties will be required to state a range of claims or be subject to a filing fee of $10,200.

Deficient Claim Filing[2]	$350
Additional Services[3]	

Fees are subject to increase if the amount of a claim or counterclaim is modified after the initial filing date. Fees are subject to decrease if the amount of a claim or counterclaim is modified before the first hearing.

The minimum fees for any case having three or more arbitrators are $2,800 for the filing fee, plus a $1,250 Case Service Fee.

Parties on cases filed under either the Flexible Fee Schedule or the Standard Fee Schedule that are held in abeyance for one year will be assessed an annual abeyance fee of $300. If a party refuses to pay the assessed fee, the other party or parties may pay the entire fee on behalf of all parties, otherwise the matter will be administratively closed.

For more information, please contact the ICDR at +212.484.4181.

Refund Schedule for Standard Fee Schedule

The ICDR offers a refund schedule on filing fees connected with the Standard Fee Schedule. For cases with claims up to $75,000, a minimum filing fee of $350 will not be refunded. For all other cases, a minimum fee of $600 will not be refunded. Subject to the minimum fee requirements, refunds will be calculated as follows:

> 100% of the filing fee, above the minimum fee, will be refunded if the case is settled or withdrawn within five calendar days of filing.

> 50% of the filing fee will be refunded if the case is settled or withdrawn between six and 30 calendar days of filing.

> 25% of the filing fee will be refunded if the case is settled or withdrawn between 31 and 60 calendar days of filing.

No refund will be made once an arbitrator has been appointed (this includes one arbitrator on a three-arbitrator panel). No refunds will be granted on awarded cases.

---

2 The Deficient Claim Filing Fee shall not be charged in cases filed by a consumer in an arbitration governed by the Supplementary Procedures for the Resolution of Consumer-Related Disputes, or in cases filed by an Employee who is submitting their dispute to arbitration pursuant to an employer promulgated plan.

3 The ICDR may assess additional fees where procedures or services outside the Rules sections are required under the parties' agreement or by stipulation.

Note: The date of receipt of the demand for arbitration with the ICDR will be used to calculate refunds of filing fees for both claims and counterclaims.

Flexible Fee Schedule

A non-refundable Initial Filing Fee is payable in full by a filing party when a claim, counterclaim, or additional claim is filed. Upon receipt of the Demand for Arbitration, the ICDR will promptly initiate the case and notify all parties as well as establish the due date for filing of an Answer, which may include a Counterclaim. In order to proceed with the further administration of the arbitration and appointment of the arbitrator(s), the appropriate, non-refundable Proceed Fee outlined below must be paid.

If a Proceed Fee is not submitted within ninety (90) days of the filing of the Claimant's Demand for Arbitration, the ICDR will administratively close the file and notify all parties.

No refunds or refund schedule will apply to the Filing or Proceed Fees once received.

The Flexible Fee Schedule below also may be utilized for the filing of counterclaims. However, as with the Claimant's claim, the counterclaim will not be presented to the arbitrator until the Proceed Fee is paid.

A Final Fee will be incurred for all claims and/or counterclaims that proceed to their first hearing. This fee will be payable in advance when the first hearing is scheduled, but will be refunded at the conclusion of the case if no hearings have occurred. However, if the administrator is not notified of a cancellation at least 24 hours before the time of the scheduled hearing, the Final Fee will remain due and will not be refunded.

All fees will be billed in accordance with the following schedule:

Amount of Claim	Initial Filing Fee	Proceed Fee	Final Fee
Above $0 to $10,000	$400	475	$200
Above $10,000 to $75,000	$625	$500	$300
Above $75,000 to $150,000	$850	$1250	$750
Above $150,000 to $300,000	$1,000	$2125	$1,250

Above $300,000 to $500,000	$1,500	$3,400	$1,750
Above $500,000 to $1,000,000	$2,500	$4,500	$2,500
Above $1,000,000 to $5,000,000	$2,500	$6,700	$3,250
Above $5,000,000 to $10,000,000	$3,500	$8,200	$4,000
Above $10,000,000	$4,500	$10,300 plus .01% of claim amount over $10,000,000 up to $65,000	$6,000
Nonmonetary[1]	$2,000	$2,000	$1,250
Deficient Claim Filing Fee	$350		

Additional Services[2]

All fees are subject to increase if the amount of a claim or counterclaim is modified after the initial filing date. Fees are subject to decrease if the amount of a claim or counterclaim is modified before the first hearing.

The minimum fees for any case having three or more arbitrators are $1,000 for the Initial Filing Fee; $2,125 for the Proceed Fee; and $1,250 for the Final Fee.

Under the Flexible Fee Schedule, a party's obligation to pay the Proceed Fee shall remain in effect regardless of any agreement of the parties to stay, postpone or otherwise modify the arbitration proceedings. Parties that, through mutual agreement, have held their case in abeyance for one year will be assessed an annual abeyance fee of $300. If a party refuses to pay the assessed fee, the other party or parties may pay the entire fee on behalf of all parties, otherwise the matter will be closed.

---

1 This fee is applicable when a claim or counterclaim is not for a monetary amount. Where a monetary claim amount is not known, parties will be required to state a range of claims or be subject to a filing fee of $3,500 and a proceed fee of $8,200.

2 The ICDR reserves the right to assess additional administrative fees for services performed by the ICDR beyond those provided for in these Rules and which may be required by the parties' agreement or stipulation.

§ 3.17 Text of the AAA/ABA Code of Ethics for Arbitrators (2004)

Preamble

The use of arbitration to resolve a wide variety of disputes has grown extensively and forms a significant part of the system of justice on which our society relies for a fair determination of legal rights. Persons who act as arbitrators therefore undertake serious responsibilities to the public, as well as to the parties. Those responsibilities include important ethical obligations.

Few cases of unethical behavior by commercial arbitrators have arisen. Nevertheless, this Code sets forth generally accepted standards of ethical conduct for the guidance of arbitrators and parties in commercial disputes, in the hope of contributing to the maintenance of high standards and continued confidence in the process of arbitration.

This Code provides ethical guidelines for many types of arbitration but does not apply to labor arbitration, which is generally conducted under the Code of Professional Responsibility for Arbitrators of Labor-Management Disputes.

There are many different types of commercial arbitration. Some proceedings are conducted under arbitration rules established by various organizations and trade associations, while others are conducted without such rules. Although most proceedings are arbitrated pursuant to voluntary agreement of the parties, certain types of disputes are submitted to arbitration by reason of particular laws.

This Code is intended to apply to all such proceedings in which disputes or claims are submitted for decision to one or more arbitrators appointed in a manner provided by an agreement of the parties, by applicable arbitration rules, or by law. In all such cases, the persons who have the power to decide should observe fundamental standards of ethical conduct. In this Code, all such persons are called "arbitrators," although in some types of proceeding they might be called "umpires," "referees," "neutrals," or have some other title.

Arbitrators, like judges, have the power to decide cases. However, unlike full-time judges, arbitrators are usually engaged in other occupations before, during, and after the time that they serve as arbitrators. Often, arbitrators are purposely chosen from the same trade or industry as the parties in order to bring special knowledge to the task of deciding. This Code recognizes these fundamental differences between arbitrators and judges.

In those instances where this Code has been approved and recommended by organizations that provide, coordinate, or administer services of arbitrators, it provides ethical standards for the members of their respective panels of arbitrators.

However, this Code does not form a part of the arbitration rules of any such organization unless its rules so provide.

THE CODE OF ETHICS FOR ARBITRATORS IN COMMERCIAL DISPUTES

Note on Neutrality

In some types of commercial arbitration, the parties or the administering institution provide for three or more arbitrators.

In some such proceedings, it is the practice for each party, acting alone, to appoint one arbitrator (a "party-appointed arbitrator") and for one additional arbitrator to be designated by the party-appointed arbitrators, or by the parties, or by an independent institution or individual. The sponsors of this Code believe that it is preferable for all arbitrators including any party-appointed arbitrators to be neutral, that is, independent and impartial, and to comply with the same ethical standards. This expectation generally is essential in arbitrations where the parties, the nature of the dispute, or the enforcement of any resulting award may have international aspects. However, parties in certain domestic arbitrations in the United States may prefer that party-appointed arbitrators be non-neutral and governed by special ethical considerations. These special ethical considerations appear in Canon X of this Code.

This Code establishes a presumption of neutrality for all arbitrators, including party-appointed arbitrators, which applies unless the parties' agreement, the arbitration rules agreed to by the parties or applicable laws provide otherwise. This Code requires all party-appointed arbitrators, whether neutral or not, to make pre-appointment disclosures of any facts which might affect their neutrality, independence, or impartiality.

This Code also requires all party-appointed arbitrators to ascertain and disclose as soon as practicable whether the parties intended for them to serve as neutral or not. If any doubt or uncertainty exists, the party-appointed arbitrators should serve as neutrals unless and until such doubt or uncertainty is resolved in accordance with Canon IX. This Code expects all arbitrators, including those serving under Canon X, to preserve the integrity and fairness of the process.

Note on Construction

Various aspects of the conduct of arbitrators, including some matters covered by this Code, may also be governed by agreements of the parties, arbitration rules to which the parties have agreed, applicable law, or other applicable ethics rules, all of which should be consulted by the arbitrators. This Code does not take the place of or supersede such laws, agreements, or arbitration rules to which the parties have agreed and should be read in conjunction with other rules of ethics. It does not establish new or additional grounds for judicial review of arbitration awards.

All provisions of this Code should therefore be read as subject to contrary provisions of applicable law and arbitration rules. They should also be read as subject to contrary agreements of the parties. Nevertheless, this Code imposes no obligation on any arbitrator to act in a manner inconsistent with the arbitrator's fundamental duty to preserve the integrity and fairness of the arbitral process.

Canons I through VIII of this Code apply to all arbitrators. Canon IX applies to all party-appointed arbitrators, except that certain party-appointed arbitrators are exempted by Canon X from compliance with certain provisions of Canons I–IX related to impartiality and independence, as specified in Canon X.

THE CODE OF ETHICS FOR ARBITRATORS IN COMMERCIAL DISPUTES

CANON I: An arbitrator should uphold the integrity and fairness of the arbitration process.

A. An arbitrator has a responsibility not only to the parties but also to the process of arbitration itself, and must observe high standards of conduct so that the integrity and fairness of the process will be preserved. Accordingly, an arbitrator should recognize a responsibility to the public, to the parties whose rights will be decided, and to all other participants in the proceeding. This responsibility may include pro bono service as an arbitrator where appropriate.

B. One should accept appointment as an arbitrator only if fully satisfied:

(1) that he or she can serve impartially;

(2) that he or she can serve independently from the parties, potential witnesses, and the other arbitrators;

(3) that he or she is competent to serve; and

(4) that he or she can be available to commence the arbitration in accordance with the requirements of the proceeding and

thereafter to devote the time and attention to its completion that the parties are reasonably entitled to expect.

C. After accepting appointment and while serving as an arbitrator, a person should avoid entering into any business, professional, or personal relationship, or acquiring any financial or personal interest, which is likely to affect impartiality or which might reasonably create the appearance of partiality. For a reasonable period of time after the decision of a case, persons who have served as arbitrators should avoid entering into any such relationship, or acquiring any such interest, in circumstances which might reasonably create the appearance that they had been influenced in the arbitration by the anticipation or expectation of the relationship or interest. Existence of any of the matters or circumstances described in this paragraph C does not render it unethical for one to serve as an arbitrator where the parties have consented to the arbitrator's appointment or continued services following full disclosure of the relevant facts in accordance with Canon II.

D. Arbitrators should conduct themselves in a way that is fair to all parties and should not be swayed by outside pressure, public clamor, and fear of criticism or self-interest. They should avoid conduct and statements that give the appearance of partiality toward or against any party.

E. When an arbitrator's authority is derived from the agreement of the parties, an arbitrator should neither exceed that authority nor do less than is required to exercise that authority completely. Where the agreement of the parties sets forth procedures to be followed in conducting the arbitration or refers to rules to be followed, it is the obligation of the arbitrator to comply with such procedures or rules. An arbitrator has no ethical obligation to comply with any agreement, procedures or rules that are unlawful or that, in the arbitrator's judgment, would be inconsistent with this Code.

F. An arbitrator should conduct the arbitration process so as to advance the fair and efficient resolution of the matters submitted for decision. An arbitrator should make all reasonable efforts to prevent delaying tactics, harassment of parties or other participants, or other abuse or disruption of the arbitration process.

G. The ethical obligations of an arbitrator begin upon acceptance of the appointment and continue throughout all stages of the proceeding. In addition, as set forth in this Code, certain ethical obligations begin as soon as a person is requested to serve as an arbitrator and certain ethical obligations continue after the decision in the proceeding has been given to the parties.

H. Once an arbitrator has accepted an appointment, the arbitrator should not withdraw or abandon the appointment unless compelled to do so by unanticipated circumstances that would render it impossible or impracticable to continue. When an arbitrator is to be compensated for his or her services, the arbitrator may withdraw if the parties fail or refuse to provide for payment of the compensation as agreed.

I. An arbitrator who withdraws prior to the completion of the arbitration, whether upon the arbitrator's initiative or upon the request of one or more of the parties, should take reasonable steps to protect the interests of the parties in the arbitration, including return of evidentiary materials and protection of confidentiality.

COMMENT TO CANON I

A prospective arbitrator is not necessarily partial or prejudiced by having acquired knowledge of the parties, the applicable law or the customs and practices of the business involved. Arbitrators may also have special experience or expertise in the areas of business, commerce, or technology which are involved in the arbitration. Arbitrators do not contravene this Canon if, by virtue of such experience or expertise, they have views on certain general issues likely to arise in the arbitration, but an arbitrator may not have prejudged any of the specific factual or legal determinations to be addressed during the arbitration.

During an arbitration, the arbitrator may engage in discourse with the parties or their counsel, draw out arguments or contentions, comment on the law or evidence, make interim rulings, and otherwise control or direct the arbitration.

These activities are integral parts of an arbitration. Paragraph D of Canon I is not intended to preclude or limit either full discussion of the issues during the course of the arbitration or the arbitrator's management of the proceeding.

CANON II: An arbitrator should disclose any interest or relationship likely to affect impartiality or which might create an appearance of partiality.

A. Persons who are requested to serve as arbitrators should, before accepting, disclose:

(1) any known direct or indirect financial or personal interest in the outcome of the arbitration;

(2) any known existing or past financial, business, professional or personal relationships which might reasonably affect impartiality or lack of independence in the eyes of any of the parties. For example, prospective arbitrators should disclose any such relationships which they personally have with any party or its lawyer, with any co-arbitrator, or with any individual whom

they have been told will be a witness. They should also disclose any such relationships involving their families or household members or their current employers, partners, or professional or business associates that can be ascertained by reasonable efforts;

(3) the nature and extent of any prior knowledge they may have of the dispute; and

(4) any other matters, relationships, or interests which they are obligated to disclose by the agreement of the parties, the rules or practices of an institution, or applicable law regulating arbitrator disclosure.

B. Persons who are requested to accept appointment as arbitrators should make a reasonable effort to inform themselves of any interests or relationships described in paragraph A.

C. The obligation to disclose interests or relationships described in paragraph A is a continuing duty which requires a person who accepts appointment as an arbitrator to disclose, as soon as practicable, at any stage of the arbitration, any such interests or relationships which may arise, or which are recalled or discovered.

D. Any doubt as to whether or not disclosure is to be made should be resolved in favor of disclosure.

E. Disclosure should be made to all parties unless other procedures for disclosure are provided in the agreement of the parties, applicable rules or practices of an institution, or by law. Where more than one arbitrator has been appointed, each should inform the others of all matters disclosed.

F. When parties, with knowledge of a person's interests and relationships, nevertheless desire that person to serve as an arbitrator, that person may properly serve.

G. If an arbitrator is requested by all parties to withdraw, the arbitrator must do so. If an arbitrator is requested to withdraw by less than all of the parties because of alleged partiality, the arbitrator should withdraw unless either of the following circumstances exists:

(1) An agreement of the parties, or arbitration rules agreed to by the parties, or applicable law establishes procedures for determining challenges to arbitrators, in which case those procedures should be followed; or

(2) In the absence of applicable procedures, if the arbitrator, after carefully considering the matter, determines that the reason for the challenge is not substantial, and that he or she can nevertheless act and decide the case impartially and fairly.

H. If compliance by a prospective arbitrator with any provision of this Code would require disclosure of confidential or privileged information, the prospective arbitrator should either:

(1) Secure the consent to the disclosure from the person who furnished the information or the holder of the privilege; or

(2) Withdraw.

CANON III: An arbitrator should avoid impropriety or the appearance of impropriety in communicating with parties.

A. If an agreement of the parties or applicable arbitration rules establishes the manner or content of communications between the arbitrator and the parties, the arbitrator should follow those procedures notwithstanding any contrary provision of paragraphs B and C.

B. An arbitrator or prospective arbitrator should not discuss a proceeding with any party in the absence of any other party, except in any of the following circumstances:

(1) When the appointment of a prospective arbitrator is being considered, the prospective arbitrator:

(a) may ask about the identities of the parties, counsel, or witnesses and the general nature of the case; and

(b) may respond to inquiries from a party or its counsel designed to determine his or her suitability and availability for the appointment. In any such dialogue, the prospective arbitrator may receive information from a party or its counsel disclosing the general nature of the dispute but should not permit them to discuss the merits of the case.

(2) In an arbitration in which the two party-appointed arbitrators are expected to appoint the third arbitrator, each party-appointed arbitrator may consult with the party who appointed the arbitrator concerning the choice of the third arbitrator;

(3) In an arbitration involving party-appointed arbitrators, each party-appointed arbitrator may consult with the party who appointed the arbitrator concerning arrangements for any compensation to be paid to the party-appointed arbitrator.

Submission of routine written requests for payment of compensation and expenses in accordance with such arrangements and written communications pertaining solely to such requests need not be sent to the other party;

(4) In an arbitration involving party-appointed arbitrators, each party-appointed arbitrator may consult with the party who appointed the arbitrator concerning the status of the arbitrator (i.e., neutral or non-neutral), as contemplated by paragraph C of Canon IX;

(5) Discussions may be had with a party concerning such logistical matters as setting the time and place of hearings or making other arrangements for the conduct of the proceedings. However, the arbitrator should promptly inform each other party of the discussion and should not make any final determination concerning the matter discussed before giving each absent party an opportunity to express the party's views; or

(6) If a party fails to be present at a hearing after having been given due notice, or if all parties expressly consent, the arbitrator may discuss the case with any party who is present.

C. Unless otherwise provided in this Canon, in applicable arbitration rules or in an agreement of the parties, whenever an arbitrator communicates in writing with one party, the arbitrator should at the same time send a copy of the communication to every other Party, and whenever the arbitrator receives any written communication concerning the case from one party which has not already been sent to every other party, the arbitrator should send or cause it to be sent to the other parties.

CANON IV: An arbitrator should conduct the proceedings fairly and diligently.

A. An arbitrator should conduct the proceedings in an even-handed manner. The arbitrator should be patient and courteous to the parties, their representatives, and the witnesses and should encourage similar conduct by all participants.

B. The arbitrator should afford to all parties the right to be heard and due notice of the time and place of any hearing. The arbitrator should allow each party a fair opportunity to present its evidence and arguments.

C. The arbitrator should not deny any party the opportunity to be represented by counsel or by any other person chosen by the party.

D. If a party fails to appear after due notice, the arbitrator should proceed with the arbitration when authorized to do so, but only after receiving assurance that appropriate notice has been given to the absent party.

E. When the arbitrator determines that more information than has been presented by the parties is required to decide the case, it is not improper for the arbitrator to ask questions, call witnesses, and request documents or other evidence, including expert testimony.

F. Although it is not improper for an arbitrator to suggest to the parties that they discuss the possibility of settlement or the use of mediation, or other dispute resolution processes, an arbitrator should not exert pressure on any party to settle or to utilize other dispute resolution processes. An arbitrator should not be present or otherwise participate in settlement discussions or act as a mediator unless requested to do so by all parties.

G. Co-arbitrators should afford each other full opportunity to participate in all aspects of the proceedings.

COMMENT TO PARAGRAPH G

Paragraph G of Canon IV is not intended to preclude one arbitrator from acting in limited circumstances (e.g., *ruling on discovery issues) where authorized by the agreement of the parties, applicable rules or law, nor does it preclude a majority of the arbitrators from proceeding with any aspect of the arbitration if an arbitrator is unable or unwilling to participate and such action is authorized by the agreement of the parties or applicable rules or law. It also does not preclude ex parte requests for interim relief.*

CANON V: An arbitrator should make decisions in a just, independent and deliberate manner.

A. The arbitrator should, after careful deliberation, decide all issues submitted for determination. An arbitrator should decide no other issues.

B. An arbitrator should decide all matters justly, exercising independent judgment, and should not permit outside pressure to affect the decision.

C. An arbitrator should not delegate the duty to decide to any other person.

D. In the event that all parties agree upon a settlement of issues in dispute and request the arbitrator to embody that agreement in an award, the arbitrator may do so, but is not required to do so unless satisfied with the propriety of the terms of settlement.

Whenever an arbitrator embodies a settlement by the parties in an award, the arbitrator should state in the award that it is based on an agreement of the parties.

CANON VI: An arbitrator should be faithful to the relationship of trust and confidentiality inherent in that office.

A. An arbitrator is in a relationship of trust to the parties and should not, at any time, use confidential information acquired during the arbitration proceeding to gain personal advantage or advantage for others, or to affect adversely the interest of another.

B. The arbitrator should keep confidential all matters relating to the arbitration proceedings and decision. An arbitrator may obtain help from an associate, a research assistant or other persons in connection with reaching his or her decision if the arbitrator informs the parties of the use of such assistance and such persons agree to be bound by the provisions of this Canon.

C. It is not proper at any time for an arbitrator to inform anyone of any decision in advance of the time it is given to all parties. In a proceeding in which there is more than one arbitrator, it is not proper at any time for an arbitrator to inform anyone about the substance of the deliberations of the arbitrators. After an arbitration award has been made, it is not proper for an arbitrator to assist in proceedings to enforce or challenge the award.

D. Unless the parties so request, an arbitrator should not appoint himself or herself to a separate office related to the subject matter of the dispute, such as receiver or trustee, nor should a panel of arbitrators appoint one of their number to such an office.

CANON VII: An arbitrator should adhere to standards of integrity and fairness when making arrangements for compensation and reimbursement of expenses.

A. Arbitrators who are to be compensated for their services or reimbursed for their expenses shall adhere to standards of integrity and fairness in making arrangements for such payments.

B. Certain practices relating to payments are generally recognized as tending to preserve the integrity and fairness of the arbitration process. These practices include:

(1) Before the arbitrator finally accepts appointment, the basis of payment, including any cancellation fee, compensation in the event of withdrawal and compensation for study and preparation time, and all other charges, should be established. Except for arrangements for the compensation of party-appointed arbitrators, all parties should be informed in writing of the terms established;

(2) In proceedings conducted under the rules or administration of an institution that is available to assist in making arrangements for payments, communication related to compensation should be made through the institution. In proceedings where no institution has been engaged by the parties to administer the arbitration, any communication with

arbitrators (other than party appointed arbitrators) concerning payments should be in the presence of all parties; and

(3) Arbitrators should not, absent extraordinary circumstances, request increases in the basis of their compensation during the course of a proceeding.

CANON VIII: An arbitrator may engage in advertising or promotion of arbitral services which is truthful and accurate.

A. Advertising or promotion of an individual's willingness or availability to serve as an arbitrator must be accurate and unlikely to mislead. Any statements about the quality of the arbitrator's work or the success of the arbitrator's practice must be truthful.

B. Advertising and promotion must not imply any willingness to accept an appointment otherwise than in accordance with this Code.

COMMENT TO CANON VIII

This Canon does not preclude an arbitrator from printing, publishing, or disseminating advertisements conforming to these standards in any electronic or print medium, from making personal presentations to prospective users of arbitral services conforming to such standards or from responding to inquiries concerning the arbitrator's availability, qualifications, experience, or fee arrangements.

CANON IX: Arbitrators appointed by one party have a duty to determine and disclose their status and to comply with this code, except as exempted by Canon X.

A. In some types of arbitration in which there are three arbitrators, it is customary for each party, acting alone, to appoint one arbitrator. The third arbitrator is then appointed by agreement either of the parties or of the two arbitrators, or failing such agreement, by an independent institution or individual. In tripartite arbitrations to which this Code applies, all three arbitrators are presumed to be neutral and are expected to observe the same standards as the third arbitrator.

B. Notwithstanding this presumption, there are certain types of tripartite arbitration in which it is expected by all parties that the two arbitrators appointed by the parties may be predisposed toward the party appointing them. Those arbitrators, referred to in this Code as "Canon X arbitrators," are not to be held to the standards of neutrality and independence applicable to other arbitrators.

Canon X describes the special ethical obligations of party-appointed arbitrators who are not expected to meet the standard of neutrality.

C. A party-appointed arbitrator has an obligation to ascertain, as early as possible but not later than the first meeting of the arbitrators and parties, whether the parties have agreed that the party-appointed arbitrators will serve as neutrals or whether they shall be subject to Canon X, and to provide a timely report of their conclusions to the parties and other arbitrators:

(1) Party-appointed arbitrators should review the agreement of the parties, the applicable rules and any applicable law bearing upon arbitrator neutrality. In reviewing the agreement of the parties, party-appointed arbitrators should consult any relevant express terms of the written or oral arbitration agreement. It may also be appropriate for them to inquire into agreements that have not been expressly set forth, but which may be implied from an established course of dealings of the parties or well-recognized custom and usage in their trade or profession;

(2) Where party-appointed arbitrators conclude that the parties intended for the party-appointed arbitrators not to serve as neutrals, they should so inform the parties and the other arbitrators. The arbitrators may then act as provided in Canon X unless or until a different determination of their status is made by the parties, any administering institution or the arbitral panel; and

(3) Until party-appointed arbitrators conclude that the party-appointed arbitrators were not intended by the parties to serve as neutrals, or if the party-appointed arbitrators are unable to form a reasonable belief of their status from the foregoing sources and no decision in this regard has yet been made by the parties, any administering institution, or the arbitral panel, they should observe all of the obligations of neutral arbitrators set forth in this Code.

D. Party-appointed arbitrators not governed by Canon X shall observe all of the obligations of Canons I through VIII unless otherwise required by agreement of the parties, any applicable rules, or applicable law.

CANON X: Exemptions for arbitrators appointed by one party who are not subject to rules of neutrality.

Canon X arbitrators are expected to observe all of the ethical obligations prescribed by this Code except those from which they are specifically excused by Canon X.

A. Obligations Under Canon I

Canon X arbitrators should observe all of the obligations of Canon I subject only to the following provisions:

(1) Canon X arbitrators may be predisposed toward the party who appointed them but in all other respects are obligated to act in good faith and with integrity and fairness. For example, Canon X arbitrators should not engage in delaying tactics or harassment of any party or witness and should not knowingly make untrue or misleading statements to the other arbitrators; and

(2) The provisions of subparagraphs B(1), B(2), and paragraphs C and D of Canon I, insofar as they relate to partiality, relationships, and interests are not applicable to Canon X arbitrators.

B. Obligations Under Canon II

(1) Canon X arbitrators should disclose to all parties, and to the other arbitrators, all interests and relationships which Canon II requires be disclosed. Disclosure as required by Canon II is for the benefit not only of the party who appointed the arbitrator, but also for the benefit of the other parties and arbitrators so that they may know of any partiality which may exist or appear to exist; and

(2) Canon X arbitrators are not obliged to withdraw under paragraph G of Canon II if requested to do so only by the party who did not appoint them.

C. Obligations Under Canon III

Canon X arbitrators should observe all of the obligations of Canon III subject only to the following provisions:

(1) Like neutral party-appointed arbitrators, Canon X arbitrators may consult with the party who appointed them to the extent permitted in paragraph B of Canon III;

(2) Canon X arbitrators shall, at the earliest practicable time, disclose to the other arbitrators and to the parties whether or not they intend to communicate with their appointing parties. If they have disclosed the intention to engage in such communications, they may thereafter communicate with their appointing parties concerning any other aspect of the case, except as provided in paragraph (3);

(3) If such communication occurred prior to the time they were appointed as arbitrators, or prior to the first hearing or other meeting of the parties with the arbitrators, the Canon X arbitrator should, at or before the first hearing or meeting of the arbitrators with the parties, disclose the fact that such communication has taken place. In complying with the provisions of this subparagraph, it is sufficient that there be

disclosure of the fact that such communication has occurred without disclosing the content of the communication. A single timely disclosure of the Canon X arbitrator's intention to participate in such communications in the future is sufficient;

(4) Canon X arbitrators may not at any time during the arbitration:

(a) disclose any deliberations by the arbitrators on any matter or issue submitted to them for decision;

(b) communicate with the parties that appointed them concerning any matter or issue taken under consideration by the panel after the record is closed or such matter or issue has been submitted for decision; or

(c) disclose any final decision or interim decision in advance of the time that it is disclosed to all parties.

(5) Unless otherwise agreed by the arbitrators and the parties, a Canon X arbitrator may not communicate orally with the neutral arbitrator concerning any matter or issue arising or expected to arise in the arbitration in the absence of the other Canon X arbitrator. If a Canon X arbitrator communicates in writing with the neutral arbitrator, he or she shall simultaneously provide a copy of the written communication to the other Canon X arbitrator;

(6) When Canon X arbitrators communicate orally with the parties that appointed them concerning any matter on which communication is permitted under this Code, they are not obligated to disclose the contents of such oral communications to any other party or arbitrator; and

(7) When Canon X arbitrators communicate in writing with the party who appointed them concerning any matter on which communication is permitted under this Code, they are not required to send copies of any such written communication to any other party or arbitrator.

D. Obligations Under Canon IV

Canon X arbitrators should observe all of the obligations of Canon IV.

E. Obligations Under Canon V

Canon X arbitrators should observe all of the obligations of Canon V, except that they may be predisposed toward deciding in favor of the party who appointed them.

F. Obligations Under Canon VI

Canon X arbitrators should observe all of the obligations of Canon VI.

G. Obligations Under Canon VII

Canon X arbitrators should observe all of the obligations of Canon VII.

H. Obligations Under Canon VIII

Canon X arbitrators should observe all of the obligations of Canon VIII.

I. Obligations Under Canon IX

The provisions of paragraph D of Canon IX are inapplicable to Canon X arbitrators, except insofar as the obligations are also set forth in this Canon.

Chapter 4

INVESTOR-STATE ARBITRATIONS UNDER BITs, FTAs, NAFTA 1994 AND USMCA 2018

Table of Sections

Sec.

PART A: INVESTOR-STATE ARBITRATIONS

Given the absence of a cohesive body of widely accepted foreign investment law, and notably the failure of the Multilateral Agreement of Investment (MAI), nations have turned to negotiation of bilateral foreign investment treaties (BITs) and/or free trade agreements (FTAs) that contain foreign investment chapters. For detailed NAFTA 1994 coverage of foreign investor-host state rules and arbitration examples, see Sections 4.10 and 4.11.

From the perspective of capital exporting countries, BITs and FTAs offer protection from host state actions that violate the foreign investor rights contained therein. From the perspective of capital importing countries, investment treaties and FTAs create incentives to invest in what may be perceived as high-risk markets.

There is a long history of foreign investors' purchasing political-risk insurance against expropriation, civil unrest and the like, sometimes from their home governments. In Latin America, the spread of "Calvo Doctrine" rules designed to limit foreign investors to host nations' judicial and administrative remedies increased the desire for protection. Investor-state dispute settlement (ISDS) by arbitration first appeared in a 1959 BIT treaty between Germany and Pakistan. Since the 1990s the signing of BITs and FTAs with investment arbitration provisions has proliferated.

§ 4.1 The Proliferation of Investor-State Arbitrations Under BITs and FTAs

Bilateral Investment Treaties

The principal focus of BITs and FTAs covering foreign investment dispute settlement is the protection and promotion of foreign investment. It is not only the United States which has emphasized these treaties. They are common features of most developed nations in their relations with developing host nations. Tracking its rise as a capital exporter, China has over 100 investment protection agreements, mostly with emerging economies, but also with such nations as Australia, Austria, Belgium/Luxembourg, Denmark, France, Germany, Japan, the Netherlands, and the United Kingdom. A benefit of such an agreement is that its provisions prevail over domestic law and remedies, although the agreements usually allow for exceptions to investment protection when in the interests of national security.

Approximately 3,000 bilateral investment treaties (BITs) lattice the globe. China and Germany have well over 100 BITs, France, Britain and the Netherlands about 100, India, Romania, Italy, The Czech Republic, Belgium/Luxembourg 75 to 85, Russia, Sweden, Poland 65, while Brazil has none and South Africa has said it will withdraw from any ISDS treaty obligations. Singapore has a number of BITs that seem to be designed to attract foreign investors to incorporate there so as to take advantage of Singaporean subsidiaries as foreign investment vehicles in the likes of Jordan and Egypt. Investment arbitrations administered by the Singapore International Arbitration Center have skyrocketed.

The United States has nearly 50 BITs, mostly with developing nations, in addition to comparable coverage of foreign investment under its free trade agreements (NAFTA 1994, CAFTA, etc.). Unlike the latter, U.S. BITs are ratified only by the Senate and do not require implementing legislation. In 2012, the United States issued a revised Model BIT, usually employed as a starting point in its BIT negotiations. This Model BIT includes a definition of "foreign investment" that reaches broadly to sovereign obligations and intellectual property rights, expressly covers indirect expropriations, and omits any balance of payments safeguard escape clause. It is reproduced in Section 4.8 of this chapter.

The United States has considered a BIT with China, which inked a BIT with Canada in 2012 that does not cover regulatory controls over permissions to invest ("pre-investment" rules). In other words, the Canada-China BIT only concerns operational and disposal aspects of foreign investment law. This approach is common in European-based BITs, which are the most prevalent around the globe.

The Netherlands is known for allowing "mailbox" companies to utilize their network of BITs by making foreign investments through them. Critics assert that this lattice allows foreign investors to engage in "treaty shopping", the making of investments in order to raise arbitral challenges to national laws. A prominent example is the Phillip Morris (Asia) acquisition of a Hong Kong firm to facilitate challenge of Australia's 2011 plain packaging (no brand) cigarette law under the 1993 Hong Kong-Australia Bilateral Investment Treaty. This arbitration was dismissed by the arbitrators in 2015 as an abuse of process.

Treaty shopping inside the European Union to avoid the dubious legitimacy of national courts in Poland, Hungary, and quite a few other EU states has been undertaken by making investments in those countries via U.K., Dutch and German companies benefiting from **intra-EU** BITs. Some 200 intra-EU member-state BIT arbitration provisions have effectively been invalidated by the European Court of Justice in its landmark 2018 *Slovak Republic v. Achmea* (Case C-284/16) decision. The logic of the Court's reasoning is that such provisions interfere with the autonomy, effectiveness and primacy of the EU legal regime. As such, awards rendered thereunder are unenforceable. This decision raises questions as to whether **extra-EU** member state BIT arbitration decisions, which are numerous, may also be unenforceable. Further, it is an open question as to whether ICSID or Energy Charter investment arbitrations (see Sections 4.5, 4.6 and 4.7) are suspect under *Achmea.*

Free Trade Agreements (FTAs) with Investment Coverage

Leading nations have gathered together networks of free trade agreements under various titles, some with foreign investment dispute settlement by arbitration coverage, and some not:

(1) **Japan** has "Economic Partnership Agreements" (that is to say free trade agreements) with Mexico, Chile, Thailand, the Philippines, Malaysia, Vietnam, Switzerland, India, Indonesia, Brunei, Singapore, Peru, Mongolia, the Association of Southeast Asian Nations (ASEAN), a major 2018 FTA with the European Union (not as yet covering foreign investment), and is a leader in the Comprehensive and Progressive Trans-Pacific Partnership (TPP-11), which provides for investor-state arbitrations and took effect in 2019. Japan and its companies have rarely participated in investor-state arbitrations.

(2) **China** has free trade agreements with its own Hong Kong and Macau Special Administrative Regions, Chile, Pakistan, Costa Rica, Peru, Singapore, New Zealand, Australia, South Korea, Iceland, Maldives and ASEAN, none of which appear to cover foreign investment. Like Japan, China and its firms have only been involved in only a few investor-state arbitrations, initiated under its very large number of BITs.

(3) The **European Union** has numerous free trade agreements, including with Algeria, Chile, Egypt, Iceland, Israel, Jordan, Lebanon, Mexico, Morocco, Norway, Serbia, South Africa, Vietnam, Singapore, Japan, Canada, Tunisia and a customs union agreement with Turkey. Traditionally, EU FTAs included foreign investment law rules and dispute settlement by arbitration. But recent FTAs with Vietnam, Singapore, Mexico and the Japan-EU 2018 Economic Partnership Agreement do not. The EU's "new generation" policy for foreign investment dispute settlement anticipates using an Investment Court system instead of arbitrators.

(4) The **United States** has 12 bilateral free trade agreements with Australia (2004), Bahrain (2006), Chile (2004), Colombia (2012), Israel and the Palestinian Authority (1985), Jordan (2001), South Korea (KORUS I 2012 and II 2018), Morocco (2006), Oman (2006), Panama (2012), Peru (2012) and Singapore (2004). It also has two multilateral agreements: The NAFTA 1994 and pending USMCA 2018 agreement with Canada and Mexico, and the Central America Free Trade Agreement (CAFTA-DR 2015)

which includes the Dominican Republic, Guatemala, Honduras, El Salvador, Nicaragua and Costa Rica.

All U.S. FTAs cover foreign investment dispute settlement by arbitration *except* those with Israel, Australia and Canada under the USMCA 2018. For examples of NAFTA 1994 investor-state arbitrations, the text of NAFTA 1994 Chapter 11 covering investment, and post-NAFTA foreign investment rules in later U.S. FTAs, see Section 4.13.

(5) **India** has free trade agreements with ASEAN, Sri Lanka, Malaysia, the Gulf Cooperation Council (GCC), Singapore, Korea, Japan, Afghanistan, Chile, MERCOSUR and leads the 7-nation South Asian FTA. Foreign investment arbitration coverage is limited.

(6) **South Korea** has free trade agreements with ASEAN, India, Australia, Canada, the United States (KORUS I and II), China, Chile, Colombia, EFTA, the European Union (KOREU), Turkey, Vietnam, Peru, and Singapore. Some of these FTAs cover foreign investment arbitrations, including KORUS I and II, but some do not.

(7) **Canada** has free trade agreements (in addition to NAFTA 1994 and its successor the USMCA of 2018) with Korea, the EU (CETA 2017), Chile, Peru, Colombia, Costa Rica, Israel, EFTA, Jordan, Panama, Honduras, and Ukraine, and is a leader in the TPP-11 Virtually all have foreign investment arbitration coverage, including NAFTA 1994.

Ratification of the Canada-EU Comprehensive Economic and Trade Agreement of 2014 (CETA) was delayed primarily due foreign investor-host state issues. These were resolved by agreeing to create a new Investment Court comprised of Canadian, European and other jurists. The Court will replace party selected arbitrators. Other EU free trade agreements (above) follow this "new generation" course for investor-state dispute settlement.

CETA raised a fundamental question: Is dispute settlement by arbitration really needed when both parties have sophisticated judicial systems and/or good diplomatic relations capable of handling foreign investor disputes? *Under the pending USMCA of 2018, Canada and the United States will eliminate ISDS arbitrations.*

(8) **Mexico** has free trade agreements in addition to NAFTA and the USMCA with Chile, Colombia, Venezuela

(dormant), Costa Rica, Bolivia, Nicaragua, Guatemala, Honduras, El Salvador, Peru, Uruguay, the European Union (see Chapter 3), Japan and Israel. It also has an enhanced Pacific Alliance with Chile, Peru, and Colombia, and participates in the TPP-11. Most Mexican FTAs embrace investor-state dispute settlement by arbitration resembling NAFTA 1994.

Under NAFTA's successor, the USMCA Agreement of 2018 (ratification pending) Mexico-Canada ISDS by arbitration is governed by TPP-11, and U.S.-Mexico investor-state arbitrations are restricted. For NAFTA 1994 arbitration rules and examples involving Mexico, see Sections 4.7 and 4.8. For USMCA arbitration rules, see Section 4.14.

For much more details on these FTAs, See Folsom, *Principles of Free Trade Agreements, From GATT 1947 through NAFTA Re-Negotiated 2018.*

§ 4.2 Foreign Investor Rights

Bilateral investment treaties and FTAs with investment coverage traditionally provide foreign investors with certain core rights:

(1) "national treatment";

(2) "most-favored-nation treatment";

(3) "fair and equitable treatment" (known as the "minimum standard);

(4) "full protection and security"; and

(5) direct and indirect expropriation rules.

Some BIT agreements also require host governments to comply with obligations undertaken with foreign investors, often via foreign investment agreements, including for example "stabilization clauses" intended to stabilize or even freeze the law of the host country at the time of the signing of the agreement. If the investor-state agreement contains a "stabilization" clause, promising no significant change in the host state's law will adversely affect the investment, such clauses may give rise to breach of contract claims which become BIT/FTA violations subject to arbitration. Veolia, a French utility, for example commenced arbitration proceedings against Egypt for raising the minimum wage.

National treatment promises nondiscriminatory, equal treatment with domestic investors. Most-favored-nation treatment means foreign investors from different nations will be treated equally, thus sometimes allowing investors to claim more generous benefits provided in other agreements. In one such dispute, an Argentinian investor in Spain obtained the benefit of a Chile-Spain BIT dispute resolution provision not requiring prior exhaustion of local judicial remedies. See Maffenzi v. Spain, ICSID Case No. ARB/97/7 (Jan. 25, 2000).

General exception clauses in some investment protection agreements, notably the Canada-EU Comprehensive Economic and Trade Agreement (CETA 2017), tend to mirror Article XX of the GATT and Article XIV of the GATS. Such clauses create state immunities for permissible policy objectives and acts, such as for the protection of human, animal or plant life or health, national security and the conservation of natural resources.

Fair and equitable treatment, and full protection and security, are notably open-ended "minimum standards" derived from customary international law. In determining fair and equitable treatment, the investor's legitimate expectations and the transparency, predictability, consistency and denial of justice under state rules have been evaluated as appropriate criteria. *See, e.g.*, Tecmed v. Mexico, 10 ICSID Reports 133 (2004); OEPC v. Ecuador, Case No. UN 3467 (London Ct. Intl. Arb. July 1, 2004); Waste Management v. Mexico, ICSID Case No. ARB/00/0 (April 30, 2004) (NAFTA 1994 dispute).

In addition, the duty of fair and equitable treatment has frequently been construed by arbitrators as protecting the stability of the legal and business framework under which the foreign investor operates. *Id.* Fair and equitable treatment has been construed as requiring that the host state respect the basic expectations of the investor at the time of the investment. In other words, the host state may not alter rules and decisions upon which the investor relied in planning its investment. Thus unilateral changes in the legal and contractual framework existing at the time of the original investment, frustrating the investor's legitimate expectations, can and have be deemed unfair and inequitable. *Id.*

Unfair and inequitable treatment has become the primary violation found by foreign investment arbitration tribunals. For an informative review of "unfair and inequitable" conduct by Argentina in connection with emergency financial measures and judicial access to remedies, see the U.S. Supreme Court case BG Group PLC v. Argentina, 134 S.Ct. 1198 (2014) (litigate first requirement in UK-Argentina BIT excused in New York Convention recognition and enforcement proceedings in the USA). If the investor obtained investment rights by unlawful means, for example corruption, dismissal of its claims is appropriate as a matter of international public policy. See World Duty Free Co. v. Kenya, ICSID Case No. ARB/00/07 (October 4, 2006).

Beyond core foreign investor rights, some agreements broadly allow arbitration of "other claims" related to the investment. Most rules on expropriation require valid public purposes and prompt, adequate and effective compensation. NAFTA 1994 rules protect foreign investors from governmental acts "tantamount to expropriation", an ambiguous term (see Section 4.7). Acts of sub-central government authorities or state-owned companies may be attributed to the state for liability purposes. See Tokios Tokeles v. Ukraine, ICSID Case No. ARB/02/18 (April 29, 2004) (local government authorities); Salini Costruttori v. Morocco, ICSID Case No. ARB/00/04 (July 16, 2001) (state-owned company).

In addition, BITs and FTAs may also protect capital movement and limit performance requirements. All of these rights may extend beyond the life of a BIT or FTA, and cannot be retroactively revoked, thus allowing for investor claims against states under "tails."

§ 4.3 Foreign Investor-Host State Dispute Settlement

BITs and FTAs covering investment provide foreign investors with designated rights, and typically establish investor-state dispute settlement procedures (ISDS) to resolve alleged violations of those rights. These may involve state-to-state dispute settlement negotiations (SSDS). Exhaustion or at least attempted utilization of host state national legal remedies (courts, agencies) may first be required, a requirement found for example in the Trans-Pacific Partnership Agreement (TPP-12), rejected by President Trump, its TPP-11 successor and the USMCA 2018 Agreement. In some jurisdictions, notably under Calvo Clauses in Latin America, foreign investor-host state disputes can only be decided pursuant to local remedies.

A highlight of many BIT and FTA foreign investment agreements is the consent in advance of host sovereign states to arbitration of foreign investor disputes; no separate consent is required. ISDS arbitrations are subject to review in the place of arbitration *and* wherever enforcement is sought.

Investor-State Arbitrations

Foreign investment provisions frequently establish mandatory, binding dispute settlement procedures allowing foreign investors to invoke arbitration procedures by filing claims for *damages* against host nations. The formulae for these provisions differ. Many channel investor-state disputes to the World Bank's International Centre for

Settlement of Investment Disputes (ICSID) in Washington, D.C., discussed below. Some BIT arbitrations have gone to the Stockholm Chamber of Commerce, the Permanent Court of Arbitration in The Hague, the U.N. Commission on International Trade Law (UNCITRAL), and the International Chamber of Commerce (ICC) in Paris.

Hundreds of investor-state arbitration claims have been filed, the largest number against Argentina (many arising out of its sovereign debt repudiations and emergency economic measures affecting utilities). The mere filing of such claims facilitates leverage in renegotiation of investment contracts as well as compensation.

Claims have been lodged against the United States, and U.S. investors abroad have very actively pursued claims against U.S. BIT and free trade partners, notably Argentina. Exxon Mobil obtained a $1.6 billion expropriation award in ICSID proceedings under the U.S.-Venezuela BIT. Dow Chemical received a $2.2 billion award in ICC proceedings against Kuwait. Under the U.S.-Ecuador BIT, in ICSID proceedings, Occidental Petroleum won a $2.3 billion award against Ecuador for termination of an oil-concession contract.

Some investor-state claims are settled, others dismissed on technical grounds. UNCTAD data indicates that arbitrated investment disputes reaching final awards favor the state by close to two to one. That said, it is clear that investors from the developed world (notably the United States, the Netherlands, the United Kingdom and Germany) comprise a large majority of the claimants against developing nations (notably Argentina, Venezuela, Ecuador and Mexico). As a general rule, investment arbitration awards can be recognized and enforced in foreign courts under the 1958 New York Convention on the Recognition and Enforcement of Arbitral Awards. See Section 3.9.

The growth of investment arbitration has in many instances overrun contract-based choice of forum clauses, including alternative arbitral proceedings. When "parallel proceedings" exist arbitrators have often declined to defer to party autonomy. For example, U.S. investors in an Argentine port terminal agreed "for all purposes" in their concession contract to the jurisdiction of Argentinian courts. They invoked instead the U.S.-Argentina BIT arbitration procedures under ICSID. The arbitrators upheld their "jurisdiction" to hear the dispute. See generally, Gus Van Harten, *Sovereign Choices and Sovereign Constraints: Judicial Restraint in Investment Treaty Arbitration* (2013).

Investor-State Arbitration Critiques, Treaty Shopping

Critics of investor-state arbitrations broadly decry the creation of a private system of justice for foreign investors. Even the U.S. Congress has frequently expressed concern that ISDS arbitrations may provide foreign investors in the United States with greater remedies than U.S. investors in their home country. Critics focus particularly on the fair and equitable treatment obligation, which has been increasingly construed by arbitrators to create "legitimate expectations" (future profits), and "specific commitments" that host governments will compensate foreign investors for changes in law, notably regulatory law. This has created a degree of foreign investment "regulatory chill." Investors have also been arguing that they are entitled to the legitimate expectation that governments will adhere to their international treaty obligations, notably under the WTO TRIPs agreement concerning intellectual property rights. Investors have also used BIT and NAFTA 1994 provisions to influence and challenge proposed host state regulations.

Additional criticisms assert there is something of a "good old boy" network of inherently biased ISDS arbitrators drawn significantly from corporate legal worlds operating with relatively little transparency. Arbitrators who simultaneously act as counsel in other ongoing arbitrations, or repeat as arbitrators for the same parties, have been particularly critiqued. Most NAFTA 1994 and ICSID awards and related documents are published, and greater transparency should be forthcoming under the UNCITRAL Mauritius Convention (2015).

"Treaty shopping" to access investor-state arbitration remedies occurs, notably in connection with the formation of "mailbox companies" for that purpose. Romanian and other companies have been reported using Dutch mailbox companies as the vehicle for investments in their own home countries in order to avoid local law and asserted corrupt local courts. Philip Morris made a strategic investment in Hong Kong so as to be able to challenge anticipated (but not yet enacted) Australian no-brand, plain packaging cigarette rules under a Hong Kong-Australia BIT dating from the British era. Philip Morris feared losing Marlboro Man and other trademarked brand names. In 2015, the arbitrators dismissed this proceeding on abuse of process grounds.

Philip Morris also utilized the Swiss-Uruguay BIT to challenge Uruguay's comparable plain packaging cigarette rules. In the first "jurisdictional" round of this ICSID dispute, Philip Morris persuaded the arbitrators that an "investment" had indeed been made in Uruguay on the basis of its economic contribution to development, despite smoking's adverse effects on the people and economy of that country. This dispute was eventually settled after Philip Morris lost its treaty shopping attempt at overcoming Australian tobacco packaging rules (above). *See* generally J. Chaisse, *The Treaty Shopping Practice: Corporate Structuring and Restructuring to Gain Access to Investment Treaties and Arbitration,* 11 Hastings Bus. L.J. 225 (2015).

Rejection or Limitation of Investor-State Arbitrations

Reacting negatively to investor-state arbitrations, some developing world BITs, for example the Indian Model BIT and the Southern African Development Community (SADC) Model BIT, require foreign investors to first exhaust local remedies. The Trans-Pacific Partnership Agreements (TPP-12 and TPP-11) as well as the pending USMCA 2018 successor to NAFTA 1994 do likewise.

South Africa is actively terminating its BITs in favor of national investment code rules. Indonesia, Brazil, Bolivia, Ecuador, Nicaragua, Venezuela and others have started moving away from investor-state arbitrations and ICSID (below), replacing arbitrations with local remedies or state-to-state dispute settlement (SSDS). The latter include use of the World Court and Permanent Court of Arbitration in The Hague, Ombudsmen, conciliation, and diplomatic remedies. State-to-state remedies force foreign investors to seek remedies via their home governments, very different from investor-state arbitration mechanisms.

Foreign investors should take note that the Canada-EU FTA of 2017 (CETA) anticipates replacing traditional party-selected arbitrators with an Investment Court system comprised of judges from both sides. Recent EU FTAs with Singapore, Vietnam, Japan and Mexico may do likewise. *Under the pending USMCA of 2018, Canada and the United States will eliminate investor-state arbitrations.* They are retained, subject to limitations, for U.S-Mexico and Canada-Mexico foreign investment arbitrations. See Section 4.14.

At Australia's insistence, the United States-Australia free trade agreement does NOT contain investor-state arbitration procedures, though the Trans-Pacific Partnership (TPP-12) vetoed by President Trump would have altered that result. However, arbitration claims regarding the regulation of tobacco were specifically excluded under the TPP-12 and remain so under TPP-11.

Growing rejection and criticism of investment dispute settlement by party-selected arbitrators has led to tune ups of procedures and rules related to them. For example, TPP-12 and TPP-11 (neither of which is the United States a party) undertake material arbitration reforms. For example, financial stability regulation falls outside indirect expropriation claims, tobacco regulation may not be challenged, mere frustration of profit expectations is insufficient to pursue investor-state arbitrations, the burden of proof falls on investor claimants, no shell companies may be used to access investor-state arbitral remedies, and state-owned enterprises along with authorized government agents are made subject to the agreement's dispute settlement regime.

In addition, the TPP agreements mandate public access to hearings and documents, allow amicus briefs, facilitate expedited dismissals of frivolous claims, and generally protect existing intellectual property license royalties and durations from alteration. All of these reforms represent an effort to rehabilitate use of investor-state arbitrations.

§ 4.4 United States BITs and Model BIT

To promote national treatment and protect U.S. investors abroad, the United States embarked on a BIT program in the early 1980s. The BIT program followed earlier extensive use of Friendship, Commerce, and Navigation (FCNs) treaties, some of which provided for diplomatic state-to-state protection for U.S. foreign investors, notably regarding expropriation. Some U.S. FCNs remain in effect, *e.g.* the U.S.-Japan FCN. Unlike the FCNs, the Model U.S. BIT distinguishes treatment of foreign-owned, domestically incorporated subsidiaries and branches of foreign firms for some provisions, particularly employment. As a result of Sumitomo Shoji America v. Avagliano, 457 U.S. 176 (1982), the Japan-U.S. FCN treaty afforded no protection to a foreign company using its nationals in hiring inside the United States. Under the typical U.S. BIT, explicit freedom to hire nationals exists in a narrow range of management provisions.

The United States has entered into approximately 45 bilateral investment treaties (BITs). *U.S. BITs are ratified only by the Senate and, unlike U.S. FTAs, do not require implementing legislation.* Most U.S. BITs have been negotiated with small developing countries, though the United States has signed a BIT with Argentina, Egypt, Turkey and a number of Eastern European countries such as Poland. Most U.S. BITs preceded NAFTA 1994 and the 1995 WTO TRIMs Agreement regarding foreign investor performance requirements. Earlier U.S. BITs thus placed particular emphasis on reducing performance requirements. Subsequent agreements generally reflect the foreign investor rights and investor-state claims procedures found in NAFTA 1994, which generated a large number of arbitrations and have been modified (particularly regarding indirect expropriations) by official interpretations and post-NAFTA U.S. FTAs. See Section 4.13.

Numerous U.S. investors have filed and frequently won arbitration awards for damages against Argentina. Under U.S. law, ICSID awards (below) are given full faith and credit in federal courts. The Federal Arbitration Act does not apply, and reliance on the New York Convention is not needed. Hence the enforcement rate of ICSID awards in U.S. courts is high. Argentina has as a rule unsuccessfully defended itself on foreign sovereign immunity grounds. One court held that Argentina waived its immunity by becoming a party to ICSID, and further noted that the U.S. Foreign Sovereign Immunities Act exempts arbitration awards. See Blue Ridge Investments v. Argentina, 902 F.Supp.2d 367 (S.D.N.Y 2012), affirmed 735 F.3d 72 (2d Cir. 2013).

United States BITs do not prohibit nations from enacting foreign investment control laws. Such laws are common in developing nations, notably in Latin America, including Mexico. But some developed nations, such as Canada, also screen foreign investments, particularly mergers and acquisitions. Most U.S. agreements provide that pre-investment laws should not interfere with any rights in the treaty, but since no rights to avoid national foreign investment controls are created, challenges to foreign investment control laws are generally not possible under U.S. BITs and FTAs.

One important provision the United States seeks to include in its BITs and FTAs is the "prompt, adequate and effective" concept of compensation subsequent to expropriation. For example, the 1994 Argentina-United States BIT uses language referring to compensation for the "fair market value. . . immediately before the expropriatory action." Many of the nations which have recently agreed to this language disputed its appropriateness during the nationalistic North-South dialogue of the 1960s and 1970s. But as they began to promote rather than restrict investment, the nations had to accept the idea that expropriated investment had to be compensated reasonably soon after the taking ("prompt"), based on a fair valuation ("adequate"), and in a realistic form ("effective").

Most U.S. BITs and FTAs do not include provisions for consultations when investment differences arise. The Argentina-United States and Sri Lanka-United States BITs are exceptions. U.S. BITs and FTAs typically provide for investor-state arbitration, sometimes with no necessary recourse to prior exhaustion of local remedies. The 2012 Model U.S. BIT is thought to have reduced the scope of foreign investor protections, but they remained very controversial in the Obama-era Trans-Pacific Partnership (TPP-12) and Transatlantic Trade and Investment (TTIP) negotiations, and in the re-negotiation of NAFTA under the Trump administration. It appears only two U.S. BITs, with Rwanda and Uruguay, have been negotiated under the 2012 Model.

The United States has considered a BIT with China, which inked a BIT with Canada in 2012 that does not cover regulatory controls over permissions to invest ("pre-investment" rules). In other words, the Canada-China BIT only concerns operational and disposal aspects of foreign investment law. This approach is common in European-based BITs, which are the most prevalent around the globe.

A linked list of U.S. BITs appears below. See: https://www.state.gov/e/eb/ifd/bit/117402.htm.

Agreement Title
Albania Bilateral Investment Treaty
Argentina Bilateral Investment Treaty
Armenia Bilateral Investment Treaty
Azerbaijan Bilateral Investment Treaty
Bahrain Bilateral Investment Treaty
Bangladesh Bilateral Investment Treaty
Bolivia Bilateral Investment Treaty
Bulgaria Bilateral Investment Treaty
Cameroon Bilateral Investment Treaty
Congo, Democratic Republic Of (Kinshasa) Bilateral Investment Treaty
Congo, Republic Of (Brazzaville) Bilateral Investment Treaty
Croatia Bilateral Investment Treaty
Czech Republic Bilateral Investment Treaty
Ecuador Bilateral Investment Treaty
Egypt Bilateral Investment Treaty
Estonia Bilateral Investment Treaty
Georgia Bilateral Investment Treaty
Grenada Bilateral Investment Treaty
Honduras Bilateral Investment Treaty
Jamaica Bilateral Investment Treaty
Jordan Bilateral Investment Treaty
Kazakhstan Bilateral Investment Treaty
Kyrgyzstan Bilateral Investment Treaty

Latvia Bilateral Investment Treaty
Lithuania Bilateral Investment Treaty
Moldova Bilateral Investment Treaty
Mongolia Bilateral Investment Treaty
Morocco Bilateral Investment Treaty
Mozambique Bilateral Investment Treaty
Panama Bilateral Investment Treaty
Poland Bilateral Investment Treaty
Poland Business and Economic Relations Treaty
Romania Bilateral Investment Treaty
Rwanda Bilateral Investment Treaty
Senegal Bilateral Investment Treaty
Slovakia Bilateral Investment Treaty
Sri Lanka Bilateral Investment Treaty
Trinidad And Tobago Bilateral Investment Treaty
Tunisia Bilateral Investment Treaty
Turkey Bilateral Investment Treaty
Ukraine Bilateral Investment Treaty
Uruguay Bilateral Investment Treaty

§ 4.5 ICSID Foreign Investment Arbitrations

Arbitration rules were adopted under the 1966 Convention on the Settlement of Investment Disputes between States and Nationals of Other States (ICSID). The text of the ICSID Convention is reproduced at the end of this chapter. Over 150 countries are parties to this Convention, but Brazil, Canada (until 2013), Mexico, Russia, Thailand and Vietnam have notably not joined the ICSID Convention. In recent years, Bolivia, Ecuador and Venezuela have withdrawn from ICSID, asserting it is biased toward investors and undermines national sovereignty.

The Convention was implemented in the United States by 22 U.S.C. § 1650 and § 1650a. An arbitral money award, rendered pursuant to the Convention, is entitled to the same full faith and credit in the United States as a final judgment of a court of general jurisdiction in a State of the United States (22 U.S.C.A. 1650a).

The 1966 Convention provided for the establishment of an International Center for the Settlement of Investment Disputes (ICSID), as a non-financial organ of the World Bank (the

International Bank for Reconstruction and Development). The ICSID Convention is reproduced in Appendix B of this chapter. ICSID is designed to serve as a forum for both conciliation and arbitration of disputes between private investors and host governments. It provides an institutional framework within which arbitrators, selected by the disputing parties from an ICSID Panel of Arbitrators or from elsewhere, conduct arbitration in accordance with ICSID Rules of Procedure for Arbitration Proceedings. Arbitrations are held in Washington D.C. unless agreed otherwise.

Under the 1966 Convention (Article 25), ICSID's jurisdiction extends only "to any legal dispute arising directly out of an investment, between a Contracting State or. . . any subdivision. . . and a national of another Contracting State, which the parties to the dispute consent in writing to submit to the Centre. Where the parties have given their consent, either in respect of future disputes or in respect of existing disputes, no party may withdraw its consent unilaterally." Consent by signatory states cannot unilaterally be withdrawn so long as that state is still a member of ICSID.

Thus, ICSID is an attempt to institutionalize dispute resolution between States and non-State foreign investors. The disputes often arise under contracts between foreign investors and member states. Many sovereign consents to ICSID arbitrations are found in bilateral investment treaties (BITs, see above) and free trade agreements (Section 4.1).

Unlike international commercial arbitrations, the law of the place of arbitration generally has no influence over ICSID arbitrations, which are therefore said to be "delocalized." If one party questions such jurisdiction (predicated upon disputes arising "directly out of" an investment, between a Contracting Party and the national of another, and written consent to submission), the issue may be decided by the arbitration tribunal (Rule 41).

A party may seek annulment of any award only by an appeal to an ad hoc committee of persons drawn by the Administrative Council of ICSID from the Panel of Arbitrators under the Convention (Article 52). An ICSID award cannot be set aside by national courts or in any other way. Annulment is available only if the ICSID Tribunal was not properly constituted, exceeded its powers, seriously departed from a fundamental procedural rule, failed to state the reasons for its award, or included a member who practiced corruption.

Divergent ad hoc Annulment Committee decisions, particularly those known as the "Argentine Gas Sector Cases", have cast doubt on the legitimacy of ICSID annulment proceedings. Those cases concern challenges by foreign investors to emergency measures converting U.

S. dollar bank deposits to pesos after Argentina's sovereign default in 2001. Depending on the Committee, with nearly identical facts, some investors have prevailed and others have lost arguments centered on whether Argentina was entitled to invoke public order and/or customary law of necessity defenses.

Enforcement of the award (with attachment of assets if needed) is automatically possible within ICSID signatory state courts, including those of the host state, without further review or consideration of setting aside the award. All member states must enforce ICSID awards as if they were final, binding judgments of their national courts. There is no need to go through the New York Convention procedures associated with international commercial arbitration awards.

§ 4.6 ICSID Additional Facility Arbitrations

The Convention's 1966 jurisdictional limitations have prompted the ICSID Administrative Counsel to establish an Additional Facility for conducting conciliations and arbitrations for disputes which do not arise directly out of an investment and for investment disputes in which one party is not a Contracting State to the Convention or the national of a Contracting State. The Additional Facility is intended for use by parties having long-term relationships of special economic importance to the State party to the dispute and which involve the commitment of substantial resources on the part of either party. The Facility is not designed to service disputes which fall within the 1966 Convention or which are "ordinary commercial transaction" disputes. ICSID's Secretary General must give advance approval of an agreement contemplating use of the Additional Facility.

Because the Additional Facility operates outside the scope of the 1966 Convention, the Facility has its own Arbitration Rules. Under them, ICSID Convention rules regarding exclusion of other remedies, denial of provisional relief in national courts, internal annulment review, and recognition and enforcement do not apply. Additional Facility awards are subject to the set aside rules of the arbitral seat, and enforceable under the New York Convention.

The ICSID Convention has been used under numerous bilateral investment treaties (BITs). Because neither Canada (until December 2013) nor Mexico are ICSID signatories, the Additional Facility Rules have been employed in most NAFTA 1994 investor-state arbitrations (see Section 4.8), and, more recently, in CAFTA-DR FTA investor-state arbitrations. Mexican-U.S. investor-state arbitrations under the pending USMCA 2018 Agreement are likely to follow this pattern.

§ 4.7 Energy Charter Treaty Arbitrations

Some 60 nations have signed the Energy Charter Treaty of 1991. Article 26 permits foreign investors to take to arbitration disputes with signatory states concerning investment treatment rights contained in the Charter. These rights focus on national treatment, protection from direct or indirect expropriation, and contract adherence duties of the host state. Such arbitrations can be conducted under ICSID, UNCITRAL or Stockholm Chamber of Commerce rules.

In 2009, the Permanent Court of Arbitration in The Hague held that Russia's signing of the Charter, without subsequent ratification, was sufficient to confer jurisdiction. In 2014, that body ordered Russia to pay billions to the shareholders of Yukos for what it described as Russia's "devious and calculated expropriation" of assets designed to bankrupt Yukos, which happened. Because Yukos had unclean hands as a result of tax abuses, the arbitrators reduced the award by 25% to roughly $50 billion. Collection efforts are expected to center on Russian state assets and Rosneft, the Russian company that gained control of most of these assets in a series of politically driven bankruptcy proceedings. As of 2016, some success has been had in the Dutch, French and Belgian courts.

Another controversial invocation of ISDS before the Permanent Court of Arbitration occurred in 2011 when Germany, following the Fukushima disaster, decided to close its nuclear power industry. Vattenfall, a Swedish operator of two nuclear power plants in Germany, is currently demanding billions in expropriation compensation under the Energy Charter Treaty.

§ 4.8 Text of United States Model BIT (2012)

CONCERNING THE ENCOURAGEMENT AND RECIPROCAL PROTECTION OF INVESTMENT

The Government of the United States of America and the Government of [Country] (hereinafter the "Parties");

Desiring to promote greater economic cooperation between them with respect to investment by nationals and enterprises of one Party in the territory of the other Party;

Recognizing that agreement on the treatment to be accorded such investment will stimulate the flow of private capital and the economic development of the Parties;

Agreeing that a stable framework for investment will maximize effective utilization of economic resources and improve living standards;

Recognizing the importance of providing effective means of asserting claims and enforcing rights with respect to investment under national law as well as through international arbitration;

Desiring to achieve these objectives in a manner consistent with the protection of health, safety, and the environment, and the promotion of internationally recognized labor rights;

Having resolved to conclude a Treaty concerning the encouragement and reciprocal protection of investment;

Have agreed as follows:

Section A

Article 1: Definitions

For purposes of this Treaty:

"central level of government" means:

(a) for the United States, the federal level of government; and

(b) for [Country],

"Centre" means the International Centre for Settlement of Investment Disputes ("ICSID") established by the ICSID Convention.

"claimant" means an investor of a Party that is a party to an investment dispute with the other Party.

"covered investment" means, with respect to a Party, an investment in its territory of an investor of the other Party in existence as of the date of entry into force of this Treaty or established, acquired, or expanded thereafter.

"disputing parties" means the claimant and the respondent.

"disputing party" means either the claimant or the respondent.

"enterprise" means any entity constituted or organized under applicable law, whether or not for profit, and whether privately or governmentally owned or controlled, including a corporation, trust, partnership, sole proprietorship, joint venture, association, or similar organization; and a branch of an enterprise.

"enterprise of a Party" means an enterprise constituted or organized under the law of a Party, and a branch located in the territory of a Party and carrying out business activities there.

"existing" means in effect on the date of entry into force of this Treaty.

"freely usable currency" means "freely usable currency" as determined by the International Monetary Fund under its *Articles of Agreement*.

"GATS" means the *General Agreement on Trade in Services*, contained in Annex 1B to the WTO Agreement. **"government procurement"** means the process by which a government obtains the use of or acquires goods or services, or any combination thereof, for governmental purposes and not with a view to commercial sale or resale, or use in the production or supply of goods or services for commercial sale or resale.

"ICSID Additional Facility Rules" means the *Rules Governing the Additional Facility for the Administration of Proceedings by the Secretariat of the International Centre for Settlement of Investment Disputes*.

"ICSID Convention" means the *Convention on the Settlement of Investment Disputes between States and Nationals of Other States*, done at Washington, March 18, 1965.

[**"Inter-American Convention"** means the *Inter-American Convention on International Commercial Arbitration*, done at Panama, January 30, 1975.]

"investment" means every asset that an investor owns or controls, directly or indirectly, that has the characteristics of an investment, including such characteristics as the commitment of capital or other resources, the expectation of gain or profit, or the assumption of risk. Forms that an investment may take include:

(a) an enterprise;

(b) shares, stock, and other forms of equity participation in an enterprise;

(c) bonds, debentures, other debt instruments, and loans;[1]

(d) futures, options, and other derivatives;

(e) turnkey, construction, management, production, concession, revenue-sharing, and other similar contracts;

(f) intellectual property rights;

---

1 Some forms of debt, such as bonds, debentures, and long-term notes, are more likely to have the characteristics of an investment, while other forms of debt, such as claims to payment that are immediately due and result from the sale of goods or services, are less likely to have such characteristics.

(g) licenses, authorizations, permits, and similar rights conferred pursuant to domestic law;[2,3]

(h) other tangible or intangible, movable or immovable property, and related property rights, such as leases, mortgages, liens, and pledges.

"investment agreement" means a written agreement[4] between a national authority[5] of a Party and a covered investment or an investor of the other Party, on which the covered investment or the investor relies in establishing or acquiring a covered investment other than the written agreement itself, that grants rights to the covered investment or investor:

(a) with respect to natural resources that a national authority controls, such as for their exploration, extraction, refining, transportation, distribution, or sale;

(b) to supply services to the public on behalf of the Party, such as power generation or distribution, water treatment or distribution, or telecommunications; or

(c) to undertake infrastructure projects, such as the construction of roads, bridges, canals, dams, or pipelines, that are not for the exclusive or predominant use and benefit of the government.

---

[2] Whether a particular type of license, authorization, permit, or similar instrument (including a concession, to the extent that it has the nature of such an instrument) has the characteristics of an investment depends on such factors as the nature and extent of the rights that the holder has under the law of the Party. Among the licenses, authorizations, permits, and similar instruments that do not have the characteristics of an investment are those that do not create any rights protected under domestic law. For greater certainty, the foregoing is without prejudice to whether any asset associated with the license, authorization, permit, or similar instrument has the characteristics of an investment.

[3] The term "investment" does not include an order or judgment entered in a judicial or administrative action.

[4] "Written agreement" refers to an agreement in writing, executed by both parties, whether in a single instrument or in multiple instruments, that creates an exchange of rights and obligations, binding on both parties under the law applicable under Article 30[Governing Law] (2). For greater certainty, (a) a unilateral act of an administrative or judicial authority, such as a permit, license, or authorization issued by a Party solely in its regulatory capacity, or a decree, order, or judgment, standing alone; and (b) an administrative or judicial consent decree or order, shall not be considered a written agreement.

[5] For purposes of this definition, "national authority" means (a) for the United States, an authority at the central level of government; and (b) for [Country],

"investment authorization"[6] means an authorization that the foreign investment authority of a Party grants to a covered investment or an investor of the other Party.

"investor of a non-Party" means, with respect to a Party, an investor that attempts to make, is making, or has made an investment in the territory of that Party, that is not an investor of either Party.

"investor of a Party" means a Party or state enterprise thereof, or a national or an enterprise of a Party, that attempts to make, is making, or has made an investment in the territory of the other Party; provided, however, that a natural person who is a dual national shall be deemed to be exclusively a national of the State of his or her dominant and effective nationality.

"measure" includes any law, regulation, procedure, requirement, or practice.

"national" means:

(a) for the United States, a natural person who is a national of the United States as defined in Title III of the Immigration and Nationality Act; and

(b) for [Country],

"New York Convention" means the United Nations Convention on the Recognition and Enforcement of Foreign Arbitral Awards, done at New York, June 10, 1958.

"non-disputing Party" means the Party that is not a party to an investment dispute.

"person" means a natural person or an enterprise.

"person of a Party" means a national or an enterprise of a Party.

"protected information" means confidential business information or information that is privileged or otherwise protected from disclosure under a Party's law.

"regional level of government" means:

(a) for the United States, a state of the United States, the District of Columbia, or Puerto Rico; and

(b) for [Country],

"respondent" means the Party that is a party to an investment dispute.

---

6 For greater certainty, actions taken by a Party to enforce laws of general application, such as competition laws, are not encompassed within this definition.

"Secretary-General" means the Secretary-General of ICSID.

"state enterprise" means an enterprise owned, or controlled through ownership interests, by a Party.

"territory" means:

(a) with respect to the United States,

(i) the customs territory of the United States, which includes the 50 states, the District of Columbia, and Puerto Rico;

(ii) the foreign trade zones located in the United States and Puerto Rico.

(b) with respect to [Country,]

(c) with respect to each Party, the territorial sea and any area beyond the territorial sea of the Party within which, in accordance with customary international law as reflected in the United Nations Convention on the Law of the Sea, the Party may exercise sovereign rights or jurisdiction.

"TRIPS Agreement" means the *Agreement on Trade-Related Aspects of Intellectual Property Rights*, contained in Annex 1C to the WTO Agreement.[7]

"UNCITRAL Arbitration Rules" means the arbitration rules of the United Nations Commission on International Trade Law.

"WTO Agreement" means the *Marrakesh Agreement Establishing the World Trade Organization*, done on April 15, 1994.

Article 2: Scope and Coverage

1. This Treaty applies to measures adopted or maintained by a Party relating to:

(a) investors of the other Party;

(b) covered investments; and

(c) with respect to Articles 8 [Performance Requirements], 12 [Investment and Environment], and 13 [Investment and Labor], all investments in the territory of the Party.

---

7 For greater certainty, "TRIPS Agreement" includes any waiver in force between the Parties of any provision of the TRIPS Agreement granted by WTO Members in accordance with the WTO Agreement.

2. A Party's obligations under Section A shall apply:

(a) to a state enterprise or other person when it exercises any regulatory, administrative, or other governmental authority delegated to it by that Party;[8] and

(b) to the political subdivisions of that Party.

3. For greater certainty, this Treaty does not bind either Party in relation to any act or fact that took place or any situation that ceased to exist before the date of entry into force of this Treaty.

Article 3: National Treatment

1. Each Party shall accord to investors of the other Party treatment no less favorable than that it accords, in like circumstances, to its own investors with respect to the establishment, acquisition, expansion, management, conduct, operation, and sale or other disposition of investments in its territory.

2. Each Party shall accord to covered investments treatment no less favorable than that it accords, in like circumstances, to investments in its territory of its own investors with respect to the establishment, acquisition, expansion, management, conduct, operation, and sale or other disposition of investments.

3. The treatment to be accorded by a Party under paragraphs 1 and 2 means, with respect to a regional level of government, treatment no less favorable than the treatment accorded, in like circumstances, by that regional level of government to natural persons resident in and enterprises constituted under the laws of other regional levels of government of the Party of which it forms a part, and to their respective investments.

Article 4: Most-Favored-Nation Treatment

1. Each Party shall accord to investors of the other Party treatment no less favorable than that it accords, in like circumstances, to investors of any non-Party with respect to the establishment, acquisition, expansion, management, conduct, operation, and sale or other disposition of investments in its territory.

2. Each Party shall accord to covered investments treatment no less favorable than that it accords, in like circumstances, to investments in its territory of investors of any non-Party with respect to the establishment, acquisition, expansion, management, conduct, operation, and sale or other disposition of investments.

---

[8] For greater certainty, government authority that has been delegated includes a legislative grant, and a government order, directive or other action transferring to the state enterprise or other person, or authorizing the exercise by the state enterprise or other person of, governmental authority.

Article 5: Minimum Standard of Treatment[9]

1. Each Party shall accord to covered investments treatment in accordance with customary international law, including fair and equitable treatment and full protection and security.

2. For greater certainty, paragraph 1 prescribes the customary international law minimum standard of treatment of aliens as the minimum standard of treatment to be afforded to covered investments. The concepts of "fair and equitable treatment" and "full protection and security" do not require treatment in addition to or beyond that which is required by that standard, and do not create additional substantive rights. The obligation in paragraph 1 to provide:

(a) "fair and equitable treatment" includes the obligation not to deny justice in criminal, civil, or administrative adjudicatory proceedings in accordance with the principle of due process embodied in the principal legal systems of the world; and

(b) "full protection and security" requires each Party to provide the level of police protection required under customary international law.

3. A determination that there has been a breach of another provision of this Treaty, or of a separate international agreement, does not establish that there has been a breach of this Article.

4. Notwithstanding Article 14 [Non-Conforming Measures] (5)(b) [subsidies and grants], each Party shall accord to investors of the other Party, and to covered investments, non-discriminatory treatment with respect to measures it adopts or maintains relating to losses suffered by investments in its territory owing to armed conflict or civil strife.

5. Notwithstanding paragraph 4, if an investor of a Party, in the situations referred to in paragraph 4, suffers a loss in the territory of the other Party resulting from:

(a) requisitioning of its covered investment or part thereof by the latter's forces or authorities; or

(b) destruction of its covered investment or part thereof by the latter's forces or authorities, which was not required by the necessity of the situation, the latter Party shall provide the investor restitution, compensation, or both, as appropriate, for such loss. Any compensation shall be prompt, adequate, and

---

[9] Article 5 [Minimum Standard of Treatment] shall be interpreted in accordance with Annex A.

effective in accordance with Article 6 [Expropriation and Compensation] (2) through (4), *mutatis mutandis*.

6. Paragraph 4 does not apply to existing measures relating to subsidies or grants that would be inconsistent with Article 3 [National Treatment] but for Article 14 [Non-Conforming Measures] (5)(b) [subsidies and grants].

Article 6: Expropriation and Compensation[10]

1. Neither Party may expropriate or nationalize a covered investment either directly or indirectly through measures equivalent to expropriation or nationalization ("expropriation"), except:

(a) for a public purpose;

(b) in a non-discriminatory manner;

(c) on payment of prompt, adequate, and effective compensation; and

(d) in accordance with due process of law and Article 5 [Minimum Standard of Treatment] (1) through (3).

2. The compensation referred to in paragraph 1(c) shall:

(a) be paid without delay;

(b) be equivalent to the fair market value of the expropriated investment immediately before the expropriation took place ("the date of expropriation");

(c) not reflect any change in value occurring because the intended expropriation had become known earlier; and

(d) be fully realizable and freely transferable.

3. If the fair market value is denominated in a freely usable currency, the compensation referred to in paragraph 1(c) shall be no less than the fair market value on the date of expropriation, plus interest at a commercially reasonable rate for that currency, accrued from the date of expropriation until the date of payment.

4. If the fair market value is denominated in a currency that is not freely usable, the compensation referred to in paragraph 1(c)—converted into the currency of payment at the market rate of exchange prevailing on the date of payment—shall be no less than:

(a) the fair market value on the date of expropriation, converted into a freely usable currency at the market rate of exchange prevailing on that date, plus

10 Article 6 [Expropriation] shall be interpreted in accordance with Annexes A and B.

(b) interest, at a commercially reasonable rate for that freely usable currency, accrued from the date of expropriation until the date of payment.

5. This Article does not apply to the issuance of compulsory licenses granted in relation to intellectual property rights in accordance with the TRIPS Agreement, or to the revocation, limitation, or creation of intellectual property rights, to the extent that such issuance, revocation, limitation, or creation is consistent with the TRIPS Agreement.

Article 7: Transfers

1. Each Party shall permit all transfers relating to a covered investment to be made freely and without delay into and out of its territory. Such transfers include:

(a) contributions to capital;

(b) profits, dividends, capital gains, and proceeds from the sale of all or any part of the covered investment or from the partial or complete liquidation of the covered investment;

(c) interest, royalty payments, management fees, and technical assistance and other fees;

(d) payments made under a contract, including a loan agreement;

(e) payments made pursuant to Article 5 [Minimum Standard of Treatment] (4) and (5) and Article 6 [Expropriation and Compensation]; and

(f) payments arising out of a dispute.

2. Each Party shall permit transfers relating to a covered investment to be made in a freely usable currency at the market rate of exchange prevailing at the time of transfer.

3. Each Party shall permit returns in kind relating to a covered investment to be made as authorized or specified in a written agreement between the Party and a covered investment or an investor of the other Party.

4. Notwithstanding paragraphs 1 through 3, a Party may prevent a transfer through the equitable, non-discriminatory, and good faith application of its laws relating to:

(a) bankruptcy, insolvency, or the protection of the rights of creditors;

(b) issuing, trading, or dealing in securities, futures, options, or derivatives;

(c) criminal or penal offenses;

(d) financial reporting or record keeping of transfers when necessary to assist law enforcement or financial regulatory authorities; or

(e) ensuring compliance with orders or judgments in judicial or administrative proceedings.

Article 8: Performance Requirements

1. Neither Party may, in connection with the establishment, acquisition, expansion, management, conduct, operation, or sale or other disposition of an investment of an investor of a Party or of a non-Party in its territory, impose or enforce any requirement or enforce any commitment or undertaking:[11]

(a) to export a given level or percentage of goods or services;

(b) to achieve a given level or percentage of domestic content;

(c) to purchase, use, or accord a preference to goods produced in its territory, or to purchase goods from persons in its territory;

(d) to relate in any way the volume or value of imports to the volume or value of exports or to the amount of foreign exchange inflows associated with such investment;

(e) to restrict sales of goods or services in its territory that such investment produces or supplies by relating such sales in any way to the volume or value of its exports or foreign exchange earnings;

(f) to transfer a particular technology, a production process, or other proprietary knowledge to a person in its territory;

(g) to supply exclusively from the territory of the Party the goods that such investment produces or the services that it supplies to a specific regional market or to the world market; or

(h) (i) to purchase, use, or accord a preference to, in its territory, technology of the Party or of persons of the Party;[12] or

(ii) that prevents the purchase or use of, or the according of a preference to, in its territory, particular technology, so as to afford protection on the basis of nationality to its own

[11] For greater certainty, a condition for the receipt or continued receipt of an advantage referred to in paragraph 2 does not constitute a "commitment or undertaking" for the purposes of paragraph 1.

[12] For purposes of this Article, the term "technology of the Party or of persons of the Party" includes technology that is owned by the Party or persons of the Party, and technology for which the Party holds, or persons of the Party hold, an exclusive license.

investors or investments or to technology of the Party or of persons of the Party.

2. Neither Party may condition the receipt or continued receipt of an advantage, in connection with the establishment, acquisition, expansion, management, conduct, operation, or sale or other disposition of an investment in its territory of an investor of a Party or of a non-Party, on compliance with any requirement:

(a) to achieve a given level or percentage of domestic content;

(b) to purchase, use, or accord a preference to goods produced in its territory, or to purchase goods from persons in its territory;

(c) to relate in any way the volume or value of imports to the volume or value of exports or to the amount of foreign exchange inflows associated with such investment; or

(d) to restrict sales of goods or services in its territory that such investment produces or supplies by relating such sales in any way to the volume or value of its exports or foreign exchange earnings.

3. (a) Nothing in paragraph 2 shall be construed to prevent a Party from conditioning the receipt or continued receipt of an advantage, in connection with an investment in its territory of an investor of a Party or of a non-Party, on compliance with a requirement to locate production, supply a service, train or employ workers, construct or expand particular facilities, or carry out research and development, in its territory.

(b) Paragraphs 1(f) and (h) do not apply:

(i) when a Party authorizes use of an intellectual property right in accordance with Article 31 of the TRIPS Agreement, or to measures requiring the disclosure of proprietary information that fall within the scope of, and are consistent with, Article 39 of the TRIPS Agreement; or

(ii) when the requirement is imposed or the commitment or undertaking is enforced by a court, administrative tribunal, or competition authority to remedy a practice determined after judicial or administrative process to be anticompetitive under the Party's competition laws.[13]

(c) Provided that such measures are not applied in an arbitrary or unjustifiable manner, and provided that such measures do not constitute a disguised restriction on international trade or investment, paragraphs 1(b), (c), (f), and (h), and 2(a) and (b),

[13] The Parties recognize that a patent does not necessarily confer market power.

shall not be construed to prevent a Party from adopting or maintaining measures, including environmental measures:

(i) necessary to secure compliance with laws and regulations that are not inconsistent with this Treaty;

(ii) necessary to protect human, animal, or plant life or health; or

(iii) related to the conservation of living or non-living exhaustible natural resources.

(d) Paragraphs 1(a), (b), and (c), and 2(a) and (b), do not apply to qualification requirements for goods or services with respect to export promotion and foreign aid programs.

(e) Paragraphs 1(b), (c), (f), (g), and (h), and 2(a) and (b), do not apply to government procurement.

(f) Paragraphs 2(a) and (b) do not apply to requirements imposed by an importing Party relating to the content of goods necessary to qualify for preferential tariffs or preferential quotas.

4. For greater certainty, paragraphs 1 and 2 do not apply to any commitment, undertaking, or requirement other than those set out in those paragraphs.

5. This Article does not preclude enforcement of any commitment, undertaking, or requirement between private parties, where a Party did not impose or require the commitment, undertaking, or requirement.

Article 9: Senior Management and Boards of Directors

1. Neither Party may require that an enterprise of that Party that is a covered investment appoint to senior management positions natural persons of any particular nationality.

2. A Party may require that a majority of the board of directors, or any committee thereof, of an enterprise of that Party that is a covered investment, be of a particular nationality, or resident in the territory of the Party, provided that the requirement does not materially impair the ability of the investor to exercise control over its investment.

Article 10: Publication of Laws and Decisions Respecting Investment

1. Each Party shall ensure that its:

(a) laws, regulations, procedures, and administrative rulings of general application; and

(b) adjudicatory decisions respecting any matter covered by this Treaty are promptly published or otherwise made publicly available.

2. For purposes of this Article, "administrative ruling of general application" means an administrative ruling or interpretation that applies to all persons and fact situations that fall generally within its ambit and that establishes a norm of conduct but does not include:

(a) a determination or ruling made in an administrative or quasi-judicial proceeding that applies to a particular covered investment or investor of the other Party in a specific case; or

(b) a ruling that adjudicates with respect to a particular act or practice.

Article 11: Transparency

1. The Parties agree to consult periodically on ways to improve the transparency practices set out in this Article, Article 10 and Article 29.

2. Publication

To the extent possible, each Party shall:

(a) publish in advance any measure referred to in Article 10(1)(a) that it proposes to adopt; and

(b) provide interested persons and the other Party a reasonable opportunity to comment on such proposed measures.

3. With respect to proposed regulations of general application of its central level of government respecting any matter covered by this Treaty that are published in accordance with paragraph 2(a), each Party:

(a) shall publish the proposed regulations in a single official journal of national circulation and shall encourage their distribution through additional outlets;

(b) should in most cases publish the proposed regulations not less than 60 days before the date public comments are due;

(c) shall include in the publication an explanation of the purpose of and rationale for the proposed regulations; and

(d) shall, at the time it adopts final regulations, address significant, substantive comments received during the comment period and explain substantive revisions that it made to the proposed regulations in its official journal or in a prominent location on a government Internet site.

4. With respect to regulations of general application that are adopted by its central level of government respecting any matter covered by this Treaty, each Party:

(a) shall publish the regulations in a single official journal of national circulation and shall encourage their distribution through additional outlets; and

(b) shall include in the publication an explanation of the purpose of and rationale for the regulations.

5. Provision of Information

(a) On request of the other Party, a Party shall promptly provide information and respond to questions pertaining to any actual or proposed measure that the requesting Party considers might materially affect the operation of this Treaty or otherwise substantially affect its interests under this Treaty.

(b) Any request or information under this paragraph shall be provided to the other Party through the relevant contact points.

(c) Any information provided under this paragraph shall be without prejudice as to whether the measure is consistent with this Treaty.

6. Administrative Proceedings

With a view to administering in a consistent, impartial, and reasonable manner all measures referred to in Article 10(1)(a), each Party shall ensure that in its administrative proceedings applying such measures to particular covered investments or investors of the other Party in specific cases:

(a) wherever possible, covered investments or investors of the other Party that are directly affected by a proceeding are provided reasonable notice, in accordance with domestic procedures, when a proceeding is initiated, including a description of the nature of the proceeding, a statement of the legal authority under which the proceeding is initiated, and a general description of any issues in controversy;

(b) such persons are afforded a reasonable opportunity to present facts and arguments in support of their positions prior to any final administrative action, when time, the nature of the proceeding, and the public interest permit; and

(c) its procedures are in accordance with domestic law.

7. Review and Appeal

(a) Each Party shall establish or maintain judicial, quasi-judicial, or administrative tribunals or procedures for the purpose of the prompt review and, where warranted, correction of final administrative actions regarding matters covered by this Treaty. Such tribunals shall be impartial and independent of the office or authority entrusted with administrative enforcement and shall not have any substantial interest in the outcome of the matter.

(b) Each Party shall ensure that, in any such tribunals or procedures, the parties to the proceeding are provided with the right to:

(i) a reasonable opportunity to support or defend their respective positions; and

(ii) a decision based on the evidence and submissions of record or, where required by domestic law, the record compiled by the administrative authority.

(c) Each Party shall ensure, subject to appeal or further review as provided in its domestic law, that such decisions shall be implemented by, and shall govern the practice of, the offices or authorities with respect to the administrative action at issue.

8. Standards-Setting

(a) Each Party shall allow persons of the other Party to participate in the development of standards and technical regulations by its central government bodies.[14] Each Party shall allow persons of the other Party to participate in the development of these measures, and the development of conformity assessment procedures by its central government bodies, on terms no less favorable than those it accords to its own persons.

(b) Each Party shall recommend that non-governmental standardizing bodies in its territory allow persons of the other Party to participate in the development of standards by those bodies. Each Party shall recommend that non-governmental standardizing bodies in its territory allow persons of the other Party to participate in the development of these standards, and the development of conformity assessment procedures by those bodies, on terms no less favorable than those they accord to persons of the Party.

(c) Subparagraphs 8(a) and 8(b) do not apply to:

[14] A Party may satisfy this obligation by, for example, providing interested persons a reasonable opportunity to provide comments on the measure it proposes to develop and taking those comments into account in the development of the measure.

(i) sanitary and phytosanitary measures as defined in Annex A of the World Trade Organization (WTO) Agreement on the Application of Sanitary and Phytosanitary Measures; or

(ii) purchasing specifications prepared by a governmental body for its production or consumption requirements.

(d) For purposes of subparagraphs 8(a) and 8(b), "central government body", "standards", "technical regulations" and "conformity assessment procedures" have the meanings assigned to those terms in Annex 1 of the WTO Agreement on Technical Barriers to Trade. Consistent with Annex 1, the three latter terms do not include standards, technical regulations or conformity assessment procedures 'for the supply of a service.

Article 12: Investment and Environment

1. The Parties recognize that their respective environmental laws and policies, and multilateral environmental agreements to which they are both party, play an important role in protecting the environment.

2. The Parties recognize that it is inappropriate to encourage investment by weakening or reducing the protections afforded in domestic environmental laws. Accordingly, each Party shall ensure that it does not waive or otherwise derogate from or offer to waive or otherwise derogate from its environmental laws[15] in a manner that weakens or reduces the protections afforded in those laws, or fail to effectively enforce those laws through a sustained or recurring course of action or inaction, as an encouragement for the establishment, acquisition, expansion, or retention of an investment in its territory.

3. The Parties recognize that each Party retains the right to exercise discretion with respect to regulatory, compliance, investigatory, and prosecutorial matters, and to make decisions regarding the allocation of resources to enforcement with respect to other environmental matters determined to have higher priorities. Accordingly, the Parties understand that a Party is in compliance with paragraph 2 where a course of action or inaction reflects a reasonable exercise of such discretion, or results from a *bona fide* decision regarding the allocation of resources.

4. For purposes of this Article, "environmental law" means each Party's statutes or regulations,[16] or provisions thereof, the primary

---

[15] Paragraph 2 shall not apply where a Party waives or derogates from an environmental law pursuant to a provision in law providing for waivers or derogations.

[16] For the United States, "statutes or regulations" for the purposes of this Article means an act of the United States Congress or regulations promulgated pursuant to

purpose of which is the protection of the environment, or the prevention of a danger to human, animal, or plant life or health, through the:

(a) prevention, abatement, or control of the release, discharge, or emission of pollutants or environmental contaminants;

(b) control of environmentally hazardous or toxic chemicals, substances, materials, and wastes, and the dissemination of information related thereto; or

(c) protection or conservation of wild flora or fauna, including endangered species, their habitat, and specially protected natural areas, in the Party's territory, but does not include any statute or regulation, or provision thereof, directly related to worker safety or health.

5. Nothing in this Treaty shall be construed to prevent a Party from adopting, maintaining, or enforcing any measure otherwise consistent with this Treaty that it considers appropriate to ensure that investment activity in its territory is undertaken in a manner sensitive to environmental concerns.

6. A Party may make a written request for consultations with the other Party regarding any matter arising under this Article. The other Party shall respond to a request for consultations within thirty days of receipt of such request. Thereafter, the Parties shall consult and endeavor to reach a mutually satisfactory resolution.

7. The Parties confirm that each Party may, as appropriate, provide opportunities for public participation regarding any matter arising under this Article.

Article 13: Investment and Labor

1. The Parties reaffirm their respective obligations as members of the International Labor Organization ("ILO") and their commitments under the *ILO Declaration on Fundamental Principles and Rights at Work and its Follow-Up*.

2. The Parties recognize that it is inappropriate to encourage investment by weakening or reducing the protections afforded in domestic labor laws. Accordingly, each Party shall ensure that it does not waive or otherwise derogate from or offer to waive or otherwise derogate from its labor laws where the waiver or derogation would be inconsistent with the labor rights referred to in subparagraphs (a) through (e) of paragraph 3, or fail to effectively enforce its labor laws through a sustained or recurring course of actions or inaction, as an

an act of the United States Congress that is enforceable by action of the central level of government.

encouragement for the establishment, acquisition, expansion, or retention of an investment in its territory.

3. For purposes of this Article, "labor laws" means each Party's statutes or regulations,[17] or provisions thereof, that are directly related to the following:

(a) freedom of association;

(b) the effective recognition of the right to collective bargaining;

(c) the elimination of all forms of forced or compulsory labor;

(d) the effective abolition of child labor and a prohibition on the worst forms of child labor;

(e) the elimination of discrimination in respect of employment and occupation; and

(f) acceptable conditions of work with respect to minimum wages, hours of work, and occupational safety and health.

4. A Party may make a written request for consultations with the other Party regarding any matter arising under this Article. The other Party shall respond to a request for consultations within thirty days of receipt of such request. Thereafter, the Parties shall consult and endeavor to reach a mutually satisfactory resolution.

5. The Parties confirm that each Party may, as appropriate, provide opportunities for public participation regarding any matter arising under this Article.

Article 14: Non-Conforming Measures

1. Articles 3 [National Treatment], 4 [Most-Favored-Nation Treatment], 8 [Performance Requirements], and 9 [Senior Management and Boards of Directors] do not apply to:

(a) any existing non-conforming measure that is maintained by a Party at:

(i) the central level of government, as set out by that Party in its Schedule to Annex I or Annex III,

(ii) a regional level of government, as set out by that Party in its Schedule to Annex I or Annex III, or

(iii) a local level of government;

[17] For the United States, "statutes or regulations" for purposes of this Article means an act of the United States Congress or regulations promulgated pursuant to an act of the United States Congress that is enforceable by action of the central level of government.

(b) the continuation or prompt renewal of any non-conforming measure referred to in subparagraph (a); or

(c) an amendment to any non-conforming measure referred to in subparagraph (a) to the extent that the amendment does not decrease the conformity of the measure, as it existed immediately before the amendment, with Article 3 [National Treatment], 4 [Most Favored-Nation Treatment], 8 [Performance Requirements], or 9 [Senior Management and Boards of Directors].

2. Articles 3 [National Treatment], 4 [Most-Favored-Nation Treatment], 8 [Performance Requirements], and 9 [Senior Management and Boards of Directors] do not apply to any measure that a Party adopts or maintains with respect to sectors, subsectors, or activities, as set out in its Schedule to Annex II.

3. Neither Party may, under any measure adopted after the date of entry into force of this Treaty and covered by its Schedule to Annex II, require an investor of the other Party, by reason of its nationality, to sell or otherwise dispose of an investment existing at the time the measure becomes effective.

4. Articles 3 [National Treatment] and 4 [Most-Favored-Nation Treatment] do not apply to any measure covered by an exception to, or derogation from, the obligations under Article 3 or 4 of the TRIPS Agreement, as specifically provided in those Articles and in Article 5 of the TRIPS Agreement.

5. Articles 3 [National Treatment], 4 [Most-Favored-Nation Treatment], and 9 [Senior Management and Boards of Directors] do not apply to:

(a) government procurement; or

(b) subsidies or grants provided by a Party, including government-supported loans, guarantees, and insurance.

Article 15: Special Formalities and Information Requirements

1. Nothing in Article 3 [National Treatment] shall be construed to prevent a Party from adopting or maintaining a measure that prescribes special formalities in connection with covered investments, such as a requirement that investors be residents of the Party or that covered investments be legally constituted under the laws or regulations of the Party, provided that such formalities do not materially impair the protections afforded by a Party to investors of the other Party and covered investments pursuant to this Treaty.

2. Notwithstanding Articles 3 [National Treatment] and 4 [Most-Favored-Nation Treatment], a Party may require an investor of the other Party or its covered investment to provide information concerning that investment solely for informational or statistical purposes. The Party shall protect any confidential business information from any disclosure that would prejudice the competitive position of the investor or the covered investment. Nothing in this paragraph shall be construed to prevent a Party from otherwise obtaining or disclosing information in connection with the equitable and good faith application of its law.

Article 16: Non-Derogation

This Treaty shall not derogate from any of the following that entitle an investor of a Party or a covered investment to treatment more favorable than that accorded by this Treaty:

1. laws or regulations, administrative practices or procedures, or administrative or adjudicatory decisions of a Party;

2. international legal obligations of a Party; or

3. obligations assumed by a Party, including those contained in an investment authorization or an investment agreement.

Article 17: Denial of Benefits

1. A Party may deny the benefits of this Treaty to an investor of the other Party that is an enterprise of such other Party and to investments of that investor if persons of a non-Party own or control the enterprise and the denying Party:

(a) does not maintain diplomatic relations with the non-Party; or

(b) adopts or maintains measures with respect to the non-Party or a person of the non-Party that prohibit transactions with the enterprise or that would be violated or circumvented if the benefits of this Treaty were accorded to the enterprise or to its investments.

2. A Party may deny the benefits of this Treaty to an investor of the other Party that is an enterprise of such other Party and to investments of that investor if the enterprise has no substantial business activities in the territory of the other Party and persons of a non-Party, or of the denying Party, own or control the enterprise.

Article 18: Essential Security

Nothing in this Treaty shall be construed:

1. to require a Party to furnish or allow access to any information the disclosure of which it determines to be contrary to its essential security interests; or

2. to preclude a Party from applying measures that it considers necessary for the fulfillment of its obligations with respect to the maintenance or restoration of international peace or security, or the protection of its own essential security interests.

Article 19: Disclosure of Information

Nothing in this Treaty shall be construed to require a Party to furnish or allow access to confidential information the disclosure of which would impede law enforcement or otherwise be contrary to the public interest, or which would prejudice the legitimate commercial interests of particular enterprises, public or private.

Article 20: Financial Services

1. Notwithstanding any other provision of this Treaty, a Party shall not be prevented from adopting or maintaining measures relating to financial services for prudential reasons, including for the protection of investors, depositors, policy holders, or persons to whom a fiduciary duty is owed by a financial services supplier, or to ensure the integrity and stability of the financial system.[18] Where such measures do not conform with the provisions of this Treaty, they shall not be used as a means of avoiding the Party's commitments or obligations under this Treaty.

2. (a) Nothing in this Treaty applies to non-discriminatory measures of general application taken by any public entity in pursuit of monetary and related credit policies or exchange rate policies. This paragraph shall not affect a Party's obligations under Article 7 [Transfers] or Article 8 [Performance Requirements].[19]

(b) For purposes of this paragraph, "public entity" means a central bank or monetary authority of a Party.

---

[18] It is understood that the term "prudential reasons" includes the maintenance of the safety, soundness, integrity, or financial responsibility of individual financial institutions, as well as the maintenance of the safety and financial and operational integrity of payment and clearing systems.

[19] For greater certainty, measures of general application taken in pursuit of monetary and related credit policies or exchange rate policies do not include measures that expressly nullify or amend contractual provisions that specify the currency of denomination or the rate of exchange of currencies.

3. Where a claimant submits a claim to arbitration under Section B [Investor-State Dispute Settlement], and the respondent invokes paragraph 1 or 2 as a defense, the following provisions shall apply:

(a) The respondent shall, within 120 days of the date the claim is submitted to arbitration under Section B, submit in writing to the competent financial authorities[20] of both Parties a request for a joint determination on the issue of whether and to what extent paragraph 1 or 2 is a valid defense to the claim. The respondent shall promptly provide the tribunal, if constituted, a copy of such request. The arbitration may proceed with respect to the claim only as provided in subparagraph (d).

(b) The competent financial authorities of both Parties shall make themselves available for consultations with each other and shall attempt in good faith to make a determination as described in subparagraph (a). Any such determination shall be transmitted promptly to the disputing parties and, if constituted, to the tribunal. The determination shall be binding on the tribunal.

(c) If the competent financial authorities of both Parties, within 120 days of the date by which they have both received the respondent's written request for a joint determination under subparagraph (a), have not made a determination as described in that subparagraph, the tribunal shall decide the issue or issues left unresolved by the competent financial authorities. The provisions of Section B shall apply, except as modified by this subparagraph.

(i) In the appointment of all arbitrators not yet appointed to the tribunal, each disputing party shall take appropriate steps to ensure that the tribunal has expertise or experience in financial services law or practice. The expertise of particular candidates with respect to the particular sector of financial services in which the dispute arises shall be taken into account in the appointment of the presiding arbitrator.

(ii) If, before the respondent submits the request for a joint determination in conformance with subparagraph (a), the presiding arbitrator has been appointed pursuant to Article 27(3), such arbitrator shall be replaced on the request of either disputing party and the tribunal shall be

---

[20] For purposes of this Article, "competent financial authorities" means, for the United States, the Department of the Treasury for banking and other financial services, and the Office of the United States Trade Representative, in coordination with the Department of Commerce and other agencies, for insurance; and for [Country].

reconstituted consistent with subparagraph (c)(i). If, within 30 days of the date the arbitration proceedings are resumed under subparagraph (d), the disputing parties have not agreed on the appointment of a new presiding arbitrator, the Secretary-General, on the request of a disputing party, shall appoint the presiding arbitrator consistent with subparagraph (c)(i).

(iii) The tribunal shall draw no inference regarding the application of paragraph 1 or 2 from the fact that the competent financial authorities have not made a determination as described in subparagraph (a).

(iv) The non-disputing Party may make oral and written submissions to the tribunal regarding the issue of whether and to what extent paragraph 1 or 2 is a valid defense to the claim. Unless it makes such a submission, the non-disputing Party shall be presumed, for purposes of the arbitration, to take a position on paragraph 1 or 2 not inconsistent with that of the respondent.

(d) The arbitration referred to in subparagraph (a) may proceed with respect to the claim:

(i) 10 days after the date the competent financial authorities' joint determination has been received by both the disputing parties and, if constituted, the tribunal; or

(ii) 10 days after the expiration of the 120-day period provided to the competent financial authorities in subparagraph (c).

(e) On the request of the respondent made within 30 days after the expiration of the 120-day period for a joint determination referred to in subparagraph (c), or, if the tribunal has not been constituted as of the expiration of the 120-day period, within 30 days after the tribunal is constituted, the tribunal shall address and decide the issue or issues left unresolved by the competent financial authorities as referred to in subparagraph (c) prior to deciding the merits of the claim for which paragraph 1 or 2 has been invoked by the respondent as a defense. Failure of the respondent to make such a request is without prejudice to the right of the respondent to invoke paragraph 1 or 2 as a defense at any appropriate phase of the arbitration.

4. Where a dispute arises under Section C and the competent financial authorities of one Party provide written notice to the competent financial authorities of the other Party that the dispute

involves financial services, Section C shall apply except as modified by this paragraph and paragraph 5.

(a) The competent financial authorities of both Parties shall make themselves available for consultations with each other regarding the dispute, and shall have 180 days from the date such notice is received to transmit a report on their consultations to the Parties. A Party may submit the dispute to arbitration under Section C only after the expiration of that 180-day period.

(b) Either Party may make any such report available to a tribunal constituted under Section C to decide the dispute referred to in this paragraph or a similar dispute, or to a tribunal constituted under Section B to decide a claim arising out of the same events or circumstances that gave rise to the dispute under Section C.

5. Where a Party submits a dispute involving financial services to arbitration under Section C in conformance with paragraph 4, and on the request of either Party within 30 days of the date the dispute is submitted to arbitration, each Party shall, in the appointment of all arbitrators not yet appointed, take appropriate steps to ensure that the tribunal has expertise or experience in financial services law or practice. The expertise of particular candidates with respect to financial services shall be taken into account in the appointment of the presiding arbitrator.

6. Notwithstanding Article 11(2)–(4) [Transparency-Publication], each Party, to the extent practicable,

(a) shall publish in advance any regulations of general application relating to financial services that it proposes to adopt and the purpose of the regulation;

(b) shall provide interested persons and the other Party a reasonable opportunity to comment on such proposed regulations; and

(c) should at the time it adopts final regulations, address in writing significant substantive comments received from interested persons with respect to the proposed regulations.

7. The terms "financial service" or "financial services" shall have the same meaning as in subparagraph 5(a) of the Annex on Financial Services of the GATS.

8. For greater certainty, nothing in this Treaty shall be construed to prevent the adoption or enforcement by a party of measures relating to investors of the other Party, or covered investments, in financial institutions that are necessary to secure compliance with

laws or regulations that are not inconsistent with this Treaty, including those related to the prevention of deceptive and fraudulent practices or that deal with the effects of a default on financial services contracts, subject to the requirement that such measures are not applied in a manner which would constitute a means of arbitrary or unjustifiable discrimination between countries where like conditions prevail, or a disguised restriction on investment in financial institutions.

Article 21: Taxation

1. Except as provided in this Article, nothing in Section A shall impose obligations with respect to taxation measures.

2. Article 6 [Expropriation] shall apply to all taxation measures, except that a claimant that asserts that a taxation measure involves an expropriation may submit a claim to arbitration under Section B only if:

(a) the claimant has first referred to the competent tax authorities[21] of both Parties in writing the issue of whether that taxation measure involves an expropriation;

and

(b) within 180 days after the date of such referral, the competent tax authorities of both Parties fail to agree that the taxation measure is not an expropriation.

3. Subject to paragraph 4, Article 8 [Performance Requirements] (2) through (4) shall apply to all taxation measures.

4. Nothing in this Treaty shall affect the rights and obligations of either Party under any tax convention. In the event of any inconsistency between this Treaty and any such convention, that convention shall prevail to the extent of the inconsistency. In the case of a tax convention between the Parties, the competent authorities under that convention shall have sole responsibility for determining whether any inconsistency exists between this Treaty and that convention.

Article 22: Entry into Force, Duration, and Termination

1. This Treaty shall enter into force thirty days after the date the Parties exchange instruments of ratification. It shall remain in force for a period of ten years and shall continue in force thereafter unless terminated in accordance with paragraph 2.

---

[21] For purposes of this Article, the "competent tax authority" means: (a) for the United States, the Assistant Secretary of Treasury (Tax Policy), Department of Treasury; (b) for [Country].

2. A Party may terminate this Treaty at the end of the initial ten-year period or at any time thereafter by giving one year's written notice to the other Party.

3. For ten years from the date of termination, all other Articles shall continue to apply to covered investments established or acquired prior to the date of termination, except insofar as those Articles extend to the establishment or acquisition of covered investments.

Section B

Article 23: Consultation and Negotiation

In the event of an investment dispute, the claimant and the respondent should initially seek to resolve the dispute through consultation and negotiation, which may include the use of non-binding, third-party procedures.

Article 24: Submission of a Claim to Arbitration

1. In the event that a disputing party considers that an investment dispute cannot be settled by consultation and negotiation:

(a) the claimant, on its own behalf, may submit to arbitration under this Section a claim

(i) that the respondent has breached

(A) an obligation under Articles 3 through 10,

(B) an investment authorization, or

(C) an investment agreement;

and

(ii) that the claimant has incurred loss or damage by reason of, or arising out of, that breach; and

(b) the claimant, on behalf of an enterprise of the respondent that is a juridical person that the claimant owns or controls directly or indirectly, may submit to arbitration under this Section a claim

(i) that the respondent has breached

(A) an obligation under Articles 3 through 10,

(B) an investment authorization, or

(C) an investment agreement;

and

(ii) that the enterprise has incurred loss or damage by reason of, or arising out of, that breach, provided that a claimant may submit pursuant to subparagraph (a)(i)(C) or (b)(i)(C) a claim for breach of an investment agreement only if the subject matter of the claim and the claimed damages directly relate to the covered investment that was established or acquired, or sought to be established or acquired, in reliance on the relevant investment agreement.

2. At least 90 days before submitting any claim to arbitration under this Section, a claimant shall deliver to the respondent a written notice of its intention to submit the claim to arbitration ("notice of intent"). The notice shall specify:

(a) the name and address of the claimant and, where a claim is submitted on behalf of an enterprise, the name, address, and place of incorporation of the enterprise;

(b) for each claim, the provision of this Treaty, investment authorization, or investment agreement alleged to have been breached and any other relevant provisions;

(c) the legal and factual basis for each claim; and

(d) the relief sought and the approximate amount of damages claimed.

3. Provided that six months have elapsed since the events giving rise to the claim, a claimant may submit a claim referred to in paragraph 1:

(a) under the ICSID Convention and the ICSID Rules of Procedure for Arbitration Proceedings, provided that both the respondent and the non-disputing Party are parties to the ICSID Convention;

(b) under the ICSID Additional Facility Rules, provided that either the respondent or the non-disputing Party is a party to the ICSID Convention;

(c) under the UNCITRAL Arbitration Rules; or

(d) if the claimant and respondent agree, to any other arbitration institution or under any other arbitration rules.

4. A claim shall be deemed submitted to arbitration under this Section when the claimant's notice of or request for arbitration ("notice of arbitration"):

(a) referred to in paragraph 1 of Article 36 of the ICSID Convention is received by the Secretary-General;

(b) referred to in Article 2 of Schedule C of the ICSID Additional Facility Rules is received by the Secretary-General;

(c) referred to in Article 3 of the UNCITRAL Arbitration Rules, together with the statement of claim referred to in Article 20 of the UNCITRAL Arbitration Rules, are received by the respondent; or

(d) referred to under any arbitral institution or arbitral rules selected under paragraph 3(d) is received by the respondent.

A claim asserted by the claimant for the first time after such notice of arbitration is submitted shall be deemed submitted to arbitration under this Section on the date of its receipt under the applicable arbitral rules.

5. The arbitration rules applicable under paragraph 3, and in effect on the date the claim or claims were submitted to arbitration under this Section, shall govern the arbitration except to the extent modified by this Treaty.

6. The claimant shall provide with the notice of arbitration:

(a) the name of the arbitrator that the claimant appoints; or

(b) the claimant's written consent for the Secretary-General to appoint that arbitrator.

Article 25: Consent of Each Party to Arbitration

1. Each Party consents to the submission of a claim to arbitration under this Section in accordance with this Treaty.

2. The consent under paragraph 1 and the submission of a claim to arbitration under this Section shall satisfy the requirements of:

(a) Chapter II of the ICSID Convention (Jurisdiction of the Centre) and the ICSID Additional Facility Rules for written consent of the parties to the dispute; [and]

(b) Article II of the New York Convention for an "agreement in writing." and

(c) Article I of the Inter-American Convention for an "agreement."]

Article 26: Conditions and Limitations on Consent of Each Party

1. No claim may be submitted to arbitration under this Section if more than three years have elapsed from the date on which the claimant first acquired, or should have first acquired, knowledge of the breach alleged under Article 24(1) and knowledge that the claimant (for claims brought under Article 24(1)(a)) or the enterprise (for claims brought under Article 24(1)(b)) has incurred loss or damage.

2. No claim may be submitted to arbitration under this Section unless:

(a) the claimant consents in writing to arbitration in accordance with the procedures set out in this Treaty; and

(b) the notice of arbitration is accompanied,

(i) for claims submitted to arbitration under Article 24(1)(a), by the claimant's written waiver, and

(ii) for claims submitted to arbitration under Article 24(1)(b), by the claimant's and the enterprise's written waivers of any right to initiate or continue before any administrative tribunal or court under the law of either Party, or other dispute settlement procedures, any proceeding with respect to any measure alleged to constitute a breach referred to in Article 24.

3. Notwithstanding paragraph 2(b), the claimant (for claims brought under Article 24(1)(a)) and the claimant or the enterprise (for claims brought under Article 24(1)(b)) may initiate or continue an action that seeks interim injunctive relief and does not involve the payment of monetary damages before a judicial or administrative tribunal of the respondent, provided that the action is brought for the sole purpose of preserving the claimant's or the enterprise's rights and interests during the pendency of the arbitration.

Article 27: Selection of Arbitrators

1. Unless the disputing parties otherwise agree, the tribunal shall comprise three arbitrators, one arbitrator appointed by each of the disputing parties and the third, who shall be the presiding arbitrator, appointed by agreement of the disputing parties.

2. The Secretary-General shall serve as appointing authority for an arbitration under this Section.

3. Subject to Article 20(3), if a tribunal has not been constituted within 75 days from the date that a claim is submitted to arbitration under this Section, the Secretary-General, on the request of a disputing party, shall appoint, in his or her discretion, the arbitrator or arbitrators not yet appointed.

4. For purposes of Article 39 of the ICSID Convention and Article 7 of Schedule C to the ICSID Additional Facility Rules, and without prejudice to an objection to an arbitrator on a ground other than nationality:

(a) the respondent agrees to the appointment of each individual member of a tribunal established under the ICSID Convention or the ICSID Additional Facility Rules;

(b) a claimant referred to in Article 24(1)(a) may submit a claim to arbitration under this Section, or continue a claim, under the ICSID Convention or the ICSID Additional Facility Rules, only on condition that the claimant agrees in writing to the appointment of each individual member of the tribunal; and

(c) a claimant referred to in Article 24(1)(b) may submit a claim to arbitration under this Section, or continue a claim, under the ICSID Convention or the ICSID Additional Facility Rules, only on condition that the claimant and the enterprise agree in writing to the appointment of each individual member of the tribunal.

Article 28: Conduct of the Arbitration

1. The disputing parties may agree on the legal place of any arbitration under the arbitral rules applicable under Article 24(3). If the disputing parties fail to reach agreement, the tribunal shall determine the place in accordance with the applicable arbitral rules, provided that the place shall be in the territory of a State that is a party to the New York Convention.

2. The non-disputing Party may make oral and written submissions to the tribunal regarding the interpretation of this Treaty.

3. The tribunal shall have the authority to accept and consider *amicus curiae* submissions from a person or entity that is not a disputing party.

4. Without prejudice to a tribunal's authority to address other objections as a preliminary question, a tribunal shall address and decide as a preliminary question any objection by the respondent that, as a matter of law, a claim submitted is not a claim for which an award in favor of the claimant may be made under Article 34.

(a) Such objection shall be submitted to the tribunal as soon as possible after the tribunal is constituted, and in no event later than the date the tribunal fixes for the respondent to submit its counter-memorial (or, in the case of an amendment to the notice of arbitration, the date the tribunal fixes for the respondent to submit its response to the amendment).

(b) On receipt of an objection under this paragraph, the tribunal shall suspend any proceedings on the merits, establish a schedule for considering the objection consistent with any schedule it has established for considering any other preliminary question, and issue a decision or award on the objection, stating the grounds therefor.

(c) In deciding an objection under this paragraph, the tribunal shall assume to be true claimant's factual allegations in support of any claim in the notice of arbitration (or any amendment thereof) and, in disputes brought under the UNCITRAL Arbitration Rules, the statement of claim referred to in Article 20 of the UNCITRAL Arbitration Rules. The tribunal may also consider any relevant facts not in dispute.

(d) The respondent does not waive any objection as to competence or any argument on the merits merely because the respondent did or did not raise an objection under this paragraph or make use of the expedited procedure set out in paragraph 5.

5. In the event that the respondent so requests within 45 days after the tribunal is constituted, the tribunal shall decide on an expedited basis an objection under paragraph 4 and any objection that the dispute is not within the tribunal's competence. The tribunal shall suspend any proceedings on the merits and issue a decision or award on the objection(s), stating the grounds therefor, no later than 150 days after the date of the request. However, if a disputing party requests a hearing, the tribunal may take an additional 30 days to issue the decision or award. Regardless of whether a hearing is requested, a tribunal may, on a showing of extraordinary cause, delay issuing its decision or award by an additional brief period, which may not exceed 30 days.

6. When it decides a respondent's objection under paragraph 4 or 5, the tribunal may, if warranted, award to the prevailing disputing party reasonable costs and attorney's fees incurred in submitting or opposing the objection. In determining whether such an award is warranted, the tribunal shall consider whether either the claimant's claim or the respondent's objection was frivolous, and shall provide the disputing parties a reasonable opportunity to comment.

7. A respondent may not assert as a defense, counterclaim, right of set-off, or for any other reason that the claimant has received or will receive indemnification or other compensation for all or part of the alleged damages pursuant to an insurance or guarantee contract.

8. A tribunal may order an interim measure of protection to preserve the rights of a disputing party, or to ensure that the tribunal's jurisdiction is made fully effective, including an order to preserve evidence in the possession or control of a disputing party or to protect the tribunal's jurisdiction. A tribunal may not order attachment or enjoin the application of a measure alleged to constitute a breach referred to in Article 24. For purposes of this paragraph, an order includes a recommendation.

9. (a) In any arbitration conducted under this Section, at the request of a disputing party, a tribunal shall, before issuing a decision or award on liability, transmit its proposed decision or award to the disputing parties and to the non-disputing Party. Within 60 days after the tribunal transmits its proposed decision or award, the disputing parties may submit written comments to the tribunal concerning any aspect of its proposed decision or award. The tribunal shall consider any such comments and issue its decision or award not later than 45 days after the expiration of the 60-day comment period.

(b) Subparagraph (a) shall not apply in any arbitration conducted pursuant to this Section for which an appeal has been made available pursuant to paragraph 10.

10. In the event that an appellate mechanism for reviewing awards rendered by investor-State dispute settlement tribunals is developed in the future under other institutional arrangements, the Parties shall consider whether awards rendered under Article 34 should be subject to that appellate mechanism. The Parties shall strive to ensure that any such appellate mechanism they consider adopting provides for transparency of proceedings similar to the transparency provisions established in Article 29.

Article 29: Transparency of Arbitral Proceedings

1. Subject to paragraphs 2 and 4, the respondent shall, after receiving the following documents, promptly transmit them to the non-disputing Party and make them available to the public:

(a) the notice of intent;

(b) the notice of arbitration;

(c) pleadings, memorials, and briefs submitted to the tribunal by a disputing party and any written submissions submitted pursuant to Article 28(2) [Non-Disputing Party submissions] and (3) [*Amicus* Submissions] and Article 33 [Consolidation];

(d) minutes or transcripts of hearings of the tribunal, where available; and

(e) orders, awards, and decisions of the tribunal.

2. The tribunal shall conduct hearings open to the public and shall determine, in consultation with the disputing parties, the appropriate logistical arrangements. However, any disputing party that intends to use information designated as protected information in a hearing shall so advise the tribunal. The tribunal shall make appropriate arrangements to protect the information from disclosure.

3. Nothing in this Section requires a respondent to disclose protected information or to furnish or allow access to information

that it may withhold in accordance with Article 18 [Essential Security Article] or Article 19 [Disclosure of Information Article].

4. Any protected information that is submitted to the tribunal shall be protected from disclosure in accordance with the following procedures:

(a) Subject to subparagraph (d), neither the disputing parties nor the tribunal shall disclose to the non-disputing Party or to the public any protected information where the disputing party that provided the information clearly designates it in accordance with subparagraph (b);

(b) Any disputing party claiming that certain information constitutes protected information shall clearly designate the information at the time it is submitted to the tribunal;

(c) A disputing party shall, at the time it submits a document containing information claimed to be protected information, submit a redacted version of the document that does not contain the information. Only the redacted version shall be provided to the non-disputing Party and made public in accordance with paragraph 1; and

(d) The tribunal shall decide any objection regarding the designation of information claimed to be protected information. If the tribunal determines that such information was not properly designated, the disputing party that submitted the information may (i) withdraw all or part of its submission containing such information, or (ii) agree to resubmit complete and redacted documents with corrected designations in accordance with the tribunal's determination and subparagraph (c). In either case, the other disputing party shall, whenever necessary, resubmit complete and redacted documents which either remove the information withdrawn under (i) by the disputing party that first submitted the information or re-designate the information consistent with the designation

5. Nothing in this Section requires a respondent to withhold from the public information required to be disclosed by its laws.

Article 30: Governing Law

1. Subject to paragraph 3, when a claim is submitted under Article 24(1)(a)(i)(A) or Article 24(1)(b)(i)(A), the tribunal shall decide the issues in dispute in accordance with this Treaty and applicable rules of international law.

2. Subject to paragraph 3 and the other terms of this Section, when a claim is submitted under Article 24(1)(a)(i)(B) or (C), or Article 24(1)(b)(i)(B) or (C), the tribunal shall apply:

(a) the rules of law specified in the pertinent investment authorization or investment agreement, or as the disputing parties may otherwise agree; or

(b) if the rules of law have not been specified or otherwise agreed:

(i) the law of the respondent, including its rules on the conflict of laws;[22] and

(ii) such rules of international law as may be applicable.

3. A joint decision of the Parties, each acting through its representative designated for purposes of this Article, declaring their interpretation of a provision of this Treaty shall be binding on a tribunal, and any decision or award issued by a tribunal must be consistent with that joint decision.

Article 31: Interpretation of Annexes

1. Where a respondent asserts as a defense that the measure alleged to be a breach is within the scope of an entry set out in Annex I, II, or III, the tribunal shall, on request of the respondent, request the interpretation of the Parties on the issue. The Parties shall submit in writing any joint decision declaring their interpretation to the tribunal within 90 days of delivery of the request.

2. A joint decision issued under paragraph 1 by the Parties, each acting through its representative designated for purposes of this Article, shall be binding on the tribunal, and any decision or award issued by the tribunal must be consistent with that joint decision. If the Parties fail to issue such a decision within 90 days, the tribunal shall decide the issue.

Article 32: Expert Reports

Without prejudice to the appointment of other kinds of experts where authorized by the applicable arbitration rules, a tribunal, at the request of a disputing party or, unless the disputing parties disapprove, on its own initiative, may appoint one or more experts to report to it in writing on any factual issue concerning environmental, health, safety, or other scientific matters raised by a disputing party in a proceeding, subject to such terms and conditions as the disputing parties may agree.

Article 33: Consolidation

1. Where two or more claims have been submitted separately to arbitration under Article 24(1) and the claims have a question of law

---

[22] The "law of the respondent" means the law that a domestic court or tribunal of proper jurisdiction would apply in the same case.

or fact in common and arise out of the same events or circumstances, any disputing party may seek a consolidation order in accordance with the agreement of all the disputing parties sought to be covered by the order or the terms of paragraphs 2 through 10.

2. A disputing party that seeks a consolidation order under this Article shall deliver, in writing, a request to the Secretary-General and to all the disputing parties sought to be covered by the order and shall specify in the request:

(a) the names and addresses of all the disputing parties sought to be covered by the order;

(b) the nature of the order sought; and

(c) the grounds on which the order is sought.

3. Unless the Secretary-General finds within 30 days after receiving a request under paragraph 2 that the request is manifestly unfounded, a tribunal shall be established under this Article.

4. Unless all the disputing parties sought to be covered by the order otherwise agree, a tribunal established under this Article shall comprise three arbitrators:

(a) one arbitrator appointed by agreement of the claimants;

(b) one arbitrator appointed by the respondent; and

(c) the presiding arbitrator appointed by the Secretary-General, provided, however, that the presiding arbitrator shall not be a national of either Party.

5. If, within 60 days after the Secretary-General receives a request made under paragraph 2, the respondent fails or the claimants fail to appoint an arbitrator in accordance with paragraph 4, the Secretary-General, on the request of any disputing party sought to be covered by the order, shall appoint the arbitrator or arbitrators not yet appointed. If the respondent fails to appoint an arbitrator, the Secretary-General shall appoint a national of the disputing Party, and if the claimants fail to appoint an arbitrator, the Secretary-General shall appoint a national of the non-disputing Party.

6. Where a tribunal established under this Article is satisfied that two or more claims that have been submitted to arbitration under Article 24(1) have a question of law or fact in common, and arise out of the same events or circumstances, the tribunal may, in the interest of fair and efficient resolution of the claims, and after hearing the disputing parties, by order:

(a) assume jurisdiction over, and hear and determine together, all or part of the claims;

(b) assume jurisdiction over, and hear and determine one or more of the claims, the determination of which it believes would assist in the resolution of the others; or

(c) instruct a tribunal previously established under Article 27 [Selection of Arbitrators] to assume jurisdiction over, and hear and determine together, all or part of the claims, provided that

(i) that tribunal, at the request of any claimant not previously a disputing party before that tribunal, shall be reconstituted with its original members, except that the arbitrator for the claimants shall be appointed pursuant to paragraphs 4(a) and 5; and

(ii) that tribunal shall decide whether any prior hearing shall be repeated.

7. Where a tribunal has been established under this Article, a claimant that has submitted a claim to arbitration under Article 24(1) and that has not been named in a request made under paragraph 2 may make a written request to the tribunal that it be included in any order made under paragraph 6, and shall specify in the request:

(a) the name and address of the claimant;

(b) the nature of the order sought; and

(c) the grounds on which the order is sought.

The claimant shall deliver a copy of its request to the Secretary-General.

8. A tribunal established under this Article shall conduct its proceedings in accordance with the UNCITRAL Arbitration Rules, except as modified by this Section.

9. A tribunal established under Article 27 [Selection of Arbitrators] shall not have jurisdiction to decide a claim, or a part of a claim, over which a tribunal established or instructed under this Article has assumed jurisdiction.

10. On application of a disputing party, a tribunal established under this Article, pending its decision under paragraph 6, may order that the proceedings of a tribunal established under Article 27 [Selection of Arbitrators] be stayed, unless the latter tribunal has already adjourned its proceedings.

Article 34: Awards

1. Where a tribunal makes a final award against a respondent, the tribunal may award, separately or in combination, only:

(a) monetary damages and any applicable interest; and

(b) restitution of property, in which case the award shall provide that the respondent may pay monetary damages and any applicable interest in lieu of restitution.

A tribunal may also award costs and attorney's fees in accordance with this Treaty and the applicable arbitration rules.

2. Subject to paragraph 1, where a claim is submitted to arbitration under Article 24(1)(b):

(a) an award of restitution of property shall provide that restitution be made to the enterprise;

(b) an award of monetary damages and any applicable interest shall provide that the sum be paid to the enterprise; and

(c) the award shall provide that it is made without prejudice to any right that any person may have in the relief under applicable domestic law.

3. A tribunal may not award punitive damages.

4. An award made by a tribunal shall have no binding force except between the disputing parties and in respect of the particular case.

5. Subject to paragraph 6 and the applicable review procedure for an interim award, a disputing party shall abide by and comply with an award without delay.

6. A disputing party may not seek enforcement of a final award until:

(a) in the case of a final award made under the ICSID Convention,

(i) 120 days have elapsed from the date the award was rendered and no disputing party has requested revision or annulment of the award; or

(ii) revision or annulment proceedings have been completed; and

(b) in the case of a final award under the ICSID Additional Facility Rules, the UNCITRAL Arbitration Rules, or the rules selected pursuant to Article 24(3)(d),

(i) 90 days have elapsed from the date the award was rendered and no disputing party has commenced a proceeding to revise, set aside, or annul the award; or

(ii) a court has dismissed or allowed an application to revise, set aside, or annul the award and there is no further appeal.

7. Each Party shall provide for the enforcement of an award in its territory.

8. If the respondent fails to abide by or comply with a final award, on delivery of a request by the non-disputing Party, a tribunal shall be established under Article 37 [State-State Dispute Settlement]. Without prejudice to other remedies available under applicable rules of international law, the requesting Party may seek in such proceedings:

(a) a determination that the failure to abide by or comply with the final award is inconsistent with the obligations of this Treaty; and

(b) a recommendation that the respondent abide by or comply with the final award.

9. A disputing party may seek enforcement of an arbitration award under the ICSID Convention or the New York Convention [or the Inter-American Convention] regardless of whether proceedings have been taken under paragraph 8.

10. A claim that is submitted to arbitration under this Section shall be considered to arise out of a commercial relationship or transaction for purposes of Article I of the New York Convention [and Article I of the Inter-American Convention].

Article 35: Annexes and Footnotes

The Annexes and footnotes shall form an integral part of this Treaty.

Article 36: Service of Documents

Delivery of notice and other documents on a Party shall be made to the place named for that Party in Annex C.

Section C

Article 37: State-State Dispute Settlement

1. Subject to paragraph 5, any dispute between the Parties concerning the interpretation or application of this Treaty, that is not resolved through consultations or other diplomatic channels, shall be submitted on the request of either Party to arbitration for a binding decision or award by a tribunal in accordance with applicable rules of international law. In the absence of an agreement by the Parties to the contrary, the UNCITRAL Arbitration Rules shall govern, except as modified by the Parties or this Treaty.

2. Unless the Parties otherwise agree, the tribunal shall comprise three arbitrators, one arbitrator appointed by each Party and the third, who shall be the presiding arbitrator, appointed by agreement of the Parties. If a tribunal has not been constituted within 75 days

from the date that a claim is submitted to arbitration under this Section, the Secretary-General, on the request of either Party, shall appoint, in his or her discretion, the arbitrator or arbitrators not yet appointed.

3. Expenses incurred by the arbitrators, and other costs of the proceedings, shall be paid for equally by the Parties. However, the tribunal may, in its discretion, direct that a higher proportion of the costs be paid by one of the Parties.

§ 4.9 Text of the ICSID Convention (1966)

CHAPTER I—INTERNATIONAL CENTRE FOR SETTLEMENT OF INVESTMENT DISPUTES

Article 1

(1) There is hereby established the International Centre for Settlement of Investment Disputes (hereinafter called the Centre).

(2) The purpose of the Centre shall be to provide facilities for conciliation and arbitration of investment disputes between Contracting States and nationals of other Contracting States in accordance with the provisions of this Convention.

Article 2

The seat of the Centre shall be at the principal office of the International Bank for Reconstruction and Development (hereinafter called the Bank). The seat may be moved to another place by decision of the Administrative Council adopted by a majority of two-thirds of its members.

Article 3

The Centre shall have an Administrative Council and a Secretariat and shall maintain a Panel of Conciliators and a Panel of Arbitrators.

Article 4

(1) The Administrative Council shall be composed of one representative of each Contracting State. An alternate may act as representative in case of his principal's absence from a meeting or inability to act.

(2) In the absence of a contrary designation, each governor and alternate governor of the Bank appointed by a Contracting State shall be *ex officio* its representative and its alternate respectively.

Article 5

The President of the Bank shall be *ex officio* Chairman of the Administrative Council (hereinafter called the Chairman) but shall have no vote. During his absence or inability to act and during any vacancy in the office of President of the Bank, the person for the time being acting as President shall act as Chairman of the Administrative Council.

Article 6

(1) Without prejudice to the powers and functions vested in it by other provisions of this Convention, the Administrative Council shall:

(a) adopt the administrative and financial regulations of the Centre;

(b) adopt the rules of procedure for the institution of conciliation and arbitration proceedings;

(c) adopt the rules of procedure for conciliation and arbitration proceedings (hereinafter called the Conciliation Rules and the Arbitration Rules);

(d) approve arrangements with the Bank for the use of the Bank's administrative facilities and services;

(e) determine the conditions of service of the Secretary-General and of any Deputy Secretary-General;

(f) adopt the annual budget of revenues and expenditures of the Centre;

(g) approve the annual report on the operation of the Centre.

The decisions referred to in sub-paragraphs (a), (b), (c) and (f) above shall be adopted by a majority of two-thirds of the members of the Administrative Council.

(2) The Administrative Council may appoint such committees as it considers necessary.

(3) The Administrative Council shall also exercise such other powers and perform such other functions as it shall determine to be necessary for the implementation of the provisions of this Convention.

Article 7

(1) The Administrative Council shall hold an annual meeting and such other meetings as may be determined by the Council, or convened by the Chairman, or convened by the Secretary-General at the request of not less than five members of the Council.

(2) Each member of the Administrative Council shall have one vote and, except as otherwise herein provided, all matters before the Council shall be decided by a majority of the votes cast.

(3) A quorum for any meeting of the Administrative Council shall be a majority of its members.

(4) The Administrative Council may establish, by a majority of two-thirds of its members, a procedure whereby the Chairman may seek a vote of the Council without convening a meeting of the Council.

The vote shall be considered valid only if the majority of the members of the Council cast their votes within the time limit fixed by the said procedure.

Article 8

Members of the Administrative Council and the Chairman shall serve without remuneration from the Centre.

Article 9

The Secretariat shall consist of a Secretary-General, one or more Deputy Secretaries-General and staff.

Article 10

(1) The Secretary-General and any Deputy Secretary-General shall be elected by the Administrative Council by a majority of two-thirds of its members upon the nomination of the Chairman for a term of service not exceeding six years and shall be eligible for re-election. After consulting the members of the Administrative Council, the Chairman shall propose one or more candidates for each such office.

(2) The offices of Secretary-General and Deputy Secretary-General shall be incompatible with the exercise of any political function. Neither the Secretary-General nor any Deputy Secretary-General may hold any other employment or engage in any other occupation except with the approval of the Administrative Council.

(3) During the Secretary-General's absence or inability to act, and during any vacancy of the office of Secretary-General, the Deputy Secretary-General shall act as Secretary-General. If there shall be more than one Deputy Secretary-General, the Administrative Council shall determine in advance the order in which they shall act as Secretary-General.

Article 11

The Secretary-General shall be the legal representative and the principal officer of the Centre and shall be responsible for its administration, including the appointment of staff, in accordance with the provisions of this Convention and the rules adopted by the Administrative Council. He shall perform the function of registrar and shall have the power to authenticate arbitral awards rendered pursuant to this Convention, and to certify copies thereof.

Article 12

The Panel of Conciliators and the Panel of Arbitrators shall each consist of qualified persons, designated as hereinafter provided, who are willing to serve thereon.

Article 13

(1) Each Contracting State may designate to each Panel four persons who may but need not be its nationals.

(2) The Chairman may designate ten persons to each Panel. The persons so designated to a Panel shall each have a different nationality.

Article 14

(1) Persons designated to serve on the Panels shall be persons of high moral character and recognized competence in the fields of law, commerce, industry or finance, who may be relied upon to exercise independent judgment. Competence in the field of law shall be of particular importance in the case of persons on the Panel of Arbitrators.

(2) The Chairman, in designating persons to serve on the Panels, shall in addition pay due regard to the importance of assuring representation on the Panels of the principal legal systems of the world and of the main forms of economic activity.

Article 15

(1) Panel members shall serve for renewable periods of six years.

(2) In case of death or resignation of a member of a Panel, the authority which designated the member shall have the right to designate another person to serve for the remainder of that member's term.

(3) Panel members shall continue in office until their successors have been designated.

Article 16

(1) A person may serve on both Panels.

(2) If a person shall have been designated to serve on the same Panel by more than one Contracting State, or by one or more Contracting States and the Chairman, he shall be deemed to have been designated by the authority which first designated him or, if one such authority is the State of which he is a national, by that State.

(3) All designations shall be notified to the Secretary-General and shall take effect from the date on which the notification is received.

Article 17

If the expenditure of the Centre cannot be met out of charges for the use of its facilities, or out of other receipts, the excess shall be borne by Contracting States which are members of the Bank in proportion to their respective subscriptions to the capital stock of the Bank, and by Contracting States which are not members of the Bank in accordance with rules adopted by the Administrative Council.

Article 18

The Centre shall have full international legal personality. The legal capacity of the Centre shall include the capacity:

(a) to contract;

(b) to acquire and dispose of movable and immovable property;

(c) to institute legal proceedings.

Article 19

To enable the Centre to fulfil its functions, it shall enjoy in the territories of each Contracting State the immunities and privileges set forth in this Section.

Article 20

The Centre, its property and assets shall enjoy immunity from all legal process, except when the Centre waives this immunity.

Article 21

The Chairman, the members of the Administrative Council, persons acting as conciliators or arbitrators or members of a Committee appointed pursuant to paragraph (3) of Article 52, and the officers and employees of the Secretariat

(a) shall enjoy immunity from legal process with respect to acts performed by them in the exercise of their functions, except when the Centre waives this immunity;

(b) not being local nationals, shall enjoy the same immunities from immigration restrictions, alien registration requirements and national service obligations, the same facilities as regards exchange restrictions and the same treatment in respect of travelling facilities as are accorded by Contracting States to the representatives, officials and employees of comparable rank of other Contracting States.

Article 22

The provisions of Article 21 shall apply to persons appearing in proceedings under this Convention as parties, agents, counsel, advocates, witnesses or experts; provided, however, that subparagraph (b) thereof shall apply only in connection with their travel to and from, and their stay at, the place where the proceedings are held.

Article 23

(1) The archives of the Centre shall be inviolable, wherever they may be.

(2) With regard to its official communications, the Centre shall be accorded by each Contracting State treatment not less favorable than that accorded to other international organizations.

Article 24

(1) The Centre, its assets, property and income, and its operations and transactions authorized by this Convention shall be exempt from all taxation and customs duties. The Centre shall also be exempt from liability for the collection or payment of any taxes or customs duties.

(2) Except in the case of local nationals, no tax shall be levied on or in respect of expense allowances paid by the Centre to the Chairman or members of the Administrative Council, or on or in respect of salaries, expense allowances or other emoluments paid by the Centre to officials or employees of the Secretariat.

(3) No tax shall be levied on or in respect of fees or expense allowances received by persons acting as conciliators, or arbitrators, or members of a Committee appointed pursuant to paragraph (3) of Article 52, in proceedings under this Convention, if the sole jurisdictional basis for such tax is the location of the Centre or the place where such proceedings are conducted or the place where such fees or allowances are paid.

CHAPTER II—JURISDICTION OF THE CENTRE

Article 25

(1) The jurisdiction of the Centre shall extend to any legal dispute arising directly out of an investment, between a Contracting State (or any constituent subdivision or agency of a Contracting State designated to the Centre by that State) and a national of another Contracting State, which the parties to the dispute consent in writing to submit to the Centre. When the parties have given their consent, no party may withdraw its consent unilaterally.

(2) "National of another Contracting State" means:

(a) any natural person who had the nationality of a Contracting State other than the State party to the dispute on the date on which the parties consented to submit such dispute to conciliation or arbitration as well as on the date on which the request was registered pursuant to paragraph (3) of Article 28 or paragraph (3) of Article 36, but does not include any person who on either date also had the nationality of the Contracting State party to the dispute; and

(b) any juridical person which had the nationality of a Contracting State other than the State party to the dispute on the date on which the parties consented to submit such dispute to conciliation or arbitration and any juridical person which had the nationality of the Contracting State party to the dispute on that date and which, because of foreign control, the parties have agreed should be treated as a national of another Contracting State for the purposes of this Convention.

(3) Consent by a constituent subdivision or agency of a Contracting State shall require the approval of that State unless that State notifies the Centre that no such approval is required.

(4) Any Contracting State may, at the time of ratification, acceptance or approval of this Convention or at any time thereafter, notify the Centre of the class or classes of disputes which it would or would not consider submitting to the jurisdiction of the Centre. The Secretary-General shall forthwith transmit such notification to all Contracting States. Such notification shall not constitute the consent required by paragraph (1).

Article 26

Consent of the parties to arbitration under this Convention shall, unless otherwise stated, be deemed consent to such arbitration to the exclusion of any other remedy. A Contracting State may require the exhaustion of local administrative or judicial remedies as a condition of its consent to arbitration under this Convention.

Article 27

(1) No Contracting State shall give diplomatic protection, or bring an international claim, in respect of a dispute which one of its nationals and another Contracting State shall have consented to submit or shall have submitted to arbitration under this Convention, unless such other Contracting State shall have failed to abide by and comply with the award rendered in such dispute.

(2) Diplomatic protection, for the purposes of paragraph (1), shall not include informal diplomatic exchanges for the sole purpose of facilitating a settlement of the dispute.

CHAPTER III—CONCILIATION

Article 28

(1) Any Contracting State or any national of a Contracting State wishing to institute conciliation proceedings shall address a request to that effect in writing to the Secretary-General who shall send a copy of the request to the other party.

(2) The request shall contain information concerning the issues in dispute, the identity of the parties and their consent to conciliation in accordance with the rules of procedure for the institution of conciliation and arbitration proceedings.

(3) The Secretary-General shall register the request unless he finds, on the basis of the information contained in the request that the dispute is manifestly outside the jurisdiction of the Centre. He shall forthwith notify the parties of registration or refusal to register.

Article 29

(1) The Conciliation Commission (hereinafter called the Commission) shall be constituted as soon as possible after registration of a request pursuant to Article 28.

(2) (a) The Commission shall consist of a sole conciliator or any uneven number of conciliators appointed as the parties shall agree.

> (b) Where the parties do not agree upon the number of conciliators and the method of their appointment, the Commission shall consist of three conciliators, one conciliator appointed by each party and the third, who shall be the president of the Commission, appointed by agreement of the parties.

Article 30

If the Commission shall not have been constituted within 90 days after notice of registration of the request has been dispatched by the Secretary-General in accordance with paragraph (3) of Article 28, or such other period as the parties may agree, the Chairman shall, at the request of either party and after consulting both parties as far as possible, appoint the conciliator or conciliators not yet appointed.

Article 31

(1) Conciliators may be appointed from outside the Panel of Conciliators, except in the case of appointments by the Chairman pursuant to Article 30.

(2) Conciliators appointed from outside the Panel of Conciliators shall possess the qualities stated in paragraph (1) of Article 14.

Article 32

(1) The Commission shall be the judge of its own competence.

(2) Any objection by a party to the dispute that that dispute is not within the jurisdiction of the Centre, or for other reasons is not within the competence of the Commission, shall be considered by the Commission which shall determine whether to deal with it as a preliminary question or to join it to the merits of the dispute.

Article 33

Any conciliation proceeding shall be conducted in accordance with the provisions of this Section and, except as the parties otherwise agree, in accordance with the Conciliation Rules in effect on the date on which the parties consented to conciliation. If any question of procedure arises which is not covered by this Section or the Conciliation Rules or any rules agreed by the parties, the Commission shall decide the question.

Article 34

(1) It shall be the duty of the Commission to clarify the issues in dispute between the parties and to endeavor to bring about agreement between them upon mutually acceptable terms. To that end, the Commission may at any stage of the proceedings and from time to time recommend terms of settlement to the parties. The parties shall cooperate in good faith with the Commission in order to enable the Commission to carry out its functions, and shall give their most serious consideration to its recommendations.

(2) If the parties reach agreement, the Commission shall draw up a report noting the issues in dispute and recording that the parties have reached agreement. If, at any stage of the proceedings, it appears to the Commission that there is no likelihood of agreement between the parties, it shall close the proceedings and shall draw up a report noting the submission of the dispute and recording the failure of the parties to reach agreement. If one party fails to appear or participate in the proceedings the Commission shall close the proceedings and shall draw up a report noting that party's failure to appear or participate.

Article 35

Except as the parties to the dispute shall otherwise agree, neither party to a conciliation proceeding shall be entitled in any other proceeding, whether before arbitrators or in a court of law or otherwise, to invoke or rely on any views expressed or statements or admissions or offers of settlement made by the other party in the conciliation proceedings, or the report or any recommendations made by the Commission.

CHAPTER IV—ARBITRATION

Article 36

(1) Any Contracting State or any national of a Contracting State wishing to institute arbitration proceedings shall address a request to that effect in writing to the Secretary-General who shall send a copy of the request to the other party.

(2) The request shall contain information concerning the issues in dispute, the identity of the parties and their consent to arbitration in accordance with the rules of procedure for the institution of conciliation and arbitration proceedings.

(3) The Secretary-General shall register the request unless he finds, on the basis of the information contained in the request that the dispute is manifestly outside the jurisdiction of the Centre. He shall forthwith notify the parties of registration or refusal to register.

Article 37

(1) The Arbitral Tribunal (hereinafter called the Tribunal) shall be constituted as soon as possible after registration of a request pursuant to Article 36.

(2) (a) The Tribunal shall consist of a sole arbitrator or any uneven number of arbitrators appointed as the parties shall agree.

> (b) Where the parties do not agree upon the number of arbitrators and the method of their appointment, the Tribunal shall consist of three arbitrators, one arbitrator appointed by each party and the third, who shall be the president of the Tribunal, appointed by agreement of the parties.

Article 38

If the Tribunal shall not have been constituted within 90 days after notice of registration of the request has been dispatched by the Secretary-General in accordance with paragraph (3) of Article 36, or such other period as the parties may agree, the Chairman shall, at the request of either party and after consulting both parties as far as possible, appoint the arbitrator or arbitrators not yet appointed. Arbitrators appointed by the Chairman pursuant to this Article shall not be nationals of the Contracting State party to the dispute or of the Contracting State whose national is a party to the dispute.

Article 39

The majority of the arbitrators shall be nationals of States other than the Contracting State party to the dispute and the Contracting State whose national is a party to the dispute; provided, however, that the foregoing provisions of this Article shall not apply if the sole arbitrator or each individual member of the Tribunal has been appointed by agreement of the parties.

Article 40

(1) Arbitrators may be appointed from outside the Panel of Arbitrators, except in the case of appointments by the Chairman pursuant to Article 38.

(2) Arbitrators appointed from outside the Panel of Arbitrators shall possess the qualities stated in paragraph (1) of Article 14.

Article 41

(1) The Tribunal shall be the judge of its own competence.

(2) Any objection by a party to the dispute that that dispute is not within the jurisdiction of the Centre, or for other reasons is not within the competence of the Tribunal, shall be considered by the Tribunal which shall determine whether to deal with it as a preliminary question or to join it to the merits of the dispute.

Article 42

(1) The Tribunal shall decide a dispute in accordance with such rules of law as may be agreed by the parties. In the absence of such agreement, the Tribunal shall apply the law of the Contracting State party to the dispute (including its rules on the conflict of laws) and such rules of international law as may be applicable.

(2) The Tribunal may not bring in a finding of *non liquet* on the ground of silence or obscurity of the law.

(3) The provisions of paragraphs (1) and (2) shall not prejudice the power of the Tribunal to decide a dispute *ex aequo et bono* if the parties so agree.

Article 43

Except as the parties otherwise agree, the Tribunal may, if it deems it necessary at any stage of the proceedings,

(a) call upon the parties to produce documents or other evidence, and

(b) visit the scene connected with the dispute, and conduct such inquiries there as it may deem appropriate.

Article 44

Any arbitration proceeding shall be conducted in accordance with the provisions of this Section and, except as the parties otherwise agree, in accordance with the Arbitration Rules in effect on the date on which the parties consented to arbitration. If any question of procedure arises which is not covered by this Section or the

Arbitration Rules or any rules agreed by the parties, the Tribunal shall decide the question.

Article 45

(1) Failure of a party to appear or to present his case shall not be deemed an admission of the other party's assertions.

(2) If a party fails to appear or to present his case at any stage of the proceedings the other party may request the Tribunal to deal with the questions submitted to it and to render an award. Before rendering an award, the Tribunal shall notify, and grant a period of grace to, the party failing to appear or to present its case, unless it is satisfied that that party does not intend to do so.

Article 46

Except as the parties otherwise agree, the Tribunal shall, if requested by a party, determine any incidental or additional claims or counterclaims arising directly out of the subject-matter of the dispute provided that they are within the scope of the consent of the parties and are otherwise within the jurisdiction of the Centre.

Article 47

Except as the parties otherwise agree, the Tribunal may, if it considers that the circumstances so require, recommend any provisional measures which should be taken to preserve the respective rights of either party.

Article 48

(1) The Tribunal shall decide questions by a majority of the votes of all its members.

(2) The award of the Tribunal shall be in writing and shall be signed by the members of the Tribunal who voted for it.

(3) The award shall deal with every question submitted to the Tribunal, and shall state the reasons upon which it is based.

(4) Any member of the Tribunal may attach his individual opinion to the award, whether he dissents from the majority or not, or a statement of his dissent.

(5) The Centre shall not publish the award without the consent of the parties.

Article 49

(1) The Secretary-General shall promptly dispatch certified copies of the award to the parties. The award shall be deemed to have been rendered on the date on which the certified copies were dispatched.

(2) The Tribunal upon the request of a party made within 45 days after the date on which the award was rendered may after notice to the other party decide any question which it had omitted to decide in the award, and shall rectify any clerical, arithmetical or similar error in the award. Its decision shall become part of the award and shall be notified to the parties in the same manner as the award. The periods of time provided for under paragraph (2) of Article 51 and paragraph (2) of Article 52 shall run from the date on which the decision was rendered.

Article 50

(1) If any dispute shall arise between the parties as to the meaning or scope of an award, either party may request interpretation of the award by an application in writing addressed to the Secretary-General.

(2) The request shall, if possible, be submitted to the Tribunal which rendered the award. If this shall not be possible, a new Tribunal shall be constituted in accordance with Section 2 of this Chapter. The Tribunal may, if it considers that the circumstances so require, stay enforcement of the award pending its decision.

Article 51

(1) Either party may request revision of the award by an application in writing addressed to the Secretary-General on the ground of discovery of some fact of such a nature as decisively to affect the award, provided that when the award was rendered that fact was unknown to the Tribunal and to the applicant and that the applicant's ignorance of that fact was not due to negligence.

(2) The application shall be made within 90 days after the discovery of such fact and in any event within three years after the date on which the award was rendered.

(3) The request shall, if possible, be submitted to the Tribunal which rendered the award. If this shall not be possible, a new Tribunal shall be constituted in accordance with Section 2 of this Chapter.

(4) The Tribunal may, if it considers that the circumstances so require, stay enforcement of the award pending its decision. If the applicant requests a stay of enforcement of the award in his application, enforcement shall be stayed provisionally until the Tribunal rules on such request.

Article 52

(1) Either party may request annulment of the award by an application in writing addressed to the Secretary-General on one or more of the following grounds:

(a) that the Tribunal was not properly constituted;

(b) that the Tribunal has manifestly exceeded its powers;

(c) that there was corruption on the part of a member of the Tribunal;

(d) that there has been a serious departure from a fundamental rule of procedure; or

(e) that the award has failed to state the reasons on which it is based.

(2) The application shall be made within 120 days after the date on which the award was rendered except that when annulment is requested on the ground of corruption such application shall be made within 120 days after discovery of the corruption and in any event within three years after the date on which the award was rendered.

(3) On receipt of the request the Chairman shall forthwith appoint from the Panel of Arbitrators an *ad hoc* Committee of three persons. None of the members of the Committee shall have been a member of the Tribunal which rendered the award, shall be of the same nationality as any such member, shall be a national of the State party to the dispute or of the State whose national is a party to the dispute, shall have been designated to the Panel of Arbitrators by either of those States, or shall have acted as a conciliator in the same dispute. The Committee shall have the authority to annul the award or any part thereof on any of the grounds set forth in paragraph (1).

(4) The provisions of Articles 41–45, 48, 49, 53 and 54, and of Chapters VI and VII shall apply *mutatis mutandis* to proceedings before the Committee.

(5) The Committee may, if it considers that the circumstances so require, stay enforcement of the award pending its decision. If the applicant requests a stay of enforcement of the award in his application, enforcement shall be stayed provisionally until the Committee rules on such request.

(6) If the award is annulled the dispute shall, at the request of either party, be submitted to a new Tribunal constituted in accordance with Section 2 of this Chapter.

Article 53

(1) The award shall be binding on the parties and shall not be subject to any appeal or to any other remedy except those provided for in this Convention. Each party shall abide by and comply with the terms of the award except to the extent that enforcement shall have been stayed pursuant to the relevant provisions of this Convention.

(2) For the purposes of this Section, "award" shall include any decision interpreting, revising or annulling such award pursuant to Articles 50, 51 or 52.

Article 54

(1) Each Contracting State shall recognize an award rendered pursuant to this Convention as binding and enforce the pecuniary obligations imposed by that award within its territories as if it were a final judgment of a court in that State. A Contracting State with a federal constitution may enforce such an award in or through its federal courts and may provide that such courts shall treat the award as if it were a final judgment of the courts of a constituent state.

(2) A party seeking recognition or enforcement in the territories of a Contracting State shall furnish to a competent court or other authority which such State shall have designated for this purpose a copy of the award certified by the Secretary-General. Each Contracting State shall notify the Secretary-General of the designation of the competent court or other authority for this purpose and of any subsequent change in such designation.

(3) Execution of the award shall be governed by the laws concerning the execution of judgments in force in the State in whose territories such execution is sought.

Article 55

Nothing in Article 54 shall be construed as derogating from the law in force in any Contracting State relating to immunity of that State or of any foreign State from execution.

CHAPTER V—REPLACEMENT AND DISQUALIFICATION OF CONCILIATORS AND ARBITRATORS

Article 56

(1) After a Commission or a Tribunal has been constituted and proceedings have begun, its composition shall remain unchanged; provided, however, that if a conciliator or an arbitrator should die, become incapacitated, or resign, the resulting vacancy shall be filled in accordance with the provisions of Section 2 of Chapter III or Section 2 of Chapter IV.

(2) A member of a Commission or Tribunal shall continue to serve in that capacity notwithstanding that he shall have ceased to be a member of the Panel.

(3) If a conciliator or arbitrator appointed by a party shall have resigned without the consent of the Commission or Tribunal of which he was a member, the Chairman shall appoint a person from the appropriate Panel to fill the resulting vacancy.

Article 57

A party may propose to a Commission or Tribunal the disqualification of any of its members on account of any fact indicating a manifest lack of the qualities required by paragraph (1) of Article 14. A party to arbitration proceedings may, in addition, propose the disqualification of an arbitrator on the ground that he was ineligible for appointment to the Tribunal under Section 2 of Chapter IV.

Article 58

The decision on any proposal to disqualify a conciliator or arbitrator shall be taken by the other members of the Commission or Tribunal as the case may be, provided that where those members are equally divided, or in the case of a proposal to disqualify a sole conciliator or arbitrator, or a majority of the conciliators or arbitrators, the Chairman shall take that decision. If it is decided that the proposal is well-founded the conciliator or arbitrator to whom the decision relates shall be replaced in accordance with the provisions of Section 2 of Chapter III or Section 2 of Chapter IV.

CHAPTER VI—COST OF PROCEEDINGS

Article 59

The charges payable by the parties for the use of the facilities of the Centre shall be determined by the Secretary-General in accordance with the regulations adopted by the Administrative Council.

Article 60

(1) Each Commission and each Tribunal shall determine the fees and expenses of its members within limits established from time to time by the Administrative Council and after consultation with the Secretary-General.

(2) Nothing in paragraph (1) of this Article shall preclude the parties from agreeing in advance with the Commission or Tribunal concerned upon the fees and expenses of its members.

Article 61

(1) In the case of conciliation proceedings the fees and expenses of members of the Commission as well as the charges for the use of the facilities of the Centre, shall be borne equally by the parties. Each party shall bear any other expenses it incurs in connection with the proceedings.

(2) In the case of arbitration proceedings the Tribunal shall, except as the parties otherwise agree, assess the expenses incurred by the

parties in connection with the proceedings, and shall decide how and by paid. Such decision shall form part of the award.

CHAPTER VII—PLACE OF PROCEEDINGS

Article 62

Conciliation and arbitration proceedings shall be held at the seat of the Centre except as hereinafter provided.

Article 63

Conciliation and arbitration proceedings may be held, if the parties so agree,

(a) at the seat of the Permanent Court of Arbitration or of any other appropriate institution, whether private or public, with which the Centre may make arrangements for that purpose; or

(b) at any other place approved by the Commission or Tribunal after consultation with the Secretary-General.

CHAPTER VIII—DISPUTES BETWEEN CONTRACTING STATES

Article 64

Any dispute arising between Contracting States concerning the interpretation or application of this Convention which is not settled by negotiation shall be referred to the International Court of Justice by the application of any party to such dispute, unless the States concerned agree to another method of settlement.

CHAPTER IX—AMENDMENT

Article 65

Any Contracting State may propose amendment of this Convention. The text of a proposed amendment shall be communicated to the Secretary-General not less than 90 days prior to the meeting of the Administrative Council at which such amendment is to be considered and shall forthwith be transmitted by him to all the members of the Administrative Council.

Article 66

(1) If the Administrative Council shall so decide by a majority of two-thirds of its members, the proposed amendment shall be circulated to all Contracting States for ratification, acceptance or approval. Each amendment shall enter into force 30 days after dispatch by the depositary of this Convention of a notification to Contracting States that all Contracting States have ratified, accepted or approved the amendment.

(2) No amendment shall affect the rights and obligations under this Convention of any Contracting State or of any of its constituent

subdivisions or agencies, or of any national of such State arising out of consent to the jurisdiction of the Centre given before the date of entry into force of the amendment.

CHAPTER X—FINAL PROVISIONS

Article 67

This Convention shall be open for signature on behalf of States members of the Bank. It shall also be open for signature on behalf of any other State which is a party to the Statute of the International Court of Justice and which the Administrative Council, by a vote of two-thirds of its members, shall have invited to sign the Convention.

PART B: NAFTA 1994 INVESTOR-STATE ARBITRATIONS

§ 4.10 Foreign Investment Rules Under NAFTA 1994

NAFTA's foreign investment law is extremely controversial and investor-state arbitrations were aggressively pursued. This generally remains a "hot area" of free trade agreement (FTA) investment law. The text of Chapter 11 of NAFTA 1994 covering Investment is reproduced in Section 4.12.

Investing in Mexico

NAFTA 1994 placed special emphasis on relaxation of Mexico's foreign investment controls. These controls find their roots in the revolutionary 1917 Mexican Constitution and the nationalization of foreign oil and gas interests in 1937 as well as the widespread adoption of foreign investment control commissions throughout Latin America during the 1970s. Under Mexican regulation of foreign investment since the 1940s, some industries were reserved for state ownership while others could only be owned by Mexicans. Foreigners were ordinarily allowed to invest in less sensitive industries, but often subject to mandatory joint venture requirements with majority Mexican ownership and "Calvo clause" rules limiting foreign investor dispute remedies to those available under Mexican law.

In 1973, Mexico promulgated an Investment Law that mandated more use of joint ventures if approved by the National Foreign Investment Commission. This Law was the most restrictive of its kind in Mexican history. By the 1980s, after years of mismanagement and corruption while awash in petroleum dollars, Mexico had a massive national debt problem. Foreign investment regulations issued by Presidential decree in 1989 shifted significantly towards allowance of wholly-owned subsidiaries. However, these regulations conflicted with the 1973 Investment Law. These uncertainties were finally resolved in 1993 as a direct consequence of NAFTA when Mexico adopted a new Law on Foreign Investment.

The 1993 Law is much more permissive of foreign investment without prior approval of by the Mexican Investment Commission. Although adopted on the eve of NAFTA, the 1993 Law opens many of the same doors to all investors, not just those from NAFTA. Investment opportunities based upon the NAFTA agreement that are not generally available include the suspension of many performance requirements, the phased removal of market share caps on financial services, and reduced thresholds triggering Investment Commission review. In addition, NAFTA investors are not subject to Mexico's mandatory joint venture rule, nor its "Calvo clause." Removal of these restrictions represents a major concession on the part of Mexico.

Acquisitions or sales of existing Mexican companies are generally subject to Commission review if exceeding $25 million U.S. This threshold increased to $150 million U.S. for NAFTA investors in 2003. For NAFTA investors, no permission from the National Commission is required to invest on a wholly-owned basis or acquire or sell Mexican companies whose values fall below this threshold.

NAFTA 1994 Investment Rights

In an unusual provision, Article 1112 subordinates all of Chapter 11 on investment to the rest of the NAFTA 1994 agreement. In other words, if there are inconsistencies between Chapter 11 and other parts of the NAFTA agreement, those other parts are supreme. That said, NAFTA 1994 provided investors and their investments with a number of important rights.

Canadian, Mexican and United States citizens, permanently resident aliens, and other designated persons are eligible to benefit from NAFTA's investment rules. In addition, most private and public, profit and nonprofit businesses "constituted or organized" under Canadian, Mexican or United States law also qualify. This coverage specifically includes businesses operating as corporations, partnerships, trusts, sole proprietorships, joint ventures and business associations.

Furthermore, in a notable change from CUSFTA, it is not necessary for such businesses to be owned or controlled by Canadian, Mexican or U.S. nationals or enterprises. As with services, this means that businesses owned by anyone which are "constituted or organized" inside NAFTA benefit from the agreement *provided* they carry on substantial business activities in North America. **Thus Asians, Europeans and Latin Americans (for example) could**

invest in North America and benefit from NAFTA 1994 investment rights and remedies. See *Corn Syrup Sweeteners* below. Exceptions were made for NAFTA businesses owned or controlled by third parties from countries lacking diplomatic relations with or economically embargoed by Canada, Mexico or the United States.

Beneficiaries of NAFTA 1994 rights enjoyed a broad definition of "investment." This definition includes most stocks, bonds, loans, and income, profit or asset interests. Real estate, tangible or intangible (intellectual) business property, turnkey or construction contracts, concessions, and licensing and franchising contracts are also generally included (Article 1139). However, under Annex III, each member state reserves certain economic activities to its state or domestic investors. Mexico has done so under its 1993 Foreign Investment Law. For purposes of Chapter 11, investment is defined so as to exclude claims to money arising solely from commercial contracts for the sale of goods or services, or trade financing, and claims for money that do not involve the interests noted above.

Treatment of Foreign Investors and Investments

The NAFTA 1994 agreement established a so-called *"minimum standard of treatment"* for NAFTA investors and investments which is "treatment in accordance with international law," including "fair and equitable treatment and full protection and security" (Article 1105.) For example, if losses occur due to armed conflict or civil strife, NAFTA investors and investments must be accorded nondiscriminatory treatment in response. An official NAFTA interpretative ruling indicates that Article 1105 embraces treatment in accordance with "customary" international law, a ruling intended to limit the scope of protection afforded to foreign investors. In addition, limiting definitions of "fair and equitable treatment" and "full protection and security" have been established in subsequent U.S free trade agreements.

Beyond this minimum, NAFTA 1994 investors and their investments are entitled to the better of national or most-favored-nation treatment from federal governments. Such treatment rights extend to establishing, acquiring, expanding, managing, conducting, operating, and selling or disposing of investments. From state or provincial governments, NAFTA investors and their investments are entitled to receive the most-favored treatment those governments grant their own investors and investments. Along these lines, United Parcel Service found Mexico lacking when it was initially limited to using smaller vans than Mexican competitors. UPS persuaded the United States to lodge a complaint under Chapter 20 (below) which led to intergovernmental consultations followed by NAFTA

Commission mediation. These efforts lasted many months but eventually UPS got permission to use larger vans.

Article 1102 of NAFTA 1994 prohibits requiring minimum levels of equity holdings by nationals of the host government. Hence the historic bias in Mexican law towards mandatory joint ventures is overcome by NAFTA. No investor can be forced on grounds of nationality to sell or dispose of a qualified investment. Mandatory appointment of senior managers on the basis of nationality is also contrary to NAFTA. However, it is permissible to require boards of directors and corporate committees with majorities from one nationality or residence, provided this does not materially impair the investor's ability to exercise control. Canadian law often makes such stipulations. Residency requirements are generally authorized if there is no impairment of the treaty rights of NAFTA investors.

Article 1106 of NAFTA 1994 prohibits various investment performance obligations, including tax-related measures, in a scope that surpasses the WTO Agreement on Trade-Related Investment Measures (TRIMS) (1995). Requirements relating to exports, domestic content, domestic purchases, trade balancing of foreign exchange inflows or earnings, import/export ratios, technology transfers, and regional or global sales exclusivity ("product mandates") are broadly prohibited. All other types of investment-related performance requirements, such as employment and research and development obligations, are not prohibited and therefore presumably lawful.

Article 1106.3 of NAFTA 1994 further prohibits conditioning the receipt or continued receipt of "an advantage" (e.g., a government subsidy or tax benefit) on compliance with requirements relating to domestic content, domestic purchases, domestic sales restraints or trade balancing. But "advantages" can be given when the requirements concern production location, provision of services, training or employing workers, constructing or expanding facilities, or carrying out research and development locally. By way of exception, domestic content or purchase requirements *and* advantages can be linked to investor compliance with: (1) Laws and regulations that are consistent with NAFTA; (2) laws necessary to protect human, animal or plant life or health; or (3) laws needed to conserve living or non-living exhaustible natural resources. However, such requirements cannot be applied arbitrarily or unjustifiably, and may not constitute a disguised restraint on trade or investment.

All monetary transfers relating to NAFTA investments are to be allowed "freely and without delay." (Article 1109) Such transfers must be possible in a "freely usable currency" at the market rate of exchange prevailing in spot transactions on the transfer date. For these purposes, monetary transfers specifically include profits, dividends, interest, capital gains, royalties, management, technical assistance and other fees, returns in kind, and funds derived from the investment. Sale or liquidation proceeds, contract payments, compensatory payments for expropriation and NAFTA dispute settlement payments are also encompassed.

Requiring investment-related monetary transfers or penalizing them is prohibited. However, such transfers can be controlled in an equitable, nondiscriminatory and good faith application of bankruptcy, insolvency, creditors' rights, securities, criminal, currency reporting and satisfaction of judgment laws. Whereas tax withholding was a justifiable basis for restricting monetary transfers under CUSFTA, this is not the case under NAFTA 1994. Special restraints may arise in connection with balance of payments problems and taxation laws.

Expropriation

Article 1110 of NAFTA 1994 generally prohibited direct or indirect nationalization or expropriation of NAFTA investments. Measures "*tantamount to*" nationalization or expropriation, such as creeping expropriation or confiscatory taxation, are also prohibited. Expropriation, nationalization or tantamount measures may occur for public purposes on a nondiscriminatory basis in accordance with due process of law and NAFTA's "minimum level of treatment" (above). Post-NAFTA U.S. free trade agreements have expressly limited the possibility of succeeding with "indirect" regulatory taking expropriation claims.

Any authorized expropriation must result in payment of compensation without delay. The amount of payment must be equivalent to the fair market value of the investment immediately prior to expropriation. In valuing the investment, going concern value, asset value (including declared tax values of tangible property) and other appropriate factors must be considered. Payment must be made in a manner that is fully realizable, such as in a "G7" currency (U.S. dollars, Canadian dollars, EUROs, British pounds sterling, Japanese yen). Interest at a commercially reasonable rate must also be included. If payment is made in Mexican pesos, this amount must be calculated as of the expropriation date in a G7 currency plus interest.

Certain governmental acts are not treated as expropriations. For example, NAFTA specifies that nondiscriminatory measures of general application that impose costs on defaulting debtors are not tantamount to expropriation of a bond or loan *solely* for that reason. Compulsory licensing of intellectual property rights is not an expropriation. Revocation, limitation or creation of such rights as allowed by Chapter 17 of NAFTA 1994 is also deemed not an expropriation.

These provisions embody an historic change in Mexico's position on expropriation law. Without explicitly saying so, Mexico has essentially embraced the U.S. position that under "international law" expropriation of foreign investments requires "prompt, adequate and effective" compensation. Mexico had specifically rejected this standard in negotiating a settlement of its oil and gas (and land) expropriations in the 1930s. Down through the years Mexico adamantly clung to its view that compensation would only be paid according to Mexican law. For investors protected under NAFTA 1994 (which are not just Canadian and U.S. investors), Chapter 11 represented the dawn of a new era.

Exceptions and Reservations, The Environment

Annexes I–IV of the NAFTA 1994 agreement reveal a host of investment-related reservations and exceptions. Many pre-existing, non-conforming regulations were grandfathered though most (not including basic telecommunications, social services and maritime services) are subject to a standstill agreement intended to avoid relapses into greater protection. In contrast, regulations promoting investment "sensitive to environmental concerns" are expressly authorized. Mexico's tradition of assessing the environmental impact of foreign investments will therefore continue. There is also a formal recognition that creating exceptions to environmental laws to encourage NAFTA investors to establish, acquire, expand or retain their investments is inappropriate. However, NAFTA's Chapter 20 dispute settlement mechanism cannot be invoked concerning this "commitment." Only intergovernmental consultations are mandatory.

Other investment-related exceptions concern government procurement, subsidies, export promotion, foreign aid and preferential trade arrangements. These exceptions apply mostly to the rules on nondiscriminatory treatment and performance requirements. Most general exceptions to NAFTA 1994, such as for Canadian cultural industries (above), also apply to its investment rules. The general national security exception, for example, allowed the United States to block the acquisition of U.S. companies by foreigners (including Canadians and Mexicans) under FINSA/FIRMMA national security ("Exon-Florio") regulations (50 U.S.C. App. § 2170).

§ 4.11 NAFTA 1994 Arbitrations of Investor-State Disputes

NAFTA 1994 created a highly innovative and increasingly controversial investment dispute settlement system. This system provides a way for foreign investors to challenge governmental and state enterprise acts and recover damages for violation of rights established in Chapter 11. Remarkably, investors may not only assert claims as individuals, but also on behalf of NAFTA enterprises they own or control directly or indirectly (Article 1117). This authorization avoids one of international law's most famous problems . . . "standing to sue" when the investor's only loss or damage is injury to its investment abroad. See *Belgium v. Spain (the "Barcelona Traction Case")*, 1970 Int'l Court of Justice 3 (preliminary objections).

Chapter 20 NAFTA 1994 dispute settlement does not apply to "investor-state disputes." Such disputes are instead subject to binding arbitration, another major concession on the part of Mexico which has always adhered to the "Calvo Doctrine." That doctrine (widely followed in Latin America) requires foreign investors to forego protection by their home governments, be treated as Mexican nationals, and pursue legal remedies exclusively in Mexico. *See* Article 27 of the Mexican Constitution.

Individual investors claiming that a government has breached NAFTA 1994 investment or state enterprise obligations, or that one of its monopolies has done so, commence the dispute resolution process. All claims are filed against the federal government even when it is state, provincial or local government action that is being challenged. This can place Canada, Mexico and the United States in the awkward position of defending sub-central governmental acts. *See Metalclad* and *Loewen* below.

The investor must allege that the breach of NAFTA 1994 caused loss or damage. Such claims must be asserted no later than three years after the date when knowledge of the alleged breach and knowledge of the loss or damage was first acquired or should have been first acquired. However, decisions by the Canadian or Mexican foreign investment control commissions, national security actions, and Canadian cultural industry reservations cannot be the basis for such a claim. Moreover, a host of reservations and exceptions contained in Chapter 11B deny access to NAFTA's investor-state arbitration remedy. Even so, as outlined below, the number of claims being filed is rising, some claims are producing unexpected results, and the process itself is under dispute.

Before submitting a claim to arbitration, individual investors must give 90 days' advance notice to the host country. Such notice must include an explanation of the issues, their factual basis and remedies sought. Claimants must also consent in writing to arbitrate under the procedures established in the NAFTA agreement. They *must waive* in writing their rights to initiate or continue any other damages proceedings. See *Commerce Group Corp. v. El Salvador* (ICSID, 2011) (CAFTA-DR tribunal dismisses complaint due to pending litigation). Individual investors need not, however, waive their rights to injunctive, declaratory or other extraordinary relief (not involving damages). These remedies may not be awarded through NAFTA arbitration of investor-state disputes.

Investment Arbitration Procedures, Appeals and Remedies

The NAFTA nations consented unconditionally in advance to the submission of investor claims to arbitration under NAFTA 1994 procedures. Furthermore, they agreed not to assert insurance payments or other investor indemnification rights as a defense, counterclaim, right of setoff or otherwise. **Arbitration of investor-state disputes continues in a more limited way as between Mexico and the United States under USMCA 2018. It is completely eliminated as between the United States and Canada.** See Section 4.14.

The investor submitting a claim to arbitration against a NAFTA state ordinarily can elect between the following arbitration rules:

(1) The ICSID Convention* if both member states adhere. (This is impossible at present since only the United States has ratified ICSID);

(2) The Additional Facility Rules of ICSID provided one-member state (i.e., the United States or more recently Canada) adheres to the ICSID Convention; or

(3) The U.N.-derived UNCITRAL Arbitration Rules.

NAFTA 1994 investor-state tribunals have three panelists. The investor and the state each choose one arbitrator. If possible, the third presiding panelist is chosen by agreement. The ICSID Secretary-General selects the presiding arbitrator if agreement is not reached within 90 days. That person is chosen from a consensus roster of acceptable names, but may not be a national from either side of the dispute.

Investor-state tribunals must decide the dispute in accordance with the NAFTA 1994 agreement and "applicable rules of international law." The responding state may raise defenses based

* The Convention on the Settlement of Investment Disputes between States and Nationals of Other States (1966). The Convention is administered through the World Bank in Washington, D.C. and has been ratified by over 150 nations.

upon reservations or exceptions contained in Annexes I–IV to the NAFTA agreement. In such instances, the NAFTA Commission (not the arbitration panel) will generally issue a binding ruling on the validity of such a defense. Defenses based upon permissible regulation of monetary transfers by financial institutions are generally decided by the NAFTA Financial Services Committee.

By agreement of the parties, the investor-state arbitration tribunal can obtain expert reports on factual issues concerning environmental, health, safety or other scientific matters. The tribunal may also order temporary relief measures to preserve rights or the full effectiveness of its jurisdiction. It may, for example, order the preservation of evidence. The tribunal cannot, however, order attachment or enjoin governmental regulations that are being challenged.

NAFTA 1994 investor-state tribunals were authorized to award investors or NAFTA enterprises actual *damages* and interest, or restitution of property, or both. At this writing, damages have been awarded against and paid by Canada and Mexico, but not the United States. See *Metalclad* and *S.D. Myers* below. If the award is to an enterprise, any person may *also* pursue relief under "applicable domestic law." If restitution is ordered, the responsible member state may provide monetary damages and interest instead. NAFTA tribunals can apportion legal fees between the parties at their discretion. Such fees routinely run into hundreds of thousands, if not millions, of dollars. The costs of administering Chapter 11 tribunals, including generous fees for the arbitrators, often exceed $500,000. The losing party is typically required to pay these costs.

The award of the tribunal is binding on the parties, but subject to revision or annulment in the courts of the arbitration's situs. See *Metalclad* and *S.D. Myers* below. Absent agreement, the arbitrators determine situs. Professor Brower and others have argued that a standing appellate body not unlike that of the WTO would provide greater legitimacy and uniformity to Chapter 11 arbitrations. See 36 *Vanderbilt J. Transnational Law* 37 (2003).

Awards are specifically not "precedent" in future NAFTA 1994 arbitrations (Article 1136), yet routinely cited and argued in Chapter 11 proceedings and decisions. NAFTA investor-state arbitration awards are supposed to be honored. Should this not occur, the investor may seek enforcement of the award. NAFTA nations agreed to provide the means for such enforcement. The NAFTA investor-state dispute settlement system meets the various requirements of the ICSID Convention, its Additional Facility Rules, the New York Convention on Recognition and Enforcement of Foreign Arbitral

Awards (1958), and the Inter-American Convention on International Commercial Arbitration (1975).

Should it become necessary to judicially enforce an investor-state arbitration award, the New York Convention provides a likely recourse as all three nations adhere to it. However, U.S. courts have held the grounds for denying enforcement of NAFTA awards under the New York Convention limited strictly to its provisions. Thus, the longstanding U.S. doctrine of denying enforcement when arbitrators "manifestly disregard the law", a doctrine not incorporated in the New York Convention, was not applied in a NAFTA 1994 award enforcement proceeding. See In re Arbitration between International Thunderbird Gaming Corp. v. United Mexican States, 473 F.Supp.2d 80 (D.C.2007).

If there is no compliance with the award and enforcement proceedings fail, the investor's government may as a last recourse commence intergovernmental dispute settlement under Chapter 20 of NAFTA 1994. This panel rules on whether noncompliance inconsistent with the NAFTA agreement has occurred and can recommend compliance. If compliance still does not follow, benefits granted under NAFTA to the noncomplying nation may be suspended.

Arbitrated Foreign Investor Claims against Host States

Investors did not hesitate to invoke the innovative investor-state arbitration procedures authorized under Section B of Chapter 11 of NAFTA 1994. Since 2001, in an official Interpretation, Chapter 11 has been construed as not imposing a general duty of confidentiality. The NAFTA governments have therefore released all documents submitted to or issued by Chapter 11 arbitration tribunals. A particularly good collection of these materials can be found at www.naftaclaims.com. Moreover, since late 2003 open Chapter 11 hearings have become the rule, as have permissive procedures for non-party submissions (amicus curiae).

Many investors alleged state action that is "tantamount to expropriation." This is a claim that Article 1110 authorizes and one which could be construed to fit many fact patterns. National treatment and the NAFTA minimum standard of treatment (see above) were also commonly disputed. Some examples of these disputes follow.

Metalclad v. Mexico. A prominent dispute involved Metalclad Corp. of California, which had acquired a hazardous waste site operated by a Mexican company in Guadalcazar, San Luis Potosi subject to various federal approvals, all of which were obtained. State and local opposition to opening the site after an expensive clean-up resulted in the denial of a building permit in a newly created "ecological zone." Metalclad claimed these acts were tantamount to expropriation, and denial of national and the NAFTA minimum standards of treatment. It sought $90 million in damages from the Mexican federal government, which despite having supported the Metalclad contract was obliged to defend the hostile local and state actions. Metalclad received an award of $16 million under NAFTA Chapter 11 in 2000. The arbitration was conducted under the ICSID Additional Facility rules.

Mexico instituted judicial proceedings to set aside the award in British Columbia, the arbitration's legal *situs*. Canada intervened in support of Mexico. The arbitrators had found the Mexican regulatory action a breach of NAFTA's minimum standard based on a lack of "transparency," and tantamount to expropriation without adequate compensation.

The British Columbia Supreme Court, ruling under the B.C. International Arbitration Act, agreed that the expropriation decision fell within the scope of the dispute submitted and was therefore valid. It rejected, however, the transparency decision as beyond the scope of the submission. The court found no transparency obligations in Chapter 11, and none as a matter of *customary* international law (which traditionally bars only "egregious," "outrageous" or "shocking" conduct). Mexico subsequently paid Metalclad approximately $16 million U.S., the first payment by a state to an investor under Chapter 11.

Ethyl v. Canada and Methanex v. United States. A second prominent dispute involved Ethyl Corp. of the USA, which claimed $250 million U.S. damages against the Canadian government as a consequence of 1997 federal legislation banning importation or interprovincial trade of the gasoline additive, MMT. Canada was the first country to ban MMT as a pollution and health hazard, although California has also done so. MMT is a manganese-based octane enhancer alleged to interfere with the proper functioning of catalytic converters. Ethyl Corp. is the sole producer of MMT in North America. Ethyl claimed that the new law was tantamount to expropriation, violated NAFTA's national treatment standards and constituted an unlawful Canadian-content performance requirement (because the ban would favor Canadian ethanol as a substitute for MMT).

A dispute resolution panel under Canada's Agreement on Internal Trade struck down the interprovincial trade ban. In 1998, Canada withdrew its ban on MMT and paid $13 million to Ethyl Corp. Ethyl then withdrew its $250 million arbitration claim. Canada noted the current lack of scientific evidence documenting MMT harm, an apparent abandonment of the "precautionary principle." Environmentalists decried evidence of NAFTA's negative impact, and Europeans cited *Ethyl* as good reason to reject multilateral investment guarantee agreements in the OECD (Organization for Economic Cooperation and Development). Both groups believe Chapter 11 has created a privileged class of "super-citizens" who are a threat to state sovereignty.

Methanex Corp. of Canada submitted a claim that was in some ways the reverse of *Ethyl*. Methanex claimed that California's ban of the MTBE gasoline additive (for which it makes feedstock) amounted to an expropriation of its business interests and violated its minimum treatment rights. It sought $970 million in damages and simultaneously filed a petition under the North American Environmental Cooperation Agreement asserting that California failed to enforce its gasoline storage regulations, which Methanex saw as the source of MTBE water pollution. In 2002, the *Methanex* panel working under the UNCITRAL Rules largely rejected the complaint on jurisdictional grounds, allowing a limited re-filing on the question of intentional injury. The *Methanex* panel notably ruled that it would accept NGO amicus briefs, in this instance from the International Institute for Sustainable Development. This position was subsequently ratified for all Chapter 11 arbitrations by the NAFTA Free Trade Commission in 2003.

Loewen v. United States. The Loewen Group of Canada was held liable by a jury in 1995 to $500 million in a Mississippi breach of a funeral home contract suit. The case was settled for $150 million after the Mississippi Supreme Court required posting a $625 million bond prior to appealing the jury's verdict, a sum in excess of Loewen's net worth. In 1998, Loewen filed a claim under NAFTA alleging discrimination, denial of the minimum NAFTA standard of treatment, and uncompensated expropriation. This claim, like that of Ethyl Corp., was destined for controversy. Among other things, it challenged the discretion of American juries in awarding punitive damages. Note that it does so in a forum that does not give the American Trial Lawyers Association an opportunity to respond.

In 2003, the *Loewen* panel, calling the Mississippi decision "a disgrace," nevertheless ruled heavily against the bankrupt funeral home giant because its status as a Canadian (versus U.S.) company entitled to NAFTA investor rights was in doubt. Watch for a re-run challenging American punitive damages in the future.

Pope & Talbot v. Canada. Pope and Talbot, Inc. of Portland, Oregon claimed that the 1996 Softwood Lumber Agreement (see Chapter 2) violated the national treatment, most-favored-nation treatment, minimum treatment and performance requirements rules of NAFTA. The claim asserted that the company's British Columbia subsidiary was the victim of discrimination in that the Canadian export restraints required under that Agreement applied only to four Canadian provinces. Pope & Talbot sought $20 million in compensation from the Canadian government. Rejecting most of the claims, the *Pope & Talbot* panel found Canada did violate the NAFTA minimum standard of treatment in denying export authorization to the company's B.C. subsidiary.

Although the award was only about $460,000 U.S., the panel's reasoning set off fireworks. In its view, Article 1105 demanded something more than the level of treatment commanded by customary international law. "Fair and equitable treatment" and "full protection and security" were seen as "additive;" new and expansive norms created by NAFTA's novel investor protection regime.

The additive reading of *Pope & Talbot* was subsequently rejected by the British Columbia Supreme Court in *Metalclad* (above), and collectively negated by a binding interpretation of Article 1105 issued by the three NAFTA parties in 2001. This controversial, defensive interpretation "clarifies" that Article 1105 corresponds to and thus does not expand the *customary* international law standard of minimum treatment (see *Metalclad* above), and that a breach of a NAFTA obligation does not ipso facto constitute a breach of that Article.

S.D. Myers v. Canada. S.D. Myers is an Ohio company specializing in hazardous waste management of PCBs. Its Canadian affiliate imported PCBs from Ontario, to the consternation of the only Canadian PCB remediation company, Chem-Security of Alberta. In 1995, Canada banned PCB exports, intentionally giving Chem-Security a monopoly. S.D. Myers asserted this export ban violated the national treatment, performance requirements, expropriation and fair and equitable treatment provisions of Chapter 11. The arbitrators found in favor of S.D. Myers on the national treatment and fair and equitable treatment claims, awarding over $6,000,000 CDN in damages. Canada appealed to the courts of Ontario, the situs of the arbitration, and lost. In Ontario, at least, considerable deference is given to arbitral decisions. Compare British Columbia in *Metalclad* below. Subsequently, S. D. Myers and Canada settled the dispute.

Mondev v. United States. Mondev is a Canadian company engaged in commercial real estate development. It pursued various claims against the City of Boston and the Boston Redevelopment Authority in the Massachusetts courts, which were denied on sovereign immunity grounds. Mondev then filed a Chapter 11 claim arguing primarily unfair and inequitable treatment in the Massachusetts courts.

In its complaint, Mondev directly challenged the 2001 Interpretation of Article 1105, arguing it was de facto an amendment of the NAFTA agreement. Mondev also argued that customary international law should be construed in light of conclusions reached under hundreds of bilateral investment treaties and modern judgments. The tribunal recognized that fair and equitable treatment had evolved by 1994 (NAFTA's effective date) beyond what is "egregious" or "outrageous," and that bad faith on the part of states need not be shown. It then ruled against Mondev's denial of justice claims.

Glamis v. United States. Glamis, a Canadian mining company, alleged that government regulations limiting the impact of open-pit mining and protecting indigenous peoples' religious sites made its *proposed* California gold mine unprofitable. Under Chapter 11, it asserted violations of the NAFTA rules against government acts tantamount to expropriation, and denial of fair and equitable treatment. In June of 2009, a Chapter 11 tribunal accepted, in principle, that "regulatory taking" measures could amount to "creeping expropriation." That said, the tribunal undertook a detailed accounting of Glamis' alleged losses and found the mine project still had a net positive value of $20 million U.S. Hence it concluded Glamis was not impacted sufficiently to support a NAFTA expropriation claim.

While the outcome once again allowed the United States to avoid paying Chapter 11 damages, the willingness of the tribunal to entertain a regulatory taking claim was controversial (to put it mildly) and once again raised concerns that foreign investors may have greater rights under NAFTA than U.S. investors possess under United States law.

Corn Syrup Sweeteners v. Mexico. Late in 2009, a third Chapter 11 tribunal ruled against Mexico concerning its 20% tax from 2002 to 2007 on the production and sale of soft drinks using High Fructose Corn Syrup (HFCS). This tax was imposed in the context of a trade dispute between the U.S. and Mexico over HFCS exports south of the border and Mexican sugar exports headed north. U.S. agribusiness giants Cargill, Corn Products International and Archer Daniels Midlands, along with British Tate and Lyle's U.S. subsidiary, successfully argued that the tax constituted a "performance requirement" in violation of NAFTA Article 1106. The Mexican government was ordered to pay a total of $170 million plus interest.

AbitibiBowater v. Canada. In August 2010, the Canadian federal government agreed to pay $130 million CDN to settle a Chapter 11 claim by a U.S. pulp and paper multinational, AbitibiBowater (AB). In 2008, AB closed a longstanding mill in Newfoundland via bankruptcy, terminating 800 workers without severance. Newfoundland passed a law returning, without compensation, the company's water and timber rights to the crown, and expropriating with compensation AB lands, buildings and dams in the province. AB asserted NAFTA expropriation violations. This settlement, along with the *Glamis* decision (above), has raised concerns that resource-related NAFTA investor claims may increase. For example, a Brazilian company with a U.S. subsidiary received a $15 million settlement form Canada after alleging permit delays for rock quarrying.

Apotex. v. Unites States. Apotex is a Canadian manufacturer of generic pharmaceuticals. It filed at least three Chapter 11 claims against the United States. These filings challenged U.S. federal court decisions denying its efforts to obtain "patent certainty" for drugs (in order to allow its generic versions to proceed), FDA denial of approval for another Apotex generic drug, and FDA import inspection practices for drugs. All of these complaints were rejected by a Chapter 11 arbitration panel in 2014.

Exxon/Mobil v. Canada. Exxon/Mobil developed off shore oil fields in Canadian waters. It first challenged Canadian Petroleum Board rules mandating fees to support R & D in Newfoundland and Labrador in the Canadian courts and lost at trial and on appeal. Exxon subsequently filed a Chapter 11 claim which a panel affirmed in 2012, holding these fees amounted to NAFTA-prohibited "performance requirements." The damages awarded amounted to nearly $15 million.

Bilcon v. Canada. Bilcon of Delaware sought to develop a quarry and marine terminal in Nova Scotia, subject to environmental review. A joint federal/province review denied approval based upon "incompatibility with community core values". Bilcon alleged NAFTA Chapter 11 violations of the national and minimum treatment standards (the latter claim focused on fair and equitable treatment). By agreement, the UNCITRAL Rules controlled before the Permanent Court of Arbitration.

In a split 2015 decision, the arbitrators held in favor of Bilcon, noting particularly an absence of fair notice and treatment in the environmental review process, and a fundamental departure from the "likely significant adverse effects after mitigation" standard of evaluation required by Canadian law.

Eli Lilly v. Canada. Eli Lilly filed a claim for damages under Chapter 11 after Canadian courts invalidated patents on two of its blockbuster drugs on grounds that their utility was not shown. Eli Lilly argued unfair, inequitable and discriminatory treatment. A 2017 arbitration panel rejected these arguments, noting that the "promise of utility" doctrine developed by Canadian courts was well established, putting Eli Lilly on notice prior to its patent claims.

This dispute was unusual because it asserted violation of NAFTA Chapter 11 by Canadian *courts*, not by Canadian legislation or regulation. Subsequently, in June of 2017, the Canadian Supreme Court overturned the "promise doctrine" under its patent law.

Windstream Energy v. Canada and Mesa Power Group v. Canada. Windstream Energy of the USA sought to participate in Ontario's green energy program, and obtained a contract to build an offshore wind farm. Subsequently, Ontario imposed a moratorium on offshore wind projects pending further scientific study. This had the effect of suspending but not terminating the Windstream contract. Other participants in the program were offered alternative opportunities to join the green energy program, but Windstream was not.

Windstream filed a Chapter 11 complaint before the Permanent Court of Arbitration arguing discrimination, indirect expropriation and unfair and inequitable treatment. A 2017 arbitration panel rejected all but the unfair and inequitable treatment claim, recognizing that Ontario had not within a reasonable time clarified the relevant science or the status of the contract, leaving Windstream in legal limbo. It assessed 21 million Euros damages, minus certain adjustments, based upon the value of comparable transactions in Europe.

Mesa Power challenged Ontario's award of power purchase contracts under its green energy program as discriminatory and unfair under Chapter 11 before the Permanent Court of Arbitration in The Hague. In a split decision, the arbitrators rejected Mesa' claims of unfair bidding rules and procedures for power contracts.

Other Foreign Investor Claims of Note. Several U.S. companies commenced Chapter 11 proceedings against Canada asserting damages based on Quebec's moratorium on "fracking", the use of water and chemicals to release sub-surface oil and gas reserves.

After President Obama's rejection in 2015 of the Keystone Pipeline from Alberta's tar sands to Texas, Trans Canada has filed a Chapter 11 claim against the United States alleging discriminatory (non-national) treatment, breach of the duty of most-favored-nation treatment, U.S. governmental acts tantamount to expropriation, and unfair and inequitable treatment. Trans Canada sought in excess of $15 billion in damages, but withdrew its claim after President Trump approved the pipeline.

Summary. These examples of investor-state claims under NAFTA 1994 represent only a partial summary of the impact of NAFTA 1994 Chapter 11. Lawyers learned that U.S. FTAs and BITs can be used to challenge or threaten to challenge all sorts of existing or proposed government actions, particularly regulatory decisions. There is leverage in these broad investor rights, and in its mandatory arbitral procedures. That said, **the United States has never lost an investment arbitration nor paid damages under NAFTA 1994.**

§ 4.12 U.S. FTA Investment Rules from NAFTA 1994 to President Trump

The United States negotiated a number of free trade agreements post-NAFTA 1994 prior to the presidency of Donald Trump. These included FTAs with Australia, Bahrain, Chile, Colombia, Jordan, South Korea (KORUS), Morocco, Oman, Panama, Peru and Singapore, plus the Dominican Republic-Central America Free Trade Agreement (DR-CAFTA) with the Dominican Republic, Guatemala, Honduras, El Salvador, Nicaragua and Costa Rica.

Mutations on the law of investor-state claims appeared in post-NAFTA U.S. free trade agreements. These mutations are in part a response to Congressional concerns expressed in the Trade Promotion Authority (fast-track) Act of 2002 that Chapter 11 of NAFTA 1994 accorded "greater substantive rights" to foreigners with respect to investment protection than enjoyed by U.S. investors in the United States.

United States free trade agreements after NAFTA 1994 evolved substantively. Changes are most evident regarding foreign investment and intellectual property. Regarding investor-state claims, for example, post-NAFTA U.S. free trade agreements insert the word "customary" before international law in defining the minimum standard of treatment to which foreign investors are entitled. This insertion tracks the official Interpretation issued in that regard under NAFTA 1994. Further, the contested terms "fair and equitable treatment" and "full protection and security" do not require treatment in addition to or beyond that customary standard, and do not create additional substantive rights. This language was defined for the first time:

> "**fair and equitable treatment**" includes the obligation not to deny justice in criminal, civil, or administrative adjudicatory

proceedings in accordance with the principle of due process embodied in the principal legal systems of the world; and

"**full protection and security**" requires each Party to provide the level of police protection required under customary international law.

More significantly perhaps, starting with the U.S.-Chile FTA, these agreements contain an Annex restricting the scope of "**indirect expropriation**" claims:

> Except in rare circumstances, nondiscriminatory regulatory actions by a Party that are designed and applied to protect legitimate public welfare objectives, such as public health, safety and the environment, do not constitute indirect expropriations.

Hence the potential for succeeding with "regulatory takings" investor-state claims has been reduced.

In sum, the United States generally used its leverage with smaller trade partners in the Americas, the Middle East and Pacific Rim to obtain more preferential treatment and expanded protection for its investors. Save for the 2012 KORUS agreement, the U.S. gave up relatively little in return, for example a modest increase in agricultural market openings.

§ 4.13 Investment Disputes Under the Pending USMCA 2018

Investor-state arbitration of disputes for damages continues in full as between Mexico and Canada under the Comprehensive and Progressive Trans-Pacific Partnership (TPP-11) effective Jan. 1, 2019. ISDS continues under revised USMCA terms as between Mexico and the United States. U.S.-Mexico claims involving *government contracts* are limited to specified capital intensive sectors (oil and gas, telecommunications, power generation, and contracts for roads, railways, bridges or canals but not apparently dams, seaports and airports). Such government contract disputes may assert the full range of NAFTA 1994 investor rights (direct and indirect expropriation, fair and equitable treatment (minimum standard), national and MFN treatment, and more).

For claims not involving government contracts, limitations are placed on ISDS by NAFTA Re-Negotiated 2018. Such claims are limited to national and most-favored nation treatment, and expropriation grounds, notably dropping out fair and equitable treatment claims. In addition, borrowing from post-NAFTA 1994 U.S free trade agreements and the Trans-Pacific Partnership (TPP-12), rejected by President Trump, "indirect" expropriation claims are also limited. Indirect expropriations are defined as situations "in which an action or series of actions by a Party has an effect equivalent to direct expropriation without formal transfer of title or outright seizure". Further, "non-discriminatory regulatory actions by a Party that are designed and applied to protect legitimate public welfare objectives, such as health, safety and the environment, do *not* constitute indirect expropriations, except in rare circumstances." This language addresses criticisms of NAFTA 1994 investor-state arbitrations challenging environmental measures as regulatory takings and/or indirect expropriations.

Furthermore, borrowing a TPP-12 rule, investor claimants under NAFTA Re-Negotiated 2018, must first exhaust local remedies or attempt to do so for 30 months prior to seeking arbitration. This rule does not appear to apply to the select government contract claimants noted above. Claimants owned or controlled by non-market economy states are barred from using NAFTA Re-Negotiated ISDS, and establishment claims prior to actual investment are generally excluded.

By agreement in USMCA Chapter 14, apart from legacy NAFTA 1994 claims (presented no later than three years after NAFTA Re-Negotiated enters into force), Canada and the United States *completely* removed the availability of arbitrations to resolve investor-state disputes. In the future, presumably such disputes will be resolved by state-to-state negotiations or the courts of either nation.

For a detailed review of the USMCA 2018 Agreement, see Folsom, *Principles of Free Trade Agreements, From GATT 1947 through NAFTA Re-Negotiated 2018.*

§ 4.14 Text of NAFTA Chapter 11

Section A. Investment

Article 1101. Scope and Coverage

1. This Chapter applies to measures adopted or maintained by a Party relating to: (a) investors of another Party; (b) investments of investors of another Party in the territory of the Party; and (c) with respect to Article 1106, all investments in the territory of the Party.

2. A Party has the right to perform exclusively the economic activities set out in Annex III and to refuse to permit the establishment of investment in such activities.

3. This Chapter does not apply to measures adopted or maintained by a Party to the extent that they are covered by Chapter Fourteen (Financial Services).

4. Nothing in this Chapter shall be construed to prevent a Party from providing a service or performing a function such as law enforcement, correctional services, income security or insurance, social security or insurance, social welfare, public education, public training, health, and child care, in a manner that is not inconsistent with this Chapter.

Article 1102. National Treatment

1. Each Party shall accord to investors of another Party treatment no less favorable than that it accords, in like circumstances, to its own investors with respect to the establishment, acquisition, expansion, management, conduct, operation, and sale or other disposition of investments.

2. Each Party shall accord to investments of investors of another Party treatment no less favorable than that it accords, in like circumstances, to investments of its own investors with respect to the establishment, acquisition, expansion, management, conduct, operation, and sale or other disposition of investments.

3. The treatment accorded by a Party under paragraphs 1 and 2 means, with respect to a state or province, treatment no less favorable than the most favorable treatment accorded, in like circumstances, by that state or province to investors, and to investments of investors, of the Party of which it forms a part.

4. For greater certainty, no Party may: (a) impose on an investor of another Party a requirement that a minimum level of equity in an enterprise in the territory of the Party be held by its nationals, other than nominal qualifying shares for directors or incorporators of corporations; or (b) require an investor of another Party, by reason of its nationality, to sell or otherwise dispose of an investment in the territory of the Party.

Article 1103. Most-Favored-Nation Treatment

1. Each Party shall accord to investors of another Party treatment no less favorable than that it accords, in like circumstances, to investors of another Party or of a non-Party with respect to the establishment, acquisition, expansion, management, conduct, operation, and sale or other disposition of investments.

2. Each Party shall accord to investments of investors of another Party treatment no less favorable than that it accords, in like circumstances, to investments of investors of another Party or of a non-Party with respect to the establishment, acquisition, expansion, management, conduct, operation, and sale or other disposition of investments.

Article 1104. Standard of Treatment

Each Party shall accord to investors of another Party and to investments of investors of another Party the better of the treatment required by Articles 1102 and 1103.

Article 1105. Minimum Standard of Treatment

1. Each Party shall accord to investments of investors of another Party treatment in accordance with international law, including fair and equitable treatment and full protection and security.

2. Without prejudice to paragraph 1 and notwithstanding Article 1108(7)(b), each Party shall accord to investors of another Party, and to investments of investors of another Party, non-discriminatory treatment with respect to measures it adopts or maintains relating to losses suffered by investments in its territory owing to armed conflict or civil strife.

3. Paragraph 2 does not apply to existing measures relating to subsidies or grants that are inconsistent with Article 1102.

Article 1106. Performance Requirements

1. No Party may impose or enforce any of the following requirements, or enforce any commitment or undertaking, in connection with the establishment, acquisition, expansion, management, conduct or operation of an investment of an investor of a Party or of a non-Party in its territory:

(a) to export a given level or percentage of goods or services; (b) to achieve a given level or percentage of domestic content; (c) to purchase, use or accord a preference to goods produced or services provided in its territory, or to purchase goods or services from persons in its territory; (d) to relate in any way the volume or value of imports to the volume or value of exports or to the amount of foreign exchange inflows associated with such investment; (e) to restrict sales of goods or services in its territory that such investment produces or provides by relating such sales in any way to the volume or value of its exports or foreign exchange earnings; (f) to transfer technology, a production process or other proprietary knowledge to a person in its territory, except when the requirement is imposed or the 4 commitment or undertaking is enforced by a court, administrative tribunal or competition authority to remedy an alleged violation of competition laws or to act in a manner not inconsistent with other provisions of this Agreement; or (g) to act as the exclusive supplier of the goods it produces or services it provides to a specific region or world market.

2. A measure that requires an investment to use a technology to meet generally applicable health, safety or environmental requirements shall not be construed to be inconsistent with paragraph (1)(f). For greater certainty, Articles 1102 and 1103 apply to the measure.

3. No Party may condition the receipt or continued receipt of an advantage, in connection with an investment in its territory of an investor of a Party or of a non-Party, on compliance with any of the following requirements:

> (a) to purchase, use or accord a preference to goods produced in its territory, or to purchase goods from producers in its territory; (b) to achieve a given level or percentage of domestic content; (c) to relate in any way the volume or value of imports to the volume or value of exports or to the amount of foreign exchange inflows associated with such investment; or (d) to restrict sales of goods or services in its territory that such investment produces or provides by relating such sales in any way to the volume or value of its exports or foreign exchange earnings.

4. Nothing in paragraph 3 shall be construed to prevent a Party from conditioning the receipt or continued receipt of an advantage, in connection with an investment in its territory of an investor of a Party or of a non-Party, on compliance with a requirement to locate production, provide a service, train or employ workers, construct or expand particular facilities, or carry out research and development, in its territory.

5. Paragraphs 1 and 3 do not apply to any requirement other than the requirements set out in those paragraphs.

6. Provided that such measures are not applied in an arbitrary or unjustifiable manner, or do not constitute a disguised restriction on international trade or investment, nothing in 5 paragraph 1(b) or (c) or 3(a) or (b) shall be construed to prevent any Party from adopting or maintaining measures, including environmental measures: (a) necessary to secure compliance with laws and regulations that are not inconsistent with the provisions of this Agreement; (b) necessary to protect human, animal or plant life or health; or (c) necessary for the conservation of living or non-living exhaustible natural resources.

Article 1107. Senior Management and Boards of Directors

1. No Party may require that an enterprise of that Party that is an investment of an investor of another Party appoint to senior management positions individuals of any particular nationality.

2. A Party may require that a majority of the board of directors, or any committee thereof, of an enterprise of that Party that is an investment of an investor of another Party, be of a particular nationality, or resident in the territory of the Party, provided that the requirement does not materially impair the ability of the investor to exercise control over its investment.

Article 1108. Reservations and Exceptions

1. Articles 1102, 1103, 1106 and 1107 do not apply to:

(a) any existing non-conforming measure that is maintained by (i) a Party at the federal level, as set out in its Schedule to Annex I or III, (ii) a state or province, for two years after the date of entry into force of this Agreement, and thereafter as set out by a Party in its Schedule to Annex I, in accordance with paragraph 2, or (iii) a local government;

(b) the continuation or prompt renewal of any non-conforming measure referred to in subparagraph (a); or

(c) an amendment to any non-conforming measure referred to in subparagraph (a) to the extent that the amendment does not decrease the conformity of the measure, as it existed immediately before the amendment, with Articles 1102, 1103, 1106 and 1107.

2. Each Party may set out in its Schedule to Annex I any existing non-conforming measure maintained by a state or province, not including a local government, within two years of the date of entry into force of this Agreement.

3. Articles 1102, 1103, 1106 and 1107 do not apply to any measure that a Party adopts or maintains with respect to sectors, subsectors or activities, as set out in its Schedule to Annex II.

4. No Party may, under any measure adopted after the date of entry into force of this Agreement and covered by its Schedule to Annex II, require an investor of another Party, by reason of its nationality, to sell or otherwise dispose of an investment existing at the time the measure becomes effective.

5. Articles 1102 and 1103 do not apply to any measure that is an exception to, or derogation from, the obligations under Article 1703 (Intellectual Property—National Treatment) as specifically provided for in that Article.

6. Article 1103 does not apply to treatment accorded by a Party pursuant to agreements, or with respect to sectors, set out in its Schedule to Annex IV.

7. Articles 1102, 1103 and 1107 do not apply to: (a) procurement by a Party or a state enterprise; or (b) subsidies or grants provided by a Party or a state enterprise, including government-supported loans, guarantees and insurance.

8. The provisions of: (a) Article 1106(1)(a), (b) and (c), and (3)(a) and (b) do not apply to qualification requirements for goods or services with respect to export promotion and foreign aid programs; (b) Article 1106(1)(b), (c), (f) and (g), and (3)(a) and (b) do not apply to procurement by a Party or a state enterprise; and (c) Article 1106(3)(a) and (b) do not apply to requirements imposed by an importing Party relating to the content of goods necessary to qualify for preferential tariffs or preferential quotas.

Article 1109. Transfers

1. Each Party shall permit all transfers relating to an investment of an investor of another Party in the territory of the Party to be made freely and without delay. Such transfers include:

> (a) profits, dividends, interest, capital gains, royalty payments, management fees, technical assistance and other fees, returns in kind and other amounts derived from the investment; (b) proceeds from the sale of all or any part of the investment or from the partial or complete liquidation of the investment; (c) payments made under a contract entered into by the investor, or its investment, including payments made pursuant to a loan agreement; (d) payments made pursuant to Article 1110; and (e) payments arising under Section B.

2. Each Party shall permit transfers to be made in a freely usable currency at the market rate of exchange prevailing on the date of transfer with respect to spot transactions in the currency to be transferred.

3. No Party may require its investors to transfer, or penalize its investors that fail to transfer, the income, earnings, profits or other amounts derived from, or attributable to, investments in the territory of another Party.

4. Notwithstanding paragraphs 1 and 2, a Party may prevent a transfer through the equitable, non-discriminatory and good faith application of its laws relating to: (a) bankruptcy, insolvency or the protection of the rights of creditors; (b) issuing, trading or dealing in securities; (c) criminal or penal offenses; (d) reports of transfers of currency or other monetary instruments; or (e) ensuring the satisfaction of judgments in adjudicatory proceedings.

5. Paragraph 3 shall not be construed to prevent a Party from imposing any measure through the equitable, non-discriminatory

and good faith application of its laws relating to the matters set out in subparagraphs (a) through (e) of paragraph 4.

6. Notwithstanding paragraph 1, a Party may restrict transfers of returns in kind in circumstances where it could otherwise restrict such transfers under this Agreement.

Article 1110. Expropriation and Compensation

1. No Party may directly or indirectly nationalize or expropriate an investment of an investor of another Party in its territory or take a measure tantamount to nationalization or expropriation of such an investment ("expropriation"), except: (a) for a public purpose; (b) on a non-discriminatory basis; (c) in accordance with due process of law and Article 1105(1); and (d) on payment of compensation in accordance with paragraphs 2 through 6.

2. Compensation shall be equivalent to the fair market value of the expropriated investment immediately before the expropriation took place ("date of expropriation"), and shall not reflect any change in value occurring because the intended expropriation had become known earlier. Valuation criteria shall include going concern value, asset value including declared tax value of tangible property, and other criteria, as appropriate, to determine fair market value.

3. Compensation shall be paid without delay and be fully realizable.

4. If payment is made in a G7 currency, compensation shall include interest at a commercially reasonable rate for that currency from the date of expropriation until the date of actual payment.

5. If a Party elects to pay in a currency other than a G7 currency, the amount paid on the date of payment, if converted into a G7 currency at the market rate of exchange prevailing on that date, shall be no less than if the amount of compensation owed on the date of expropriation had been converted into that G7 currency at the market rate of exchange prevailing on that date, and interest had accrued at a commercially reasonable rate for that G7 currency from the date of expropriation until the date of payment.

6. On payment, compensation shall be freely transferable as provided in Article 1109.

7. This Article does not apply to the issuance of compulsory licenses granted in relation to intellectual property rights, or the revocation, limitation or creation of intellectual property rights, to the extent that such issuance, revocation, limitation or creation is consistent with Chapter Seventeen (Intellectual Property).

8. For purposes of this Article and for greater certainty, a non-discriminatory measure of general application shall not be considered a measure tantamount to an expropriation of a debt security or loan covered by this Chapter solely on the ground that the measure imposes costs on the debtor that cause it to default on the debt.

Article 1111. Special Formalities and Information Requirements

1. Nothing in Article 1102 shall be construed to prevent a Party from adopting or maintaining a measure that prescribes special formalities in connection with the establishment of investments by investors of another Party, such as a requirement that investors be residents of the Party or that investments be legally constituted under the laws or regulations of the Party, provided that such formalities do not materially impair the protections afforded by a Party to investors of another Party and investments of investors of another Party pursuant to this Chapter.

2. Notwithstanding Articles 1102 or 1103, a Party may require an investor of another Party, or its investment in its territory, to provide routine information concerning that investment solely for informational or statistical purposes. The Party shall protect such business information that is confidential from any disclosure that would prejudice the competitive position of the investor or the investment. Nothing in this paragraph shall be 10 construed to prevent a Party from otherwise obtaining or disclosing information in connection with the equitable and good faith application of its law.

Article 1112. Relation to Other Chapters

1. In the event of any inconsistency between a provision of this Chapter and a provision of another Chapter, the provision of the other Chapter shall prevail to the extent of the inconsistency.

2. A requirement by a Party that a service provider of another Party post a bond or other form of financial security as a condition of providing a service into its territory does not of itself make this Chapter applicable to the provision of that cross-border service. This Chapter applies to that Party's treatment of the posted bond or financial security.

Article 1113. Denial of Benefits

1. A Party may deny the benefits of this Chapter to an investor of another Party that is an enterprise of such Party and to investments of such investor if investors of a non-Party own or control the enterprise and the denying Party: (a) does not maintain diplomatic relations with the non-Party; or (b) adopts or maintains measures

with respect to the non-Party that prohibit transactions with the enterprise or that would be violated or circumvented if the benefits of this Chapter were accorded to the enterprise or to its investments.

2. Subject to prior notification and consultation in accordance with Articles 1803 (Notification and Provision of Information) and 2006 (Consultations), a Party may deny the benefits of this Chapter to an investor of another Party that is an enterprise of such Party and to investments of such investors if investors of a non-Party own or control the enterprise and the enterprise has no substantial business activities in the territory of the Party under whose law it is constituted or organized.

Article 1114. Environmental Measures

1. Nothing in this Chapter shall be construed to prevent a Party from adopting, maintaining or enforcing any measure otherwise consistent with this Chapter that it considers appropriate to ensure that investment activity in its territory is undertaken in a manner sensitive to environmental concerns.

2. The Parties recognize that it is inappropriate to encourage investment by relaxing domestic health, safety or environmental measures. Accordingly, a Party should not waive or otherwise derogate from, or offer to waive or otherwise derogate from, such measures as an encouragement for the establishment, acquisition, expansion or retention in its territory of an investment of an investor. If a Party considers that another Party has offered such an encouragement, it may request consultations with the other Party and the two Parties shall consult with a view to avoiding any such encouragement.

Section B—Settlement of Disputes Between a Party and an Investor of Another Party

Article 1115. Purpose

Without prejudice to the rights and obligations of the Parties under Chapter Twenty (Institutional Arrangements and Dispute Settlement Procedures), this Section establishes a mechanism for the settlement of investment disputes that assures both equal treatment among investors of the Parties in accordance with the principle of international reciprocity and due process before an impartial tribunal.

Article 1116. Claim by an Investor of a Party on Its Own Behalf

1. An investor of a Party may submit to arbitration under this Section a claim that another Party has breached an obligation under: (a) Section A or Article 1503(2) (State Enterprises); or (b) Article

1502(3)(a) (Monopolies and State Enterprises) where the monopoly has acted in a manner inconsistent with the Party's obligations under Section A, and that the investor has incurred loss or damage by reason of, or arising out of, that breach.

2. An investor may not make a claim if more than three years have elapsed from the date on which the investor first acquired, or should have first acquired, knowledge of the alleged breach and knowledge that the investor has incurred loss or damage.

Article 1117. Claim by an Investor of a Party on Behalf of an Enterprise

1. An investor of a Party, on behalf of an enterprise of another Party that is a juridical person that the investor owns or controls directly or indirectly, may submit to arbitration under this Section a claim that the other Party has breached an obligation under:

> (a) Section A or Article 1503(2) (State Enterprises); or (b) Article 1502(3)(a) (Monopolies and State Enterprises) where the monopoly has acted in a manner inconsistent with the Party's obligations under Section A, and that the enterprise has incurred loss or damage by reason of, or arising out of, that breach.

2. An investor may not make a claim on behalf of an enterprise described in paragraph 1 if more than three years have elapsed from the date on which the enterprise first acquired, or should have first acquired, knowledge of the alleged breach and knowledge that the enterprise has incurred loss or damage.

3. Where an investor makes a claim under this Article and the investor or a noncontrolling investor in the enterprise makes a claim under Article 1116 arising out of the same events that gave rise to the claim under this Article, and two or more of the claims are submitted to arbitration under Article 1120, the claims should be heard together by a Tribunal established under Article 1126, unless the Tribunal finds that the interests of a disputing party would be prejudiced thereby.

4. An investment may not make a claim under this Section.

Article 1118. Settlement of a Claim through Consultation and Negotiation

The disputing parties should first attempt to settle a claim through consultation or negotiation.

Article 1119. Notice of Intent to Submit a Claim to Arbitration

The disputing investor shall deliver to the disputing Party written notice of its intention to submit a claim to arbitration at least 90 days before the claim is submitted, which notice shall specify: (a) the name and address of the disputing investor and, where a claim is made under Article 1117, the name and address of the enterprise; (b) the provisions of this Agreement alleged to have been breached and any other relevant provisions; (c) the issues and the factual basis for the claim; and (d) the relief sought and the approximate amount of damages claimed.

Article 1120. Submission of a Claim to Arbitration

1. Except as provided in Annex 1120.1, and provided that six months have elapsed since the events giving rise to a claim, a disputing investor may submit the claim to arbitration under: (a) the ICSID Convention, provided that both the disputing Party and the Party of the investor are parties to the Convention; (b) the Additional Facility Rules of ICSID, provided that either the disputing Party or the Party of the investor, but not both, is a party to the ICSID Convention; or (c) the UNCITRAL Arbitration Rules.

2. The applicable arbitration rules shall govern the arbitration except to the extent modified by this Section.

Article 1121. Conditions Precedent to Submission of a Claim to Arbitration

1. A disputing investor may submit a claim under Article 1116 to arbitration only if: (a) the investor consents to arbitration in accordance with the procedures set out in this Agreement; and (b) both the investor and an enterprise of another Party that is a juridical person that the investor owns or controls directly or indirectly, waive their right to initiate or continue before any administrative tribunal or court under the law of any Party any proceedings with respect to the measure of the disputing Party that is alleged to be a breach referred to in Article 1116, except for proceedings for injunctive, declaratory or other extraordinary relief, not involving the payment of damages, before an administrative tribunal or court under the law of the disputing Party.

2. A disputing investor may submit a claim under Article 1117 to arbitration only if both the investor and the enterprise: (a) consent to arbitration in accordance with the procedures set out in this Agreement; and (b) waive their right to initiate or continue before any administrative tribunal or court under the law of any Party any proceedings with respect to the measure of the disputing Party that

is alleged to be a breach referred to in Article 1117, except for proceedings for injunctive, declaratory or other extraordinary relief, not involving the payment of damages, before an administrative tribunal or court under the law of the disputing Party.

3. A consent and waiver required by this Article shall be in writing, shall be delivered to the disputing Party and shall be included in the submission of a claim to arbitration.

Article 1122. Consent to Arbitration

1. Each Party consents to the submission of a claim to arbitration in accordance with the procedures set out in this Agreement.

2. The consent given by paragraph 1 and the submission by a disputing investor of a claim to arbitration shall satisfy the requirement of: (a) Chapter II of the ICSID Convention (Jurisdiction of the Centre) and the Additional Facility Rules for written consent of the parties; (b) Article II of the New York Convention for an agreement in writing; and (c) Article I of the Inter-American Convention for an agreement.

Article 1123. Number of Arbitrators and Method of Appointment

Except in respect of a Tribunal established under Article 1126, and unless the disputing parties otherwise agree, the Tribunal shall comprise three arbitrators, one arbitrator appointed by each of the disputing parties and the third, who shall be the presiding arbitrator, appointed by agreement of the disputing parties.

Article 1124. Constitution of a Tribunal When a Party Fails to Appoint an Arbitrator or the Disputing Parties Are Unable to Agree on a Presiding Arbitrator

1. The Secretary-General shall serve as appointing authority for an arbitration under this Section.

2. If a Tribunal, other than a Tribunal established under Article 1126, has not been constituted within 90 days from the date that a claim is submitted to arbitration, the Secretary-General, on the request of either disputing party, shall appoint, in his discretion, the arbitrator or arbitrators not yet appointed, except that the presiding arbitrator shall be appointed in accordance with paragraph 3.

3. The Secretary-General shall appoint the presiding arbitrator from the roster of presiding arbitrators referred to in paragraph 4, provided that the presiding arbitrator shall not be a national of the disputing Party or a national of the Party of the disputing investor. In the event that no such presiding arbitrator is available to serve, the Secretary-General shall appoint, from the ICSID Panel of

Arbitrators, a presiding arbitrator who is not a national of any of the Parties.

4. On the date of entry into force of this Agreement, the Parties shall establish, and thereafter maintain, a roster of 45 presiding arbitrators meeting the qualifications of the Convention and rules referred to in Article 1120 and experienced in international law and investment matters. The roster members shall be appointed by consensus and without regard to nationality.

Article 1125. Agreement to Appointment of Arbitrators

For purposes of Article 39 of the ICSID Convention and Article 7 of Schedule C to the ICSID Additional Facility Rules, and without prejudice to an objection to an arbitrator based on Article 1124(3) or on a ground other than nationality:

(a) the disputing Party agrees to the appointment of each individual member of a Tribunal established under the ICSID Convention or the ICSID Additional Facility Rules;

(b) a disputing investor referred to in Article 1116 may submit a claim to arbitration, or continue a claim, under the ICSID Convention or the ICSID Additional Facility Rules, only on condition that the disputing investor agrees in writing to the appointment of each individual member of the Tribunal; and

(c) a disputing investor referred to in Article 1117(1) may submit a claim to arbitration, or continue a claim, under the ICSID Convention or the ICSID Additional Facility Rules, only on condition that the disputing investor and the enterprise agree in writing to the appointment of each individual member of the Tribunal.

Article 1126. Consolidation

1. A Tribunal established under this Article shall be established under the UNCITRAL Arbitration Rules and shall conduct its proceedings in accordance with those Rules, except as modified by this Section.

* * *

Article 1128. Participation by a Party

On written notice to the disputing parties, a Party may make submissions to a Tribunal on a question of interpretation of this Agreement.

Article 1129. Documents

1. A Party shall be entitled to receive from the disputing Party, at the cost of the requesting Party a copy of: (a) the evidence that has

been tendered to the Tribunal; and (b) the written argument of the disputing

2. A Party receiving information pursuant to paragraph 1 shall treat the information as if it were a disputing Party.

Article 1130. Place of Arbitration

Unless the disputing parties agree otherwise, a Tribunal shall hold an arbitration in the territory of a Party that is a party to the New York Convention, selected in accordance with: (a) the ICSID Additional Facility Rules if the arbitration is under those Rules or the ICSID Convention; or (b) the UNCITRAL Arbitration Rules if the arbitration is under those Rules.

Article 1131. Governing Law

1. A Tribunal established under this Section shall decide the issues in dispute in accordance with this Agreement and applicable rules of international law.

2. An interpretation by the Commission of a provision of this Agreement shall be binding on a Tribunal established under this Section.

Article 1132. Interpretation of Annexes

1. Where a disputing Party asserts as a defense that the measure alleged to be a breach is within the scope of a reservation or exception set out in Annex I, Annex II, Annex III or Annex IV, on request of the disputing Party, the Tribunal shall request the interpretation of the Commission on the issue. The Commission, within 60 days of delivery of the request, shall submit in writing its interpretation to the Tribunal.

2. Further to Article 1131(2), a Commission interpretation submitted under paragraph 1 shall be binding on the Tribunal. If the Commission fails to submit an interpretation within 60 days, the Tribunal shall decide the issue.

Article 1133. Expert Reports

Without prejudice to the appointment of other kinds of experts where authorized by the applicable arbitration rules, a Tribunal, at the request of a disputing party or, unless the disputing parties disapprove, on its own initiative, may appoint one or more experts to report to it in writing on any factual issue concerning environmental, health, safety or other scientific matters raised by a disputing party in a proceeding, subject to such terms and conditions as the disputing parties may agree.

Article 1134. Interim Measures of Protection

A Tribunal may order an interim measure of protection to preserve the rights of a disputing party, or to ensure that the Tribunal's jurisdiction is made fully effective, including an order to preserve evidence in the possession or control of a disputing party or to protect the Tribunal's jurisdiction. A Tribunal may not order attachment or enjoin the application of the measure alleged to constitute a breach referred to in Article 1116 or 1117. For purposes of this paragraph, an order includes a recommendation.

Article 1135. Final Award

1. Where a Tribunal makes a final award against a Party, the Tribunal may award only: (a) monetary damages and any applicable interest; or (b) restitution of property, in which case the award shall provide that the disputing Party may pay monetary damages and any applicable interest in lieu of restitution.

2. Subject to paragraph 1, where a claim is made under Article 1117(1): (a) an award of restitution of property shall provide that restitution be made to the enterprise; (b) an award of monetary damages and any applicable interest shall provide that the sum be paid to the enterprise; and (c) the award shall provide that it is made without prejudice to any right that any person may have in the relief under applicable domestic law.

3. A Tribunal may not order a Party to pay punitive damages.

Article 1136. Finality and Enforcement of an Award

1. An award made by a Tribunal shall have no binding force except between the disputing parties and in respect of the particular case.

2. Subject to paragraph 3 and the applicable review procedure for an interim award, a disputing party shall abide by and comply with an award without delay.

3. A disputing party may not seek enforcement of a final award until: (a) in the case of a final award made under the ICSID Convention (i) 120 days have elapsed from the date the award was rendered and no disputing party has requested revision or annulment of the award, or (ii) revision or annulment proceedings have been completed; and (b) in the case of a final award under the ICSID Additional Facility Rules or the UNCITRAL Arbitration Rules (i) three months have elapsed from the date the award was rendered and no disputing party has commenced a proceeding to revise, set aside or annul the award, or (ii) a court has dismissed or allowed an application to revise, set aside or annul the award and there is no further appeal.

4. Each Party shall provide for the enforcement of an award in its territory.

5. If a disputing Party fails to abide by or comply with a final award, the Commission, on delivery of a request by a Party whose investor was a party to the arbitration, shall establish a panel under Article 2008 (Request for an Arbitral Panel). The requesting Party may seek in such proceedings: (a) a determination that the failure to abide by or comply with the final award is inconsistent with the obligations of this Agreement; and (b) a recommendation that the Party abide by or comply with the final award.

6. A disputing investor may seek enforcement of an arbitration award under the ICSID Convention, the New York Convention or the Inter-American Convention regardless of whether proceedings have been taken under paragraph 5.

7. A claim that is submitted to arbitration under this Section shall be considered to arise out of a commercial relationship or transaction for purposes of Article I of the New York Convention and Article I of the Inter-American Convention.

* * *

Article 1138. Exclusions

1. Without prejudice to the applicability or non-applicability of the dispute settlement provisions of this Section or of Chapter Twenty (Institutional Arrangements and Dispute Settlement Procedures) to other actions taken by a Party pursuant to Article 2102 (National Security), a decision by a Party to prohibit or restrict the acquisition of an investment in its territory by an investor of another Party, or its investment, pursuant to that Article shall not be subject to such provisions.

2. The dispute settlement provisions of this Section and of Chapter Twenty shall not apply to the matters referred to in Annex 1138.2.

Article 1139. Definitions

For purposes of this Chapter:

> **disputing investor** means an investor that makes a claim under Section B;
>
> **disputing parties** means the disputing investor and the disputing Party;
>
> **disputing party** means the disputing investor or the disputing Party;
>
> **disputing Party** means a Party against which a claim is made under Section B;

enterprise means an "enterprise" as defined in Article 201, and a branch of an enterprise;

enterprise of a Party means an enterprise constituted or organized under the law of a Party, and a branch located in the territory of a Party and carrying out business activities there;

equity or debt securities includes voting and non-voting shares, bonds, convertible debentures, stock options and warrants;

G7 Currency means the currency of Canada, France, Germany, Italy, Japan, the United Kingdom of Great Britain and Northern Ireland or the United States;

ICSID means the International Centre for Settlement of Investment Disputes;

ICSID Convention means the Convention on the Settlement of Investment Disputes between States and Nationals of other States, done at Washington, March 18, 1965;

Inter-American Convention means the Inter-American Convention on International Commercial Arbitration, done at Panama, January 30, 1975;

investment means: (a) an enterprise; (b) an equity security of an enterprise; (c) a debt security of an enterprise (i) where the enterprise is an affiliate of the investor, or (ii) where the original maturity of the debt security is at least three years, but does not include a debt security, regardless of original maturity, of a state enterprise; (d) a loan to an enterprise (i) where the enterprise is an affiliate of the investor, or (ii) where the original maturity of the loan is at least three years, but does not include a loan, regardless of original maturity, to a state enterprise; (e) an interest in an enterprise that entitles the owner to share in income or profits of the enterprise; (f) an interest in an enterprise that entitles the owner to share in the assets of that enterprise on dissolution, other than a debt security or a loan excluded from subparagraph (c) or (d); (g) real estate or other property, tangible or intangible, acquired in the expectation or used for the purpose of economic benefit or other business purposes; and (h) interests arising from the commitment of capital or other resources in the territory of a Party to economic activity in such territory, such as under (i) contracts involving the presence of an investor's property in the territory of the Party, including turnkey or construction contracts, or concessions, or (ii) contracts where remuneration depends substantially on the production, revenues or profits of an enterprise;

but investment does not mean, (i) claims to money that arise solely from (i) commercial contracts for the sale of goods or services by a national or enterprise in the territory of a Party to an enterprise in the territory of another Party, or (ii) the extension of credit in connection with a commercial transaction, such as trade financing, other than a loan covered by subparagraph (d); or (j) any other claims to money, that do not involve the kinds of interests set out in subparagraphs (a) through (h);

investment of an investor of a Party means an investment owned or controlled directly or indirectly by an investor of such Party;

investor of a Party means a Party or state enterprise thereof, or a national or an enterprise of such Party, that seeks to make, is making or has made an investment;

investor of a non-Party means an investor other than an investor of a Party, that seeks to make, is making or has made an investment;

New York Convention means the United Nations Convention on the Recognition and Enforcement of Foreign Arbitral Awards, done at New York, June 10, 1958;

Secretary-General means the Secretary-General of ICSID;

transfers means transfers and international payments;

Tribunal means an arbitration tribunal established under Article 1120 or 1126; and

UNCITRAL Arbitration Rules means the arbitration rules of the United Nations Commission on International Trade Law, approved by the United Nations General Assembly on December 15, 1976.

Annex 1120.1—Submission of a Claim to Arbitration

Mexico

With respect to the submission of a claim to arbitration: (a) an investor of another Party may not allege that Mexico has breached an obligation under: (i) Section A or Article 1503(2) (State Enterprises), or (ii) Article 1502(3)(a) (Monopolies and State Enterprises) where the monopoly has acted in a manner inconsistent with the Party's obligations under Section A, both in an arbitration under this Section and in proceedings before a Mexican court or administrative tribunal; and

(b) where an enterprise of Mexico that is a juridical person that an investor of another Party owns or controls directly or indirectly alleges in proceedings before a Mexican court or administrative tribunal that Mexico has breached an obligation under:(i) Section A or Article 1503(2) (State Enterprises), or (ii) Article 1502(3)(a) (Monopolies and State Enterprises) where the monopoly has acted in a manner inconsistent with the Party's obligations under Section A, the investor may not allege the breach in an arbitration under this Section.

* * *

Annex 1138.2—Exclusions from Dispute Settlement

Canada

A decision by Canada following a review under the Investment Canada Act, with respect to whether or not to permit an acquisition that is subject to review, shall not be subject to the dispute settlement provisions of Section B or of Chapter Twenty (Institutional Arrangements and Dispute Settlement Procedures).

Mexico

A decision by the National Commission on Foreign Investment ("Comision Nacional de Inversiones Extranjeras") following a review pursuant to Annex I, page I–M–4, with respect to whether or not to permit an acquisition that is subject to review, shall not be subject to the dispute settlement provisions of Section B or of Chapter Twenty (Institutional Arrangements and Dispute Settlement Procedures).

Chapter 5

INTERNATIONAL BUSINESS LITIGATION: JURISDICTION

Table of Sections

§ 5.1 Introduction

Each of the topics covered in this chapter, such as personal jurisdiction and subject matter jurisdiction, should be familiar. But that familiarity is likely based upon transactions between persons from different U.S. states rather than different nations. Each of these areas will be revisited emphasizing international business litigation and the very different issues it generates. I am indebted to Professor Michael Gordon of Florida for his original work on Sections 5.2, 5.3 and 5.4 of this chapter.

Special attention is given to "extraterritorial" U.S. antitrust jurisdiction, a subject of great international controversy for more than a century. It has caused the adoption of "blocking statutes" by many nations concerned with extraterritorial U.S. antitrust jurisdiction, discovery and enforcement of judgments. A comparison with European Union (EU) extraterritorial antitrust, known as business competition law, is undertaken, along with a review of the efforts by the U.S. and EU to cooperate on antitrust matters. These topics appear in Sections 5.5 through 5.8.

§ 5.2 Personal Jurisdiction, Due Process

Jurisdiction to adjudicate the rights and obligations of persons and business entities, or to determine their property interests, is referred to as personal jurisdiction under United States law. Two personal jurisdiction categories have been recognized in the case law: Specific and General. Specific personal jurisdiction involves litigation that arises out of or relates to the defendant's contacts with the U.S. forum. Specific jurisdiction, for example, is the basis for most international product liability and contract suits. General personal jurisdiction concerns causes of action that do *not* arise out of or relate to contacts with the U.S. forum (typically arising instead from activities outside the United States). General personal jurisdiction over foreign corporations derives from, in the aggregate, substantial, continuous operations and affiliations within a U.S. forum.

Personal jurisdiction is a decidedly American legal doctrine, one that often comes into play when foreign defendants are sued in United States courts. Choice of a U.S. court by agreement of the parties (see Section 2.2) will likely constitute waiver of personal jurisdiction. Where a suit is initiated in the United States and the defendant believes a *forum non conveniens* motion (see Section 2.4) will prevail, possible defects in jurisdiction are overlooked for the moment, or deferred pending the resolution of the motion. The reason may be that predicting answers to questions of personal jurisdiction is less certain than predicting answers to *forum non conveniens*.

A parallel situation arises when a foreign state or state-controlled entity is sued in a U.S. court. The court will turn to the Foreign Sovereign Immunities Act of 1976 (FSIA) and address the questions whether the party is a state or state agency or instrumentality, and whether there is a commercial activity, waiver or other immunity exception. The FSIA creates its own unique service of process requirements, and unique personal and subject matter jurisdiction rules. See Section 7.5.

U.S. Supreme Court Case Law

Both state and federal courts are bound by federal Constitutional due process limitations on personal jurisdiction. State courts may be further constrained by state constitutional rules. Some U.S. states have long-arm statutes which explicitly extend to the federal limits. California Civil Procedure Code Section 410.10, for example, authorizes jurisdiction "on any basis not inconsistent with the constitution of this state or of the United States." Similarly, FRCP Rule 4(k)(2) grants federal courts personal jurisdiction in federal question cases (when there is no basis for general state jurisdiction) "consistent with the Constitution and laws of the United States."

For many years, the controlling doctrine of personal jurisdiction law in the United States mandated that the defendant be physically present in the forum state at the time the lawsuit was commenced.[1] The reversal of that doctrine came in a 1945 U.S. Supreme Court decision, *International Shoe*. There is no other way to present personal jurisdiction in international litigation than to start with the classic due process test of minimum contacts and reasonableness discussed in that venerable decision.[2] Perhaps in no other area of constitutional law have the courts been able to adopt varying approaches to the meaning of due process than in the progeny of *International Shoe*. Having an office or employees in the state, frequent and voluminous in-state business, and use of services in the state (such as banking) are often cited when analyzing the minimum contacts necessary to assert personal jurisdiction without offending fair play and substantial justice.

Although *International Shoe* did not involve a foreign defendant, foreign defendants benefit from the Fifth Amendment due process requirements.[3] In a 1980 domestic case, *Worldwide Volkswagen,*[4] the Supreme Court held that a defendant must have "purposefully directed" its activities toward the forum state. In other words, the defendant must have anticipated being subjected to the forum state's courts, and there should be some link between the injuries and the defendant's activities in the state. The Supreme Court listed several factors to examine, emphasizing the number, nature, and quality of contacts, as well as the source and connection of the action with these contacts.

General Personal Jurisdiction

In 1984, in a major Supreme Court case examining general personal jurisdiction over foreign defendants, the Court emphasized that only "continuous and systematic" contacts give rise to general personal jurisdiction.[5] In this decision, a Colombian company was sued in tort by U.S. plaintiffs who were injured when its Texas-made

---

1 Pennoyer v. Neff, 95 U.S. 714 (1877).

2 International Shoe Co. v. Washington, 326 U.S. 310, 66 S.Ct. 154, 90 L.Ed. 95 (1945).

3 *See, e.g.*, Mathews v. Diaz, 426 U.S. 67, 96 S.Ct. 1883, 48 L.Ed.2d 478 (1976), Wong Wing v. United States, 163 U.S. 228, 16 S.Ct. 977, 41 L.Ed. 140 (1896).

4 World-Wide Volkswagen Corp. v. Woodson, 444 U.S. 286, 100 S.Ct. 559, 62 L.Ed.2d 490 (1980). It is essentially a domestic case, the German parent was not a defendant.

5 Helicopteros Nacionales de Colombia v. Hall, 466 U.S. 408, 104 S.Ct. 1868, 80 L.Ed.2d 404 (1984) (general personal jurisdiction not found). *See* Perkins v. Benguet Consolidated Mining Co., 342 U.S. 437 (1952).

helicopter crashed in Peru. A jury awarded $1.1 million in damages. The Colombian company had various contacts with Texas, including contract negotiations, banking, equipment purchases and training sessions. Nevertheless, the Supreme Court deemed these insufficient for general jurisdiction purposes: They were not continuous and systematic. In 2011, the Supreme Court came to a similar conclusion in *Goodyear Dunlop Tires Operations S.A. v. Brown.*[6] In this case, the exercise of general jurisdiction by North Carolina courts over foreign corporations concerning a bus accident near Paris attributed to a defective tire manufactured in Turkey by a Goodyear subsidiary was rejected as not continuous and systematic.

In *Daimler AG v. Bauman,*[7] the U.S. Supreme Court held that general jurisdiction over foreign firms rests on an analysis of their "continuous and systematic" affiliations with the jurisdiction, in other words whether those firms are "essentially at home" in a state. The Court suggested that being incorporated or having a principal place of business would likely meet this more demanding standard. In *Daimler*, Argentinian plaintiffs sued a German company doing business in the USA via its Delaware subsidiary (MBUSA) whose principal place of business was in New Jersey. Suit was filed in a California federal district court predicated for personal jurisdiction purposes on MBUSA's contacts in California.

The suit by foreign plaintiffs alleged multiple human rights violations during Argentina's "Dirty War". Defendant successfully moved to dismiss for want of general personal jurisdiction under California's long-arm statute, which is limited only by federal due process law. Employing an "agency" test, the Ninth Circuit affirmed general jurisdiction over Daimler because of the "special importance" of the services its New Jersey subsidiary provided to it in California. Reversing the Ninth Circuit, the Supreme Court held that MBUSA's contacts with California were insufficient to establish general personal jurisdiction over Daimler, admonished that court for paying little heed to international comity, and noted its decisions limiting the scope of the Alien Tort Claims Act and Torture Victim Protection Act. See Section 5.3.

Specific Personal Jurisdiction

Another major Supreme Court decision with foreign defendants came in 1987, *Asahi.*[8] This decision involved an assertion specific personal jurisdiction. In this case, a motorcycle tire failed and the

---

[6] 131 S.Ct. 2846 (2011).

[7] 134 S.Ct. 746 (2014).

[8] Asahi Metal Industry Co., Ltd. v. Superior Court of California, Solano County, 480 U.S. 102, 107 S.Ct. 1026, 94 L.Ed.2d 92 (1987).

driver and passenger were respectively injured and killed in California. The valve stem was allegedly the defective part of the tire, and had been made by Asahi, a company in Japan. It was purchased by the Taiwan tire manufacturer. The tire manufacturer was sued in California state court, and cross-complained against Asahi.[9] The California Supreme Court upheld specific jurisdiction over Asahi, but the U.S. Supreme Court reversed. The Court was unanimous in its ruling that specific personal jurisdiction over Asahi was unreasonable. But the reasoning was not unanimous.

There was general agreement that the *International Shoe* decision applied, and that there must be *both* minimum contacts and constitutional due process. But there was disagreement regarding the standard to determine minimum contacts. Four justices found the "stream of commerce" theory insufficient, rejecting proof of this step by finding the product was brought into the forum by the consumer. Some action by the defendant was needed to satisfy a substantial connection theory. The defendant would have to take some action "*purposefully directed toward the state*."[10] Four other justices preferred the stream of commerce theory without additional conduct. The split of opinion regarding minimum contacts has not helped subsequent cases. Federal circuits and state courts have also split on which side they favor.[11]

If the minimum contacts test is satisfied, the court next considers reasonableness—whether exercising jurisdiction meets the *International Shoe* and *World-Wide Volkswagen* "notions of fair play and substantial justice." It is not easy to establish unreasonableness. Simply listing minimum contacts and assuming that they are somehow weighed will not suffice. The minimum contacts must be sufficient to conclude that the defendant "purposely availed itself of the benefits and burdens of doing business" in the subject state. "Purposely availed" has become a new term of art to be debated

---

[9] The result might have been different had the action been initiated directly by the California parties against the valve manufacturer. See Restatement (Third) of Foreign Relations Law, § 421, reporters' note 2, at 310.

[10] 480 U.S. at 112 (emphasis in original).

[11] *See, e.g.*, Gould v. P.T. Krakatau Steel, 957 F.2d 573 (8th Cir. 1992), *cert. denied*, 506 U.S. 908, 113 S.Ct. 304, 121 L.Ed.2d 227 (1992) (sale of Indonesian company's product to N.Y. corporation with subsequent sending of product to Arkansas does not meet test), Mason v. F. LLI Luigi & Franco Dal Maschio, 832 F.2d 383 (7th Cir. 1987) (sale of Italian goods to Maryland with subsequent sending of product to Illinois does meet test), Microsoft Corp. v. Very Competitive Computer Prod. Corp., 671 F.Supp. 1250 (N.D.Cal.1987) (sale of Taiwanese product to California through another Taiwanese company does meet test) and Glencore Grain Rotterdam BV v. Shivnath Rai Harnarian Co., 284 F.3d 1114 (9th Cir. 2002) (despite systematic and continuous contacts, purposeful interjection into California was slight, and hence unreasonable for personal jurisdiction analysis). Compare the rejection of "stream of commerce" jurisdiction in J. McIntyre Machery Ltd. v. Nicastro, 131 S.Ct. 2780 (2011).

seemingly without end, in the same manner as "stream of commerce."[12] In 2011, the Supreme Court held that mere knowledge by a foreign manufacturer that its products would be nationally distributed, without advertising in, sending goods to or in any relevant sense targeting the New Jersey market, did not constitute purposeful availment.[13]

The finding of minimum contacts seems to imply that reasonableness exists. But *Asahi* suggests that a weighing of comity interests is also required. There must be consideration of the burden on the defendant of litigating in the forum state, the interests of the foreign state, the interests of the plaintiff in obtaining relief, the interests of the judicial system in efficient resolution of cases, and the shared interests of the states in furthering substantive social policies.[14] The Court in *Asahi* was notably concerned with the burden placed on Asahi in defending the action in a foreign (U.S.) forum. It additionally noted that "great care and reserve should be exercised when extending our notions of personal jurisdiction in the international field."[15] Thus due process standards appear heightened when the defendants are foreigners.

With these principal cases providing guidelines, however conflicting and confusing, the state and federal courts have been left to work out the details when the defendant is foreign. E-commerce has brought use of the Internet into the debate over minimum contacts.[16] An international contract's connections (negotiations, communications, visits, agents, delivery, choice of law) with a jurisdiction must be evaluated.[17] There is a trend in the courts towards assessing specific personal jurisdiction as a balancing of contacts and reasonableness: The stronger the contacts, the more likely reasonableness will be found. The weaker the contacts, the more likely unreasonableness will be determined.[18]

---

12 *See, e.g.*, Frederick Juenger, A Shoe Unfit for Globetrotting, 28 Univ. Calif. Davis L.J. 1027 (1995).

13 131 S.Ct. 2730 (2011).

14 *See also* Burger King Corp. v. Rudzewicz, 471 U.S. 462, 105 S.Ct. 2174, 85 L.Ed.2d 528 (1985).

15 480 U.S. at 114. *See* Meier v. Sun Int'l Hotels, 288 F.3d 1264 (11th Cir. 2002) (minimum contacts and fair play and substantial justice provide basis for Florida jurisdiction over Bahamian boat accident).

16 *See, e.g.*, Toys "R" Us, Inc v. Step Two S.A., 318 F.3d 446 (3rd Cir. 2003) (allowing jurisdictional discovery focused on E-commerce contacts).

17 *See* Afram Export Corp. v. Metallurgiki Halyps, 772 F.2d 1358 (7th Cir. 1985); Benton v. Cameco Corp., 375 F.3d 1070 (10th Cir. 2004).

18 *See, e.g.*, O.M.I. Holdings v. Royal Ins. Co., 149 F.3d 1086 (10th Cir. 1998); Benton v. Cameco Corp., 375 F.3d 1070 (10th Cir. 2004).

Quasi-In-Rem Jurisdiction, Attachments

Pre-trial attachments of property within a court's territory traditionally provided a basis for personal jurisdiction in U.S. federal and state courts. In 1977, however, the Supreme Court cast doubt on the constitutionality of quasi-in-rem jurisdiction, indicating that such assertions must conform to the minimum contacts analysis on *International Shoe*.[19] Furthermore, when the assets are located outside the United States, federal courts generally lack the equitable power to issue injunctions against their transfer.[20]

However, U.S. state laws may permit "*Mareva*-like" injunctions regarding assets unrelated to the cause of action.[21] The reference is to English law where the leading cases[22] allow such pre-trial orders. In exceptional circumstances *Mareva* injunctions can apply to assets anywhere in the world. They can be obtained for litigation pending in the U.K. or outside it. *Mareva* injunctions are normally issued *ex parte* without notice, and thousands of them are sought every month. They are known as "freezing injunctions".

Veil Piercing to Obtain Jurisdiction

When a foreign defendant is the parent of a subsidiary corporation located in the United States, a court may extend personal jurisdiction to the parent in what is often called piercing the corporate veil. The Supreme Court upheld this practice in 1948 when "constant supervision and intervention beyond normal exercise of shareholder rights" of the subsidiary by the parent is proven.[23] More recently, the Supreme Court has acknowledged a split of authority regarding whether affiliate-based jurisdiction requires a subsidiary to be an alter ego of the parent, or merely an agent performing some important service.[24] In either case, the Court affirmed that general personal jurisdiction rules (discussed above) must be met.

Veil piercing usually involves linking two enterprises, but in jurisdiction cases, the analysis can be less demanding, using agency

---

19 Shaffer v. Heitner, 433 U.S. 186 (1977).

20 Grupo Mexicano de Desarrollo SA v. Alliance Bond Fund Inc., 527 U.S. 308 (1999). Compare prior allowance of global asset freezes in Republic of Philippines v. Marcos, 806 F.2d 344 (9th Cir. 1988).

21 *See* CIBC Mellon Trust Co. v. Mora Hotel Corp. 296 App.Div.2d 81 (N.Y. App. Div. 2002) (*Mareva* injunction does not violate due process so as to bar enforcement of a UK judgment).

22 *See* Mareva Compania Navierra SA v. Int'l Bulkcarriers SA, 2 Lloyd's Rep. 509 (1975) and Derby & Co. Ltd. v. Weldon, 1988 WL 622901 (Ct. App.1988).

23 United States v. Scophony Corp., 333 U.S. 795 (1948). *See generally,* Cannon Mfg. Co. v. Cudahy Packing Co., 267 U.S. 33 (1925).

24 Daimler AG v. Bauman, 143 S.Ct. 746 (2014). *See* Wiwa v. Royal Dutch Petroleum Co., 226 F.3d 88 (2d Cir. 2009) (one person investor relations office in New York sufficient for affiliate jurisdiction).

concepts more freely and replacing "formal relationships" with "economic realities."[25] A conclusion that pierces the veil of the U.S. entity means that jurisdictional factors of minimum contacts and due process are less complex. Additionally, because the parent and subsidiary are one, service of process on the U.S. entity will constitute service on the whole entity, including the foreign parent. See Section 6.1.

International Law and Personal Jurisdiction

International law limitations on extraterritorial extensions of jurisdiction may conflict with U.S. personal jurisdiction rules. U.S. courts considering personal jurisdiction in international cases generally have ignored international law, instead focusing on traditional minimum contacts and due process issues.[26] U.S. administrative agencies have similarly attempted to assert jurisdiction beyond what appear to be acceptable international limits. When *foreign* courts or tribunals have considered U.S. extraterritorial assertions of personal jurisdiction, the U.S. rules have not been well received.[27] The Restatement of Foreign Relations in its *jurisdiction to adjudicate* provisions suggests "reasonableness" as the standard in asserting personal jurisdiction, but this Restatement provision has received at best limited acceptance by U.S. courts.[28]

The U.S. Supreme Court has addressed the issue whether one must first challenge personal jurisdiction before a *forum non conveniens* motion, ruling that there is no mandate to first establish jurisdiction.[29] Transient U.S. personal "tag jurisdiction", considered by many nations to be exorbitant and inconsistent with international law, has been upheld by the Supreme Court.[30] In other words, tag

---

25 Andrulonis v. United States, 526 F.Supp. 183, 188 (N.D.N.Y.1981). *See also* Meyers v. ASICS Corp., 711 F.Supp. 1001, 1004 (C.D.Cal.1989). Compare Anderson v. Dassault Aviation, 361 F.3d 449 (8th Cir. 2004) (rejecting veil piercing).

26 *See, e.g.*, Dieter Lange & Gary B. Born, The Extraterritorial Application of National Laws (1989); Harold G. Maier, Resolving Extraterritorial Conflicts, or "There and Back Again," 25 Va. J. Int'l L. 7 (1984); Harold G. Maier, Extraterritorial Jurisdiction at a Crossroads: An Intersection Between Public and Private International Law, 76 A. J. Int'l L. 280 (1982).

27 *See* Compagnie Euro des Petroles SA v. Sensor Nederland BV reprinted in 22 I.L.M. 66 (1983), Fruehauf Corp. v. Massardy, Court of Appeals Paris reprinted in 5 I.L.M. 476 (1966).

28 The Restatement on Foreign Relations Law is often more aspirational than a reflection of the current status of the law. It is as essential to know its limitations as it is important to be familiar with its substance. It reflects a great deal of effort by some exceptionally capable scholars and practitioners.

29 Sinochem Int'l Co., Ltd. v. Malaysia Int'l Shipping Corp., 549 U.S. 422, 127 S.Ct. 1184, 167 L.Ed.2d 15 (2007).

30 Burnham v. Superior Court, 495 U.S. 604 (1990). Accord, Kadic v. Karadzic, 70 F.3d 232 (2d Cir. 1995).

jurisdiction, even aboard aircraft flying over the United States,[31] is not subject to minimum contacts due process. The courts are split on whether corporations can be tagged via their officers,[32] or are subject to jurisdiction if registered to do business in a U.S. state.[33]

Jurisdiction in Foreign Nations

Jurisdiction in other nations, in particular civil law countries, is fundamentally different. For example, the nations within the European Union have harmonized jurisdiction under the EU Regulation on Jurisdiction and the Recognition and Enforcement of Judgments in Civil and Commercial Matters (the Brussels Regulation, see Sections 8.2 and 8.7). There is no distinction between personal and subject matter jurisdiction in the Brussels Regulation, but there is a distinction between jurisdiction and special jurisdiction. Special jurisdiction involves exceptions to the general principal that jurisdiction is vested in courts of a particular state where the defendant is domiciled, and that jurisdiction issues must be interpreted restrictively. Jurisdiction based upon a French plaintiff's citizenship (regardless of whether the defendant has any contacts with France), and jurisdiction in Germany based upon the presence of assets (however illusory) are examples of special jurisdictional exceptions that are permitted.

There is no concept within the EU that allows a court to first determine whether it has jurisdiction. Jurisdiction in the EU is often said to be a relationship between the court and the claim, whereas in the United States it is between the court and the defendant. This has ramifications in such areas as *forum non conveniens* as it exists in common law nations. *Forum non conveniens* allows a court to dismiss a case because it is allegedly better heard in an alternative and adequate forum. See Section 2.4. In Europe the rule is essentially that if jurisdiction is present, the court must go forward and address the claim.

Another comparison is Japan, which after WWII adopted a code of civil procedure influenced by the then existing German code. But Japan has developed in case law a concept called "jōri", which

---

[31] *See* Grace v. MacArthur, 170 F.Supp. 442 (E.D.Ark.1959).

[32] Compare Oyuela v. Seacor Marine (Nigeria), 290 F.Supp.2d 713 (E.D.La. 2003) (corporate officer tagging upheld) with Martinez v. Aero Caribbean, 764 F.3d 1062 (9th Cir. 2014) and Schulz v. Research and Development v. Kruse, 720 F.Supp. 710 (N.D. Ill. 1989) (corporate officer tagging rejected).

[33] Compare King v. American Family Mut Ins. Co., 632 F.3d 570 (9th Cir. 2011) (no jurisdiction) with Knowlton v. Allied Van Lines, 900 F.2d 713 (8th Cir. 1990) (jurisdiction upheld).

introduces a fairness discussion that is closer to U.S. due process analysis.[34]

§ 5.3 International Human Rights and Environmental Claims Against Businesses in U.S. Courts

Foreign investors have always faced possible litigation in the host nation. Jurisdiction in the host nation is rarely a problem because the company is clearly there and doing business. But the subsidiary in the host nation often has few assets. While they may be sufficient to satisfy judgments dealing with such common issues as a job related injury to an employee, or a contract breach, they are insufficient when multiple plaintiff actions are brought for alleged large scale injury such as environmental damage or labor abuses. In such actions the defendants typically include both the parent and the host nation subsidiary, leading to jurisdiction issues over the parent if the suit is brought in the host nation.

Such suits are also brought in the United States, often in state courts where juries are perceived as hostile to multinational corporations, such as South Texas or Mississippi.[35] Initiated by attorneys' with contingent fee contracts and who demand punitive damages, human rights abuses, environmental damages and even cultural genocide have been the charges in an increasing number of suits against some of the largest corporations in the United States, including Del Monte, DuPont, Exxon Mobil Corp., Ford Motor Company, Texaco, Union Carbide, and United Technologies. The principal basis for these suits has been alleged violations of international law and specifically of the Alien Tort Claims Act (ACTA) of 1789.[36] The Act gives U.S. district courts jurisdiction over "any civil action by an alien for a tort only, committed in violation of the law of nations or a treaty of the United States."

Early U.S. Supreme Court Case Law

Much of the ACTA litigation has evolved since the *Filártiga v. Peña-Irala* decision by the U.S. Supreme Court in 1980.[37] *Filártiga* did not involve a corporate defendant. It was brought by a Paraguayan citizen, Filártiga, residing in the United States, against one Peña, another Paraguayan citizen in the United States on a

---

[34] Goto v. Malaysia Airline, 35 Minshū (No. 7) 1224 (Supreme Court, Oct. 16, 1981), *translated in* 26 Japanese Annual of International Law 122 (1983).

[35] The U.S. parent will usually argue lack of jurisdiction over the parent because it operates in the foreign host nation solely through a host nation corporation. This usually leads to veil piercing issues, discussed above.

[36] 28 U.S.C.A. Section 1350.

[37] 630 F.2d 876 (2d Cir. 1980).

tourist visa. Peña had been the Inspector General of the Police in Asunción, Paraguay, and allegedly tortured and killed the son of Filártiga. The case was based principally on violations of the Alien Tort Claims Act, a 1789 enactment of Congress addressing quite different concerns, such as acts of piracy. It was rarely used until *Filártiga*. But its brevity and breadth provided the court a foundation to find Peña in violation. The court had little trouble in holding that death by torture constituted a violation of international law.

The Court indicated that private claims under federal common law should not be recognized for violations of international law norms with "less definite content and acceptance among civilized nations than the historical paradigms familiar when the ACTA was enacted." Nevertheless, when the court rendered its opinion in 1980 the floodgates opened for many suits that tried to enlarge upon the scope of violations of international law.

How expansive an interpretation should be given the ATCA's "violation of the law of nations" language is yet undetermined. Certainly torture and extra-judicial killing are such violations. So perhaps are hostage taking and aircraft sabotage, and acts of terrorism. But the cases have tested the ATCA's language in two ways. One is the scope of acts within a category that appear at first glance to constitute international law violations, but may encompass less clear violations, such as torture (e.g., cutting off hands versus sleep deprivation) and human rights (extra-judicial killing of political dissidents versus "cultural genocide" relocating indigenous people to build a dam).[38]

The second debate is whether to bring within violations of international law areas where there is uncertainty about whether acts violate treaties or customary international law. The most frequently litigated may be violations of environmental laws. While there are many domestic environmental laws, there is considerable debate as to whether there is any international environmental law, especially customary law. Several federal Circuit courts have rejected environmental ACTA claims.[39]

Sosa v. Alvarez-Machain, a 2004 U.S. Supreme Court decision, limited ATCA.[40] *Sosa* involved an individual claiming that his

---

[38] *See*, for example, Abagninin v. AMVAC Chemical Corp., 545 F.3d 733 (9th Cir. 2008) (Ivory Coast genocide complaint rejected); Khulumani v. Barclay Nat'l Bank, 504 F.3d 254 (2d Cir. 2007) (torture and extrajudicial killing in apartheid South Africa complaint upheld); Sarei v. Rio Tinto, 550 F.3d 822 (9th Cir. 2008) (Papua New Guinea war crimes complaint dismissed).

[39] *See* Flores v. Southern Peru Copper Corp., 343 F.3d 140 (2d Cir. 2003) and Beanal v. Freeport McMoran Inc., 197 F.3d 161 (5th Cir. 1999).

[40] 542 U.S. 692, 124 S.Ct. 2739 (2004).

abduction in Mexico by U.S. federal authorities constituted a violation of international law under the ATCA. The case brought the U.S. Supreme Court into the debate over the limits of the ATCA. The Court rejected the defendant's argument that the ATCA does not provide a cause of action, but found that the abduction of Alvarez-Machain in Mexico and his transportation to the United States for trial did not violate the law of nations. The Court urged judicial caution in applying too broad an interpretation of the ATCA.

While these issues could be debated and litigated in cases against officials of the foreign nations, subject to jurisdiction in U.S. courts, the far deeper pockets are those of multinational corporations. It was inevitable that suits would be brought against corporate defendants. The first to establish corporate liability was *Doe v. Unocal*, brought by Burmese nationals charging human rights violations by the defendant for complicity with the government in using forced labor in the construction of an oil pipeline.[41] Subsequent Federal Circuit opinions stress the need to prove that corporations share the intent of government acts causing harm to ATCA plaintiffs.[42]

Recent U.S. Supreme Court Case Law

In 2012, the Supreme Court held that only natural persons could be liable under the federal Torture Victim Protection Act of 1992.[43] The issue of corporate liability under the ATCA was raised but not decided by the U.S. Supreme Court in *Kiobel v. Royal Dutch Petroleum Co.*[44] This 2013 opinion involved human rights claims by Nigerian refugees against British and Dutch oil companies and their Nigerian subsidiaries for allegedly aiding and abetting human rights violations by the government in Nigeria. Declining to rule on a Second Circuit decision that corporations are not subject to ACTA[45] as a matter of customary international law, the Supreme Court instead ruled unanimously that the ATCA could not be used because there is a presumption against extraterritorial application of U.S. law. See Section 5.4. That presumption is not easily displaced, and the mere presence of a corporation in a foreign country is not a sufficient reason.

---

41 110 F.Supp.2d 1294 (C.D.Cal. 2000); 395 F.3d 932 (9th Cir. 2002).

42 *See* Presbyterian Church of Sudan v. Talisman Energy Inc., 582 F.3d 244 (2d Cir. 2009) and Aziz v. Alcolac Inc., 658 F.3d 388 (4th Cir. 2011) (Iraq).

43 Mohamad v. Palestinian Authority, 132 S.Ct 1702 (2012). *See generally*, Kadic v. Karadzic, 70 F.3d 232 (2d Cir. 1995) (upholding claim in the Balkans).

44 132 S.Ct. 1738 (2013).

45 Kiobel v. Royal Dutch Petroleum Co., 621 F.3d 111 (2d Cir. 2011). *See*, contra, Flomo v. Firestone National Rubber Co., 643 F.3d 1014 (7th Cir. 2011).

The *Kiobel* Court held: "And even where the claims touch and concern the territory of the United States, they must do so with sufficient force to displace the presumption against extraterritorial application."[46] While the decision was unanimous, four justices believed that corporations may be "today's pirates." Immediate reaction was that the decision would substantially eliminate ACTA litigation by foreign plaintiffs based on nothing more than a U.S. corporation's presence in a foreign nation. And indeed in *Jesner v. Arab Bank,* the Supreme Court by vote of 5 to 4 explicitly held that corporations cannot be sued under ACTA "when all the relevant conduct took place outside the United States."[47] Jesner was an action brought by 6,000 plaintiffs against a Jordanian bank for injuries perpetrated by Hamas and other terrorists in Israel.

These Supreme Court decisions have not ended suits against international business parties. Other U.S. grounds remain, such as the Racketeer Influenced and Corrupt Organizations Act (RICO) (18 U.S.C. 1961), the Anti-Terrorism Act (18 U.S.C. 2333), the Torture Victims Protection Act (28 U.S.C. 1350 Note), and traditional actions such as wrongful death, false imprisonment, assault, intentional infliction of emotional distress, and negligence.[48] And the United States is not the only country to permit suits based upon the law of nations. Belgium, for example, has legislation permitting suits for "Grave Breaches on International Humanitarian Law."

§ 5.4 Subject Matter Jurisdiction, Extraterritorial Jurisdiction

Subject matter jurisdiction is another decidedly American legal doctrine, though it has some foreign parallels. Subject matter jurisdiction concerns the nature, scope and jurisdiction (competence) of a court under the law being litigated. It is fundamentally focused on the power of nations to apply their law to persons and acts inside and beyond their territorial limits. U. S. statutes may express an intention to apply only to interstate commerce, and/or additionally to foreign commerce. Difficult questions of subject matter jurisdiction arise when no clear legislative intent is stated. A U.S. court may

---

[46] *Id. See* al Shimari v. CACI Premier Technology, 758 F.3d 516 (4th Cir. 2014) (allowing claims against a U.S. contractor for the Abu Ghraib prison in Iraq). Compare Balintulo v. Daimler AG, 727 F.3d 174 (2d Cir. 2013) (*Kiobel* bars suits for foreign conduct against U.S. corporations); Cardona v. Chiquita Brands Int'l, 760 F.3d 1185 (11th Cir. 2014) (*Kiobel* bars foreign conduct suits against U.S. corporations).

[47] 138 S.Ct. 1386 (2018).

[48] The ATCA and each of these examples of causes of action were grounds in Doe v. Unocal Corp., 110 F.Supp.2d 1294 (C.D.Cal.2000). The case was appealed, 395 F.3d 932 (9th Cir. 2002). After a majority of the 9th Circuit voted to have an en banc rehearing, and a few months after the Sosa decision, a settlement was reached.

avoid the issue of subject matter jurisdiction by refusing to hear the matter for *forum non conveniens* reasons. See Section 2.4.

The general rule fashioned by the Supreme Court is that a U.S. federal statute is to be applied to conduct only within United States territory, unless there is clear Congressional intent that it should apply to conduct abroad.[49] In other words, there is a presumption against "extraterritorial" subject matter jurisdiction. But there are statutes which do express such legislative intent. For example, Title VII of the Civil Rights Act of 1964, as amended in 1991, and the Americans with Disabilities Act of 1990, apply prohibitions against workplace discriminations extraterritorially to U.S. corporations operating abroad. Another example is the Securities Exchange Act of 1934, which has been be applied to international parties using U.S. security exchanges and/or engaging in security transactions in the United States. But in 2010 the Supreme Court held that Section 10 (b) of the 1934 Act does not apply, in most cases, extraterritorily.[50] This decision involved foreign plaintiffs, foreign defendants and securities traded on a foreign exchange. Congress subsequently amended the Act, applying a conduct and effects test, but only in SEC or DOJ public enforcement actions.[51]

Still another example is the extraterritorial enforcement of U.S. export controls over goods and technology, memorably by President Reagan against the building of the gas pipeline from the Soviet Union to Europe. Other trade-related laws are specifically and intentionally directed to extraterritorial conduct: The anti-boycott provisions of the Export Administration Act and the Foreign Corrupt Practices Act. The former provisions were enacted exclusively to address the Arab boycott of Israel; the latter to address what are referred to as "corrupt" payments made by U.S. persons and businesses to foreign officials. These two laws by their language *were* intended to correct cross-border issues, and they have been so applied for decades. See R. Folsom, *Principles of International Trade Law.*

The best example may be the Sherman (Antitrust) Act, which expressly states that it governs trade with foreign nations.[52] Although there was little foreign commerce when the Act was passed in 1890, and foreign commerce was not an issue in its debate, the

---

[49] *See* EEOC v. Arabian Am. Oil Co., 499 U.S. 244, 111 S.Ct. 1227, 113 L.Ed.2d 274 (1991). Accord, RJR Nabisco v. European Community, 136 S.Ct. 2090 (2016) (RICO statute does not apply extraterritorily). Compare Steele v. Bulova Watch Co., 344 U.S. 280 (1952) (Lanham Trademark Act construed to apply extraterritorily).

[50] Morrison v. National Australia Bank, 130 S.Ct. 2869 (2010) (Section 10(b) of the 1934 Act does not apply extraterritorially). Accord, City of Pontiac Policemen's & Firemen's Retirement System v. UBS AG, 752 F.3d 173 (2d Cir. 2014).

[51] "Dodd-Frank" Act, Title IX, Section 929P(b) (2010).

[52] 15 U.S.C.A. § 1.

Sherman Act has a substantial and controversial history of extraterritorial jurisdictional application. For that reason, the subject matter jurisdiction of the Sherman Act is covered below in its own section, along with the similarly controversial extraterritorial jurisdiction of European Union business competition law. See Sections 5.5 and 5.6. As noted below, the Sherman Act has generated numerous "blocking statutes" in countries hostile to U.S. extraterritorial subject matter jurisdiction. For the application of such statutes to international antitrust discovery, see Section 6.7.

§ 5.5 Extraterritorial U.S. Antitrust Jurisdiction, Blocking Statutes

The first federal antitrust statute was the Sherman Act of 1890. The early state statutes and the Sherman Act reflected a "populist" movement in United States society in the late 19th Century. This movement opposed the formation of large and economically powerful "trusts" by the captains of the American industrial revolution. Perhaps the most famous of all trusts was that put together by the Rockefellers to control the oil industry.

The Sherman Act contains two basic prohibitions. Section 1 prohibits every contract, combination or conspiracy in restraint of trade. Section 2 prohibits monopolization, attempts to monopolize, and combinations or conspiracies to monopolize. Both of these prohibitions extend to interstate commerce within the United States and, under Section 7 of the Sherman Act, to United States foreign commerce. Section 7 concerns the "extraterritorial" application of the Sherman Act to foreign enterprises and restraints of trade undertaken outside the limits of the United States which have "direct, substantial and reasonably foreseeable" effects on U.S. commerce. Extraterritorial U.S. antitrust jurisdiction has always been controversial and is discussed below.

Originally enacted as misdemeanors, the Sherman Act prohibitions have now become felony criminal offenses. Among the family of nations with antitrust-type laws, the United States is almost unique in criminally sanctioning anticompetitive behavior. Persons violating either Section 1 or Section 2 of the Sherman Act may be imprisoned up to three years or fined up to $350,000. Corporations held to violate those sections may be fined up to $10,000,000. In fact, criminal prosecutions under the Sherman Act are rare. Perhaps the most common kind of activity which is criminally prosecuted is bid-rigging on government contracts.

The Sherman Act also created a powerful private remedy, treble the actual damages suffered as a result of an antitrust violation. This remedy has been carried forward and is now found in Section 4 of the

Clayton Act. When combined with class action and *parens patriae* procedures before federal and state courts, and the constitutional right to a jury trial in civil litigation, treble damages is transformed into an incredibly powerful remedy. Private treble damages actions account for approximately 85 percent of all antitrust litigation. No other nation permits the bulk of its antitrust law enforcement to be accomplished by private parties.

In the United States, this result is rationalized as promoting the enforcement of extremely important, almost quasi-constitutional law. The Supreme Court has repeatedly referred to the Sherman Act as "the economic constitution of the United States" or the "Magna Carta of free enterprise." Private antitrust litigants are often said to function as "attorneys general" when seeking to obtain treble damages relief.

Extraterritorial U.S. Antitrust in Perspective

After some initial hesitation,[53] United States courts have long asserted the right to apply the Sherman Antitrust Act to foreign commerce intended to or affecting the United States market. Perhaps the most famous application of this approach was by Judge Learned Hand in the *Alcoa* case.[54] This decision is the origin of the "effects test" governing extraterritorial U.S. antitrust jurisdiction. It was affirmatively applied in *Alcoa* to a foreign cartel acting almost entirely outside the United States but with clear restraint upon U.S. imports. In some cases, this approach has been tempered to allow consideration and balancing of the interests of comity and foreign countries in the outcome.[55] This results in a kind of jurisdictional "rule of reason" and is supported by the American Law Institute's Third Restatement of Foreign Relations Law.[56]

In 1982, Congress amended the Sherman Act and the Federal Trade Commission Act by enacting the Foreign Trade Antitrust Improvements Act.[57] Section 402 of the Act added a new Section 6a to the Sherman Act, which states:

---

53 *See especially*, American Banana Co. v. United Fruit Co., 213 U.S. 347, 29 S.Ct. 511, 53 L.Ed. 826 (1909).

54 United States v. Aluminum Co. of America, 148 F.2d 416 (2d Cir. 1945).

55 *See especially*, Timberlane Lumber Co. v. Bank of America, 549 F.2d 597 (9th Cir. 1976); Mannington Mills, Inc. v. Congoleum Corp., 595 F.2d 1287 (3d Cir. 1979); Compare Laker Airways Ltd. v. Sabena, Belgian World Airlines, 731 F.2d 909 (D.C.Cir. 1984) and Uranium Antitrust Litigation, 617 F.2d 1248 (7th Cir. 1980) (jurisdictional rule of reason rejected).

56 Section 403 (1987).

57 Pub. L. No. 97–290, 96 Stat. 1233 (1982) (codified in scattered sections of 12 and 15 U.S.C.). The Foreign Trade Antitrust Improvements Act [hereinafter FTAIA] was part of the Export Trading Company Act. The Export Trading Company Act consists of four separate titles, each of which applies to a different type of activity.

This Act shall not apply to conduct involving trade or commerce (other than import trade or import commerce) with foreign nations unless—

(1) such conduct has direct, substantial, and reasonably foreseeable effect—

(A) on trade or commerce which is not trade or commerce with foreign nations, or on import trade or import commerce with foreign nations; or

(B) on export trade or export commerce with foreign nations, of a person engaged in such trade or commerce in the United States; and

(2) such effect gives rise to a claim under the provisions of this Act, other than this section.

If this Act applies to such conduct only because of the operation of paragraph (1)(B), then this Act shall apply to such conduct only for injury to export business in the United States.[58]

The FTAIA has been construed as not applying to criminal price-fixing prosecutions,[59] and more generally to federal antitrust enforcement actions.[60] The FTAIA makes it clear that the Sherman Act no longer applies to transactions the principal effects of which are felt in markets wholly outside the United States.[61] The Act accomplishes this by first laying down a "general rule placing *all* (non-import) activity involving foreign commerce outside the Sherman Act's reach."[62] Then, the FTAIA creates an exception to the general rule; that exception brings such conduct back within the Sherman Act's reach *provided that* the conduct *both* (i) sufficiently affects American commerce, *i.e.*, it has a "direct, substantial, and reasonable foreseeable effect" on American domestic, import or

---

Title IV, the Foreign Trade Antitrust Improvements Act of 1982, deals with the extraterritorial reach of the antitrust laws.

[58] 15 U.S.C. § 6a.

[59] United States v. Hui Hsiung, 758 F.3d 1074 (9th Cir. 2014).

[60] *See* Motorola Mobility LLC v. AU Optronics Corp., 2014 U.S. App. LEXIS 22408 (7th Cir. 2014).

[61] *See* F. Hoffmann-La Roche Ltd. v. Empagran S.A., 542 U.S. 155, 161, 124 S.Ct. 2359, 159 L.Ed.2d 226 (2004) ("The FTAIA seeks to make clear to American exporters (and to firms doing business abroad) that the Sherman Act does not prevent them from entering into business arrangements (say, joint-selling arrangements), however anticompetitive, as long as those arrangements adversely affect only foreign markets.") *See also* United States v. Anderson, 326 F.3d 1319, 1329, *reh'g, en banc, denied,* (11th Cir.), *cert. denied,* 540 U.S. 825, 124 S.Ct. 178, 157 L.Ed.2d 46 (2003) ("In 1982, Congress enacted the Foreign Trade Antitrust Improvements Act . . . to limit American courts' jurisdiction over international commerce to transactions that affect the American economy.").

[62] F. Hoffmann-La Roche Ltd. v. Empagran S.A., 542 U.S. 155, 162, 124 S.Ct. 2359, 159 L.Ed.2d 226 (2004) (emphasis in original).

(certain) export commerce, *and* (2) has an effect of a kind that antitrust law considers harmful, *i.e.*, the "effect" must "give ris[e] to a [Sherman Act] claim.[63]

The extraterritorial reach of the antitrust laws was addressed by the U.S. Supreme Court in a divided decision in *Hartford Fire Insurance Co. v. California*.[64] The majority opted for an extraterritorial application unless there was a "true conflict." What a true conflict means was left to future debate, but it appeared to mean that the Sherman Act would be applied unless the foreign law required the American party to act in a manner which is in violation of U.S. law, or compliance with the laws of both nations is impossible. The case raises doubt about the status of interest balancing in any situation where U.S. laws are applied extraterritorially and create a conflict.[65] The Circuit Courts have been divided on the impact of *Hartford Fire* on comity analysis. Predictably, the Ninth Circuit has resisted abandonment of its *Timberlane* approach.[66] The Second Circuit, on the other hand, has fully embraced the true conflict doctrine.[67] Most courts and commentators see comity as "more an aspiration than a fixed rule" after *Hartford Fire*.[68]

Principles of comity significantly influenced the Supreme Court's decision in the *Empagran* decision[69] which held that the FTAIA did not permit a plaintiff injured by independent foreign effects of conduct occurring in foreign commerce to sue under the Sherman Act. One basis for its decision was that in construing the FTAIA, deemed ambiguous, the Court said it must "avoid unreasonable interference with the sovereign authority of other

---

63 542 U.S. at 162 (emphasis in original). Whether the FTAIA imposes substantive or merely jurisdictional bars has been much debated. *See* Animal Science Products v. China Minerals Corp., 654 F.3d 462 (3d Cir. 2011); Minn-Chem Inc. v. Agrium Inc., 683 F.3d 845 (7th Cir. en banc 2012) (FTAIA relates to the merits of the claim, not subject matter jurisdiction, and is governed by FRCP 12(b)(6) not FRCP 12(b)(1)).

64 509 U.S. 764, 113 S.Ct. 2891, 125 L.Ed.2d 612 (1993).

65 For a debate regarding the meaning of the decision, *see* Andreas F. Lowenfeld, Conflict, Balancing of Interests, and the Exercise of Jurisdiction to Prescribe: Reflections on the Insurance Antitrust Case, 89 Am.J. Int'l L. 42 (1995); Phillip R. Trimble, The Supreme Court and International Law: The Demise of Restatement Section 403, 89 Am.J.Int'l L. 53 (1995); Larry Kramer, Extraterritorial Application of American Law after the Insurance Antitrust Case: a Reply to Professors Lowenfeld and Trimble, 89 Am.J.Int'l L. 750 (1995).

66 Metro Industries, Inc. v. Sammi Corp., 82 F.3d 839 (9th Cir. 1996), *cert. denied*, 519 U.S. 868, 117 S.Ct. 181, 136 L.Ed.2d 120 (1996).

67 In re Maxwell Communication Corp., 93 F.3d 1036 (2d Cir. 1996).

68 United States v. Nippon Paper Indus. Co., Ltd., 109 F.3d 1 (1st Cir. 1997), *cert. denied*, 522 U.S. 1044, 118 S.Ct. 685, 139 L.Ed.2d 632 (1998) (*criminal* extraterritorial antitrust jurisdiction affirmed).

69 F. Hoffman-La Roche Ltd. v. Empagran S.A., 542 U.S. 155, 124 S.Ct. 2359, 159 L.Ed.2d 226 (2004).

nations" and consider international disagreements with U.S. antitrust polices and remedies.[70]

Some limits on the extraterritorial reach of the Sherman Act are created by the act of state doctrine, the Foreign Sovereign Immunities Act and the foreign sovereign compulsion (they forced me to do it) defense.[71] But in the main, United States antitrust law has been applied to foreigners and overseas activities with a zeal sometimes approaching religious fervor. Amendments to the Sherman Act in 1984 stress the "direct, substantial and reasonably foreseeable" nature of effects on United States foreign commerce as a prerequisite to antitrust jurisdiction.

Nevertheless, the potential for conflict in this field is enormous. For example, a multinational enterprise (MNE) headquartered in the U.S. but doing business in England could be constrained by United States antitrust law from fixing prices, yet permitted by EU competition law to do exactly that. Assuming that the price fixing in question has effects in both markets, what course of action is to be followed? There is no easy answer. When the MNE is located within a country other than one of the Member States of the EU or the United States, but engages in activity having effects within those markets, the problem potential of extraterritoriality may be even more acute. See Section 5.5. Reconciling a conflict of antitrust laws applied extraterritorially by these two jurisdictions could become a flashpoint in international business transactions.

Blocking Statutes

Extraterritoriality is a matter of balance. The executive, legislative, and judicial branches of government in the United States have reached out extraterritorially in the law of admiralty, antitrust, crime, labor, securities regulation, taxation, torts, trademarks and wildlife management. A balance drawn wrongly by one nation invites retaliatory action by others. In the case of antitrust judgments emanating from courts in the United States, most notably the

---

[70] 542 U.S. at 164. *See* Motorola Mobility LLC v. AU Optronics Corp., 2014 U.S. App. LEXIS 22408 (7th Cir. 2014) (damages claims via foreign subsidiaries precluded).

[71] For coverage of the act of state doctrine and the FSIA, see Chapter 7. Foreign sovereign compulsion as an antitrust defense has been recognized in a few U.S. court decisions, but not yet affirmed by the U.S. Supreme Court. *See* Matsushita Electric Industries v. Zenith Radio Corp., 475 U.S. 574 (1986); Hartford Fire Insurance v. California, 509 U.S. 764, 113 S.Ct. 2891, 125 L.Ed.2d 612 (1993).

Even when there are effects in the U.S.A., extraterritorial antitrust conspiracies are not actionable unless those effects "give rise" to the plaintiff's antitrust claim. No subject matter jurisdiction exists. *See* Den Norske Stats Oljeselskap As v. HeereMac Vof, 241 F.3d 420 (5th Cir. 2001), *cert. denied*, 534 U.S. 1127, 122 S.Ct. 1059, 151 L.Ed.2d 967 (2002), *reh'g denied*, 535 U.S. 1012, 122 S.Ct. 1597, 152 L.Ed.2d 512 (2002) (Norwegian oil company claims fail).

"Uranium Cartel" treble damages litigation of the late 1970s,[72] many nations consider that the balance has been wrongly drawn. At least nine nations (Australia, Canada, France, Germany, Netherlands, New Zealand, Philippines, South Africa and the United Kingdom) have taken retaliatory action by enacting "blocking statutes." In addition, the 41 Commonwealth nations have resolved general support for a position similar to that of the United Kingdom.

The United Kingdom blocking statute is the Protection of Trading Interests Act of 1980, reproduced in Section 5.8. This Act (without specifying United States antitrust law) makes it difficult to depose witnesses, obtain documents or enforce multiple liability judgments extraterritorially in the U.K. Violation of the 1980 Act may result in criminal penalties. Furthermore, under the "clawback" provision of the Act, parties with outstanding multiple liabilities in foreign jurisdictions (e.g., U.S. treble damages defendants) may recoup the punitive element of such awards in Britain against assets of the successful plaintiff. The British Act invites other nations to adopt clawback provisions by offering clawback reciprocity. United States attorneys confronted with a blocking statute need to understand that multiple liability judgments combined with contingency fee arrangements are virtually unknown elsewhere.

The extensive array of pre-trial discovery mechanisms allowed in U.S. civil litigation rarely, if ever, have a counterpart in foreign law. Discovery subpoenas originating in United States litigation often "shock" many foreign defendants. And the U.S. Supreme Court has ruled that use of letters rogatory under the Hague Convention is not obligatory.[73] It is the blocking of discovery that potentially most threatens the extraterritorial application of United States laws, especially antitrust. See Chapter 6. Since U.S. courts may sanction parties who in bad faith fail to respond to discovery requests and foreign defendants requesting help from their home governments under blocking statutes are especially at risk. Particularly if there is little or no risk of foreign blocking statutes actually being enforced,[74] U.S. discovery court orders and sanctions are likely to apply. On the other hand, good faith efforts to modify or work around discovery blockades may favor foreign defendants. Such defendants are often caught in a "no win" situation. Either way they will be penalized.

---

[72] *See* Uranium Antitrust Litigation (Westinghouse Electric Corp. v. Rio Algom Limited), 617 F.2d 1248 (7th Cir. 1980).

[73] Société Nationale Industrielle Aérospatiale v. U.S. District Court, 482 U.S. 522, 107 S.Ct. 2542, 96 L.Ed.2d 461 (1987).

[74] *See* Re Air Cargo Shipping Services Antitrust Litigation, 2014 WL 7882100 (E.D.N.Y.).

The reasons advanced to support an extraterritorial application of United States antitrust laws are founded on the idea that some extraterritorial extension is necessary to prevent their circumvention by multinational corporations which have the business sagacity to ensure that anticompetitive transactions are consummated beyond the territorial borders of the United States. An extraterritorial extension of antitrust laws can also help to ensure that the U.S. consumer receives the benefit of competing imports, which in turn may spur complacent domestic industries. The effect of foreign auto imports on the car manufacturers in the United States may be cited as an example. In an increasingly internationalized world, extraterritorial antitrust may merely reflect economic reality.

On the other hand, the British argue that extraterritoriality permits the United States to unjustifiably "mold the international economic and trading world to its own image." In particular, the "effects test" doctrine creates legal uncertainty for international traders, and U.S. courts pay little attention to the competing policies (interests) of other concerned governments. As the House of Lords has stated: "It is axiomatic that in anti-trust matters the policy of one state may be to defend what it is the policy of another state to attack."[75] The British also argue, not without some support, that customary international law does not permit extraterritorial application of national laws. In making this argument, the British have a convenient way of forgetting about the extraterritorial scope of Articles 101 and 102, which are now part of their law. See Section 5.6.

Moreover, in a curious reversal of roles illustrating the extremes of the debate, the British government applied the Protection of Trading Interests Act to block the pursuit of treble damages in U.S. courts by the liquidator of Laker Airway against British Airways and other defendants. A House of Lords decision reversed this ban, but retained government restrictions on discovery related to the case.[76] In sequel litigation, British banks successfully obtained an injunction against the liquidator's pursuit of U.S. antitrust remedies.[77] See Chapter 6.

§ 5.6 Extraterritorial EU Antitrust Jurisdiction

In Europe, the field of law that Americans call "antitrust" is generally referred to as "competition law." Although some nations in Europe have active competition law policies (notably Britain and

---

[75] Rio Tinto Zinc Corp. v. Westinghouse Electric Corp., 2 W.L.R. 81 (1978).

[76] British Airways Board v. Laker Airways, 3 W.L.R. 413 (1984).

[77] Midland Bank v. Laker Airways Ltd., 1 Q.B. 689 (Ct App. 1986).

Germany), none surpass the embracement of competition as a public good by the European Union.

Articles 101 and 102—Restraints of Trade and Abuses of Dominant Positions

Article 101(1) of the Treaty on the Functioning of the European Union (TFEU) deals with concerted business practices, business agreements and trade association decisions. When they have the potential to affect trade between member states *and* have the object or effect of preventing, restricting or distorting competition *within* Europe, such business activities are deemed incompatible with the Common Market and are prohibited. The focus of Article 101(1) is thus on cartels. By way of example, Article 101(1) lists certain prohibited activities:

(1) The fixing of prices or trading conditions;

(2) The limitation of production, markets, technical development or investment;

(3) The sharing of markets or sources of supply;

(4) The application of unequal terms to equivalent transactions, creating competitive disadvantages; and

(5) The conditioning of a contract on the acceptance of commercially unrelated additional supplies.

Article 101(2) voids agreements and decisions (or severable parts thereof) prohibited by Article 101(1). Thus the prohibitions of Article 101(1) against anticompetitive activity are absolute and immediately effective under 101(2) without prior judicial or administrative action. The open-ended text of 101(1) gives considerable leeway for interpretation and enforcement purposes. It has, for example, been interpreted to cover nonbinding "gentlemen's agreements."[78] Trade association "recommendations" influencing competition are caught.[79] It also generates considerable uncertainty as to the validity of many business agreements, since full market analyses of their competitive and trade impact are often required.

Article 102 of the Treaty on the Functioning of the European Union (TFEU) prohibits abuses by one or more undertakings of a dominant position within a substantial part of the Common Market insofar as the abuses may affect trade between member states. The existence of a dominant position is not prohibited by European law. Only its abuse is proscribed.

---

78 ACF Chemiefarma v. Commission (1970) Eur.Comm.Rep. 661.

79 Re ANSEAU-NAVEWA (1983) Eur.Comm.Rep. 3369.

Article 102 proceeds to list certain examples of what constitute abuses by dominant enterprises:

(1) The imposition of unfair prices or other trading conditions;

(2) The limitation of production, markets or technical development which prejudices consumers;

(3) The application of dissimilar conditions to equivalent transactions, thereby engendering competitive disadvantages; and

(4) The subjection of contracts to commercially unrelated supplementary obligations.

*The Extraterritorial Reach of Articles **101** and **102***

There is a question about the extent to which the competition rules of Europe extend to activity anywhere in the world, including activity occurring entirely or partly within the territorial limits of the United States, Mexico or Canada. Decisions by the Commission and the Court of Justice suggest that the territorial reach of Articles 101 and 102 is expanding and may extend to almost any international business transaction.

For an agreement to be incompatible with the Common Market and prohibited under Article 101(1), it must be "likely to affect trade between Member States" and have the object or effect of impairing "competition within the Common Market." Taken together, these requirements amount to an "effects test" for extraterritorial application of Article 101. This test is similar to that which operates under the Sherman Act of the United States. See Section 5.4.

The Court has repeatedly held that the fact that one of the parties to an agreement is domiciled in a third country does not preclude the applicability of Article 101(1). Swiss and British chemical companies, for example, argued that the Commission was not competent to impose competition law fines for acts committed in Switzerland and Britain (before joining the EU) by enterprises domiciled outside its scope even if the acts had effects within the Common Market.[80] Nevertheless, the Court held those companies in violation of Article 101 because they owned subsidiary companies within the Union and controlled their behavior. The foreign parent and its subsidiaries were treated as a "single enterprise" for purposes of service of process, judgment, and collection of fines and penalties. In doing so, the Court observed that the fact that a subsidiary

[80] *See* ICI v. Commission (1972) Eur.Comm.Rep. 619.

company has its own legal personality does not rule out the possibility that its conduct is attributable to the parent company.

The Court has extended its reasoning to the extraterritorial application of Article 102. A United States parent company, for example, was held potentially liable for acquisitions by its subsidiary which affected market conditions within the Common Market.[81] In another decision, the Court held that a Maryland company's refusal to sell its product to a competitor of its affiliate company was a result of united "single enterprise" action.[82] It proceeded to state that extraterritorial conduct merely having "repercussions on competitive structures" in the Common Market fell within the parameters of Article 102. The Court ordered Commercial Solvents, through its Italian affiliate, to supply the competitor at reasonable prices.

In 1988, the Court of Justice widened the extraterritorial reach of Article 101 in a case where wood pulp producers from the U.S., Canada, Sweden and Finland were fined for price fixing activities affecting Union trade and competition. These firms did not have substantial operations within Common Market; they were primarily exporters to it. This decision's utilization of a place of implementation "effects test" is quite similar to that used under the Sherman Act.[83] And the reliance by the U.S. exporters upon a traditional Webb-Pomerene export cartel exemption from United States antitrust law carried no weight in European law. The Court has also affirmed the extraterritorial reach of Articles 101 and 102 to airfares in and out of Europe.[84] The EU Mergers regulation clearly applies to firms located outside the Common Market.

§ 5.7 United States-EU Antitrust Cooperation

In 1991 the European Community (of which Britain is still a member) and the United States reached an antitrust cooperation agreement. This accord commits the parties to notify each other of imminent enforcement action, to share relevant information and consult on potential policy changes. It was prominently used in 1994 to jointly settle charges of restrictive trade practices with the Microsoft Corporation. An innovative feature is the inclusion of "comity" principles, each side promising to take the other's interests into account when considering antitrust prosecutions. Since the Commission has traditionally permitted U.S. lawyers to appear

---

81 *See* Europemballage Corp. and Continental Can Co., Inc. v. Commission (1973) Eur.Comm.Rep. 215.

82 *See* Commercial Solvents Corp. v. Commission (1974) Eur.Comm.Rep. 223.

83 Woodpulp Producers v. Commission (1988) Eur.Comm.Rep. 5193.

84 Ahmed Saeed Flugreisen v. Zentrale zur Bekämpfung unlauteren Wettbewerbs (1989) Eur.Comm.Rep. 838.

before it on competition law matters, the FTC announced on the same day as the signing of the antitrust cooperation agreement that European lawyers would be permitted to appear before it on a reciprocal basis.

The agreement has had a significant effect on mergers of firms doing business in North America and Europe. Each side has agreed to notify and consult with the other regarding antitrust matters, including mergers and acquisitions, that "may affect important interests." In its first six months of operation, about 45 notifications were exchanged between the Commission, the U.S. Federal Trade Commission, and the Antitrust Division of the U.S. Justice Department. A large portion of these notifications concerned international mergers and acquisitions. Since both Europe and the U.S. have pre-merger notification systems, the exchange of such information has increased rapidly. In the first year after the cooperation agreement, U.S. antitrust enforcers sent 37 such notifications to the European Commission and received 15 in return. About 20 percent of all the mergers reviewed by the Commission under its competition law were simultaneously being reviewed by U.S. antitrust authorities.

In April of 1997 the Justice Department made its first "positive comity" request to the European Commission under the U.S.-E.U. Antitrust Cooperation Agreement. The Justice Department has asked the Commission to investigate alleged anticompetitive conduct by European airlines regarding U.S.-based airline computer reservation systems (CRS). In 1998, the European Union and the United States signed a "Positive Comity Agreement." This agreement reinforces the 1991 Cooperation Agreement by establishing procedures for positive comity requests and responses, including parallel investigations such as against Microsoft. The Agreement can be found at http://www.usdoj.gov/.

In the more recent round of public prosecutions of Microsoft focused on Windows as a monopoly, the United States settlement reached in 2001 is less demanding than the Commission abuse of a dominant position judgment of 2004, which requires an unbundling of media playback capabilities. This example reaffirms that transatlantic antitrust "cooperation" need not necessarily result in similar outcomes. In 2007, the Court of First Instance (now the General Court) broadly confirmed the Commission's 2004 decision. Shortly thereafter, Microsoft settled the prosecution by altering its operating systems' licensing arrangements to favor "open source" software developers (e.g., Linux). Prior to settlement, Microsoft had been fined, including daily noncompliance penalties, in excess of 2 billion EUROs. By 2008, the Commission was investigating

Microsoft's bundling of its web browser with Windows, and the compatibility of its Office software with rival programs. A quick settlement "unbundled" web browsers on Windows . . . creating a dozen or more choices. But, in 2013, the Commission fined Microsoft over 500 million Euros for breach of this settlement agreement.

Other U.S. technology firms are also under the EU competition law microscope: Qualcomm, Intel, Google and Apple included. In 2009, the Commission fined Intel a massive 1.06 billion EUROs for abusing its dominant position in microprocessors for PCs. Intel's price discounts and loyalty rebates are the center of this judgment. In 2017, Facebook paid a 110 million Euro fine for providing "misinformation" in the review of its acquisition of WhatsApp. In the same year, Google set a record by paying a 2.42 *billion* Euro fine for abusing its dominance (90% market share) in Internet shopping searches by favoring its own price-comparison results. Microsoft was one of the complaining parties.

§ 5.8 The U.K. Protection of Trading Interests Act ("Blocking Statute") (1980)

Ch. 11.

An Act to provide protection from requirements, prohibitions and judgments imposed or given under the laws of countries outside the United Kingdom and affecting the trading or other interests of persons in the United Kingdom

1. Overseas Measures Affecting United Kingdom Trading Interests

(1) If it appears to the Secretary of State—

(a) that measures have been or are proposed to be taken by or under the law of any overseas country for regulating or controlling international trade; and

(b) that those measures, in so far as they apply or would apply to things done or to be done outside the territorial jurisdiction of that country by persons carrying on business in the United Kingdom, are damaging or threaten to damage the trading interests of the United Kingdom,

the Secretary of State may by order direct that this section shall apply to those measures either generally or in their application to such cases as may be specified in the order.

(2) The Secretary of State may by order make provision for requiring, or enabling the Secretary of State to require, a person in the United Kingdom who carries on business there to give notice to the Secretary of State of any requirement or prohibition imposed or

threatened to be imposed on that person pursuant to any measures in so far as this section applies to them by virtue of an order under subsection (I) above.

(3) The Secretary of State may give to any person in the United Kingdom who carries on business there such directions for prohibiting compliance with any such requirement or prohibition as aforesaid as he considers appropriate for avoiding damage to the trading interests of the United Kingdom.

(4) The power of the Secretary of State to make orders under subsection (I) or (2) above shall be exercisable by statutory instrument subject to annulment in pursuance of a resolution of either House of Parliament.

(5) Directions under subsection (3) above may be either general or special and may prohibit compliance with any requirement or prohibition either absolutely or in such cases or subject to such conditions as to consent or otherwise as may be specified in the directions; and general directions under that subsection shall be published in such manner as appears to the Secretary of State to be appropriate.

(6) In this section "trade" includes any activity carried on in the course of a business of any description and "trading interests" shall be construed accordingly.

2. Documents and Information Required by Overseas Courts and Authorities

(1) If it appears to the Secretary of State—

(a) that a requirement has been or may be imposed on a person or persons in the United Kingdom to produce to any court, tribunal or authority of an overseas country any commercial document which is not within the territorial jurisdiction of that country or to furnish any commercial information to any such court, tribunal or authority; or

(b) that any such authority has imposed or may impose a requirement on a person or persons in the United Kingdom to publish any such document or information,

the Secretary of State may, if it appears to him that the requirement is inadmissible by virtue of subsection (2) or (3) below, give directions for prohibiting compliance with the requirement.

(2) A requirement such as is mentioned in subsection (I)(a) or (b) above is inadmissible—

(a) if it infringes the jurisdiction of the United Kingdom or is otherwise prejudicial to the sovereignty of the United Kingdom; or

(b) if compliance with the requirement would be prejudicial to the security of the United Kingdom or to the relations of the government of the United Kingdom with the government of any other country.

(3) A requirement such as is mentioned in subsection (I)(a) above is also inadmissible—

(a) if it is made otherwise than for the purposes of civil or criminal proceedings which have been instituted in the overseas country; or

(b) if it requires a person to state what documents relevant to any such proceedings are or have been in his possession, custody or power or to produce for the purposes of any such proceedings any documents other than particular documents specified in the requirement.

(4) Directions under subsection (I) above may be either general or special and may prohibit compliance with any requirement either absolutely or in such cases or subject to such conditions as to consent or otherwise as may be specified in the directions; and general directions under that subsection shall be published in such manner as appears to the Secretary of State to be appropriate.

(5) For the purposes of this section the making of a request or demand shall be treated as the imposition of a requirement if it is made in circumstances in which a requirement to the same effect could be or could have been imposed; and

(a) any request or demand for the supply of a document or information which, pursuant to the requirement of any court, tribunal or authority of an overseas country, is addressed to a person in the United Kingdom; or

(b) any requirement imposed by such a court, tribunal or authority to produce or furnish any document or information to a person specified in the requirement,

shall be treated as a requirement to produce or furnish that document or information to that court, tribunal or authority.

(6) In this section "commercial document" and "commercial information" mean respectively a document or information relating to a business of any description and "document" includes any record or device by means of which material is recorded or stored.

3. Offences Under ss. 1 and 2

(1) Subject to subsection (2) below, any person who without reasonable excuse fails to comply with any requirement imposed under subsection (2) of section I above or knowingly contravenes any directions given under subsection (3) of that section or section 2(I) above shall be guilty of an offence and liable—

(a) on conviction on indictment, to a fine;

(b) on summary conviction, to a fine not exceeding the statutory maximum.

(2) A person who is neither a citizen of the United Kingdom and Colonies nor a body corporate incorporated in the United Kingdom shall not be guilty of an offence under subsection (I) above by reason of anything done or omitted outside the United Kingdom in contravention of directions under section I(3) or 2(I) above.

(3) No proceedings for an offence under subsection (I) above shall be instituted in England, Wales or Northern Ireland except by the Secretary of State or with the consent of the Attorney General or, as the case may be, the Attorney General for Northern Ireland.

(4) Proceedings against any person for an offence under this section may be taken before the appropriate court in the United Kingdom having jurisdiction in the place where that person is for the time being.

* * *

4. Restriction of Evidence (Proceedings in Other Jurisdictions) Act 1975

A court in the United Kingdom shall not make an order under section 2 of the Evidence (Proceedings in Other Jurisdictions) Act 1975 for giving effect to a request issued by or on behalf of a court or tribunal of an overseas country if it is shown that the request infringes the jurisdiction of the United Kingdom or is otherwise prejudicial to the sovereignty of the United Kingdom; and a certificate signed by or on behalf of the Secretary of State to the effect that it infringes that jurisdiction or is so prejudicial shall be conclusive evidence of that fact.

5. Restriction on Enforcement of Certain Overseas Judgments

(1) A judgment to which this section applies shall not be registered under Part II of the Administration of Justice Act 1920 or Part I of the Foreign Judgments (Reciprocal Enforcement) Act 1933 and no

court in the United Kingdom shall entertain proceedings at common law for the recovery of any sum payable under such a judgment.

(2) This section applies to any judgment given by a court of an overseas country, being—

(a) a judgment for multiple damages within the meaning of subsection (3) below;

(b) a judgment based on a provision or rule of law specified or described in an order under subsection (4) below and given after the coming into force of the order; or

(c) a judgment on a claim for contribution in respect of damages awarded by a judgment falling within paragraph (a) or (b) above.

(3) In subsection (2)(*a*) above a judgment for multiple damages means a judgment for an amount arrived at by doubling, trebling or otherwise multiplying a sum assessed as compensation for the loss or damage sustained by the person in whose favour the judgment is given.

(4) The Secretary of State may for the purposes of subsection (2)(*b*) above make an order in respect of any provision or rule of law which appears to him to be concerned with the prohibition or regulation of agreements, arrangements or practices designed to restrain, distort or restrict competition in the carrying on of business of any description or to be otherwise concerned with the promotion of such competition as aforesaid.

(5) The power of the Secretary of State to make orders under subsection (4) above shall be exercisable by statutory instrument subject to annulment in pursuance of a resolution of either House of Parliament.

(6) Subsection (2)(*a*) above applies to a judgment given before the date of the passing of this Act as well as to a judgment given on or after that date but this section does not affect any judgment which has been registered before that date under the provisions mentioned in subsection (I) above or in respect of which such proceedings as are there mentioned have been finally determined before that date.

6. Recovery of Awards of Multiple Damages

(1) This section applies where a court of an overseas country has given a judgment for multiple damages within the meaning of section 5(3) above against—

(a) a citizen of the United Kingdom and Colonies; or

(b) a body corporate incorporated in the United Kingdom or in a territory outside the United Kingdom for whose international relations Her Majesty's Government in the United Kingdom are responsible; or

(c) a person carrying on business in the United Kingdom,

(in this section referred to as a "qualifying defendant") and an amount on account of the damages has been paid by the qualifying defendant either to the party in whose favour the judgment was given or to another party who is entitled as against the qualifying defendant to contribution in respect of the damages.

(2) Subject to subsections (3) and (4) below, the qualifying defendant shall be entitled to recover from the party in whose favour the judgment was given so much of the amount referred to in subsection (I) above as exceeds the part attributable to compensation; and that part shall be taken to be such part of the amount as bears to the whole of it the same proportion as the sum assessed by the court that gave the judgment as compensation for the loss or damage sustained by that party bears to the whole of the damages awarded to that party.

(3) Subsection (2) above does not apply where the qualifying defendant is an individual who was ordinarily resident in the overseas country at the time when the proceedings in which the judgment was given were instituted or a body corporate which had its principal place of business there at that time.

(4) Subsection (2) above does not apply where the qualifying defendant carried on business in the overseas country and the proceedings in which the judgment was given were concerned with activities exclusively carried on in that country.

(5) A court in the United Kingdom may entertain proceedings on a claim under this section notwithstanding that the person against whom the proceedings are brought is not within the jurisdiction of the court.

(6) The reference in subsection (I) above to an amount paid by the qualifying defendant includes a reference to an amount obtained by execution against his property or against the property of a company which (directly or indirectly) is wholly owned by him; and references in that subsection and subsection (2) above to the party in whose favour the judgment was given or to a party entitled to contribution include references to any person in whom the rights of any such party have become vested by succession or assignment or otherwise.

(7) This section shall, with the necessary modifications, apply also in relation to any order which is made by a tribunal or authority of an overseas country and would, if that tribunal or authority were a court, be a judgment for multiple damages within the meaning of section 5(3) above.

(8) This section does not apply to any judgment given or order made before the passing of this Act.

7. Enforcement of Overseas Judgment under Provision Corresponding to s. 6

(1) If it appears to Her Majesty that the law of an overseas country provides or will provide for the enforcement in that country of judgments given under section 6 above, Her Majesty may by Order in Council provide for the enforcement in the United Kingdom of judgments given under any provision of the law of that country corresponding to that section.

(2) An Order under this section may apply, with or without modification, any of the provisions of the Foreign Judgments (Reciprocal Enforcement) Act 1933.

Chapter 6

INTERNATIONAL BUSINESS LITIGATION: PROCEDURE

Table of Sections

Procedure, both pre-trial and during trial, is a critical element in international business litigation. Procedural issues are generally determined by the law of the forum, though the U.S. Supreme Court has ruled that quantification of damages is not a procedural issue, and therefore is governed by the substantive law controlling the claim.[1] Like jurisdiction, U.S. law on civil procedure is not generally in the mainstream of global practice. The wide scope and extraterritorial reach of U.S. pre-trial discovery, along with anti-suit injunctions attempting to bar litigation outside the United States, are two prime examples. In contrast, U.S. participation in the Hague Convention on Service Abroad and the Inter-American Convention on Letters Rogatory, has brought a modicum of harmony to service of process law.

1 Gasperini v. Center for Humanities Inc., 518 U.S. 415 (1996).

To illustrate international business litigation procedural issues, Sections 6.5, 6.6, 6.7 and 6.8 focus in detail on U.S. and EU antitrust litigation. The opening four Sections are of general applicability, and I am indebted to Professor Michael Gordon of Florida for his original work on them.

§ 6.1 Service of Process, The Hague and Inter-American Service Conventions

The law that governs service of process in the various U.S. states may be different, but resonate with similar characteristics. For domestic purposes, process is usually effective when actually given to the defendant. Once again, due process constitutional law requirements matter. Service of process must provide adequate informed notice of the lawsuit, the parties involved and the right to be heard. In the absence knowing the whereabouts of defendants after exercising due diligence, the Supreme Court has held that published notice suffices.[2] Under such circumstances, U.S. state laws tend to focus on substituted service by such means as a registered letter. In contrast, other nations allow service by posting a notice on the courthouse door, or by service on a willing neighbor or a public official (e.g., *notification au parquet* in France). Fortunately, quite a few nations, including the United States, have adopted what is known as The Hague Service Convention. This Convention attempts to articulate acceptable rules for international service of process.

Service of process will be ineffective if it is not in conformance with the law of the forum. There may be options, but whichever method is used must conform. U.S. plaintiffs pursuing litigation in the United States against foreign defendants too often attempt to use shortcuts that ultimately prove to be the plaintiff's downfall. For example the U.S. plaintiff may not adequately provide translations of the papers required abroad for a recognized claim. The U.S. concept of "tag" jurisdiction obtained by the U.S. party, perhaps by serving the foreign party while in a New York City airport awaiting the final leg on a flight to Europe from Brazil, will almost never be recognized abroad despite its approval by the U.S. Supreme Court.[3] The fortuities perceived to be gained by the U.S. party in tracking down the defendant during a layover in the airport may not seem so clever when an attempt is made to enforce a resulting judgment abroad. And luring foreign parties or their representatives in bad faith to the United States for mediation or a settlement conference

---

2 Mullane v. Central Hanover Bank & Trust, 339 U.S. 306 (1950).

3 Burnham v. Superior Court, 495 U.S. 604 (1990). Accord, Kadic v. Karadzic, 70 F.3d 232 (2d Cir. 1995).

that amounts to a mere artifice for purposes of service of process will not be tolerated.[4]

The party seeking service may have various options for serving the defendants in the home forum or elsewhere. Plaintiff's lawyers must be cautious when deciding to minimize costs by using such methods as substituted or constructive service. The cost of service abroad may be considerably higher than in the United States, especially if documents have to be translated. Service elsewhere may mean service in a foreign nation. If so, there will be rules of the foreign forum for service of process that may be very different in comparison to those of a U.S. forum. In Germany and Switzerland, for example, service by return receipt mail is insufficient. Service might be done in person, perhaps via local counsel or a process-server, but even that may be prohibited (it is a crime in Switzerland). Service by mail or substituted service of an investigatory subpoena by a U.S. administrative agency may be invalidated as a breach of customary international law.[5] There are no significant U.S. restrictions on service of foreign process in the United States, which can be accomplished with or without court assistance, subject of course to The Hague Convention when applicable, and attention to U.S. rules for enforcing foreign judgments. See Chapter 8.

Additionally, there may be international rules that are applicable. For example, European Union Regulation 1393/2007 establishes common service of process rules among its member states. Attorneys must determine the best method of providing effective service on the defendants, wherever they may be. If the defendants have assets in the United States, greater liberties might be taken than if assets are only available abroad. If the latter, short-cutting plaintiffs run the risk they may not be able to have a judgment obtained against a foreign party enforced in the defendant's national courts, or in the courts of *any* other nation.

Rule 4 of the Federal Rules of Civil Procedure outlines methods of service and procedural requirements to establish jurisdiction over foreign parties to litigation in U.S. courts. Rule 4(d) permits waivers of service, with the cost of service shifted to non-waiving defendants located in the United States, but not those located outside the USA. Rule 4(k) authorizes for federal question jurisdiction the use of federal long-arm jurisdiction where the defendants cannot be served under any state law, but can be constitutionally subjected to

---

4 Citrexsa SA v. Landsman, 528 So.2d 517 (Fla. Dist. Ct. App. 1988).

5 FTC v. SGPM, 636 F.2d 1300 (D.C.Cir. 1980); Commodity Futures Trading Comm. v. Nahas, 738 F.2d 487 (D.C.Cir. 1984); Rio Properties Inc. v. Rio International Interlink, 284 F.3d 1007 (9th Cir. 2002) (service by email). Compare Mapping Your Future Services Ltd., 266 F.R.D. 305 (D.S.D. 2009).

jurisdiction of the federal courts. For diversity based jurisdiction, Rules 4(e) and (h) provide that state law service rules apply to service upon individuals and corporations, whether foreign or domestic, within a judicial district of the United States.

Rule 4(f) provides alternative means of service upon individuals in a foreign country, including the Hague or other Conventions, or if no international agreement is applicable, by letters rogatory (a request by a court for assistance from a foreign court in achieving service), the service rules of the country where the defendant is found and, *unless prohibited by that country*, personal delivery and signed receipt mail. Rule 4(f)(3) allows service "by other means not prohibited by international agreements, as the court orders." Under this provision, for example, service by email on a foreign Internet company has been authorized.[6] When plaintiffs sought to serve OPEC in Austria by return receipt mail without its consent, this was determined to violate Austrian law and dismissal of the complaint for insufficient service was ordered.[7]

Effective use of the Conventions does not eliminate the need to acquire valid personal jurisdiction over persons "doing business" in the United States, including adherence to state "long arm" jurisdiction requirements. See Section 5.2. Special service of process rules apply to foreign states and their entities under the Foreign Sovereign Immunities Act. See Section. 7.4. The U.S Department of State website details how to serve process in various foreign countries.

The Hague and Inter-American Conventions on Service Abroad

Service of Process abroad is effectively regulated by two conventions. The larger in scope is the Hague Convention on the Service Abroad of Judicial and Extrajudicial Documents (Hague Service Convention), reproduced in Section 6.9.[8] The second is the Inter-American Convention, reproduced in Section 6.10.[9] Rule 4(f) of the Federal Rules of Civil Procedure provides for the service of process abroad, requiring use of the treaties. If service is not available under treaty agreements, the Rule provides for alternative

---

6 *See* Rio Properties v. Rio Int'l Interlink, 284 F.3d 1007 (9th Cir. 2002). *See* FTC v. Pecon Software Ltd., 2013 WL 5288897 (S.D.N.Y. 2013) (permitting service on foreign defendants via Facebook messaging and email accounts).

7 Prewitt Enterprises v. OPEC, 353 F.3d 916 (11th Cir. 2003).

8 Hague Convention on the Service Abroad of Judicial and Extrajudicial Documents in Civil or Commercial Matters, done Nov. 15, 1965, 20 U.S.T. 362.

9 Inter-American Convention on Letters Rogatory, *done* Jan 30, 1975, *entered into force for the U.S.*, Aug. 27, 1988, S. Treaty Doc. 98–27, 98th Cong., 2d Sess. (1984); Additional Protocol to the Inter-American Convention on Letters Rogatory, *done* May 8, 1979, *entered into force for the U.S.*, Aug. 27, 1988, S. Treaty Doc. 98–27, 98th Cong., 2d Sess (1984).

means of service. Use of the treaty process should result in service acceptable to the foreign country, but use of the alternative means may not. When using alternative means, consideration must be given to the rules in the country where service is to be made. Ineffective service will make enforcement of a judgment very unlikely in a foreign nation, such as Japan.[10]

Service under the Hague Convention is available in some 70 participating countries, including such major nations as Belgium, Canada, China, France, Germany, Italy, Japan, Netherlands, Poland, Spain, Switzerland, the United Kingdom and the United States. Some participating countries have made special reservations which affect the method of service. The service is exclusive, stating in Art. 1 that the Convention "shall apply in all cases, in civil or commercial matters, where there is occasion to transmit a judicial or extrajudicial document for service abroad."[11] Service is made upon a "central authority" in the foreign nation, which subsequently transmits the documents to the proper location.

As with so many conventions, certain provisions become a major problem in applying the Convention. So it has been with Article 10 of The Hague Service Convention, which allows "sending" judicial documents by postal channels. Many Convention states (but not the United States or Japan) have made reservations or declarations prohibiting service by mail to be made within their nation. Thus there is some limited authority to send documents by mail absent a reservation against this by participating countries,[12] but whether such "sending" constitutes acceptable service has been debated in the United States courts.[13] The U.S. Supreme Court has unanimously held that Article 10(a) of the Hague Service Convention does not prohibit service by mail.[14] As long as the receiving state does not

---

10 *See* Bankston v. Toyota Motor Corp., 889 F.2d 172 (8th Cir. 1989).

11 Sheets v. Yamaha Motors, 891 F.2d 533 (5th Cir. 1990). *See* Société Nationale Industrielle Aerospatiale v. United States Dist. Court, 482 U.S. 522, 107 S.Ct. 2542, 96 L.Ed.2d 461 (1987) (comparing Hague Service Convention with Hague Evidence Convention).

12 Hague Service Convention, art. 10(a).

13 *See, e.g.*, Ackermann v. Levine, 788 F.2d 830 (2d Cir. 1986) (upholding mail service of German complaint against U.S. defendant resulting in default judgment). Accord, Brockmeyer v. May, 383 F.3d 798 (9th Cir. 2004) (U.S. service on English defendant); Shoei Kako Co. v. Superior Court, 33 Cal.App.3d 808, 109 Cal.Rptr. 402 (1973) (sending of U.S. complaint by mail to Japanese defendant upheld as valid service of process); Ackermann v. Levine, 788 F.2d 830 (2d Cir. 1086). Compare Bankston v. Toyota Motor Corp., 889 F.2d 172 (8th Cir. 1989) (sending of U.S. complaint to Japanese defendant by mail does not constitute service of process). Accord, Nuovo Pignone v. Storman Asia, 310 F.3d 374 (5th Cir. 2002); Honda Motor Co., Ltd. v. Superior Court, 10 Cal.App.4th 1043, 12 Cal.Rptr.2d 861 (1992); Suzuki Motor Co., Ltd. v. Superior Court, 200 Cal.App.3d 1476, 249 Cal.Rptr. 376 (1988).

14 Water Splash, Inc. v. Menon, 137 S.Ct. 1504 (2017).

object, the Convention does not affect lawful service of documents by mail.[15] But a federal court order must be first obtained.[16] Mail service is thus a form that should be used very carefully, with knowledge of the interpretation of Article 10 in the foreign forum.

While acknowledging the exclusive nature of the Convention governs both state and federal lawsuits requiring "service abroad", the U.S. Supreme Court has suggested it is inapplicable (though optional) if service may be made on a U.S. subsidiary, agent or statutory agent, or at a U.S. address or mail box of a foreign corporation. In *Volkswagenwerk, A.G. v. Schlunk,*[17] service made on Volkswagen of America (VWOA—a U.S. corporation) was held proper to reach Volkswagenwerk (VWAG—the German parent corporation). The Convention was held not to be applicable in a decision applying veil piercing alter ego theory, but without the usual substantive analysis that accompanies veil piercing cases.

The Inter-American Convention and its Additional Protocol have been ratified by the United States and a number of Latin American nations: Argentina, Brazil, Chile, Colombia, Ecuador, Guatemala, Mexico, Panama, Peru, Uruguay and Venezuela. The Convention is limited to letters rogatory, essentially requests from one country through its courts to another country through its courts to assist the administration of justice. Its purpose is similar but less encompassing than The Hague Service Convention. If both are applicable, the Inter-American Convention applies. Unlike the Hague Convention, the Inter-American Convention is not exclusive.[18] A party thus might use state methods of service that if transmitted to an Inter-American Convention nation would be effective, but that if transmitted to a Hague Service Convention nation not a party to the Inter-American Convention would fail because the Hague Service Convention would be applicable and exclusive.

Fears that being "*Schlunked*" would cause retaliation abroad have largely proven unfounded, but avoidance of the Hague Service Convention's procedures may well render resulting judgments unenforceable abroad. The German government made it very clear in the *Schlunk* case that unless service was made on VWAG under the Convention that German courts would not enforce a judgment.[19] There is thus a certain coercive effect to these service conventions,

---

15 *Id.*

16 *See* Brockmeyer v. May, 383 F.3d 798 (9th Cir. 2004).

17 486 U.S. 694, 108 S.Ct. 2104, 100 L.Ed.2d 722 (1988).

18 Kreimerman v. Casa Veerkamp, 22 F.3d 643 (5th Cir. 1994).

19 Brief for Volkswagenwerk, A.G. at 16, Volkswagenwerk, A.G. v. Schlunk, 486 U.S. 694, 108 S.Ct. 2104, 100 L.Ed.2d 722 (1988).

whether or not they are viewed as exclusive. If they are not followed, enforcement of a judgment will likely be denied.

§ 6.2 Parallel Proceedings, Anti-Suit Injunctions and *Lis Pendens*

The doctrine of *forum non conveniens* may apply regardless of whether foreign legal proceedings exist. See Section 2.4. But international business litigation frequently results in litigation before several jurisdictions, a phenomenon known as parallel litigation.

Anti-Suit Injunctions

Complex international litigation may create a situation where a suit is initiated in one nation by a foreign plaintiff against several defendants, including one or more from the foreign plaintiff's nation. Such was the case when Laker Airways initiated litigation in the United States against several U.S. and foreign airlines, including two from the United Kingdom.[20] The British defendants asked an English court to enjoin Laker Airways from pursuing the suit in the United States against the two British airlines because such litigation had only one proper forum—England. The injunction is called an "anti-suit injunction." The U.S. Court of Appeals rejected the injunction granted by the English court. Indeed, the D.C. Circuit Court in *Laker* affirmed a "counter anti-suit injunction" against the anti-injunction proceedings in the UK. A serious conflict was avoided only after the House of Lords overturned the UK anti-suit injunction, although preserving the concept.

Although the U.S. court in *Laker* rejected the English anti-suit injunction, such injunctions had been accepted in some U.S. courts. Some federal circuits have granted anti-suit injunctions against foreign litigation, generally applying a multi-part test which considers such issues as: Would the foreign litigation frustrate a policy of the U.S. forum, be vexatious or oppressive, threaten the court's jurisdiction, or prejudice other considerations.[21] *Laker*, however, narrowed the concept, allowing it to protect the jurisdiction of the court or prevent the litigant from evading public policies of the forum. The federal Circuit Courts are split in their willingness to

---

[20] *See* Laker Airways, Ltd. v. Sabena, Belgian World Airlines, 731 F.2d 909 (D.C.Cir. 1984).

[21] In re Unterweser Reederei, GmbH, 428 F.2d 888 (5th Cir. 1970), *affirmed en banc*, 446 F.2d 907 (5th Cir. 1971), *vacated on other grounds sub nom.*, M/S Bremen v. Zapata Off-Shore Co., 407 U.S. 1, 92 S.Ct. 1907, 32 L.Ed.2d 513 (1972). *See also* Seattle Totems Hockey Club, Inc. v. National Hockey League, 652 F.2d 852 (9th Cir. 1981), *cert. denied*, 457 U.S. 1105, 102 S.Ct. 2902, 73 L.Ed.2d 1313 (1982); Re Apple Inc., 2017 CCH Trade Cas. 80,129 (S.D.Cal. 2017) (Qualcomm anti-suit injunctions against Apple in multiple jurisdictions denied).

affirm anti-suit injunctions, including those issued in aid of arbitration agreements.[22]

Australia and Canada will also consider issuance of anti-suit injunctions.[23] U.S. anti-suit injunctions are unusual because U.S. courts often allow parallel proceedings to continue in two jurisdictions. A judgment of a U.S. court will be considered *res judicata.* So may the foreign judgment. Thus, which party receives the first judgment may have the advantage, encouraging a race to judgment. But, however undesirable it is to encourage such a race, U.S. courts have not granted anti-suit injunctions just to stop a race.

Lis Pendens

Civil law courts reasonably often stay, under the doctrine of *lis pendens*, parallel proceedings brought after another court is first seised of the matter. Article 27 of the EU Jurisdiction and Judgments Regulation (see Section 8.2) bars parallel proceedings in member states after the first EU court is seised, even if not all of the parties are from the Union and regardless of choice of court clauses. This rule generates race incentives within the EU, notably favoring first suits by debtors in jurisdictions with extremely slow collection procedures (think Italy).[24] EU courts are further prohibited from issuing anti-suit injunctions against proceedings, however vexacious and in bad faith, in another member state, even when the injunction would support courts or arbitrations that have been selected by agreement of the parties.[25] U.S. courts may be hesitant to invoke *lis pendens* to

---

[22] For decisions subsequent to *Laker* stringently opposed to anti-suit injunctions, *see* China Trade & Dev. Corp. v. M.V. Choong Yong, 837 F.2d 33 (2d Cir. 1987) (reversing an injunction); Gau Shan Co. v. Bankers Trust Co., 956 F.2d 1349 (6th Cir. 1992), *appeal after remand,* 966 F.2d 1452 (6th Cir. 1992) (reversing an injunction); General Electric Co. v. Deutz, 270 F.3d 144 (3d Cir. 2001) (denying injunction); Goss Int'l Corp. v. Man Roland D.A., 491 F.3d 355 (8th Cir. 2007) (reversing an injunction). *See also* Quaak v. Klynveld Peat Marwick Goerdeler, 361 F.3d 11 (1st Cir. 2004). For more sympathetic treatment of anti-suit injunctions, *see* Seattle Totems Hockey Club v. National Hockey League, 652 F.2d 852 (9th Cir. 1981); Allendale Mut. Ins. Co. v. Bull Data Sys., Inc., 10 F.3d 425 (7th Cir. 1993); Kaepa Inc. v. Achilles Corp., 76 F.3d 624 (5th Cir. 1996); E.J. Gallo Winery v. Andina Licores, 446 F.3d 984 (9th Cir. 2006) (injunction in aid of forum selection clause).

On anti-suit injunctions in aid of arbitration, *see* Paramedics Electromedicina Comercial Ltda v. GE Medical Systems Information Technologies, 369 F.3d 645 (2d Cir. 2004) (injunction upheld) and Ibeto Petrochemical Indus. Ltd. v. M/T Beffen, 475 F.3d 56 (2d Cir. 2007) (injunction upheld); Karaha Bodas Co. v. Perusahaan Pertambangan, 335 U.S. F.3d 357 (5th Cir. 2003) (injunction denied). Compare Allianz SpA v. West Tankers Inc., 2009 E.C.R. I–00663 (EC Court of Justice denies injunction in aid of arbitration).

[23] *See* Amchem Products v. British Columbia, 102 D.L.R.4th 96 (Canada S.Ct. 1993); CSR Ltd. v. Cigna Insur. Australia, 146 A.L.R. 402 (High Ct of Austl).

[24] *See* Erich Gasser GmbH v. MISAT SRL, 2003 Eur.Comm.Rep. I–14693 (ECJ, 2003).

[25] Turner v. Grovit, 20004 Eur.Comm.Rep. I–3565 (ECJ, 2004); Allianz SpA v. West Tankers Inc., 2009 Eur.Comm.Rep. Case C–185/07 (ECJ, 2009).

stay proceedings when parallel foreign actions are underway.[26] The race then continues. But there is U.S. state and federal precedent for invoking *lis pendens* when parallel proceedings exist abroad.[27] Indeed, the Laker decision explicitly acknowledges this discretionary possibility.[28] U.S. Supreme Court domestic rulings on *lis pendens* are confusing, most recently emphasizing the "unflagging" obligation of U.S. courts to exercise jurisdiction conferred upon them,[29] but in the past stressing the waste inherent in parallel proceedings and supporting stays.[30] Cases involving international parallel proceedings, sometimes noting that comity considerations may favor stays, are equally split.[31]

The impact of parallel proceedings will occur when the judgment is enforced. If the winner of the race's victory is accepted abroad and the judgment is enforced, the judgment was given *res judicata* effect. But it is not clear that it will be so recognized. The foreign court may reject the U.S. decision for traditional reasons justifying non-recognition and enforcement of foreign judgments (see Chapter 8), which may incorporate some of the justifications for granting *lis pendens* stays or anti-suit injunctions. A U.S. judgment entered after an anti-suit judgment is granted abroad will not be enforced in the foreign court. The intention of the British anti-suit injunction *Laker* was to block enforcement of a U.S. judgment from U.S. assets of the foreign defendant.

§ 6.3 Proving Foreign Law

Unfortunately, many cases are filed in U.S. courts with a complaint drafted without any thought that foreign law might be applicable. The complaint may include several counts that may correctly make reference to U.S. law, but have no relevance if foreign law applies. For example, most civil law nations do not provide causes of action based on an alleged civil conspiracy or unjust enrichment. Additionally, most foreign courts do not grant punitive damages. Sometimes the plaintiff will attempt to equate a foreign concept as

---

26 *See, e.g.*, Neuchatel Swiss Gen Ins. Co. v. Lufthansa, 925 F.2d 1193 (9th Cir. 1991).

27 *See, e.g.*, Turner Entertainment v. Aegeto Film, 25 F.3d 1512 (11th Cir. 1994); Barclays Bank v. Tsakos, 543 A.2d 802 (D.C. App. 1988).

28 Laker Airways, Ltd. v. Sabena, Belgian World Airlines, 731 F.2d 909 (D.C.Cir. 1984).

29 Colorado River Water Conservation District v. United States, 424 U.S. 800 (1976); Quackenbush v. Allstate Ins. Co., 517 U.S. 706 (1996).

30 Landis v. North American Co., 299 U.S. 248 (1936).

31 Compare Ingersoll Milling Machine Co. v. Granger, 833 F.2d 680 (7th Cir. 1987) (stay denied, exceptional circumstances required) with Posner v. Essex Ins. Co., 178 F.3d 1209 (11th Cir. 1999) (stay granted) and Continental Tire v. Swiss Credit Bank, 543 F.Supp. 408 (S.D.N.Y. 1982) (U.S. action dismissed).

being the same as a U.S. concept. For example, when a plaintiff has asked for punitive damages, and the law of Mexico is to apply, Mexico's "moral damage" law may be misconstrued to be the same as punitive damages.

Questions regarding proving foreign law in U.S. *forum non conveniens* proceedings are pivotal. See Section 2.4. Proving foreign law in a U.S. court very likely will include various forms of written and oral testimony. Often affidavits of experts are submitted,[32] with the experts appearing at trial to support and respond to questions about their opinions.[33] Usually when foreign law must be proved, experts will be practitioners or academics from the foreign country. But often those persons, unless they have received some of their legal education in the United States, may not be effective in explaining a very different legal system to an American judge. In such case U.S. comparative law experts may be helpful in explaining to the judge the nature of the perceived differences between the laws of the two nations.

If the opposing lawyers do not recognize that the case involves the application of foreign law, and proceed on the assumption that U.S. law applies, they may be asked by the court to present opinions on the foreign law. If the lawyers fail to do so, there is a split of authority regarding whether the U.S. judge may or must undertake the proof of foreign law. A court may conduct its own research, which also may be helpful when the experts are divided on the meaning of the foreign law. That is usually the case.

Proof of foreign law often requires obtaining translations. Some foreign laws are available in English, especially constitutions and important codes such as civil and commercial codes. If there is a published version of the foreign statutes, it is likely to have been translated objectively and thus will be accepted by the court. Where the parties have to translate foreign statutes or cases, they may do so with a choice of words favoring their case. The court may have to choose between two versions. Translations of foreign cases are not often undertaken, sometimes because of their length and thus expense, and sometimes because they are written very abstractly and are difficult to understand by a U.S. judge without experience with foreign materials. When they do exist, they may be very helpful because a U.S. judge may not wish to interpret a foreign statute in a manner that is not clear from the language unless a foreign court has already given a similar or consistent interpretation.

---

[32] *See* Bing v. Halstead, 495 F.Supp. 517 (S.D.N.Y.1980) (affidavits resulting in granting summary judgment).

[33] *See* John R. Brown, 44.1 Ways to Prove Foreign Law, 9 Marq. Law. 179 (1984).

§ 6.4 Depositions and Document Discovery Abroad, The Hague Evidence Convention

For a trial in the United States gathering evidence is far easier when both the defendant and the evidence are in the United States. But when the evidence is located abroad, and especially when the defendant resides abroad, obtaining evidence may become very difficult.[34]

The rules for obtaining evidence are the rules of procedure of the forum and any applicable international conventions or treaties such as the Hague Evidence Convention. Unlike service of process (see Section 6.1), the United States does not participate in the Inter-American Convention on Evidence. When personal jurisdiction has been obtained by use of disputed extraterritorial application of U.S. law, gathering evidence abroad under the court's authority may conflict with foreign laws blocking the production of evidence. See Section 6.6. Numerous suits are filed by U.S. lawyers who proceed under the forum's rules of evidence only to discover they need a short-course in obtaining evidence abroad to save their suit. Part of that short-course must be learning that some practices of obtaining evidence from parties and non-parties permitted in the United States constitute *criminal* conduct in foreign nations.[35]

If U.S. notions of proper evidence paralleled those in foreign nations there would be far less trouble. The problem in gathering evidence abroad is not that all foreign nations prevent other nations from obtaining evidence in their nations. The problem is that the U.S. concept of evidence extends beyond nearly all other nations' rules regarding what may be obtained. Furthermore, U.S. sanctions for failure to follow pretrial discovery orders and discovery orders issued to determine jurisdiction (called "jurisdictional discovery") can be severe, particularly in the absence of good faith on the part of defendants.[36] In most civil law tradition nations, judges with substantial discretion closely regulate gathering evidence. Attorneys

---

[34] If the defendant is a U.S. citizen or resident, however, a U.S. court may subpoena the defendant to appear in the United States, and produce specified documents. 28 U.S.C.A. § 1783(a).

[35] Especially in France and Switzerland. *See, e.g.*, Strauss v. Credit Lyonnais SA, 242 F.R.D. 199 (E.D.N.Y. 2007) (France).

[36] *See* Insurance Corp of Ireland v. Compagnie des Bauxites de Guinee, 456 U.S. 694 (1982) (jurisdictional discovery sanctions upheld); Societe Internationale Pour Participations Indutrielles et Commerciales SA v. Rogers, 357 U.S. 197 (1958) (pretrial sanctions explored when blocking statutes apply). The important *Rogers* case is discussed at length in Section 6.7. *See also* In re Westinghouse Corp., 563 F.2d 992 (10th Cir. 1977) (seeking of foreign government waivers for release of documents demonstrates good faith, contempt sanctions reversed); United States v. Westinghouse Electric Corp., 648 F.2d 642 (9th Cir. 1981) (failure to comply per diem monetary sanctions upheld).

are for the most part not left on their own to collect what they think would be useful, with occasional forays into court for new orders of production.

Civil law judges determine who may be witnesses. The judges ask questions they originate or those referred to them by the lawyers which they have approved. Requests for documents must be specific, disallowing requests, for example, for any documents that might have affected the design and manufacture of a product involved in an injury. If we sometimes think of our own process as condoning "fishing expeditions" for evidence, other nations are likely to interpret our method of fishing as using drift nets miles long that catch everything that the net surrounds. Other nations have effectively banned our nets.

As a civil process unfolds in the United States, the search for evidence begins at an early stage, well before the trial. Much that the lawyers are seeking will help in the further development of the case. There may have been very little, if any, evidence present when a brief and general complaint was filed. Much of what *is* subsequently obtained will never be used. This pretrial discovery is neither fully understood nor accepted by many civil law tradition nations. They sometimes think that "pretrial" means before the suit is filed.[37] Obviously, evidence needs to be gathered before the day of the trial, just as it is gathered over a period of time in a civil law nation and not all presented at one time for the judge's consideration. The dislike for pretrial evidence is made apparent in The Hague Evidence Convention,[38] allowing a convention participant to make a declaration that disallows letters of request seeking "pretrial discovery of documents."[39]

Obtaining evidence abroad comes in two general areas, deposing witnesses and obtaining physical evidence, principally written documents. If depositions are permitted by the foreign nation, they are sometimes taken before a person commissioned by the U.S. court.[40] U.S. consular officers are ordinarily used as the designated commissioners to take the testimony, but a foreign official or private person may be appointed. In some countries the testimony may only be taken under rules of the country that disallow the use of a commissioner appointed by the U.S. court. The foreign rules may even prohibit taking any testimony by deposition. In such case the

---

37 Their misunderstanding is perhaps because they view the stage like a grand jury proceeding, where evidence is gathered and presented before an indictment.

38 Hague Convention on the Taking of Evidence Abroad in Civil or Commercial Matters, Mar. 18, 1970, 8 I.L.M. 37 (1965).

39 *Id.*, Art. 23. Most signatories have issued such a declaration.

40 Fed. R. Civ. P. 28(b)(4).

U.S. court may be able to issue a letter of request to a court in the foreign nation asking that it issue an order to take the testimony.[41] The letter may be accepted under notions of comity. Foreign plaintiffs in U. S. courts may be ordered to appear for depositions in the United States.[42]

When the court in the United States approves discovery of documents abroad, the laws of the foreign nation may admit or block such discovery. See Section 6.6. This may occur even though the foreign company is a subsidiary of a U.S. parent corporation. Most U.S. courts will order "controlled" foreign subsidiaries of U.S. companies to produce documents.[43] In general, parties and nonparties can be compelled to produce non-privileged documents and materials located outside the United States when properly served with a *subpoena duces tecum* and subject to personal jurisdiction of a U.S. court.[44] Whether foreign-based documents and communications are covered by attorney-client privilege is a critical issue. U.S. courts are increasingly finding that communications between in-house counsel and companies in China, India, the Netherlands and Russia do not enjoy protection from disclosure. These decisions generally focus corporate counsel's lack of professional licenses to practice law. Furthermore, the U.S. Supreme Court has ruled that the Foreign Sovereign Immunities Act (see Chapter 7, Part A) does not limit a court's power to order *post-judgment, worldwide* discovery in aid of sovereign debt collection efforts.[45]

The Hague Convention on Evidence

In addition to use of procedural rules of various nations, and the application of comity, another route is present. About 40 countries, including the United States, China, Germany, Russia, France, Italy, Korea, Mexico and India, are parties to the Hague Evidence Convention. Most African and Middle East countries are not. This Convention provides for three methods of obtaining evidence abroad. First is use of a letter of request to the "Central Authority" in the foreign nation. That authority sends the request to the appropriate court. Second is by means of a request to take evidence before a

---

[41] Some nations require the letters of request to be submitted through diplomatic channels rather than court-to-court.

[42] *See, e.g.*, Dubai Islamic Bank v. Citibank, 2002 WL 1159699 (S.D.N.Y. 2002).

[43] *See, e.g.*, United States v. Vetco, 691 F.2d 1281 (9th Cir. 1981).

[44] *See, e.g.*, In re Citric Acid Litig., 191 F.3d 1090 (9th Cir. 1999).

[45] Argentina v. NML Capital Ltd., 134 S.Ct. 2250 (2014). Compare Reinsurance Co. of America v. Administratia Asigurarilor de Stat, 902 F.2d 1275 (7th Cir. 1990) (post-judgment discovery to locate assets not allowed as it would violate Romanian state secrets). *See* Richmark Corp. v. Timber Falling Consultants, 959 F.2d 1468 (9th Cir. 1992) (post-judgment discovery ordered despite Chinese criminal sanctions).

diplomatic or consular officer in the foreign country. Third, a request may be made to have a commissioner appointed to take evidence. These three methods parallel those outlined above under the Federal Rules of Civil Procedure, but there are variations. One most important question for nations adhering to the Convention is whether it is the exclusive method of taking evidence abroad.

For the United States, at least as to document discovery to be produced in the United States, the Supreme Court answered that it is not the exclusive method in *Societe Nationale Industrielle Aerospatiale v. United States.*[46] Hence, since this decision, most discovery in international business litigation is undertaken via the Federal Rules of Civil Procedure. Use of the Convention would seem to be a form approved by participating countries, and more likely therefore to be respected. The majority of decisions since *Aerospatiale* have not required use of the Convention as a necessary first option for document discovery,[47] but some have suggested it is mandatory for depositions or other discovery physically taking place on foreign territory.[48] The fact remains that the view of the United States is the view of only one side, the requirements of the foreign nation in which discovery is sought have to be considered, and as noted above most Hague Convention adherents have opted out of coverage for pretrial discovery of documents.

By way of example, the next two sections detail discovery abroad issues in the context of U.S. antitrust jurisdiction under the Sherman (Antitrust) Act, and taking evidence in the United States in aid of foreign proceedings. Coverage of extraterritorial U.S. antitrust subject matter jurisdiction can be found in Section 5.5.

---

46 482 U.S. 522, 107 S.Ct. 2542, 96 L.Ed.2d 461 (1987).

47 *See, e.g.*, In re Automotive Refinishing Paint Antitrust Litigation, 358 F.3d 288 (3d Cir. 2004).

48 *See, e.g.*, Belmont Textile Machinery v. Superba, 48 F.Supp.2d 521 (W.D.N.C. 1999).

§ 6.5 Using The Hague Convention on Evidence[49]

The United States and about 40 other nations[50] are parties to the Hague Evidence Convention.[51] The purpose of Hague Evidence Convention is to minimize the difficulties in obtaining evidence from countries with differing legal systems by establishing standards and procedures for the taking of evidence among member states.[52] The Hague Convention procedures are generally considered to be less burdensome and time consuming than traditional Letters Rogatory. The United States Supreme Court has ruled the Evidence Convention is *optional*, not mandatory,[53] and that all other avenues of international discovery can be pursed.[54]

All Evidence Convention states, plus others, are parties to the 1965 Hague Convention on the Service Abroad of Judicial and Extrajudicial Documents in Civil or Commercial Matters.[55] The "Hague Service Convention" allows service directly via each state's "Central Authority," which eliminates the traditional need to use Evidence Convention Letters of Request (detailed below) for service purposes. Letters Rogatory are analogous to Letters of Request. Service via Letters Rogatory is still common in Central and South America.[56]

The Hague Evidence Convention provides two methods for taking evidence in Convention states. Chapter I of the Convention permits a court in one state to direct a letter of request to the designated authority in a foreign state. The letter of request specifies

---

[49] Adapted from R. Folsom, "International Discovery in Antitrust Litigation", Chapter 15, in von Kalinowski, *Antitrust Litigation and Counseling Techniques* (Matthew-Bender Co.)

[50] The Hague Evidence Convention is in force in the following countries: Albania, Argentina, Armenia, Australia, Barbados, Belarus, Bosnia, Bulgaria, Cyprus, Colombia, Croatia, Czech Republic, Denmark, Estonia, Finland, France, Germany, Greece, Herzegovina, Hungary, Iceland, India, Israel, Italy, Kuwait, Latvia, Liechtenstein, Lithuania, Luxembourg, Macedonia, Malta, Montenegro, Mexico, Monaco, Morocco, Netherlands, Norway, People's Republic of China, Poland, Portugal, Romania, Russian Federation, Serbia, Seychelles, Singapore, Slovakia, Slovenia, South Africa, South Korea, Spain, Sri Lanka, Sweden, Switzerland, Turkey, Ukraine, United Kingdom, United States, and Venezuela. As between European Union states (save Denmark), the Evidence Convention has largely been supplanted by Council Regulation (EC) No. 1206/2001.

[51] 23 U.S.T. 2555, T.I.A.S. No. 7444, reprinted in 28 U.S.C.A. § 1781.

[52] Preamble to the Hague Evidence Convention.

[53] Société Nationale Industrielle Aérospatiale v. United States District Court for the Southern District of Iowa, 482 U.S. 522, 107 S.Ct. 2542, 96 L.Ed.2d 641 (1987).

[54] See Section 6.4.

[55] 20 U.S.T. 361; 658 U.N.T.S. 163, T.I.A.S. No. 6638.

[56] See the Inter-American Convention on Letters Rogatory (Panama, 1975), applicable to service of process and taking evidence. It is force in the United States and 18 other countries of the Americas.

the evidence to be obtained or the judicial act to be performed. The foreign state then may perform the requested act. Chapter II of the Convention permits a court in one state to obtain evidence in a foreign state through the use of its own diplomatic or consular officers located in the foreign state or through a person the court has commissioned to take evidence.

Article 23 of the Hague Evidence Convention

Probably the most important provision of the Hague Evidence Convention is Article 23. Article 23 permits any state which is a party to the Convention to declare that it will not execute letters of request for the purpose of obtaining pretrial discovery of documents. Most of the Convention states have made such declarations.[57]

The Article 23 reservation is a significant impediment to obtaining evidence through the Hague Evidence Convention procedures. In most instances counsel may have only a general idea of the type of documents which are relevant to a given action. If, however, a broad request is made for all documents relating to a certain subject, the enforcing state is likely to view such a request as not restricted to evidence to be used at trial.[58] This significantly limits the ability of counsel to use the Hague Evidence Convention procedures as an investigative or trial preparation vehicle.

Letters of Request

Scope and Issuance of Letter. The letter of request is the principal method for obtaining evidence under The Hague Evidence Convention. Both documentary and testimonial evidence may be obtained by means of a letter of request. However, there are some significant *limitations* on the use of letters of request in addition to its general unavailability for American-style document discovery.

First, a letter of request may be employed only to obtain evidence for use in judicial proceedings,[59] for example in patent litigation.[60] The focus on obtaining evidence for use in judicial proceedings arguably is much narrower than the discovery obtainable under Rule

---

[57] Albania, Serbia, Slovakia, Malta, Morocco, Israel, Russia, Slovenia, Latvia, The Czech Republic, Bulgaria, Bosnia and Herzegovina, Belarus and the United States have not made declarations pursuant to Article 23.

[58] This occurred in the *Rio Tinto Zinc* case, Note 32 *infra.* In *Rio Tinto Zinc,* the letter of request asked for the production of all documents relating to the operation of the alleged cartel. The English court pared down the request so that it would comply with English law relating to discovery. In re Westinghouse Electric Corporation Uranium Contract Litigation, [1977] 3 W.L.R. 430, 439 (C.A.).

[59] Hague Evidence Convention, article 1. *See also* Hague Evidence Convention, article 23.

[60] Tulip Computers Int'l B.V. v. Dell Computer Corp., 254 F.Supp.2d 469 (D. Del. 2003).

26 of the Federal Rules of Civil Procedure, which permits parties to request and receive information which may be used as evidence at trial and any other information which may tend to provide leads to relevant, admissible evidence.[61]

Second, the letter must request the performance of a judicial act.[62] If the requested act is beyond the power of the judiciary in the foreign country, cooperation may be denied.[63] Further, the Hague Evidence Convention specifically excludes the request of certain judicial acts. These include the service of judicial documents, the enforcement of outstanding judgments or orders and the issuance of orders for provisional or protective measures.[64]

Third, a foreign state may refuse to execute a letter of request if the action requested would be prejudicial to the foreign state's sovereignty.[65] This limitation could conceivably prove troublesome in the context of antitrust litigation. There has been substantial friction between the United States and foreign countries concerning what other nations perceive to be extraterritorial application of American antitrust laws.[66] There is a possibility that discovery requests in connection with antitrust litigation could be construed as prejudicial to national sovereignty.[67] This should be kept in mind when considering the use of the Hague Evidence Convention as a possible avenue of discovery.

---

[61] Rule 26 of the Federal Rules of Civil Procedure provides:

"Parties may obtain discovery regarding any matter, not privileged, which is relevant to the subject matter involved in the pending action, whether it relates to the claim or defense of the party seeking discovery or to the claim or defense of any other party. . . . It is not ground for objection that the information sought will be inadmissible at the trial if the information sought appears reasonably calculated to lead to the discovery of admissible evidence."

[62] Hague Evidence Convention, article 1.

[63] Hague Evidence Convention, article 12.

[64] Hague Evidence Convention, article 1.

[65] Hague Evidence Convention, article 12.

[66] An example of the friction between the United States and a foreign state concerning the reach and effect of the antitrust law is the *Laker Airways* case. Laker, a British company, brought an antitrust action in the United States against several domestic and foreign airlines, including two other British carriers. While Laker's action was pending in the district court, two of the British defendants, British Caledonian Airlines and British Airways, applied to a British court for an order enjoining Laker from proceeding with the American action against them. The British court granted the application. *See* British Airways v. Laker Airways, [1983] 5 W.L.R. 545 (C.A.). This provoked the American court to issue an injunction of its own forbidding the other defendants from seeking relief in the British courts. *See* Laker Airways Ltd. v. Pan American World Airways, 577 F.Supp. 348 (D.D.C. 1983). The British injunction was later vacated by the House of Lords. British Airways v. Laker Airways, [1984] 3 All E.R. 39.

[67] Hague Evidence Convention, article 12.

Once it has determined that the evidence to be obtained falls within the permissible scope of the letter of request provisions of the Convention, counsel then must apply to the district court for issuance of the letter.[68] It is recommended that the application be accompanied by an affidavit setting forth the reasons for the letter of request and a draft letter in compliance with the terms of the Convention. This may facilitate the issuance of the letter and narrow the issues for litigation concerning execution of the letter.

Article 3 of the Convention requires that a letter of request specify: (1) the authority requesting execution of the letter and the authority requested to execute the letter; (2) the names and addresses of the parties to the proceedings and their representatives; (3) the nature of the proceedings for which the evidence is required; and (4) the evidence to be obtained or other judicial act to be performed. Depending on the evidence to be obtained, the letter must also specify: (1) the names and addresses of persons to be examined; (2) the questions to be put to the persons to be examined; (3) the documents or other property to be inspected; and (4) any special form required for the evidence (e.g., testimony given under oath).[69]

Once the court has determined the need for and the appropriate contents of the letter, the court will issue the letter and transmit it to the central authority designated by the foreign state.[70] In some cases, it may be helpful to retain knowledgeable foreign counsel to assist in shepherding the letter through the foreign system.[71]

Enforcement of Letter. Enforcement of the letter of request is left to the central authority of the requested state. Although the Convention limits the power of the foreign state in refusing to enforce a letter of request,[72] the Convention allows the enforcing state wide latitude in determining the manner in which the letter will be enforced and the procedures by which evidence will be obtained.

Once the letter is received, the foreign authority will make its own independent determination of whether the letter complies with

---

[68] Article 1 of the Hague Evidence Convention requires a "judicial authority" to issue the letter of request. This is analogous to the traditional procedure of issuing letters rogatory under Fed. R. Civ. P. 28(b).

[69] Hague Evidence Convention, article 3.

[70] Each country which has ratified the treaty has designated a central authority for receiving letters of request. A complete list of designated authorities can be found at 28 U.S.C.A. § 1783.

[71] Platto, "Taking Evidence Abroad for Use in Civil Cases in the United States—A Practical Guide," 13 Int'l Law. 575 (1979).

[72] See text of Convention in Section 6.11.

the Convention. If the foreign state objects to the letter, it must promptly inform the requesting state.[73]

If the foreign authority determines that the letter conforms to the provisions of the Convention, it will execute the letter according to its own procedures.[74] This may mean that a request will be executed in a manner radically different from that employed with respect to United States discovery requests. In some civil law countries, for example, it is traditionally the function of the judge to examine witnesses and then prepare a written summary of the testimony.[75] A letter of request which contemplates a deposition by counsel of a witness with a verbatim transcript of the proceedings may be executed by a judicial examination of the witness with a written summary. Although an American court might admit into evidence testimony elicited in this form,[76] the testimony may prove to be of only limited utility to counsel.

The court issuing the letter of request may specify a special method or procedure be followed in taking evidence.[77] For example, a letter seeking testimony in a civil law country may request that U.S. deposition procedures be followed, including examination by counsel and the preparation of a verbatim record. The executing state is obligated to follow the special procedure unless it is incompatible with its own internal law, which often may be the case.[78] Thus even if a special procedure is requested, there is no assurance that this procedure will be employed.

In some cases, it may be possible to reach an informal accommodation which will meet the needs of counsel while not compromising the foreign state's procedures. In *Corning Glass Works v. International Telephone and Telegraph Corp.*,[79] for example, a

---

[73] Hague Evidence Convention, article 5.

[74] Hague Evidence Convention, article 9.

[75] The Federal Republic of Germany, France and Switzerland, for example, follow this procedure. For a description of procedures in these countries *see* Heck, "U.S. Misinterpretation of the Hague Evidence Convention," 24 Colum. J. Trans. L. 231 (1986) (German procedures); "Symposium/Transnational Litigation: Switzerland," 18 Int'l Law. 789 (1984); Borel and Boyd, "Opportunities for and Obstacles to Obtaining Evidence in France for Use in Litigation in the United States," 16 Int'l Law. 35 (1982).

[76] Fed. R. Civ. P. 28(b) provides: "Evidence obtained in response to a letter rogatory need not be excluded merely for the reason that it is not a verbatim transcript or that the testimony was not taken under oath or for any similar departure from the requirements for depositions taken within the United States under these rules."

[77] Hague Evidence Convention, article 9.

[78] In many countries, only authorized persons may take testimony. Unauthorized depositions are strictly prohibited and those involved subject to criminal penalties. *See, e.g.*, Section 271, Swiss Penal Code of December 21, 1937 as amended; Code de Procedure Civile, Title VII, Art. 214.

[79] Civil Action No. 76–0144 (W.D. Va. 1977). A complete account of the international discovery issues in this case can be found in Platto, "Taking Evidence

German court adhered to the traditional procedure of judicial examination of witnesses but allowed counsel for the parties to conduct extensive "follow up" examination. In addition, the court allowed a verbatim transcript to be taken. In complex cases, it may be advisable to pursue some accommodation which will allow counsel at least a limited role in examining witnesses.

Compulsory Process. The Hague Evidence Convention provides that persons may be compelled to give evidence pursuant to a letter of request. Here again, however, the executing state will apply its own law in determining the appropriate measures of compulsion.[80] It is therefore recommended that counsel be well informed about methods, procedures and sanctions before the letter is issued in order to arrange for the expeditious use of proper means of compelling testimony or production of documents.

Privileges. A person from whom evidence is sought may refuse to provide evidence on the ground of privilege. Under the Convention, the privileges permitted under the laws of both the state issuing the letter and the state enforcing the letter may be invoked by the witness.[81] A state may also declare that it will honor privileges existing under the laws of states other than the issuing state.[82]

Since an unwilling witness may be able to invoke a broad range of privileges in order to delay or avoid providing evidence in a given matter, counsel should prepare a strategy to meet the claims of privilege that may possibly be raised. As a first step, counsel should be well aware of the privileges available to any given witness. Many foreign privileges may completely foreclose counsel from obtaining relevant evidence. Thus all the effort expended in obtaining a letter of request may be for naught.

Second, counsel must consider privileges which may be invoked under United States law and develop a strategy to quickly resolve privilege issues. It is not uncommon for a witness to invoke an U.S. privilege during examination in a foreign country thousands of miles from American courts. If some mechanism is not in place for dealing with these issues, such as the presence of a court-appointed master or a means by which counsel can appeal directly to the judge, counsel may be put in the position of adjourning the examination and returning to the court for a ruling on the privilege issues. This undoubtedly will be both time-consuming and expensive.

Abroad for Use in Civil Cases in the United States—A Practical Guide," 13 Int'l Law. 575 (1979).

80 Hague Evidence Convention, article 1.

81 Hague Evidence Convention, article 11.

82 *Id.*

Rio Tinto Zinc Corp. v. *Westinghouse Electric Corp.*[83] is a good illustration of the thicket in which counsel may find themselves concerning privilege issues when attempting to obtain information in sensitive antitrust cases. In 1977, Westinghouse Electric Corp. sought to examine present and former employees of Rio Tinto Zinc Corp. ("RTZ") concerning the alleged formation of an international cartel to manipulate the price of uranium.[84] Judge Merhige, the federal district judge assigned to the Westinghouse case, issued a letter to the High Court in England requesting the examinations.

In the English court, the RTZ witnesses opposed enforcement of the letter on two grounds. First, the RTZ witnesses claimed that the letter requested information that could not conceivably be used as evidence at trial. Thus it was outside the permissible scope of a letter of request. Second, the RTZ witnesses claimed that the information sought was protected by the Fifth Amendment privilege against self-incrimination and by a somewhat analogous privilege under British law.[85]

The U.K. Court of Appeal[86] rejected the RTZ witnesses' claim that the letter was unenforceable because it was an attempt to obtain pretrial discovery which is prohibited under English law.[87] The court, however, slightly narrowed its scope, allowing enforcement with respect only to those documents which were specified with such distinctiveness as would be sufficient for a *subpoena duces tecum*.[88] The court also declared that the information might be privileged under British and United States law.[89]

---

83 A description of the English proceedings in Rio Tinto Zinc v. Westinghouse Electric Corp. may be found in the House of Lords decision and opinion reported at [1978] 1 All E.R. 434.

84 The *Rio Tinto Zinc* affair grew out of Westinghouse's attempt to defend itself in a number of lawsuits stemming from Westinghouse's failure to perform contracts for the delivery of uranium. *See* In re Westinghouse Electric Corp. Uranium Contracts Litigation, 405 F.Supp. 316 (E.D. Va. 1975). In the *Uranium Contract Litigation*, Westinghouse claimed that a number of uranium producers had formed a cartel to control the supply of uranium. It contended that the cartel's manipulation of the uranium market caused the price of uranium to rise dramatically, thus making it commercially impracticable for Westinghouse to deliver on its fixed price contracts. Rio Tinto Zinc Corp. was allegedly a member of the uranium cartel.

85 Civil Evidence Act of 1968, Pub. Gen. Acts Vol. 2, C. 64, § 14. The Act recognizes a "right of a person in any legal proceeding (other than criminal proceedings) to refuse to answer any question or produce any document or thing if to do so would tend to expose that person to proceedings for an offense or for the recovery of a penalty. . . ."

86 In re Westinghouse Electric Corporation Uranium Contract Litigation, [1977] 3 W.L.R. 430 (C.A.).

87 *Id.* at 434.

88 *Id.* at 438.

89 *Id.*

When the RTZ witnesses were called to testify each refused to answer questions on the grounds that the information was privileged under British law and the Fifth Amendment. The privilege claim under the Fifth Amendment was referred to Judge Merhige, who upheld the claim.[90]

At this point the United States Department of Justice entered the case. The Department of Justice informed Judge Merhige that the information sought to be obtained through the letter of request was required by it for a grand jury investigation into possible antitrust violations by the cartel. The Department of Justice offered immunity from criminal prosecution to all witnesses. Judge Merhige issued an order compelling the witnesses to testify.[91]

In the meantime, the RTZ witnesses appealed the Court of Appeal's decision to enforce the letter of request to the House of Lords.[92] The House of Lords agreed with the original order. Despite this, however, the House of Lords ultimately decided that the letters should not now be given effect in view of the intervention of the Department of Justice in the case. The offer of immunity to the witnesses had essentially changed the nature of the proceedings. With the grant of immunity, it became clear that the evidence sought to be obtained would be used in the grand jury investigation of the cartel. As a result, the evidence requested no longer fell within the scope of The Hague Evidence Convention.[93] Therefore the letters could not be given effect.

The decisions in *Rio Tinto Zinc* point up two issues concerning the invocation of privilege which the practitioner must keep in mind when attempting to obtain evidence by means of a letter of request. First, it is important to be fully conversant with the privileges available under the law of the country in which the letter is to be enforced. In *Rio Tinto Zinc,* the RTZ witnesses claimed that their testimony could expose them to a penalty under the antitrust provisions of the Treaty on the Functioning of the European Union

---

[90] In re Westinghouse Electric Corp. Uranium Contract Litigation, [1978] 2 W.L.R. 81 (H.L.).

[91] *See* Augustine, "Obtaining International Judicial Assistance Under the Federal Rules and the Hague Evidence Convention on Taking Evidence Abroad in Civil and Commercial Matters: An Exposition of the Procedures and a Practical Example: In re Westinghouse Uranium Contract Litigation," 10 Ga. J. Int'l & Comp. L. 101, 153 n. 252 (1980).

[92] Rio Tinto Zinc Corporation v. Westinghouse Electric Corporation, [1978] 1 All E.R. 434.

[93] [1978] 1 All E.R. 434, 448 (Opinion of Lord Wilberforce). The House of Lords also upheld the claim of privilege under British law.

(formerly the Treaty of Rome).[94] The Court of Appeal upheld the witnesses' claims of privilege under English law on this basis.[95]

Second, the practitioner must be prepared to litigate in both the United States court and the foreign court the question of whether privileges available under U.S. law are properly invoked. In its decision in *Rio Tinto Zinc,* the House of Lords implied that it had the power to determine whether the Fifth Amendment privilege was properly invoked by the RTZ witnesses.[96] Since the enforcing state may well determine the scope of privileges available under American law, it is imperative that the practitioner devise some means by which the practice under United States law may be presented to the foreign court.

Right to Decline Enforcement. Aside from Article 23, which permits a foreign state to refuse enforcement of a request designed to obtain pretrial discovery of documents,[97] the right of a state to decline enforcement of a letter of request is strictly limited. Under Article 12 of the Convention, an enforcing state may decline to enforce a letter of request only if the requested act does not fall within the function of the judiciary or the requested act would prejudice the sovereignty or security of the enforcing state.

There are, however, other methods by which a state can effectively limit the utility of a letter of request. First, if the letter requests a special method for obtaining evidence a state may decline to use such special procedures if it is in conflict with the state's own internal law and procedure.[98] This may significantly limit the utility of the request or negate the letter altogether.

Second, the letter and circumstances surrounding issuance of the letter may be interpreted by the enforcing state in such a way as to render the request outside the scope of the Hague Evidence Convention. In *Rio Tinto Zinc,* for example, the House of Lords found that the Justice Department's intervention had in essence converted the request into one for evidence to be used in a criminal proceeding which was outside the scope of The Hague Evidence Convention.[99]

---

94 Article 101 of the Treaty provides: "all agreements. . . and concerted practices which affect trade between member states and which have as their object or effect the prevention, restriction or distortion of competition within the Common Market, and in particular those which (a) directly or indirectly fix purchase or selling prices or any other trading conditions, (b) limit or control production, markets, technical developments, or investments. . . are prohibited." Violations of this provision are punishable by a fine.

95 [1977] 3 W.L.R. 430, 440 (C.A.).

96 [1978] 1 All E.R. 434, 437.

97 Article 23, Hague Evidence Convention.

98 Hague Evidence Convention, article 9.

99 [1978] 1 All E.R. 434, 448.

Use of Diplomatic Officers, Consular Agents and Commissioners

Chapter II of the Convention allows diplomatic officers, consular agents and persons appointed as commissioners to take evidence within a Convention state.[100] Evidence may be taken either from nationals or foreign citizens located within the state.[101] Diplomatic consular officers and commissioners may take all types of evidence.[102]

The person from whom evidence is sought to be obtained must be given notice to appear before the consular agent, diplomatic officer or commissioner.[103] The notice must be in the language of the state where the evidence is to be obtained.[104] Further, the notice must clearly state that the person is under no compulsion to appear and may be represented by counsel if desired.[105] Finally, the person requested to appear may invoke the privileges permitted by the law of the place where the examination is to take place or by the laws of the place where the action is pending.[106]

Although this method appears to be an attractive method of obtaining discovery, there are several limitations on its use which severely restrict its utility. First, the Convention provides that any state may reserve the right to place conditions on the use of this method or exclude this method as a means of discovery within its borders.[107] Several states which have ratified the Convention have done so.[108]

Second, this method of taking evidence is, for the most part, noncompulsory. Although a state may declare that it will use compulsory process to compel unwilling witnesses to appear before consular or diplomatic officers for the purposes of obtaining evidence, this is not often allowed.[109] Further, only the methods of compulsion

---

[100] *See* Tulip Computers Int'l B.V. v. Dell Computer Corp., 254 F.Supp.2d 469 (D. Del. 2003); Reiss v. Société Centrale du Groupe des Assurances Nationales, 246 F.Supp.2d 285 (S.D.N.Y. 2003).

[101] Hague Evidence Convention, article 16.

[102] Hague Evidence Convention, article 21.

[103] *Id.*

[104] *Id.*

[105] *Id.*

[106] *Id.*

[107] Hague Evidence Convention, article 33.

[108] For example, Norway, Portugal and Sweden have declared that prior permission from the appropriate local authority is required before evidence may be taken pursuant to Chapter II of The Hague Evidence Convention. For other reservations and conditions by Convention countries on the use of Chapter II see 28 U.S.C.A. § 1781.

[109] Hague Evidence Convention, article 18. The United States has so declared. 28 U.S.C.A. § 1781.

prescribed by the law of the place where the proceedings are to take place will apply.[110]

Third, evidence may be taken only in a manner consistent with the law of the state in which the proceedings are to take place.[111] Therefore, in convention states where testimony may be taken only by an authorized judicial officer, this method may not be available for the taking of depositions in the usual manner.

Finally, even if a state may be willing to allow this method of obtaining evidence within its boundaries, it may impose certain conditions on its use.[112] These conditions may be applied either generally or on a case-by-case basis.[113] Even though a state may permit this method and not have general conditions on its use, special conditions may be imposed on attempts to use this method in connection with an antitrust case.

§ 6.6 International Discovery in Antitrust Litigation[114]

The evidence needed to litigate an antitrust case with international aspects ordinarily will be no different from that needed to litigate domestic antitrust cases. Information must be gathered from adverse parties, non-party witnesses and experts. The difference lies primarily in where the evidence is located. The ability to obtain evidence from abroad, and the means available to obtain it, will depend significantly on whether the individual or corporation from whom evidence is sought is a party to the action and subject to the jurisdiction of U.S. courts, or a non-party having relevant information to the action.

In the case of a foreign party, discovery in most cases may proceed according to the Federal Rules of Civil Procedure. In the case of a non-party witness, discovery may be subject to the local laws of the place in which the witness is located or to the Convention on the Taking of Evidence Abroad in Civil or Commercial Matters (the "Hague Evidence Convention") (above).[115]

The Impact of Twombly. The U.S. Supreme Court's 2007 decision in *Bell Atl. Corp. v. Twombly*,[116] creating a more demanding standard

---

110 Hague Evidence Convention, article 18.

111 Hague Evidence Convention, article 21.

112 Hague Evidence Convention, articles 16 and 17.

113 *Id.*

114 Adapted from R. Folsom, "International Discovery in Antitrust Litigation", Chapter 15, in von Kalinowski, *Antitrust Litigation and Counseling Techniques* (Matthew-Bender Co.)

115 23 U.S.T. 2555, T.I.A.S. No. 7444, reprinted in 28 U.S.C.A. § 1781.

116 550 U.S. 544, 127 S.Ct. 1955, 167 L.Ed.2d 929 (2007).

for pleading antitrust cases, has notable implications for discovery, including international discovery. The Court's concerns with the burden and cost of discovery were central to its decision mandating that complaints must allege enough factual matter to suggest an unlawful agreement or conspiracy plausibly entitled to relief. As the Court noted, proceeding to antitrust discovery can be sprawling, costly, hugely time consuming, and expensive. It also noted that judicial supervision of the discovery process has been modest.

One of the effects of *Twombly* has been increased pressure on plaintiffs to seek early discovery, even before the filing of an operative complaint. Courts in the past have generally rejected such efforts under FRCP 26(b).[117] Likewise, in both domestic and international cases, they have generally rejected discovery efforts post-complaint but prior to decisions on motions to dismiss.[118] For example, one court delayed discovery of Lufthansa documents seized by the European Commission until it could determine if the pleading met *Twombly's* standards.[119]

Privacy Law Limitations on Discovery. Privacy law limitations in foreign jurisdictions, notably the European Union, may impact international antitrust discovery. Many such rules focus on the retention and transfer (by discovery or otherwise) of personal data, including business obligations. Rapid requests for retention of such data may avoid its routine destruction.

In 2018, the U.S. Clarifying Lawful Overseas Use of Data ("CLOUD") Act (H.R. 4943), was adopted. The Act clarifies, over opposition by Microsoft, that lawful orders issued under the U.S. Stored Communications Act may reach data located in other countries. By agreement with the United States, foreign governments may be pre-qualified to make foreign law enforcement data requests, subject to challenge, directly to U.S. service providers rather than by invoking U.S. government assistance.

International Agreements and Treaties Affecting Discovery. The United States has entered into bilateral treaties, agreements, and understandings concerning the exchange of information relating to anticompetitive business practices. Canada and the United States, for example, have been exchanging antitrust information since 1969.

Mutual Assistance Treaties. The International Antitrust Enforcement Assistance Act of 1994 (P.L. 103–438) authorizes mutual assistance agreements between the DOJ and FTC and their foreign counterparts. Such assistance includes the disclosure and

117 *See, e.g.*, Little v. Seattle, 863 F.2d 681 (9th Cir. 1988).

118 *See, e.g.*, DSM Desotech Inc. v. 3D Systems Corp., 2008 WL 4812440.

119 McLafferty v. Deutsche Lufthansa A.G., 2008 WL 4612856.

sharing of evidence. The first International Antitrust Enforcement Assistance Agreement was completed between Australia and the United States in 1997. Its focus is on mutual assistance for criminal investigations. Additional antitrust cooperation agreements were negotiated with Israel, Japan and Brazil in 1999, Mexico in 2000, Russia in 2009, Chile and China in 2010, and India in 2012. The DOJ maintains a list of such agreements at http://www.justice.gov/. Several of these agreements are selectively reviewed below. In August of 1995, the United States and Canada signed an antitrust and deceptive practices cooperation agreement, followed by a "positive comity" agreement in 2004 not unlike that between the EU and the United States.

In addition, the United States has over 60 Mutual Legal Assistance Treaties (MLAT) with other countries. The U.S. State department maintains a list of such treaties at http://www.state.gov/. The MLAT treaties focuses on *criminal* law enforcement, notably tax, securities, and antitrust. They generally *require* each country, upon request, to summon witness testimony, compel document production for trial use, issue search warrants, freeze assets, and assist in obtaining forfeitures. Hence, documents and depositions provided to U.S. authorities can end up in the hands of foreign antitrust officials. MLATs are treated as self-executing, and not limited by 28 U.S.C. § 1782 (see § 15.07).[120] The information sought need not be discoverable in the requesting jurisdiction.[121] Requests for assistance are made via each nation's "Central Authority" (usually Justice Departments).

Although these agreements and treaties focus on the disclosure of information related to governmental investigations and proceedings concerning anticompetitive conduct, they can have some effect on private antitrust actions in U.S. courts.

Discovery against Foreign Parties

In considering discovery against a foreign party to a U.S. antitrust case, the starting point is the Federal Rules of Civil Procedure. The Federal Rules permit the same discovery devices and sanctions (including default judgments)[122] employed in domestic civil litigation to be used to obtain discovery from a foreign national even

---

[120] *See* In re Commissioner's Subpoenas, 325 F.3d 1287 (11th Cir. 2003) (subpoenas issued to persons in the U.S. to compel testimony not discoverable in Canadian criminal proceedings, nor obtainable under Section 1782); United States v. Erato (In re Erato), 2 F.3d 11 (2d Cir. 1993).

[121] *See* In re Commissioner's Subpoenas, 325 F.3d 1287 (11th Cir. 2003).

[122] *See* United Nuclear Corp. v. General Atomic Co., 629 P. 2d 231 (N.M. 1980); Compagnie Francaise d' Assurance v. Phillips Petroleum Co., 105 F.R.D. 16 (S.D.N.Y. 1984).

when the information is located abroad.[123] Indeed, under the expansive "control test," U.S. courts can even compel production of evidence from foreign subsidiaries and affiliates of a U.S. party.[124]

The Relationship between the Optional Hague Convention and U.S. Discovery Procedures. The Federal Rules provide a broader range of discovery devices and require production of a broader range of information than is permitted under The Hague Evidence Convention. Many foreign litigants therefore have sought to resist or limit discovery in United States litigation by contending that the Hague Evidence Convention is the exclusive means of obtaining evidence located in Convention countries.

Prior to 1987, courts and commentators took differing views as to whether the Hague Evidence Convention was the exclusive means of obtaining evidence located in a Convention country.[125] The Supreme Court ultimately dealt with this issue in *Societe Nationale Industrielle Aerospatiale v. United States District Court for the*

---

[123] *See, e.g.*, In re Uranium Antitrust Litigation, 480 F.Supp. 1138, 1980–1 Trade Cas. (CCH) P63124 (N.D. Ill. 1979); In re Auto. Refinishing Paint Antitrust Litigation, 358 F.3d 288 (3d Cir. 2004).

[124] United States v. First Nat'l City Bank, 396 F.2d 897 (2d Cir. 1968).

[125] The following cases held that the Hague Evidence Convention is not the exclusive means of obtaining evidence located in convention countries: Société Nationale Industrielle Aerospatiale v. United States District Court for the Southern District of Iowa, 482 U.S. 522, 107 S.Ct. 2542, 96 L.Ed.2d 461 (1987); In re Messerschmitt Bolkow Blohm & GmbH, 757 F.2d 729 (5th Cir. 1985), *cert. vacated*, 483 U.S. 1002, 107 S.Ct. 3223, 97 L.Ed.2d 730 (1987) (vacated in light of *Societe Nationale Industrielle Aerospatiale*, supra); Testerion, Inc. v. Skoog, Civ. No. 4–84–911 slip op. (M.D. Tenn. 1986); Work v. Bier, 106 F.R.D. 45 (D.D.C. 1985); Compagnie Francaise D'Assurance Pour Le Commerce Exterieur v. Phillips Petroleum Co., 105 F.R.D. 16 (S.D.N.Y. 1984); Graco, Inc. v. Kremlin, Inc., 101 F.R.D. 503 (N.D. Ill. 1984); Murphy v. Reifenhauser KG Maschinenfabrik, 101 F.R.D. 360 (D. Vt. 1984); Lasky v. Continental Products Corp., 569 F.Supp. 1227 (E.D. Pa. 1983); Slavenwhite v. Ekim Machinenfabriken, GmbH, 104 F.R.D. 616 (D. Mass. 1985); International Society for Krishna Consciousness v. Lee, 105 F.R.D. 435 (S.D.N.Y. 1984); Beckman Instruments, Inc. v. LKB Produkter AB, 229 U.S.P.Q. 78 (D. Md. 1986).

The following cases held the Hague Evidence Convention is the exclusive means of obtaining discovery in Convention countries: Philadelphia Gear Corp. v. American Pfauter Corp., 100 F.R.D. 58 (E.D. Pa. 1983); Schroder v. Lufthansa German Airlines, 1983 U.S. Dist. LEXIS 13735 (N.D. Ill. 1983); Volkswagenwerk, A.G. v. Superior Court, 123 Cal. App.3d 840, 176 Cal. Rptr. 874 (1979); Pierburg, GmbH v. Superior Court, 137 Cal. App. 3d 238, 186 Cal. Rptr. 876 (1982).

Commentators also urged that the Hague Evidence Convention be treated as the exclusive means of obtaining discovery in Convention countries. *See* Comment, "The Hague Evidence Convention on the Taking of Evidence Abroad in Civil or Commercial Matters: The Exclusive and Mandatory Procedures for Discovery Abroad," 132 U. Pa. L. Rev. 1461 (1984); Heck, "U.S. Misinterpretation of the Hague Evidence Convention," 24 Colum. J. Transnat'l L. 231 (1986).

The issue of whether the Hague Evidence Convention preempts state rules of discovery has been raised in two cases. Dorin v. Club Mediterranee, S.A., 93 A.D.2d 1007, 462 N.Y.S.2d 524 (1st Dep't 1983), *cert. denied and appeal dismissed*, 469 U.S 913 (1984); Falzon v. Volkswagen Mfg. Corp., 417 Mich. 889 (1983), *appeal dismissed*, 465 U.S. 1014, 104 S.Ct. 1260, 79 L.Ed.2d 668 (1984).

Southern District of Iowa (*'Aerospatiale'*),[126] holding that the Hague Convention is not the sole means of obtaining evidence located in a Convention country.

As to Parties Subject to Court Jurisdiction. The Supreme Court ruled in *Aerospatiale* that discovery may proceed according to the Federal Rules against nationals of other Convention states where the U.S. court has jurisdiction over the foreign parties.[127] In *Aerospatiale*, the plaintiffs sued a French airplane manufacturer and others for damages as a result of personal injuries caused by the crash of a plane sold and manufactured by the defendants. After the plaintiffs served the defendants with discovery under the Federal Rules of Civil Procedure, the defendants asked for a ruling that the Hague Evidence Convention procedures were mandatory because the evidence sought was located in France. The District Court denied the motion. The defendants then sought a writ of mandamus to compel the trial court to use the Convention's discovery procedures. The Eighth Circuit denied the writ.[128] The defendants then sought a writ of certiorari from the Supreme Court. The Court granted the writ, but ruled against the plaintiffs on the merits, holding that the Hague Convention is not the sole means of obtaining evidence located in a Convention courtry.[129]

In reaching its decision the Supreme Court looked to the language of the Convention, finding numerous instances in which permissive rather than mandatory terms were used.[130] This indicated to the Court that the Convention was not intended to be the exclusive means of obtaining information located abroad. Despite this conclusion, the Court did not discard the Convention. Instead, it held that considerations of international comity should be utilized in deciding whether to use the Federal Rules or the Hague Evidence Convention. Comity, the Court stated, requires "a particularized analysis of the respective interests of the foreign nation and the requesting nation."[131] The Court listed the following factors as being relevant to any comity analysis:

(1) The importance to the litigation of the documents or other information requested;

(2) The degree of specificity of the request;

---

126 482 U.S. 522, 107 S.Ct. 2542, 96 L.Ed.2d 461 (1987).

127 107 S.Ct. at 2552.

128 782 F.2d 120 (5th Cir. 1985).

129 107 S.Ct. at 2553.

130 *Id.*

131 107 S.Ct. at 556.

(3) Whether the information originated in the United States;

(4) The availability of alternative means of securing the information; and

(5) The extent to which noncompliance with the request would undermine important interests of the United States, or compliance with the request would undermine important interests of the state in which the information is located.[132]

The Court also said that the degree of a discovery request's intrusiveness should be considered in a comity analysis.[133] After applying this comity analysis to the *Aerospatiale* facts, the Court held that the plaintiffs would be allowed to conduct discovery pursuant to the Federal Rules of Civil Procedure. Although *Aerospatiale* suggests that discovery against foreign parties subject to U.S. jurisdiction often, or even usually, will proceed according to the Federal Rules of Civil Procedure, the Court's comity discussion leaves room for argument that the Hague Convention should be used in a particular case.

As to Parties Challenging Jurisdiction. Different concerns arise when the court's jurisdiction over a foreign national is challenged. While courts in this instance usually require a plaintiff to make a prima facie showing of jurisdiction before discovery on this issue will be compelled, the party seeking to establish jurisdiction often wishes to conduct discovery on the jurisdictional issue. The propriety of discovery in these circumstances is well established.

In *Insurance Corporation of Ireland v. Compagnie de Bauxites de Guinee,*[134] the Supreme Court held that an American court may compel discovery from foreign nationals on the question of jurisdiction and impose sanctions if they do not comply. But the question remained whether a national of a Convention state may be subjected to discovery pursuant to the Federal Rules before jurisdiction is established, or whether the Hague Evidence Convention is the exclusive vehicle in that situation. A Subsequent

---

132 *Id.*, n. 28, citing the *Restatement of Foreign Relations Law of the United States* (Revised) § 437(1)(C) (Tent. Draft No. 7, 1986) (Approved May 14, 1986). *See* In re Baycol Products Litigation, 348 F.Supp.2d 1058 (D. Minn. 2004); Tulip Computers Int'l BV v. Dell Computer Corp., 254 F.Supp.2d 469 (D. Del. 2003); First American Corp. v. Price Waterhouse LLP, 154 F.3d 16 (2nd Cir. 1998).

133 107 S.Ct. at 2556.

134 456 U.S. 694, 102 S.Ct. 2099, 72 L.Ed.2d 492 (1982).

decisions suggest that the Evidence Convention is not mandatory for discovery in connection with jurisdictional issues.[135]

Depositions

As far as the Federal Rules are concerned, deposition practice involving efforts to obtain discovery from foreign nationals or to obtain evidence located abroad can be the same as in domestic cases. If the party or witness is within the court's jurisdiction or if the deposition is to be conducted in the United States, a deposition may be conducted in the usual way. Although the Federal Rules do not explicitly say so, a corporation subject to the court's jurisdiction may be directed to appear by an officer, director or managing agent and may be subjected to Rule 37 sanctions if the individual fails to appear.[136]

The Federal Rules also contemplate the conduct of depositions abroad. Apart from evidence treaties or conventions, like the Hague Convention discussed above, Rule 28(b) prescribes three methods by which the deposition of a party or non-party may be taken in a foreign country: (1) on notice (as within U.S. territory); (2) by commission which involves the appointment by the U.S. court of a person before whom the deposition will take place; and (3) by letter rogatory which is a formal request by the U.S. court to the foreign court for assistance in obtaining evidence. Where the parties agree and the witness is willing to testify, the parties may stipulate to a deposition under the Federal Rules on foreign soil.[137] Where the deponent is from a Hague or other Evidence Convention country, those procedures should be used.

Deposition on Notice. The notice procedure is a voluntary private arrangement between the parties with no intervention of either foreign or U.S. courts. FRCP Rule 28(b)(1)(C) permits such depositions before persons authorized to administer oaths by federal law or the law in the place of examination. In some countries, deposition by notice is limited or even prohibited.[138] Hence, persuading a witness to come to the United States for a deposition on notice is preferable.

Deposition by Commission. FRCP Rule 28(b)(1)(D) authorizes U.S. courts to designate individuals to administer oaths and take depositions outside the United States. Such commissions are

[135] In re Automotive Refinishing Paint Antitrust Litigation, 358 F.3d 288 (3rd Cir. 2004); In re Vitamins Antitrust Litigation, 120 F.Supp.2d 45 (D.D.C. 2000); Fishel v. BASF Group, 175 F.R.D. 525 (S.D. Iowa 1997).

[136] E.g., 8 C. Wright & A. Miller, *Federal Practice & Procedure: Civil* §§ 2103, 2107 (1970).

[137] Fed. R. Civ. P. 29.

[138] *See, e.g.*, Article 271 of the Swiss Penal Code.

typically issued to U.S. consular officers. Advance planning with the U.S. State Department's Office of Overseas Citizens Services is advisable. In most countries, there is no power to compel a witness to give a deposition by commission and in certain jurisdictions, such as Switzerland, they are absolutely prohibited. In the United Kingdom, however, the order for a commission deposition can be filed with a local court, which may elect to compel testimony and rule on disputed responses.[139]

Deposition by Letters of Request/Letters Rogatory. FRCP Rule 28(b)(2) permits letters of request (often referred to as letters rogatory) to obtain evidence. Such letters are essentially request by U.S. courts to foreign courts to take the deposition of witnesses within their territories, and to transmit such testimony to the U.S. court. All U.S. courts have inherent authority to issue such letters, regardless of whether they are addressed to jurisdictions that does not participate in the Hague Convention on Evidence. The requesting party may ask for specific procedures to be followed, but procedural issues are generally decided under the law of the receiving country.[140] Letters rogatory should be detailed as to questions to be posed (including cross-examination or supplementary questions), and indicate if document production is requested. They should be translated as needed and are normally delivered via diplomatic channels. In civil law jurisdictions, the deposition is likely to be taken by a local judge, not counsel. A transcript may not necessarily be generated, with the judge instead producing a summary of the testimony.

Legality of Depositions Abroad. Notwithstanding our Federal Rules, some countries regard the conduct of U.S. discovery proceedings on their soil as an infringement of their sovereignty and, indeed, as a criminal offense.[141] Since foreign law may have a serious impact on conducting a deposition abroad, the practitioner should be well aware of the scope and nature of laws relating to depositions. This may be determinative in deciding where to hold the deposition and the method by which the deposition is taken.

---

139 Take note of the UK "blocking statute" reproduced in Section 5.8.

140 *See* In re Clerici, 481 F.3d 1324 (11th Cir. 2007).

141 *See, e.g.,* In re Messerschmitt Bolkow Blohm GmbH, 757 F.2d 729 (5th Cir. 1985), *cert. vacated,* 107 S.Ct. 3223 (1987) (vacated in light of Société Nationale Industrielle Aerospatiale v. United States Dist. Court for Southern Dist., 482 U.S. 522, 107 S.Ct. 2542, 96 L.Ed.2d 461 (1987)). The unauthorized taking of depositions in Switzerland, for example, is a crime. See Section 271, Swiss Penal Code of December 21, 1937 as amended. It is also prohibited in Brazil, Japan, Venezuela, Luxembourg, Denmark, Afghanistan, Russia and China. In contrast, Belgium, France and Germany permit voluntary testimony taken by commission.

Location. In order to avoid the problems that may be associated with taking a deposition abroad, it is advisable at the outset to attempt to notice the depositions of employees, officers or agents of a foreign party for a site within the United States. As a general rule, a foreign plaintiff will be compelled to produce its employees, officers and agents for deposition in the United States.[142] A foreign defendant often will not be compelled to do so.

If the deposition must be taken abroad, the law of the country in which the deposition is to be conducted may make it be advisable to arrange to have the deposition taken at the local U.S. Embassy or Consulate, since these locations are considered to be within the territory of the United States.

If the U.S. Embassy is not available and the conduct of a deposition is illegal under applicable foreign law, the practitioner should consider either changing the site of the deposition to a nearby country which does not prohibit the taking of American-style depositions or utilizing the procedures of the Hague Evidence Convention.

If all else fails, the practitioner should consider applying to the court for an order compelling production of the witness in the United States.

Administration of Oaths. Rule 28(b) provides that depositions taken on foreign soil may be conducted either before a person authorized to administer oaths in the place in which the examination is to be held, or by the laws of the United States, or before a person commissioned by the court to administer the necessary oaths and take evidence.

The practices of foreign countries vary widely on who is permitted to administer oaths. Therefore, before embarking on the deposition in a foreign country, the practitioner should consult counsel in the country where the deposition is to take place concerning the legality of the administration of the oath by a court-ordered commissioner or United States notary.

Discovery by Letters Rogatory

The letter rogatory is analogous to the letter of request procedure prescribed by the Hague Evidence Convention (see § 15.02). It can be used with any jurisdiction. The letter rogatory seeks assistance from a foreign tribunal in obtaining compliance with a discovery request. This procedure may be utilized in any situation,

---

142 *See, e.g.*, de Dalmady v. Price Waterhouse & Co., 62 F.R.D. 157 (D.P.R. 1973); Grotrian, Helfferich, Schulz, Th. Steinweg Nachf. v. Steinway & Sons, 54 F.R.D. 280 (S.D.N.Y. 1971).

but is most useful in the situation where evidence is sought from a witness over whom the U.S. court lacks jurisdiction and who is located in a *non-Convention* country.

Issuance. The letter rogatory may be issued by any court of the United States.[143] As with The Hague Convention letter of request procedure, the practitioner must apply directly to the court, stating the reasons for issuance of the letter, the information sought and the witness from whom the party proposes to obtain the information.

Once the court has determined that the judicial assistance of another country is necessary[144] and the letter has been prepared, it is transmitted to the foreign tribunal either directly[145] or through the Department of State.[146] Several countries require transmittal of the letter rogatory through diplomatic channels only.[147] Therefore, the practitioner should be aware of the foreign country's policy for receiving letters rogatory before applying to the court for assistance.

Enforcement. A letter rogatory is a request for judicial assistance and does not obligate a foreign tribunal to provide such assistance, particularly where doing so would violate its own law or national policy.[148]

If a foreign tribunal agrees to lend its assistance in compelling discovery, it need not adopt U.S.-style discovery procedures.[149] A request by means of a letter rogatory for a deposition of a witness may not result in an American-style deposition, but in an examination by the judicial authority and the preparation of a written summary. Parties to the litigation should all include their questions, for example cross-examination questions, in the letters rogatory to avoid possible rejection by the local judicial authority.

The Federal Rules provide that evidence obtained by means of a letter rogatory need not be excluded solely on the ground that it does not conform to the standard form of evidence obtained in a wholly domestic proceeding.[150] Although this is meant to ease the burden on the party who must depend upon evidence obtained abroad, it does not guarantee that the evidence so obtained will be useful. Thus the

---

143 United States v. Staples, 256 F.2d 290, 292 (9th Cir. 1958).

144 For rejection of a deposition letter rogatory, *see* U.S. v. Rosen, 240 F.R.D. 204 (E.D. Va. 2007). As to the expense of letters rogatory, *see* Anglo American Ins. Group v. CalFed Inc., 940 F.Supp. 554 (1996)

145 28 U.S.C. § 1781(b)(2).

146 28 U.S.C. § 1781(a)(2).

147 22 C.F.R. § 92.66(b).

148 *See, e.g.*, Gulf Oil Corp. v. Gulf Canada, Ltd., 111 D.L.R.3d 73 (Sup. Ct. 1980).

149 *See* United States v. Parrafin Wax, 23 F.R.D. 289 (E.D.N.Y. 1959).

150 Fed. R. Civ. P. 28(b).

letter rogatory procedure presents many of the same problems as the letter of request procedure under the Hague Evidence Convention.

Documents and Interrogatories

Rule 34 permits one party to serve upon another party a request for documents within the scope of Rule 26(b) that are within "the possession, custody or control of the party upon whom the request is served."[151] The key concept is "control." The control issue frequently arises in the context of efforts to obtain documents from multinational enterprises, one of the constituent entities of which is a party to a U.S. litigation.

If the parent company, whether a U.S. or a foreign corporation, is a party to the U.S. litigation and subject to jurisdiction, there is little problem so far as the Federal Rules are concerned. The parent ordinarily controls its foreign subsidiaries and therefore a court usually will compel production of documents in the possession of those subsidiaries despite the fact that they are abroad.[152]

The problem becomes more difficult where the party to the U.S. litigation is a subsidiary of a foreign parent company and a Rule 34 request seeks documents in the hands of the parent. In such circumstances, it cannot be said that the subsidiary controls the parent. So U.S. courts typically proceed in a manner analogous to piercing the corporate veil. If the American subsidiary and the foreign parent are so intertwined as to give the appearance of a pattern of control or stand in such a relationship to the litigation that to deny the Rule 34 request would frustrate discovery, production may be required.[153]

In *In re Uranium Antitrust Litigation,*[154] for example, the issue was whether one of the defendants, Rio Algom Corporation, could be compelled to produce documents in the custody of its foreign parent, Rio Algom Ltd. In analyzing the relationship between the subsidiary and parent, the court focused on formal mechanisms of corporate control: ownership of shares, interlocking directorates and common management systems. The court found that the subsidiary and parent were so intertwined as to constitute a single business

---

151 Fed. R. Civ. P. 34(a).

152 *See* In re Uranium Antitrust Litigation, 480 F.Supp. 1138, 1144–1145 (N.D. Ill. 1979), citing In re Investigation of World Arrangements, 13 F.R.D. 280, 285 (D.D.C. 1952).

153 *See* In re Uranium Antitrust Litigation, 480 F.Supp. at 1145; Compagnie Francaise D'Assurance pour Le Commerce Exterieur v. Phillips Petroleum Co., 105 F.R.D. 16, 33–34 (S.D.N.Y. 1984). *See also* Smalley, *How to Conduct International Discovery* 71 Am. Jur. Trials 1 (1999).

154 480 F.Supp. 1138 (N.D. Ill. 1979).

entity.[155] The court held that the subsidiary could be compelled to produce documents in the custody of its foreign parent.

Compagnie Francaise D'Assurance Pour Le Commerce Exterieur (COFACE) v. Phillips Petroleum[156] presented a roughly analogous situation. COFACE there argued that it could not produce documents in the hands of the French Ministry of Finance and Economy. The court held that COFACE could be compelled to produce the documents. The court noted that the French government owned 85% of COFACE. COFACE was acting merely as an agent for the government. Indeed, the court found that the French government would ultimately receive the benefits of a successful outcome of COFACE's litigation. Therefore, COFACE could be deemed to have control over the documents.[157]

Rule 33 permits parties to serve interrogatories upon one another. The same control limitations apply under this provision as under Rule 34, as the answering party is only obliged to answer to the extent "such information is available to the [answering] party."[158]

Discovery against Foreign Non-Parties

The Federal Rules do not permit a litigant to use the same range of discovery techniques against non-parties as are available against parties.[159] Generally, discovery against non-parties is limited to the taking of testimony by deposition and the production of documents pursuant to a subpoena. A subpoena can be issued to a non-party witness in a foreign country only if that witness is a national or resident of the United States and the court determines that his or her testimony or documents are "necessary in the interest of justice" and not otherwise obtainable.[160] In the case of a foreign national, evidence can only be obtained if permitted by foreign law or by treaty or convention, and the deposition procedures allowed by FRCP Rule 28(b) are followed. These Rules are detailed below. Non-party discovery can be compelled even in the face of foreign statutes specifically opposed to it.[161]

---

155 *Id.* at 1153.

156 105 F.R.D. 16 (S.D.N.Y. 1984).

157 *Id.* at 32–34.

158 Fed. R. Civ. P. 33(a). For a case using the Hague Convention for service of interrogatories, *see* Hudson v. Hermann Pfauter GmbH, 117 F.R.D. 33 (N.D.N.Y. 1987).

159 Fed. R. Civ. P. 34(a) limits requests for the production of documents to parties. Similarly Fed. R. Civ. P. 33 permits interrogatories to be served only on parties.

160 228 U.S.C. § 1783; Fed. R. Civ. P. 45(b)(3).

161 Linde v. Arab Bank PLC, 463 F.Supp.2d 310 (E.D.N.Y. 2006).For a non-party discovery of documents case under The Hague Convention, *see* S & S Screw Machinery Corp. v. Cosa Corp., 647 F.Supp. 600 (M.D. Tenn. 1986).

Non-Parties Having a Presence in the United States. If a foreign non-party witness can be served with a subpoena in the United States, a U.S. court may compel it to submit to depositions and produce documents much as it can compel discovery against a foreign party over whom it has jurisdiction.[162]

Compelling Production of Documents Located Abroad. In order to obtain documents from a non-party witness over whom the court has jurisdiction, be it an American or a foreign person or entity, it is necessary to serve a subpoena directing the witness to appear and to bring designated documents for inspection and copying. If the non-party witness objects to discovery he or she may move to have the subpoena quashed or file objections pursuant to Rule 45.

The cases are divided on whether a foreign entity having offices in the United States will be required to produce documents located abroad.[163] In *United States v. Bank of Nova Scotia,*[164] the Bank of Nova Scotia, a Canadian bank with offices in the United States, refused to comply with a subpoena for documents located in its Bahamian branch offices. The subpoena related to the financial records of a bank customer who was the target of a federal criminal grand jury investigation. The district court cited the bank for contempt for failure to comply with the subpoena. On appeal of the contempt citation, the bank argued that the principle of comity among nations precluded enforcement of the subpoena. The bank argued that its compliance with the subpoena would be illegal under the Bahamian bank secrecy laws[165] and therefore suggested that the proper means of seeking the information was to apply for assistance to the Bahamian courts rather than compel the bank to produce the documents pursuant to the subpoena.

The court of appeals rejected the Bank's arguments and affirmed the lower court's order. The court found that the U.S. interest protecting the grand jury's investigative function outweighed the privacy interest protected by the bank secrecy laws. The court also rejected the Bank's argument that a request for judicial assistance

---

[162] In re Grand Jury Proceedings, 691 F.2d 1384 (11th Cir. 1982); United States v. First National City Bank, 396 F.2d 897 (2d Cir. 1968).

[163] The following courts have required production of documents pursuant to subpoena: United States v. First National City Bank, 396 F.2d 897 (2d Cir. 1968); In re Grand Jury Proceedings, 691 F.2d 1384 (11th Cir. 1982); First National City Bank v. Internal Revenue Service, 271 F.2d 616 (2d Cir. 1959).

The following courts have not required production of documents pursuant to a subpoena: Ings v. Ferguson, 282 F.2d 149 (2d Cir. 1960); Laker Airways Ltd. v. Pan American World Airways, 607 F.Supp. 324 (S.D.N.Y. 1985).

[164] 691 F.2d 1384 (11th Cir. 1982).

[165] *Id.* at 1391.

was proper means of obtaining the information because that procedure did not accord proper deference to American interests.[166]

In *Laker Airways Ltd. v. Pan American World Airways,*[167] however, the court came out the other way. In *Laker,* two English banks moved to quash subpoenas served on their New York offices. Neither bank was a party to the litigation. The subpoenas sought documents related to loan applications that had been made to the banks in England and had subsequently been denied.

The court granted the banks' motion to quash the subpoenas. The court reasoned that the subpoena was being used to circumvent the Hague Evidence Convention procedures in order to compel production of documents in violation of British law. It therefore concluded that the subpoena power was being abused.[168] The court was particularly sensitive to the nature of the litigation in which evidence was sought. The court noted that antitrust litigation involving foreign corporations was a sensitive issue with foreign governments and particularly so in *Laker* because the case implicated British governmental policy.[169] Although the court did not reach the question of whether the Hague Evidence Convention was the exclusive means by which discovery could be obtained, it strongly indicated that in the situation presented it was probably the preferable means of obtaining the desired information.

Although the *Laker* court and the *Bank of Nova Scotia* court reached contradictory results, the courts' analyses were similar. In both cases, the courts had jurisdiction over the foreign witness by virtue of the fact that the companies had offices in the United States and transacted business here. Both courts, however, weighed the interests of the United States in enforcing the subpoena against those of a foreign country in furthering its policy in determining whether to enforce the subpoena. In this respect both decisions are consistent with the Supreme Court's opinion in *Aerospatiale* which mandates a comity analysis in resolving conflicts between The Hague Evidence Convention and the Federal Rules of Civil Procedure.[170]

Compelling Testimony of Witnesses Located Abroad. Is it possible to obtain the testimony of a witness located abroad who is

---

[166] *Id.*

[167] 607 F.Supp. 324 (S.D.N.Y. 1985). Accord First Am. Corp. v. Price Waterhouse LLP, 154 F.3d 16 (2d Cir. 1998) (foreign accounting firm properly served with document subpoena on a partner residing in Connecticut). 607 F.Supp. 324 (S.D.N.Y. 1985). Accord First Am. Corp. v. Price Waterhouse LLP, 154 F.3d 16 (2d Cir. 1998) (foreign accounting firm properly served with document subpoena on a partner residing in Connecticut).

[168] *Id.* at 326.

[169] *Id.* at 327.

[170] 482 U.S. 522, 107 S.Ct. 2542, 96 L.Ed.2d 461 (1987).

an employee of a foreign corporation by serving a subpoena on the U.S. office of the corporation?

Rule 45 is silent on this question.[171] Rule 30, however, does shed some light on it. Rule 30 provides that a party may name a corporation as deponent in a notice of deposition and subpoena.[172] The party seeking to depose the corporation may then designate an officer, director or managing agent to testify on behalf of the corporation.[173] If the corporation refuses to produce the witness to testify on its behalf, sanctions may be imposed for its failure to do so.[174]

The courts have interpreted Rule 30 strictly in determining who will be considered to speak on behalf of a corporation. An employee who is not an officer, director or managing agent of the corporation will not be considered to speak on behalf of the corporation.[175] Some courts have refused to compel corporations to produce unwilling employees who are not officers, directors or managing agents for deposition.[176]

Practice under Rule 30(b) suggests that Rule 45 may be construed to require a non-party corporation to produce an officer, director or managing agent for examination, at least if the examination relates to matters within the scope of employment. This finds support in a decision by the New York Court of Appeals which held that a corporation was obliged to produce out-of-state officers and employees having knowledge about the events at issue pursuant to an investigatory subpoena.[177]

Non-Parties Lacking a Presence in the United States. If the non-party from whom discovery is sought lacks a presence in the United States, one can proceed only by arrangement with the non-party witness or by seeking the judicial assistance, through The Hague Evidence Convention or another means, of the country in which the witness is located.

---

171 Fed. R. Civ. P. 45(a).

172 Fed. R. Civ. P. 30(b)(6).

173 Advisory Committee Note of 1970 to Amended Subdivision [30](b), reprinted in 4A J. Moore, *Moore's Federal Practice* ¶ 30.01[19] at 30–27 (2d ed. 1984).

174 Bon Air Hotel, Inc. v. Time, Inc., 376 F.2d 118 (5th Cir. 1967).

175 Cleveland v. Palmby, 75 F.R.D. 654 (W.D. Okla. 1977); Burns Bros. v. The B. & O. No. 177, 21 F.R.D. 142 (E.D.N.Y. 1957).

176 Cleveland v. Palmby, 75 F.R.D. 654 (W.D. Okla. 1977); Banks v. Travelers Insurance Co., 60 F.R.D. 158 (E.D. Pa. 1973); Mattingly v. Boston Woven Hose & Rubber Co., 12 F.R.D. 266 (S.D.N.Y. 1952).

177 Standard Fruit & Steamship Co. v. Waterfront Com. of New York Harbor, 43 N.Y.2d 11, 400 N.Y.S.2d 732, 371 N.E.2d 453 (1977); *see also* Stanford v. Kuwait Airlines Corp. et al., 1987 WL 26829 (court may order foreign non-party corporation to produce witnesses subject to Fed. R. Civ. P. 45(d) (a)).

Willing Witnesses. If a non-party is willing to testify or produce documents, discovery may be arranged in the same way as for a willing adverse party. The practitioner should be aware, however, that even in the case of a willing witness foreign law may pose problems. As has been pointed out already, these problems can range from the illegality of taking testimony or producing documents on foreign soil to the illegality of revealing certain privileged information. In some cases, these problems may be avoidable by arranging to have discovery take place outside of the foreign country's jurisdiction or obtaining a waiver of privilege. In other cases, the problems may well be unavoidable.

Unwilling Witnesses. If the non-party witness is unwilling to appear or produce documents, some means of compulsion will be required in order to obtain the information sought. Since the witness is beyond the power of the U.S. court,[178] foreign judicial assistance will be required. Thus counsel must apply to the U.S. court under Rule 28(b) for foreign judicial assistance.[179]

Once the United States court has determined that the discovery sought is appropriate, the court will issue a letter requesting the assistance of the foreign judicial authority. If the witness is located in a Hague Evidence Convention country, a letter of request will be directed to the appropriate judicial authority.[180] The manner of enforcement will be subject to the limitations of the law of both the requesting state and the state from which assistance is requested.[181]

If the witness resides in a non-Convention country, a letter rogatory may be issued by the U.S. court and transmitted through the proper channels. Enforcement of the letter, however, will be determined solely by the law of the country in which the witness resides.

Discovery against U.S. Citizens or Residents Living Abroad (Section 1783)

If discovery is sought from an U.S. citizen or resident living abroad, a subpoena may be obtained to compel either testimony or the production of documents.[182] In order to obtain the subpoena, the party seeking discovery must show that the information sought is necessary and that it is not possible to obtain the information in any

---

178 U.S. v. Korolkov, 870 F.Supp. 60 (S.D.N.Y. 1994) (subpoena not possible); Air Turbine Technology, Inc. v. Atlas Copco AB, 217 F.R.D. 545 (S.D. Fla 2003) (video conference testimony not possible).

179 See text above.

180 Hague Evidence Convention, article 1.

181 Hague Evidence Convention, articles 9, 10, 11, 12.

182 28 U.S.C. § 1783.

other manner. The court, in the exercise of its discretion, will determine whether the proper showing in the interest of justice has been made.[183]

The subpoena will specify the time and place of the examination, in the case of a deposition, or for the production of documents.[184] Once the court has issued the subpoena, it may be served in accordance with the Federal Rules.[185] Counsel should bear in mind, however, that service in a foreign country may violate local law. Accordingly, it may be necessary to obtain a letter rogatory requesting the foreign authority to serve the subpoena.[186]

When service of the subpoena is made, the person serving the subpoena shall also tender all necessary travel and attendance expenses.[187] These expenses will generally be borne by the party seeking discovery.

U.S. Discovery by Persons Interested in Foreign Legal Proceedings (Section 1782)

Section 1782 of Title 28 of the United States Code allows tribunals and persons interested in existing or contemplated legal proceedings *outside* the United States to apply to an American court to obtain evidence for use in the non-U.S. proceeding. The full name of Section 1782 is "Assistance to foreign and international tribunals and to litigants before such tribunals."[188] In essence, an applicant under Section 1782 needs to show three things: (a) It is an "interested person" in a foreign proceeding, (b) the proceeding is before a foreign "tribunal," and (c) the person from whom evidence is sought resides or is found in the district of the court before which the application

---

[183] Blackmer v. United States, 284 U.S. 421, 52 S.Ct. 252, 76 L.Ed. 375 (1932); Klesch & Co. Ltd. v. Liberty Media Corp., 217 F.R.D. 517 (D. Colo. 2003); Estate of Ungar v. Palestinian Authority, 412 F.Supp.2d 328 (S.D.N.Y. 2006).

[184] 28 U.S.C. § 1783(b).

[185] 28 U.S.C. § 1783(b). For foreign service of process procedures, see Fed. R. Civ. P. 4(i).

[186] Estate of Ungar v. Palestinian Authority, 412 F.Supp.2d 328 (S.D.N.Y. 2006).

[187] 28 U.S.C. § 1783(b).

[188] The text of Section 1782(a) reads as follows:

> The district court of the district in which a person resides or is found may order him to give his testimony or statement or to produce a document or other thing for use in a proceeding in a foreign or international tribunal, including criminal investigations conducted before formal accusation. The order may be made pursuant to a letter rogatory issued, or request made, by a foreign or international tribunal or upon the application of any interested person. . . . The order may prescribe the practice and procedure, which may be in whole or part the practice and procedure of the foreign country or the international tribunal, for taking the testimony or statement or producing the document or other thing. To the extent that the order does not prescribe otherwise, the testimony or statement shall be taken, and the document or other thing produced, in accordance with the Federal Rules of Civil Procedure.

has been filed. Either U.S. or foreign parties can use Section 1782,[189] and non-parties can be compelled under it.[190]

Service of a Section 1782 order can be done while an individual is visiting the United States,[191] or a business has systematic and continuous activities in the relevant judicial district.[192] Both documentary evidence and testimonial evidence may be obtained under Section 1782, though at the court's broad discretion reciprocal exchanges of information may be required.[193] The material sought need not be discoverable in the foreign jurisdiction, though its admissibility in evidence is a relevant consideration[194] as is its unavailability to the foreign tribunal.[195] Foreign discovery procedures need not be exhausted to invoke Section 1782.[196]

For many years, federal district and appellate courts disagreed as to the scope of permitted evidence-taking under Section 1782, who may request Section 1782 discovery, at what stage of a non-U.S. proceeding a Section 1782 order may be granted, the meaning of the term "tribunal," and whether an applicant under Section 1782 needed to show that the requested evidence would be "discoverable" in the foreign jurisdiction. These issues were significantly clarified by the Supreme Court in *Intel Corp. v. Advanced Micro Devices, Inc.*[197]

The Supreme Court held that Section 1782 discovery may be sought not just by litigants but by any "interested person," such discovery may be sought prior to the initiation of formal proceedings outside the United States, and a "tribunal" within the meaning of the section is any tribunal that acts as a "first instance decision-maker." The Court also largely rejected any requirement of "discoverability"

---

189 Lancaster Factoring Co. v. Mangone, 90 F.3d 38 (2d Cir. 1996); Weber v. Finker, 554 F.3d 1379 (11th Cir. 2009) (MLAT no barrier to Swiss criminal defendant getting discovery in U.S.).

190 *Intel*, infra, at 2476.

191 Edelman v. Taittinger (In re Edelman), 295 F.3d 171 (2d Cir. 2002).

192 In re Inversiones y Gasolinera Petroleos Valenzuela, 2011 WL 181311.

193 *See* Euromepa, S.A. v. R. Esmerian, Inc., 51 F.3d 1095 (2d Cir. 1995).

194 John Deere, Ltd. v. Sperry Corp., 754 F.2d 132 (3d Cir. 1985).

195 Fleischmann v. McDonald's Corp. (In re Application for an Order for Judicial Assistance in a Foreign Proceeding in the Labor Court of Braz.), 466 F.Supp.2d 1020 (N.D. Ill. 2006).

196 Fleischmann v. McDonald's Corp. (In re Application for an Order for Judicial Assistance in a Foreign Proceeding in the Labor Court of Braz.), 466 F.Supp.2d 1020 (N.D. Ill. 2006).

197 542 U.S. 241, 124 S.Ct. 2466, 159 L.Ed.2d 355 (2004). Intel was an antitrust complainant before the Commission of the European Community. Compare In re Microsoft Corp., 428 F.Supp.2d 188 (S.D.N.Y. 2006) (EC antitrust respondent denied discovery of documents submitted by rivals to European Commission). Accord In re Microsoft Corp., 2006 U.S. Dist. LEXIS 24870 (N.D. Cal. Mar. 29, 2006); In re Microsoft Corp., 428 F.Supp.2d 188 (S.D.N.Y. 2006).

before the non-U.S. tribunal. Hence, Section 1782 discovery is available almost as freely as with lawsuits pending before a court in the United States, subject always to that court's discretion. It does not appear that Section 1782 can be used to discover documents located outside the United States.[198] Nor must the applicant first exhaust discovery under the rules of the foreign forum state.[199]

In the post-*Intel* era, most applications under Section 1782 have been filed by companies from Britain, Germany, and other European countries. There has also been an increase in recent years in applications from Middle Eastern countries. Arbitration proceedings abroad can trigger Section 1782 discovery.[200] Following the Supreme Court's listing of factors to consider,[201] it has been said that in determining whether to grant application for discovery for use in a foreign proceeding, courts should consider: (1) whether the documents or testimony sought are within the foreign tribunal's jurisdictional reach; (2) the nature of the foreign tribunal, the character of the proceedings underway abroad, and the receptivity of the foreign government or the court or agency abroad to federal court judicial assistance;[202] (3) whether the request for discovery conceals an attempt to circumvent foreign proof-gathering restrictions or other policies of a foreign country or the United States;[203] and (4) whether the subpoena contains unduly intrusive or burdensome requests.[204]

---

198 In re Godfrey, 526 F.Supp.2d 417 (S.D.N.Y. 2007); Norex Petroleum Ltd. v. Chubb Ins. Co. of Can., 384 F.Supp.2d 45 (D.D.C. 2005); In re Microsoft Corp., 428 F.Supp.2d 188 (S.D.N.Y. 2006).

199 Malev Hungarian Airlines v. United Technologies, 964 F.2d 97 (2d Cir. 1992).

200 In re Roz Trading Ltd., 469 F.Supp.2d 1221 (N.D. Ga. 2006); In re Hallmark Capital Corp., 534 F.Supp.2d 951 (D. Minn. 2007); In re Consorcio Ecuatoriano de Telecommunicaciones SA v. JAS Forwarding USA, 685 F.3d 987 (11th Cir. 2012). *But see*, prior to *Intel*, NBC v. Bear Stearns & Co., 165 F.3d 184 (2d Cir. 1999); Republic of Kazakhstan v. Biedermann Int'l, 168 F.3d 880 (5th Cir. 1999). *See also* In re Gemeinshcaftspraxis Dr. Med. Schottdorf, 2006 WL 3844464; In re Application of Babcock Borsig AG, 583 F.Supp.2d 233 (D. Mass. 2008).

201 *Intel, supra*, at 264–65.

202 *See* In re Application of Servicio Pan Americano de Proteccion, C.A., 354 F.Supp.2d 269 (S.D.N.Y. 2004).

203 *See generally* In re Microsoft Corp., 428 F.Supp.2d 188 (S.D.N.Y. 2006) (defendant to EC Commission antitrust proceedings not entitled to discovery).

204 *See* In re Godfrey, 526 F.Supp.2d 417 (S.D.N.Y. 2007); Edelman v. Taittinger (In re Edelman), 295 F.3d 171 (2d Cir. 2002); Norex Petroleum Ltd. v. Chubb Ins. Co. of Can., 384 F.Supp.2d 45 (D.D.C. 2005); In re Digitechnic, 2007 U.S. Dist. LEXIS 33708 (W.D. Wash. May 8, 2007) (sweeping requests); In re Management Servs., 2005 U.S. Dist. LEXIS 17025 (E.D.N.Y. Aug. 16, 2005) (confidentiality agreement facilitates use of Section 1782); In re Gemeinshcaftspraxis Dr. Med. Schottdorf, 2006 U.S. Dist. LEXIS 94161 (S.D.N.Y. Dec. 29, 2006) (Translation requirements imposed on producing parties are not burdensome). *See generally* In re Microsoft Corp., 428 F.Supp.2d 188 (S.D.N.Y. 2006) (defendant to EU Commission antitrust proceedings not entitled to circumvent EU discovery rules).

Provided such applications are not abusive, discovery has generally been ordered.[205] Mutual legal assistance treaties of the United States may circumscribe Section 1782 discovery requests.[206] A person may not be compelled to reveal legally privileged information unless that privilege has been waived.[207] Section 1782 applications are normally considered ex parte, with any resulting subpoena subject to a motion to quash,[208] reviewed under an abuse of discretion standard.[209]

§ 6.7 International Discovery in U.S. Antitrust Litigation: Foreign Blocking Statutes[210]

United States antitrust laws and litigation are viewed with hostility by much of the world. This hostility is based upon both substantive and procedural factors. Many foreign countries, including a significant number of America's trading partners, do not share the policy views reflected in U.S. antitrust laws.[211] Procedurally, many countries view U.S. discovery requests as an infringement on their sovereignty and look with dismay upon broad pretrial discovery.[212]

---

[205] *See* In re Clerici, 481 F.3d 1324 (11th Cir. 2007); Heraeus Kulzer, GmbH v. Biomet, Inc., 633 F.3d 591 (7th Cir. 2011) (in aid of German trade secrets litigation); Chevron Corp. v. Berlinger, 629 F.3d 297 (2d Cir. 2011) (Chevron obtains movie outtakes); In re Gemeinshcaftspraxis Dr. Med. Schottdorf, 2006 U.S. Dist. LEXIS 94161 (S.D.N.Y. Dec. 29, 2006). *But see* Schmitz v. Bernstein Liebhard & Lifshitz, LLP, 376 F.3d 79 (2d Cir. 2004) (German court stated allowing discovery would interfere with German law.); Kestrel Coal PTY. LTD. v. Joy Global, Inc., 362 F.3d 401 (7th Cir. 2004); Four Pillars Enterprises Co. v. Avery Dennison, 308 F.3d 1075 (9th Cir. 2002) (request denied since material already produced in another U.S. lawsuit).

[206] United States v. Global Fishing, Inc. (In re Premises Located at 840 140th Ave. NE, Bellevue), 634 F.3d 557 (9th Cir. 2011) (Russia).

[207] In re Chevron Corp., 633 F.3d 153 (3d Cir. 2011) (work-product privileges waived).

[208] In re Letters Rogatory from Tokyo Dist., 539 F.2d 1216 (9th Cir. 1976).

[209] U.K. v. United States, 238 F.3d 1312 (11th Cir. 2001).

[210] Adapted from R. Folsom, "International Discovery in Antitrust Litigation", Chapter 15, in von Kalinowski, *Antitrust Litigation and Counseling Techniques* (Matthew-Bender Co.)

[211] In In re Westinghouse and Duquesne Light Co., 78 D.L.R.3d 3 (Ont. S.Ct. 1977), for example, a Canadian court refused to enforce letters rogatory requesting information in connection with the U.S. uranium litigation. The court found that, notwithstanding the existence of the purported anticompetitive conduct of the uranium cartel, the Canadian government's policy regarding information about the uranium information prohibited enforcement of the letters.

[212] As has been noted, Article 23 of the Hague Evidence Convention expressly permits signatories to declare that they will not execute letters of request for the purpose of obtaining pretrial discovery. All but a few countries have chosen to do so.

In *Rio Tinto Zinc*, § 15.02, Note 32 *supra*, the House of Lords also expressed their disapproval with U.S. style discovery in the antitrust context: "The use of wide investigatory procedures under the United States antitrust legislation against persons outside of the United States who are not United States citizens constitute an

Extraterritoriality is a matter of balance. The executive, legislative, and judicial branches of government in the United States have reached out extraterritorially in the law of admiralty, antitrust, crime, labor, securities regulation, taxation, torts, trademarks and wildlife management. A balance drawn wrongly by one nation invites retaliatory action by others. In the case of antitrust judgments emanating from courts in the United States, most notably the "Uranium Cartel" treble damages litigation of the late 1970s,[213] many nations consider that the balance has been wrongly drawn. At least nine nations (Australia, Canada, France, Germany, Netherlands, New Zealand, Philippines, South Africa and the United Kingdom) have taken retaliatory action by enacting "blocking statutes." In addition, the 41 Commonwealth nations have resolved general support for a position similar to that of the United Kingdom.

In response to what many perceive as the overreaching of United States law, some blocking statutes prohibit the production of documents and the taking of testimony in connection with foreign inquiries. With increasing frequency, these blocking statutes have been invoked to limit the scope of pretrial discovery in United States antitrust litigation. This of course has created a unique set of problems for litigants seeking to obtain information located in a foreign country.

Many of the United States' principal trading partners have enacted blocking statutes. In some cases, these statutes represent a long standing policy by a foreign government.[214] In other cases, these statutes have been enacted specifically in response to U.S. discovery and the extraterritorial application of American antitrust law.[215] The terms of blocking legislation vary from country to country.

---

infringement of the proper jurisdiction and sovereignty of the United Kingdom." Rio Tinto Zinc, [1978] 1 All E.R. 434, 442. *See also* Radio Corporation of America v. Rauland, [1956] 1 All E.R. 260.

[213] *See* Uranium Antitrust Litigation (Westinghouse Electric Corp.) v. Rio Algom Limited, 617 F.2d 1248 (7th Cir. 1980).

[214] The Swiss bank secrecy laws, for example, represent a long-standing policy on the part of the Swiss government to protect the privacy and assets of persons subject to governmental persecution. *See* Meyer, "Swiss Banking Secrecy and Its Legal Implications in the United States," 14 New Eng. L. Rev. 18 (1978); Rosdeitcher, "Foreign Blocking Statutes and U.S. Discovery: A Conflict of National Policies," 16 N.Y.U. J. Int'l L. and Pol. 1061 (1984).

[215] The French blocking legislation, for example, was designed to preclude pretrial discovery of French nationals involved in U.S. litigation. *See* Batista, "Confronting Foreign "Blocking" Legislation: A Guide to Securing Disclosure from Non-Resident Parties to American Litigation," 17 Int'l Law. 61 (1983).

Canada enacted blocking legislation prohibiting the disclosure of information relating to the uranium industry in response to American antitrust litigation concerning the industry. *See* Regulations Respecting the Security of Uranium Information, 3 Can. Stat. O. & Reg. Ch. 366 (1977).

One of the broadest blocking statutes was enacted in France in 1980 in response to what was viewed as a threat to French sovereignty posed by United States policy. The French blocking statute makes it unlawful to seek information from French companies or individuals by means other than those prescribed by French law.[216] If a company or an individual fails to comply with the statute, criminal sanctions may be imposed.[217] Since the only means prescribed by French law to discover information from French companies and individuals is the Hague Evidence Convention and since France has reserved the right under Article 23 of the Convention to prohibit the execution of letters of request in connection with pretrial document discovery, the ability to obtain information is severely limited.

South Africa has also passed a wide-ranging blocking statute.[218] The South African statute prohibits the disclosure of any information relating to the transaction of business in South Africa.[219] The South African government has taken the position that its blocking statute prohibits disclosure of business information regardless of where the information is located. Thus the statute may affect the disclosure of information even outside the territorial limits of South Africa. Failure to comply with the South African blocking statute is subject to a fine and imprisonment.[220]

Other countries have passed narrower statutes related to specific types of information. For example, Canadian law bars the disclosure of information relating to the export or marketing of uranium or its derivatives.[221]

Australia and Britain have enacted a third type of blocking legislation.[222] They permit government officials to forbid disclosure of particular information on a case-by-case basis. The United Kingdom blocking statute is the Protection of Trading Interests Act of 1980. This Act (without specifying United States antitrust law)

See also Canadian Foreign Extraterritorial Measures (2 ILM 794 (1985) and Australian Foreign Proceedings (Excess of Jurisdiction) Act of 1984 (23 ILM 1038).

216 Law Relating to the Communication of Economic, Commercial, Industrial, Financial or Technical Documents or Information to Foreign Natural of Legal Persons, No. 80–538 J.O. 8799 (1980).

217 *Id.*

218 Protection of Business Act, S. Africa Stat. Ch. 681 (1978).

219 *Id.*

220 *Id.*

221 Regulations Respecting the Security of Uranium Information, 3 Can. Stat. O. & Reg. Ch. 366 (1977). In addition, two Canadian provinces, Ontario and Quebec, have enacted blocking statutes of broad application. Business Records Protection Act, Ont. Rev. Stat. C. 54 (1970), Business Concerns Records Act, Que. Rev. Stat. Ch. 278 (1964).

222 Protection of Trading Interests Act, C. 11, S. 1–4 (1980); Foreign Proceedings Act (Prohibition of Certain Evidence), Austl. Acts. No. 121 (1976).

makes it difficult to depose witnesses, obtain documents or enforce multiple liability judgments extraterritorially in the U.K. Violation of the 1980 Act may result in criminal penalties. Furthermore, under the "clawback" provision of the Act, parties with outstanding multiple liabilities in foreign jurisdictions (e.g., U.S. treble damages defendants) may recoup the punitive element of such awards in Britain against assets of the successful plaintiff. The British Act invites other nations to adopt clawback provisions by offering clawback reciprocity. For example, the Australian Foreign Proceedings (Excess of Jurisdiction) Act of 1984 permits recovery of the entire amount of an antitrust judgment deemed "contrary to international law or inconsistent with international comity or international practice" by its Attorney General. United States attorneys confronted with such a blocking statute need to understand that multiple liability judgments combined with contingency fee arrangements are virtually unknown elsewhere.

Effects of Blocking Statutes in Antitrust Litigation. Foreign blocking statutes raise a number of problems. First, they may prevent discovery of evidence from witnesses or others who are otherwise willing to provide the information requested. Second, they limit the extent to which the judicial mechanisms of a foreign nation may be used to compel discovery. Finally, they may affect whether or not U.S. courts will order a party to produce evidence located in a foreign nation or impose sanctions for failure to comply with such orders.

In recent years, there has been increasing uncertainty concerning the effect these foreign statutes will have in American courts. This is actually a two-fold problem. First, there is a question as to whether foreign blocking legislation prohibits U.S. courts from compelling a foreign party to produce information in violation of foreign law. Second, there is a question as to whether it is appropriate to impose sanctions on a party who refuses to comply with discovery requests or orders where compliance would violate foreign law.

Societe Internationale Pour-Participations Industrielles et Commerciales, S.A. v. Rogers

The first Supreme Court decision to address these issues was *Societe Internationale Pour-Participations Industrielles et Commerciales, S.A. v. Rogers.*[223] In *Rogers,* a Swiss company sought to recover property seized by the Alien Property Custodian during World War II in accordance with the Trading with The Enemy Act.[224] The government challenged the Swiss company's claim of ownership

[223] 357 U.S. 197, 78 S.Ct. 1087, 2 L.Ed.2d 1255 (1958).

[224] 357 U.S. at 198–199.

and asserted that the Swiss company in any event could not recover the property because it was merely a shell set up to protect the interests of I.G. Farben, an "enemy" within the meaning of the Act.

During discovery, the government obtained a court order requiring Societe to produce certain Swiss bank records. Production of these records would have been a direct violation of the Swiss bank secrecy law. Societe sought to obtain a waiver from the Swiss government in order to comply with the discovery request. Although the Swiss government permitted production of some records, it refused permission to produce and took constructive possession of other records. The district court eventually dismissed Societe's action on the ground that it had failed to comply with the discovery order. The court of appeals affirmed the lower court decision.

On appeal, the Supreme Court began by considering the propriety of the district court order to produce the records in the face of the Swiss legislation. It held that Swiss law did not automatically make the issuance of an order compelling discovery inappropriate. Rather, the Court balanced the U.S. interests in enforcing the Trading with the Enemy Act and the critical nature of the documents to those interests against the Swiss policy of bank secrecy. The Court concluded that the American interests weighed heavily in favor of requiring Societe to produce the records. Thus the lower court's order compelling discovery was valid.[225]

The Court then turned to the issue of whether dismissal of Societe's claims was an appropriate sanction for failure to comply with the order. It began its analysis by noting that the district court's power to impose sanctions was limited by the requirements of due process.[226] Although the Court did not find that the district court's order of dismissal violated the Due Process Clause, it noted that due process requirements were seriously implicated in this case. In order to regain the assets seized under the Act, Societe had to show that it was the rightful owner of the property and that it was not an "enemy" within the meaning of the Act. Thus with respect to the question of whether or not it was a captive of "enemy" interests, the plaintiff was essentially in the position of a defendant who is entitled to a hearing before it may be deprived of its property. The implication of the Court's distinction is that a party who seeks the benefits of an American forum may be subject to the burdens which go along with the choice.

Thus the requirements of the Due Process Clause are not necessarily violated when the claims of a party seeking the benefits

---

225 *Id.* at 205.

226 *Id.* at 210.

of the American forum are dismissed because of that party's failure to comply with a court's discovery order. A party who unwillingly becomes subject to an American court's jurisdiction, however, may not be bound in the same way. In such a case, it may violate due process requirements to dismiss the claims of a party which is subject to a foreign blocking statute but which has no choice but to litigate in an American court.

In view of these considerations, as well as Societe's extensive efforts to comply with the court order, the Court held that dismissal was not appropriate.[227] It never nevertheless refused to hold that sanctions were entirely prohibited.[228] Instead, it remanded the case to the district court and directed it "to proceed in whatever manner it seems most effective"—implying that the district court could impose other less drastic sanctions.[229]

The Supreme Court's decision in *Rogers* has not dispelled the problems which an American court encounters when faced with a foreign blocking statute. Rather, the Supreme Court's approach—focusing on the unique facts of the *Rogers* case—has engendered a good deal of uncertainty.

Compelling Discovery. Since the *Rogers* decision, courts have taken markedly different views of whether they may order discovery from a foreign entity in violation of a blocking statute. In a line of cases decided immediately following *Rogers,* the Second Circuit held that a court did not have the power to compel discovery from a foreign party in violation of a blocking statute.[230] More recent decisions in the Second Circuit have backed away from the approach.[231]

Other courts have taken a different view. In *In re Westinghouse Electric Corporation Uranium Contracts Litigation,*[232] for example, the court of appeals held that the local court has the power to order a party to produce foreign documents despite the fact that such production may subject the party to criminal sanctions in a foreign

---

[227] *Id.* at 211.

[228] *Id.* at 212–213.

[229] *Id.*

[230] Application of Chase Manhattan Bank, 297 F.2d 611 (2d Cir. 1962); Ings v. Ferguson, 282 F.2d 149 (2d Cir. 1960); First National City Bank of New York v. Internal Revenue Service, 271 F.2d 616 (2d Cir. 1959).

[231] *See* United States v. First National City Bank, 396 F.2d 897 (2d Cir. 1968); Strauss v. Credit Lyonnais, S.A., 242 F.R.D. 199 (E.D.N.Y. 2007); Compagnie Francaise D'Assurance v. Phillips Petroleum Co., 105 F.R.D. 16 (S.D.N.Y. 1984); Securities & Exchange Commission v. Banca Della Svizzera Italiana, 92 F.R.D. 111 (S.D.N.Y. 1981).

[232] 563 F.2d 992 (10th Cir. 1977). Accord Arthur Andersen & Co. v. Finesilver, 546 F.2d 338 (10th Cir. 1976).

country.[233] The blocking statute, in that court's view, only becomes important at the stage when sanctions are considered.[234] A court then must consider the blocking statute and other factors in determining whether sanctions are appropriate in a given case.

The Restatement Second of Foreign Relations Law takes a similar approach.[235] It assumes that the court may order a foreign party to comply with discovery despite a blocking statute. It then requires a balancing of several factors before determining whether, in the interests of comity, sanctions should be imposed for failure to comply with the order.[236] These factors include:

1. The vital interests of the United States and of the foreign state;

2. The extent and nature of the hardship that inconsistent enforcement actions would impose upon the party for whom discovery is sought;

3. The extent to which the required conduct is to take place in a foreign country;

4. The nationality from whom discovery is sought; and

5. The extent to which enforcement by action of either state can reasonably be expected to achieve compliance with the rule prescribed by that state.

Several other courts have adopted a balancing approach using the factors similar to those enumerated in the Restatement in determining whether an order to compel discovery is appropriate.[237]

The Supreme Court addressed the blocking statute issue again in *Aerospatiale*.[238] There the Court reiterated the *Rogers* holding that blocking statutes do not deprive American courts of the power to order parties subject to their jurisdiction to produce evidence even though the act of production may violate the statute.[239] The Court also further minimized the significance of blocking statutes by

---

[233] *Id.* at 997.

[234] *Id.*

[235] Restatement (Second) of the Foreign Relation Law of the United States § 40 (1965).

[236] *Id.*

[237] United States v. Vetco, Inc., 644 F.2d 1324 (9th Cir. 1981); United States v. First National City Bank, 396 F.2d 897 (2d Cir. 1968); In re Uranium Antitrust Litigation, 480 F.Supp. 1138 (N.D. Ill. 1979); Compagnie Francaise D'Assurance v. Phillips Petroleum Co., 105 F.R.D. 16 (S.D.N.Y. 1984); Graco, Inc. v. Kremlin, Inc., 101 F.R.D. 503 (N.D. Ill. 1984); Minepeco, S.A. v. Conticommodity Services, Inc., slip. op., 81 Civ. 7619 (MEL) (S.D.N.Y. January 6, 1988); Securities & Exchange Commission v. Banca Della Svizzera Italiana, 92 F.R.D. 111 (S.D.N.Y. 1981).

[238] 107 S.Ct. 2542, 96 L.Ed.2d 461 (1987).

[239] 107 S.Ct. at 2556, n. 29.

holding that blocking statutes are relevant to courts' particularized comity analysis only to the extent that they identify the nature of the foreign sovereign's interest in non-disclosure of specific kinds of material.[240]

Sanctions for Non-Compliance Based on Blocking Statutes. In *Rogers,* the Court sent conflicting signals as to whether an order dismissing a party's claims is an appropriate sanction for failure to comply with a discovery order where compliance would violate foreign law. On the one hand, the Court noted that dismissal may run afoul of the Due Process Clause, at least where the party against whom the sanction is sought is a defendant.[241] On the other hand, the Court noted that dismissal may be appropriate when a party deliberately courts impediments to discovery.[242]

Recent decisions have taken varying approaches. Some courts have required a finding of willful noncompliance to justify dismissal.[243] At least one court has required that the party seeking sanctions establish not only bad faith in failure to comply, but that the party is prejudiced by noncompliance and that the sanction is commensurate with the prejudice incurred.[244] Another court has implied that a party who deliberately courts impediments to discovery may be subject to harsh sanctions.[245] Still other courts have excused compliance once the party establishes a direct conflict with foreign law and a good faith effort to obtain a waiver from the foreign government.[246] The *Aerospatiale* Court did not address this issue.

Representing a Client Subject to Conflicting Demands by a Blocking Statute and Discovery

As is evident, representing a client subject to the conflicting demands of an American discovery order and a foreign blocking statute poses unique problems. The key however is to develop a record establishing that the client is faced with the Hobson's choice of suffering the risk of sanctions for failure to comply with a discovery

---

240 *Id.*

241 Societe Internationale v. Rogers, N. 12 supra, 357 U.S. at 210.

242 *Id.* at 211.

243 Flaks v. Koegel, 504 F.2d 702 (2d Cir. 1974); Sapiro v. Hartford Fire Insurance Co., 452 F.2d 215 (7th Cir. 1971).

244 General Atomic Co. v. Exxon Nuclear Co., Inc., 90 F.R.D. 290 (S.D. Cal. 1981).

245 In re Ampicillin Antitrust Litigation, 81 F.R.D. 395 (D.D.C. 1978). *See* Richmark Corp. v. Timber Falling Consultants, 959 F.2d 1468 (9th Cir. 1992) (contempt sanctions) and In re Marc Rich & Co., A.G., 707 F.2d 663 (2d Cir. 1983) (contempt sanctions).

246 In re Westinghouse Electric Corporation Uranium Contracts Litigation, 563 F.2d 992 (10th Cir. 1977); Federal Maritime Com. v. A. T. Desmedt, 268 F.Supp. 972 (S.D.N.Y. 1967).

order or suffering the risk of criminal or other penalties for complying with a discovery order.

In order to develop the record, it is important to keep in mind three critical factors. First, it must be apparent that there is a direct conflict between American law and foreign law. Therefore, it is important that counsel be well versed in the scope of the foreign blocking legislation. Second, there must be no appearance of collusion between the foreign party subject to the blocking statute and the foreign government since this may be used as evidence of bad faith. Finally, it is essential that the foreign party make a good faith effort to comply with discovery.

From the outset, counsel must keep in mind the scope of the foreign blocking law. In some cases, the foreign law will prohibit the party from producing all of the requested documents. However, not every blocking statute completely prohibits a party from producing all documents relative to an issue. When only private interests are involved, the foreign law may not demand that a party absolutely comply.[247] Penalties for production of information may vary with the circumstances.[248] Further, it is often the case that the practice under a foreign blocking statute may be different than what appears on the face of the statute. It is recommended that an expert be retained who can assist in explaining, both for the benefit of counsel and the court, the pattern of enforcement of the foreign statute. In any event, it is important at the outset to determine whether the information requested falls within the blocking statute and to what extent the foreign party will be subject to criminal or civil penalty.

It is also important to avoid the appearance of collusion with a foreign government. As the Court noted in *Rogers,* the courting of impediments to production may be a sufficient reason for imposing sanctions.[249]

Finally, it is helpful to establish that the foreign party has made a good faith effort to comply with discovery. One important way of establishing good faith is to demonstrate that the foreign party has attempted to solicit a waiver of the blocking statute from the foreign government. Further, the foreign entity should be encouraged to disclose all documents that may be disclosed without incurring liability under the foreign blocking statute. Finally, the foreign entity may try to develop the requested information from sources not subject to the blocking statute. For example, information concerning

---

247 For a good discussion of this principle in the context of German law *see* United States v. First National City Bank 396 F.2d 897 (2d Cir. 1968).

248 *See* United States v. First National City Bank, 396 F.2d 897 (2d Cir. 1968).

249 Societe Internationale v. Rogers, N. 27 supra, 357 U.S. at 211.

production of certain commodities may be available from public documents such as government reports and corporate reports on file with governmental agencies or trade associations.

Representing a Client Seeking Discovery Barred by a Blocking Statute. Given American courts' disenchantment with foreign blocking statutes, the job of representing a client who seeks discovery from a foreign entity is somewhat easier. In this case, it is important to demonstrate that the information sought is critical to the litigation and that the party has exhausted all other means of obtaining the information.

One way of demonstrating that the party has used all means possible to obtain this information is to develop information in spite of the blocking statutes. This may mean attempting to obtain documents from another party in another foreign country where blocking statutes are not applicable, or trying to develop the information through public information and the use of experts. Once this is done, it will be easier to demonstrate a good faith attempt to obtain this information without violating the laws of the foreign state. In addition, the use of an expert can help establish the importance of the documents that are being sought.

Another important factor to keep in mind is that of collusion between the foreign government and the foreign party. In such a case, if collusion is demonstrated, the court may be willing to impose drastic sanctions.

§ 6.8 EU Investigation, Discovery, and Privilege Issues

For coverage of European Union business competition law substance and jurisdiction, see Section 5.6.

In March of 1962 the EU Council of Ministers adopted Regulation 17, which became the major enforcement regime for Articles 101 and 102. Effective May 1, 2004, Regulation 17 was replaced by Regulation 1/2003. No private remedies are established. The European Commission, for the most part its Competition Directorate-General (department), has a wide range of powers.

The regulations confer investigatory powers in the Commission to conduct general studies into economic sectors and to review the affairs of individual businesses and trade associations. The Commission may investigate in response to a complaint or upon its own initiative. These powers are particularly significant because (except in the case of mergers) notification of restrictive agreements, decisions, and practices to the Commission, although at times beneficial, is not mandatory. The Commission may request all information *it* considers necessary, and examine and make copies of record books and business documents.

Written communications with external EU-licensed lawyers undertaken for defense purposes are confidential and need not be disclosed.[250] Written communications with in-house lawyers are *not* exempt from disclosure, nor are communications with external *non*-EU counsel.[251] Thus, communications with North American attorneys (who are not also EU-licensed attorneys) are generally discoverable. For example, the Commission obtained in-house counsel documents from John Deere, Inc., a Belgian subsidiary of the United States multinational. These documents were drafted as advice to management on how to avoid competition law liability for export prohibition restraints. They were used by the Commission to justify the finding of an intentional Article 101 violation and a fine of 2 million Euros.[252] United States attorneys have followed these developments with trepidation. Disclaimers of possible non-confidentiality are one option to consider in dealing with clients. At a minimum, U.S. attorneys ought to advise their clients that the usual U.S. rules on attorney-client privilege may not apply. Engaging *outside* counsel in Europe would be prudent.

In conducting its investigations, the Commission may ask for verbal explanations on the spot and have access to premises. One author refers to these powers as "dawn raids and other nightmares." Nevertheless, the Court of Justice has affirmed this right of hostile access.[253] Effective May 1, 2004, subject to the issuance of a local court warrant, this right of access extends to private homes and motor vehicles of corporate directors, managers, and other staff. In these matters the Commission acts on its own authority provided there are reasonable grounds to believe that relevant books or records are kept in these locations. It must, however, inform member states prior to taking such steps and may request their assistance. The member states must render assistance when businesses fail to comply with competition law investigations of the Commission.

---

250 AM & S Europe Ltd. v. Commission (1982) Eur.Comm.Rep. 1575.

251 AM & S Europe Ltd. v. Commission (1982) Eur.Comm.Rep. 1575.

252 John Deere v. Commission (1985) 28 Off. J. Eur. Comm. L/35, 58.

253 Hoechst v. Commission (1987) Eur.Comm.Rep. 1549; Dow Chemical Nederland BV v. Commission (1987) Eur.Comm.Rep. 4367; E. Hoechst v. Commission (1987) Eur.Comm.Rep. 1549; Dow Chemical Nederland BV v. Commission (1987) Eur.Comm.Rep. 4367; NV Samenwerkende Elektriciteits-produktiebedrijven (SEP) v. Commission (1991) Eur.Comm.Rep. II–1497 (Case T–39/90).ur. Comm. Rep. II–1497 (Case T–39/90).

Businesses involved in the Commission's investigatory process have limited rights to notice and hearing.[254] They do not have access to the Commission's files. Any failure on the part of an enterprise to provide information requested by the Commission or to submit to its investigation can result in the imposition of considerable fines and penalties. For example, the Belgian and French subsidiaries of the Japanese electrical and electronic group, Matsushita, were fined by the Commission for supplying it with false information about whether Matsushita recommended retail prices for its products. These sanctions are civil in nature and run against the corporation, not its directors or management.

The Commission has increased the use of its investigatory powers. Several procedural requirements for Commission investigations and hearings have been discussed by the Court of Justice. One notable Court decision upheld the authority of the Commission to conduct searches of corporate offices without notice or warrant when it has reason to believe that pertinent evidence may be lost.[255] Another notable decision permitted a Swiss "whistle blower" who once worked for Hoffmann-La Roche (a defendant in competition law proceedings) to sue the Community in tort for disclosure of his identity as an informant.[256]

Regulation 17 and Regulation 1 envision significant cooperation and information sharing between European and national authorities in the field of competition law. Effective May 1, 2004, enforcement of Articles 101 and 102 has been shared with the competition agencies and national courts of the member states. A new European Competition Network was established to facilitate cooperative law enforcement, share information, and minimize divergent application of competition law principles, with the Commission to act as final arbiter on substantive matters.

---

[254] Commission Regulation 99/63. *See generally* Hoffmann-La Roche v. Commission (1979) Eur.Comm.Rep. 461.

[255] Re National Panasonic (1980) Eur.Comm.Rep. 2033.

[256] Adams v. Commission (1985) Eur.Comm.Rep. 3539.

§ 6.9 Text of The Hague Convention on Service Abroad of Judicial and Extrajudicial Documents (1965)

20 U.S.T. 361, 1969 WL 97765 (U.S. Treaty), T.I.A.S. No. 6638

Article 1

The present Convention shall apply in all cases, in civil or commercial matters, where there is occasion to transmit a judicial or extrajudicial document for service abroad.

This Convention shall not apply where the address of the person to be served with the document is not known.

CHAPTER I—JUDICIAL DOCUMENTS

Article 2

Each contracting State shall designate a Central Authority which will undertake to receive requests for service coming from other contracting States and to proceed in conformity with the provisions of articles 3 to 6.

Each State shall organise the Central Authority in conformity with its own law.

Article 3

The authority or judicial officer competent under the law of the State in which the documents originate shall forward to the Central Authority of the State addressed a request conforming to the model annexed to the present Convention, without any requirement of legalisation or other equivalent formality.

The document to be served or a copy thereof shall be annexed to the request. The request and the document shall both be furnished in duplicate.

Article 4

If the Central Authority considers that the request does not comply with the provisions of the present Convention it shall promptly inform the applicant and specify its objections to the request.

Article 5

The Central Authority of the State addressed shall itself serve the document or shall arrange to have it served by an appropriate agency, either—

(a) by a method prescribed by its internal law for the service of documents in domestic actions upon persons who are within its territory, or

(b) by a particular method requested by the applicant, unless such a method is incompatible with the law of the State addressed.

Subject to sub-paragraph (b) of the first paragraph of this article, the document may always be served by delivery to an addressee who accepts it voluntarily.

If the document is to be served under the first paragraph above, the Central Authority may require the document to be written in, or translated into, the official language or one of the official languages of the State addressed.

That part of the request, in the form attached to the present Convention, which contains a summary of the document to be served, shall be served with the document.

Article 6

The Central Authority of the State addressed or any authority which it may have designated for that purpose, shall complete a certificate in the form of the model annexed to the present Convention.

The certificate shall state that the document has been served and shall include the method, the place and the date of service and the person to whom the document was delivered. If the document has not been served, the certificate shall set out the reasons which have prevented service.

The applicant may require that a certificate not completed by a Central Authority or by a judicial authority shall be countersigned by one of these authorities.

The certificate shall be forwarded directly to the applicant.

Article 7

The standard terms in the model annexed to the present Convention shall in all cases be written either in French or in English. They may also be written in the official language, or in one of the official languages, of the State in which the documents originate.

The corresponding blanks shall be completed either in the language of the State addressed or in French or in English.

Article 8

Each contracting State shall be free to effect service of judicial documents upon persons abroad, without application of any compulsion, directly through its diplomatic or consular agents.

Any State may declare that it is opposed to such service within its territory, unless the document is to be served upon a national of the State in which the documents originate.

Article 9

Each contracting State shall be free, in addition, to use consular channels to forward documents, for the purpose of service, to those authorities of another contracting State which are designated by the latter for this purpose.

Each contracting State may, if exceptional circumstances so require, use diplomatic channels for the same purpose.

Article 10

Provided the State of destination does not object, the present Convention shall not interfere with—

(a) the freedom to send judicial documents, by postal channels, directly to persons abroad,

(b) the freedom of judicial officers, officials or other competent persons of the State of origin to effect service of judicial documents directly through the judicial officers, officials or other competent persons of the State of destination,

(c) the freedom of any person interested in a judicial proceeding to effect service of judicial documents directly through the judicial officers, officials or other competent persons of the State of destination.

Article 11

The present Convention shall not prevent two or more contracting States from agreeing to permit, for the purpose of service of judicial documents, channels of transmission other than those provided for in the preceding articles and, in particular, direct communication between their respective authorities.

Article 12

The service of judicial documents coming from a contracting State shall not give rise to any payment or reimbursement of taxes or costs for the services rendered by the State addressed.

The applicant shall pay or reimburse the costs occasioned by—

(a) the employment of a judicial officer or of a person competent under the law of the State of destination,

(b) the use of a particular method of service.

Article 13

Where a request for service complies with the terms of the present Convention, the State addressed may refuse to comply therewith only if it deems that compliance would infringe its sovereignty or security.

It may not refuse to comply solely on the ground that, under its internal law, it claims exclusive jurisdiction over the subject-matter of the action or that its internal law would not permit the action upon which the application is based.

The Central Authority shall, in case of refusal, promptly inform the applicant and state the reasons for the refusal.

Article 14

Difficulties which may arise in connection with the transmission of judicial documents for service shall be settled through diplomatic channels.

Article 15

Where a writ of summons or an equivalent document had to be transmitted abroad for the purpose of service, under the provisions of the present Convention, and the defendant has not appeared, judgment shall not be given until it is established that—

(a) the document was served by a method prescribed by the internal law of the State addressed for the service of documents in domestic actions upon persons who are within its territory, or

(b) the document was actually delivered to the defendant or to his residence by another method provided for by this Convention,

and that in either of these cases the service or the delivery was effected in sufficient time to enable the defendant to defend.

Each contracting State shall be free to declare that the judge, notwithstanding the provisions of the first paragraph of this article, may give judgment even if no certificate of service or delivery has been received, if all the following conditions are fulfilled—

(a) the document was transmitted by one of the methods provided for in this Convention,

(b) a period of time of not less than six months, considered adequate by the judge in the particular case, has elapsed since the date of the transmission of the document,

(c) no certificate of any kind has been received, even though every reasonable effort has been made to obtain it through the competent authorities of the State addressed.

Notwithstanding the provisions of the preceding paragraphs the judge may order, in case of urgency, any provisional or protective measures.

Article 16

When a writ of summons or an equivalent document had to be transmitted abroad for the purpose of service, under the provisions of the present Convention, and a judgment has been entered against a defendant who has not appeared, the judge shall have the power to relieve the defendant from the effects of the expiration of the time for appeal from the judgment if the following conditions are fulfilled—

(a) the defendant, without any fault on his part, did not have knowledge of the document in sufficient time to defend, or knowledge of the judgment in sufficient time to appeal, and

(b) the defendant has disclosed a prima facie defence to the action on the merits.

An application for relief may be filed only within a reasonable time after the defendant has knowledge of the judgment.

Each contracting State may declare that the application will not be entertained if it is filed after the expiration of a time to be stated in the declaration, but which shall in no case be less than one year following the date of the judgment.

This article shall not apply to judgments concerning status or capacity of persons.

CHAPTER II—EXTRAJUDICIAL DOCUMENTS

Article 17

Extrajudicial documents emanating from authorities and judicial officers of a contracting State may be transmitted for the purpose of service in another contracting State by the methods and under the provisions of the present Convention.

CHAPTER III—GENERAL CLAUSES

Article 18

Each contracting State may designate other authorities in addition to the Central Authority and shall determine the extent of their competence.

The applicant shall, however, in all cases, have the right to address a request directly to the Central Authority.

Federal States shall be free to designate more than one Central Authority.

Article 19

To the extent that the internal law of a contracting State permits methods of transmission, other than those provided for in the preceding articles, of documents coming from abroad, for service within its territory, the present Convention shall not affect such provisions.

Article 20

The present Convention shall not prevent an agreement between any two or more contracting States to dispense with—

(a) the necessity for duplicate copies of transmitted documents as required by the second paragraph of article 3,

(b) the language requirements of the third paragraph of article 5 and article 7,

(c) the provisions of the fourth paragraph of article 5,

(d) the provisions of the second paragraph of article 12.

Article 21

Each contracting State shall, at the time of the deposit of its instrument of ratification or accession, or at a later date, inform the Ministry of Foreign Affairs of the Netherlands of the following—

(a) the designation of authorities, pursuant to articles 2 and 18,

(b) the designation of the authority competent to complete the certificate pursuant to article 6,

(c) the designation of the authority competent to receive documents transmitted by consular channels, pursuant to article 9.

Each contracting State shall similarly inform the Ministry, where appropriate, of—

(a) opposition to the use of methods of transmission pursuant to articles 8 and 10,

(b) declarations pursuant to the second paragraph of article 15 and the third paragraph of article 16,

(c) all modifications of the above designations, oppositions and declarations.

* * *

Designations and Declarations Made on the Part of the United States in Connection with the Deposit of the United States Ratification

1. In accordance with Article 2, the United States Department of State is designated as the Central Authority to receive requests for

service from other Contracting States and to proceed in conformity with Articles 3 to 6.

§ 6.10 Text of the Inter-American Convention on Letters Rogatory (1975) and Its Additional Protocol (1979)

The Governments of the Member States of the Organization of American States, desirous of concluding a convention on letters rogatory, have agreed as follows:

I. USE OF TERMS

Article 1

For the purposes of this Convention the terms "exhortos" and "cartas rogatorias" are synonymous in the Spanish text. The terms "letters rogatory", "commissions rogatoires", and "cartas rogatórias" used in the English, French and Portuguese texts, respectively, cover both "exhortos" and "cartas rogatorias".

II. SCOPE OF THE CONVENTION

Article 2

This Convention shall apply to letters rogatory, issued in conjunction with proceedings in civil and commercial matters held before the appropriate judicial or other adjudicatory authority of one of the States Parties to this Convention, that have as their purpose:

(a) The performance of procedural acts of a merely formal nature, such as service of process, summonses or subpoenas abroad;

(b) The taking of evidence and the obtaining of information abroad, unless a reservation is made in this respect.

Article 3

This Convention shall not apply to letters rogatory relating to procedural acts other than those specified in the preceding article; and in particular it shall not 1 apply to acts involving measures of compulsion.

III. TRANSMISSION OF LETTERS ROGATORY

Article 4

Letters rogatory may be transmitted to the authority to which they are addressed by the interested parties, through judicial channels, diplomatic or consular agents, or the Central Authority of the State of origin or of the State of destination, as the case may be.

Each State Party shall inform the General Secretariat of the Organization of American States of the Central Authority competent to receive and distribute letters.

IV. REQUIREMENTS FOR EXECUTION

Article 5

Letters rogatory shall be executed in the States Parties provided they meet the following requirements:

(a) The letter rogatory is legalized, except as provided for in Articles 6 and 7 of this Convention. The letter rogatory shall be presumed to be duly legalized in the State of origin when legalized by the competent consular or diplomatic agent;

(b) The letter rogatory and the appended documentation are duly translated into the official language of the State of destination.

Article 6

Whenever letters rogatory are transmitted through consular or diplomatic channels or through the Central Authority, legalization shall not be required.

Article 7

Courts in border areas of the States Parties may directly execute the letters rogatory contemplated in this Convention and such letters shall not require legalization.

Article 8

Letters rogatory shall be accompanied by the following documents to be delivered to the person on whom process, summons or subpoena is being served:

(a) An authenticated copy of the complaint with its supporting documents, and of other exhibits or rulings that serve as the basis for the measure requested;

(b) Written information identifying the judicial or other adjudicatory authority issuing the letter, indicating the time-limits allowed the person affected to act upon the request, and warning of the consequences of failure to do so;

(c) Where appropriate, information on the existence and address of the court-appointed defense counsel or of competent legal-aid societies in the State of origin.

Article 9

Execution of letters rogatory shall not imply ultimate recognition of the jurisdiction of the judicial or other adjudicatory authority issuing the letter rogatory or a commitment to recognize the validity of the judgment it may render or to execute it.

V. EXECUTION

Article 10

Letters rogatory shall be executed in accordance with the laws and procedural rules of the State of destination.

At the request of the judicial or other adjudicatory authority issuing the letter rogatory, the authority of the State of destination may execute the letter through a special procedure, or accept the observance of additional formalities in performing the act requested, provided this procedure or the observance of those formalities is not contrary to the law of the State of destination.

Article 11

The authority of the State of destination shall have jurisdiction to determine any issue arising as a result of the execution of the measure requested in the letter rogatory. Should such authority find that it lacks jurisdiction to execute the letter rogatory, it shall *ex officio* forward the documents and antecedents of the case to the authority of the State **which has jurisdiction.**

Article 12

The costs and other expenses involved in the processing and execution of letters rogatory shall be borne by the interested parties.

The State of destination may, in its discretion, execute a letter rogatory that does not indicate the person to be held responsible for costs and other expenses when incurred. The identity of the person empowered to represent the applicant for legal purposes may be indicated in the letter rogatory or in the documents relating to its execution.

The effects of a declaration in forma pauperis shall be regulated by the law of the State of destination.

Article 13

Consular or diplomatic agents of the States Parties to this Convention may perform the acts referred to in Article 2 in the State in which they are accredited, provided the performance of such acts is not contrary to the laws of that State. In so doing, they shall not perform any acts involving measures of compulsion.

VI. GENERAL PROVISIONS

Article 14

States Parties belonging to economic integration systems may agree directly between themselves upon special methods and procedures more expeditious than those provided for in this Convention. These agreements may be extended to include other States in the manner in which the parties may agree.

Article 15

This Convention shall not limit any provisions regarding letters rogatory in bilateral or multilateral agreements that may have been signed or may be signed in the future by the States Parties or preclude the continuation of more favorable practices in this regard that may be followed by these States.

Article 16

The States Parties to this Convention may declare that its provisions cover the execution of letters rogatory in criminal, labor, and "contentious-administrative" cases, as well as in arbitrations and other matters within the jurisdiction of special courts. Such declarations shall be transmitted to the General Secretariat of the Organization of American States.

Article 17

The State of destination may refuse to execute a letter rogatory that is manifestly contrary to its public policy ("ordre public").

Article 18

The States Parties shall inform the General Secretariat of the Organization of American States of the requirements stipulated in their laws for the legalization and the translation of letters rogatory.

VII. FINAL PROVISIONS

Article 19

This Convention shall be open for signature by the Member of the Organization of American States.

Article 20

This Convention is subject to ratification. The instruments of ratification shall be deposited with the General Secretariat of the Organization of American States.

Article 21

This Convention shall remain open for accession by any other State. The instrument of accession shall be deposited with the General Secretariat of the Organization of American States.

Article 22

This Convention shall enter into force on the thirtieth day following the date of deposit of the second instrument of ratification.

For each State ratifying or acceding to the Convention after the deposit of the second instrument of ratification, the Convention shall enter into force on the thirtieth day after deposit by such State of its instrument of ratification or accession

Article 23

If a State Party has two or more territorial units in which different systems' of law apply in relation to the matters dealt with in this Convention, it may, at the time of signature, ratification or accession, declare that this Convention shall extend to all its territorial units or only to one or more of them.

Such declaration may be modified by subsequent declarations, which shall expressly indicate the territorial unit or units to which the Convention applies. Such subsequent declarations shall be transmitted to the General Secretariat of the Organization of American States and shall become effective thirty days after the. This Convention shall remain in force indefinitely, but any of the States Parties may denounce it. The instrument of denunciation shall be deposited with l the General Secretariat of the Organization of American States. After one year from the date of deposit of the instrument of denunciation~ the Convention shall no longer be in effect for the denouncing State, but shall remain in effect for the other States Parties.

Article 25

The original instrument of this Convention, the English, French, Portuguese and Spanish texts of which are equally authentic, shall be deposited with the General Secretariat of the Organization of American States. The Secretariat shall notify the Member States of the Organization of American States and the States that have acceded to the Convention of the signatures, deposits of instruments of ratification, accession, and denunciation as well as of reservations, if any. It shall also transmit the information mentioned in the second paragraph of Article 4 and in Article 18 and the declarations referred to in Articles 16 and 23 of this Convention.

IN WITNESS WHEREOF the undersigned Plenipotentiaries, being duly authorized thereto by their respective Governments, have signed this Convention.

DONE AT PANAMA CITY, Republic of Panama, this thirtieth day of January one thousand nine hundred and seventy-five.

Additional Protocol to the Inter American Convention on Letters Rogatory

The Governments of the Member States of the Organization of American States, desirous of strengthening and facilitating international cooperation in judicial procedures as provided for in the Inter-American Convention on Letters Rogatory done in Panama on January 30, 1975, have agreed as follows:

I. SCOPE OF PROTOCOL

Article 1

This Protocol shall apply only to those procedural acts set forth in Article 2 (a) of the Inter-American Convention on Letters Rogatory, hereinafter referred to as "the Convention". For the purposes of this Protocol, such acts shall be understood to mean procedural acts (pleadings, motions, orders, and subpoenas) that are served and requests for information that are made by a judicial or other adjudicatory authority of a State Party to a judicial or administrative authority of another State Party and are transmitted by a letter rogatory from the Central Authority of the State of origin to the Central Authority of the State of destination.

II. CENTRAL AUTHORITY

Article 2

Each State Party shall designate a central authority that shall perform the functions assigned to it in the Convention and in this Protocol. At the time of deposit of their instruments of ratification or accession to this Protocol, the States Parties shall communicate the designations to the General Secretariat of the Organization of American States, which shall distribute to the States Parties to the Convention a list containing the designations received. The Central Authority designated by a State Party in accordance with Article 4 of the Convention may be changed at any time. The State Party shall inform the above-mentioned Secretariat of such change as promptly as possible.

III. PREPARATION OF LETTERS ROGATORY

Article 3

Letters rogatory shall be prepared on forms that are printed in the four official languages of the Organization of American States or in the languages of the State of origin and of the State of destination and conform to Form A contained in the Annex to this Protocol.

Letters rogatory shall be accompanied by the following:

(a) Copy of the complaint or pleading that initiated the action in which the letter rogatory was issued, as well as a translation thereof into the language of the State of destination;

(b) Untranslated copy of the documents attached to the complaint or pleading;

(c) Untranslated copy of any rulings ordering issuance of the letter rogatory;

(d) Form conforming to Form B annexed to this Protocol and containing essential information for the person to be served or the authority to receive the documents; and

(e) Certificate conforming to Form C annexed to this Protocol on which the Central Authority of the State of destination shall attest to execution or non-execution of the letter rogatory.

The copies shall be regarded as authenticated for the purposes of Article 8(a) of the Convention if they bear the seal of the judicial or other adjudicatory authority that issued the letter rogatory.

A copy of the letter rogatory together with Form B and the copies referred to in items a, b, and c of this Article shall be delivered to the person notified or to the authority to which the request is addressed. One of the copies of the letter rogatory and the documents attached to it shall remain in the possession of the State of destination; the untranslated original, the certificate of execution and the documents attached to them shall be returned to the Central Authority of the State of origin through appropriate channels.

If a State Party has more than one official language, it shall, at the time of signature, ratification or accession to this Protocol, declare which language or languages shall be considered official for the purposes of the Convention and of this Protocol. If a State Party comprises territorial units that have different official languages, it shall, at the time of signature, ratification or accession to this Protocol, declare which language or languages in each territorial unit shall be considered official for the purposes of the Convention and of this Protocol The General Secretariat of the Organization of

American States shall distribute to the States Parties to this Protocol the information contained in such declarations.

IV. TRANSMISSION AND PROCESSING OF LETTERS ROGATORY

Article 4

Upon receipt of a letter rogatory from the Central Authority in another State Party, the Central Authority in the State of destination shall transmit the letter rogatory to the appropriate judicial or administrative authority for processing in accordance with the applicable local law.

Upon execution of the letter rogatory, the judicial or administrative authority or authorities that processed it shall attest to the execution thereof in the manner prescribed in their local law, and shall transmit it with the relevant documents to the Central Authority. The Central Authority of the State Party of destination shall certify execution of the letter rogatory to the Central Authority of the State Party of origin on a form conforming to Form C of the Annex, which shall not require legalization. In addition, the Central Authority of the State of destination shall return the letter rogatory and attached documents to the Central Authority of the State of origin for delivery to the judicial or other adjudicatory authority that issued it.

V. COSTS AND EXPENSES

Article 5

The processing of letters rogatory by the Central Authority of the State Party of destination and its judicial or administrative authorities shall be free of charge. However, this State Party may seek payment by parties requesting execution of letters rogatory for those services which, in accordance with its local law, are required to be paid for directly by those parties.

The party requesting the execution of a letter rogatory shall, at its election, either select and indicate in the letter rogatory the person who is responsible in the State of destination for the cost of such services or, alternatively, shall attach to the letter rogatory a check for the fixed amount that is specified in Article 6 of this Protocol for its processing by the State of destination and will cover the cost of such services or a document proving that such amount has been transferred by some other means to the Central Authority of the State of destination.

The fact that the cost of such services ultimately exceeds the fixed amount shall not delay or prevent the processing or execution of the letter rogatory by the Central Authority or the judicial or administrative authorities of the State of destination. Should the cost exceed that amount, the Central Authority of the State of destination may, when returning the executed letter rogatory, seek payment of the outstanding amount due from the party requesting execution of the letter rogatory.

Article 6

At the time of deposit of its instrument of ratification or accession to this Protocol with the General Secretariat of the Organization of American States, each State Party shall attach a schedule of the services and the costs and other expenses that, in accordance with its local law, shall be paid directly by the party requesting execution of the letter rogatory. In addition, each State Party shall specify in the above-mentioned schedule the single amount which it considers will reasonably cover the cost of such services, regardless of the number or nature thereof. This amount shall be paid when the person requesting execution of the letter rogatory has not designated a person responsible for the payment of such services in the State of destination but has decided to pay for them directly in the manner provided for in Article 5 of this Protocol.

The General Secretariat of the Organization of American States shall distribute the information received to the States Parties to this Protocol. A State Party may at any time notify the General Secretariat of the Organization of American States of changes in the above-mentioned schedules, which shall be communicated by the General Secretariat to the other States Parties to this Protocol.

Article 7

States Parties may declare in the schedules mentioned in the foregoing articles that, provided there is reciprocity, they will not charge parties requesting execution of letters rogatory for the services necessary for executing them, or will accept in complete satisfaction of the cost of such services either the single fixed amount specified in Article 6 or another specified amount.

Article 8

This Protocol shall be open for signature and subject to ratification or accession by those Member States of the Organization of American States that have signed, ratified, or acceded to the Inter-American Convention on Letters Rogatory signed in Panama on January 30, 1975.

This Protocol shall remain open for accession by any other State that accedes or has acceded to the Inter-American Convention on Letters Rogatory, under the conditions set forth in this article.

The instruments of ratification and accession shall be deposited with the General Secretariat of the Organization of American States.

Article 9

This Protocol shall enter into force on the thirtieth day following the date on which two States Parties to the Convention have deposited their instruments of ratification or accession to this Protocol.

For each State ratifying or acceding to the Protocol after its entry into force, the Protocol shall enter into force on the thirtieth day following deposit by such State of its instrument of ratification or accession, provided that such State is a Party to the Convention.

Article 10

If a State Party has two or more territorial units in which different systems of law apply in relation to matters dealt with in this Protocol, it may, at the time of signature, ratification or accession, declare that this Protocol shall extend to all its territorial units or only to one or more of them.

Such declaration may be modified by subsequent declarations that shall expressly indicate the territorial unit or units to which this Protocol applies. Such subsequent declarations shall be transmitted to the General Secretariat of the Organization of American States, and shall become effective thirty days after the date of their receipt.

Article 11

This Protocol shall remain in force indefinitely, but any of the States Parties may denounce it. The instrument of denunciation shall be deposited with the General Secretariat of the Organization of American States. After one year from the date of deposit of the instrument of denunciation, the Protocol shall no longer be in effect for the denouncing State, but shall remain in effect for the other States Parties.

Article 12

The original instrument of this Protocol and its Annex (Forms A, B and C), the English, French, Portuguese and Spanish texts of which are equally authentic, shall be deposited with the General Secretariat of the Organization of American States, which will forward an authenticated copy of the text to the Secretariat of the United Nations for registration and publication in accordance with Article 102 of its Charter. The General Secretariat of the Organization of American States shall notify the Member States of that Organization and the States that have acceded to the Protocol of the signatures, deposits of instruments of ratification, accession and denunciation, as well as of reservations, if any. It shall also transmit to them the information mentioned in Article 2, the last paragraph of Article 3, and Article 6 and the declarations referred to in Article 10 of this Protocol.

IN WITNESS WHEREOF the undersigned Plenipotentiaries, being duly authorized thereto by their respective Governments, have signed this Protocol.

DONE AT MONTEVIDEO, Republic of Uruguay, this eighth day of May, one thousand nine hundred and seventy-nine.

§ 6.11 Text of The Hague Convention on Taking Evidence Abroad in Civil and Commercial Matters (1968) and Model Letters of Request

23 U.S.T. 2555, 1972 WL 122493 (U.S. Treaty), T.I.A.S. No. 7444

CHAPTER I—LETTERS OF REQUEST

Article 1

In civil or commercial matters a judicial authority of a Contracting State may, in accordance with the provisions of the law of that State, request the competent authority of another Contracting State, by means of a Letter of Request, to obtain evidence, or to perform some other judicial act.

A Letter shall not be used to obtain evidence which is not intended for use in judicial proceedings, commenced or contemplated.

The expression "other judicial act" does not cover the service of judicial documents or the issuance of any process by which judgments or orders are executed or enforced, or orders for provisional or protective measures.

Article 2

A Contracting State shall designate a Central Authority which will undertake to receive Letters of Request coming from a judicial authority of another Contracting State and to transmit them to the authority competent to execute them. Each State shall organize the Central Authority in accordance with its own law.

Letters shall be sent to the Central Authority of the State of execution without being transmitted through any other authority of that State.

Article 3

A Letter of Request shall specify—

(a) the authority requesting its execution and the authority requested to execute it, if known to the requesting authority;

(b) the names and addresses of the parties to the proceedings and their representatives, if any;

(c) the nature of the proceedings for which the evidence is required, giving all necessary information in regard thereto;

(d) the evidence to be obtained or other judicial act to be performed.

Where appropriate, the Letter shall specify, inter alia—

(e) the names and addresses of the persons to be examined;

(f) the questions to be put to the persons to be examined or a statement of the subject-matter about which they are to be examined;

(g) the documents or other property, real or personal, to be inspected;

(h) any requirement that the evidence is to be given on oath or affirmation, and any special form to be used;

(i) any special method or procedure to be followed under Article 9.

A Letter may also mention any information necessary for the application of Article 11.

No legalization or other like formality may be required.

Article 4

A Letter of Request shall be in the language of the authority requested to execute it or be accompanied by a translation into that language.

Nevertheless, a Contracting State shall accept a Letter in either English or French, or a translation into one of these languages, unless it has made the reservation authorized by Article 33.

A Contracting State which has more than one official language and cannot, for reasons of internal law, accept Letters in one of these languages for the whole of its territory, shall, by declaration, specify the language in which the Letter or translation thereof shall be expressed for execution in the specified parts of its territory. In case of failure to comply with this declaration, without justifiable excuse, the costs of translation into the required language shall be borne by the State of origin.

A Contracting State may, by declaration, specify the language or languages other than those referred to in the preceding paragraphs, in which a Letter may be sent to its Central Authority.

Any translation accompanying a Letter shall be certified as correct, either by a diplomatic officer or consular agent or by a sworn translator or by any other person so authorized in either State.

Article 5

If the Central Authority considers that the request does not comply with the provisions of the present Convention, it shall promptly inform the authority of the State of origin which transmitted the Letter of Request, specifying the objections to the Letter.

Article 6

If the authority to whom a Letter of Request has been transmitted is not competent to execute it, the Letter shall be sent forthwith to the authority in the same State which is competent to execute it in accordance with the provisions of its own law.

Article 7

The requesting authority shall, if it so desires, be informed of the time when, and the place where, the proceedings will take place, in order that the parties concerned, and their representatives, if any, may be present. This information shall be sent directly to the parties or their representatives when the authority of the State of origin so requests.

Article 8

A Contracting State may declare that members of the judicial personnel of the requesting authority of another Contracting State may be present at the execution of a Letter of Request. Prior authorization by the competent authority designated by the declaring State may be required.

Article 9

The judicial authority which executes a Letter of Request shall apply its own law as to the methods and procedures to be followed.

However, it will follow a request of the requesting authority that a special method or procedure be followed, unless this is incompatible with the internal law of the State of execution or is impossible of performance by reason of its internal practice and procedure or by reason of practical difficulties.

A Letter of Request shall be executed expeditiously.

Article 10

In executing a Letter of Request the requested authority shall apply the appropriate measures of compulsion in the instances and to the same extent as are provided by its internal law for the execution of orders issued by the authorities of its own country or of requests made by parties in internal proceedings.

Article 11

In the execution of a Letter of Request the person concerned may refuse to give evidence in so far as he has a privilege or duty to refuse to give the evidence—

(a) under the law of the State of execution; or

(b) under the law of the State of origin, and the privilege or duty has been specified in the Letter, or, at the instance of the requested authority, has been otherwise confirmed to that authority by the requesting authority.

A Contracting State may declare that, in addition, it will respect privileges and duties existing under the law of States other than the State of origin and the State of execution, to the extent specified in that declaration.

Article 12

The execution of a Letter of Request may be refused only to the extent that—

(a) in the State of execution the execution of the Letter does not fall within the functions of the judiciary; or

(b) the State addressed considers that its sovereignty or security would be prejudiced thereby.

Execution may not be refused solely on the ground that under its internal law the State of execution claims exclusive jurisdiction over the subject-matter of the action or that its internal law would not admit a right of action on it.

Article 13

The documents establishing the execution of the Letter of Request shall be sent by the requested authority to the requesting authority by the same channel which was used by the latter.

In every instance where the Letter is not executed in whole or in part, the requesting authority shall be informed immediately through the same channel and advised of the reasons.

Article 14

The execution of the Letter of Request shall not give rise to any reimbursement of taxes or costs of any nature.

Nevertheless, the State of execution has the right to require the State of origin to reimburse the fees paid to experts and interpreters and the costs occasioned by the use of a special procedure requested by the State of origin under Article 9, paragraph 2.

The requested authority whose law obliges the parties themselves to secure evidence, and which is not able itself to execute the Letter, may, after having obtained the consent of the requesting authority, appoint a suitable person to do so. When seeking this consent the requested authority shall indicate the approximate costs which would result from this procedure. If the requesting authority gives its consent it shall reimburse any costs incurred; without such consent the requesting authority shall not be liable for the costs.

CHAPTER II—TAKING OF EVIDENCE BY DIPLOMATIC OFFICERS, CONSULAR AGENTS AND COMMISSIONERS

Article 15

In a civil or commercial matter, a diplomatic officer or consular agent of a Contracting State may, in the territory of another Contracting State and within the area where he exercises his functions, take the evidence without compulsion of nationals of a State which he represents in aid of proceedings commenced in the courts of a State which he represents.

A Contracting State may declare that evidence may be taken by a diplomatic officer or consular agent only if permission to that effect is given upon application made by him or on his behalf to the appropriate authority designated by the declaring State.

Article 16

A diplomatic officer or consular agent of a Contracting State may, in the territory of another Contracting State and within the area where he exercises his functions, also take the evidence, without compulsion, of nationals of the State in which he exercises his functions or of a third State, in aid of proceedings commenced in the courts of a State which he represents, if—

(a) a competent authority designated by the State in which he exercises his functions has given its permission either generally or in the particular case, and

(b) he complies with the conditions which the competent authority has specified in the permission.

A Contracting State may declare that evidence may be taken under this Article without its prior permission.

Article 17

In a civil or commercial matter, a person duly appointed as a commissioner for the purpose may, without compulsion, take evidence in the territory of a Contracting State in aid of proceedings commenced in the courts of another Contracting State if—

(a) a competent authority designated by the State where the evidence is to be taken has given its permission either generally or in the particular case; and

(b) he complies with the conditions which the competent authority has specified in the permission.

A Contracting State may declare that evidence may be taken under this Article without its prior permission.

Article 18

A Contracting State may declare that a diplomatic officer, consular agent or commissioner authorized to take evidence under Articles 15, 16 or 17, may apply to the competent authority designated by the declaring State for appropriate assistance to obtain the evidence by compulsion. The declaration may contain such conditions as the declaring State may see fit to impose.

If the authority grants the application it shall apply any measures of compulsion which are appropriate and are prescribed by its law for use in internal proceedings.

Article 19

The competent authority, in giving the permission referred to in Articles 15, 16 or 17, or in granting the application referred to in Article 18, may lay down such conditions as it deems fit, inter alia, as to the time and place of the taking of the evidence. Similarly it may require that it be given reasonable advance notice of the time, date and place of the taking of the evidence; in such a case a representative of the authority shall be entitled to be present at the taking of the evidence.

Article 20

In the taking of evidence under any Article of this Chapter persons concerned may be legally represented.

Article 21

Where a diplomatic officer, consular agent or commissioner is authorized under Articles 15, 16 or 17 to take evidence—

(a) he may take all kinds of evidence which are not incompatible with the law of the State where the evidence is taken or contrary to any permission granted pursuant to the above Articles, and shall have power within such limits to administer an oath or take an affirmation;

(b) a request to a person to appear or to give evidence shall, unless the recipient is a national of the State where the action is pending, be drawn up in the language of the place where the evidence is taken or be accompanied by a translation into such language;

(c) the request shall inform the person that he may be legally represented and, in any State that has not filed a declaration under Article 18, shall also inform him that he is not compelled to appear or to give evidence;

(d) the evidence may be taken in the manner provided by the law applicable to the court in which the action is pending provided that such manner is not forbidden by the law of the State where the evidence is taken;

(e) a person requested to give evidence may invoke the privileges and duties to refuse to give the evidence contained in Article 11.

Article 22

The fact that an attempt to take evidence under the procedure laid down in this Chapter has failed, owing to the refusal of a person to give evidence, shall not prevent an application being subsequently made to take the evidence in accordance with Chapter I.

CHAPTER III—GENERAL CLAUSES

Article 23

A Contracting State may at the time of signature, ratification or accession, declare that it will not execute Letters of Request issued for the purpose of obtaining pre-trial discovery of documents as known in Common Law countries.

Article 24

A Contracting State may designate other authorities in addition to the Central Authority and shall determine the extent of their competence. However, Letters of Request may in all cases be sent to the Central Authority.

Federal States shall be free to designate more than one Central Authority.

Article 25

A Contracting State which has more than one legal system may designate the authorities of one of such systems, which shall have exclusive competence to execute Letters of Request pursuant to this Convention.

Article 26

A Contracting State, if required to do so because of constitutional limitations, may request the reimbursement by the State of origin of fees and costs, in connection with the execution of Letters of Request, for the service of process necessary to compel the appearance of a person to give evidence, the costs of attendance of such persons, and the cost of any transcript of the evidence.

Where a State has made a request pursuant to the above paragraph, any other Contracting State may request from that State the reimbursement of similar fees and costs.

Article 27

The provisions of the present Convention shall not prevent a Contracting State from—

(a) declaring that Letters of Request may be transmitted to its judicial authorities through channels other than those provided for in Article 2;

(b) permitting, by internal law or practice, any act provided for in this Convention to be performed upon less restrictive conditions;

(c) permitting, by internal law or practice, methods of taking evidence other than those provided for in this Convention.

Article 28

The present Convention shall not prevent an agreement between any two or more Contracting States to derogate from—

(a) the provisions of Article 2 with respect to methods of transmitting Letters of Request;

(b) the provisions of Article 4 with respect to the languages which may be used;

(c) the provisions of Article 8 with respect to the presence of judicial personnel at the execution of Letters;

(d) the provisions of Article 11 with respect to the privileges and duties of witnesses to refuse to give evidence;

(e) the provisions of Article 13 with respect to the methods of returning executed Letters to the requesting authority;

(f) the provisions of Article 14 with respect to fees and costs;

(g) the provisions of Chapter II.

* * *

Article 33

A State may, at the time of signature, ratification or accession exclude, in whole or in part, the application of the provisions of paragraph 2 of Article 4 and of Chapter II. No other reservation shall be permitted.

Each Contracting State may at any time withdraw a reservation it has made; the reservation shall cease to have effect on the sixtieth day after notification of the withdrawal.

When a State has made a reservation, any other State affected thereby may apply the same rule against the reserving State.

Article 34

A State may at any time withdraw or modify a declaration.

Article 35

A Contracting State shall, at the time of the deposit of its instrument of ratification or accession, or at a later date, inform the Ministry of Foreign Affairs of the Netherlands of the designation of authorities, pursuant to Articles 2, 8, 24 and 25.

A Contracting State shall likewise inform the Ministry, where appropriate, of the following—

(a) the designation of the authorities to whom notice must be given, whose permission may be required, and whose assistance may be invoked in the taking of evidence by diplomatic officers and consular agents, pursuant to Articles 15, 16 and 18 respectively;

(b) the designation of the authorities whose permission may be required in the taking of evidence by commissioners pursuant to Article 17 and of those who may grant the assistance provided for in Article 18;

(c) declarations pursuant to Articles 4, 8, 11, 15, 16, 17, 18, 23 and 27;

(d) any withdrawal or modification of the above designations and declarations;

(e) the withdrawal of any reservation.

Article 36

Any difficulties which may arise between Contracting States in connection with the operation of this Convention shall be settled through diplomatic channels.

* * *

HAGUE EVIDENCE CONVENTION

DECLARATIONS PURSUANT TO ARTICLE 23

Standard Declaration (made by all states except the United States, Czechoslovakia, and Israel, and those states following the British example):

[The Federal Republic of Germany] declares in pursuance of Article 23 of the Convention that it will not, in its territory, execute Letters of Request issued for the purpose of obtaining pre-trial discovery of documents as known in Common Law countries.

British Declaration (made by the United Kingdom and Singapore):

In accordance with Article 23 Her Majesty's Government declare that the United Kingdom will not execute Letters of Request issued for the purpose of obtaining pre-trial discovery of documents. Her Majesty's Government further declare that Her Majesty's Government understand "Letters of Request issued for the purpose of obtaining pre-trial discovery of documents" for the purposes of the foregoing Declaration as including any Letter of Request which requires a person:—

a. to state what documents relevant to the proceedings to which the Letter of Request relates are, or have been, in his possession, custody, or power; or

b. to produce any documents other than particular documents specified in the Letter of Request as being documents appearing to the requesting court to be, or to be likely to be, in his possession, custody or power.

LETTER FROM MINISTRY OF JUSTICE FEDERAL REPUBLIC OF GERMANY

(October 16, 1990)

. . . With reference to the issuance of an order concerning discovery of documents pursuant to Section 14(2) of the German Law for the Implementation of the Hague Evidence Convention of 1970, I hereby inform you that there is hardly any prospect for the issuance of such an order. It can only be suggested to counsel for German firms which are supposed to produce documents to apply to the American court for appointment of a commissioner, so that the document production in Germany may take place in accordance with the rules of the judicial administration of the respective states . . .

MODEL FOR LETTERS OF REQUEST RECOMMENDED FOR USE IN APPLYING THE HAGUE CONVENTION OF 18 MARCH 1970 ON THE TAKING OF EVIDENCE ABROAD IN CIVIL OR COMMERCIAL MATTERS

REQUEST FOR INTERNATIONAL JUDICIAL ASSISTANCE PURSUANT TO THE HAGUE CONVENTION OF 18 MARCH 1970 ON THE TAKING OF EVIDENCE IN CIVIL OR COMMERCIAL MATTERS

N.B. Under the first paragraph of article 4, the Letter of Request shall be in the language of the authority requested to execute it or be accompanied by a translation into that language. However, the provisions of the second and third paragraphs may permit use of other languages.

In order to avoid confusion, please spell out the name of the month in each date.

1.	Sender	____*(identity and address)*
2.	Central Authority of the Requested State	____*(identity and address)*
3.	Person to whom the executed request is to be returned	____*(identity and address)*

4.	Specification of the date by which the requesting authority requires receipt of the response to the Letter of Request	
	Date	______________
		______________
	Reason for Urgency[257]	______________
		______________
		______________

In conformity with article 3 of the Convention, the undersigned applicant has the honour to submit the following request:

5.	a.	Requesting judicial authority (article 3, a)	____*(identity and address)*
	b.	To the competent authority of (article 3, a)	____*(the requested State)*
	c.	Names of the case and any identifying number	______________

[257] Omit if not applicable.

6. Names and addresses of the parties and their representatives (including representatives in the requesting state*) (article 3, b)

a.	Plaintiff	__________________
		__________________
		__________________
b.	Defendant	__________________
		__________________
		__________________
c.	Other parties	__________________
		__________________
		__________________

7. a. Nature of the proceedings (divorce, paternity, breach of contract, product liability, etc.) (article 3, c) __________________

	b.	Summary of complaint	____________
	c.	Summary of defence and counterclaim*	____________
	d.	Other necessary information or documents*	____________
8.	a.	Evidence to be obtained or other judicial act to be performed (article 3, d)	____________

	b. Purpose of the evidence or judicial act sought	____ ____ ____
9.	Identity and address of any person to be examined (article 3, e)*	____
10.	Questions to be put to the persons to be examined or statement of the subject-matter about which they are to be examined (article 3, f)*	____*(or see attached list)*
11.	Documents or other property to be inspected (article 3, g)*	____*(specify whether it is to be produced, copied, valued, etc.)*
12.	Any requirement that the evidence be given on oath or affirmation and any special form to be used (article 3, h)*	____*(In the event that the evidence cannot be taken in the manner requested, specify whether it is to be taken in such manner as provided by local law for the formal taking of evidence.)*
13.	Special methods or procedure to be followed (e.g., oral or in writing, verbatim, transcript or summary, cross-	____

	examination, etc.) (articles 3, i and 9)*	
14.	Request for notification of the time and place for the execution of the Request and identity and address of any person to be notified (article 7)*	________________
15.	Request for attendance or participation of judicial personnel of the requesting authority at the execution of the Letter of Request (article 8)*	________________
16.	Specification of privilege or duty to refuse to give evidence under the law of the State of origin (article 11, b)*	____*(attach copies of relevant laws or regulations)*
17.	The fees and costs incurred which are reimbursable under the second paragraph of article 14 or under article 26 of the Convention will be borne by	____*(identity and address)*

Date of request ________________

Signature and seal of the

requesting authority ________________

____

Chapter 7

INTERNATIONAL BUSINESS LITIGATION: SOVEREIGN DEFENSES

Table of Sections

Sec.

Two affirmative defenses frequently arise in U.S. courts when international business disputes involving sovereign states and their entities are before them. The first, replacing a long common law history, is provided by the U.S. Foreign Sovereign Immunities Act of

1976 (FSIA). The second is the result of judicial precedent under the "act of state doctrine." I am indebted to Professor Michael Gordon of Florida for his original work on material appearing in this chapter and to USD Professor Herbert Lazerow for additional insights.

PART A: SOVEREIGN IMMUNITY

§ 7.1 Introduction to Foreign Sovereign Immunity

When the circumstances for foreign state immunity are present, the court relinquishes jurisdiction to adjudicate or enforce over the foreign state. In other words, both personal and subject matter jurisdiction are absent. See Sections 5.2 and 5.4. Because foreign sovereign immunity is influenced by concepts of separation of powers and notions of comity, immunity theory assumes different forms in different nations. Somewhat paradoxically, foreign sovereign immunity is contained in statutes in several common law nations, but is found only in the case law of many civil law nations.

Sovereign immunity theory in the United States developed in case law exclusively until the enactment of the Foreign Sovereign Immunities Act of 1976 (FSIA),[1] reproduced in Section 7.16. The experience in the United Kingdom is similar; case law prevailed until the enactment of the State Immunity Act of 1978.[2] On the continent, sovereign immunity theory long remained in case law, but is covered at least partly now under the 1972 European Convention on State Immunity and its Additional Protocol.

§ 7.2 History and Rationale

The roots of U.S. foreign sovereign immunity precedent go back to *The Schooner Exchange v. McFaddon.*[3] Chief Justice Marshall stated in this Supreme Court decision that the courts of the United States lacked jurisdiction over an armed ship of a foreign state (France) located in a U.S. port. When engaged in official acts (*jure imperii*) the sovereign (whether ancient prince or modern state):

> [b]eing in no respect amenable to another; and being bound by obligations of the highest character not to degrade the dignity of his nation, by placing himself or its sovereign rights within the jurisdiction of another, can be supposed to enter a foreign territory only under an express license, or in

---

1 28 U.S.C.A. §§ 1330, 1602–1611.

2 *See* M. Gordon, Foreign State Immunity in Commercial Transactions § 17 (1991).

3 11 U.S. (7 Cranch) 116, 3 L.Ed. 287 (1812).

> the confidence that the [absolute] immunities belonging to his independent sovereign station, though not expressly stipulated, are reserved by implication, and will be extended to him.[4]

But Chief Justice Marshall was also aware of the logic of limits on immunity, acknowledging a distinction between the private property of a person who happens to be a prince, and the military force of a sovereign power. Had he been confronted with a case of commercial activity by a sovereign, the long struggle with state immunity theory in the United States might have been prevented.

Immunity of a sovereign was nevertheless consistently found to be absolute, regardless of the nature of the activity. Although it may have appeared from *The Schooner Exchange* that sovereign immunity is domestic law, it is as well an accepted principle of customary international law.[5] The doctrine of state immunity would have caused little difficulty had sovereigns engaged only in "sovereign" acts. But modern nations engage in many private transactions (*jure gestionis*). The doctrine of absolute and unqualified immunity gave way to a restrictive theory which denied immunity when the sovereign descended into the market place. The evolution from absolute to restrictive sovereign immunity was less influenced by international law than developing concepts of the role of the state in modern society.

Many states became private traders, engaging in the operation of transportation, telegraph and telephone services, radio and television communications, and the production of goods (extraction of natural resources, tobacco and matches, etc.). Commercial transactions gave rise to disputes and brought into the courts of one nation the trading sovereigns of another. National courts were slow to alter the absolute immunity doctrine. Rather surprisingly, the evolution from absolute theory to restrictive theory occurred in civil law nations in European case law. As early as 1857 in Belgium, in *Etat du Perou v. Krelinger,*[6] restrictive theory began to be accepted on the Continent. An Italian decision in 1882, *Morellet C. Goveruo Danese,*[7] continued the movement, as did Austrian and German courts in the 20th century.

---

[4] 11 U.S. (7 Cranch) at 137.

[5] *See* Berizzi Brothers Co. v. The Pesaro, 271 U.S. 562, 46 S.Ct. 611, 70 L.Ed. 1088 (1926).

[6] P.B. 1857–II–348.

[7] (1882) Guir. It. 1883–I–25.

The Tate Letter

In common law nations, courts struggled with such evolution and the restrictive theory only took root clearly with the enactment of legislation. The Department of State regularly requested immunity when friendly nations were sued in U.S. courts. The U.S. Supreme Court affirmed that courts were required to defer to the State department.[8] In 1952, the Department of State sent what became known as the "Tate Letter" to the Department of Justice, announcing that Department of State policy was "to follow the restrictive theory of sovereign immunity in the consideration of requests of foreign governments for a grant of sovereign immunity."[9] The letter stated:

> It is realized that a shift in policy by the executive cannot con trol the courts but it is felt that the courts are less likely to al low a plea of sovereign immunity where the executive has de clined to do so. There have been indications that at least some Justices of the Supreme Court feel that in this matter courts should follow the branch of the Government charged with re sponsibility for the conduct of foreign relations.

Although the Tate Letter announced an acceptance of the restrictive theory of sovereign immunity, it offered no guidelines or criteria to distinguish a state's public acts from its private acts. Until the passage of the Foreign Sovereign Immunities Act (FSIA) twenty-four years later, the application of the restrictive theory proved troublesome. The courts generally complied with "suggestions" of immunity from the Department of State, and foreign sovereigns were often successful in urging the Department to support immunity for the kind of private acts the restrictive theory was intended to address.

But even when state immunity was codified in the 1976 FSIA, it was uncertain to what degree separation of powers principles would induce judicial caution about embarrassing the executive branch in its role as the primary organ of international policy. Moreover, and "(p)erhaps more importantly, in the chess game that is diplomacy, only the executive has a view of the entire board and an understanding of the relationship between isolated moves."[10]

---

[8] Ex parte Republic of Peru, 318 U.S. 578 (1943); Republic of Mexico v. Hoffman, 324 U.S. 30 (1945).

[9] 24 Dept. State Bull. 984 (1952).

[10] Spacil v. Crowe, 489 F.2d 614 (5th Cir. 1974).

§ 7.3 The Foreign Sovereign Immunities Act of 1976

The enactment of the Foreign Sovereign Immunities Act was intended to relieve the government of diplomatic pressures, "thereby eliminating the role of the State Department in such questions and bringing the United States into conformity with the immunity practice of virtually every other country."[11] The FSIA additionally illustrated to litigants that sovereign immunity decisions would be made on legal rather than political grounds. The old suggestion of immunity made by the executive was abrogated by the FSIA.[12] The FSIA is the sole basis for obtaining jurisdiction over a foreign state in U.S. courts.[13]

In adopting the restrictive theory, the FSIA established exclusive legal standards applicable to claims of immunity made by foreign sovereigns, whether the litigation is in a state or federal court in the United States. The Act applies retroactively to conduct prior to 1976.[14] It bars jury trials, but allows punitive damages under state or federal common law actions in suits against foreign state agencies or instrumentalities, but not the states themselves.[15]

Unless one of the FSIA exceptions to sovereign immunity applies, the state and its entities remains immune from suit in the United States. These exceptions are detailed below. The burden of proof, by a preponderance of the evidence, that an exception is inapplicable rests with the sovereign state.[16] If an exception is held to apply, then under the FSIA there is personal and subject matter jurisdiction over the sovereign and its entities.

The FSIA also guarantees foreign states the right to remove civil actions from a state court to a federal court, thus allaying fears of "local" treatment and contemplating the development of a fairly uniform body of law in the federal courts. That body has proven to be less than uniform. One court has described it as a "statutory labyrinth that, owing to the numerous interpretive questions engendered by its bizarre structure . . . has . . . been a financial boon for the private bar but a constant bane of the federal judiciary."[17]

---

[11] Martropico Compania Naviera S.A. v. Perusahaan Pertambangan Minyak Dan Gas Bumi Negara (Pertamina), 428 F.Supp. 1035, 1037 (S.D.N.Y.1977).

[12] Republic of Philippines v. Marcos, 665 F.Supp. 793 (N.D.Cal.1987).

[13] Argentine Republic v. Amerada Hess Shipping Corp., 488 U.S. 428 (1989).

[14] Republic of Austria v. Altmann, 541 U.S. 677 (2004); Argentina v. Amerada Hess Shipping Corp., 488 U.S. 428 (1989).

[15] 28 U.S.C.A. 1441(d); 28 U.S.C.A. 1606.

[16] Aquamar v. Del Monte, 179 F.3d 1279 (11th Cir. 1999).

[17] Gibbons v. Udaras na Gaeltachta, 549 F.Supp. 1094, 1105 (S.D.N.Y.1982).

A further goal of the FSIA was to provide procedures for service of process and obtaining *in personam* jurisdiction, thus avoiding the past practices of plaintiffs seizing property of foreign states to force an appearance. And finally, the FSIA allows execution upon commercial assets, although the requirements for execution are stricter than those for jurisdiction to adjudicate.

§ 7.4 Who Is a Sovereign?

Sovereign immunity is a defense that is the patrimony of foreign states. A "foreign state" includes "a political subdivision of a foreign state or an agency or instrumentality of a foreign state."[18] An "agency or instrumentality of a foreign state" is any entity:

> (1) which is a separate legal person, corporate or otherwise, and
>
> (2) which is an organ of a foreign state or political subdivision thereof, or a majority of whose shares or other ownership in terest is owned by a foreign state or political subdivision there-of, and
>
> (3) which is neither a citizen of a State of the United States [as defined in the Act], . . . nor created under the laws of any third country.[19]

The distinction between a foreign state and agency or instrumentality is important. Section 1608 of the FSIA creates different rules for service of process for states versus their entities. Section 1606 provides that punitive damages may be had against state entities, but not foreign states. The distinction may also be important when service of default judgments is at issue.[20] Purely fictional separations of entities from states will be ignored when assessing immunity and allowing counterclaims.[21] The public functions that an entity performs are critical to determining if it, whether incorporated or not, is an agency or instrumentality of the state.[22]

The Vatican has been held to be a foreign state, thus facilitating claims against it for abuses by priests.[23] The PLO has been denied

---

[18] 28 U.S.C.A. § 1603(a).

[19] 28 U.S.C.A. § 1603(b).

[20] Compare Antoine v. Atlas Turner, 66 F.3d 105 (6th Cir. 1995) with Straub v. A.P. Green, 38 F.3d 448 (9th Cir. 1994).

[21] First Nat'l City Bank v. Banco Para El Comercio Exterior De Cuba (Bancec), 462 U.S.611, 103 S.Ct.2591, 77 L.Ed.2d 46 (1983).

[22] *See* Kelly v. Syria Shell Petroleum, 213 F.3d 841 (5th Cir. 2000); Byrd v. Corp. Forestal y Industrial de Olancho, 182 F.3d 380 (5th Cir. 1999).

[23] English v. Thorne, 676 F.Supp. 761 (S.D.Miss.1987); Doe v. Holy See, 557 F.3d 1066 (9th Cir. 2009); O'Bryan v. Holy See, 556 F.3d 361 (6th Cir. 2009).

such status.[24] Foreign trade organizations of nonmarket nations have usually been held to be instrumentalities, as have state controlled corporations engaged in a wide variety of activities, such as airlines, mining, oil and gas, shipping, banking and production such as steel. A 2003 decision of the U.S. Supreme Court determined that corporations are agencies or instrumentalities of a foreign state when the state owns a majority of its shares at the time of suit versus the time of an alleged tort.[25] Since it has no direct ownership interests, a foreign state may not be liable for the acts of subsidiaries of its corporate agencies or instrumentalities,[26] unless they are deemed "organs" of the state,[27] such as the Long Term Credit Bank of Japan.[28]

The FSIA does not address the status of international organizations as foreign states. Courts have denied such status to OPEC,[29] granted it to the British West Indies Central Labour Organization,[30] and in other cases suggested that it did not have to reach a decision because immunity would exist (or not exist) depending on whether absolute or restrictive theory applied. In 2010 the Supreme Court held that the FSIA does not apply to government officials, leaving that issue to federal common law.[31] Acting heads of state, for example, traditionally have benefited from sovereign immunity when the President concurs.[32]

§ 7.5 Jurisdictional and Procedural Issues, Attachments

The FSIA is federal law based on the theory that a foreign state is "presumptively immune" from the jurisdiction of a U.S. court. The

[24] National Petrochemical Co. of Iran v. M/T Stolt Sheaf, 860 F.2d 551 (2d Cir. 1988).

[25] Dole Food Co. v. Patrickson, 538 U.S. 468 (2003).

[26] *Id.*

[27] *See* California Department of Water Resources v. Powerex Corp., 533 F.3d 1087 (9th Cir. 2008). *Compare* Patrickson v. Dole Food Co., 251 F.3d 795 (9th Cir. 2001).

[28] EIE Guam Corp. v. The Long Term Credit Bank of Japan, 322 F.3d 635 (9th Cir. 2003).

[29] International Ass'n of Machinists and Aerospace Workers v. OPEC, 477 F.Supp. 553, 560 (C.D.Cal.1979), *aff'd*, 649 F.2d 1354 (9th Cir. 1981), *cert. denied*, 454 U.S. 1163, 102 S.Ct. 1036, 71 L.Ed.2d 319 (1982).

[30] Rios v. Marshall, 530 F.Supp. 351 (S.D.N.Y.1981).

[31] Yousuf v. Samantar, 560 U.S. 305, 130 S.Ct. 2278, 176 L.Ed.2d 1047 (2010) and Yousuf v. Samantar, 699 F.3d 763 (4th Cir. 2012) (no common law immunity for alleged violations of *jus cogens* customary international law against torture, killings and arbitrary imprisonment in Somalia).

[32] *See, e.g.*, Ye v. Zemin, 383 F.3d 620 (7th Cir. 2004) (President of China immune from Falun Gong claims). Compare United States v. Noriega, 117 F.3d 1206 (11th Cir. 1997) (immunity denied) and Samantar, *supra*, (head of state and foreign official immunity denied).

court lacks subject matter jurisdiction unless a specific exception applies.[33] Subject matter jurisdiction is conferred by § 1330(a) to permit a nonjury civil action against a foreign state not entitled to immunity. The FSIA does not create a cause of action; it merely permits all causes of action brought after its enactment regardless of their historical basis.[34] Actions brought in state courts may be removed to federal courts.[35] If the court has subject matter jurisdiction under § 1330(a), and if service of process is made in strict accordance with § 1608[36], and if constitutional due process requirements are met (see Section 5.2), then the court has specific (not general)[37] personal jurisdiction over the foreign state under § 1330(b). Aliens may avail themselves of FSIA jurisdiction to file suit against foreign sovereigns,[38] which may be dismissed on *forum non conveniens* grounds (see Section 2.4).[39]

The principal function of the FSIA is to confer immunity upon a defendant foreign state or state entity. A court clearly lacks jurisdiction unless one of the exceptions applies. It should thus be apparent that "(u)nder the analytic structure of the Act, the existence of subject matter and personal jurisdiction, the requisites for service of process, and the availability of sovereign immunity as a defense are intricately coordinated inquiries."[40] Understanding the Congressional pattern of subject matter and personal jurisdiction under the FSIA requires one additional essential comment, that the "Act cannot create personal jurisdiction where the Constitution forbids it. Accordingly, each finding of personal jurisdiction under the FSIA requires, in addition, a due process scrutiny of the court's power to exercise its authority over a particular defendant."[41] The FSIA "is designed to embody the 'requirements of minimum jurisdictional

---

33 *See* Saudi Arabia v. Nelson, 507 U.S. 349, 113 S.Ct. 1471, 123 L.Ed.2d 47 (1993); Argentine Republic v. Amerada Hess Shipping Corp., 488 U.S. 428, 109 S.Ct. 683, 102 L.Ed.2d 818 (1989); Verlinden B.V. v. Central Bank of Nigeria, 461 U.S. 480, 103 S.Ct. 1962, 76 L.Ed.2d 81 (1983).

34 Austria v. Altmann, 541 U.S. 677 (2004) (WWII claims).

35 28 U.S.C. § 1441(d).

36 Magness v. Russian Federation, 247 F.3d 609 (5th Cir. 2001). Service of process rules differ for agencies and instrumentalities of foreign states. See Section 1608(b) and Transaero Inc. v. La Fuerza Aerea Boliviana, 30 F.3d 148 (D.C.Cir. 1994) (Air Force is part of sovereign state, not an instrumentality).

37 Santos v. Air France, 934 F.3d 890 (7th Cir. 1991). See Section 5.2 for coverage of specific versus general personal jurisdiction.

38 Verlinden BV v. Nigeria, 461 U.S. 480 (1983).

39 *See, e.g.*, Forsythe v. Saudi Arabia, 885 F.3d 285 (5th Cir. 1989). See generally Section 2.3.

40 Velidor v. L/P/G Benghazi, 653 F.2d 812, 817 (3d Cir. 1981).

41 Texas Trading & Milling Corp. v. Federal Republic of Nigeria, 647 F.2d 300, 308 (2d Cir. 1981), *cert. denied*, 454 U.S. 1148, 102 S.Ct. 1012, 71 L.Ed.2d 301 (1982).

contacts and adequate notice."[42] Acts of U.S. subsidiaries may not be attributed to foreign parents for jurisdictional purposes when applying the commercial activity exception (discussed in Section 7.7).[43] Discovery orders in aid of determining whether FSIA jurisdiction exists have been issued.[44]

Motions to dismiss on grounds of sovereign immunity that are denied are subject to immediate interlocutory appeal.[45] Special rules apply under FSIA Sections 1609 and 1610 to attachments of state property. Section 1609 establishes a presumption of immunity from attachment, and Section 1611 bars attachment of central bank or monetary authority assets and designated military use property. Prejudgment attachments are allowed only if the state has explicitly waived that immunity, for example by contract,[46] and cannot be used to obtain jurisdiction. But the U.S. Supreme Court has ruled that *post-judgment, world-wide discovery* in aid of collection of sovereign debts is permissible, and not limited by the FSIA.[47]

Attachments

Section 1610 of the FSIA mandates that attachments in aid of execution of judgments against foreign sovereigns require a court order. There must be a finding of one of the following: That immunity has been waived explicitly or implicitly, the property sought to be attached was used for commercial activity excepted from FSIA immunity, the execution relates to establishing certain property rights, the property consists of insurance proceeds indemnifying or holding a state harmless, the judgment is based on confirmation of an arbitral award against the state, or the judgment relates to non-immune terrorist acts. In the latter case, attachments may be made to foreign state assets frozen by the United States, with U.S. government assistance, unless the President determines that U.S. national security interests demand otherwise.

Attachments in aid of execution of judgments against foreign state agencies or instrumentalities are less demanding. All of the grounds for post-judgment attachment noted above apply, and no nexus to the underlying claim is required when invoking the

---

42 East Europe Domestic Int'l Sales Corp. v. Terra, 467 F.Supp. 383, 387 (S.D.N.Y.1979).

43 Federal Insurance Co. v. Rubin, 12 F.3d 1270 (3rd Cir. 1994).

44 Doe v. Bin Laden, 663 F.3d 64 (2d Cir. 2011).

45 United States v. Moats, 961 F.2d 1198 (5th Cir. 1992); Compania Mexicana de Aviation SA v. U.S. Dist. Ct., 859 F.3d 1354 (9th Cir. 1988).

46 Compare Libra Bank v. Banco National de Costa Rica, 676 F.3d 47 (2d Cir. 1982) (waiver found) and O'Connell Mach. Co. v. M.V. Americana 734 F.3d 115 (2d Cir. 1984) (waiver not found).

47 Argentina v. NML Capital Ltd., 134 S.Ct. 2250 (2014).

commercial activity, rights in property, insurance proceeds and terrorist act grounds. International discovery orders in aid of executing on judgments against sovereigns are permissible.[48]

Because the FSIA contains its own attachment rules, there is a distinct possibility that although the sovereign is not immune, a judgment against it cannot be enforced.[49] This result is particularly probable when jurisdiction is based on the noncommercial tort exception to foreign sovereign immunity. See Section 7.9. To quote the Second Circuit regarding a political assassination judgment against Chile: "Congress did in effect create a right without a remedy".[50]

Numerous judgments against Iran resulting from the hostage crisis and bombings in Beirut have never been executed upon. In 2000, Congress responded to complaints by adopting the Victims of Trafficking and Violence Protection Act.[51] This Act permits collection of compensatory (but not punitive) damages from the U.S. government, which then seeks to recoup these sums from the foreign state. Some monies have been paid under this Act to judgment creditors of Iran.[52]

§ 7.6 Exceptions to Sovereign Immunity—Waiver

A foreign state is not immune in any case "in which [it] has waived its immunity either explicitly or by implication, notwithstanding any withdrawal of the waiver . . . except in accordance with the terms of waiver."[53]

Implied waivers are not easily established, though becoming a party to the ICSID Convention on foreign investment disputes (see Chapter 4) implies a waiver of sovereign immunity.[54] Entering into a treaty with the United States does not imply a waiver.[55] A foreign state does not waive its state immunity by entering into a contract with parties from another nation. But if that contract contains a choice of U.S. forum or U.S. law clause, then a waiver may be found.[56] That contract may give rise to a commercial exception issue, but a

---

[48] *Id.*

[49] *See, e.g.*, De Letelier v. Chile, 748 F.2d 790 (2d Cir. 1984); Alejandre v. Telefonica de Puerto Rico, 183 F.3d 1277 (11th Cir. 1999).

[50] De Letelier, *supra.*

[51] Public Law 106–386, 114 Stat. 1464.

[52] *See* Section 7.11.

[53] 28 U.S.C.A. § 1605(a)(1).

[54] Blue Ridge Investments LLC v. Argentina, 735 F.3d 72 (2d Cir. 2013).

[55] *See* Foremost-McKesson Inc. v. Iran, 905 F.2d 438 (D.C.Cir. 1990).

[56] *See* Eckert Int'l Inc. v. Fiji, 32 F.3d 77 (4th Cir. 1994); Joseph v. Consulate of Nigeria, 830 F.2d 1018 (9th Cir. 1987).

waiver must be intentional and knowing.[57] Implied waivers will not be found when violations of *jus cogens* customary international law are alleged.[58] How a foreign state responds to a complaint is important to determining the existence of an implicit waiver. Entering a general appearance without reservation of immunity may constitute a waiver, as might failure to appear altogether.[59] Foreign states filing actions in U.S. courts may be deemed to have waived their immunity to related counterclaims that otherwise might have been subject to immunity.[60] But failing to timely answer or file motions, such as a motion to dismiss, will not automatically waive immunity.[61]

Explicit waivers are more readily identifiable, such as those found in treaties. For example, the United States has waived immunity with respect to commercial and other activities in some of its treaties of Friendship, Commerce and Navigation (FCN). The language used in the waiver is important—a commonly used provision in FCN treaties that immunity shall not be claimed from "suit, execution or judgment or other liability" is not an explicit waiver from prejudgment attachment.[62]

A second source of explicit waivers is in private agreements. For example, a loan document providing that "The Borrower can sue and be sued in its own name and does not have any right of immunity from suit with respect to the Borrower's obligations under this Letter or the Notes," has been held to be an explicit waiver of a right to raise the defense of sovereign immunity for a prejudgment attachment.[63] Waivers of immunity are common in sovereign debt instruments,[64] but judgments against defaulting sovereign debtors are hard to enforce in the absence of non-immune assets to execute upon.

---

57 Transamerican Steamship Corp. v. Somali Democratic Republic, 767 F.2d 998 (D.C.Cir. 1985).

58 *See* Sampson v. Federal Republic of Germany, 250 F.3d 1145 (7th Cir. 2001); Princz v. Germany, 26 F.3d 1166 (D.C.Cir. 1994).

59 Von Dardel v. USSR, 623 F.Supp. 246 (D.D.C.1985), *vacated,* 736 F.Supp. 1 (D.D.C. 1990). *See also* Frolova v. USSR, 761 F.2d 370 (7th Cir. 1985).

60 *See* Siderman de Blake v. Republic of Argentina, 965 F.2d 699 (9th Cir. 1992).

61 *See* Shapiro v. Bolivia, 930 F.3d 1013 (2d Cir. 1991).

62 Libra Bank Ltd. v. Banco Nacional De Costa Rica, S.A., 676 F.2d 47 (2d Cir. 1982).

63 Id at 49.

64 *See* Capital Ventures Int'l v. Republic of Argentina, 552 F.3d 289 (2d Cir. 2009) (bonds issued under German law).

§ 7.7 Exceptions to Sovereign Immunity—Commercial Activity

The commercial activity exception is the reason the FSIA was enacted. Law prior to the passage of the Act was unclear about whether a restrictive theory of sovereign immunity excluded acts which were commercial in *nature* or commercial in *purpose*. The FSIA chooses those commercial in *nature*, by defining "commercial activity" as:

> either a regular course of commercial conduct or a particular commercial transaction or act. The commercial character of an activity shall be determined by reference to the nature of the course of conduct or particular transaction or act, rather than by reference to its purpose.[65]

There are three statutory classes of commercial activity which deny immunity to the foreign state. The FSIA defines those three classes:

> A foreign state shall not be immune from the jurisdiction of courts of the United States or of the States in any case . . . (1) in which the action is based upon a commercial activity carried on in the United States by the foreign state; or (2) upon an act performed in the United States in connection with a commercial activity of the foreign state elsewhere; or (3) upon an act outside the territory of the United States in connection with a comercial activity of the foreign state elsewhere and that act causes a direct effect in the United States.[66]

The legislative history of the FSIA suggests that a commercial activity is one which an individual might customarily carry on for profit. If the activity is one which normally could be engaged in by a private party, it is commercial and a foreign state is not immune, but if the activity is one in which only a state can engage, it is noncommercial under the FSIA. The focus is not on whether the defendant generally engages in commercial activities, but on the particular conduct giving rise to the action.[67]

Commercial Activity Interpreted

The U. S. Supreme Court held that Argentina's default on its sovereign bonds was a commercial not governmental activity with a

---

65 28 U.S.C.A. § 1603(d).

66 28 U.S.C.A. § 1605(a)(2).

67 *See* Texas Trading & Milling Corp. v. Nigeria, 647 F.2d 300 (2d Cir. 1981); Brazosport Towing Co., Inc. v. 3,838 Tons of Sorghum Laden on Board, 607 F.Supp. 11 (S.D.Tex.1984).

direct effect in the United States.[68] But funds of Argentina for repayment of its IMF obligations were not property of a foreign state used for commercial activity, and hence could not be attached.[69] Cases have found commercial activity to include purchasing grain from a U.S. company under a U.S. government program, a Republic of Ireland joint venture with two U.S. citizens to manufacture plastic cosmetic containers, a Turkish government-owned gun manufacturer selling in the United States, artistic contracts for tours of USSR artists to the United States and Great Britain, offering a reward for a fugitive, and a Polish government-owned company selling golf carts in the United States. Noncommercial activities have included nationalizing plaintiff's corporation, establishing terms and conditions for removal of natural resources from its territory, and granting and revoking a license to export a natural resource.[70] Likewise, sales of military equipment to sovereign states are not commercial activities.[71]

The proper focus is on the *nature* of the activity rather than its *purpose*. In 1992 the U.S. Supreme Court addressed the definition of commercial activity and came down strongly against any interpretation based on the *purpose* of the activity.[72] The court said the issue is whether the actions that the foreign state "performs (whatever the motive behind them) are the type of actions by which a private party engages in 'trade and traffic or commerce' ", such as issuing bonds.

The FSIA and pleas of sovereign immunity after expropriations are important. Since considerable U.S. litigation against foreign sovereigns follows non-compensated nationalizations, the view that a "nationalization is the quintessentially sovereign act, never viewed as having a commercial character," obviously is a disappointment to many subjects of nationalization.[73] The exception contained in § 1605(a)(3), rights taken in violation of international law, may apply to some nationalizations, depending on the relation of the property located in the United States to the property nationalized. See Section 7.8.

The three-part commercial activity test of § 1605(a)(2) requires the activity to bear some relationship to the United States. The first

---

[68] Republic of Argentina v. Weltover Inc., 504 U.S. 607 (1992).

[69] EM Ltd. v. Argentina, 473 F.3d 463 (2d Cir. 2007).

[70] *See, e.g.*, MOL Inc. v. Bangladesh, 736 F.2d 1326 (9th Cir. 1984) (termination of natural resource license a sovereign not commercial act).

[71] Triple A Int'l v. Democratic Republic of the Congo, 721 F.3d 415 (6th Cir. 2013).

[72] Republic of Argentina v. Weltover, Inc., 504 U.S. 607, 112 S.Ct. 2160, 119 L.Ed.2d 394 (1992) (issuance of sovereign bonds not immune, commercial activity exception applies).

[73] Alberti v. Empresa Nicaraguense De La Carne, 705 F.2d 250 (7th Cir. 1983).

part is "action based upon a commercial activity carried on in the United States by the foreign state." This is the easiest part of the test and essentially involves how much commercial activity was done in the United States, and what is the link between the cause of action and the commercial activity. "Substantial contact" with the United States is sufficient.[74] The second part of the test deals with an "act performed in the United States in connection with a commercial activity of the foreign state performed elsewhere." It is the least used of the three parts since many of the acts complained of occur outside the United States. When they do occur in the United States the matter is often considered under or in combination with part one of the test.

It is the third part of the test, an "act outside . . . the United States in connection with a commercial activity of the foreign state and that act causes a direct effect in the United States," that has been the most difficult to define. Since many acts do occur abroad, the "direct effect" language is often the focus of attention. The federal Circuit Courts have been split on what constitutes a direct effect. Some followed the view that it must be "substantial and foreseeable", drawing upon the Restatement of Foreign Relations on jurisdiction to prescribe.[75] Others have rejected this approach and believe direct effect to be satisfied where there is some financial loss.[76]

This division in the Circuits was answered by the Supreme Court in 1992, when it rejected the House Report and Restatement views that direct effect meant both "substantial" and "foreseeable" and ruled that an effect is direct if it "follows 'as an immediate consequence of the defendant's . . . activity.' "[77]

§ 7.8 Exceptions to Sovereign Immunity—Takings of Property in Violation of International Law

Customary international law generally permits sovereign takings of property if they serve a public purpose, do not discriminate against foreigners, and are followed by just compensation. Rights in

---

[74] *See* Sachs v. Austria, 695 F.3d 1021 (9th Cir. 2012) (rail ticket agency in U.S. sufficient).

[75] *See, e.g.*, Maritime Int'l Nominees Establishment v. Republic of Guinea, 693 F.2d 1094 (D.C.Cir. 1982).

[76] *See, e.g.*, Texas Trading & Milling Corp. v. Federal Republic of Nigeria, 647 F.2d 300 (2d Cir. 1981).

[77] Republic of Argentina v. Weltover, Inc., 504 U.S. 607, 112 S.Ct. 2160, 2168, 119 L.Ed.2d 394 (1992), citing Texas Trading & Milling Corp. v. Federal Republic of Nigeria, 647 F.2d 300, 311 (2d Cir. 1981), *cert. denied*, 454 U.S. 1148, 102 S.Ct. 1012, 71 L.Ed.2d 301 (1982). *See* Adler v. Nigeria, 107 F.3d 720 (9th Cir. 1997) (mere financial loss is not sufficient).

property taken in violation of international law may preclude the defense of sovereign immunity under the FSIA only if:

> that property or any property exchanged for such property is present in the United States in connection with a commercial activity carried on in the United States by the foreign state; or that property or any property exchanged for such property is owned or operated by an agency or instrumentality of the for eign state and that agency or instrumentality is engaged in a commercial activity in the United States.[78]

This section may be used to respond to non-compensated expropriations of property.[79] The U.S. commercial activity requirement limits the use of this provision of the FSIA, although an Austrian gallery in possession of paintings taken by the Nazis did meet this test by publishing and advertising books in the USA containing pictures of those paintings.[80] National remedies may first need to be exhausted.[81] In general, the FSIA is not a helpful statute to persons whose property has been expropriated by a foreign state, though some decisions suggest relief for owners of intellectual or contract rights.[82]

§ 7.9 Exceptions to Sovereign Immunity—Noncommercial Torts

FSIA Section 1605 (a)(5), derived from the U.S. Federal Tort Claims Act, creates an exception to sovereign immunity for tortious acts or omissions *causing injury in the United States* that were undertaken outside commercial activity, such as traffic accidents by foreign officials. Suits against the Vatican alleging negligent supervision of priests have benefited from this exception to sovereign immunity.[83] The Supreme Court has stressed the importance of finding injury in the United States, not just effects.[84] Hence foreign sovereigns have been immune from suits by U.S. tourists injured

---

[78] 28 U.S.C.A. § 1605(a)(3).

[79] *See* Cassirer v. Spain, 616 F.3d 1019 (9th Cir. 2010) (takings need not be by foreign government in possession of a painting) and Aguadas Chasidei Chabad v. Russian Federation, 528 F.3d 934 (D.C.Cir. 2008) (takings of books). *But see* Dayton v. Czechoslovakia, 834 F.3d 203 (D.C.Cir. 1987) (takings exception not applied); Chuidan v. Philipine National Bank, 912 F.2d 1095 (9th Cir. 1990).

[80] Altmann v. Austria, 317 F.3d 954 (9th Cir. 2002).

[81] Abellesz v. Magyar Nemzeti Bank, 692 F.3d 691 (7th Cir. 2012).

[82] *See* Zappia Middle East Construction v. Abu Dhabi, 215 F.3d 247 (2d Cir. 2000).

[83] *See* O'Bryan v. Holy See, 556 F.3d 361 (6th Cir. 2009).

[84] Argentina v. Amerada Hess Shipping, 488 U.S. 428 (1989).

abroad,[85] and supporting terrorist conduct outside the United States,[86] but subject to suit for New York building code violations.[87]

Intentional torts such as libel, misrepresentation, interference with contracts, malicious prosecution and the like are excluded from this exception. Tortious interference with contract claims may be allowed under the FSIA commercial activities exception, but disallowed under the tort exception, which remain analytically distinct.[88] Acts constituting "discretionary functions" of sovereigns undertaking policy judgments are also excluded from the noncommercial torts exception of the FSIA.[89] This exclusion helped save Mexico from having to respond to tort claims for polluting Texas beaches while exploiting its oil resources.[90] But politically driven assassinations in the United States have not benefited from the discretionary function exclusion.[91]

§ 7.10 Exceptions to Sovereign Immunity—Arbitration Agreements and Awards

Many sovereigns have ratified bilateral investment treaties (BITs), and/or trade agreements that incorporate mandatory foreign investment arbitration rules and procedures. See Chapter 4. Section 1610(a)(6) of the FSIA creates an exception to sovereign immunity for actions to enforce arbitral agreements agreed to by states, or an order confirming an arbitral award rendered against a foreign state, provided there is a nexus to the United States.

If the U.S. was the place of arbitration, that is sufficient nexus. Or if the agreement or award is subject to a U.S. treaty such as the New York Convention on Recognition and Enforcement of Foreign Arbitral Awards or the Inter-American Convention on International Commercial Arbitration (see Section 3.8), sufficient nexus is again present.[92] Thus this FSIA exception reinforces the widely adopted

---

85 *See, e.g.*, Upton v. Iran, 459 F.Supp. 264 (D.D.C. 1978) *aff'd*, 607 F.2d 494 (D.C. Cir 1978).

86 In re Terrorist Attacks on Sept. 11, 2001, 714 F.3d 109 (2d Cir. 2013).

87 USAA Casualty Insurance Co. v. Permanent Mission of the Republic of Namibia, 681 F.3d 103 (2d Cir. 2011).

88 *See* Export Group v. Reef Indus., 54 F.3d 1466 (9th Cir. 1995)

89 *See* United States v. VARIG Airlines, 467 U.S. 797 (1984).

90 *See* In re Sedco, 543 F.Supp. 561 (S.D.Tex. 1982).

91 *See* De Letelier v. Chile, 488 F.Supp. 665 (D.D.C. 1980) and Liu v. China, 892 F.2d 1419 (9th Cir. 1989).

92 *See* Employers Ins. of Wausau v. Banco De Seguros Del Estado, 199 F.3d 937 (7th Cir. 1999) (New York Convention).

New York Convention.[93] But enforcement of arbitral awards against foreign sovereigns can still fail for want of due process.[94]

Section 15 of the U.S. Federal Arbitration Act adopting the New York Convention specifically denies judicial application of the Act of State doctrine, covered in Part B below.

§ 7.11 Exceptions to Sovereign Immunity—Terrorism

In 2008, reformulating existing provisions, the FSIA was amended to add Section 1605A creating an exception to sovereign immunity when damages are sought by U.S. nationals, members of its armed forces, and U.S. employees or contractors for personal injury or wrongful death caused by acts of torture, extrajudicial killing, aircraft sabotage, and hostage taking or provision of material support or resources for the same by foreign states or their officials, employees or agents. This provision specifically targets claims against states designated by the United States as sponsors of terrorism (Cuba, Iran, Iraq, Libya, Syria, Sudan and North Korea have been so designated).

Section 1605A creates a private right of action (subject to a 10 year statute of limitations) against such states with liens of *lis pendens* against foreign state property subject to attachment. Such judgments may face extreme enforcement difficulties. Allegations of torture by Saudi Arabia against an American working in a state hospital failed in a 1993 Supreme Court case focused on whether the commercial activity exception applied.[95] Torture allegations under Section 1605A failed in 2008 against Saudi Arabia absent designation as a state sponsor of terrorism.[96] But numerous other Section 1605A FSIA exceptions have been recognized,[97] though collection against Iranian assets in the USA has been difficult.[98]

§ 7.12 Exceptions to Sovereign Immunity—Admiralty

FSIA Section 1605(b) creates an exception to sovereign immunity for admiralty claims to enforce liens against vessels or cargo of a foreign state based upon the commercial activity of that

---

93 *See* In re Arbitration between: Trans Chem. Ltd. & China Nat'l Mach. Import & Export Corp., 978 F.Supp. 266 (S.D. Tex. 1997).

94 *See* Creighton v. Ltd v. Qatar, 181 F.2d 118 (D.C.Cir. 1999).

95 Saudi Arabia v. Nelson, 507 U.S. 349 (1993).

96 In re Terrorist Attacks, 538 F.3d 71 (2d Cir. 2008).

97 *See, e.g.*, Leibovitch v. Iran, 697 F.3d 561 (7th Cir. 2011) (Palestinian group attacks on U.S. and Isreali citizens in Israel); Rubin v. Iran, 709 F.3d 49 (1st Cir. 2013).

98 *But see* Peterson v. Iran, 758 F.3d 185 (2d Cir. 2014) (bank assets seized).

state. Notice must be given to the person or agent in possession of the vessel, followed within 10 days by notice to the foreign state.

§ 7.13 Exceptions to Sovereign Immunity—Directly Disputed U.S. Property

FSIA Section 1605(a)(4) establishes another exception to foreign sovereign immunity when directly disputed U.S. property rights have been inherited or gifted, or U.S. real estate is at stake. This exception has been narrowly construed.[99]

§ 7.14 Text of Foreign Sovereign Immunities Act of 1976 (FSIA)

90 Stat. 2891, 28 U.S.C.A. §§ 1330, 1332, 1391, 1441, 1602–1611 (1976), as amended by Public Law 100–640, 102 Stat. 3333 (1988); Public Law 100–669, 102 Stat. 3969 (1988); Public Law 104–132, 110 Stat. 1241 (1986); Public Law 105–11, 111 Stat. 22 (1997) and Public Law 4986–10 (2008).

> An Act to define the jurisdiction of United States courts in suits against foreign states, the circumstances in which foreign states are immune from suit and in which execution may not be levied on their property, and for other purposes.

Be it enacted by the Senate and House of Representatives of the United States of America in Congress assembled, That this Act may be cited as the "Foreign Sovereign Immunities Act of 1976."

Sec. 2. (a) That chapter 85 of title 28, United States Code, is amended by inserting immediately before section 1331 the following new section:

§ 1330. Actions against Foreign States

> (a) The district courts shall have original jurisdiction without regard to amount in controversy of any nonjury civil action against a foreign state as defined in section 1603(a) of this title as to any claim for relief in personam with respect to which the foreign state is not entitled to immunity either under sections 1605–1607 of this title or under any applicable international agreement.
>
> (b) Personal jurisdiction over a foreign state shall exist as to every claim for relief over which the district courts have jurisdiction under subsection (a) where service has been made under section 1608 of this title.

---

[99] *See, e.g.*, MacArthur Area Citizens Assn v. Peru, 809 F.2d 918 (D.C.Cir. 1987) (alleged zoning violations do not involve directly disputed property disputes).

(c) For purposes of subsection (b), an appearance by a foreign state does not confer personal jurisdiction with respect to any claim for relief not arising out of any transaction or occurrence enumerated in sections 1605–1607 of this title."

Sec. 4. (a) That title 28, United States Code, is amended by inserting after chapter 95 the following new chapter:

CHAPTER 97—JURISDICTIONAL IMMUNITIES OF FOREIGN STATES

§ 1602. Findings and Declaration of Purpose

The Congress finds that the determination by United States courts of the claims of foreign states to immunity from the jurisdiction of such courts would serve the interests of justice and would protect the rights of both foreign states and litigants in United States courts. Under international law, states are not immune from the jurisdiction of foreign courts insofar as their commercial activities are concerned, and their commercial property may be levied upon for the satisfaction of judgments rendered against them in connection with their commercial activities. Claims of foreign states to immunity should henceforth be decided by courts of the United States and of the States in conformity with the principles set forth in this chapter.

§ 1603. Definitions

For purposes of this chapter—

(a) A 'foreign state' except as used in section 1608 of this title, includes a political subdivision of a foreign state or an agency or instrumentality of a foreign state as defined in subsection (b).

(b) An 'agency or instrumentality of a foreign state' means any entity—

(1) which is a separate legal person, corporate or otherwise, and

(2) which is an organ of a foreign state or political subdivision thereof, or a majority of whose shares or other ownership interest is owned by a foreign state or political subdivision thereof, and

(3) which is neither a citizen of a State of the United States as defined in section 1332(c) and (d) of this title, nor created under the laws of any third country.

(c) The 'United States' includes all territory and waters, continental or insular, subject to the jurisdiction of the United States.

(d) A 'commercial activity' means either a regular course of commercial conduct or a particular commercial transaction or act. The commercial character of an activity shall be determined by reference to the nature of the course of conduct or particular transaction or act, rather than by reference to its purpose.

(e) A 'commercial activity carried on in the United States by a foreign state' means commercial activity carried on by such state and having substantial contact with the United States.

§ 1604. Immunity of a Foreign State from Jurisdiction

Subject to existing international agreements to which the United States is a party at the time of enactment of this Act a foreign state shall be immune from the jurisdiction of the courts of the United States and of the States except as provided in sections 1605 to 1607 of this chapter.

§ 1605. General Exceptions to the Jurisdictional Immunity of a Foreign State

(a) A foreign state shall not be immune from the jurisdiction of courts of the United States or of the States in any case—

(1) in which the foreign state has waived its immunity either explicitly or by implication, notwithstanding any withdrawal of the waiver which the foreign state may purport to effect except in accordance with the terms of the waiver;

(2) in which the action is based upon a commercial activity carried on in the United States by the foreign state; or upon an act performed in the United States in connection with a commercial activity of the foreign state elsewhere; or upon an act outside the territory of the United States in connection with a commercial activity of the foreign state elsewhere and that act causes a direct effect in the United States;

(3) in which rights in property taken in violation of international law are in issue and that property or any property exchanged for such property is present in the United States in connection with a commercial activity carried on in the United States by the foreign state; or that property or any property exchanged for such property is owned or operated by an agency or instrumentality of the foreign state and that agency or instrumentality is engaged in a commercial activity in the United States;

(4) in which rights in property in the United States acquired by succession or gift or rights in immovable property situated in the United States are in issue;

(5) not otherwise encompassed in paragraph (2) above, in which money damages are sought against a foreign state for personal injury or death, or damage to or loss of property, occurring in the United States and caused by the tortious act or omission of that foreign state or of any official or employee of that foreign state while acting within the scope of his office or employment; except this paragraph shall not apply to—

(A) any claim based upon the exercise or performance or the failure to exercise or perform a discretionary function regardless of whether the discretion be abused, or

(B) any claim arising out of malicious prosecution, abuse of process, libel, slander, misrepresentation, deceit, or interference with contract rights;

(6) in which the action is brought, either to enforce an agreement made by the foreign State with or for the benefit of a private party to submit to arbitration all or any differences which have arisen or which may arise between the parties with respect to a defined legal relationship, whether contractual or not, concerning a subject matter capable of settlement by arbitration under the laws of the United States, or to confirm an award made pursuant to such an agreement to arbitrate, if (A) the arbitration takes place or is intended to take place in the United States, (B) the agreement or award is or may be governed by a treaty or other international agreement in force for the United States calling for the recognition and enforcement of arbitral awards, (C) the underlying claim, save for the agreement to arbitrate, could have been brought in a United States court under this section or section 1607, or (D) paragraph (1) of this subsection is otherwise applicable.

(b) A foreign state shall not be immune from the jurisdiction of the courts of the United States in any case in which a suit in admiralty is brought to enforce a maritime lien against a vessel or cargo of the foreign state, which maritime lien is based upon a commercial activity of the foreign state: *Provided,* That—

(1) notice of the suit is given by delivery of a copy of the summons and of the complaint to the person, or his agent, having possession of the vessel or cargo against which the

maritime lien is asserted; and if the vessel or cargo is arrested pursuant to process obtained on behalf of the party bringing the suit, the service of process of arrest shall be deemed to constitute valid delivery of such notice, but the party bringing the suit shall be liable for any damages sustained by the foreign state as a result of the arrest if the party bringing the suit had actual or constructive knowledge that the vessel or cargo of a foreign state was involved; and

(2) notice to the foreign state of the commencement of suit as provided in section 1608 of this title is initiated within ten days either of the delivery of notice as provided in paragraph (1) of this subsection or, in the case of a party who was unaware that the vessel or cargo of a foreign state was involved, of the date such party determined the existence of the foreign state's interest.

(c) Whenever notice is delivered under subsection (b)(1), the suit to enforce a maritime lien shall thereafter proceed and shall be heard and determined according to the principles of law and rules of practice of suits in rem whenever it appears that, had the vessel been privately owned and possessed, a suit in rem might have been maintained. A decree against the foreign state may include costs of the suit and, if the decree is for a money judgment, interest as ordered by the court, except that the court may not award judgment against the foreign state in an amount greater than the value of the vessel or cargo upon which the maritime lien arose. Such value shall be determined as of the time notice is served under subsection (b)(1). Decrees shall be subject to appeal and revision as provided in other cases of admiralty and maritime jurisdiction. Nothing shall preclude the plaintiff in any proper case from seeking relief in personam in the same action brought to enforce a maritime lien as provided in this section.

(d) A foreign state shall not be immune from the jurisdiction of the courts of the United States in any action brought to foreclose a preferred mortgage, as defined in the Ship Mortgage Act 1920, (46 U.S.C. § 911 and following). Such action shall be brought, heard, and determined in accordance with the provisions of that Act and in accordance with the principles of law and rules of practice of suits in rem, whenever it appears that had the vessel been privately owned and possessed a suit in rem might have been maintained.

* * *

§ 1605A. Terrorism exception to jurisdictional immunity of a foreign state

(a) IN GENERAL.—

(1) NO IMMUNITY.—A foreign state shall not be immune from the jurisdiction of courts of the United States or of the States in any case not otherwise covered by this chapter in which money damages are sought against a foreign state for personal injury or death that was caused by an act of torture, extrajudicial killing, aircraft sabotage, hostage taking, or the provision of material support or resources for such an act if such act or provision of material support or resources is engaged in by an official, employee, or agent of such foreign state while acting within the scope of his or her office, employment, or agency.

(2) CLAIM HEARD.—The court shall hear a claim under this section if—

(A)(i)

(I) the foreign state was designated as a state sponsor of terrorism at the time the act described in paragraph (1) occurred, or was so designated as a result of such act, and, subject to subclause (II), either remains so designated when the claim is filed under this section or was so designated within the 6-month period before the claim is filed under this section; or

(II) in the case of an action that is refiled under this section by reason of section 1083(c)(2)(A) of the National Defense Authorization Act for Fiscal Year 2008 or is filed under this section by reason of section 1083(c)(3) of that Act, the foreign state was designated as a state sponsor of terrorism when the original action or the related action under section 1605(a)(7) (as in effect before the enactment of this section) or section 589 of the Foreign Operations, Export Financing, and Related Programs Appropriations Act, 1997 (as contained in section 101(c) of division A of Public Law 104–208) was filed;

(ii) the claimant or the victim was, at the time the act described in paragraph (1) occurred—

(I) a national of the United States;

(II) a member of the armed forces; or

(III) otherwise an employee of the Government of the United States, or of an individual performing a contract awarded by the United States Government, acting within the scope of the employee's employment; and

(iii) in a case in which the act occurred in the foreign state against which the claim has been brought, the claimant has afforded the foreign state a reasonable opportunity to arbitrate the claim in accordance with the accepted international rules of arbitration; or

(B) the act described in paragraph (1) is related to Case Number 1:00CV03110 (EGS) in the United States District Court for the District of Columbia.

(b) LIMITATIONS.—An action may be brought or maintained under this section if the action is commenced, or a related action was commenced under section 1605(a)(7) (before the date of the enactment of this section) or section 589 of the Foreign Operations, Export Financing, and Related Programs Appropriations Act, 1997 (as contained in section 101(c) of division A of Public Law 104–208) not later than the latter of—"(1) 10 years after April 24, 1996; or "(2) 10 years after the date on which the cause of action arose.

(c) PRIVATE RIGHT OF ACTION.—A foreign state that is or was a state sponsor of terrorism as described in subsection (a)(2)(A)(i), and any official, employee, or agent of that foreign state while acting within the scope of his or her office, employment, or agency, shall be liable to—"(1) a national of the United States, "(2) a member of the armed forces, "(3) an employee of the Government of the United States, or of an individual performing a contract awarded by the United States Government, acting within the scope of the employee's employment, or "(4) the legal representative of a person described in paragraph (1), (2), or (3), for personal injury or death caused by acts described in subsection (a)(1) of that foreign state, or of an official, employee, or agent of that foreign state, for which the courts of the United States may maintain jurisdiction under this section for money damages. In any such action, damages may include economic damages, solatium, pain and suffering, and punitive damages. In any such action, a foreign state shall be vicariously liable for the acts of its officials, employees, or agents.

(d) ADDITIONAL DAMAGES.—After an action has been brought under subsection (c), actions may also be brought for reasonably foreseeable property loss, whether insured or uninsured, third party liability, and loss claims under life and property insurance policies, by reason of the same acts on which the action under subsection (c) is based.

(e) SPECIAL MASTERS.—

(1) IN GENERAL.—The courts of the United States may appoint special masters to hear damage claims brought under this section.

(2) TRANSFER OF FUNDS.—The Attorney General shall transfer, from funds available for the program under section 1404C of the Victims of Crime Act of 1984 (42 U.S.C. 10603c), to the Administrator of the United States district court in which any case is pending which has been brought or maintained under this section such funds as may be required to cover the costs of special masters appointed under paragraph (1). Any amount paid in compensation to any such special master shall constitute an item of court costs.

(f) APPEAL.—In an action brought under this section, appeals from orders not conclusively ending the litigation may only be taken pursuant to section 1292(b) of this title.

(g) PROPERTY DISPOSITION.—

(1) IN GENERAL.—In every action filed in a United States district court in which jurisdiction is alleged under this section, the filing of a notice of pending action pursuant to this section, to which is attached a copy of the complaint filed in the action, shall have the effect of establishing a lien of lis pendens upon any real property or tangible personal property that is—

(A) subject to attachment in aid of execution, or execution, under section 1610;

(B) located within that judicial district; and

(C) titled in the name of any defendant, or titled in the name of any entity controlled by any defendant if such notice contains a statement listing such controlled entity.

(2) NOTICE.—A notice of pending action pursuant to this section shall be filed by the clerk of the district court in the same manner as any pending action and shall be indexed

by listing as defendants all named defendants and all entities listed as controlled by any defendant.

(3) ENFORCEABILITY.—Liens established by reason of this subsection shall be enforceable as provided in chapter 111 of this title.

(h) DEFINITIONS.—For purposes of this section—

(1) the term 'aircraft sabotage' has the meaning given that term in Article 1 of the Convention for the Suppression of Unlawful Acts Against the Safety of Civil Aviation;

(2) the term 'hostage taking' has the meaning given that term in Article 1 of the International Convention Against the Taking of Hostages;

(3) the term 'material support or resources' has the meaning given that term in section 2339A of title 18;

(4) the term 'armed forces' has the meaning given that term in section 101 of title 10;

(5) the term 'national of the United States' has the meaning given that term in section 101(a)(22) of the Immigration and Nationality Act (8 U.S.C. 1101(a)(22));

(6) the term 'state sponsor of terrorism' means a country the government of which the Secretary of State has determined, for purposes of section 6(j) of the Export Administration Act of 1979 (50 U.S.C. App. 2405(j)), section 620A of the Foreign Assistance Act of 1961 (22 U.S.C. 2371), section 40 of the Arms Export Control Act (22 U.S.C. 2780), or any other provision of law, is a government that has repeatedly provided support for acts of international terrorism; and

(7) the terms 'torture' and 'extrajudicial killing' have the meaning given those terms in section 3 of the Torture Victim Protection Act.

§ 1606. Extent of Liability

As to any claim for relief with respect to which a foreign state is not entitled to immunity under section 1605 or 1607 of this chapter, the foreign state shall be liable in the same manner and to the same extent as a private individual under like circumstances; but a foreign state except for an agency or instrumentality thereof shall not be liable for punitive damages; if, however, in any case wherein death was caused, the law of the place where the action or omission occurred provides, or has been construed to provide, for damages only punitive in nature, the foreign state shall be liable for actual or compensatory damages measured by the pecuniary injuries resulting from such death which were incurred by the persons for whose benefit the action was brought.

§ 1607. Counterclaims

In any action brought by a foreign state, or in which a foreign state intervenes, in a court of the United States or of a State, the foreign state shall not be accorded immunity with respect to any counterclaim—

(a) for which a foreign state would not be entitled to immunity under section 1605 of this chapter had such claim been brought in a separate action against the foreign state; or

(b) arising out of the transaction or occurrence that is the subject matter of the claim of the foreign state; or

(c) to the extent that the counterclaim does not seek relief exceeding in amount or differing in kind from that sought by the foreign state.

* * *

§ 1609. Immunity from Attachment and Execution of Property of a Foreign State

Subject to existing international agreements to which the United States is a party at the time of enactment of this Act the property in the United States of a foreign state shall be immune from attachment arrest and execution except as provided in sections 1610 and 1611 of this chapter.

§ 1610. Exceptions to the Immunity from Attachment or Execution

(a) The property in the United States of a foreign state, as defined in section 1603(a) of this chapter, used for a commercial activity in the United States, shall not be immune from attachment in aid of execution, or from execution, upon a judgment entered by a court of the United States or of a State after the effective date of this Act, if—

(1) the foreign state has waived its immunity from attachment in aid of execution or from execution either explicitly or by implication, notwithstanding any withdrawal of the waiver the foreign state may purport to effect except in accordance with the terms of the waiver, or

(2) the property is or was used for the commercial activity upon which the claim is based, or

(3) the execution relates to a judgment establishing rights in property which has been taken in violation of international law or which has been exchanged for property taken in violation of international law, or

(4) the execution relates to a judgment establishing rights in property—

(A) which is acquired by succession or gift, or

(B) which is immovable and situated in the United States: *Provided,* That such property is not used for purposes of maintaining a diplomatic or consular mission or the residence of the Chief of such mission, or

(5) the property consists of any contractual obligation or any proceeds from such a contractual obligation to indemnify or hold harmless the foreign state or its employees under a policy of automobile or other liability or casualty insurance covering the claim which merged into the judgment;

(6) the judgment is based on an order confirming an arbitral award rendered against the foreign State, provided that attachment in aid of execution, or execution, would not be inconsistent with any provision in the arbitral agreement, or

(7) the judgment relates to a claim for which the foreign state is not immune under section 1605(a)(7), regardless of whether the property is or was involved with the act upon which the claim is based.

(b) In addition to subsection (a), any property in the United States of an agency or instrumentality of a foreign state engaged in commercial activity in the United States shall not be immune from attachment in aid of execution, or from execution, upon a judgment entered by a court of the United States or of a State after the effective date of this Act, if—

(1) the agency or instrumentality has waived its immunity from attachment in aid of execution or from execution either explicitly or implicitly, notwithstanding any withdrawal of the waiver the agency or instrumentality may purport to effect except in accordance with the terms of the waiver, or

(2) the judgment relates to a claim for which the agency or instrumentality is not immune by virtue of section 1605(a)(2), (3), (5) or (7) 1605(b) of this chapter, regardless

of whether the property is or was used for the activity upon which the claim is based.

(c) No attachment or execution referred to in subsections (a) and (b) of this section shall be permitted until the court has ordered such attachment and execution after having determined that a reasonable period of time has elapsed following the entry of judgment and the giving of any notice required under section 1608(e) of this chapter.

(d) The property of a foreign state, as defined in section 1603(a) of this chapter, used for a commercial activity in the United States, shall not be immune from attachment prior to the entry of judgment in any action brought in a court of the United States or of a State, or prior to the elapse of the period of time provided in subsection (c) of this section, if—

(1) the foreign state has explicitly waived its immunity from attachment prior to judgment, notwithstanding any withdrawal of the waiver the foreign state may purport to effect except in accordance with the terms of the waiver, and

(2) the purpose of the attachment is to secure satisfaction of a judgment that has been or may ultimately be entered against the foreign state, and not to obtain jurisdiction.

(e) The vessels of a foreign State shall not be immune from arrest in rem, interlocutory sale, and execution in actions brought to foreclose a preferred mortgage as provided in section 1605(d). * * *

(g) PROPERTY IN CERTAIN ACTIONS.—

(1) IN GENERAL.—Subject to paragraph (3), the property of a foreign state against which a judgment is entered under section 1605A, and the property of an agency or instrumentality of such a state, including property that is a separate juridical entity or is an interest held directly or indirectly in a separate juridical entity, is subject to attachment in aid of execution, and execution, upon that judgment as provided in this section, regardless of—

(A) the level of economic control over the property by the government of the foreign state;

(B) whether the profits of the property go to that government;

(C) the degree to which officials of that government manage the property or otherwise control its daily affairs;

(D) whether that government is the sole beneficiary in interest of the property; or

(E) whether establishing the property as a separate entity would entitle the foreign state to benefits in United States courts while avoiding its obligations.

(2) UNITED STATES SOVEREIGN IMMUNITY INAPPLICABLE.—Any property of a foreign state, or agency or instrumentality of a foreign state, to which paragraph (1) applies shall not be immune from attachment in aid of execution, or execution, upon a judgment entered under section 1605A because the property is regulated by the United States Government by reason of action taken against that foreign state under the Trading With the Enemy Act or the International Emergency Economic Powers Act.

(3) THIRD-PARTY JOINT PROPERTY HOLDERS.—Nothing in this subsection shall be construed to supersede the authority of a court to prevent appropriately the impairment of an interest held by a person who is not liable in the action giving rise to a judgment in property subject to attachment in aid of execution, or execution, upon such judgment." * * *

§ 1611. Certain Types of Property Immune from Execution

(a) Notwithstanding the provisions of section 1610 of this chapter, the property of those organizations designated by the President as being entitled to enjoy the privileges, exemptions and immunities provided by the International Organizations Immunities Act shall not be subject to attachment or any other judicial process impeding the disbursement of funds to, or on the order of, a foreign state as the result of an action brought in the courts of the United States or of the States.

(b) Notwithstanding the provisions of section 1610 of this chapter, the property of a foreign state shall be immune from attachment and from execution, if—

(1) the property is that of a foreign central bank or monetary authority held for its own account, unless such bank or authority, or its parent foreign government, has explicitly waived its immunity from attachment in aid of execution, or from execution, notwithstanding any

withdrawal of the waiver which the bank, authority or government may purport to effect except in accordance with the terms of the waiver; or

(2) the property is, or is intended to be, used in connection with a military activity and

(A) is of a military character, or

(B) is under the control of a military authority or defense agency."

(c) Notwithstanding the provisions of section 1610 of this chapter, the property of a foreign state shall be immune from attachment and from execution in an action brought under section 302 of the Cuban Liberty and Democratic Solidarity (LIBERTAD) Act of 1996 to the extent that the property is a facility or installation used by an accredited diplomatic mission for official purposes.

PART B: ACT OF STATE DOCTRINE

§ 7.15 The Act of State Doctrine

The defense of sovereignty immunity often is accompanied by the separate defense of "act of state", although a number of purely private litigations seek to invoke the act of state doctrine.[100] Acceptance of either defense generates judicial abstention. The sovereign immunity doctrine mandates that a foreign sovereign may not be sued in the courts of other nations, thus focusing on who should or should not be sued. It is concerned with the *status* of the defendant. Contrastingly, the act of state doctrine suggests that courts of one nation will not sit in judgment of the acts of a foreign sovereign that occurred *in* the foreign state, thus focusing on what is or is not a proper subject matter. It is concerned with the *acts* of the defendant inside its territory.

It has been said that act of state "operates as an issue preclusion device."[101] Sovereign immunity is jurisdictional in nature. If immunity exists, the court lacks jurisdiction. But the act of state doctrine does not deprive a court of jurisdiction. Where the act of state doctrine is at issue, the court has jurisdiction but opts, for act of state reasons, not to decide the issue. Sovereign immunity in the United States is governed by the FSIA (above), which *inter alia* has exemption provisions for commercial activity, waivers and violations

---

[100] *See, e.g.*, Oetjen v. Central Leather, 246 U.S. 297 (1918).

[101] National American Corp. v. Federal Republic of Nigeria, 448 F.Supp. 622, 640 (S.D.N.Y.1978), *aff'd*, 597 F.2d 314 (2d Cir. 1979).

of international law. See Sections 7.6, 7.7 and 7.8. Those issues have not escaped the act of state doctrine. See Sections 7.16 and 7.19.

The act of state doctrine in the United States is not governed by statute but rather by federal common law cases. That case law includes debate regarding its application to violations of international law. Congressional anger over *Banco Nacional de Cuba v. Sabbatino*[102] led to legislation (discussed below) mandating that courts not accept the defense in some instances where there are alleged violations of international law. But of most concern to those engaged in international business transactions is the debate regarding the existence of a commercial exception to the doctrine.

§ 7.16 History of Act of State Doctrine

The act of state doctrine resembles the "political question" doctrine in U.S. constitutional law. The doctrine can be traced to the 1674 English case of *Blad v. Bamfield.*[103] It also exists in the jurisprudence of France, Germany, Greece, Italy, The Netherlands, Switzerland and other countries. The initial important U.S. decision is *Underhill v. Hernandez.*[104] There the Supreme Court stated that:

> Every sovereign state is bound to respect the independence of every other state, and the courts of one country will not sit in judgment on the acts of the government of another, done with in its own territory. Redress of grievances by reason of such acts must be obtained through the means open to be availed of by sovereign powers as between themselves.[105]

The *Underhill* litigation arose from claimed damages suffered by the plaintiff (Underhill) at the hands of a Venezuelan revolutionary army commander (Hernandez) during an alleged false arrest in Venezuela. The United States had subsequently recognized the revolutionary government. The doctrine as expressed in *Underhill* was reaffirmed in the modern classic, *Sabbatino.*

§ 7.17 Act of State and Expropriation

Banco Nacional de Cuba v. Sabbatino began the contemporary history of the act of state doctrine and its applicability to

---

102 376 U.S. 398, 84 S.Ct. 923, 11 L.Ed.2d 804 (1964).

103 36 All E.Eng.Rep. 992, applied in 1981 in Buttes Gas and Oil Co. v. Hammer (No. 3), [1981] 3 All E.R. 616.

104 168 U.S. 250, 18 S.Ct. 83, 42 L.Ed. 456 (1897).

105 *Id.* at 252, 18 S.Ct. at 84.

expropriations.[106] The case involved rights to property affected by the Cuban nationalization of property in 1960. Justice Harlan stated:

> [T]he Judicial Branch will not examine the validity of a taking of property within its own territory by a foreign sovereign, ex tant and recognized by this country at the time of suit, *in the absence of a treaty or other unambiguous agreement regarding controlling legal principles,* even if the complaint alleges that the taking violates customary international law.[107] (*emphasis added*).

Justice White dissented, stating:

> I do not believe that the act of state doctrine, as judicially fash ioned in the Court, and the reasons underlying it, require American courts to decide cases in disregard of international law and of the rights of litigants to a full determination on the merits.[108]

The Supreme Court decision was not well received by many members of Congress. The Sabbatino Amendment to the Foreign Assistance Act was quickly passed, and stated:

> Notwithstanding any other provisions of law, no court in the United States shall decline on the ground of the federal act of state doctrine to make a determination on the merits giving ef fect to the principles of international law in a case in which a claim of title or other right [to property] is asserted by any par ty including a foreign state . . . based upon . . . a confisca tion or other taking . . . by an act of that state in violation of the principles of international law, including the principles of compensation and the other standards set out in this subsec tion: *Provided*, That this subparagraph shall not be applicable . . . (2) in any case with respect to which the President deter mines that application of the act of state doctrine is required in that particular case by the foreign policy interests of the Unit ed States and a suggestion to this effect is filed on his behalf in that case with the court.[109]

This Sabbatino Amendment (also called the Second Hickenlooper Amendment) led to a reversal of the *Sabbatino* decision

---

106 376 U.S. 398, 84 S.Ct. 923, 11 L.Ed.2d 804 (1964).

107 *Id.* at 428, 84 S.Ct. at 940. For an expropriation case rejecting application of the act of state doctrine because of a BIT treaty between the Ethiopia and the United States, *see* Kalamazoo Spice Extraction Co. v. Ethiopia, 729 F.2d 422 (6th Cir. 1984).

108 *Id.* at 441, 84 S.Ct. at 946.

109 22 U.S.C.A. § 2370(e)(2). The bracketed words were added in 1965 to clarify that the doctrine continued to apply to acts not involving the taking of property.

on remand.[110] But in the years that followed, the courts have not applied it very enthusiastically.[111]

§ 7.18 Limitations on Act of State Doctrine

The act of state doctrine, subsequent to the formation of much of its characteristics in expropriation cases, was for several years expanded in scope, but in 1990 encountered a Supreme Court contraction in *W.S. Kirkpatrick & Co. v. Environmental Tectonics Corp., Int'l.*[112] In the *Kirkpatrick* case Environmental Tectonics learned that the reason it had lost a contract with Nigeria was that Kirkpatrick had bribed Nigerian government officials. Environmental Tectonics sought damages against Kirkpatrick, which raised the act of state doctrine alleging that proof of the bribe might require the court to consider an act of the foreign state. The Circuit Court declined to apply the act of state doctrine because the Department of State said that such inquiry would not cause embarrassment to U.S. foreign relations.

But the Supreme Court rejected that reasoning, refusing instead to apply the doctrine because it did not involve an inquiry into the validity of an official act (statute, decree, order or resolution) of the foreign government, but merely the consideration of the motivations of foreign officials. *Kirkpatrick* is an important decision, suggesting a method by which the act of state doctrine may be diminished in application. Later decisions have stressed the need for public or official acts of state to be involved, not merely a pattern of conduct by a foreign government's agents[113] or occupying powers.[114] Nevertheless, the doctrine continues to be frequently invoked, shielding Mexico for example from suit on a certificate of deposit after default was triggered under its foreign exchange control regulations,[115] and sheltering Brazil from taxpayer disputes.[116]

---

[110] Banco Nacional de Cuba v. Farr, 243 F.Supp. 957 (S.D.N.Y.1965), *aff'd*, 383 F.2d 166 (2d Cir. 1967), *cert. denied*, 390 U.S. 956, 88 S.Ct. 1038, 19 L.Ed.2d 1151 (1968).

[111] *See, e.g.*, Glen v. Club Mediterranee SA, 450 F.3d 1251 (11th Cir. 2006) (Cuban expropriation covered by act of state doctrine) and FOGADE v. ENB Revocable Trust, 263 F.3d 1274 (11th Cir. 2001) (Hickenlooper not applicable).

[112] 493 U.S. 400, 110 S.Ct. 701, 107 L.Ed.2d 816 (1990).

[113] *See* McKesson Corp. v. Islamic Republic of Iran, 672 F.3d 1066 (D.C.Cir. 2012).

[114] *See* Aguidas Chasidei Chabad v. Russia, 528 F.3d 934 (D.C.Cir. 2008).

[115] Braka v. Bancomer, 762 F.2d 222 (2d Cir. 1985). Accord, Allied Bank Int'l v. Banco Credito Agricola, 757 F.2d 516 (2d Cir. 1985) (Costa Rican suspensión of debt payments no bar to collection of state-owned bank promissory notes) and Optopics Lab. Corp. v. Savannah Bank of Nigeria, 816 F.Supp. 898 (S.D. N.Y. 1993) (Nigerian exchange controls).

[116] Riggs Nat'l Corp. v. IRS, 163 F.3d 1363 (D.C.Cir. 1999). *See also* World Wide Minerals Ltd. v. Kazakhstahn, 296 F.2d 1154 (D.C.Cir. 2000); Grupo Protexa SA v. All Amer. Marine Slip, 20 F.3d 1224 (2d Cir. 1994).

§ 7.19 Act of State and Separation of Powers

The act of state doctrine is punctuated by unclear contours, debatable exceptions and an unsympathetic Congressional response. The cases illustrate that the doctrine is deliberate but flexible. There is general agreement that the doctrine is grounded in self-imposed judicial restraint, analogous to the "political question" doctrine.[117] The doctrine rests upon considerations of international comity and separation of powers between the executive and judicial branches of the government. It is intended to avoid embarrassment in the conduct of the nation's foreign relations. One has only to envision a justice of peace court in the United States proclaiming the illegality of actions taken in a foreign country by the highest officers of that government to sense the international prudence of such a doctrine.[118]

Bernstein Exception, The Role of the Executive Branch

The act of state doctrine's interface with the separation of powers between the executive and judicial branches of the U.S. government has been discussed by courts for over twenty years in large part because of *Bernstein v. N.V. Nederlandsche-Amerikaansche Stoomvaart-Maatschappij.*[119] In *Bernstein* the court was inclined to apply the act of state doctrine, but the Department of State urged the court to refrain and to proceed with an examination of the legal issues. The court concluded:

> [I]n the prior appeal in this case . . . because of the lack of a definitive expression of Executive Policy, we felt constrained to follow . . . [the act of state doctrine] . . . Following our deci sion, however, the State Department issued . . . [a policy statement intended] . . . to relieve American courts from any [such] restraint upon the exercise of their jurisdiction. . . . In view of this supervening expression of Executive Policy, we amend our mandate . . . [that the act of state doctrine pre cludes judicial inquiry].[120]

The validity of this "*Bernstein* exception" to the act of state doctrine was before the Supreme Court in *First National City Bank v. Banco Nacional de Cuba.*[121] Reversing the lower court, three justices, as a plurality, wrote:

---

[117] *See* Baker v. Carr, 369 U.S. 186 (1962); Zivotofsky v. Clinto, 132 S.Ct. 1421 (2012); Alperin v. Vatican Bank, 410 F.3d 532 (9th Cir. 2005).

[118] *See* DeRoburt v. Gannett Co., Inc., 548 F.Supp. 1370, 1380 (D.Haw.1982).

[119] 210 F.2d 375 (2d Cir. 1954).

[120] *Id.* at 375–376.

[121] 406 U.S. 759, 92 S.Ct. 1808, 32 L.Ed.2d 466 (1972), *reh'g denied,* 409 U.S. 897, 93 S.Ct. 92, 34 L.Ed.2d 155 (1972).

> [W]here the Executive Branch, charged as it is with primary responsibility for the conduct of foreign affairs, expressly rep resents to the Court that application of the act of state doctrine would not advance the interests of American foreign policy, that doctrine should not be applied by the courts. In so doing, we of course adopt and approve the so-called *Bernstein* excep tion to the act of state doctrine. We believe this to be no more than an application of the classical common-law maxim that "[t]he reason of the law ceasing, the law itself also ceases". . . . Our holding is in no sense an abdication of the judicial func tion to the Executive Branch.[122]

Two concurring Justices and four dissenting Justices disagreed, however, the latter writing:

> As six members of this Court recognize today, . . . [it] is clear that the representations of the Department of State are enti tled to weight for the light they shed on the permutation and combination of factors underlying the act of state doctrine. But they cannot be determinative. . . .
>
> The task of defining the contours of a political question such as the act of state doctrine is exclusively the function of this Court. . . . The "*Bernstein*" exception relinquishes the function to the Executive by requiring blind adherence to its requests that foreign acts of state be reviewed. Conversely, it politicizes the judiciary.[123]

Four years later, in *Alfred Dunhill of London, Inc. v. Republic of Cuba*,[124] four dissenting justices wrote:

> [S]ix members of the Court in *First National* . . . disapproved finally the so-called *Bernstein* exception to the act of state doctrine, thus minimizing the significance of any letter from the Department of State . . . the task of defining the role of the judiciary is for this court, not the Executive Branch.

Constitutional effect aside, a *Bernstein* letter from the Department of State to a court may be quite persuasive in providing the court a reason to avoid application of the doctrine. Lack of such a letter may not result in a reverse conclusion. In 1982, the Department of State advised the Solicitor General that "courts should not infer from the silence of the Department of State that adjudication in . . . (a

---

[122] *Id.* at 768, 92 S.Ct. at 1813.

[123] *Id.* at 790, 92 S.Ct. at 1824.

[124] 425 U.S. 682, 725, 96 S.Ct. 1854, 48 L.Ed.2d 301 (1976).

pending) case would be harmful to the foreign policy of the United States."[125]

The *Kirkpatrick* decision discussed in Section 7.17 supports the view of *Dunhill* that it is the function of the judiciary rather than the executive to define the role of courts in addressing acts of foreign states. The Supreme Court in *Kirkpatrick* did not reject any role for the executive, but clearly rejected the Circuit Court's giving "full, faith and credit" to the letter from the Department of State.

§ 7.20 Act of State Exceptions

As in the case of the application of sovereign immunity, there are exceptions to the act of state doctrine. One exception, where the act violates international law, has been considered in Section 7.16. Another involves disavowed acts of foreign governments that no longer exist.[126] Two other actions that are debated as constituting exceptions, analogous to those under the FSIA, are waiver and commercial activity.

Waiver

A sovereign sometimes appears to expressly waive its right to raise the act of state defense. One question is whether the imposition of a counterclaim by a defendant sovereign constitutes a waiver. A majority of the Court in the *First National* decision (reviewed in Section 7.18) suggested no, but it was not part of the opinion. If the sovereign brings an action in a U.S. court, it is not stripped of its right to invoke the act of state as a defense to a counterclaim just because it thereby waives its right to avoid a counterclaim on grounds of sovereign immunity. A clear and unambiguous statement by a foreign state that it does not object to judicial scrutiny of a state act may influence a court, but other factors may also be considered.[127] And there is support for arguing that treaties of the sovereign being sued may provide exceptions to the act of state doctrine, even in expropriation cases, and particularly if the United States government agrees.[128]

Commercial Activity

Uncertainty also clouds the issue of the existence of a commercial activity exception to the act of state doctrine. The Supreme Court

---

[125] *See* 22 Int'l Legal Mat. 207 (1983).

[126] *See, e.g.*, Bigio v. Coca-Cola Co., 239 F.3d 440 (2d Cir. 2001) (Egypt) and Philippines v. Marcos, 806 F.2d 344 (2d Cir. 1986).

[127] Compania de Gas de Nuevo Laredo, S.A. v. Entex, Inc., 686 F.2d 322 (5th Cir. 1982).

[128] *See* Kalamazoo Spice Extraction Co. v. Provisional Military Government of Socialist Ethiopia, 729 F.2d 422 (6th Cir. 1984).

decided the *Dunhill* case (see Section 7.17), another Cuban expropriation dispute, close to the adoption of the commercial activity exception in the FSIA of 1976. In *Dunhill*, the Supreme Court stated:

> [T]he concept of an act of state should not be extended to in clude the repudiation of a purely commercial obligation owed by a foreign sovereign or by one of its commercial instrument talities. . . . In their commercial capacities, foreign govern ments do not exercise powers peculiar to sovereigns. . . . Subjecting them in connection with such acts to the same rules of law that apply to private citizens is unlikely to touch very sharply on "national nerves."[129]

The *Dunhill* case has become known as the "commercial exception" to the act of state doctrine notwithstanding that only four justices joined in that part of the opinion, and that four other justices wrote:

> [I]t does not follow that there should be a commercial act ex ception to the act of state doctrine. . . .

The carving out of broad exceptions to the doctrine is fundamentally at odds with the careful case-by-case approach adopted in *Sabbatino*.[130] The ambiguity of the court has led to different views expressed in lower federal courts. One court stated:

> consideration of the commercial nature of a given act is com pelled if the doctrine is to be applied correctly. In this connec tion, attention is owed not to the purpose of the act but to its nature. The goal of the inquiry is to determine if denial of the act of state defense in the case under consideration will thwart the policy concerns in which the doctrine is rooted.[131]

But the Ninth Circuit, applying the act of state doctrine to shelter OPEC activities from challenge, observed:

> While purely commercial activity may not rise to the level of an act of state, certain seemingly commercial activities will trigger act of state considerations. . . . When the state *qua* state acts in the public interest, its sovereignty is asserted. The Courts must proceed cautiously to avoid an affront to that sov ereignty. . . . [W]e find that the act of state doctrine remains available when such caution is

---

129 Alfred Dunhill of London, Inc. v. Republic of Cuba, 425 U.S. 682, 695, 704, 96 S.Ct. 1854, 48 L.Ed.2d 301 (1976).

130 *Id.* at 725, 96 S.Ct. at 1876.

131 Sage Int'l, Ltd. v. Cadillac Gage Co., 534 F.Supp. 896, 905 (E.D.Mich.1981). Compare Honduras Aircraft Registry Ltd. v. Honduras, 129 F.3d 543 (11th Cir. 1997) (commercial exception to act of state rejected) and Virtual Defense & Dev. Int'l v. Moldova, 133 F.Supp.2d 1 (D.D.C. 1999) (commercial exception recognized).

> appropriate regardless of any commercial component of the activity involved.[132]

If a commercial exception is denied, determining that the *situs* of the activity (commercial or not) is not *in* the foreign state may cause judicial rejection of the doctrine. This has proven important to the international debt issue. If nonpayment is held to have occurred as required by contract at the office of the lending bank in the United States, the doctrine may be rejected as a defense.[133] But sovereign acts undertaken in a commercial context without such an agreement fall outside the scope of the act of state doctrine.[134]

---

[132] IAM v. OPEC, 649 F.2d 1354, 1360 (9th Cir. 1981) (disposition of natural resources not commercial activity).

[133] Allied Bank Int'l v. Banco Credito Agricola de Cartago, 757 F.2d 516 (2d Cir. 1985), *cert. denied,* 473 U.S. 934, 106 S.Ct. 30, 87 L.Ed.2d 706 (1985) (Costa Rican debt).

[134] Braka v. Bancomer, 762 F.2d 222 (2d Cir. 1985).

Chapter 8

INTERNATIONAL BUSINESS LITIGATION: ENFORCEMENT OF JUDGMENTS

Table of Sections

There is an important distinction between recognizing versus enforcing foreign judgments. Recognition of a foreign judgment ensures that it will not have to be re-litigated abroad . . . it is *res judicata*. Enforcement of a foreign judgment provides the relief anticipated by the source court, typically by attachment of local assets. Despite much effort, there is no international convention or treaty facilitating the recognition and enforcement of judgments across borders. In other words, there is no international law principle embodying the "full faith and credit" given to U.S. state court judgments.

Britain has bilateral treaties providing for nearly automatic, reciprocal recognition of court judgments with Australia, Canada, and India. But, in the absence of an international convention in the area, many nations simply have no provisions for enforcing foreign judgments. While more nations are adding such a process, in many countries the operational reality of foreign judgment enforcement is next to nil.

One example experienced by Professor Michael Gordon of Florida involved taking (with the help of a very prominent Spanish lawyer) a U.S. judgment to Spain for enforcement. Under then applicable Spanish law, the matter was properly started in the Supreme Court. The Supreme Court rejected enforcement, stating incorrectly that it had to go to a lower court. Although that was clearly contrary to Spanish law, the case was taken to that first instance court, which stated that the matter was within the exclusive jurisdiction of the Spanish Supreme Court. Enforcement was again sought before the Supreme Court without success, other than to realize that the court did not really want to enforce the U.S. judgment despite its own law. A lesson slowly learned.

The material in this chapter covers enforcement of foreign judgments in the states of the United States and within the European Union. These jurisdictions, especially U.S. states, are well ahead of the curve in recognizing and enforcing foreign judgments. See Section 8.1. Most of the more developed civil law nations have a process of *exaquator* that allows enforcement, although bringing an enforcement action may appear to be little different from a new action on the merits. But some decisions of the source court may be respected by a civil law court under a theory comparable to *res judicata*.

The European Union has harmonized the enforcement process among its members. Regulation 1215/212 (the Brussels Regulation, reproduced in Section 8.7) governs jurisdiction as well as judgment recognition and enforcement, and mandates recognition unless a designated defense is proven. See Section 8.2. Those defenses are not unlike the defenses available in many states of the United States that have adopted the Uniform Foreign-Money Judgments Recognition Act (reproduced in Section 8.15), or its successor, the Uniform Foreign-Country Money Judgments Recognition Act (reproduced in Section 8.6). See Section 8.1.

Jurisdictional and procedural issues examined in Chapters 5 and 6 may return with a vengeance to deny recognition and enforcement of judgments abroad. This risk reinforces the need for compliance with such issues in a manner that anticipates future enforcement actions. I am indebted to Professor Gordon for his original work on materials appearing Sections 8.1, 8.3 and 8.4 of this chapter.

§ 8.1 Recognition and Enforcement of Foreign Judgments in the States of the United States

Judgments in one state of the United States are recognized in other states under the "full faith and credit" clause of Article IV of the U.S. Constitution. But there is no application of this doctrine to foreign judgments. Foreign judgments are recognized and enforced in many nations, but often only under strict rules that allow careful scrutiny of many aspects of the original judgment. No rule exists in the United States prohibiting enforcement. Indeed, as noted below, the Supreme Court in *Hilton v. Guyot* suggested long ago that considerations of international comity (recognition and deferral to foreign legislative, executive and judicial acts) may provide a basis for U.S. foreign judgment enforcement.

Enforcement is currently a matter for separate national decision. Negotiations at The Hague for an international convention on jurisdiction and the enforcement of foreign judgments have been underway for years. They are yet to conclude with a final document. Even if that is accomplished, there is no certainty that it will be adopted in the United States.[1] It is unlikely, for example, that judgments from nations with corrupt or poorly developed legal systems will be enforced by U.S. courts. For example, several judgments in Nicaraguan courts against U.S. corporations for alleged injuries to Nicaraguan workers resulted in awards of many millions of dollars. The decisions were riddled with inequities and failure to include the most fundamental due process. They have been uniformly rejected by U.S. courts.[2]

The common law rule in England was that a judgment for money rendered by a court in a foreign country was only *prima facie* evidence of the subject matter it purported to decide, and was subject to impeachment before English courts. Thus, foreign judgments were not conclusive on the merits of the dispute, and could act as neither *res judicata* nor collateral estoppel to actions in English courts by the loser in the foreign court.

The U.S. Supreme Court did not follow the English approach. The leading case remains *Hilton v. Guyot*.[3] The Court denied enforcement of a French judgment, announcing:

> Where there has been an opportunity for a full and fair trial abroad before a court of competent jurisdiction, conducting the trial upon regular proceedings, after due citation or voluntary appearance of the defendant, and under a system of jurisprudence likely to secure an

---

[1] *See generally* Russell Weintraub, How Substantial is Our Need for a Judgments-Recognition Convention and What Should We Bargain Away to Get It?, 24 Brook. L. Rev. 167 (1998); Cromie, A Choice Between Evils, New Law Journal, at 1244 (Aug. 16, 1996); Yoav Oestreicher, *"We're on a Road to Nowhere"—Reasons for the Continuing Failure to Regulate Recognition and Enforcement of Foreign Judgments*, 42 Int'l Law. 59 (2008).

[2] *See* Osorio v. Dole Food Co., 665 F.Supp.2d 130 (S.D. Fla.2009).

[3] 159 U.S. 113, 16 S.Ct. 139, 40 L.Ed. 95 (1895).

impartial administration of justice between the citizens of its own country and those of other countries, and there is nothing to show either prejudice * * * or fraud * * *, the merits of the case should not, in an action brought in this country upon the judgment, be tried afresh. * * *

The Court did not find any prejudice, fraud or lack of due process in the French courts, but it did find that the defendants had alleged that French courts would not give conclusive effect to judgments of U.S. courts. Since "mutuality and reciprocity" were not available for U.S. judgments in France, the Court refused to hold that the French judgment was conclusive in the United States.

Hilton may remain the leading case on the subject, but it is seldom controlling. Even actions brought in federal court are dependent, under the subsequent doctrine of *Erie v. Tompkins*,[4] upon state law. State courts have felt free to pursue other analyses and doctrines. For example, in 1926 the New York Court of Appeals, with Pound on the bench, gave conclusive effect to the judgment of a French court despite the known lack of reciprocity and comity.[5] The court deliberately stated that it was not bound by the *Hilton* decision or doctrine.

Uniform State Laws

Inconsistent and sparse state law ultimately led to the National Conference of Commissioners on Uniform State Laws (NCCUSL—the same people who brought you the UCC) to produce the 1962 Uniform Foreign Money-Judgments Recognition Act (UFMJRA). It expressly adopts full faith and credit principles, subject to defenses noted below, for foreign money judgments recognition and enforcement. Many states, however, enacted variations of the 1962 Unifrom Act, including in some states a reciprocity requirement. Absent adoption of the UFMJRA or its successor the UFCMJRA, re-litigation of the dispute may follow.[6] Note that both of these Uniform Acts apply largely to commercial or investor money judgments, not taxation judgments or criminal fines.

The purpose of the Act was to attempt to bring uniformity of result to such cases, and to furnish many states with a coherent and consistent set of rules on the problem involved. But even with the significant creation of the UFMJRA, many states adopted variations, including the requirement of reciprocity in a few states. Consider the perplexed state of the foreign possessor of a judgment against a

---

[4] 304 U.S. 6 (1938).

[5] Johnston v. Compagnie Générale Transatlantique, 242 N.Y. 381, 152 N.E. 121 (1926).

[6] *See* Society of Lloyd's v. Reinhart, 402 F.3d 982 (10th Cir. 2005) (Utah).

person or corporation in the United States trying to understand how foreign judgments are recognized and enforced in a multi-state system. Should the suit be brought in a federal court or state court? Is the judgment debtor in a state which has adopted the Uniform Act, or one which has not?

The Uniform Act was not based on the *Hilton* doctrine, but upon an independent analysis of the problems conducted by the National Conference. The Commissioners in 2005 promulgated a revision of the 1962 Act, the Uniform Foreign-Country Money Judgments Recognition Act (UFCMJRA). It is very similar to the 1962 version, with five primary clarifications. They are: (1) Judgments entitled to internal U.S. sister-state full faith and credit are not enforceable under the Act; (2) the party seeking recognition has the burden of proving the judgment is subject to the Act; (3) the party objecting to recognition and raising specific grounds has the burden of proving those grounds; (4) the establishment of procedures for seeking enforcement depending on whether it is an original action or part of a pending action; and (5) the prohibition of the action if the judgment may no longer be enforced in the country of the judgment, with a maximum of 15 years from its date of effectiveness.

As of 2019, the UFCMJRA was the preferred form, adopted in over 20 states plus the District of Columbia, and was replacing the UFMJRA. Another 13 states continue to rely on UFMJRA. These uniform Acts are reproduced in Sections 8.5 and 8.6. The NCCUSL provides a very useful commentary on the 2005 Act.

Utilization of the UFMJRA and UFCMJRA

Before turning to the cases, it should be noted that U.S. courts may give one of two effects to a foreign decision. The court may recognize the judgment, or it may additionally enforce it. If it limits its action to recognition, it decides that there is an issue, or issues, which do not need to be re-litigated. If it enforces the judgment, it goes further and grants to the successful party some part or all of the judgment decreed by the foreign court. In trying to predict what a U.S. court will do, one should consider that (1) the governing law is for the most part state rather than federal, (2) enforcement first requires recognition, (3) direct enforcement is unusual—the process to expect is reduction of the foreign judgment to a judgment of the enforcing court in the United States, and (4) since there is little statutory law on the subject—one ought to look to the cases. Courts will almost never enforce the revenue or criminal laws of a foreign nation.[7]

---

[7] *See* Overseas Inns SA v. United States, 911 F.2d 1146 (5th Cir. 1990); British Columbia v. Gilbertson, 597 F.2d 1161 (9th Cir. 1979).

The UFMJRA and UFCMJRA provide for recognition and enforcement unless one of the listed defenses is met. They are classified under two headings, situations where foreign judgments should not be recognized, and situations where they need not be recognized. Non-recognition and non-enforcement is mandatory if in the original proceedings there was a lack of an impartial tribunal, respect for procedural due process, personal jurisdiction (six examples of sufficient personal jurisdiction bases, known as safe harbors, are included in the Act), or a lack of subject matter jurisdiction.

Non-recognition and non-enforcement is discretionary if in those proceedings there was a lack of adequate notice, extrinsic fraud in obtaining the judgment, repugnance to the public policy of the enforcing state,[8] inconsistency with another final judgment, violation of a choice of forum agreement (including arbitrations), or serious inconvenience of the trial forum when personal service was made in the state of the originating court. The burden of proving one of these defenses rests with the party seeking to avoid recognition and enforcement.[9] Lack of personal jurisdiction and inadequate notice are the most commonly pursued defenses, and U.S. statutory and constitutional due process standards are sometimes applied.[10] Default foreign judgments are generally enforceable.[11]

The fact that recognition and enforcement in the United States remains state law (even in federal courts) creates problems for foreign nations, especially where they have adopted reciprocity as a norm for enforcement. For example, Spain requires reciprocity. Will a Spanish court enforce a Texas judgment if (a) Texas has enforced Spanish judgments, (b) Texas has never either enforced or rejected a Spanish judgment, but has a record of enforcing judgments from other civil law nations, or (c) Texas has never enforced any foreign judgments but other U.S. states have? It is likely that only in (a) might Spain enforce the Texas judgment. Thus, Spain and other foreign nations may tend to view enforcement of judgments from the United States as though it were dealing with 50 different nations.

In a United States court, success is primarily dependent upon whether (1) the foreign court had jurisdiction over the person or

---

8 *See* Southwest Livestock and Trucking Co. v. Ramon, 169 F.3d 317 (5th Cir. 1999) (recognizing Mexican judgment despite Texas usury public policy argument).

9 *See* Banque Libanaise v. Khreich, 915 F.2d 1000 (5th Cir. 1990).

10 *See, e.g.*, Choi v. Kim, 50 F.3d 244 (3d Cir. 1995) (inadequate notice); Koster v. Automark Ind., Inc., 640 F.2d 77 (7th Cir. 1981) (no minimum contacts). Compare The Society of Lloyd's v. Ashenden, 233 F.3d 473 (7th Cir. 2000) (following lesser "international due process" standards).

11 *See* Bank of Montreal v. Kough, 612 F.2d 467 (9th Cir. 1980); Somportex Ltd. v. Philadelphia Chewing Gum Corp., 318 F.2d 435 (3d Cir. 1971).

subject matter, (2) adequate notice was given, (3) there was no fraud in obtaining the judgment, and (4) whether the public policy of the United States will be harmed. Finally, the issue of reciprocity may be raised. States courts have differed on the issue of reciprocity as a requirement for recognition and enforcement of foreign judgments. Similarly state legislatures adopting uniform foreign judgment statutes have differed on including reciprocity as a requirement for enforcement. Reciprocity is required by statute in Idaho, North Carolina, New Hampshire Texas, Florida, Georgia, Maine, Massachusetts and Ohio.[12]

Those states that have not adopted the UFMJRA or UFCMRA either reject foreign judgments and require a de novo trial, or they recognize and enforce judgments after applying tests not usually at great variance with the U.S. Supreme Court's *Hilton* decision quoted above.[13] Conditions imposed may include reciprocity, acceptable personal and subject matter jurisdiction (see Chapter 5) of the foreign court, adequate notice to and proper service of the defendant (see Chapter 6), absence of fraud, fairness (bias) or due process (see Section 1.1, *Questionable Judicial Systems*), and absence of any conflict with public policy.[14] For example, public policy and free speech considerations have denied enforcement of English libel judgments,[15] a policy now allied with the federal SPEECH ACT prohibiting enforcement of foreign judgments that violate U.S. free speech or press principles.[16] And Judge Posner may have diluted U.S. due process law in upholding the enforceability of English money judgments against Lloyd's "names" in Illinois.[17] Those states that have adopted the UFMJRA or UFCMJRA follow a procedure that includes considerations of some of these very same factors,[18] with or without a reciprocity requirement depending on the state.

---

12 *See* Royal Bank of Canada v. Trentham Corp., 665 F.2d 515 (5th Cir. 1981) (Texas).

13 *See, e.g.*, Koster v. Automark Ind., Inc., 640 F.2d 77 (7th Cir. 1981) (Dutch judgment not enforceable for want of personal jurisdiction).

14 *See, e.g.*, Hunt v. BP Exploration Co. (Libya) Ltd., 492 F.Supp. 885 (N.D.Tex.1980) (suggesting there are "favored" and "unfavored" legal systems). *See also* Ackermann v. Levine, 788 F.2d 830 (2d Cir. 1986) (award in default German judgment of documented attorneys' fees not in violation of public policy).

15 *See* An Account of Telnikoff v. Matusevitch, 347 Md. 561 (1997). *See also Ackermann, supra,* upholding German judgment based on statutory claim for attorneys' fees, and Southwest Livestock and Trucking v. Ramon 169 F.3d 317 (5th Cir. 1999) recognizing Mexican judgment despite usurious interest rates.

16 28 U.S.C. 4102.

17 *See* The Society of Lloyd's v. Ashenden, 233 F.3d 473 (7th Cir. 2000).

18 *See, e.g.*, Bank of Nova Scotia v. Tschabold Equipment Ltd., 51 Wash.App. 749, 754 P.2d 1290 (1988); Society of Lloyd's v. Turner, 303 F.3d 325 (5th Cir. 2002) (public policy issues under Texas UFMJRA explored; enforcement of English judgments

A related issue to the enforcement of a foreign judgment is what the enforcing state should do when the original judgment is in a foreign currency. Judgments are usually given in the currency of the forum, and in some cases this is a mandatory rule, but judgments in U.S. courts may be in foreign currencies. The principal issue for courts has been establishing the time of conversion of the currency of the judgment to the currency of the enforcing forum. Some jurisdictions use the time of the act establishing the cause of action, others such as New York use the date of the judgment, and others use the date of payment. The Uniform Foreign Money Claims Act, adopted in over 20 states, utilizes the date of payment. The Restatement of Foreign Relations, Section 823, suggests use of the date which would best "serve the ends of justice in the circumstances."

Enforcing Mass Tort Judgments from Questionable Legal Systems

Several decades ago large multinationals began to be sued in U.S. courts by groups of plaintiffs who were almost all from another country and complained about use of U.S. designed or manufactured products allegedly causing injury in their country. Litigation strategy initially was to defend the suit in the same manner as a totally domestic case—that was to at most seek to remove the case from a state to federal court and go forth applying U.S. law. When lawyers for the defendants learned more about other legal systems and discovered that most foreign nations allowed quite limited damages, and permitted neither contingent fees nor punitive damages, they began to argue that choice of law pointed to the law of the foreign country where the acts occurred. The long-recognized doctrine of *lex loci delicti* (see Section 2.1) helped their strategy.

But that meant there would be a trial in the United States. Perhaps that trial could be avoided altogether by moving to dismiss on *forum non conveniens* grounds. See Section 2.4. When many of the cases were so dismissed, and especially when that effectively ended the matter, *forum non conveniens* became the motion of choice. Some Latin American nations responded by trying to keep mass tort cases out of their courts. For example, Ecuador enacted a law that attempted to govern the U.S. courts *forum non conveniens* argument, by disallowing any Ecuadorian who had first sued abroad (read—in the United States) from being able to bring the suit in Ecuador if the suit were dismissed abroad. The law attempted to remove local jurisdiction, although there were usually escape holes that would

upheld); Somportex Ltd. v. Philadelphia Chewing Gum Corp., 453 F.2d 435 (3d Cir. 1971) (upholding English breach of contract money judgment); Southwest Livestock & Trucking Co., Inc. v. Ramon, 169 F.3d 321 (5th Cir. 1999) (upholding enforcement in Texas of Mexican money judgments against usury claims).

allow such a suit if it benefitted the local party. Because of the relatively minimal development of tort law theory in most of the plaintiffs' nations, the existence of few lawyers who were "tort attorneys," the lack of punitive damages and the prohibition of contingent fees, few cases were taken home for trial. Winning the *forum non conveniens* motion to dismiss essentially meant ending the litigation.

Some nominal settlement often was the last nail in the coffin. But lawyers are creative beings and it was only a matter of time before they worked out the fee problems. As for punitive damages, why couldn't the foreign nation allow punitive damages, or some variant thereof, only where the defendant was a large foreign multinational. As to the actual trial, that could be abbreviated by presumptions of injury and overlooking causation. And one further characteristic of many of these nations didn't hurt the plaintiffs, a corrupt and nationalistic judiciary.

Thus, not very long ago, a few of these cases began to be brought abroad, ending with large judgments against the U.S. defendants. But the putatively successful plaintiffs face one serious obstacle. Since the defendants were usually careful not to have significant assets in the foreign country, the foreign judgment would have to be taken abroad for recognition and enforcement—usually to the United States. Attempts at enforcing a $97 million Nicaraguan judgment in Florida under its UFMJR brought this result:

This court holds that Defendants have established multiple, independent grounds under the Florida Recognition Act that compel non-recognition of the $97 million Nicaraguan judgment. Because the judgment was "rendered under a system which does not provide impartial tribunal or procedures compatible with the requirements of due process of law," and the rendering court did not have jurisdiction over Defendants, the judgment is not considered conclusive, and cannot be enforced under the Florida Recognition Act. Fla. Stat. § 55.605(1)(a)–(c). Additionally, the judgment will not be enforced because "the cause of action or claim for relief on which the judgment is based is repugnant to the public policy of this state." Fla. Stat. § 55.605(2)(c). The Court, therefore, orders that Plaintiffs' judgment shall be neither recognized nor enforced.[19]

Compare the *Osorio* ruling with that of the Fifth Circuit regarding recognition of a Moroccan judgment under Texas law:

"Morroco's judicial system is not in a state of complete collapse, and there is no evidence that Moroccan courts or the Moroccan

[19] Osorio v. Dole Food Co., 665 F.Supp.2d 1307, *aff'd*, 635 F.3d 1277 (11th Cir. 2011).

government routinely disregard constitutional provisions or the rule of law. Because Morocco's judicial system is not in such a dire situation, it does not present the unusual case of a foreign judicial system that "offended against basic fairness." * * *

The Texas Recognition Act's due process standard requires only that the foreign proceedings be fundmentally unfair and inoffensive to "basic fairness." This standard sets a high bar for non-recognition. The Morrocan judicial system does not present an exceptional case of "serious injustice" that renders the entire system fundamentally unfair and incompatible with due process. The district court thus erred in concluding that non-recognition was justified under Section 36.005(a)(1) of the Texas recognition Act."[20]

For additional examples of U.S. decisions concerned with questionable foreign court systems, see Section 2.1. See especially the *Chevron* case discussed in Section 2.4.

§ 8.2 Jurisdiction and the Recognition and Enforcement of Civil and Commercial Judgments in the European Union

The 1968 Jurisdiction and Enforcement of Judgments Convention (Brussels Convention) (now EU Regulation 1215/2012, Recast Jan. 10, 2015) regulates jurisdiction among the member states and facilitates enforcement of civil and commercial judgments of the 28 EU member states' courts. In other words, the Brussels Convention introduced "full faith and credit" principles to the European Union. Much of its substance is reproduced in the Lugano Convention on Jurisdiction and Enforcement of Judgments in Civil and Commercial Matters (1988). The Lugano Convention extends these principles to all ratifying EFTA countries, such as Switzerland.

The Brussels Convention was converted for all but Denmark from an international agreement into legislation by Council Regulation 44/2001. A number of amendments were added at that time, and an agreement choosing the courts of one of the member states is enforceable if one or more of the parties is domiciled in the Union. Regulation 44/2001 was succeeded by Regulation 1215/2012. Effective in 2015, under a re-casted version of Regulation 2015/2012, an agreement choosing the courts of an EU member state will be enforceable regardless of the domicile of the parties. In addition, Regulation 1393/2007) establishes speedy and reliable means for service of civil or commercial process. Regulation 1206/2001 facilitates the cross-border taking of evidence in civil and commercial

[20] DeJoria v. Maghreb Petroleum Exploration, S.A., 804 F.3d 373 (5th Cir. 2015) reversing 38 F.Supp.3d 805 (W.D. Texas 2014).

matters. These regulations take the 1965 and 1970 Hague Conventions as their inspirations. See Chapter 6.

It is important to remember that the Brussels Convention and its successor Regulations govern jurisdiction as well as enforcement of national court judgments. This means, as a practical matter, that it applies from the outset of the litigation once a jurisdictional challenge is raised and not just after judgment has been reached. Interpreting the Brussels Convention and Regulation 1215/2012 thus initially is the task of national trial courts. One elementary issue is the scope of applicability of the Convention/Regulation to "civil and commercial matters." These terms are not defined, except by exclusion. Most revenue, customs and administrative litigation along with legal status, capacity, matrimonial property, wills, succession, bankruptcy, social security, arbitration matters and intellectual property licensing contracts are not covered.[21]

In 1998, however, a separate EU Convention on Jurisdiction, Recognition and Enforcement of Judgments in Matrimonial matters was concluded.[22] In 2000, Regulation 1346/2000 established jurisdictional, procedural and recognition rules for insolvency proceedings. In 2007, Regulation 864/2007 detailed conflict-of-law rules applicable to non-contractual obligations (torts) throughout the European Union ("Rome II Regulation"), while Regulation 593/2008 ("Rome I Regulation") did likewise for contractual obligations.

The ECJ has adopted an independent approach to the meaning of civil and commercial matters drawn from the Convention/Regulation purposes and the general principles of relevant law found in the member states. Special attention has been given to the original six EU civil law jurisdictions and their distinction between public and private law. Thus, most exercises of public authority by administrative bodies do not fall within the Convention or its successor Regulations.[23] Marital dissolution property settlements are not covered,[24] but suits against estates by third parties over title to realty are.[25] Employment contracts fall within its scope.[26] The rules of jurisdiction thus mandate

---

[21] Falco Privatstiftung & Rabitsch v. Weller-Lindhorst, (2009) Eur.Comm.Rep. ___ (Case C–533/07).

[22] O.J. C221 (July 16, 1998).

[23] *See* Lufttransportunternehmen GmbH & Co. K.G. v. Eurocontrol (1976) Eur.Comm.Rep. 1541 (recovery of route charges); Netherlands v. Rüffer (1980) Eur.Comm.Rep. 3807.

[24] de Cavel v. de Cavel (1979) Eur.Comm.Rep. 1055.

[25] CHW v. GJH (1982) Eur.Comm.Rep. 1189.

[26] Sanicentral v. Collin (1979) Eur.Comm.Rep. 3423.

classification of the litigation in terms of the exclusions to civil and commercial matters.

Jurisdiction

The Brussels Convention and Regulation 1215/2012 apply to all persons who are domiciled in a member state even if they are not citizens thereof. Thus, a United States-owned subsidiary incorporated in an EU state benefits from these provisions, whereas its parent would not. This coverage is important regarding the application of so-called "exorbitant jurisdiction" (below) and enforcement of judgments derived therefrom which will *not* apply to the subsidiary but will apply to the parent. Furthermore, generally speaking, defendants are to be sued where they are domiciled. The concept of "domicile" is thus critical. As this term is not defined, the issue is left to national law. National courts must be satisfied that jurisdiction is taken in accordance with EU rules.[27] Co-defendants may be sued in non-domiciliary jurisdictions so closely connected that expediency requires suit to avoid the risk of irreconcilable judgments.

Persons may be sued in forums outside their state of domicile only if the Convention/Regulation so provides. These provisions provide for a number of special jurisdictions as alternatives to domicile. Contract disputes can ordinarily be litigated where the "place" of performance of the obligation occurs as determined by the law controlling the contract.[28] This includes disputes as to the existence of contracts.[29] Regulation 1215/2012 replacing the Brussels Convention renders the place of performance of the obligation as that agreed, or in the case of sale of goods, the place of delivery of the goods, or in the case of provision of services, the place of provision. Special new rules govern employment contracts and favor employees.[30] Torts may be litigated at the place where the event or damage occurred.[31] This has been construed to mean either the place where the defendant acted (*e.g.*, manufactured a product) or where the injury was suffered.

---

[27] Group Josi Reinsurance Company SA v. Universal General Insurance Co (2000) Eur.Comm.Rep. I–5925; Duijnstee v. Goderbauer (1983) Eur.Comm.Rep. 3663.

[28] Industrie Tessili Italiana Como v. Dunlop A.G. (1976) Eur.Comm.Rep. 1473. *See also* Ivenel v. Schwab (1982) Eur.Comm.Rep. 1891 (commercial agency contracts also where work performed) and Leathertex v. Bodetex (1999) Eur.Comm.Rep. I–6747 (commercial agency)

[29] Effer v. Kantner (1982) Eur.Comm.Rep. 825.

[30] *See* Mulrox IBC Ltd. v. Hendrick Geels (1993) Eur.Comm.Rep. I–4075 (employment contract place of performance is where employee works).

[31] Dumez France SA and Tacoba SARL v. Hessische Landesbank, (1990) Eur.Comm.Rep. I–49; Handelskerij G.J. Bier B.V. v. Mines de Potasse d'Alsace (1976) Eur.Comm.Rep. 1735; Bier B.V. v. Mines de Potasse d'Alsace SA (1976) Eur.Comm.Rep. 1735.

The contract rules of the Brussels Convention and Regulation 1215/2012 do not apply to damages' actions between manufacturers and purchasers of their products with whom they have no privity of contract, even when the chain of sale is through wholly-owned subsidiaries.[32] Such actions are ordinarily governed by the rules applicable to non-contractual (tortious) liability. If there are several contractual obligations in question, the national court must distinguish between principal and secondary obligations. In one case, a German architect sued a Dutch client over fees for plans for construction of buildings located in Germany. The principal obligation at issue was payment, not the plans or construction, which could be pursued in the courts of the Netherlands where the fees were to be paid. However, employment and consumer contracts come under special provisions designed to protect the weaker party. For example, the focus may be upon the place of work and not the place of the payment obligation when that would favor employees.[33]

Civil damages or restitution flowing from criminal acts are to be litigated in the forum of the crime. Cases involving branches, agencies or other establishments may be pursued where the branch, agency or other establishment is located or in the domicile of the principal. The mere appointment of a commercial agent does not appear to trigger this rule.[34] Suits for recovery of family and other support obligations ("maintenance") may be brought where the creditor is domiciled or "habitually resident," another undefined term.[35] Additional Convention/Regulation rules for jurisdiction which operate as alternatives to the general rule of suit where the defendant is domiciled have been created for trusts, admiralty, insurance (policy-holder, insured and beneficiary domicile options) and consumer contracts (consumer domicile). The rules on jurisdiction favor only ordinary consumers, not business consumers.[36] Consumers, for these purposes, are economically weaker and less experienced private persons not engaged in commercial or professional activities. A German company trading currency futures could not, therefore, benefit from the consumer domicile option of the Brussels Convention in its suit against a New York broker.[37]

---

[32] Jakob Handte & Co. GmbH v. Traitements Mécano-chimiques des Surfaces (1992) Eur.Comm.Rep. I–03967 (Case C–26/91).

[33] Ivenel v. Schwab (1982) Eur.Comm.Rep. 1981.

[34] Blanckaert & Willems v. Trost (1981) Eur.Comm.Rep. 819.

[35] *See* Delvaux v. Commission (1976) Eur.Comm.Rep. 167.

[36] Société Bertrand v. Paul Ott KG (1978) Eur.Comm.Rep. 1431.

[37] Shearson Lehmann Hutton Inc. v. TVB Treuhandgesellschaft für Vermögensverwaltung und Beteiligungen mbH (1993) Eur.Comm.Rep. I–139 (Case C–89/91).

In a few areas, the Brussels Convention and Regulation 1215/2012 convey exclusive jurisdiction to specified courts regardless of domicile or party agreement on choice of forum. These concern real property, company validity, public register, intellectual property validity, and enforcement of judgment litigations. As exceptions to the general rule, they have been narrowly construed. For example, although disputes between landlords and tenants (including unpaid rent)[38] are treated as subject to exclusive jurisdictional rules, disputes between tenants and sub-tenants are not.[39]

The Brussels Convention and Regulation 1215/2012 deny enforcement by EU domiciliaries against EU domiciliaries of certain judgments deemed to be based on "exorbitant jurisdiction" (*e.g.* French jurisdiction based solely on plaintiff's citizenship or German asset-based *in personam* jurisdiction). But, in a discriminatory measure of importance, it permits EU domiciliaries to enforce judgments based upon exorbitant jurisdiction against non-EU domiciliaries. Thus, a North American trader with assets somewhere in the Union could find itself at the wrong end of such discrimination. Other grounds for denial of enforcement of a judgment that is subject to the Brussels Convention or Regulation 1215/2012 include public policy, violation of defendant's procedural rights (service, notice), and the existence of an irreconcilable judgment of the enforcement court or another court (even one of a nation not party to the Brussels Convention).

The Brussels Convention and Regulation 1215/2012 provide that when the same cause of action is being litigated before the courts of two member states, the second court to be seised with litigation must stay or dismiss the proceeding pending resolution of the jurisdiction of the first court seised. This is the case even if the defendant is not domiciled in a member state, such as when the defendant is a U.S. insurance carrier.[40] The first seised rule has generated defensive suits by debtors, sometimes referred to as "Italian torpedoes," in EU jurisdictions known to have very slow procedures.[41] Likewise, even a court designated by the parties must await resolution of the first court's jurisdiction.[42] It is in this sense that the doctrine of *forum non conveniens* (see Section 2.4) is said to be precluded by European

---

38 Rösler v. Rottwinkel (1985) Eur.Comm.Rep. 99 (Case 241/83).

39 Sanders v. van der Putte (1977) Eur.Comm.Rep. 2383. *See* Dansommer A/S v. Götz (2000) Eur.Comm.Rep. I–393 (tour operator and tenancy).

40 Overseas Union Insurance v. New Hampshire Insurance (1991) Eur.Comm.Rep. I–03317 (Case C–351/89).

41 *See, e.g.*, Tatry v. Owners of Ship Maciej Rataj, (1994) Eur.Comm.Rep. I–5439.

42 Erich Gasser GmbH v. MISAT (2003) Eur.Comm.Rep. I–00000 (Case C–116/02).

Union, an analysis similarly confirmed by the ECJ in 2005 as regards courts *outside* Brussels Convention states.[43] Likewise, anti-suit injunctions (see Section 6.2) cannot interfere with the jurisdictional rules of the Convention or Regulation.[44]

Party Autonomy

The Brussels Convention and Regulation 1215/2012 affirm party autonomy to choose in writing a dispute settlement forum. This freedom does not apply regarding the insurance, consumer contract and exclusive jurisdiction areas. The affirmation of party autonomy overrides national rules contrary to such autonomy, even in the employment area. The provisions on party autonomy have been construed rather narrowly, and party awareness and appreciation of the significance of choice of forum clauses must be proved. There must be, in other words, informed written consent. Company statute clauses adopted by shareholders designating jurisdiction can meet these criteria.[45] However, when international trade contracts are involved, compliance with custom and practice is sufficient to enforce the choice of forum.[46] The parties may avoid the stringency of EU rules by designating determinative issues (e.g., place of performance of contracts) in their contract. The chosen place of performance will have jurisdiction.[47] Such choices notwithstanding, if a party appears in another forum other than to contest jurisdiction, acquiescence to that forum will allow the litigation to proceed.[48]

Parties from outside the Union are allowed to join in the selection of a member state court without fear of an exercise of jurisdiction elsewhere (*e.g.*, the place of performance) in the EU. If any judicial forum selection was concluded for the benefit of only one party, *that* party may sue elsewhere. The idea of permitting the sole beneficiary of what some might see as an adhesion clause to escape from its forum selection obligations has not been found compelling.[49]

---

[43] Omusu v. Jackson (Case C–281/02) (March 1, 2005).

[44] Allianz SpA v. West Tankers Inc. (2009) Eur.Comm.Rep. I–663; Turner v. Grovit (2004) Eur.Comm.Rep. I–3565.

[45] Powell Duffryn v. Wolfgang Peteriet (1992) Eur.Comm.Rep. I–01745 (Case 214/89).

[46] *See, e.g.*, Estasis Solotti v. RuWa (1976) Eur.Comm.Rep. 1831 (placement of choice of court clause on reverse side of offer insufficient); Galeries Segoura SPRL v. Rahim Bonakdarian (1976) Eur.Comm.Rep. 1851; MS Tilly Russ (1984) Eur.Comm.Rep. 02417 (Case 71/83); Berghoefer GmbH v. ASA SA (1986) Eur.Comm.Rep. 02699 (Case 221/84).

[47] Zelger v. Salinitri (1980) Eur.Comm.Rep. 89.

[48] Elefanten Schuh v. Jacqmain (1981) Eur.Comm.Rep. 1671; Spitzley v. Sommer (1985) Eur.Comm.Rep. 00787 (Case 48/84).

[49] *See* Anterist v. Crédit Lyonnais (1986) Eur.Comm.Rep. 1951 (selection of bank's domicile court insufficient proof of intent to benefit bank exclusively).

Recognition and Enforcement

The regulatory regime governing jurisdiction established in the Brussels Convention and Regulation 1215/2012 makes recognition and enforcement of subsequent civil and commercial judgments in the EU nearly automatic. This is true for money and non-money judgments, settlements and authentications. Moreover, recognition and enforcement of national court judgments falling within the jurisdictional scope of these provisions occurs regardless of the nationality or domicile of the parties. To facilitate their use, *full* legal aid in the enforcing state must be given to anyone who obtained full *or* partial legal aid in the source state. Recognition (but not enforcement)[50] of the judgment is possible as soon as it is enforceable in its state of origin, even if appeals or further review are pending or available.

The *ex parte* enforcement procedures of the Brussels Convention and Regulation 1215/2012 are exclusive and must be undertaken "without delay." This means that no collateral attack by the parties to the judgment may occur in another EU state and that the successful plaintiff must adhere to Convention/Regulation procedures even if there are alternative means at less cost of obtaining enforcement.[51] National courts are prohibited from charging a sliding scale of fees.

To obtain enforcement, the applicant need only provide supporting documentation on the original judgment and its enforceability under the law of the state of origin and, if required, translations. At this stage, the defendant is not summoned to appear. The decision on grant or denial of recognition and enforcement must be notified to the defendant and can be appealed by the losing party. The defendant may also appeal on points of law. But there is a presumption of recognition for judgments falling within the Convention/Regulation which can only be rebutted on specific grounds. The enforcing court may issue whatever interim protective relief measures it deems necessary to secure assets while appeals are pending even if such protection is not generally available under national law.[52]

There are five grounds under for refusing full or partial recognition and enforcement of judgments under the Brussels Convention and Regulation 1215/2012. These are reviewed *ex parte* by the enforcing court, subject to appeal, and include:

---

50 *See* Industrial Diamond Supplies v. Riva (1977) Eur.Comm.Rep. 2175.

51 DeWolf v. Cox (1976) Eur.Comm.Rep. 1759.

52 Capeloni and Anor v. Pelkmans (1985) Eur.Comm.Rep. 3147 (Case 119/84).

- Public policy (but not as applied to jurisdictional rules).[53]
- Protection of defendants' rights (*e.g.* service, opportunity to be heard, and adequate time to prepare a defense).[54]
- Irreconcilable conflict with an existing judgment in the enforcing state.
- Conflict with an earlier judgment between the same parties and on the same cause of action in a state not party to the Convention.
- An agreement with a third party nation not to enforce judgments based upon exorbitant jurisdiction.

Since recognition and enforcement will be granted absent an *existing* judgment to the contrary in the enforcing state, the Convention/Regulation essentially gives *res judicata* effect to civil and commercial judgments throughout the European Union. But this does not mean that third party creditors interested in the enforcement because it might affect their own claims may not seek independent legal redress rescinding execution of an enforcement order.[55] Proper service of process under the law of the country of the defendant is a prerequisite to enforcement of a default commercial judgment even when the defendant becomes aware by other means of the lawsuit and could have taken advantage of procedural rights in the courts of the judgment country.[56]

§ 8.3 Recognition and Enforcement of Judgments in Canada

Anyone seeking the recognition of a foreign money judgment will have to seek its enforcement before a competent provincial court. In 1990 the Canadian Supreme Court ruled that one province must enforce the judgment of another province if the basis for personal jurisdiction was sufficient for obtaining personal jurisdiction in the recognizing province.[57] But Quebec, following the French customs

---

[53] Rohr v. Ossberger (1981) Eur.Comm.Rep. 2431. *See* Krombach v. Bambersk (2000) Eur.Comm.Rep. I–1935 (denial of fair hearing violates public policy).

[54] *See* Klomps v. Michel (1981) Eur.Comm.Rep. 1593; Pendy Plastic Products B.V. v. Pluspunkt Handelsgesellschaft mbH (1982) Eur.Comm.Rep. 2723; Debaecker and Plouvier v. Bouwman (1986) Eur.Comm.Rep. 01779 (Case 49/84).

[55] *See* Deutsche Genossenschaftsbank v. Brasserie du Pcheur (1985) Eur.Comm.Rep. 1981 (Case 148/84).

[56] Minalmet GmbH v. Brandeis Ltd. (1992) Eur.Comm.Rep. I–5661 (Case C–123/91).

[57] De Savoye v. Morguard Investments Ltd., 76 D.L.R.4th 256 (Can. 1990).

established by the Code Michaud of 1629, denies conclusive effect to foreign judgments as a matter of law.[58]

General Canadian practice calls for the recognition of foreign money judgments on "comity" principles similar to those used by the U.S. Supreme Court in *Hilton v. Guyot,* discussed in Section 8.1, that a foreign judgment ought to be treated as equally binding as a domestic judgment if rendered by a competent court having proper jurisdiction over the defendant. But the understanding of jurisdiction used in the recognition of foreign judgments is different from the standards used by Canadian courts to determine their own jurisdiction.

For example, Ontario does not project its jurisdictional rules onto the foreign court. The courts will instead use an "international" standard which limits recognized jurisdiction to five bases: 1) where defendant is a subject of the country in which the judgment is rendered, 2) where he was a resident of the country when the action began, 3) where the defendant, in the character of plaintiff, selected the forum in which he was sued, 4) where he voluntarily appeared, 5) where he has contracted to submit himself to the judgment of the foreign court.[59] Thus, Canadian courts are not as likely to recognize foreign judgments as would be expected, since concepts of jurisdiction exercised by U.S. courts may not be recognized by Canadian courts. However, contractual specifications of submission to U.S. courts in contracts entered into with Canadians seems to be recognized.

A Canadian court will sometimes recognize a U.S. decision enforcing a legal obligation voluntarily undertaken even when there is no jurisdiction based strictly on the above principles. In *Allen v. Standard Trusts Company,*[60] a Manitoba court recognized a U.S. judgment (in this case a double liability upon stock assessed by a Minnesota court against the executors of a British subject resident in Manitoba) that arose from a legal obligation assumed by the defendant on purchase of the stock. But generally there will be a distinct imbalance between the extent of the recognition given to Canadian judgments in U.S. courts and U.S. judgments in Canadian courts.

---

[58] *See* Nadelman, *Enforcement of Foreign Judgments in Canada,* 38 Can.Bar Rev. 68 (1960).

[59] Rousillon v. Rousillon, 14 Ch.D. 351, 371 (1880); Ontario Power Co. v. Niagara etc. Power Co., 52 Ont.L.R. 168, 173 (C.A.1922); Metropolitan Trust & Savings Co. v. Osborne, 14 Ont.W.R. 135, 140, affd. 16 L.W.R. 226 (C.A.1909); Curtis v. Curtis, [1943] Ont.W.N. 382.

[60] [1920] 57 D.L.R. 105.

For example, in *Gyonyo v. Sanjenki*,[61] a default judgment obtained in a Montana court against a resident of Alberta was not recognized in that province. The court held that the U.S. tribunal lacked the required *in personam* jurisdiction over the defendant under the "international" rules discussed above. It made no reference to the Montana statutes that allowed the state court jurisdiction in the case (in this instance, the action arose from a traffic action in Montana involving the Alberta defendant) despite considerable similarity between the Montana and Alberta jurisdictional statutes. Further, the defendant's promise to return to Montana was held not to be a contract to submit to the Montana courts. Such a contractual agreement could not be implied absent a written undertaking. Thus, only written agreements to be subject to the jurisdiction of U.S. courts will subject a Canadian resident to their jurisdiction.

§ 8.4 Recognition and Enforcement of Judgments in France

"Absent an international agreement to the contrary, a foreign judgment, in order to have res judicata effect or to be enforceable in France, needs a so-called *exequatur*."[62]

> Hence, a foreign judgment that has not received the *exequatur* may be used as evidence in a French proceeding involving the same subject matter. However, since it does not have *res judicata* effect, it is not binding and conclusive evidence. Furthermore, a foreign judgment without *exequatur* may be considered sufficient evidence of a claim to entitle its holder to obtain an appropriate provisional remedy, such as an attachment, in France. An *exequatur* must, however, be obtained before the actual execution takes place.[63]

Five requirements must be met for a foreign judgment to be given an *exequatur*. First, the judgment must have been rendered by a court having jurisdiction under pertinent French rules. If the French courts had jurisdiction to adjudicate the original dispute, and that jurisdiction was not waived by the party against whom enforcement is sought, the foreign judgment will not receive an *exequatur*. "Similarly, if the parties had agreed to give exclusive competence to a French court, a foreign judgment rendered in disregard of that agreement will not be granted an *exequatur*."[64] Where no French court is competent, the law is unsettled. Logic has

---

61 23 D.L.R.3d 695 (Alta.S.C.1971).

62 Herzog, Civil Procedure in France, at 586 (1967).

63 *Id.* at 588.

64 *Id.* at 589.

guided some courts to rely on the foreign court's findings of jurisdiction under foreign law. But in cases of migratory divorce, some judgments are denied effect if the defendant were French.

The second requirement is that the foreign judgment comply with the minimum standards of procedural fairness prescribed by *ordre public.* The defendant must have been given actual notice. "French courts will not enforce a foreign judgment in an action in which the defendant was served only by publication, if the plaintiff knew the defendant's address and could have used a method of service better calculated to give the defendant actual notice.[65] "If the defendant actually receives timely notice * * * it is not too important what method of service is used, provided it complies with the laws applicable where the action is pending.[66] The defendant must also have been given adequate time to appear and to prepare his defense.

Third, the foreign court must have applied the "correct" law. That is, the foreign court must have applied that law which would have been applicable in a French court under the French choice of law rules. Some more "liberal" decisions have given effect to foreign judgments if the law actually applied and the law applicable under French choice of law rules lead to the same result. For example, a judgment in New York granting a divorce to a French couple under New York law, because of a finding of adulterous acts, will be given force in France, if under French law those same acts are adulterous and adultery is a ground for divorce.[67]

Fourth, even where French choice of law rules are satisfied, a judgment that violates public policy will not be given effect. An example of this might be where a party temporarily changes his residence, or even nationality, to effect a decision other than that which would have followed under the applicable law before the change. Finally, a foreign judgment need not be final, but "the judgment must be *executoire*—in other words * * * it must be capable of immediate enforcement in the place of its origin."[68] Neither the possibility, nor the actual solicitation, of an appeal prevents an *exequatur,* but, in practical effect, it might stay it.

---

[65] Cie Naviera Baracaldesa v. Lloyd de France, Trib. Seine, Jan. 18, 1929, 56 Clunet 1056 (1929)." *Id.* at 590.

[66] E.g., S.A. Wouters et Cie. v. Robert-Berin, Trib.Gde Inst. Seine Dec. 12, 1961, 89 Clunet 1032 (1962)." *Id.*

[67] Dame Cureau v. Cureau, Trib.Seine, May 14, 1956, 8 Clunet 146 (1957).

[68] *Id.* at 593.

§ 8.5 Text of Uniform Foreign-Money Judgments Recognition Act (1962)

§ 1. [Definitions]

As used in this Act:

(1) "foreign state" means any governmental unit other than the United States, or any state, district, commonwealth, territory, insular possession thereof, or the Panama Canal Zone, the Trust Territory of the Pacific Islands, or the Ryukyu Islands;

(2) "foreign judgment" means any judgment of a foreign state granting or denying recovery of a sum of money, other than a judgment for taxes, a fine or other penalty, or a judgment for support in matrimonial or family matters.

§ 2. [Applicability]

This Act applies to any foreign judgment that is final and conclusive and enforceable where rendered even though an appeal therefrom is pending or it is subject to appeal.

§ 3. [Recognition and Enforcement]

Except as provided in section 4, a foreign judgment meeting the requirements of section 2 is conclusive between the parties to the extent that it grants or denies recovery of a sum of money. The foreign judgment is enforceable in the same manner as the judgment of a sister state which is entitled to full faith and credit.

§ 4. [Grounds for Non-recognition]

(a) A foreign judgment is not conclusive if

(1) the judgment was rendered under a system which does not provide impartial tribunals or procedures compatible with the requirements of due process of law;

(2) the foreign court did not have personal jurisdiction over the defendant; or

(3) the foreign court did not have jurisdiction over the subject matter.

(b) A foreign judgment need not be recognized if

(1) the defendant in the proceedings in the foreign court did not receive notice of the proceedings in sufficient time to enable him to defend;

(2) the judgment was obtained by fraud;

(3) the [cause of action] [claim for relief] on which the judgment is based is repugnant to the public policy of this state;

(4) the judgment conflicts with another final and conclusive judgment;

(5) the proceeding in the foreign court was contrary to an agreement between the parties under which the dispute in question was to be settled otherwise than by proceedings in that court; or

(6) in the case of jurisdiction based only on personal service, the foreign court was a seriously inconvenient forum for the trial of the action.

§ 5. [Personal Jurisdiction]

(a) The foreign judgment shall not be refused recognition for lack of personal jurisdiction if

(1) the defendant was served personally in the foreign state;

(2) the defendant voluntarily appeared in the proceedings, other than for the purpose of protecting property seized or threatened with seizure in the proceedings or of contesting the jurisdiction of the court over him;

(3) the defendant prior to the commencement of the proceedings had agreed to submit to the jurisdiction of the foreign court with respect to the subject matter involved;

(4) the defendant was domiciled in the foreign state when the proceedings were instituted or, being a body corporate had its principal place of business, was incorporated, or had otherwise acquired corporate status, in the foreign state;

(5) the defendant had a business office in the foreign state and the proceedings in the foreign court involved a [cause of action] [claim for relief] arising out of business done by the defendant through that office in the foreign state; or

(6) the defendant operated a motor vehicle or airplane in the foreign state and the proceedings involved a [cause of action] [claim for relief] arising out of such operation.

(b) The courts of this state may recognize other bases of jurisdiction.

§ 6. [Stay in Case of Appeal]

If the defendant satisfies the court either that an appeal is pending or that he is entitled and intends to appeal from the foreign judgment, the court may stay the proceedings until the appeal has been determined or until the expiration of a period of time sufficient to enable the defendant to prosecute the appeal.

§ 7. [Saving Clause]

This Act does not prevent the recognition of a foreign judgment in situations not covered by this Act.

§ 8. [Uniformity of Interpretation]

This Act shall be so construed as to effectuate its general purpose to make uniform the law of those states which enact it.

§ 9. [Short Title]

This Act may be cited as the Uniform Foreign Money-Judgments Recognition Act.

§ 8.6 Text of Uniform Foreign-Country Money Judgments Recognition Act (2005) (with Commentary)

TABLE OF CONTENTS

UNIFORM FOREIGN-COUNTRY MONEY JUDGMENTS RECOGNITION ACT

PREFATORY NOTE

This Act is a revision of the Uniform Foreign Money-Judgments Recognition Act of 1962. That Act codified the most prevalent common law rules with regard to the recognition of money judgments rendered in other countries. The hope was that codification by a state of its rules on the recognition of foreign-country money judgments, by satisfying reciprocity concerns of foreign courts, would make it more likely that money judgments rendered in that state would be recognized in other countries. Towards this end, the Act sets out the circumstances in which the courts in states that have adopted the Act must recognize foreign-country money judgments. It delineates a minimum of foreign-country judgments that must be recognized by the courts of adopting states, leaving those courts free to recognize other foreign-country judgments not covered by the Act under principles of comity or otherwise. Since its promulgation over forty years ago, the 1962 Act has been adopted in a majority of the states and has been in large part successful in carrying out it purpose of establishing uniform and clear standards under which state courts will enforce the foreign-country money judgments that come within its scope.

This Act continues the basic policies and approach of the 1962 Act. Its purpose is not to depart from the basic rules or approach of the 1962 Act, which have withstood well the test of time, but rather to update the 1962 Act, to clarify its provisions, and to correct problems created by the interpretation of the provisions of that Act by the courts over the years since its promulgation. Among the more significant issues that have arisen under the 1962 Act which are addressed in this Revised Act are (1) the need to update and clarify the definitions section; (2) the need to reorganize and clarify the scope provisions, and to allocate the burden of proof with regard to establishing application of the Act; (3) the need to set out the procedure by which recognition of a foreign-country money judgment under the Act must be sought; (4) the need to clarify and, to a limited extent, expand upon the grounds for denying recognition in light of differing interpretations of those provisions in the current case law; (5) the need to expressly allocate the burden of proof with regard to the grounds for denying recognition; and (6) the need to establish a statute of limitations for recognition actions.

In the course of drafting this Act, the drafters revisited the decision made in the 1962 Act not to require reciprocity as a condition to recognition of the foreign-country money judgments covered by the Act. After much discussion, the drafters decided that the approach of the 1962 Act continues to be the wisest course with regard to this issue. While recognition of U.S. judgments continues to be problematic in a number of foreign countries, there was insufficient evidence to establish that a reciprocity requirement would have a greater effect on encouraging foreign recognition of U.S. judgments than does the approach taken by the Act. At the same time, the certainty and uniformity provided by the approach of the 1962 Act, and continued in this Act, creates a stability in this area that facilitates international commercial transactions.

UNIFORM FOREIGN-COUNTRY MONEY JUDGMENTS RECOGNITION ACT

Section 1. Short Title

This [act] may be cited as the [Uniform Foreign-Country Money Judgments Recognition Act].

COMMENT

Source: This section is an updated version of Section 9 of the Uniform Foreign Money-Judgments Recognition Act of 1962.

Section 2. Definitions

In this [act]:

(1) "Foreign country" means a government other than:

(A) the United States;

(B) a state, district, commonwealth, territory, or insular possession of the United States; or

(C) any other government with regard to which the decision in this state as to whether to recognize a judgment of that government's courts is initially subject to determination under the Full Faith and Credit Clause of the United States Constitution.

(2) "Foreign-country judgment" means a judgment of a court of a foreign country.

COMMENT

Source: This section is derived from Section 1 of the Uniform Foreign Money-Judgments Recognition Act of 1962.

1. The defined terms "foreign state" and "foreign judgment" in the 1962 Act have been changed to "foreign country" and "foreign-country judgment" in order to make it clear that the Act does not apply to recognition of sister-state judgments. Some courts have noted that the "foreign state" and "foreign judgment" definitions of the 1962 Act have caused confusion as to whether the Act should apply to sister-state judgments because "foreign

state" and "foreign judgment" are terms of art generally used in connection with recognition and enforcement of sister-state judgments. *See, e.g.*, Eagle Leasing v. Amandus, 476 N.W.2d 35 (S.Ct. Iowa 1991) (reversing lower court's application of UFMJRA to a sister-state judgment, but noting lower court's confusion was understandable as "foreign judgment" is term of art normally applied to sister-state judgments). *See also,* Uniform Enforcement of Foreign Judgments Act § 1 (defining "foreign judgment" as the judgment of a sister state or federal court).

The 1962 Act defines a "foreign state" as "any governmental unit other than the United States, or any state, district, commonwealth, territory, insular possession thereof, or the Panama Canal Zone, the Trust Territory of the Pacific Islands, or the Ryuku Islands." Rather than simply updating the list in the 1962 Act's definition of "foreign state," the new definition of "foreign country" in this Act combines the "listing" approach of the 1962 Act's "foreign state" definition with a provision that defines "foreign country" in terms of whether the judgments of the particular government's courts are initially subject to the Full Faith and Credit Clause standards for determining whether those judgments will be recognized. Under this new definition, a governmental unit is a "foreign country" if it is (1) not the United States or a state, district, commonwealth, territory or insular possession of the United States; and (2) its judgments are not initially subject to Full Faith and Credit Clause standards.

The Full Faith and Credit Clause, Art. IV, section 1, provides that "Full Faith and Credit shall be given in each State to the public Acts, Records, and judicial Proceedings of every other State. And the Congress may by general Laws prescribe the Manner in which such Acts, Records, and Proceedings shall be proved, and the Effect thereof." Whether the judgments of a governmental unit are subject to the Full Faith and Credit Clause may be determined by judicial interpretation of the Full Faith and Credit Clause or by statute, or by a combination of these two sources. For example, pursuant to the authority granted by the second sentence of the Full Faith and Credit Clause, Congress has passed 28 U.S.C.A. § 1738, which provides *inter alia* that court records from "any State, Territory, or Possession of the United States" are entitled to full faith and credit under the Full Faith and Credit Clause. In Stoll v. Gottlieb, 305 U.S. 165, 170 (1938), the United States Supreme Court held that this statute also requires that full faith and credit be given to judgments of federal courts. States also have made determinations as to whether certain types of judgments are subject to the Full Faith and Credit Clause. *E.g.* Day v. Montana Dept. of Social & Rehab. Servs., 900 P.2d 296 (Mont. 1995) (tribal court judgment not subject to Full Faith and Credit, and should be treated with same deference shown foreign-country judgments). Under the definition of "foreign country" in this Act, the determination as to whether a governmental unit's judgments are subject to full faith and credit standards should be made by reference to any relevant law, whether statutory or decisional, that is applicable "in this state."

The definition of "foreign country" in terms of those judgments not subject to Full Faith and Credit standards also has the advantage of more effectively coordinating the Act with the Uniform Enforcement of Foreign

Judgments Act. That Act, which establishes a registration procedure for the enforcement of sister state and equivalent judgments, defines a "foreign judgment" as "any judgment, decree, or order of a court of the United States or of any other court which is entitled to full faith and credit in this state." Uniform Enforcement of Foreign Judgments Act, § 1 (1964). By defining "foreign country" in the Recognition Act in terms of those judgments not subject to full faith and credit standards, this Act makes it clear that the Enforcement Act and the Recognition Act are mutually exclusive—if a foreign money judgment is subject to full faith and credit standards, then the Enforcement Act's registration procedure is available with regard to its enforcement; if the foreign money judgment is not subject to full faith and credit standards, then the foreign money judgment may not be enforced until recognition of it has been obtained in accordance with the provisions of the Recognition Act.

2. The definition of "foreign-country judgment" in this Act differs significantly from the 1962 Act's definition of "foreign judgment." The 1962 Act's definition served in large part as a scope provision for the Act. The part of the definition defining the scope of the Act has been moved to section 3, which is the scope section.

3. The definition of "foreign-country judgment" in this Act refers to "a judgment" of "a court" of the foreign country. The foreign-country judgment need not take a particular form—any order or decree that meets the requirements of this section and comes within the scope of the Act under Section 3 is subject to the Act. Similarly, any competent government tribunal that issues such a "judgment" comes within the term "court" for purposes of this Act. The judgment, however, must be a judgment of an adjudicative body of the foreign country, and not the result of an alternative dispute mechanism chosen by the parties. Thus, foreign arbitral awards and agreements to arbitrate are not covered by this Act. They are governed instead by federal law, Chapter 2 of the U.S. Arbitration Act, 9 U.S.C. §§ 201–208, implementing the United Nations Convention on the Recognition and Enforcement of Foreign Arbitral Awards and Chapter 3 of the U.S. Arbitration Act, 9 U.S.C. §§ 301–307, implementing the Inter-American Convention on International Commercial Arbitration. A judgment of a foreign court confirming or setting aside an arbitral award, however, would be covered by this Act.

4. The definition of "foreign-country judgment" does not limit foreign-country judgments to those rendered in litigation between private parties. Judgments in which a governmental entity is a party also are included, and are subject to this Act if they meet the requirements of this section and are within the scope of the Act under Section 3.

Section 3. Applicability

(a) Except as otherwise provided in subsection (b), this [act] applies to a foreign-country judgment to the extent that the judgment:

(1) grants or denies recovery of a sum of money; and

(2) under the law of the foreign country where rendered, is final, conclusive, and enforceable.

(b) This [act] does not apply to a foreign-country judgment, even if the judgment grants or denies recovery of a sum of money, to the extent that the judgment is:

(1) a judgment for taxes;

(2) a fine or other penalty; or

(3) a judgment for divorce, support, or maintenance, or other judgment rendered in connection with domestic relations.

(c) A party seeking recognition of a foreign-country judgment has the burden of establishing that this [act] applies to the foreign-country judgment.

COMMENT

Source: This section is based on Section 2 of the 1962 Act. Subsection (b) contains material that was included as part of the definition of "foreign judgment" in Section 1(2) of the 1962 Act. Subsection (c) is new.

1. Like the 1962 Act, this Act sets out in subsection 3(a) two basic requirements that a foreign-country judgment must meet before it comes within the scope of this Act—the foreign-country judgment must (1) grant or deny recovery of a sum of money and (2) be final, conclusive and enforceable under the law of the foreign country where it was rendered. Subsection 3(b) then sets out three types of foreign-country judgments that are excluded from the coverage of this Act, even though they meet the criteria of subsection 3(a)—judgments for taxes, judgments constituting fines and other penalties, and judgments in domestic relations matters. These exclusions are comparable to those contained in Section 1(2) of the 1962 Act.

2. This Act applies to a foreign-country judgment only to the extent the foreign-country judgment grants or denies recovery of a sum of money. If a foreign-country judgment both grants or denies recovery of a sum money and provides for some other form of relief, this Act would apply to the portion of the judgment that grants or denies monetary relief, but not to the portion that provides for some other form of relief. The U.S. court, however, would be left free to decide to recognize and enforce the non-monetary portion of the judgment under principles of comity or other applicable law. See Section 11.

3. In order to come within the scope of this Act, a foreign-country judgment must be final, conclusive, and enforceable under the law of the foreign country in which it was rendered. This requirement contains three distinct, although inter-related concepts. A judgment is final when it is not subject to additional proceedings in the rendering court other than execution. A judgment is conclusive when it is given effect between the parties as a determination of their legal rights and obligations. A judgment is enforceable when the legal procedures of the state to ensure that the judgment debtor

complies with the judgment are available to the judgment creditor to assist in collection of the judgment.

While the first two of these requirements—finality and conclusiveness—will apply with regard to every foreign-country money judgment, the requirement of enforceability is only relevant when the judgment is one granting recovery of a sum of money. A judgment denying a sum of money obviously is not subject to enforcement procedures, as there is no monetary award to enforce. This Act, however, covers both judgments granting and those denying recovery of a sum of money. Thus, the fact that a foreign-country judgment denying recovery of a sum of money is not enforceable does not mean that such judgments are not within the scope of the Act. Instead, the requirement that the judgment be enforceable should be read to mean that, if the foreign-country judgment grants recovery of a sum of money, it must be enforceable in the foreign country in order to be within the scope of the Act.

Like the 1962 Act, subsection 3(b) requires that the determinations as to finality, conclusiveness and enforceability be made using the law of the foreign country in which the judgment was rendered. Unless the foreign-country judgment is final, conclusive, and (to the extent it grants recovery of a sum of money) enforceable in the foreign country where it was rendered, it will not be within the scope of this Act.

4. Subsection 3(b) follows the 1962 Act by excluding three categories of foreign-country money judgments from the scope of the Act—judgments for taxes, judgments that constitute fines and penalties, and judgments in domestic relations matters. The domestic relations exclusion has been redrafted to make it clear that all judgments in domestic relations matters are excluded from the Act, not just judgments "for support" as provided in the 1962 Act. This is consistent with interpretation of the 1962 Act by the courts, which extended the "support" exclusion in the 1962 Act beyond its literal wording to exclude other money judgments in connection with domestic matters. *E.g.*, Wolff v. Wolff, 389 A.2d 413 (Md. App. 1978) ("support" includes alimony).

Recognition and enforcement of domestic relations judgments traditionally has been treated differently from recognition and enforcement of other judgments. The considerations with regard to those judgments, particularly with regard to jurisdiction and finality, differ from those with regard to other money judgments. Further, national laws with regard to domestic relations vary widely, and recognition and enforcement of such judgments thus is more appropriately handled through comity than through use of this uniform Act. Finally, other statutes, such as the Uniform Interstate Family Support Act and the federal International Child Support Enforcement Act, 42 U.S.C. § 659a (1996), address various aspects of the recognition and enforcement of domestic relations awards. Under Section 11 of this Act, courts are free to recognize money judgments in domestic relations matters under principles of comity or otherwise, and U.S. courts routinely enforce money judgments in domestic relations matters under comity principles.

Foreign-country judgments for taxes and judgments that constitute fines or penalties traditionally have not been recognized and enforced in U.S. courts. *See, e.g.*, Restatement Third of the Foreign Relations Law of the United States § 483 (1986). Both the "revenue rule," under which the courts of one country will not enforce the revenue laws of another country, and the prohibition on enforcement of penal judgments seem to be grounded in the idea that one country does not enforce the public laws of another. *See id.* Reporters' Note 2. The exclusion of tax judgments and judgments constituting fines or penalties from the scope of the Act reflects this tradition. Under Section 11, however, courts remain free to consider whether such judgments should be recognized and enforced under comity or other principles.

A judgment for taxes is a judgment in favor of a foreign country or one of its subdivisions based on a claim for an assessment of a tax. Thus, a judgment awarding a plaintiff restitution of the purchase price paid for an item would not be considered in any part a judgment for taxes, even though one element of the recovery was the sales tax paid by the plaintiff at the time of purchase. Such a judgment would not be one designed to enforce the revenue laws of the foreign country, but rather one designed to compensate the plaintiff. Courts generally hold that the test for whether a judgment is a fine or penalty is determined by whether its purpose is remedial in nature, with its benefits accruing to private individuals, or it is penal in nature, punishing an offense against public justice. *E.g.*, Chase Manhattan Bank, N.A. v. Hoffman, 665 F.Supp. 73 (D. Mass. 1987) (finding that Belgium judgment was not penal even though the proceeding forming the basis of the suit was primarily criminal where Belgium court considered damage petition a civil remedy, the judgment did not constitute punishment for an offense against public justice of Belgium, and benefit of the judgment accrued to private judgment creditor, not Belgium). Thus, a judgment that awards compensation or restitution for the benefit of private individuals should not automatically be considered penal in nature and therefore outside the scope of the Act simply because the action is brought on behalf of the private individuals by a government entity. *Cf.* U.S.-Australia Free Trade Agreement, art. 14.7.2, U.S.-Austl., May 18, 2004 (providing that when government agency obtains a civil monetary judgment for purpose of providing restitution to consumers, investors, or customers who suffered economic harm due to fraud, judgment generally should not be denied recognition and enforcement on ground that it is penal or revenue in nature, or based on other foreign public law).

5. Under subsection 3(b), a foreign-country money judgment is not within the scope of this Act "to the extent" that it comes within one of the excluded categories. Therefore, if a foreign-country money judgment is only partially within one of the excluded categories, the non-excluded portion will be subject to this Act.

6. Subsection 3(c) is new. The 1962 Act does not expressly allocate the burden of proof with regard to establishing whether a foreign-country judgment is within the scope of the Act. Courts applying the 1962 Act generally have held that the burden of proof is on the person seeking

recognition to establish that the judgment is final, conclusive and enforceable where rendered. *E.g.*, Mayekawa Mfg. Co. Ltd. v. Sasaki, 888 P.2d 183, 189 (Wash. App. 1995) (burden of proof on creditor to establish judgment is final, conclusive, and enforceable where rendered); Bridgeway Corp. v. Citibank, 45 F.Supp.2d 276, 285 (S.D.N.Y. 1999) (party seeking recognition must establish that there is a final judgment, conclusive and enforceable where rendered); S.C. Chimexim S.A. v. Velco Enterprises, Ltd., 36 F.Supp.2d 206, 212 (S.D.N.Y. 1999) (Plaintiff has the burden of establishing conclusive effect). Subsection (3)(c) places the burden of proof to establish whether a foreign-country judgment is within the scope of the Act on the party seeking recognition of the foreign-country judgment with regard to both subsection (a) and subsection (b).

Section 4. Standards for Recognition of Foreign-Country Judgment

(a) Except as otherwise provided in subsections (b) and (c), a court of this state shall recognize a foreign-country judgment to which this [act] applies.

(b) A court of this state may not recognize a foreign-country judgment if:

(1) the judgment was rendered under a judicial system that does not provide impartial tribunals or procedures compatible with the requirements of due process of law;

(2) the foreign court did not have personal jurisdiction over the defendant; or

(3) the foreign court did not have jurisdiction over the subject matter.

(c) A court of this state need not recognize a foreign-country judgment if:

(1) the defendant in the proceeding in the foreign court did not receive notice of the proceeding in sufficient time to enable the defendant to defend;

(2) the judgment was obtained by fraud that deprived the losing party of an adequate opportunity to present its case;

(3) the judgment or the [cause of action] [claim for relief] on which the judgment is based is repugnant to the public policy of this state or of the United States;

(4) the judgment conflicts with another final and conclusive judgment;

(5) the proceeding in the foreign court was contrary to an agreement between the parties under which the dispute in

question was to be determined otherwise than by proceedings in that foreign court;

(6) in the case of jurisdiction based only on personal service, the foreign court was a seriously inconvenient forum for the trial of the action;

(7) the judgment was rendered in circumstances that raise substantial doubt about the integrity of the rendering court with respect to the judgment; or

(8) the specific proceeding in the foreign court leading to the judgment was not compatible with the requirements of due process of law.

(d) A party resisting recognition of a foreign-country judgment has the burden of establishing that a ground for nonrecognition stated in subsection (b) or (c) exists.

COMMENT

Source: This section is based on Section 4 of the 1962 Act.

1. This Section provides the standards for recognition of a foreign-country money judgment. Section 7 sets out the effect of recognition of a foreign-country money judgment under this Act.

2. Recognition of a judgment means that the forum court accepts the determination of legal rights and obligations made by the rendering court in the foreign country. *See, e.g.*, Restatement (Second) of Conflicts of Laws, Ch. 5, Topic 3, Introductory Note (recognition of foreign judgment occurs to the extent the forum court gives the judgment "the same effect with respect to the parties, the subject matter of the action and the issues involved that it has in the state where it was rendered.") Recognition of a foreign-country judgment must be distinguished from enforcement of that judgment. Enforcement of the foreign-country judgment involves the application of the legal procedures of the state to ensure that the judgment debtor obeys the foreign-country judgment. Recognition of a foreign-country money judgment often is associated with enforcement of the judgment, as the judgment creditor usually seeks recognition of the foreign-country judgment primarily for the purpose of invoking the enforcement procedures of the forum state to assist the judgment creditor's collection of the judgment from the judgment debtor. Because the forum court cannot enforce the foreign-country judgment until it has determined that the judgment will be given effect, recognition is a prerequisite to enforcement of the foreign-country judgment. Recognition, however, also has significance outside the enforcement context because a foreign-country judgment also must be recognized before it can be given preclusive effect under res judicata and collateral estoppel principles. The issue of whether a foreign-country judgment will be recognized is distinct from both the issue of whether the judgment will be enforced, and the issue of the extent to which it will be given preclusive effect.

3. Subsection 4(a) places an affirmative duty on the forum court to recognize a foreign-country money judgment unless one of the grounds for nonrecognition stated in subsection (b) or (c) applies. Subsection (b) states three mandatory grounds for denying recognition to a foreign-country money judgment. If the forum court finds that one of the grounds listed in subsection (b) exists, then it must deny recognition to the foreign-country money judgment. Subsection (c) states eight nonmandatory grounds for denying recognition. The forum court has discretion to decide whether or not to refuse recognition based on one of these grounds. Subsection (d) places the burden of proof on the party resisting recognition of the foreign-country judgment to establish that one of the grounds for nonrecognition exists.

4. The mandatory grounds for nonrecognition stated in subsection (b) are identical to the mandatory grounds stated in Section 4 of the 1962 Act. The discretionary grounds stated in subsection 4(c)(1) through (6) are based on subsection 4(b)(1) through (6) of the 1962 Act. The discretionary grounds stated in subsection 4(c)(7) and (8) are new.

5. Under subsection (b)(1), the forum court must deny recognition to the foreign-country money judgment if that judgment was "rendered under a judicial system that does not provide impartial tribunals or procedures compatible with the requirements of due process of law." The standard for this ground for nonrecognition "has been stated authoritatively by the Supreme Court of the United States in Hilton v. Guyot, 159 U.S. 113, 205 (1895). As indicated in that decision, a mere difference in the procedural system is not a sufficient basis for nonrecognition. A case of serious injustice must be involved." Cmt. § 4, Uniform Foreign Money-Judgment Recognition Act (1962). The focus of inquiry is not whether the procedure in the rendering country is similar to U.S. procedure, but rather on the basic fairness of the foreign-country procedure. Kam-Tech Systems, Ltd. v. Yardeni, 74 A.2d 644, 649 (N.J. App. 2001) (interpreting the comparable provision in the 1962 Act); *accord*, Society of Lloyd's v. Ashenden, 233 F.3d 473 (7th Cir. 2000) (procedures need not meet all the intricacies of the complex concept of due process that has emerged from U.S. case law, but rather must be fair in the broader international sense) (interpreting comparable provision in the 1962 Act). Procedural differences, such as absence of jury trial or different evidentiary rules are not sufficient to justify denying recognition under subsection (b)(1), so long as the essential elements of impartial administration and basic procedural fairness have been provided in the foreign proceeding. As the U.S. Supreme Court stated in *Hilton*:

> Where there has been opportunity for a full and fair trial abroad before a court of competent jurisdiction conducting the trial upon regular proceedings, after due citation or voluntary appearance of the defendant, and under a system of jurisprudence likely to secure an impartial administration of justice between the citizens of its own country and those of other countries, and there is nothing to show either prejudice in the court, or in the system of laws under which it was sitting, or fraud in procuring the judgment, or any other special reason why the comity of this

nation should not allow it full effect then a foreign-country judgment should be recognized. *Hilton*, 159 U.S. at 202.

6. Under section 4(b)(2), the forum court must deny recognition to the foreign-country judgment if the foreign court did not have personal jurisdiction over the defendant. Section 5(a) lists six bases for personal jurisdiction that are adequate as a matter of law to establish that the foreign court had personal jurisdiction. Section 5(b) makes clear that other grounds for personal jurisdiction may be found sufficient.

7. Subsection 4(c)(2) limits the type of fraud that will serve as a ground for denying recognition to extrinsic fraud. This provision is consistent with the interpretation of the comparable provision in subsection 4(b)(2) of the 1962 Act by the courts, which have found that only extrinsic fraud—conduct of the prevailing party that deprived the losing party of an adequate opportunity to present its case—is sufficient under the 1962 Act. Examples of extrinsic fraud would be when the plaintiff deliberately had the initiating process served on the defendant at the wrong address, deliberately gave the defendant wrong information as to the time and place of the hearing, or obtained a default judgment against the defendant based on a forged confession of judgment. When this type of fraudulent action by the plaintiff deprives the defendant of an adequate opportunity to present its case, then it provides grounds for denying recognition of the foreign-country judgment. Extrinsic fraud should be distinguished from intrinsic fraud, such as false testimony of a witness or admission of a forged document into evidence during the foreign proceeding. Intrinsic fraud does not provide a basis for denying recognition under subsection 4(c)(2), as the assertion that intrinsic fraud has occurred should be raised and dealt with in the rendering court.

8. The public policy exception in subsection 4(c)(3) is based on the public policy exception in subsection 4(b)(3) of the 1962 Act, with one difference. The public policy exception in the 1962 Act states that the relevant inquiry is whether "the [cause of action] [claim for relief] on which the judgment is based" is repugnant to public policy. Based on this "cause of action" language, some courts interpreting the 1962 Act have refused to find that a public policy challenge based on something other than repugnancy of the foreign cause of action comes within this exception. *E.g.*, Southwest Livestock & Trucking Co., Inc. v. Ramon, 169 F.3d 317 (5th Cir. 1999) (refusing to deny recognition to Mexican judgment on promissory note with interest rate of 48% because cause of action to collect on promissory note does not violate public policy); Guinness PLC v. Ward, 955 F.2d 875 (4th Cir. 1992) (challenge to recognition based on post-judgment settlement could not be asserted under public policy exception); The Society of Lloyd's v. Turner, 303 F.3d 325 (5th Cir. 2002) (rejecting argument legal standards applied to establish elements of breach of contract violated public policy because cause of action for breach of contract itself is not contrary to state public policy); *cf.* Bachchan v. India Abroad Publications, Inc., 585 N.Y.S.2d 661 (N.Y. Sup. Ct. 1992) (judgment creditor argued British libel judgment should be recognized despite argument it violated First Amendment because New York recognizes a cause of action for libel). Subsection 4(c)(3) rejects this narrow focus by providing that the forum court may deny recognition if either the cause of

action or the judgment itself violates public policy. *Cf.* Restatement (Third) of the Foreign Relations Law of the United States, § 482(2)(d) (1986) (containing a similarly-worded public policy exception to recognition).

Although subsection 4(c)(3) of this Act rejects the narrow focus on the cause of action under the 1962 Act, it retains the stringent test for finding a public policy violation applied by courts interpreting the 1962 Act. Under that test, a difference in law, even a marked one, is not sufficient to raise a public policy issue. Nor is it relevant that the foreign law allows a recovery that the forum state would not allow. Public policy is violated only if recognition or enforcement of the foreign-country judgment would tend clearly to injure the public health, the public morals, or the public confidence in the administration of law, or would undermine "that sense of security for individual rights, whether of personal liberty or of private property, which any citizen ought to feel." Hunt v. BP Exploration Co. (Libya) Ltd., 492 F.Supp. 885, 901 (N.D. Tex. 1980).

The language "or of the United States" in subsection 4(c)(3), which does not appear in the 1962 Act provision, makes it clear that the relevant public policy is that of both the State in which recognition is sought and that of the United States. This is the position taken by the vast majority of cases interpreting the 1962 public policy provision. E.g., Bachchan v. India Abroad Publications, Inc., 585 N.Y.S.2d 661 (Sup.Ct. N.Y. 1992) (British libel judgment denied recognition because it violates First Amendment).

9. Subsection 4(c)(5) allows the forum court to refuse recognition of a foreign-country judgment when the parties had a valid agreement, such as a valid forum selection clause or agreement to arbitrate, providing that the relevant dispute would be resolved in a forum other than the forum issuing the foreign-country judgment. Under this provision, the forum court must find both the existence of a valid agreement and that the agreement covered the subject matter involved in the foreign litigation resulting in the foreign-country judgment.

10. Subsection 4(c)(6) authorizes the forum court to refuse recognition of a foreign-country judgment that was rendered in the foreign country solely on the basis of personal service when the forum court believes the original action should have been dismissed by the court in the foreign country on grounds of *forum non conveniens.*

11. Subsection 4(c)(7) is new. Under this subsection, the forum court may deny recognition to a foreign-country judgment if there are circumstances that raise substantial doubt about the integrity of the rendering court with respect to that judgment. It requires a showing of corruption in the particular case that had an impact on the judgment that was rendered. This provision may be contrasted with subsection 4(b)(1), which requires that the forum court refuse recognition to the foreign-country judgment if it was rendered under a judicial system that does not provide impartial tribunals. Like the comparable provision in subsection 4(a)(1) of the 1962 Act, subsection 4(b)(1) focuses on the judicial system of the foreign country as a whole, rather than on whether the particular judicial proceeding leading to the foreign-country judgment was impartial and fair. *See, e.g.,* The

Society of Lloyd's v. Turner, 303 F.3d 325, 330 (5th Cir. 2002) (interpreting the 1962 Act); CIBC Mellon Trust Co. v. Mora Hotel Corp., N.V., 743 N.Y.S.2d 408, 415 (N.Y. App. 2002) (interpreting the 1962 Act); Society of Lloyd's v. Ashenden, 233 F.3d 473, 477 (7th Cir. 2000) (interpreting the 1962 Act). On the other hand, subsection 4(c)(7) allows the court to deny recognition to the foreign-country judgment if it finds a lack of impartiality and fairness of the tribunal in the individual proceeding leading to the foreign-country judgment. Thus, the difference is that between showing, for example, that corruption and bribery is so prevalent throughout the judicial system of the foreign country as to make that entire judicial system one that does not provide impartial tribunals versus showing that bribery of the judge in the proceeding that resulted in the particular foreign-country judgment under consideration had a sufficient impact on the ultimate judgment as to call it into question.

12. Subsection 4(c)(8) also is new. It allows the forum court to deny recognition to the foreign-country judgment if the court finds that the specific proceeding in the foreign court was not compatible with the requirements of fundamental fairness. Like subsection 4(c)(7), it can be contrasted with subsection 4(b)(1), which requires the forum court to deny recognition to the foreign-country judgment if the forum court finds that the entire judicial system in the foreign country where the foreign-country judgment was rendered does not provide procedures compatible with the requirements of fundamental fairness. While the focus of subsection 4(b)(1) is on the foreign country's judicial system as a whole, the focus of subsection 4(c)(8) is on the particular proceeding that resulted in the specific foreign-country judgment under consideration. Thus, the difference is that between showing, for example, that there has been such a breakdown of law and order in the particular foreign country that judgments are rendered on the basis of political decisions rather than the rule of law throughout the judicial system versus a showing that for political reasons the particular party against whom the foreign-country judgment was entered was denied fundamental fairness in the particular proceedings leading to the foreign-country judgment.

Subsections 4(c)(7) and (8) both are discretionary grounds for denying recognition, while subsection 4(b)(1) is mandatory. Obviously, if the entire judicial system in the foreign country fails to satisfy the requirements of impartiality and fundamental fairness, a judgment rendered in that foreign country would be so compromised that the forum court should refuse to recognize it as a matter of course. On the other hand, if the problem is evidence of a lack of integrity or fundamental fairness with regard to the particular proceeding leading to the foreign-country judgment, then there may or may not be other factors in the particular case that would cause the forum court to decide to recognize the foreign-country judgment. For example, a forum court might decide not to exercise its discretion to deny recognition despite evidence of corruption or procedural unfairness in a particular case because the party resisting recognition failed to raise the issue on appeal from the foreign-country judgment in the foreign country, and the evidence establishes that, if the party had done so, appeal would have been an adequate mechanism for correcting the transgressions of the lower court.

13. Under subsection 4(d), the party opposing recognition of the foreign-country judgment has the burden of establishing that one of the grounds for nonrecognition set out in subsection 4(b) or (c) applies. The 1962 Act was silent as to who had the burden of proof to establish a ground for nonrecognition and courts applying the 1962 Act took different positions on the issue. *Compare* Bridgeway Corp. v. Citibank, 45 F.Supp.2d 276, 285 (S.D.N.Y. 1999) (plaintiff has burden to show no mandatory basis under 4(a) for nonrecognition exists; defendant has burden regarding discretionary bases) *with* The Courage Co. LLC v. The ChemShare Corp., 93 S.W.3d 323, 331 (Tex. App. 2002) (party seeking to avoid recognition has burden to prove ground for nonrecognition). Because the grounds for nonrecognition in Section 4 are in the nature of defenses to recognition, the burden of proof is most appropriately allocated to the party opposing recognition of the foreign-country judgment.

Section 5. Personal Jurisdiction

(a) A foreign-country judgment may not be refused recognition for lack of personal jurisdiction if:

(1) the defendant was served with process personally in the foreign country;

(2) the defendant voluntarily appeared in the proceeding, other than for the purpose of protecting property seized or threatened with seizure in the proceeding or of contesting the jurisdiction of the court over the defendant;

(3) the defendant, before the commencement of the proceeding, had agreed to submit to the jurisdiction of the foreign court with respect to the subject matter involved;

(4) the defendant was domiciled in the foreign country when the proceeding was instituted or was a corporation or other form of business organization that had its principal place of business in, or was organized under the laws of, the foreign country;

(5) the defendant had a business office in the foreign country and the proceeding in the foreign court involved a [cause of action] [claim for relief] arising out of business done by the defendant through that office in the foreign country; or

(6) the defendant operated a motor vehicle or airplane in the foreign country and the proceeding involved a [cause of action] [claim for relief] arising out of that operation.

(b) The list of bases for personal jurisdiction in subsection (a) is not exclusive. The courts of this state may recognize bases of personal jurisdiction other than those listed in subsection(a) as sufficient to support a foreign-country judgment.

COMMENT

Source: This provision is based on Section 5 of the 1962 Act. Its substance is the same as that of Section 5 of the 1962 Act, except as noted in Comment 2 below with regard to subsection 5(a)(4).

1. Under section 4(b)(2), the forum court must deny recognition to the foreign-country judgment if the foreign court did not have personal jurisdiction over the defendant. Section 5(a) lists six bases for personal jurisdiction that are adequate as a matter of law to establish that the foreign court had personal jurisdiction. Section 5(b) makes it clear that these bases of personal jurisdiction are not exclusive. The forum court may find that the foreign court had personal jurisdiction over the defendant on some other basis.

2. Subsection 5(a)(4) of the 1962 Act provides that the foreign court had personal jurisdiction over the defendant if the defendant was "a body corporate" that "had its principal place of business, was incorporated, or had otherwise acquired corporate status, in the foreign state." Subsection 5(a)(4) of this Act extends that concept to forms of business organization other than corporations.

3. Subsection 5(a)(3) provides that the foreign court has personal jurisdiction over the defendant if the defendant agreed before commencement of the proceeding leading to the foreign-country judgment to submit to the jurisdiction of the foreign court with regard to the subject matter involved. Under this provision, the forum court must find both the existence of a valid agreement to submit to the foreign court's jurisdiction and that the agreement covered the subject matter involved in the foreign litigation resulting in the foreign-country judgment.

Section 6. Procedure for Recognition of Foreign-Country Judgment

(a) If recognition of a foreign-country judgment is sought as an original matter, the issue of recognition shall be raised by filing an action seeking recognition of the foreign-country judgment.

(b) If recognition of a foreign-country judgment is sought in a pending action, the issue of recognition may be raised by counterclaim, cross-claim, or affirmative defense.

COMMENT

Source: This section is new.

1. Unlike the 1962 Act, which was silent as to the proper procedure for seeking recognition of a foreign-country judgment, Section 6 of this Act expressly sets out the ways in which the issue of recognition may be raised. Under section 6, the issue of recognition always must be raised in a court proceeding. Thus, section 6 rejects decisions under the 1962 Act holding that

the registration procedure found in the Uniform Enforcement of Foreign Judgments Act could be utilized with regard to recognition of a foreign-country judgment. *E.g.* Society of Lloyd's v. Ashenden, 233 F.3d 473 (7th Cir. 2000). The Enforcement Act deals solely with the *enforcement* of sister-state judgments and other judgments entitled to full faith and credit, not with the *recognition* of foreign-country judgments.

More broadly, section 6 rejects the use of any registration procedure in the context of the foreign-country judgments covered by this Act. A registration procedure represents a balance between the interest of the judgment creditor in obtaining quick and efficient recognition and enforcement of a judgment when the judgment debtor has already been provided with an opportunity to litigate the underlying issues, and the interest of the judgment debtor in being provided an adequate opportunity to raise and litigate issues regarding whether the foreign-country judgment should be recognized. In the context of sister-state judgments, this balance favors use of a truncated procedure such as that found in the Enforcement Act. Recognition of sister-state judgments normally is mandated by the Full Faith and Credit Clause. Courts recognize only a very limited number of grounds for denying full faith and credit to a sister-state judgment—that the rendering court lacked jurisdiction, that the judgment was procured by fraud, that the judgment has been satisfied, or that the limitations period has expired. Thus, the judgment debtor with regard to a sister-state judgment normally does not have any grounds for opposing recognition and enforcement of the judgment. The extremely limited grounds for denying full faith and credit to a sister-state judgment reflect the fact such judgments will have been rendered by a court that is subject to the same due process limitations and the same overlap of federal statutory and constitutional law as the forum state's courts, and, to a large extent, the same body of court precedent and socio-economic ideas as those shaping the law of the forum state. Therefore, there is a strong presumption of fairness and competence attached to a sister-state judgment that justifies use of a registration procedure.

The balance between the benefits and costs of a registration procedure is significantly different, however, in the context of recognition and enforcement of foreign-country judgments. Unlike the limited grounds for denying full faith and credit to a sister-state judgment, this Act provides a number of grounds upon which recognition of a foreign-country judgment may be denied. Determination of whether these grounds apply requires the forum court to look behind the foreign-country judgment to evaluate the law and the judicial system under which the foreign-country judgment was rendered. The existence of these grounds for nonrecognition reflects the fact there is less expectation that foreign-country courts will follow procedures comporting with U.S. notions of fundamental fairness and jurisdiction or that those courts will apply laws viewed as substantively tolerable by U.S. standards than there is with regard to sister-state courts. In some situations, there also may be suspicions of corruption or fraud in the foreign-country proceedings. These differences between sister-state judgments and foreign-country judgments provide a justification for requiring judicial involvement in the decision whether to recognize a foreign-country judgment in all cases in which that issue is raised. Although the threshold for establishing that a foreign-country judgment is not entitled to recognition under Section 4 is high, there is a sufficiently greater likelihood that significant recognition issues will be raised so as to require a judicial proceeding.

2. This Section contemplates that the issue of recognition may be raised either as an original matter or in the context of a pending proceeding. Subsection 6(a) provides that in order to raise the issue of recognition of a foreign-country judgment as an initial matter, the party seeking recognition must file an action for recognition of the foreign-country judgment. Subsection 6(b) provides that when the recognition issue is raised in a pending proceeding, it may be raised by counterclaim, cross-claim or affirmative defense, depending on the context in which it is raised. These rules are consistent with the way the issue of recognition most often was raised in most states under the 1962 Act.

3. An action seeking recognition of a foreign-country judgment under this Section is an action on the foreign-country judgment itself, not an action on the underlying cause of action that gave rise to that judgment. The parties to an action under Section 6 may not relitigate the merits of the underlying dispute that gave rise to the foreign-country judgment.

4. While this Section sets out the ways in which the issue of recognition of a foreign-country judgment may be raised, it is not intended to create any new procedure not currently existing in the state or to otherwise effect existing state procedural requirements. The parties to an action in which recognition of a foreign-country judgment is sought under Section 6 must comply with all state procedural rules with regard to that type of action. Nor does this Act address the question of what constitutes a sufficient basis for jurisdiction to adjudicate with regard to an action under Section 6. Courts have split over the issue of whether the presence of assets of the debtor in a state is a sufficient basis for jurisdiction in light of footnote 36 of the U.S. Supreme Court decision in Shaffer v. Heitner, 433 U.S. 186, 210 n.36 (1977). This Act takes no position on that issue.

5. In states that have adopted the Uniform Foreign-Money Claims Act, that Act will apply to the determination of the amount of a money judgment recognized under this Act.

Section 7. Effect of Recognition of Foreign-Country Judgment

If the court in a proceeding under Section 6 finds that the foreign-country judgment is entitled to recognition under this [act] then, to the extent that the foreign-country judgment grants or denies recovery of a sum of money, the foreign-country judgment is:

(1) conclusive between the parties to the same extent as the judgment of a sister state entitled to full faith and credit in this state would be conclusive; and

(2) enforceable in the same manner and to the same extent as a judgment rendered in this state.

COMMENT

Source: The substance of subsection 7(1) is based on Section 3 of the 1962 Act. Subsection 7(2) is new.

1. Section 5 of this Act sets out the standards for the recognition of foreign-country judgments within the scope of this Act, and places an affirmative duty on the forum court to recognize any foreign-country judgment that meets those standards. Section 6 of this Act sets out the procedures by which the issue of recognition may be raised. This Section sets out the consequences of the decision by the forum court that the foreign-country judgment is entitled to recognition.

2. Under subsection 7(1), the first consequence of recognition of a foreign-country judgment is that it is treated as conclusive between the parties in the forum state. Section 7(1) does not attempt to establish directly the extent of that conclusiveness. Instead, it provides that the foreign-country judgment is treated as conclusive to the same extent that a judgment of a sister state that had been determined to be entitled to full faith and credit would be conclusive. This means that the foreign-country judgment generally will be given the same effect in the forum state that it has in the foreign country where it was rendered. Subsection 7(1), however, sets out the minimum effect that must be given to the foreign-country judgment once recognized. The forum court remains free to give the foreign-country judgment a greater preclusive effect in the forum state than the judgment would have in the foreign country where it was rendered. *Cf.* Restatement (Third) of the Foreign Relations Law of the United States, § 481 cmt. *c* (1986).

3. Under subsection 7(2), the second consequence of recognition of a foreign-country judgment is that, to the extent it grants a sum of money, it is enforceable in the forum state in accordance with the procedures for enforcement in the forum state and to the same extent that a judgment of the forum state would be enforceable. *Cf.* Restatement (Third) of the Foreign Relations Law of the United States § 481 (1986) (judgment entitled to recognition is enforceable in accordance with the procedure for enforcement of judgments applicable where enforcement is sought). Thus, under subsection 7(2), once recognized, the foreign-country judgment has the same effect and is subject to the same procedures, defenses and proceedings for reopening, vacating, or staying a judgment of a comparable court in the forum state, and can be enforced or satisfied in the same manner as such a judgment of the forum state.

Section 8. Stay of Proceedings Pending Appeal of Foreign-Country Judgment

If a party establishes that an appeal from a foreign-country judgment is pending or will be taken, the court may stay any proceedings with regard to the foreign-country judgment until the appeal is concluded, the time for appeal expires, or the appellant has had sufficient time to prosecute the appeal and has failed to do so.

COMMENT

Source: This section is the same substantively as section 6 of the 1962 Act, except that it adds as an additional measure for the duration of the stay "the time for appeal expires."

1. Under Section 3 of this Act, a foreign-country judgment is not within the scope of this Act unless it is conclusive and enforceable where rendered. Thus, if the effect of appeal under the law of the foreign country in which the judgment was rendered is to prevent it from being conclusive or enforceable between the parties, the existence of a pending appeal in the foreign country would prevent the application of this Act. Section 8 addresses a different situation. It deals with the situation in which either (1) the party seeking a stay has demonstrated that it intends to file an appeal in the foreign country, although the appeal has not yet been filed or (2) an appeal has been filed in the foreign country, but under the law of the foreign country filing of an appeal does not affect the conclusiveness or enforceability of the judgment. Section 8 allows the forum court in those situations to determine in its discretion that a stay of proceedings is appropriate.

Section 9. Statute of Limitations

An action to recognize a foreign-country judgment must be commenced within the earlier of the time during which the foreign-country judgment is effective in the foreign country or 15 years from the date that the foreign-country judgment became effective in the foreign country.

COMMENT

Source: This Section is new. The 1962 Act did not contain a statute of limitations. Some courts applying the 1962 Act have used the state's general statute of limitations, *e.g.*, Vrozos v. Sarantopoulos, 552 N.E.2d 1053 (Ill. App. 1990) (as Recognition Act contains no statute of limitations, general five-year statute of limitations applies), while others have used the statute of limitations applicable with regard to enforcement of a domestic judgment, *e.g.*, La Societe Anonyme Goro v. Conveyor Accessories, Inc., 677 N.E. 2d 30 (Ill. App. 1997).

1. Under Section 3 of this Act, this Act only applies to foreign-country judgments that are conclusive, and if the judgment grants recovery of a sum of money, enforceable where rendered. Thus, if the period of effectiveness of the foreign-country judgment has expired in the foreign country where the judgment was rendered, the foreign-country judgment would not be subject to this Act. This means that the period of time during which a foreign-country judgment may be recognized under this Act normally is measured by the period of time during which that judgment is effective (that is, conclusive and, if applicable, enforceable) in the foreign country that rendered the judgment. If, however, the foreign-country judgment remains effective for more than fifteen years after the date on which it became effective in the foreign country, Section 9 places an additional time limit on recognition of a foreign-country judgment. It provides that, if the foreign-country judgment

remains effective between the parties for more than fifteen years, then an action to recognize the foreign-country judgment under this Act must be commenced within that fifteen year period.

2. Section 9 does not address the issue of whether a foreign-country judgment that can no longer be the basis of a recognition action under this Act because of the application of the fifteen-year limitations period in Section 9 may be used for other purposes. For example, a common rule with regard to judgments barred by a statute of limitations is that they still may be used defensively for purposes of offset and for their preclusive effect. The extent to which a foreign-country judgment with regard to which a recognition action is barred by Section 9 may be used for these or other purposes is left to the other law of the forum state.

Section 10. Uniformity Of Interpretation

In applying and construing this uniform act, consideration must be given to the need to promote uniformity of the law with respect to its subject matter among states that enact it.

COMMENT

Source: This Section is substantively the same as Section 8 of the 1962 Act. The section has been rewritten to reflect current NCCUSL practice.

Section 11. Saving Clause

This [act] does not prevent the recognition under principles of comity or otherwise of a foreign-country judgment not within the scope of this [act].

COMMENT

Source: This section is based on Section 7 of the 1962 Act.

1. Section 3 of this Act provides that this Act applies only to certain foreign-country judgments that grant or deny recovery of a sum of money. The purpose of this Act is to establish the minimum standards for recognition of those judgments. Section 11 makes clear that no negative implication should be read from the fact that this Act does not provide for recognition of other foreign-country judgments. Rather, this Act simply does not address the issue of whether foreign-country judgments not within its scope under Section 3 should be recognized. Courts are free to recognize those foreign-country judgments not within the scope of this Act under common law principles of comity or other applicable law.

Section 12. Effective Date

[(a) This [act] takes effect _______.]

[(b) This [act] applies to all actions commenced on or after the effective date of this [act] in which the issue of recognition of a foreign-country judgment is raised.]

COMMENT

Source: Subsection 12(a) is the same as Section 11 of the 1962 Act. Subsection 12(b) is new.

1. Subsection 12(b) provides that this Act will apply to all actions in which the issue of recognition of a foreign-country judgment is raised that are commenced on or after the effective date of this Act. Thus, the application of this Act is measured not from the time the original action leading to the foreign-country judgment was commenced in the foreign country, but rather from the time the action in which the issue of recognition is raised is commenced in the forum court. Subsection 12(b) does not distinguish between whether the purpose of the action commenced in the forum court was to seek recognition as an original matter under Subsection 6(a) or was an action that was already pending when the issue of recognition was raised under Subsection 6(b).

Section 13. Repeal

The following [acts] are repealed:

Uniform Foreign Money-Judgments Recognition Act,

COMMENT

Source: This Section is an updated version of Section 10 of the 1962 Act.

§ 8.7 Text of EU Regulation 1215/2012 on Jurisdiction and the Recognition and Enforcement of Civil and Commercial Matters (Brussels Regulation, Recast Jan. 10, 2015)

CHAPTER I—SCOPE AND DEFINITIONS

Article 1

1. This Regulation shall apply in civil and commercial matters whatever the nature of the court or tribunal. It shall not extend, in particular, to revenue, customs or administrative matters or to the liability of the State for acts and omissions in the exercise of State authority (*acta iure imperii*).

2. This Regulation shall not apply to:

(a) the status or legal capacity of natural persons, rights in property arising out of a matrimonial relationship or out of a relationship deemed by the law applicable to such relationship to have comparable effects to marriage;

(b) bankruptcy, proceedings relating to the winding-up of insolvent companies or other legal persons, judicial arrangements, compositions and analogous proceedings;

(c) social security;

(d) arbitration;

(e) maintenance obligations arising from a family relationship, parentage, marriage or affinity;

(f) wills and succession, including maintenance obligations arising by reason of death.

* * *

CHAPTER II—JURISDICTION

Section 1. General Provisions

Article 4

1. Subject to this Regulation, persons domiciled in a Member State shall, whatever their nationality, be sued in the courts of that Member State.

2. Persons who are not nationals of the Member State in which they are domiciled shall be governed by the rules of jurisdiction applicable to nationals of that Member State.

Article 5

1. Persons domiciled in a Member State may be sued in the courts of another Member State only by virtue of the rules set out in Sections 2 to 7 of this Chapter.

2. In particular, the rules of national jurisdiction of which the Member States are to notify the Commission pursuant to point (a) of Article 76(1) shall not be applicable as against the persons referred to in paragraph 1.

Article 6

1. If the defendant is not domiciled in a Member State, the jurisdiction of the courts of each Member State shall, subject to Article 18(1), Article 21(2) and Articles 24 and 25, be determined by the law of that Member State.

2. As against such a defendant, any person domiciled in a Member State may, whatever his nationality, avail himself in that Member State of the rules of jurisdiction there in force, and in particular those of which the Member States are to notify the Commission pursuant to point (a) of Article 76(1), in the same way as nationals of that Member State.

Section 2. Special Jurisdiction

Article 7

A person domiciled in a Member State may be sued in another Member State:

(1) (a) in matters relating to a contract, in the courts for the place of performance of the obligation in question;

(b) for the purpose of this provision and unless otherwise agreed, the place of performance of the obligation in question shall be:

— in the case of the sale of goods, the place in a Member State where, under the contract, the goods were delivered or should have been delivered,

— in the case of the provision of services, the place in a Member State where, under the contract, the services were provided or should have been provided;

(c) if point (b) does not apply then point (a) applies;

(2) in matters relating to tort, delict or quasi-delict, in the courts for the place where the harmful event occurred or may occur;

(3) as regards a civil claim for damages or restitution which is based on an act giving rise to criminal proceedings, in the court seised of those proceedings, to the extent that that court has jurisdiction under its own law to entertain civil proceedings;

(4) as regards a civil claim for the recovery, based on ownership, of a cultural object * * *, in the courts for the place where the cultural object is situated at the time when the court is seised;

(5) as regards a dispute arising out of the operations of a branch, agency or other establishment, in the courts for the place where the branch, agency or other establishment is situated;

(6) as regards a dispute brought against a settlor, trustee or beneficiary of a trust created by the operation of a statute, or by a written instrument, or created orally and evidenced in writing, in the courts of the Member State in which the trust is domiciled;

(7) as regards a dispute concerning the payment of remuneration claimed in respect of the salvage of a cargo or freight, in the court under the authority of which the cargo or freight in question:

(a) has been arrested to secure such payment; or

(b) could have been so arrested, but bail or other security has been given;

provided that this provision shall apply only if it is claimed that the defendant has an interest in the cargo or freight or had such an interest at the time of salvage.

Article 8

A person domiciled in a Member State may also be sued:

(1) where he is one of a number of defendants, in the courts for the place where any one of them is domiciled, provided the claims are so closely connected that it is expedient to hear and determine them together to avoid the risk of irreconcilable judgments resulting from separate proceedings;

(2) as a third party in an action on a warranty or guarantee or in any other third-party proceedings, in the court seised of the original proceedings, unless these were instituted solely with the object of removing him from the jurisdiction of the court which would be competent in his case;

(3) on a counter-claim arising from the same contract or facts on which the original claim was based, in the court in which the original claim is pending;

(4) in matters relating to a contract, if the action may be combined with an action against the same defendant in matters relating to rights *in rem* in immovable property, in the court of the Member State in which the property is situated.

Article 9

Where by virtue of this Regulation a court of a Member State has jurisdiction in actions relating to liability from the use or operation of a ship, that court, or any other court substituted for this purpose by the internal law of that Member State, shall also have jurisdiction over claims for limitation of such liability.

* * *

Section 4. Jurisdiction Over Consumer Contracts

Article 17

1. In matters relating to a contract concluded by a person, the consumer, for a purpose which can be regarded as being outside his trade or profession, jurisdiction shall be determined by this Section, without prejudice to Article 6 and point 5 of Article 7, if:

(a) it is a contract for the sale of goods on instalment credit terms;

(b) it is a contract for a loan repayable by instalments, or for any other form of credit, made to finance the sale of goods; or

(c) in all other cases, the contract has been concluded with a person who pursues commercial or professional activities in the Member State of the consumer's domicile or, by any means, directs such activities to that Member State or to several States including that Member State, and the contract falls within the scope of such activities.

2. Where a consumer enters into a contract with a party who is not domiciled in a Member State but has a branch, agency or other establishment in one of the Member States, that party shall, in disputes arising out of the operations of the branch, agency or establishment, be deemed to be domiciled in that Member State.

3. This Section shall not apply to a contract of transport other than a contract which, for an inclusive price, provides for a combination of travel and accommodation.

Article 18

1. A consumer may bring proceedings against the other party to a contract either in the courts of the Member State in which that party is domiciled or, regardless of the domicile of the other party, in the courts for the place where the consumer is domiciled.

2. Proceedings may be brought against a consumer by the other party to the contract only in the courts of the Member State in which the consumer is domiciled.

3. This Article shall not affect the right to bring a counter-claim in the court in which, in accordance with this Section, the original claim is pending.

Article 19

The provisions of this Section may be departed from only by an agreement:

(1) which is entered into after the dispute has arisen;

(2) which allows the consumer to bring proceedings in courts other than those indicated in this Section; or

(3) which is entered into by the consumer and the other party to the contract, both of whom are at the time of conclusion of the contract domiciled or habitually resident in the same Member State, and which confers jurisdiction on the courts of that Member State, provided that such an agreement is not contrary to the law of that Member State.

* * *

Section 6. Exclusive Jurisdiction

Article 24

The following courts of a Member State shall have exclusive jurisdiction, regardless of the domicile of the parties:

(1) in proceedings which have as their object rights *in rem* in immovable property or tenancies of immovable property, the courts of the Member State in which the property is situated.

However, in proceedings which have as their object tenancies of immovable property concluded for temporary private use for a maximum period of six consecutive months, the courts of the Member State in which the defendant is domiciled shall also have jurisdiction, provided that the tenant is a natural person and that the landlord and the tenant are domiciled in the same Member State;

(2) in proceedings which have as their object the validity of the constitution, the nullity or the dissolution of companies or other legal persons or associations of natural or legal persons, or the validity of the decisions of their organs, the courts of the Member State in which the company, legal person or association has its seat. In order to determine that seat, the court shall apply its rules of private international law;

(3) in proceedings which have as their object the validity of entries in public registers, the courts of the Member State in which the register is kept;

(4) in proceedings concerned with the registration or validity of patents, trade marks, designs, or other similar rights required to be deposited or registered, irrespective of whether the issue is raised by way of an action or as a defence, the courts of the Member State in which the deposit or registration has been applied for, has taken place or is under the terms of an instrument of the Union or an international convention deemed to have taken place.

Without prejudice to the jurisdiction of the European Patent Office under the Convention on the Grant of European Patents, signed at Munich on 5 October 1973, the courts of each Member State shall have exclusive jurisdiction in proceedings concerned with the registration or validity of any European patent granted for that Member State;

(5) in proceedings concerned with the enforcement of judgments, the courts of the Member State in which the judgment has been or is to be enforced.

Section 7. Prorogation of Jurisdiction

Article 25

1. If the parties, regardless of their domicile, have agreed that a court or the courts of a Member State are to have jurisdiction to settle any disputes which have arisen or which may arise in connection with a particular legal relationship, that court or those courts shall have jurisdiction, unless the agreement is null and void as to its substantive validity under the law of that Member State. Such jurisdiction shall be exclusive unless the parties have agreed otherwise. The agreement conferring jurisdiction shall be either:

(a) in writing or evidenced in writing;

(b) in a form which accords with practices which the parties have established between themselves; or

(c) in international trade or commerce, in a form which accords with a usage of which the parties are or ought to have been aware and which in such trade or commerce is widely known to, and regularly observed by, parties to contracts of the type involved in the particular trade or commerce concerned.

2. Any communication by electronic means which provides a durable record of the agreement shall be equivalent to 'writing'.

3. The court or courts of a Member State on which a trust instrument has conferred jurisdiction shall have exclusive jurisdiction in any proceedings brought against a settlor, trustee or beneficiary, if relations between those persons or their rights or obligations under the trust are involved.

* * *

5. An agreement conferring jurisdiction which forms part of a contract shall be treated as an agreement independent of the other terms of the contract.

The validity of the agreement conferring jurisdiction cannot be contested solely on the ground that the contract is not valid.

Article 26

1. Apart from jurisdiction derived from other provisions of this Regulation, a court of a Member State before which a defendant enters an appearance shall have jurisdiction. This rule shall not apply where appearance was entered to contest the jurisdiction, or where another court has exclusive jurisdiction by virtue of Article 24.

* * *

CHAPTER III—RECOGNITION AND ENFORCEMENT

Section 1. Recognition

Article 36

1. A judgment given in a Member State shall be recognised in the other Member States without any special procedure being required.

2. Any interested party may, in accordance with the procedure provided for in Subsection 2 of Section 3, apply for a decision that there are no grounds for refusal of recognition as referred to in Article 45.

3. If the outcome of proceedings in a court of a Member State depends on the determination of an incidental question of refusal of recognition, that court shall have jurisdiction over that question.

Article 37

1. A party who wishes to invoke in a Member State a judgment given in another Member State shall produce:

(a) a copy of the judgment which satisfies the conditions necessary to establish its authenticity; and

(b) the certificate issued pursuant to Article 53.

2. The court or authority before which a judgment given in another Member State is invoked may, where necessary, require the party invoking it to provide, in accordance with Article 57, a translation or a transliteration of the contents of the certificate referred to in point (b) of paragraph 1. The court or authority may require the party to provide a translation of the judgment instead of a translation of the contents of the certificate if it is unable to proceed without such a translation.

Article 38

The court or authority before which a judgment given in another Member State is invoked may suspend the proceedings, in whole or in part, if:

(a) the judgment is challenged in the Member State of origin; or

(b) an application has been submitted for a decision that there are no grounds for refusal of recognition as referred to in Article 45 or for a decision that the recognition is to be refused on the basis of one of those grounds.

Section 2. Enforcement

Article 39

A judgment given in a Member State which is enforceable in that Member State shall be enforceable in the other Member States without any declaration of enforceability being required.

Article 40

An enforceable judgment shall carry with it by operation of law the power to proceed to any protective measures which exist under the law of the Member State addressed.

Article 41

1. Subject to the provisions of this Section, the procedure for the enforcement of judgments given in another Member State shall be governed by the law of the Member State addressed. A judgment given in a Member State which is enforceable in the Member State addressed shall be enforced there under the same conditions as a judgment given in the Member State addressed.

2. Notwithstanding paragraph 1, the grounds for refusal or of suspension of enforcement under the law of the Member State addressed shall apply in so far as they are not incompatible with the grounds referred to in Article 45.

3. The party seeking the enforcement of a judgment given in another Member State shall not be required to have a postal address in the Member State addressed. Nor shall that party be required to have an authorised representative in the Member State addressed unless such a representative is mandatory irrespective of the nationality or the domicile of the parties.

Article 42

1. For the purposes of enforcement in a Member State of a judgment given in another Member State, the applicant shall provide the competent enforcement authority with:

(a) a copy of the judgment which satisfies the conditions necessary to establish its authenticity; and

(b) the certificate issued pursuant to Article 53, certifying that the judgment is enforceable and containing an extract of the judgment as well as, where appropriate, relevant information on the recoverable costs of the proceedings and the calculation of interest.

2. For the purposes of enforcement in a Member State of a judgment given in another Member State ordering a provisional,

including a protective, measure, the applicant shall provide the competent enforcement authority with:

(a) a copy of the judgment which satisfies the conditions necessary to establish its authenticity;

(b) the certificate issued pursuant to Article 53, containing a description of the measure and certifying that:

(i) the court has jurisdiction as to the substance of the matter;

(ii) the judgment is enforceable in the Member State of origin; and

(c) where the measure was ordered without the defendant being summoned to appear, proof of service of the judgment.

3. The competent enforcement authority may, where necessary, require the applicant to provide, in accordance with Article 57, a translation or a transliteration of the contents of the certificate.

4. The competent enforcement authority may require the applicant to provide a translation of the judgment only if it is unable to proceed without such a translation.

Article 43

1. Where enforcement is sought of a judgment given in another Member State, the certificate issued pursuant to Article 53 shall be served on the person against whom the enforcement is sought prior to the first enforcement measure. The certificate shall be accompanied by the judgment, if not already served on that person.

2. Where the person against whom enforcement is sought is domiciled in a Member State other than the Member State of origin, he may request a translation of the judgment in order to contest the enforcement if the judgment is not written in or accompanied by a translation into either of the following languages:

(a) a language which he understands; or

(b) the official language of the Member State in which he is domiciled or, where there are several official languages in that Member State, the official language or one of the official languages of the place where he is domiciled.

Where a translation of the judgment is requested under the first subparagraph, no measures of enforcement may be taken other than protective measures until that translation has been provided to the person against whom enforcement is sought.

This paragraph shall not apply if the judgment has already been served on the person against whom enforcement is sought in one of the languages referred to in the first subparagraph or is accompanied by a translation into one of those languages.

3. This Article shall not apply to the enforcement of a protective measure in a judgment or where the person seeking enforcement proceeds to protective measures in accordance with Article 40.

Article 44

1. In the event of an application for refusal of enforcement of a judgment pursuant to Subsection 2 of Section 3, the court in the Member State addressed may, on the application of the person against whom enforcement is sought:

(a) limit the enforcement proceedings to protective measures;

(b) make enforcement conditional on the provision of such security as it shall determine; or

(c) suspend, either wholly or in part, the enforcement proceedings.

2. The competent authority in the Member State addressed shall, on the application of the person against whom enforcement is sought, suspend the enforcement proceedings where the enforceability of the judgment is suspended in the Member State of origin.

Section 3. Refusal of Recognition and Enforcement

Subsection 1

REFUSAL OF RECOGNITION

Article 45

1. On the application of any interested party, the recognition of a judgment shall be refused:

(a) if such recognition is manifestly contrary to public policy (ordre public) in the Member State addressed;

(b) where the judgment was given in default of appearance, if the defendant was not served with the document which instituted the proceedings or with an equivalent document in sufficient time and in such a way as to enable him to arrange for his defence, unless the defendant failed to commence proceedings to challenge

(c) if the judgment is irreconcilable with a judgment given between the same parties in the Member State addressed;

(d) if the judgment is irreconcilable with an earlier judgment given in another Member State or in a third State involving the same cause of action and between the same parties, provided that the earlier judgment fulfils the conditions necessary for its recognition in the Member State addressed; or

(e) if the judgment conflicts with:

(i) Sections 3, 4 or 5 of Chapter II where the policyholder, the insured, a beneficiary of the insurance contract, the injured party, the consumer or the employee was the defendant; or

(ii) Section 6 of Chapter II.

2. In its examination of the grounds of jurisdiction referred to in point (e) of paragraph 1, the court to which the application was submitted shall be bound by the findings of fact on which the court of origin based its jurisdiction.

3. Without prejudice to point (e) of paragraph 1, the jurisdiction of the court of origin may not be reviewed. The test of public policy referred to in point (a) of paragraph 1 may not be applied to the rules relating to jurisdiction.

4. The application for refusal of recognition shall be made in accordance with the procedures provided for in Subsection 2 and, where appropriate, Section 4.

Subsection 2

REFUSAL OF ENFORCEMENT

Article 46

On the application of the person against whom enforcement is sought, the enforcement of a judgment shall be refused where one of the grounds referred to in Article 45 is found to exist.

Article 47

1. The application for refusal of enforcement shall be submitted to the court which the Member State concerned has communicated to the Commission pursuant to point (a) of Article 75 as the court to which the application is to be submitted.

2. The procedure for refusal of enforcement shall, in so far as it is not covered by this Regulation, be governed by the law of the Member State addressed.

3. The applicant shall provide the court with a copy of the judgment and, where necessary, a translation or transliteration of it.

The court may dispense with the production of the documents referred to in the first subparagraph if it already possesses them or if it considers it unreasonable to require the applicant to provide them. In the latter case, the court may require the other party to provide those documents.

4. The party seeking the refusal of enforcement of a judgment given in another Member State shall not be required to have a postal address in the Member State addressed. Nor shall that party be required to have an authorised representative in the Member State addressed unless such a representative is mandatory irrespective of the nationality or the domicile of the parties.

Article 48

The court shall decide on the application for refusal of enforcement without delay.

Article 49

1. The decision on the application for refusal of enforcement may be appealed against by either party.

2. The appeal is to be lodged with the court which the Member State concerned has communicated to the Commission pursuant to point (b) of Article 75 as the court with which such an appeal is to be lodged.

* * *

Section 4. Common Provisions

Article 52

Under no circumstances may a judgment given in a Member State be reviewed as to its substance in the Member State addressed.

* * *

Article 55

A judgment given in a Member State which orders a payment by way of a penalty shall be enforceable in the Member State addressed only if the amount of the payment has been finally determined by the court of origin.

* * *

Chapter 9

LITIGATING EU BUSINESS LAW

Table of Sections

Under NAFTA 1994, virtually all dispute settlement resembles arbitration. See Chapter 4. There is no North American Court of Justice. In Europe, there has been an explosive growth in litigation of European Union business law. EU legislation and administrative decisions present fertile fields of European law litigation. The range of EU business law issues being litigated is vast. The bulk of this growth has taken place in private litigation before national courts and tribunals. They are vested with wide (but not final) authority to resolve EU legal issues. That authority rests with the European Court of Justice and its associated General Court, supreme arbiters of the enormous body of EU business law.

For example, contracts disputes can raise a host of Union law questions. Is an exclusive dealing distribution contract enforceable as a matter of competition law? Can goods to which a sales contract applies be freely traded in the Common Market? Is payment for sales across borders protected by EU law? Is there strict product liability under EU law? Does an employment contract fail to provide equal pay for equal work? Can employees be terminated because of their nationality? May patent licensing agreements contain grant-back clauses? Can franchisees be limited to certain geographic markets? What joint ventures can be established for research and development purposes? Just how far can EU business competition law reach jurisdictionally? See Section 5.6. How is the EU Regulation on Jurisdiction and Recognition and Enforcement of Judgments in Civil and Commercial Matters (see Chapter 8) to be interpreted? How uniform is EU customs law? When can customs officers seize goods in transit between member states? Can national authorities deny EU nationals the right to establish a business? What about foreign investors? Can they require residency or work permits?

These questions only scratch the surface of EU business law litigation. Here is an abbreviated listing of business law fields impacted by EU law: VAT, excise and corporate taxation, government subsidies, procurement, products liability, consumer protection, advertising, securities, company law and corporate governance, environmental policy, energy, broadcasting, computer software and databases, biotechnology, telecommunications, research and development, occupational health and safety, employment law, agriculture, fisheries, intellectual property rights, e-commerce, e-privacy, pharmaceuticals, food products, banking, insurance, investment services, transportation, customs duties and regulations, international trade and foreign investment agreements, mergers and acquisitions, hostile takeovers and more. . . . lots more! Rare is the field of business law not touched by European Union law.

Coverage of all these areas of EU law, along with the Treaty on the European Union (TEU) and the Treaty on the Functioning of the European Union (TFEU), can be found in R. Folsom, *Principles of European Union Law including BREXIT*.

§ 9.0 Supremacy Doctrine

None of the European Union treaties addresses the question of what to do when national and Union laws are in conflict. There is no supremacy clause analogous to that found in the United States constitution. The issue is absolutely critical to the success or failure of European Union law in all its manifestations; the founding treaties, directives, regulations, ECJ and GC decisions, international obligations, the general principles of Union law, etc. Its omission from the treaties was perhaps necessary to secure their passage through various national parliaments. But the issue did not disappear, it was merely left to the European Court to resolve.

In a very famous 1964 decision, the Court ruled that it simply had to be the case that Union law is supreme.[1] The Court reasoned that the whole of the Common Market edifice would be at risk if national laws at variance with regional law could be retained or enacted:

"The transfer by the states from their domestic legal systems to the Community [Union] legal system of the rights and obligations arising under the Treaty carries with it a permanent limitation of their sovereign rights, against which a subsequent unilateral act incompatible with the concept of the Community cannot prevail."

The Reform Treaty of 2009, via Declaration No. 17, confirms the supremacy of EU law when undertaken within its conferred powers.

Invalidity of National Laws

Under its supremacy doctrine, the European Court of Justice has (effectively speaking) invalidated countless national laws as in conflict with EU law. It is conceivable that such laws could retain validity in cases not involving a conflict, although this would be a rare event. Supremacy notwithstanding, one of the Declarations to the 1993 Maastricht Accord indicates that European Union does not prevent member states from maintaining or introducing more stringent law on working conditions, social policy, consumer protection and the environment, provided those laws are compatible with the TFEU. This Declaration is consistent with the relevant provisions of the Treaty on these subjects.

Repeal or amendment of conflicting national law is a duty of the member states that can be reviewed by the Court of Justice in further legal proceedings.[2] An alternative growing in use and encouraged by the European Court is creative judicial interpretation by national courts so as to incorporate Union law requirements and avoid conflicts.[3] For quite some time after *Costa v. ENEL,* and even somewhat today, national courts, legislatures and executive branches have resented the supremacy doctrine. They adhere, in the end, to this judge-made law because of their mutual interest in the success of the Union enterprise and their respect for the rule of law by its prestigious Court. That said, it is certainly the case that avoiding the jurisdiction of the ECJ and its supremacy doctrine was one reason behind the BREXIT movement. See R. Folsom, *Principles of European Union Law including BREXIT,* Chapter 1.

---

1 Costa v. ENEL (1964) Eur.Comm.Rep. 585.

2 Commission v. France (1981) Eur.Comm.Rep. 2299.

3 Von Colson and Kamann v. Land Nordrhein-Westfalen (1984) Eur.Comm.Rep. 1891.

§ 9.1 Direct Effects Doctrine

The right to commence litigation in national forums must be given to the plaintiff by national law. In other words, European Union law has not (as yet) been interpreted to create national causes of action.[4] What it does do, according to the "direct effects doctrine," is give litigants the right to raise many issues ("Euro-defenses" and "Euro-offenses") in national courts and tribunals. In doing so, individuals often function as guardians of the founding treaties. When challenging member state governments, private parties rely on the "vertical direct effect" of EU law. When asserting rights against other private parties, the "horizontal direct effect" of EU law applies. Americans might analogize this role to that of "private attorneys general," a law enforcement technique adopted in a number of United States statutes. The Court of Justice has noted that the vigilance of private litigants enforcing their rights is an important element in the Union's legal system.[5]

The direct effects ("*l'effet utile*") doctrine is, to a very large degree, a product of the jurisprudence of the European Court of Justice. It can apply to EU treaties, directives, regulations, decisions and international agreements. When any of these measures are of direct effect, this impact generally commences from the date of its entry into force.[6] But the direct effects doctrine is not automatically applied. For example, although the General Agreement on Tariffs and Trade (GATT) is binding upon the Union and its member states, it has typically been construed by the Court not to have direct legal effects.[7] Likewise, WTO agreements are unlikely to have direct effect.[8] Both the Council of Ministers and the European Council tend to issue resolutions or declarations when there is a political consensus but no desire to adopt legislation. For the most part, the

---

4 *See* Wöhrmann v. Commission, 1962 Eur.Comm.Rep. 501 (Plea of illegality does not amount to an independent cause of action).

5 Van Gend en Loos v. Nederlandse Administratie der Belastingen (1963) Eur.Comm.Rep. 585.

6 Amministrazione delle Finanze v. Salumi (1980) Eur.Comm.Rep. 1237.

7 *See* International Fruit Company v. Produktschap voor Groenten en Fruit (1972) Eur.Comm.Rep. 1219; FEDIOL v. Commission (1989) Eur.Comm.Rep. 1781 (Case 70/87); Germany v. Council (1994) Eur.Comm.Rep. I–4973 (bananas). Compare Bresciani v. Amministrazione delle Finanze (1976) Eur.Comm.Rep. 129 (Yaoundé Convention trade agreements directly effective and thus override conflicting national law); Hauptzollamt Mainz v. Kupferberg (1982) Eur.Comm.Rep. 3641 (EC-Portugal Free Trade Agreement has direct effect).

8 Portuguese Republic v. Council, (1998) Eur.Comm.Rep. I–7379. *See* Schieving-Nijstad Vof v. Groeneveld (2001) Eur.Comm.Rep. I–5851.

Court of Justice has held such acts incapable of creating direct legal effects in the member states.[9]

Regulations

The legal effects of regulations are the easiest to understand. Article 288 TFEU provides that regulations are "directly applicable in all member states." In other words, regulations have immediate, unconditional legal effect without any need for national implementation. They are law in the member states from the moment of issuance, binding upon all individuals, business organizations and governments.[10] For litigants, when regulations are applicable, they control the outcome. This is true under the supremacy doctrine even in the face of contrary national law.[11]

Directives

Directives are more difficult to understand. Article 288 does *not* specify that they shall have "direct applicability." In part, their design prohibits this. Directives are addressed to member states, instructing them to implement (in whatever way is required) certain Union policies within a fixed timetable. These policies do not become law in the member states until implemented or, if timely implementation does not follow, until the European Court rules that the directive is of "direct effect." Some national courts, notably in France, have opposed this judge-made doctrine.[12]

Not all directives have direct effect. The Court of Justice has selectively ruled that only those directives that establish clear and unconditional legal norms and do not leave normative discretion to the member states are of direct effect.[13] Most "framework" (action plan) directives will not meet these criteria. Once the ECJ has decided that a European Union directive has direct effect, litigants can rely on it to the full extent of its application to member states,

---

[9] Pubblico Ministero v. Manghera (1976) Eur.Comm.Rep. 91; Schülter v. Hauptzollamt Lörrach (1973) Eur.Comm.Rep. 1135.

[10] *See, e.g.*, Politi SAS v. Ministry of Finance of the Italian Republic (1971) Eur.Comm.Rep. 1039; Fratelli Zerbone SNC v. Amministrazione delle Finanze (1978) Eur.Comm.Rep. 99.

[11] *See especially*, Variola v. Amministrazione delle Finanze dello Stato (1973) Eur.Comm.Rep. 981 (no member state legislation necessary or permissible after EU regulation).

[12] *See especially*, In re Cohn-Bendit (1978) 1979 Common Mkt.L.Rep. 702 (French Conseil d'Etat); German Federal Tax Court (Bundesfinanzhof) V.B. 51/80 (July 16, 1980), *reversed on appeal* In re Application of Frau Kloppenburg (1988) 3 Comm.Mkt.L.Rep. 1 (Fed.Constit.Ct.1987).

[13] Van Duyn v. Home Office (1974) Eur.Comm.Rep. 1337; Becker v. Finanzamt Münster-Innenstadt (1982) Eur.Comm.Rep. 53.

public service entities,[14] and local governments.[15] Litigants can challenge contrary national law, including defective implementing measures if required, and can challenge criminal laws.[16]

Interpretative Duties

Unlike regulations, directives cannot be used to challenge private activities. Thus it is said that directives do not have "horizontal" direct effects.[17] Even so, the Court of Justice has held that in applying national law the national courts and tribunals are required by Article 4(3) TEU to interpret their law in light of the wording and purposes of all EU directives.[18] National law must be interpreted in the light of regional directives even if the directive has not yet been implemented.[19] Some commentators have characterized these duties as involving the "indirect effect" of directives.

The obligation to interpret national law in view of EU directives "is limited by the general principles of law which form part of Union law and in particular the principles of legal certainty and non-retroactivity."[20] Even so, in considerable private litigation before the tribunals and courts of member states, directives will be given effect through judicial interpretations of national law. This is likely to have the same practical impact as would adoption of a "horizontal" direct effects doctrine at the regional level. Morseover, it has been argued that Article 4(3) TEU mandates that *all* provisions of national law (not just those touched by Union directives) must be interpreted in conformity with all European Union law (not just directives).[21] If this argument becomes binding law, the doctrine of direct effects will reach a zenith which few would have ever dreamed.

---

[14] Foster v. British Gas (1990) 1 Eur.Comm.Rep. 3313.

[15] Fratelli Costanzo v. Milano (1989) Eur.Comm.Rep. 1839.

[16] Pubblico Ministero v. Ratti (1979) Eur.Comm.Rep. 1629; Criminal Proceedings against Bordessa (1995) Eur.Comm.Rep. I–361.

[17] Marshall v. Southampton and South West Hampshire Area Health Authority (teaching) (1986) Eur.Comm.Rep. 723. Faccini Dori v. RECREB SRL (1994) Eur.Comm.Rep. I–3325 (consumer contract rights denied because of state failure to timely implement directive).

[18] *See* Von Colson v. Land Nordrhein-Westfalen (1984) Eur.Comm.Rep. 1891; Oberkreisdirektor des Kreises Borken v. Moormann (1988) Eur.Comm.Rep. 4869; Lister v. Forth Dry Dock Engineering Co., 1 All Eng.Rep. 1194 (House of Lords, 1989) (*Von Colson* principles followed in employee rights case).

[19] Marleasing SA v. La Comercial Internacional de Alimentación SA (1990) 1 Eur.Comm.Rep. 4135 (Compare Duke v. GEC Reliance, 1 All Eng.Rep. 626 (House of Lords, 1988) (*Von Colson* principles not followed in equal treatment case)).

[20] Case 80/86, Officier van Justitie v. Kolpinghuis Nijmegen (1987) Eur.Comm.Rep. 3969.

[21] *See* Barber v. Guardian Royal Exchange Assurance Group (1990) 1 Eur.Comm.Rep. 1889 (Advocate General's Opinion). *See also* Grimaldi v. Fonds des Maladies Professionnelles (1990) Eur.Comm.Rep. I–04407 (Case 322/88) (EU Recommendations have indirect effect).

§ 9.2 Directly Effective EU Treaty Provisions

The third major category of directly effective law originates in the founding treaties. The Court of Justice has ruled that parts of these treaties are capable of having immediate, binding legal effect in the member states. Here again the Court has been selective, sorting out which treaty provisions establish clear, unconditional and nondiscretionary legal norms. Those many articles of the treaties that are largely aspirational, procedural or written as guidelines for the exercise of member state discretion are unlikely to have direct effect.[22]

The Court of Justice has consistently refused to view the treaties as merely creating obligations among the contracting states. Citing Article 267 TFEU, the Court finds acknowledgment that the TFEU was intended to have effect in national legal regimes:

"The conclusion to be drawn. . . is that the Community [Union] constitutes a new legal order of international law for the benefit of which the States have limited their sovereign rights, albeit within limited fields, and the subjects of which comprise not only Member States but also their nationals. Independently of the legislation of Member States, Community law therefore not only imposes obligations on individuals but is also intended to confer upon them rights which become part of their legal heritage. These rights arise not only where they are expressly granted by the Treaty, but also by reason of obligations which the Treaty imposes in a clearly defined way upon individuals as well as upon the Member States and the institutions of the Community."[23]

Once the Court has held a TFEU term directly effective in the member states, litigants before national courts and tribunals can rely fully upon it. They can, under the supremacy doctrine, use it to set aside contradictory national law. Like regulations, directly effective Treaty provisions can apply horizontally to private parties.[24] This follows, in the court's view, because national courts are an arm of the states that signed the Treaty and therefore bound to apply the law in all cases. The same logic has not been carried over to directives.[25]

---

[22] *See* Spa Salgoil v. Italian Ministry for Foreign Trade (1968) Eur.Comm.Rep. 453 (Articles 33(1) and (2) discretionary and not directly effective).

[23] Van Gend en Loos v. Nederlandse Administratie der Belastingen (1963) Eur.Comm.Rep. 1.

[24] Defrenne v. Sabena (1976) Eur.Comm.Rep. 455.

[25] Marshall v. Southampton and South West Hampshire Area Health Authority (teaching) (1986) Eur.Comm.Rep. 723.

Directly Effective Treaty Provisions

The following is a partial list of the articles of the TFEU that have been held directly effective by the European Court of Justice. Many of these decisions are qualified.

Article 18	no discrimination on grounds of nationality
Articles 28–29	customs union free trade rules
Article 30	no internal customs duties or measures of equivalent effect
Article 34	no internal trade quotas or measures of equivalent effect
Article 36	no disguised restraints on internal trade
Article 37	state trading monopolies cannot discriminate between nationals
Article 45	free movement and employment of workers without nationality discriminations
Article 49	right of establishment for self-employed
Article 55	no discrimination on capital participation in companies
Article 56(1)	freedom to provide services across borders
Article 57(3)	national treatment of cross-border service providers
Articles 63–65	current payments and capital transfers
Articles 92, 95, 96	transport discriminations prohibited
Articles 101, 106	competition law prohibitions
Articles 107(1), 108(3)	state subsidies cannot distort competition without Commission approval
Article 110	national treatment on taxation of goods
Article 111	no excessive tax rebates upon exports
Article 157	equal pay for equal work, equal treatment

The following treaty provisions have generally been held *not* to have direct legal effect. Again, many of these ECJ decisions are qualified.

Article 4(3), TEU	member state obligations to facilitate and not jeopardize Treaty
Article 108	state subsidies
Article 117	harmonization of laws
Article 130	balance of payments

§ 9.3 National Legal Remedies for Directly Effective EU Law

Directly effective European Union law creates national legal rights and obligations. What remedies can be secured in national courts and tribunals when European law has these effects? The TFEU does not provide a ready answer. In general, the Court of Justice has held that directly effective rights must be enforceable in the national courts by means of remedies that are real, effective and non-discriminatory.[26] Interim or preliminary judicial and administrative remedies may be required to protect directly effective rights when national *or* Union law is challenged.[27]

The precise determination of those remedies is a matter for the national courts to decide. For example, one British court issued a notable interim order requiring public authorities to promise to pay damages if that country's Sunday trading bans ultimately were found invalid under Union law as the "price" for interlocutory injunctions sought by the authorities against Sunday traders.[28] In another British case, the House of Lords referred equal treatment remedial issues concerning a ceiling on recovery of damages and denial of interest to the Court of Justice. The Court ruled against both limitations as inadequate to restore equality of treatment.

---

[26] Rewe Zentralfinanz v. Landwirtschaftskammer Saarland (1976) Eur.Comm.Rep. 1989; Amministrazione delle Finanze v. San Giorgio (1983) Eur.Comm.Rep. 3595; Marshall v. Southampton and South West Hampshire Area Health Authority (1993) Eur.Comm.Rep. I–4367 (Case C–271/91).

[27] Regina v. Secretary of State for Transport (1990) Eur.Comm.Rep. I–2433 (Case C–213/89); Zuckerfabrik Süderdithmarschen v. Hauptzollamt Itzehoe (1991) Eur.Comm.Rep. I–415 (Cases 143/88 and C–92/89).

[28] Kirklees BC v. Wickes Building Supplies, 4 All Eng.Rep. 240 (Court of Appeal, 1991). *See* Torfaen Borough Council v. B & Q PLC Ltd. (1989) Eur.Comm.Rep. 3851.

In Britain, the Court of Appeal ruled that a failure on the part of the government to adhere to TFEU obligations does *not* give rise to an action for damages even when directly effective rights are involved.[29] This litigation was commenced by French turkey producers who lost sales when Britain imposed import restraints, allegedly for animal health reasons. The Court of Justice had previously ruled that the restraints were unlawful under Article 31 as measures of equivalent effect to quotas. The British restraints were not subject to the animal health exception created by Article 30 because they were economically motivated, *i.e.* they were disguised restraints on internal free trade. The plaintiffs in *Bourgoin* apparently could have obtained injunctive relief had Britain continued to impose its restrictions after the European Court's decision.[30]

There was some question whether *Bourgoin* meets the general criteria of the Court of Justice for real, effective and nondiscriminatory national legal remedies when directly effective EU rights are at stake. The case was settled before reaching the House of Lords by payment to Bourgoin of 3.5 million Pounds Sterling for damages, costs and interest by the UK government. Similar remedial issues have been litigated in Britain concerning directly effective European Union competition law.[31] In contrast, the French Conseil d'Etat has awarded damages against the French government for harm caused by a breach of Union law.[32] Dutch law also permits such recoveries,[33] and Spanish law.[34]

Member State Liability for Damages

In a major decision, *Francovich*, the Court of Justice has ruled that member state liability for damages to individuals caused by the state's infringement of Union law is inherent in the scheme of the TFEU.[35] This obligation follows from member state duties under Article 4(3) TEU to ensure fulfillment of EU law. The case involved an Italian failure to implement a directly effective EU directive on employee benefits in the event of insolvency. Whether or not the unimplemented directive is of direct effect does not matter, and

---

29 Bourgoin SA v. Ministry of Agriculture, Fisheries and Food (1985) 3 All Eng.Rep. 585, (1986) 1 Common Mkt.L.Rep. 267.

30 Commission v. United Kingdom (1982) Eur.Comm.Rep. 2793. Accord, Regina v. Secretary of State for Transport (1990) 3 Common Mkt.L.Rep. 375 (House of Lords).

31 Articles 101 and 102.

32 Ministre du Commerce Extérieur v. Alivar (March 23, 1984).

33 Roussel Laboratories (Hague District Court, July 18, 1984).

34 *See* Canal Satélite Digital, Case 1/46/1999 (Spanish Tribunal Supremo, June 12, 2003).

35 Francovich + Ors v. Italian Republic (1991) Eur.Comm.Rep. I–5357 (Cases C–6 and C–9/90).

faulty implementation or retention of contrary domestic law also gives rise to state liability whenever three conditions are met: (1) the law infringed is intended to confer individual rights; (2) the infringement is sufficiently serious; and (3) there is a direct causal link between the breach and damages sustained.[36]

Member state liability for damages generally tracks Community tort liability under Article 340[37] and extends to administrative as well as legislative acts and omissions.[38] In a second major decision, *Kobler*, the Court of Justice has indicated that it is possible for individuals to sue member states for damages when *national courts* exceptionally breach EU law.[39] The Commission has also challenged member state judicial interpretations that run contrary to EU law.[40]

In the absence of precise European Union rules on remedies for directly effective legal rights, the results vary from country to country and context to context. Many cases involve the question of repayment of custom duties, customs charges and taxes paid to governments under national laws that are invalidated by Union law. Others concern national laws implementing EU law which is subsequently invalidated by the Court of Justice.[41] The Court has reiterated in these decisions that the means of recovery for monies unlawfully paid to governments are controlled by national law. Thus, statutes of limitations,[42] the forum, interest on the amounts paid and related issues are national legal questions. The Court has also reiterated that procedural hurdles which discriminate against recoveries based upon EU rights when measured against procedures for similar domestic recoveries do not satisfy the requirements of the TFEU.[43] And, in general, national rules on recovery of unlawful payments to governments cannot have the practical result of making it impossible to recover such sums.[44]

---

[36] Brasserie du Pecheur SA v. Germany, joined Cases C–46, 48/93 (1996) Eur.Comm.Rep. I–1029.

[37] See Section 3.10, R. Folsom, *Principles of European Union Law including BREXIT.*

[38] R. v. Ministry of Agriculture, Fisheries and Food (Hedley Lomas) (1996) Eur.Comm.Rep. I–2553.

[39] Köbler v. Austrian Republic (2003) Eur.Comm.Rep. I–00000 (Case C–224/01).

[40] Commission v. Italy, (2003) Eur.Comm.Rep. I–8003.

[41] Deville v. Administration des Impôts (1988) Eur.Comm.Rep. 3513. *See* Marshall v. Southampton and South West Hampshire Area Health Authority (1993) Eur.Comm.Rep. 4367 (equal treatment remedies).

[42] *But see* Emmott v. Minister for Social Welfare (1991) Eur.Comm.Rep. 4269 (national statutes of limitations do not run until member state has fulfilled Directive duties).

[43] Express Dairy Foods Ltd. v. Intervention Board for Agricultural Produce (1980) Eur.Comm.Rep. 1887.

[44] Compare Re Jules Borker (1980) Eur.Comm.Rep. 1975 (Bar Council of Cour de Paris not a tribunal preliminary ruling request rejected); with Broekmeulen v.

§ 9.4 Article 267—Referrals by National Courts and Preliminary ECJ Rulings

The European Court of Justice derived its doctrine of directly effective law partly from Article 267 TFEU. This article is the linchpin that joins the national legal systems of the member states to the European Court.

Article 267 vests jurisdiction in the European Court to give "preliminary rulings" (sometimes called "advisory rulings") on the interpretation of the Treaty, the validity and interpretation of acts by the Union's institutions and other matters. These rulings occur when national courts or tribunals (faced with an issue of Union law) request them. Professional bodies may or may not constitute "tribunals of a member state" for these purposes.[45] Since the Treaty of Nice (2003), the ECJ has the power to allow some Article 267 cases to go to the Court of First Instance (now the General Court, below). Article 267 proceedings commonly last about 18 months. However, since 2008, highly expedited proceedings are possible regarding police and judicial cooperation in criminal matters, and freedom, security and justice cases.[46]

Discretionary References

Article 267 requests or "references" are discretionary with the judges of the lower-level courts and tribunals of the member states. They cannot be initiated as a matter of right by litigants, nor by arbitrators designated by contract to resolve a dispute when those arbitrators are not functioning as a court or tribunal of a member state.[47] This is a particularly notable decision because ever increasing numbers of business disputes are being taken to binding arbitration. The only recourse for review of an arbitrator's interpretation of Union law is through ancillary or enforcement proceedings in the national courts.

Whenever a national court considers a reference necessary to enable judgment, it may seek the advice of the European Court by posing questions to it. It may do so even when the European Court or

---

Huisgarts Registratie Commissie (1981) Eur.Comm.Rep. 2311 (Dutch Appeals Committee for General Medicine is a tribunal of the state; request accepted).

45 Nordsee v. Reederei Mond (1982) Eur.Comm.Rep. 1095 (German arbitration court reference rejected). *See* Corbiau v. Administration des Contributions (1993) Eur.Comm.Rep. I–1277 (Case C–24/92) (Luxembourg Director of Taxes cannot refer questions under Article 234).

46 Decision 2008/79, OJ L24/42.

47 Nordsee v. Reederei Mond (1982) Eur.Comm.Rep. 1095 (German arbitration court reference rejected). *See* Corbiau v. Administration des Contributions (1993) Eur.Comm.Rep. I–1277 (Case C–24/92) (Luxembourg Director of Taxes cannot refer questions under Article 234).

a higher national court has already ruled on the question of EU law at hand. In other words, the common law doctrine of binding precedent does not remove the discretion of lower courts to invoke Article 267.[48] Similarly, the fact that appeals are mandatory under national law does not block utilization of Article 267 references to the ECJ if the lower court believes such a reference is necessary to enable it to give judgment.[49]

In practice, lower courts refer EU law issues to the ECJ quite regularly. However, these referral decisions may be subject to an interlocutory appeal within the national legal system.[50] Such an appeal will not ordinarily require the ECJ to suspend its review of and decision on the reference.[51] But if the appeal of the referral has the effect under national law of suspending the referral decision, then the Court of Justice will suspend its Article 267 proceeding.[52] Thus, in most cases, the national interlocutory appeal of the referral decision, and the ECJ's Article 267 proceeding, will move forward simultaneously. Should the decision to refer be reversed on appeal, the Court of Justice will terminate its proceeding and not rule under Article 267.[53]

Assuming the request comes from a proper national court or tribunal, the European Court of Justice cannot refuse the reference, even when it has already ruled on the EU legal issue.[54] Once underway, the Commission almost always files a written brief expressing its opinion in Article 267 proceedings. The government of the member state whose court or tribunal is the source of the reference typically does so as well. Private parties "interested" in the questions being referred may not intervene.[55] After a preliminary ruling of the European Court is secured, the national court is obliged to implement that ruling in its final judgment.[56] The ruling is also

---

48 Rheinmühlen-Düsseldorf v. Einfuhr-und Vorratsstelle für Getreide und Futtermittel (1974) Eur.Comm.Rep. 33. *But see* to the contrary Duke v. GEC Reliance Systems Ltd. (1987) 2 Common Mkt.L.Rep. 24 (English Court of Appeal).

49 Mecanarte-Metalurgica da Lagoa Lda v. Chefe do Servico da Conferencia final da Alfandega do Porto (1991) Eur.Comm.Rep. I–3277 (Case C–348/89).

50 Rheinmühlen-Düsseldorf v. Einfuhr-und Vorratsstelle für Getreide und Futtermittel (1974) Eur.Comm.Rep. 33. *But see* Campus Oil Ltd. v. Minister for Industry and Energy (1984) 1 Common Mkt.L.Rep. 479 (Irish Supreme Court, 1983) (Article 234 references not subject to interlocutory appeal under Irish law).

51 *Id.*

52 SA Chanel v. Cepeha Handels Maatschappij NV (1970) Eur.Comm.Rep. 404.

53 Rheinmühlen, *supra.*

54 Re Da Costa en Schaake (1963) Eur.Comm.Rep. 11.

55 Biogen Inc. v. Smithkline Beecham Biological S.A. (1996) Eur.Comm.Rep. I–717.

56 Rewe Zentralfinanz v. Landwirtschaftskammer Saarland (1976) Eur. Comm.Rep. 1989.

binding on appeal of that judgment, and (at a minimum) persuasive in courts of other nations.[57]

Validity of EU and National Laws

The discretion of national courts to refer EU law questions to the European Court is largely removed whenever the question is one of the *invalidity* (not interpretation) of Union law. Such invalidity is ordinarily retrospective, nullifying EU law *ab initio*.[58] The Court of Justice has ruled that only it and not the national courts can determine the invalidity of an EU legal measure. The Court reasoned that divergent invalidity determinations could place the unity of the Union's legal order in jeopardy and detract from the general principle of legal certainty. However, national courts can declare EU legislation valid and proceed accordingly.[59]

There is a dispute as to whether the European Court can pronounce without request upon the effects of an invalid Union measure, *e.g.* whether monies paid previously can be recovered. The Court asserts the power to spell out the consequences of its invalidity rulings under Article 267 TFEU.[60] It draws upon the analogy to Article 264 which conveys to the ECJ the power to determine the effects of decisions made in the context of Article 263 challenges to Council, Commission, Parliamentary or other EU action.[61]

The highest French courts have been split as to the duty to follow the Court's Article 267 rulings on the consequences of invalid Union law. The Cour de Cassation has adhered, while the Conseil d'Etat has rejected. The Conseil d'Etat limits adherence to ECJ rulings to the scope of the questions posed by the national courts. The Court's rulings on repayment in *Roquette* were treated as gratuitous and not controlling since not requested.[62] This dispute illustrates, more generally, the distinct tendency on the part of the European Court not to see itself confined by the limits of the questions posed by national forums under Article 267. Rarely, however, has such a hostile national response been received upon delivery of the ruling.

On questions of the validity of *national* laws under the EU legal regime, the lower courts retain complete discretion to use the Article

---

57 International Chemical Corp. v. Amministrazione delle Finanze (1983) Eur.Comm.Rep. 119; SpA Int'l Chemical Corp. v. Amministrazione delle Finanze dello Stato (1981) Eur.Comm.Rep. 1191.

58 Roquette Frères SA v. Hauptzollamt Geldern (1994) Eur.Comm.Rep. I–01445 (Case C–228/92). *See* Firma Foto-Frost v. Hauptzollamt Lübeck-Ost (1987) Eur.Comm.Rep. 4199.

59 *Id.*

60 Roquette v. French Customs (1980) Eur.Comm.Rep. 2917.

61 See Section 9.7, *Principles of European Union Law including BREXIT*.

62 Conseil d'Etat (1985) Rec. des Décisions 233.

267 reference procedure, or to immediately set aside national laws under the supremacy doctrine.[63] Genuine disputes as to the compatibility of the national law of another member state may be referred to the European Court under Article 267. The Court will provide criteria for interpreting Union law so as to enable the referring court to solve the legal problem it faces. For example, in one decision on reference from a German court, by implication the European Court suggested that an Italian law conflicted with Directive 76/768 on cosmetics.[64]

Nevertheless, the Court's preliminary ruling jurisdiction cannot be invoked through "sham litigation" where there is no genuine dispute before the national court, only a desire to challenge the validity of national law.[65] Purely hypothetical questions, and questions the ECJ believes are not connected to the underlying dispute, will not be answered by Court when responding under Article 267.[66] The Court of Justice has also begun to reject Article 267 references that fail to provide adequate factual and legal information to enable it to respond.

Mandatory References

In the early years, lower courts and tribunals in the member states hesitated to invoke the preliminary ruling procedure of Article 267. In some cases, this was a matter of ignorance, in others a matter of national pride. Over the years, Article 267 references of EU law issues have risen dramatically. Today, they amount to about half of the Court's caseload. Article 267 references are undertaken not only out of need for advice, but also a growing sense of judicial cooperation in the Union. Absent such cooperation, there is a great risk that different interpretations of European law would proliferate among member state forums.

For the lower courts, Article 267 references are discretionary. For courts of last resort (no appeal as a matter of right), Article 267 *requires* a reference to the European Court except in interlocutory proceedings.[67] This requirement insures that the European Court will have the last and supreme word on EU legal issues. Thus, if a litigant is willing to exhaust his or her national judicial remedies,

---

[63] See Section 2.12, R. Folsom, *Principles of European Union Law including BREXIT.*

[64] Kommanditgesellschaft Eau de Cologne et al. v. Provide SRI (1989) Eur. Comm.Rep. 3891.

[65] Foglia v. Novello (1980) Eur.Comm.Rep. 745; (1981) Eur.Comm.Rep. 3045.

[66] *See* Wienand Meilicke v. ADV/ORGA F.A. Meyer AG (1992) Eur.Comm.Rep. I–04871 (Case C–83/91); Manuel José Lourenço Dàz v. Director da Alfânndega do Porto (1992) Eur.Comm.Rep. I–04673 (Case C–343/90); Re der Weduwe (2002) Eur.Comm.Rep. I–11319 (Case C–153/00).

[67] Hoffmann LaBroche v. Centrafarm (1977) Eur.Comm.Rep. 957.

access to the European Court is supposed to be guaranteed. In many instances, this is exactly what happens. In others, the doctrine of "acte clair" has been invoked so as to avoid mandatory Article 267 references.

§ 9.5 Acte Clair

"Acte clair" originates in the French law. It posits that appeals need not be taken whenever the law and result in the case at hand are clear. Appeals in such circumstances are wasteful of judicial and litigant time and energy. The problem in the European Union context, of course, is that differences of opinion as to the clarity of EU law will often exist. Indeed, since the Court of Justice has on occasion reversed itself,[68] one could argue that absolute clarity in EU Law never exists. If abused by national courts of last resort, acte clair could break rather than occasionally remove the linchpin of Article 267.

Entreprises Garoche Case

The *Entreprises Garoche* case provides a good example of French invocation of acte clair so as to totally avoid an Article 267 reference. A Dutch boat builder entered into a three-year exclusive dealing agreement with a French agent concerning France, Belgium, Switzerland, Monaco, and Corsica. The Dutch builder undertook to refrain from selling in these territories directly or indirectly through agents. Shortly thereafter he sold two boats through an Italian dealer to two customers domiciled in Monaco. The French agent sued for breach of the exclusive dealing contract. The Tribunal de Commerce de Paris awarded him damages.

The Cour d'Appel de Paris and then the Cour de Cassation held that the contract was void under Article 101 TFEU and not subject (for lack of notification to the Commission) to individual exemption under Article 101(3). Furthermore, the contract was outside the protection afforded by group exemption Regulation 67/67 because the isolation of national markets from other distributors resulted in high prices being charged by the French agent and hence did not allow consumers "a fair share of the resulting benefit." Thus the principle of the illegality under Article 101(1) of absolute territorial protection clauses prevailed.[69] Moreover, the direct effect of EU competition law in the French courts was not in doubt. The Dutch builder could rely on it as a matter of right.

---

[68] *See* In re Keck and Mithouard, Joined Cases C–267, 268/91, 1993 Eur.Comm.Rep. I–6097 and Metock v. Minister for Justice, Equality Law Reform, (2008) Eur.Comm.Rep. I–6241 (Case C–127/08).

[69] *See* Chapter 7, R. Folsom, *Principles of European Union Law including BREXIT*.

None of these three French courts found it necessary to refer any of the issues in *Entreprises Garoche* to the European Court of Justice. Both the Tribunal de Commerce and the Cour d'Appel invoked the acte clair doctrine while noting that their decisions were subject to appeal and hence not mandatorily referable. The Cour de Cassation, from which no appeal lies under the French legal system, agreed that the dispute was fundamentally centered on an interpretation of Article 3 of Regulation 67/67. That Regulation was clear to the highest French court in light of a 1971 European Court of Justice opinion. Consequently a "fresh interpretation" by way of reference in 1973 to the European Court was not required.[70] Although it is difficult to criticize the actual results of the *Garoche* case in the French courts, their application of acte clair illustrates how dependent European Union law is on national courts and national legal principles.

CILFIT Case

Despite an initial annoyance at French invocations of acte clair,[71] courts in other member states soon became converts. By 1982, when the European Court ruled definitively on the validity of this practice, it was faced with widespread but not particularly abusive utilization of acte clair. In *CILFIT,* the Italian Corte Suprema di Cassazione made a mandatory referral of the acte clair issue to the European Court. That is to say, the question it posed to the European Court was whether it was absolutely obliged to refer all issues of interpretation of EU law to the Court. The European Court deferentially incorporated acte clair into Union law as a gloss on the otherwise straightforward language of Article 267. In doing so, however, it was able to spell out the terms and conditions for its invocation:

> "The correct application of Community [Union] law may be so obvious as to leave no scope for any reasonable doubt as to the manner in which the question raised is to be resolved. Before it comes to the conclusion that such is the case, the national court or tribunal must be convinced that the matter is equally obvious to the courts of the other Member States and to the Court of Justice. Only if those conditions are satisfied may the national court or tribunal refrain from submitting the question to the Court of Justice and take upon itself the responsibility for resolving it. . . .

---

[70] Entreprises Garoche v. Société Striker Boats (1973) 1974 Common Mkt.L.Rep. 469.

[71] *See especially,* Re Société des Pétroles Shell-Barre (1964) Common Mkt.L.Rep. 462 (Conseil d'Etat).

> It must be borne in mind that Community legislation is drafted in several languages and that the different language versions are all equally authentic. An interpretation of a provision of Community law thus involves a comparison of the different language versions. . . . Even where the different language versions are entirely in accord with one another, Community law uses terminology which is peculiar to it. Furthermore, it must be emphasized that legal concepts do not necessarily have the same meaning in Community law and in the law of the various Member States."[72]

§ 9.6 Multiple Official Languages

In *CILFIT,* the European Court issues a reminder of the problems of language in interpreting European Union law. The Coal and Steel Treaty sought to avoid these problems by making French the only official language of that treaty.[73] There are over 20 official EU languages. Each working language can be consulted on questions of interpretation. However, with Treaty terms (such as Article 267) it is important to remember that English was *not* an official language prior to 1973 when the British joined. Thus, with reference to older legal documents *and* the EEC Treaty of Rome (now TFEU), French, German, Dutch or Italian versions are arguably more authoritative. The French version is considered the most authoritative of all because the Treaty of Rome was originally drafted in French. At a minimum, reference to different versions will promote greater understanding of European law. Attorneys practicing EU law routinely consult different language versions of European regulations, directives, decisions and treaties. North American attorneys should note that British legal English does not always correspond to American or Canadian legal language. Even when the words are the same, the concepts and doctrine may differ.

The European Court of Justice, when confronted with linguistic difficulties, has stressed the need to reconcile different official texts without giving preference to any one language.[74] Difficulties of this kind are minimized in the foreign policy arena (which operates outside the TFEU)[75] by using only English and French in the European Council. To the same effect, in Court of Justice or General Court proceedings, the plaintiff generally gets to choose the official language of the case unless the defendant is from or is a member

[72] CILFIT v. Ministro della Santa (1982) Eur.Comm.Rep. 3415.

[73] Article 100 of the Treaty of Paris.

[74] Regina v. Bouchereau (1977) Eur.Comm.Rep. 425.

[75] *See* Chapter 1, R. Folsom, *Principles of European Union Law including BREXIT.*

state (in which case the language of that member state prevails). When Article 267 proceedings are involved, the language of the nation whose court or tribunal is making the reference is official. The official language of the case is used in the pleadings, documents and oral hearings.

The Court's decision will be published in all working Union languages but only the language of the case is authentic. By custom, French is the internal working language of the Court of Justice. This means that judgments are debated and drafted in French. All other versions are translations, even when French is not the language of the case. Parliament, the Commission and the Court in public session, on the other hand, are a veritable babble of languages with simultaneous translations occurring. There are over 200 different possible pairs of official languages.

§ 9.7 Articles 263 and 265—Challenging Regional Institutions

In *CILFIT,* the Court of Justice also warned against the transferability of legal concepts within the Union. Article 263 TFEU provides a good example of these kinds of problems.

Article 263 gives the Court the power to review the legality of acts of the Council of Ministers, Commission, European Central Bank, acts jointly undertaken by the Parliament and Council, and acts of Parliament intended to produce legal effects on third parties. In unusual circumstances, individual acts of Parliament may also be challenged.[76] Acts which are merely preparatory, such as the commencement of a competition law investigation by the Commission, cannot be challenged.[77] To be challengeable, the "legal interests" of those under investigation must have been affected.[78] Member states, the Commission or Council, and directly concerned individuals may challenge regulations, directives or enforcement decisions on specified grounds.

Prior to the Maastricht Treaty on European Union, Parliament had no express authority to challenge Council or Commission action under Article 263. Now it and the European Central Bank may make such challenges for the purpose of protecting their prerogatives. No challenges may be brought against Council or Commission recommendations or opinions, but "soft" legal instruments (communications, instructions) that impose legal burdens or obligations can be challenged.

---

76 Les Verts v. Parliament (1986) Eur.Comm.Rep. 1339.

77 IBM Corp. v. Commission (1981) Eur.Comm.Rep. 2639.

78 *Id.*

Challenging Acts

There are four grounds for challenging (often called "appealing") acts of Union institutions. These are specified in Article 263 and originate in French administrative law governing "*action en recours pour excès de pouvoir.*" The same grounds apply to challenges under Article 265 TFEU, which concern failures to act as required by the Treaty ("*action en carence*"). The four grounds are:

(1) Lack of competence (*i.e., ultra vires,* or lack of jurisdiction or authority to act)[79];

(2) Infringement of an essential procedure ("administrative due process")[80];

(3) Infringement of the TFEU or any related rule of law (including general principles of EU law[81] and international law); and

(4) Misuse of powers.

Each of these grounds for challenging acts or failures to act has been extensively and uniquely developed in the jurisprudence of the European Court. For example, the term "misuse of powers" in Article 263 originated in the French administrative law concept of *détournement de pouvoir.* Research on and an understanding of French administrative law thus becomes important to Article 263.[82] Misuse of powers is a term of art in British administrative law which is narrower than the U.S. concept of abuse of administrative discretion. The original French concept is generally limited to situations of "subjective wrong" as when public institutions or personnel use their powers for personal benefit, such as to favor a relative or for financial gain. Thus the concept of *détournement de pouvoir* does not transfer easily from French into British or United States law and language. Moreover, as *CILFIT* suggests, the Court of Justice is entirely free to develop its own doctrine in this area independent of its French origins.[83]

Article 263 TFEU litigation must be brought within two months of the publication of the act that is being challenged or its notification

---

[79] See the discussion of "legal bases" for legislative acts in Section 2.9, R. Folsom, *Principles of European Union Law including BREXIT.*

[80] Article 296 TFEU. *See, e.g.*, Transocean Marine Paint Assn. v. Commission, (1974) Eur.Comm.Rep. 1063; Germany v. Commission (1963) Eur.Comm.Rep. 63.

[81] *See, e.g.*, Bela-Mühle Josef Bergmann v. Grows-Farm GmbH (1977) Eur.Comm.Rep. 1211 (principle of equal treatment voids agricultural regulation).

[82] *See* ASSIDER v. High Authority (1954–56) Eur.Comm.Rep. 63 (Advocate-General's opinion).

[83] *See* Guiffrida v. Council (1976) Eur.Comm.Rep. 1395 (sham competition for EC job is misuse of power).

to the appellant (in the absence of notice, two months from the day when that person had knowledge of it), as the case may be. Article 264 authorizes the Court to declare acts of Union institutions null and void if the appeal is well founded. This explains why Article 263 litigation is sometimes referred to as "actions for annulment." Regulations may be partially or fully annulled, or retain validity until replaced, at the Court's discretion.[84] Article 263 cannot be used to challenge the validity of national legislation.[85]

Challenging Failures to Act

Challenges for failure to act under Article 265 TFEU can only be brought if the relevant EU institution has first been called upon to act, and only if it fails to "define its position" within two months thereafter. This definition is not necessarily an act that can itself be challenged under Article 263.[86] The challenge for failure to act may then be brought in two additional months provided the institution's duty to act was owed to the plaintiff.[87] If an Article 265 challenge is well founded, Article 266 in essence authorizes the Court to order action by the institution. In both Article 263 and 265 litigations, Article 264 imposes a duty on the EU institution, as appropriate, to "take the necessary measures to comply with the judgment of the Court of Justice."

§ 9.8 Articles 263 and 265—Standing to Challenge Regional Institutions, Pleas of Illegality

Standing Issues

One limitation on Article 263 actions before the Court concerns the appeal rights of natural and legal persons. Such persons may only challenge decisions addressed to them, or regulations or decisions addressed to others which are of "direct and individual concern" to them. The Court for the most part narrowly construed the concept of "directly concerned individuals" so as to effectively limit the number of private challenges capable of being raised under Articles 263.[88]

---

84 Article 264(2), TFEU; Commission v. Council (1989) Eur.Comm.Rep. 259.

85 Oleificio Borelli v. Commission (1992) Eur.Comm.Rep. I–06313 (Case C–97/91).

86 GEMA v. Commission (1979) Eur.Comm.Rep. 3173.

87 Lord Bethell v. Commission (1982) Eur.Comm.Rep. 2277.

88 *See, e.g.*, Commission v. Jégo-Quéré & Cie SA, 2004 Eur.Comm.Rep. I–2365; Union de Pequenos Agricultores v. Council (2002) Eur.Comm.Rep. I–06677 (Case C–50/00); France v. Comafrica SpA and Dole (1999) Eur.Comm.Rep. I–185; Confédération Nationale des Producteurs de Fruits et Legumes (1962) Eur.Comm.Rep. 471; Calpak SpA v. Commission (1980) Eur.Comm.Rep.1949; Union Deutsche Lebensmittelwerke v. Commission (1987) Eur.Comm.Rep. 2265. *But see* Les Verts v.

However, in the competition law area where private interests are at stake when individual exemptions are issued by the Commission,[89] the Court was more liberal in its allowance of challenges by concerned third parties.[90] Jurisdiction to hear competition law challenges by private parties to Commission actions in the competition field has been transferred since 1989 to the European General Court.

The selectively liberal approach to Article 263 standing was also followed regarding Commission decisions on antidumping duties, internal state aids, countervailable subsidies applicable to Union imports, and illicit commercial practices of non-member nations.[91] The Reform Treaty of 2009 eased the conditions for individuals to obtain Article 263 relief. The requirement of "individual concern" is dropped. It is sufficient that individuals are directly affected by EU decisions or acts, and no implementing measures are involved.

The four grounds for appeal found in Article 263 are repeated in Article 265 which governs the failure of an EU institution to undertake actions required by the TFEU or other Union law. Actions by individuals and enterprises challenge the failure to address an act to the appellant. They cannot be used to compel discretionary Commission acts, such as Article 258 prosecutions of member states or competition law prosecutions of anticompetitive practices.[92]

Pleas of Illegality

The expiration of the two months' period for challenges to acts under Article 263 is not a firm statute of limitations. Article 277 allows any party to a proceeding where a regulation is in issue to plead the grounds for challenge specified in Article 263 in order to claim its inapplicability before the Court of Justice. This means, as a practical matter, that European Union regulations can be challenged

---

Parliament (1986) Eur.Comm.Rep. 1339 (political group has standing to challenge electoral budget decision).

[89] *See* Chapter 7, R. Folsom, *Principles of European Union Law including BREXIT*.

[90] Metro SB-Grossmärkte GmbH & Co. KG v. Commission (1977) Eur. Comm.Rep. 1875 (complainant allowed to challenge).

[91] Phillip Morris Holland v. Commission (1980) Eur.Comm.Rep. 2671 (prospective recipient of state aid may challenge denial of authorization by Commission); COFAZ SA v. Commission (1986) Eur.Comm.Rep. 391 (complainant allowed to challenge aid authorization by Commission); Allied Corp. v. Commission (1984) Eur.Comm.Rep. 1005 (named exporters may challenge imposition of dumping duties); Timex Corp. v. Council and Commission (1985) Eur.Comm.Rep. 849 (complainant may challenge antidumping decisions); FEDIOL v. Commission (1983) Eur.Comm.Rep. 2913 (complainant may challenge countervailing duties decision); FEDIOL v. Commission (1989) Eur.Comm.Rep. 1781 (Case 70/87) (complainant may challenge illicit commercial practices decision).

[92] Alfons Lütticke GmbH v. Commission (1966) Eur.Comm.Rep. 19; Lord Bethell v. Commission (1982) Eur.Comm.Rep. 2277.

at any time by what is called a "plea of illegality." Moreover, the European Court has extended this plea to directives, decisions and other acts of the Union institutions.[93]

Private parties may thus wait until the implementation of Union law is of immediate concern to them without losing an ability to test the legality of that law. Pleas of illegality are frequently made in EU torts and contracts litigation, and can be made before national courts and tribunals which must refer such issues to the Court of Justice or General Court.[94] Pleas of illegality are not allowed if the complainant had standing to challenge the act of the Union under Article 263 but failed to do so in a timely manner.[95] Under this approach, it is unclear whether member states can plea illegality since they always have Article 263 standing.[96]

Institutional Litigation

Articles 263 and 265 have spawned an interesting series of institutional litigations. In these cases, the Council, Commission and Parliament end up suing each before the European Court of Justice. These suits reflect the struggle for power and influence among these institutions. One major limitation upon them had been the absence of a general authority for Parliamentary suits under Article 263 against Council or Commission acts.[97] Prior to the Treaty of Nice of 2003, such suits could only be filed only when Parliamentary legislative prerogatives were at stake.[98] The Nice Treaty removed that limitation.

The Parliament is authorized by the TFEU to file Article 265 suits when the Council or Commission has failed to act. The Parliament successfully sued the Council over its failure to act in accordance with Treaty obligations to implement a Common Transport Policy.[99] The Council in turn has successfully sued the Parliament for excessive budgetary allocations.[100] The Commission has challenged the Council frequently before the European Court. Sometimes several institutions gang up on one. For example, the Commission (with Council and Parliamentary support) successfully

---

93 Simmenthal v. Commission (1979) Eur.Comm.Rep. 777.

94 Universität Hamburg v. HZA Hamburg-Kehrwieder (1983) Eur.Comm.Rep. 2771; Foto Frost v. HZA Lubeck Ost (1987) Eur.Comm.Rep. 4199.

95 Simmenthal v. Commission (1977) Eur.Comm.Rep. 777.

96 *See* Italy v. Commission (1966) Eur.Comm.Rep. 389; Commission v. Belgium (1978) Eur.Comm.Rep. 1881.

97 European Parliament v. Council (1988) Eur.Comm.Rep. 5615 (Comitology).

98 European Parliament v. Council (1990) Eur.Comm.Rep. 2041 (Chernobyl). Article 173, Treaty of Rome as amended by TEU.

99 European Parliament v. Council (1985) Eur.Comm.Rep. 1513.

100 Council v. European Parliament (1986) Eur.Comm.Rep. 288.

challenged the European Central Bank's creation of an independent anti-fraud unit.[101] Some of its most important victories concern the proper "legal basis" for Union legislation and international agreements.[102]

Articles 263 and 265 also provide the member states with the means to challenge the Commission. This is the reverse of the type of litigation that flows from Article 258 prosecutions of member states by the Commission.[103] Member state challenges of legislative acts by the Council seem likely to rise as more qualified majority voting occurs, and the minority seeks legal redress.[104] Article 269 TFEU allows member states to challenge the legality on serious infringement of human rights grounds of European Council and Council of Ministers acts.

§ 9.9 Article 258—Commission Prosecutions of Member States

Article 258 authorizes the Commission (alone) to bring an action before the Court of Justice against member states that have failed to fulfill their obligations under the TFEU. This authority is reinforced by some basic normative rules. In Article 4(3) TEU, the member states undertake to adopt "all appropriate measures" to ensure the fulfillment of obligations arising out of the founding treaties or resulting from action taken by the institutions of the Union. They "shall facilitate" achievement of its tasks and "shall abstain" from jeopardizing its objectives.

These fundamental principles have frequently been the subject of litigation as the Commission seeks to enforce member state duties under European law. Although it has not yet done so, it appears that the Commission could prosecute a member state *court* for failure to fulfill its treaty obligations (e.g., mandatory Article 267 references). Government passivity in the face of private conduct (angry French farmer blockades) creating obstacles to internal trade has been successfully prosecuted.[105] Informal promises to comply with EU

---

[101] Commission v. European Central Bank, 2003 Eur.Comm.Rep. I–1651.

[102] Commission v. Council (1989) Eur.Comm.Rep. 1493 (GSP preferences); (1971) Eur.Comm.Rep. 263 (the *ERTA* decision).

[103] *See, e.g.*, Germany v. Commission (1987) Eur.Comm.Rep. 3203 (lack of competence to act); Ireland v. Commission (1987) Eur.Comm.Rep. 5041 (violation of EU law); Netherlands v. Commission (1971) Eur.Comm.Rep. 639 (failure to act). The Council can likewise be challenged by the member states under Articles 230 and 232. *See* United Kingdom v. Council (1988) Eur.Comm.Rep. 855 (infringement of essential procedural requirement).

[104] *See* Chapter 2, R. Folsom, *Principles of European Union Law including BREXIT*.

[105] *See* Commission v. France, 1997 Eur.Comm.Rep. I–6959. See Regulation 2679/98.

regulations can be prosecuted, in this case repeatedly over decades against France.[106]

The Commission's prosecutorial powers under Article 258 must be distinguished from its ability in selected other circumstances to "directly" file actions against member states before the Court of Justice. Such direct actions do not involve the lengthy procedures described below in connection with Article 258 prosecutions. The Commission is authorized to sue the member states "directly" when they infringe Union rules on government subsidies to enterprises.[107] This can also be done when the member states "improperly" invoke Article 36 exceptions to single market legislation adopted by qualified majority voting in the Council of Ministers.[108]

Procedures and Penalties

Prior to commencing any Article 258 prosecutions before the Court of Justice, the Commission first delivers notice and the member state may submit a reply. Hundreds of such infringement notices are issued annually. The next stage involves issuance by the Commission of a reasoned opinion setting time limits for compliance. These time limits must be reasonable.[109] The member state can submit a reply if it wishes. The burden of proof shifts to the Commission when a member state claims to have conformed to the opinion within the stipulated time limits.[110] Negotiations may ensue at any time, and settlements frequently result. Almost 80 percent of all formal proceedings under Article 258 are settled.

If no settlement is reached, the Commission commences suit before the Court of Justice. Compliance after this point does not moot or remove the suit.[111] The most common type of Article 258 enforcement action actually filed with the Court of Justice concerns member state failures to implement directives. Constitutional, political or legal problems are unacceptable excuses for such failures.[112] Nor is the failure of other member states to implement

---

106 Commission v. France (1974) Eur.Comm.Rep. 359; Commission v. France (1996) Eur.Comm.Rep. I–1307 (French merchant seaman).

107 *See* Chapter 5, R. Folsom, *Principles of European Union Law including BREXIT*.

108 *See* Chapter 4, R. Folsom, *Principles of European Union Law including BREXIT*.

109 Commission v. Belgium (1988) Eur.Comm.Rep. 305.

110 Commission v. Italy (1973) Eur.Comm.Rep. 101; Commission v. Italy (1987) 3 Common Mkt.L.Rep. 483.

111 Commission v. Italy (1988) 2 Common Mkt.L.Rep. 951.

112 Commission v. Italy (1979) Eur.Comm.Rep. 771; Commission v. Belgium (1980) Eur.Comm.Rep. 1473 (Type approval directives).

the directive.[113] All Article 258 prosecutions are discretionary with the Commission and cannot be forced by individual complaints.[114]

Article 258 specifically requires member states to take the measures necessary to remedy failures identified by the Court in Article 258 proceedings. Prior to 1993, there were no obvious means by which the Court could enforce its judgments under Article 258 against member states. This contrasted with the power of the Court and the Commission in some areas of Union law to levy fines and penalties against individuals and corporations. Such fines and penalties can be collected in judgments enforced in the national courts.[115] To compel a member state to follow Union law, the Commission had little alternative but to bring yet another enforcement proceeding for determination before the Court. It has actually done this on occasion.[116] However, the Maastricht Treaty on European Union authorized the ECJ to levy fines and daily penalties against member states that do not take the measures necessary to remedy their Treaty failures.[117] Private litigants may also remedy member state failures, functioning in effect as attorneys general of Union law.[118]

The unwillingness of member states to carry out Court rulings under Article 258 is a problem. It could test the very fabric of the TFEU. The Commission has commenced thousands of infringement proceedings against member states and won over 90% of the time. An additional enforcement option would be to allow the Court to authorize the withholding of EU subsidies and benefits from nonconforming states. Sanctions of this kind were possible under the Coal and Steel Treaty by joint Commission and Council action.[119]

Article 273 allows member states to submit (by special agreement) disputes concerning the TFEU to the European Court. In Article 344, the member states have agreed not to submit such

---

[113] Commission v. France (1979) Eur.Comm.Rep. 2729; Commission v. Blanguernon (1990) Eur.Comm.Rep. I–00083 (Case C–38/89).

[114] Alfons Lütticke GmbH v. Commission (1966) Eur.Comm.Rep. 19.

[115] Article 299, TFEU.

[116] Commission v. Italy (1972) Eur.Comm.Rep. 527; Commission v. France (1979) Eur.Comm.Rep. 2729; Commission v. Italy (1993) Eur.Comm.Rep. I–00191 (Case C–101/91).

[117] *See* Commission v. Greece (2000) Eur.Comm.Rep. I–5047 (rubbish tip II); Commission v. France (1991) Eur.Comm.Rep. I–2727 (daily penalties, fisheries) confirmed case C–304/02 (July 12, 2005). In 2009, France was ordered by the ECJ to pay a 10 million EURO fine for failure to timely implement GMO directive 2001/118. Commission v. France (2008) Eur.Comm.Rep. I–9159.

[118] *See* Minister for Fisheries v. Schoenenberg (1978) Eur.Comm.Rep. 473 (Irish law invalid); Meijer v. Department of Trade (1979) Eur.Comm.Rep. 1387 (British law invalid).

[119] *See* Article 88 of ECSC Treaty of Paris.

disputes to any method of settlement other than those of the Treaty. Article 259 authorizes member states to prosecute each other before the European Court for failure to fulfill Treaty obligations. For diplomatic and institutional reasons, these options are almost never pursued.[120] The preferred approach is to persuasively complain to the Commission and then allow it to commence an Article 258 prosecution. Article 259 supports this approach by mandating a cooling off period of three months during which the Commission considers the arguments of both member states and issues a reasoned opinion.

§ 9.10 Contract and Tort Litigation—Court of First Instance (General Court)

Article 47 TEU provides that the European Union is a legal person. As such, it can sue and be sued like most corporations or governments. These disputes can involve employees of the Union, parties with whom it has contracted and those who are victims of its negligence or other tortious behavior.

The TFEU conveys exclusive jurisdiction to the Court of Justice over employment and non-contractual liability disputes.[121] It also can function as an arbitrator pursuant to dispute settlement clauses of contracts.[122] Contract disputes involving the Union may otherwise be entertained in the national courts.[123] The contractual liability is governed by the law applicable to the contract in question.[124]

General Court (formerly Court of First Instance)

Much of the work of the Court of Justice in employment and non-contractual liability litigation is now handled by the European General Court (GC) (formerly Court of First Instance (CFI). This court was authorized by 1987 Single European Act amendments. The CFI/GC has been "attached" to the European Court of Justice. Its general jurisdiction now extends to most EU litigation, including since the Treaty of Nice, preliminary rulings as authorized. However, the Court cannot hear Article 258 prosecutions of member states by the Commission, nor Article 263 or 265 challenges to EU institutional acts or failures to act when these are initiated by member states or Union institutions. It can hear such challenges and related "pleas of

---

120 *But see* Ireland v. France (1977) Case 58/77 (withdrawn); France v. United Kingdom (1979) Eur.Comm.Rep. 2923 (fisheries dispute).

121 Articles 268–270, TFEU.

122 Article 272, TFEU.

123 Articles 274–276, TFEU.

124 Article 340, TFEU.

illegality" when they are privately initiated, for example, in the business competition law area.[125]

In 1993, the Council extended the jurisdiction of the GC to all direct actions brought by natural or legal persons except antidumping cases.[126] In 1994, antidumping and countervailing duty cases were also brought within the scope of its jurisdiction. The GC has additionally been granted jurisdiction over Union trademark disputes arising out of the Office for Harmonization in the Internal Market (OHIM). For example, Wrigley was denied registration of its Doublemint trademark because it described one of the product's common characteristics, a ruling upheld by the Court. It is widely perceived that the General Court is now overloaded, even with staff cases heard before the Civil Service Tribunal. The TFEU anticipates an offloading other areas to "specialized courts," for which the GC would function as an appeals court.

The purpose, in general, behind creation of the CFI/GC was to relieve the Court of Justice of some of its caseload. It commenced doing this in November of 1989. However, there is a right of appeal on points of law from the GC to the Court of Justice. Article 51 of the Council Decision establishing the General Court indicates that such appeals lie on the grounds of lack of competence, procedural failures that adversely affect the appellants' interests, and infringement of Union law by the GC. In addition, the Treaty of Nice amendments to Article 256 specify that GC preliminary rulings posing a serious risk to the unity or consistency of Union law may be reviewed by the ECJ. Any failure by the GC to follow prior ECJ decisions could amount to such an infringement.

To distinguish between the judgments of these Union courts, some law reporters now prefix Court of Justice case numbers with a "C" (Case C–213/89) (Court) and Court of First Instance/General Court cases with a "T" (Case T–81/90) (Tribunal). In the official European Court Reports, ECJ judgment page numbers are preceded by "I-." CFI/GC judgment page numbers are preceded by "II-."

Non-contractual Liability

The General Court is partially heir to an interesting body of law on non-contractual (tort) liability created by the Court of Justice. In this area, the Court's role as a law-maker was fully anticipated by the treaties. Article 340 provides that the non-contractual liability of the European Union is governed by the "general principles common to the laws of the member states." Under these principles, the Union

---

[125] *See* Chapter 7, R. Folsom, *Principles of European Union Law including BREXIT.*

[126] Council Decision 93/350, O.J. 1993 L144/21.

is obliged to "make good any damage caused by its institutions or servants in the performance of their duties." For example, the negligent disclosure by the Commission of the identity of an informant who was a former employee of a company subject to EU competition law sanctions was an actionable tort.[127] In this case, a Swiss informant was arrested, held in solitary confinement, interrogated, and convicted under Swiss law for economic espionage. While in prison, his wife was interrogated by Swiss police officers and then committed suicide.

The European Court of Justice, and now the General Court when damages are sought in litigation properly before it, has had to determine just what general principles of non-contractual liability are common to the laws of the member states. At first, of course, there were only six civil law states to consider. Now there are 27 member states, including two common law jurisdictions. The Court of Justice has ruled that Article 340 does not require adherence to the highest common denominator of liability law in the member states. Rather, the Court's duty is to track down in the national laws the elements or measures necessary to create liability principles which are fair and viable.[128] Such principles can include no-fault under the founding treaties.[129]

It is now generally recognized that the Union is liable in non-contractual cases whenever its tortious conduct causes actual damages.[130] Such conduct includes faults of its officers and agents committed within the scope of their duties, including negligence, bad faith, and intentional misconduct. Drawing from French administrative law, the Court has also recognized torts resembling "faute de service." These liabilities occur when the Union fails to function in the reasonably efficient manner expected of a well-run government even if such a fault cannot be traced to negligence or misconduct by specific officials.[131]

Tortious conduct giving rise to liability also includes unlawful legal measures, e.g., EU regulations and directives, and unlawful failures to adopt such measures. The "plea of illegality" is used to challenge such activities. At first, the Court of Justice held that damages actions on these bases could only be pursued if successful challenges had been previously undertaken under Articles 263 or

---

[127] Adams v. Commission (1985) Eur.Comm.Rep. 3539. See Article 214 of the Treaty of Rome creating an EU duty of confidentiality.

[128] Plaumann & Co. v. Commission (1963) Eur.Comm.Rep. 95.

[129] *See* Article 40 of the Treaty of Paris mandating a finding of fault in coal and steel cases.

[130] Alfons Lütticke GmbH v. Commission (1971) Eur.Comm.Rep. 325.

[131] *See* Compagnie Continentale France v. Council (1975) Eur.Comm.Rep. 117.

265.[132] In a good demonstration of its willingness to reverse itself, the Court has since held the opposite.[133] Similarly, private parties need not challenge the validity of EU acts in national litigation prior to seeking damages relief before the Court. Here again the Court of Justice reversed its initial ruling to the contrary in the interest of the "proper administration of justice. . . and procedural efficiency."[134]

Nevertheless, the chances of obtaining individual damages relief for legislative acts of the European Union are not great. The Court has limited this possibility to manifest and grave disregard by EU institutions of the limits of their powers amounting to a breach of superior rules of law protecting individuals.[135] This is known as the "*Schöppenstedt* formula." And when directives are implemented at the national level in ways which cause damages, national remedies (if available and effective) must first be pursued.[136] Directives that partly harmonize an area of law intended for total harmonization are not actionable even if discriminatory.[137]

§ 9.11 EU Judicial Practice and Procedure

The structure and procedures of the European Court of Justice (ECJ) and the General Court (GC) are quite similar. Each presently has, for example, 28 judges who serve six-year renewable terms upon appointment by the member states acting in common accord. There is one judge from each member state, plus (traditionally when an odd number was required) an additional judge who rotates from the five largest member states. The GC sits in chambers of three to five judges.

The Court of Justice is also divided into chambers, but may sit *en banc* or as a "grand chamber" of 14 judges when cases are brought before it by member states or Union institutions, and in many Article 267 preliminary rulings. Some case reporters now identify the Court's opinions by chamber number. To an American, the Court's most distinguishing features are its emphasis on written (versus oral) procedures, the dominance of the Court (not the parties) over development of the evidence, and the absence of dissenting opinions.

---

132 Plaumann & Co. v. Commission (1963) Eur.Comm.Rep. 95.

133 Alfons Lütticke, supra; Aktien-Zuckerfabrik Schöppenstedt v. Council (1971) Eur.Comm.Rep. 975.

134 Merkur-Aussenhandels GmbH v. Commission (1973) Eur.Comm.Rep. 1055.

135 Bayerische HNL Vermehrungsbetriebe GmbH & Co. KG v. Council and Commission (1978) Eur.Comm.Rep. 1209; Amylum NV v. Council and Commission (1979) Eur.Comm.Rep. 3497.

136 Krohn & Co. Import-Export GmbH v. Commission (1986) Eur.Comm.Rep. 753; Asteris AE + Ors v. Hellenic Republic (1990) Eur.Comm.Rep. 5515.

137 Les Assurances du Crédit S.A. v. Council and Commission (1991) Eur.Comm.Rep. I–01799 (Case C–63/89).

Proceedings

The Protocol on the Statute of the Court of Justice and the Courts' Rules of Procedure (approved by the Council) establish a two-part proceeding. The written part commences with an application to the Court's registrar and designation of an agent or legal representative. This designation must occur. In other words, litigants may not represent themselves before the Court. Any lawyer entitled to practice before a national court of a member state may act before the Court of Justice or General Court. The application serves as a "complaint" for notice purposes and thereby limits (in most cases) the issues and evidence that can be raised in the proceeding. Its filing also triggers the assignment of a reporting judge ("juge rapporteur") and an Advocate-General to the case. The fact of the application and a summary of the issues presented is published in the Official Journal.

The application is also sent to the respondent who has one month to file a written "defense." Plaintiff may then reply, to which the defendant may submit a rejoinder. All of these written submissions to the court resemble full evidentiary and legal briefs more than pleadings. When the Article 267 preliminary ruling procedure is being used, the parties, member states, the Commission and (where appropriate) the Council may submit written briefs to the Court. The Parliament does not appear to have this right of submission, but the member states and the EU institutions (including Parliament) always have a right to intervene in cases before the Court. Individuals and enterprises with an interest in the litigation have the same right. Trade and professional associations, consumer groups and unions have also been particularly active.

At the discretion of the Court, a preliminary inquiry may be held. The Court (typically acting through the reporting judge) can pose questions to the litigants. The role of a court in posing questions is part of the civil law tradition which predominates on the Court. It is a procedure that most common law students familiar with a more adversarial system will find a bit unusual. The Court also has the power to examine witnesses, call experts and generally develop the evidence before it. Limited rights of cross-examination are allowed to counsel when this occurs.

The second part of the proceeding before the Court is oral. The Court first hears the views of the reporting judge in charge of the case and then counsel for both sides. At the end of the oral procedure, the Court hears the *Advocate-General,* a special lawyer employed by the Union to analyze and evaluate all cases before the Court and give public opinions on the proper result under EU law. Americans are typically unfamiliar with the role of an Advocate-General since there is no parallel in United States procedure. The closest parallel is the French Commissaire du Gouvernement at the Conseil d'Etat. The Advocate-General does not represent anyone and is a kind of permanent *amicus curiae* on behalf of justice.

Advocates-General (AG) are appointed for six-year terms to the Court of Justice and General Court by the member states acting in common accord. Their opinions are often much more informative than those of the Court in any given case. Whereas the Advocate-General is willing to spin out various hypotheticals and consider the broader ramifications of the legal principles at issue, the Court tends to write its opinions in a terse and summary fashion. It should be stressed that lawyers working with EU law commonly use the opinions of the Advocate-General in their practice to forecast future developments and to better understand the judgments issued by the Court. Some of the most controversial cases in European Union law have involved instances where the Court has declined to agree with the opinions of the Advocate-General.[138]

Judgments

The Court's judgment is drafted in French by the reporting judge. This draft is then discussed by the full court or chamber. The Court's decision is rendered *without dissent* in the language of the case. The absence of dissenting opinions shelters the judges from nationalistic pressures and critics. But it also makes analysis of opinions and projection of trends in the case law more difficult.

Costs are normally borne by the losing party. Costs, for these purposes, generally include the Court's expenses, witnesses and experts, travel and subsistence of the parties to the Court's proceedings, and reasonable legal fees.[139] The Court's assessment powers on costs are wide, and substantial litigation over costs has ensued. However, most litigation results in a settlement agreement as between the parties on payment of costs. The loser must also pay the costs of intervenors supporting the successful litigant.[140] The Court may make cash legal aid awards in appropriate cases and in the absence of national legal aid.[141]

---

[138] *See* Van Gend en Loos v. Nederlandse Administratie der Belastingen (1963) Eur.Comm.Rep. 1; Consten and Grundig v. Commission (1966) Eur.Comm.Rep. 299; Defrenne v. Sabena (1976) Eur.Comm.Rep. 455; Commission v. Council (1971) Eur.Comm.Rep. 263 (*ERTA*).

[139] *See* Article 72 of the ECJ Rules of Procedure.

[140] Hoogovens v. High Authority (1962) Eur.Comm.Rep. 253.

[141] Lee v. Minister for Agriculture (1980) Eur.Comm.Rep. 1495 (Article 234 reference in a civil case from Ireland). *See* DEB Deutsche Energiehandels v. Germany (2010) Eur.Comm.Rep. ___ (Case 279/09) (legal aid for companies).

Litigation brought before the Court does not automatically suspend the act being challenged. It continues to operate pending the Court's decision. The Court (*i.e.*, the President of the Court) may order suspension when it considers this necessary, along with any "interim measures." This is done only in exceptional circumstances of harm to the applicant.[142] Pecuniary judgments of the Court against persons (not member states) are enforceable under the terms of Article 299 TFEU. Once authenticated, the Court's judgment is enforced according to the ordinary judgment-creditor procedures of the member state where it is executed.

The Rules of Procedure permit revisions of Court judgments.[143] No revision can occur more than ten years after judgment, and requests for revisions must be submitted within three months of the knowledge of new facts of decisive importance justifying revision. Such facts must have originally been unknown to both the Court and the litigant.[144] Moreover, if the information could have been easily obtained during litigation, no revision of judgment will be allowed.[145]

Article 102 of the Rules of Procedure permits requests for interpretation of Court judgments when there are "difficulties" as to its meaning or scope. Such requests can be made by the parties or any Union institution with an interest in the judgment. They are granted when the effect of the judgment on the parties is uncertain, not when the consequences for others are at issue.[146] Finally, third parties may seek reconsideration of Court judgments which will cause them damage. Requests for reconsideration must be made within two months of judgment, and the applicant must demonstrate no prior notice of the litigation.[147]

---

[142] United Kingdom v. Commission (1996) Eur.Comm.Rep. I–3903 (interim ban on British beef upheld in "mad cow" crisis); NTN Toyo Bearing Co. Ltd. v. Council (1977) Eur.Comm.Rep. 1721; Commission v. Ireland (1977) Eur.Comm.Rep. 1411.

[143] Articles 92–94.

[144] Acciaieria di Roma v. High Authority (1960) Eur.Comm.Rep. 165.

[145] Fonderie Acciarierie Giovanni Mandelli v. Commission (1971) Eur.Comm.Rep. 1.

[146] High Authority and European Court v. Collotti (1965) Eur.Comm.Rep. 275.

[147] Re Breedband (1962) Eur.Comm.Rep. 145.

Chapter 10

TRADE DISPUTES: INTERGOVERNMENTAL SETTLEMENT

Table of Sections

General Agreement on Tariffs and Trade (GATT 1947 and 1994) and World Trade Organization (WTO) disputes are purely intergovernmental. That said, almost inevitably there are private and publicly controlled business interests at stake in the dispute. Indeed, those interests probably pushed hard for their government to take up their cause before the WTO. Many of the various WTO procedures and disputes referenced below, adapted from the author's *Principles of International Trade Law*, reflect these realities.

NAFTA 1994 employs a range of dispute settlement procedures. Chapter 20 of NAFTA 1994 creates general intergovernmental dispute settlement procedures that apply unless there are more specific provisions in the agreement. For example, Section B of Chapter 11 establishes investor-state arbitration procedures that operate outside Chapter 20. See Chapter 4. In addition, Chapter 19 concerns antidumping and countervailing duty disputes, uniquely resolved via Binational Panel and Extraordinary Challenge procedures that replace national judicial review. This dispute system has been retained at Canadian insistence under the pending USMCA

2018 agreement. *See* Folsom, *Principles of Free Trade Agreements, From GATT 1947 through NAFTA Re-Negotiated 2018.*

In most instances, Chapter 20 allows the complaining NAFTA government to elect as between WTO *or* NAFTA dispute settlement procedures. ***This right of election has been retained in the pending USMCA 2018 agreement intended to replace NAFTA 1994.***

For the right of election between NAFTA 1994 and WTO intergovernmental dispute settlement to be meaningful, the dispute must be covered by a WTO agreement. In other words, there must be WTO jurisdiction. To help make this assessment, the following table compares provisions of NAFTA 1994 with the WTO package of agreements:

NAFTA 1994 Chapters and WTO Agreements

The right of NAFTA governments to elect as between NAFTA and WTO remedies is limited by the substantive content of the NAFTA 1994 and WTO agreements. The NAFTA 1994 Chapters chart below indicates the closest parallel WTO agreements.

NAFTA 1994	WTO AGREEMENTS
Chapter 3, Trade in Goods	General Agreement on Tariffs and Trade 1994, Agreement on Textiles and Clothing
Chapter 4, Rules of Origin	Agreement on Rules of Origin
Chapter 5, Customs Procedures	No parallel
Chapter 6, Energy and Basic Petrochemicals	No parallel
Chapter 7, Agriculture and SPS Measures	Agreement on Agriculture, Agreement on SPS Measures
Chapter 8, Emergency Action	Agreement on Safeguards
Chapter 9, Product and Service Standards	Agreement on Technical Barriers to Trade
Chapter 10, Procurement	Agreement on Government Procurement (optional)
Chapter 11, Investment	Agreement on Trade-Related Investment Measures (TRIMs)
Chapter 12, Cross-Border Trade in Services	General Agreement on Trade in Services (GATS)
Chapter 13, Enhanced Telecommunications	See GATS, Basic Telecommunications Covered

Chapter 14, Financial Services	See GATS
Chapter 15, Competition Policy, Monopolies and State Enterprises	No parallel, but see Understanding on Interpretation of GATT Article XVII
Chapter 16, Temporary Entry for Business Persons	No parallel
Chapter 17, Intellectual Property	Agreement on Trade-Related Aspects of Intellectual Property Rights (TRIPs)
Chapter 18, Administrative Provisions	Not applicable
Chapter 19, Antidumping and Countervailing Duty Dispute Settlement	No parallel, but see DSU and Agreement on Implementation of GATT Article VI
Chapter 20, Dispute Settlement	Understanding on Rules and Procedures Governing the Settlement of Disputes (DSU)
Chapter 21, Exceptions	See GATT Articles XX, XXI and Understanding on GATT Balance of Payments Provisions
Agreement on Environmental Cooperation	No parallel
Agreement on Labor Cooperation	No parallel

Business sector interests tend to drive the choice of forum, with many NAFTA 1994 disputes resolved under the WTO procedures. In the United States, petitions to commence WTO or NAFTA 1994 dispute settlement proceedings are lodged with the United States Trade Representative (USTR).

§ 10.1 Intergovernmental NAFTA 1994 Dispute Settlement

Intergovernmental disputes under NAFTA 1994 are "resolved" by three-member arbitral panels. First, the chair is selected by consensus or by lot. The chair cannot be from the selecting country, but can come from outside NAFTA. For example, in the first Chapter 20 panel the chair came from Britain and in the second from Australia. Two panelists are chosen by both parties. Each side must select persons who are citizens of the *other* country. In other words, failure of one party to select panelists could stop the Chapter 20 process.

Any member state with a substantial interest in a Chapter 20 dispute can join as a complaining party and thereby participate in solutions to the dispute. However, in all cases, NAFTA 1994's general dispute settlement procedures are *not* binding. Consultations are followed by mediation by the NAFTA Free Trade Commission followed by arbitration before a 5-member panel. A "reverse selection" process is used to select the arbitration panel from a roster of acceptable panelists. It is possible to propose a panelist from off the roster, but such nominees can be vetoed without cause by the other side.

Chapter 20 reports should be completed 120 days after the request for arbitration. There is no appeal to a higher body such as the Extraordinary Challenge Committee under Chapter 19. If the dispute is not resolved, the prevailing party can pursue equivalent compensatory action within 30 days. Normally this should be in the same economic sector, but cross-sector retaliation can occur, and all retaliation can be challenged by panel review only if "manifestly excessive." Compensatory action cannot be undertaken by a member state that failed to join the dispute as a complaining party. The third NAFTA partner may not "normally" commence WTO or NAFTA proceedings on substantially equivalent grounds absent a significant change in economic or commercial circumstances.

The intergovernmental dispute resolution procedures found in Chapter 20 of the NAFTA 1994 agreement apply absent more specific provisions. These procedures were intended to be an alternative to GATT 1947 dispute settlement (since replaced by much more effective World Trade Organization (WTO) procedures). Private parties do not participate in Chapter 20 dispute settlement. Moreover, Article 2021 expressly prohibits private rights of action asserting inconsistency with NAFTA 1994 against a member state. The United States Trade Representative (USTR), however, does afford interested persons the opportunity to comment on Chapter 20 proceedings. Private parties can and have lodged complaints with the USTR about member state measures that adversely affect them. Whether to proceed to Chapter 20 dispute settlement is strictly a matter of USTR discretion.

The right of each member state to elect between NAFTA and WTO dispute settlement is generally preserved. However, once made, the election is exclusive and final. Use of Chapter 20 under NAFTA 1994 will be denied if the complainant takes the issue to the WTO. That said, as part of a broad evaluation of NAFTA/WTO choice of forum opportunities and risks, Professor David Gantz has noted that nations may sometimes judiciously frame their disputes so as to gain access to both NAFTA and WTO forums.[1] Preserving the option of WTO dispute settlement allowed the U.S. in the celebrated *Sports Illustrated* case[2] to successfully challenge Canadian cultural industry trade restraints that have been excluded from CUSFTA 1989 and NAFTA 1994. For any complaint that the remaining NAFTA nation wishes to join, the two complainants must resolve the choice of forum. Absent resolution, the dispute "normally" will be heard under NAFTA 1994 procedures.

The right to elect as between NAFTA 1994 or WTO dispute settlement is qualified. If the dispute falls in certain categories, the responding nation may force the issue to be heard under Chapter 20. This is the case when the dispute concerns:

- Specified environmental or conservation agreements;
- Sanitary and phytosanitary (SPS) health regulations; or
- Environmental, health, safety or conservation product or service standards (SRM)[3].

Why are these categories the only disputes where the responding nation may insist on the NAFTA forum? One reason may be the perception that these areas involve unusually sensitive trade matters. Another may be the desire to ensure that national standards are absolutely respected (as NAFTA 1994 requires) and insulated from potentially global challenges at the WTO.

A third may be the "lessons" learned in the pre-NAFTA challenge by Mexico under GATT 1947 of the U.S. Marine Mammal Protection Act (dolphin-safe tuna).[4] The United States certainly wanted no repetition of that adverse GATT Panel ruling, which it "blocked" by pressuring Mexico into a negotiated settlement under the 1995 Panama Declaration. Congress authorized the importation of tuna from Panama Declaration adherents in 1997. Nevertheless, in 2008, Mexico initiated WTO dispute proceedings against U.S. "dolphin-safe" label rules and a Ninth Circuit decision requiring no usage of purse seine nets for tuna labeled dolphin-safe[5]. In 2010, the U.S. instituted NAFTA Chapter 20 dispute proceedings seeking to force Mexico to withdraw its WTO complaint and re-file it under NAFTA, which Mexico declined to do. In 2011, a WTO panel ruled in

[1] *See* 14 American U. Law Rev. 1025 (1999) (citing Mexico-U.S. sugar/corn syrup trade complaints and the Canada-U.S. farm products blockade dispute).

[2] WT/DS31/AB/R 1997.

[3] NAFTA 1994, Article 2005.

[4] *See* BISD 39 Supp. 155 (1993).

[5] Earth Island Institute v. Hogarth, 494 F.3d 757 (2007).

favor of Mexico's complaint, which the WTO Appellate Body subsequently confirmed.

Recourse to Chapter 20 dispute settlement may ordinarily be had if an actual or proposed act is or would be inconsistent with NAFTA 1994 obligations. Canada and Mexico have, for example, threatened to carry to arbitration their challenge of the 1996 U.S. "Helms-Burton" law[6] against trafficking in U.S. property confiscated by Cuba. For some provisions of the agreement, Chapter 20 can also be used to challenge measures that are consistent with the NAFTA but cause "nullification or impairment" of expected benefits. But the government procurement, investment, telecommunications, financial services, competition law and monopolies, temporary entry of business persons, Canada's cultural industries exclusion, and automotive trading (Annex 300–A) provisions in NAFTA 1994 typically *cannot* be challenged in this way.

Professor David Lopez has provided a revealing portrait of early Chapter 20 dispute settlement, one which emphasizes just how few disputes are pushed to arbitration.[7] Of the eight complaints he cites as lodged by the end of 1996, only three went to arbitration: Canadian agricultural tariffication, U.S. escape clause restraints on Mexican brooms, and U.S. refusal to admit Mexican trucks.[8] The trucking dispute endured for years, and after several failed attempts at resolution, Mexico imposed retaliatory tariffs on about $2.4 billion on U.S. exports, arguably an example of cross-sector retaliation (discussed below under the WTO). These tariffs were removed in 2011 after the U.S. finally complied with its cross-border trucking service obligations.

To this date, the three disputes cited by Prof. Lopez remain the only Chapter 20 arbitration decisions. Professor Lopez suggests that complaints linger at the consultation/mediation stages of Chapter 20 dispute settlement because there is no compulsion to move the dispute forward and because political realities temper that decision. Some disputes are settled (e.g., tomatoes above) while others just keep on lingering (Helms-Burton). The refusal of the parties to create NAFTA Chapter 20 panels has also limited intergovernmental NAFTA 1994 dispute settlement. There is no such prerogative under WTO dispute settlement.

---

6 110 Stat. 785.

7 *See* 32 Texas Int'l Law J. 163 (1997).

8 For details, *see* R. Folsom, *Principles of Free Trade Agreements, From GATT 1947 through NAFTA Re-Negotiated 2018.*

§ 10.2 Introduction to GATT/WTO Dispute Settlement

GATT 1947 did not have an institutional charter, and was not intended to become an international organization on trade. It did later develop institutional structures and acquired quasi-organizational status, but there was always a lack of structure. This lack was most often perceived in the somewhat over-stated inability of GATT to resolve disputes which were brought to it. Indeed, GATT 1947 members could block the formation of a panel to hear a dispute. Moreover, GATT panel decisions could be blocked by the losing state! Hence most GATT 1947 dispute settlement panel reports were un-adopted, and as such "the GATT acquis" is said to merely provide guidance in the context of WTO dispute settlement.[9]

The WTO provides a unified, mandatory, and exclusive intergovernmental system for settling trade disputes governed by WTO law through the Dispute Settlement Understanding (DSU), reproduced in Section 10.10. There are no private remedies, though business sector interests are often affected by the outcomes. In the United States, private parties and their attorneys can attempt to trigger WTO dispute settlement proceedings by filing complaints with the U.S. Trade Representative (USTR), a presidential appointee. Whether to pursue WTO trade law complaints is entirely discretionary for the USTR. Under the terms of the DSU, the USTR can pursue complaints of breach of WTO agreement obligations, or nullification or impairment of benefits accruing under WTO agreements.

The Dispute Settlement Body (DSB) is a special assembly of the WTO General Council, and includes all WTO members. There are six stages in the resolution of disputes under WTO:

1) Consultation;
2) Panel establishment, investigation and report;
3) Appellate review of the panel report;
4) Adoption of the panel and appellate decision;
5) Implementation of the decision adopted; or
6) Compensation or authorized retaliation.

There is also a parallel process for binding arbitration, if both parties agree to submit this dispute to arbitration, rather than to a DSB panel. In addition, the party subject to an adverse decision may

---

[9] *See* Japan-Alcoholic Beverages II, WTO/DS/R 8, 10, 11 (1996).

seek arbitration as a matter of right on issues of compliance and authorized retaliation.

Although the DSU offers a unified dispute resolution system that is applicable across all sectors and all WTO Covered Agreements, there are many specialized rules for disputes which arise under them. Such specialized rules appear in the Agreements on Textiles, Antidumping, Subsidies and Countervailing Measures, Technical Barriers to Trade, Sanitary and Phytosanitary Measures, Customs Valuation, General Agreement on Trade in Services, Financial Services and Air Transport Services. The special provisions in these individual Covered Agreements govern, where applicable, and prevail in any conflict with the general provisions of the DSU.

Under WTO, unlike under GATT 1947, the DSU practically assures that panels will be established upon request by a member state. Further, under WTO, unlike GATT 1947, the DSU virtually ensures the adoption of unmodified panel and appellate body decisions. It accomplishes this by requiring the DSB to adopt panel reports and appellate body decisions automatically and without amendment unless they are rejected by a consensus of all members. This "inverted consensus" requires that all members of the DSB, including the state that prevailed in the dispute, decide to reject the dispute resolution decision. Not surprisingly, this has never happened because if any member formally favors that decision (the winner in the dispute for example), it becomes binding. This inverted consensus requirement is imposed on both the adoption of panel reports or appellate body decisions and also on the decision to establish a panel.

The potential resolutions of a dispute under DSU range from a "mutually satisfactory solution" agreed to by the parties under the first, or consultation phase, to authorized retaliation under the last, or implementation phase. The preferred solution is always any resolution that is mutually satisfactory to the parties. After a panel decision, there are three types of remedies available to the prevailing party, if a mutually satisfactory solution cannot be obtained. One is for the respondent to bring the measure found to violate a Covered Agreement into conformity with the Agreement. A second is for the prevailing Member to receive compensation from the respondent which both parties agree is sufficient to compensate for any injury caused by the measure found to violate a Covered Agreement.

Finally, if no such agreement can be reached, a prevailing party can be authorized to suspend some of its concessions under the Covered Agreements to the respondent. These suspended concessions, called "retaliation," can be authorized within the same trade sector and agreement; or, if that will not create sufficient compensation, can be authorized across trade sectors and agreements.

The entire WTO dispute resolution process, from filing a complaint to authorized retaliation, can take roughly three years. One perspective on WTO dispute settlement seeks a rule-oriented use of the "rule of law". The other seeks a power-oriented use of diplomacy. The United States and less developed countries have traditionally sought to develop a rule-oriented approach to international trade disputes. The European Union and Japan have traditionally sought to use the GATT/WTO primarily as a forum for diplomatic negotiations, although the EU now ranks second in number of WTO dispute proceedings. These different views created part of the conflict at the December 1999 Seattle WTO meeting (which failed to launch the Millennium Round) and the barely ongoing Doha Round. If the DSB is a court, its proceedings should be open and "transparent." However, if it is just another form of government-to-government diplomacy, that has always been held in secret.

§ 10.3 Consultation

Any WTO Member who believes that the Measures of another Member are not in conformity with the Covered Agreements may call for consultations on those measures. The respondent has ten days to reply and must agree to enter into consultation within 30 days. If the respondent does not enter into consultations within the 30-day period, the party seeking consultations can immediately request the establishment of a panel under DSU, which puts the dispute into Phase 2.

Once consultations begin, the parties have 60 days to achieve a settlement. The goal is to seek a positive solution to the dispute, and the preferred resolution is to reach whatever solution is mutually satisfactory to the parties. If such a settlement cannot be obtained after 60 days, the party seeking consultations may request the establishment of a panel under DSU, which moves the dispute into Phase 2.

WTO member third parties with an interest in the subject-matter of the consultations may seek to be included in them. If such inclusion is rejected, they may seek their own consultations with the other member state. Alternatives to consultations may be provided through the use of conciliation, mediation or good offices, where all parties agree to use the alternative process. Any party can terminate the use of conciliation, mediation or good offices and then seek the establishment of a panel under DSU, which also will move the dispute into Phase 2.

§ 10.4 Panel Establishment, Investigation and Report

If consultations between the parties fail, the party seeking the consultations (the complainant) may request the DSB to establish a panel to investigate, report and resolve the dispute. The DSB must establish such a panel upon request, unless the DSB expressly decides by consensus not to establish the panel. Since an "inverted consensus" is required to reject the establishment of the panel and the complainant member must be part of that consensus, it is almost guaranteed that a panel will be established. Roughly 100 panels were established in the first five years of operation of the DSU, and many more since then.

Almost any WTO member state may intervene in the dispute. No specific legal or trade interest in the dispute is required since every WTO member has a legal interest in seeing that WTO rules are observed. Hence, for example, the United States intervened in the *Bananas* dispute[10] between Latin American exporters and the European Union. One measure of the significance of the dispute is how many and which WTO members join either side of the dispute . . . resulting in say seven states against ten.

The WTO Secretariat maintains a list of well-qualified persons who are available to serve as panelists, mainly international trade law specialists drawn from the world of law practice, the academe and government service. The panels are usually composed of three individuals from that list who are not citizens of either party. If the parties agree, a panel can be composed of five such individuals. The parties can also agree to appoint citizens of a party to a panel. Panelists may be either nongovernmental individuals or governmental officials, but they are to be selected so as to ensure their independence. Thus, there is a bias towards independent individuals who are not citizens of any party. If a citizen of a party is appointed, his government may not instruct that citizen how to vote, for the panelist must be independent. By the same reasoning, a governmental official of a non-party member state who is subject to instructions from his or her government would not seem to fit the profile of an independent panelist.

The WTO Secretariat proposes nominations of the panelists. Parties may not normally oppose the nominations, except for "compelling reasons." The parties are given twenty days to agree on the panelists and the composition of the panel. If such agreement is

10 WT/DS 27 (1997).

not forthcoming, the WTO Director-General is authorized to appoint the panelists, in consultation with other persons in the Secretariat.

Complaints brought to DSB panels can involve either violations of Covered Agreements, or non-violation nullification and impairment of benefits under the Covered Agreements. A prima facie case of nullification impairment arises when one member infringes upon the "obligations assumed under a Covered Agreement." Such infringement creates a presumption against the infringing member, but the presumption can be rebutted by a showing that the complaining member state has suffered no adverse effect from the infringement. A classic nullification and impairment complaint concerns use of government subsidies after tariff reductions cause increased imports.[11]

The panels receive pleadings and rebuttals and hear oral arguments. Panels can also engage in fact development from sources outside those presented by the parties. Thus, the procedure has aspects familiar to civil law courts. A panel can, on its own initiative, request information, including from experts selected by the panel. It can also obtain confidential information in some circumstances from an administrative body which is part of the government of a member state, without any prior consent from that state. A panel can establish its own group of experts to provide reports on factual or scientific issues. In a series of rulings commencing with the *Shrimp-Turtles* decision in 1998,[12] the WTO Appellate Body has affirmed the right of panels and itself to elect to receive unsolicited informational and argumentative briefs or letters from non-governmental organizations (NGOs), business groups and law firms representing persons interested in the dispute.

A panel is obligated to produce two objectively assessed written reports—an interim and a final report. These reports are normally drafted by the WTO Secretariat, subject to review by the panelists. A panel is supposed to submit a final written report to the DSB within six months of its establishment. The report will contain its findings of fact, findings of law, a decision and the rationale for its decision. Before the final report is issued, the panel is supposed to provide an interim report to the parties. The purpose of this interim report is to apprize the parties of the panel's current analysis of the issues and to permit the parties to comment on that analysis. The final report of the panel need not change any of the findings or conclusions in its interim report, unless the panel is persuaded to do so by a party's comments. However, if it is not so persuaded, it is obligated to explain

---

11 See the Australian Subsidy case, 2 GATT Panel B.I.S.D. 188 (1950).

12 WT/DS 58 (1998).

in its final report why not. At this writing, well over 200 WTO panel reports have been issued.

The decisions in panel reports are final as to issues of fact. The decisions in panel reports are not necessarily final as to issues of law. Panel decisions on issues of law are subject to review by the Appellate Body, which is Phase 3, and explained below. Any party can appeal a panel report, and appeals are usually taken.

§ 10.5 Appellate Review of the WTO Panel Report

Appellate review of panel reports is available at the request of any party, unless the DSB rejects that request by an "inverted consensus." There is no threshold requirement for an appellant to present a substantial substantive legal issue. Thus, most panel decisions are appealed as a matter of course. However, the Appellate Body can only review the panel reports on questions of law or legal interpretation.

The Appellate Body is a new institution in the international trade organization and its process. GATT 1947 had nothing comparable to it. The Appellate Body is composed of seven members (or judges) who are appointed by the DSB to four-year terms. Each judge may be reappointed, but only once, to a second four-year term. Each judge is to be a recognized authority on international trade law and the Covered Agreements. To date, Appellate Body members have been drawn mostly from the academe and retired justices. They have come from Germany, Japan, Egypt, India, New Zealand, the Philippines, Argentina, China, the United States and other WTO member nations.

The review of any panel decision must be performed by three judges out of the seven. At this writing, the Trump Administration has been vetoed three appointments to the Appellate Body. Should this trend continue there will be only two AB members by late 2019 and it will not be able to function. Many consider this to be a "stealth war" by the United States against the rules-based multilateral WTO system and a way to avoid WTO review of highly debatable Trump tariffs. For details, see See R. Folsom, *Principles of Free Trade Agreements, From GATT 1947 through NAFTA Re-Negotiated 2018.*

The review of any panel decision must be performed by three judges out of the seven. The parties do not have any influence over which judges are selected to review a particular panel report. There is a schedule, created by the Appellate Body, for the rotation for sitting of each of the judges. Thus, a party might try to appear before a favored judge by timing the start of the dispute settlement process to arrive at the Appellate Body at the right moment on the rotation schedule, but this limited approach has major difficulties.

The Appellate Body receives written submissions from the parties and has 60, or in some cases 90, days in which to render its decision. The Appellate Body review is limited to issues of law and legal interpretation. The panel decision may be upheld, modified, or reversed by the Appellate Body decision. Appellate Body decisions are anonymous, and ex parte communications are not permitted. Appellate Body decisions do not represent binding precedent. That said, many have observed a desire on the part of the Appellate Body to achieve consistency and a willingness to discuss its prior rulings when rendering decisions.

§ 10.6 Adoption of the Panel or Appellate Body Decision

Appellate Body determinations are submitted to the DSB. Panel decisions which are not appealed are also submitted to the DSB. Once either type of decision is submitted, the DSB must automatically adopt them without modification or amendment at its next meeting unless the decision is rejected by all members of the DSB acting by "inverted consensus", which has never happened.

An alternative to Phases 2 through 4 is arbitration, if both parties agree. The arbitration must be binding on the parties, and there is no appeal from the arbitral tribunal's decision to the DSB or Appellate Body.

§ 10.7 Implementation of the WTO Decision

Once a panel or Appellate Body decision is adopted by the DSB, implementation is a three-step process. In the first step, the member found to have a measure which violates its WTO obligations has "a reasonable time" (usually 15 months) to bring those measures into conformity with its WTO obligations. That remedy is the preferred one, and this form of implementation is the principal goal of the WTO dispute settlement system. To date, most disputes have resulted in compliance in this manner. If the adequacy of compliance is disputed, such disputes typically return to the WTO panel that rendered decision on the merits. The panel then determines, acting as an arbitrator, the amount (if any) of authorized retaliation. The retaliation process is discussed below.

§ 10.8 Compensation or Authorized Retaliation

Compensation

If the violating measures are not brought into conformity within a reasonable time, the parties proceed to the second step. In that second step, the parties negotiate to reach an agreement upon a form of compensation which will be granted by the party in violation to the injured party. Such compensation may be monetary or comprise trade concessions by the violating party to the injured party, which are over and above those already available under the WTO and Covered Agreements. The nature, scope, amount and duration of these additional concessions is at the negotiating parties' discretion, but each side must agree that the final compensation package is fair and is properly related to the injury caused by the violating measures.

Few such compensation agreements have ever been achieved, though the United States compensated most of the membership after losing a dispute to Antigua about whether it had "reserved" (excepted) Internet gambling from coverage under the GATS. The United States also compensated the EU in a copyright dispute involving small business use of music, and Brazil after losing a subsidies dispute concerning cotton.

Both "compensation" and "retaliation" provide only for indirect enforcement of DSB decisions. There is no mechanism for direct enforcement by the WTO of its decisions through WTO orders to suspend trade obligations. Commentators differ on whether retaliation will be an effective implementation device. The division represented by these conflicting views represents two different approaches to the nature of both international law and international trade law.

Authorized Retaliation

If the parties cannot agree on an appropriate amount of compensation within twenty days, the party injured by the violating measures typically seeks authority from the DSB to retaliate against the party whose measures violated its WTO obligations. Thus complainant seeks authority to suspend some of its WTO obligations in regard to the respondent. The retaliation must ordinarily be within the same sector and agreement as the violating measure. "Sector" is sometimes broadly defined, as all trade in goods, and sometimes narrowly defined, as in individual services in the Services Sectoral Classification List. "Agreement". All the agreements listed in Annex IA to the WTO Agreement are considered a single agreement. If retaliation within the sector and agreement of the violating measure is considered insufficient compensation, the complainant may seek suspension of its obligations across sectors and agreements. This is known as "*cross-sector retaliation*."

The DSB must grant the complainant's request to retaliate within 30 days unless all WTO members reject it through an "inverted consensus." (Article 22.6, D.S.U.) However, the respondent may object to the level or scope of the retaliation. The issues raised by the objection will be examined by either the Appellate Body or by an arbitrator. The respondent has a right, even if arbitration was not used in Phases 2 through 4, to have an arbitrator review in Phase 5 the appropriateness of the complainant's proposed level and scope of retaliation. The arbitrator will also examine whether the proper procedures and criteria to establish retaliation have been followed. The Phase 5 arbitration is final and binding, and the arbitrator's decision is not subject to DSB review.

In addition to objecting to the level of authorized retaliation, the responding WTO member may simultaneously challenge the assertion of noncompliance (Article 21.5, D.S.U.). This challenge will ordinarily be heard by the original panel and must be resolved within 90 days. Thus the request for authorized retaliation and objections thereto could conceivably be accomplished before noncompliance is formally determined. In practice, WTO dispute settlement has melded these conflicting procedures such that compliance and retaliation issues are decided together, typically by the original panel.

Retaliation in Action

Retaliation has rarely been authorized and even less rarely imposed. The amount of a U.S. retaliation permitted against the EU after the WTO *Bananas* and *Beef Hormones* decisions[13] were not implemented by the EU was contested. The arbitration tribunals for this issue were the original WTO panels, which did not allow the entire amount of the almost $700 million in retaliatory tariffs proposed by the United States. The U.S. was authorized and levied retaliatory tariffs amounting to about $300 million against European goods because of the EU failure to implement those WTO decisions.

Since 2000, Congress has authorized rotating WTO retaliatory tariffs in "carousel" fashion upon different goods. The threat of carousel retaliation contributed to an April 2001 settlement of the *Bananas* dispute. In 2009, a four-year settlement of the *Beef Hormones* dispute was reached. The U.S. gets a higher quota to export hormone-free beef to the EU in return for phasing out its

---

[13] WT/DS 27 (1997) (Bananas) and WT/DS 26 (1998) (Beef Hormones).

retaliatory tariffs on EU goods. The U.S. threat of carousel sanctions was again instrumental to this settlement.

Perhaps the most dramatic use of retaliation occurred in a tax subsidy dispute. The amount of EU retaliation permissible after the U.S. lost (for the second time) under WTO subsidy rules concerning Internal Revenue Code extraterritorial export tax preferences (FISCs) was disputed. A WTO panel, serving as an arbitrator, authorized approximately $4 *billion* in EU retaliation against U.S. exports.[14] This retaliation commenced in March of 2004 and escalated monthly until the U.S. capitulated by amending the I.R.C. late in 2004.

Cross-Sector Retaliation

In a landmark ruling, a WTO panel acting as an arbitrator authorized Ecuador to remove protection of intellectual property rights regarding geographical indicators, copyrights and industrial designs on European Union goods for sale in Ecuador. This authorization was part of Ecuador's $200 million compensation in the *Bananas* dispute. The WTO panel acknowledged that Ecuador imports mostly capital goods and raw materials from the European Union and that imposing retaliatory tariffs on them would adversely harm its manufacturing industries. This risk supported "cross-retaliation" under Article 22.3 of the DSU outside the sector of the EU trade violation.

Allowance of cross-sector IP retaliation was probably the most critical driver behind the 2001 settlement of the *Bananas* dispute. Cross-sector retaliation was also authorized against the U.S. after losing a GATS dispute to Antigua on Internet gambling restraints. The United States settled this dispute with nearly all WTO members save Antigua via compensation. At this writing, Antigua is still debating whether and how to retaliate.

§ 10.9 U.S. Involvement in WTO Disputes

The WTO dispute resolution process has been invoked more frequently than many expected. The United States has been a complainant or a respondent in hundreds of disputes since 1995. It has won about 86% of the disputes when filing complaints, and has lost about 75% when responding to WTO complaints. The U.S. track record on compliance with WTO decisions is generally good, though not always with alacrity despite repeated losses on the same issue (notably zeroing in antidumping proceedings, see Folsom, *Principles of International Trade Law*). The U.S. occasionally has complied only

[14] WT/DS 108 (2000).

after authorized retaliation by the complaining party. And, the U.S. has also sometimes avoided compliance by paying compensation.

The U.S. and the EU have been involved as the complainant or respondent in roughly 80% of all WTO disputes. The sampling of disputes summarized below illustrates the WTO dispute settlement process in action.

United States WTO Disputes

The United States lost a dispute initiated by Venezuela and Brazil concerning U.S. standards for reformulated and conventional gasoline. The offending U.S. law was amended to conform to the WTO ruling. It won on a complaint initiated jointly with Canada and the European Union regarding Japanese taxes on alcoholic beverages. Japan subsequently changed its law. When Costa Rica complained about U.S. restraints on imports of underwear, the U.S. let the restraints expire prior to any formal DSB ruling at the WTO. Similar results were reached when India complained of U.S. restraints on wool shirts and blouses. The United States won a major dispute with Canada concerning trade and subsidies for periodicals This celebrated *Sports Illustrated* dispute proved that WTO remedies can be used to avoid Canada's cultural industries exclusion under NAFTA. See R. Folsom and W.D. Folsom, *NAFTA Re-Negotiated and Its Business Implications* (forthcoming).

In the longstanding *Bananas* dispute noted above, the United States joined Ecuador, Guatemala, Honduras and Mexico in successfully challenging EU import restraints against so-called "dollar bananas." The EU failed to comply with the Appellate Body's ruling, and retaliatory measures were authorized and imposed. . . . tariffs on EU goods by the United States and cross-sector IP retaliation by Ecuador and others. In April 2001, the *Bananas* dispute was settled on terms that generally converted EU quotas to tariffs by 2006, though limited preferential quotas for ACP exporters were retained. A patent law complaint by the U.S. against India prevailed in the DSB and ultimately brought changes in Indian law regarding pharmaceuticals and agricultural chemicals.

In *Beef Hormones,* also noted above, the European Union lost twice before the Appellate Body for want of proof of a "scientific basis" for its ban on hormone beef. It refused to alter its import restraints and absorbed $200 million in retaliatory tariffs on selected exports to Canada and the United States. In 2009, an arguably pro-European settlement was reached. The U.S. effectively got a higher quota to export hormone-free beef to the EU, in return for phasing out over four years its retaliatory tariffs on EU goods. The U.S. threat of carousel sanctions, i.e. rotating goods subject to retaliation, was instrumental to this settlement. Meanwhile, because the U.S. beef industry failed to timely ask for a continuation of the retaliatory tariffs, the Federal Circuit ruled in 2010 that they expired in 2007. Refunds were given to importers of EU products who paid those tariffs.

The United States prevailed against Argentina regarding tariffs and taxes on footwear, textiles and apparel. It lost a challenge (strongly supported by Kodak) to Japan's distribution rules regarding photo film and paper. In this dispute the U.S. elected *not* to appeal the adverse WTO panel ruling to the Appellate Body. In contrast, the European Union took an appeal which reversed an adverse panel ruling on its customs classification of computer equipment. The U.S. had commenced this proceeding. Opponents in many disputes, Japan, the United States and the European Union united to complain that Indonesia's National Car Program was discriminatory and in breach of several WTO agreements. They prevailed and Indonesia altered its program.

India, Malaysia, Pakistan and Thailand teamed up to challenge U.S. shrimp import restraints enacted to protect endangered sea turtles. The WTO Appellate Body generally upheld their complaint and the U.S. has moved to comply. The adequacy of U.S. compliance is being challenged by Malaysia. The European Union and the United States jointly opposed Korea's discriminatory taxes on alcoholic beverages. This challenge was successful and Korea now imposes flat non-discriminatory taxes. The United States also complained of Japan's quarantine, testing and other agricultural import rules. The U.S. won at the WTO and Japan has changed its procedures.

In a semiconductor dumping dispute, Korea successfully argued that the U.S. was not in compliance with the WTO Antidumping Agreement. The United States amended its law, but Korea has instituted further proceedings alleging that these amendments are inadequate. The United States did likewise after Australia lost a subsidies dispute relating to auto leather. The reconvened WTO panel ruled that Australia had indeed failed to conform to the original adverse DSB decision. A U.S. challenge concerning India's quotas on imports of agricultural, textile and industrial products was upheld. India and the United States subsequently reached agreement on a timeline for removal of these restraints.

Closer to home, New Zealand and the United States complained of Canada's import/export rules regarding milk. Losing at the WTO, Canada agreed to a phased removal of the offending measures. The United States also won against Mexico in an antidumping dispute involving corn syrup, but lost a "big one" when the Appellate Body determined that export tax preferences granted to "Foreign Sales

Corporations" of U.S. companies were illegal. Another "big one" went in favor of the United States. The European Union challenged the validity under the DSU of unilateral retaliation under Section 301 of the Trade Act of 1974. Section 301 has been something of a bete noire in U.S. trade law (see Chapter 14), but the WTO panel affirmed its legality in light of Presidential undertakings to administer it in accordance with U.S. obligations to adhere to multilateral WTO dispute settlement.

U.S. involvement in WTO dispute settlement continues to be extensive. The Appellate Body ruled that U.S. countervailing duties against British steel based upon pre-privatization subsidies were unlawful. The European Union prevailed before a WTO panel in its challenge of the U.S. Antidumping Act of 1916, since repealed. U.S. complaints against Korean beef import restraints and procurement practices were upheld. Canada's patent protection term was also invalidated by the WTO under a U.S. complaint. European Union complaints concerning U.S. wheat gluten quotas and the royalty free small business provisions of the Fairness in Music Licensing Act of 1998 have been sustained. The *Wheat Gluten* dispute questions the legality of U.S. "causation" rules in escape clause proceedings under Section 201 of the Trade Act of 1974.

A WTO Panel ruled in 2002 that the Byrd Amendment violates the WTO antidumping and subsidy codes. The Byrd Amendment (Continued Dumping and Subsidy Act of 2000) authorizes the Customs Service to forward AD and CVD duties to affected domestic producers for qualified expenses. Eleven WTO members including the EU, Canada and Mexico challenged the Amendment. This ruling was affirmed by the WTO Appellate Body and retaliation was authorized. Late in 2005, the U.S. repealed the Byrd Amendment, subject to a contested two-year phase out. The Appellate Body also ruled against Section 211 of the Omnibus Appropriations Act of 1998 denying trademark protection in connection with confiscated assets (the "HAVANA CLUB" dispute). U.S. compliance with these rulings has been slow in forthcoming. The United States and other complainants prevailed in a 2002 WTO proceeding against Indian local content and trade balancing requirements for foreign auto manufacturers. These requirements violated the TRIMs agreement.

In March of 2004, the European Union commenced raising tariffs against U.S. goods under the WTO retaliation authorized out of the FSC/export tax subsidy dispute. Monthly increments were planned until either the U.S. complied or the EU reached the maximum of roughly $4 billion annually it was authorized to retaliate. In the Fall of 2004, the United States repealed the extraterritorial income exclusion and the EU subsequently removed its retaliatory tariffs. In 2004, also, Antigua-Barbuda won a WTO panel ruling under the GATS against certain U.S. Internet gambling restraints. Retaliation was authorized, and the U.S. settled with nearly all members by offering compensation. The U.S. won a panel decision against Mexico's exorbitant telecom interconnection rates, but lost a 2004 cotton subsidy challenge by Brazil. Retaliation by Brazil was authorized.

The United States also lost a second dispute with the EU about pre-privatization countervailable subsidies, in particular the legality of the U.S. "same person" methodology. The U.S. won a SPS dispute against Japanese quarantine of U.S. apples, while losing an important softwood lumber "zeroing" methodology complaint brought by Canada. The U.S. repeatedly lost zeroing disputes brought by other WTO members before grudgingly amending its antidumping rules.

In 2006, the Mexico-United States "sugar war" came to a head before the Appellate Body. Mexico's 20% soft drink tax on beverages not using cane sugar, its 20% distribution tax on those beverages, and related bookkeeping requirements were found to violate GATT Article III and not exempt under Article XX(d). Subsequently, the two countries settled their dispute by agreeing, effective in 2008, to free trade in sugar and high fructose corn syrup. Sugar remains one of the most highly protected sectors of the U.S. economy sheltered behind quotas dating back to the 1930s. Commonly triple the world commodity price of sugar, U.S. sugar quotas drove Hershey Chocolates among others to move its factories abroad. The CIA reports that sugar producers in Jamaica switched to marijuana as a consequence of U.S. sugar import quotas.

The U.S. failed to persuade the Appellate Body to require the European Union under GATT Article X (3) to undertake a major overhaul of its customs law system targeting inconsistencies therein among the 28 member states. In 2010, the United States agreed to pay $147 million annually to provide technical assistance to Brazilian cotton farmers. In return, Brazil has suspended retaliatory tariffs and cross-sector IP sanctions authorized by the WTO because of U.S. cotton subsidy violations.

In 2009, a WTO panel ruled that Airbus had received $20 billion in illegal EU "launch" subsidies. By 2010, that same panel found Boeing the recipient of $5 billion in federal research contract subsidies that violated the WTO Subsidies Code. Appeals taken in both disputes resulted in affirmations by the WTO Appellate Body. These disputes remain ongoing and are frequently cited by Trump administration critics of the WTO dispute settlement process.

The United States has also settled a number of disputes prior to WTO panel decisions, and remains in consultation on other disputes that may be decided by a WTO panel. For the latest summary of all WTO disputes, including many not involving the United States, see www.wto.org.

§ 10.10 China Involvement in WTO Disputes

China, a member since 2001, is involved in a growing number of WTO disputes. China has lost nearly all the complaints filed against it, and won relatively few WTO disputes it has filed. China's compliance record with WTO decisions has been spotty. Here is a sampling of WTO disputes involving China.

Canada, the European Union and the United States complained against Chinese duties on imported auto parts (10 percent) that rose to those on complete autos (25 percent) if the imported parts exceeded a fixed percentage of the final vehicle content or price, or if specific combinations of imported auto parts were used in the final vehicle. In addition, extensive record keeping, reporting and verification requirements were imposed when Chinese auto companies used imported parts. In July of 2008, a WTO panel ruled that these "internal charges" violated Articles III (2) and III (4) of the GATT and China's accession commitments. The core Panel ruling, affirmed by the Appellate Body, found China's auto parts measures discriminatory in favor of domestic producers, a violation of the national treatment standard for taxes and regulations. This ruling marked the first time since China's admission in 2001 that it was held in breach of its WTO commitments and obligations.

Less than one month after losing this dispute, China enacted a clever "green tax" on gas-guzzling autos, most of which just happen to be imported. The sales tax on cars with engine capacities over 4.1 litres has been doubled to 40%. Autos with engines between 3 and 4.1 litres are taxed at 25%, up from 15%. Most Chinese-made cars have engines with 2.5 litres or less. Autos with engines between 1 and 3 litres remain taxed at 8% and 10%. The smallest cars with engines below 1 litre have their sales tax reduced from 3 to 1 percent. This green tax seemingly was intended to protective results similar to China's Auto Parts tariff structure.

Other disputes challenging China's compliance with WTO law are pending. They concern China's auto export subsidies and CVDs on auto imports, protection and enforcement of intellectual property rights (2009 WTO panel ruled against China), trade and distribution of publications and audiovisual entertainment products and services (2009 Appellate Body ruled against China), commodity export tariffs and restrictions (2012 WTO Appellate Body ruled against China), application of Chinese AD to U.S. grain-oriented flat rolled steel (GOES) (2012 WTO Appellate Body ruled against China), discriminatory treatment of foreign electronic payment services (2012 WTO panel ruled against China) and rare earth export restraints (2014 WTO Panel ruled against China). The United States is a complaining party to all of these disputes. China's record of compliance with these WTO rulings resembles that of the U.S. noted above, somewhat spotty and not always prompt.

China, in turn, has challenged U.S. safeguard measures applied to Chinese steel exports (2010 WTO Panel rejected challenge) and tires (2011 WTO Panel rejected challenge). It has challenged U.S. antidumping and countervailing duties on paper products from China (2011 WTO Panel ruled against U.S. dual assessment of AD and CVD duties), as well as U.S. AD on Chinese solar panels. China has also applied AD duties to U.S. exports, e.g. chicken.

In a major dispute, China challenged in 2017 continued U.S. and EU application of nonmarket economy rules in antidumping disputes. China has also challenged President Trump's solar panel and clothes washers Safeguard tariffs, as well as Trump's "national security" steel and aluminum tariffs. Numerous U.S. CVDs against a range of Chinese goods were successfully challenged in 2018 on procedural grounds by China before a WTO panel. Meanwhile, the United States is challenging Chinese export restrictions on raw materials and alleged unlawful subsidization of aluminum, rice, wheat and corn.

The Trump Administration filed in 2018 a WTO complaint, joined by Japan and the European Union, against alleged patent violations of Articles 3 and 28 of TRIPs. These allegations assert that foreign patent holders are unable to stop Chinese licensees from continuing to use patented technology after licenses expire. They also assert Chinese discrimination against and less favorable mandatory adverse contract terms for imported foreign technology. The U.S. specifically cites four Chinese laws as the source of these TRIPs violations: The PRC Foreign Trade Law, Contract Law, Chinese-Foreign Equity Joint Venture Law, and the PRC Regulations on the Administration of the Import and Export of Technologies.

§ 10.11 Text of WTO Understanding on Rules and Procedures Governing the Settlement of Disputes (1995) (DSU)

(Annex 2 to the Agreement Establishing the World Trade Organization)

(Selected Provisions)

Article 1. Coverage and Application

1. The rules and procedures of this Understanding shall apply to disputes brought pursuant to the consultation and dispute settlement provisions of the agreements listed in Appendix 1 to this Understanding (referred to in this Understanding as the "covered agreements"). The rules and procedures of this Understanding shall also apply to consultations and the settlement of disputes between Members concerning their rights and obligations under the provisions of the Agreement Establishing the World Trade Organization (referred to in this Understanding as the "WTO Agreement") and of this Understanding taken in isolation or in combination with any other covered agreement.

2. The rules and procedures of this Understanding shall apply subject to such special or additional rules and procedures on dispute settlement contained in the covered agreements as are identified in Appendix 2 to this Understanding. To the extent that there is a difference between the rules and procedures of this Understanding and the special or additional rules and procedures set forth in Appendix 2, the special or additional rules and procedures in Appendix 2 shall prevail. In disputes involving rules and procedures under more than one covered agreement, if there is a conflict between special or additional rules and procedures of such agreements under review, and where the parties to the dispute cannot agree on rules and procedures within 20 days of the establishment of the panel, the Chairman of the Dispute Settlement Body provided for in paragraph 1 of Article 2 (referred to in this Understanding as the "DSB"), in consultation with the parties to the dispute, shall determine the rules and procedures to be followed within 10 days after a request by either Member. The Chairman shall be guided by the principle that special or additional rules and procedures should be used where possible, and the rules and procedures set out in this Understanding should be used to the extent necessary to avoid conflict.

Article 2. Administration

1. The Dispute Settlement Body is hereby established to administer these rules and procedures and, except as otherwise provided in a covered agreement, the consultation and dispute

settlement provisions of the covered agreements. Accordingly, the DSB shall have the authority to establish panels, adopt panel and Appellate Body reports, maintain surveillance of implementation of rulings and recommendations, and authorize suspension of concessions and other obligations under the covered agreements. With respect to disputes arising under a covered agreement which is a Plurilateral Trade Agreement, the term "Member" as used herein shall refer only to those Members that are parties to the relevant Plurilateral Trade Agreement. Where the DSB administers the dispute settlement provisions of a Plurilateral Trade Agreement, only those Members that are parties to that Agreement may participate in decisions or actions taken by the DSB with respect to that dispute.

2. The DSB shall inform the relevant WTO Councils and Committees of any developments in disputes related to provisions of the respective covered agreements.

3. The DSB shall meet as often as necessary to carry out its functions within the time-frames provided in this Understanding.

4. Where the rules and procedures of this Understanding provide for the DSB to take a decision, it shall do so by consensus.[15]

Article 3. General Provisions

1. Members affirm their adherence to the principles for the management of disputes heretofore applied under Articles XXII and XXIII of GATT 1947, and the rules and procedures as further elaborated and modified herein.

2. The dispute settlement system of the WTO is a central element in providing security and predictability to the multilateral trading system. The Members recognize that it serves to preserve the rights and obligations of Members under the covered agreements, and to clarify the existing provisions of those agreements in accordance with customary rules of interpretation of public international law. Recommendations and rulings of the DSB cannot add to or diminish the rights and obligations provided in the covered agreements.

3. The prompt settlement of situations in which a Member considers that any benefits accruing to it directly or indirectly under the covered agreements are being impaired by measures taken by another Member is essential to the effective functioning of the WTO and the maintenance of a proper balance between the rights and obligations of Members.

[15] The DSB shall be deemed to have decided by consensus on a matter submitted for its consideration, if no Member, present at the meeting of the DSB when the decision is taken, formally objects to the proposed decision.

4. Recommendations or rulings made by the DSB shall be aimed at achieving a satisfactory settlement of the matter in accordance with the rights and obligations under this Understanding and under the covered agreements.

5. All solutions to matters formally raised under the consultation and dispute settlement provisions of the covered agreements, including arbitration awards, shall be consistent with those agreements and shall not nullify or impair benefits accruing to any Member under those agreements, nor impede the attainment of any objective of those agreements.

6. Mutually agreed solutions to matters formally raised under the consultation and dispute settlement provisions of the covered agreements shall be notified to the DSB and the relevant Councils and Committees, where any Member may raise any point relating thereto.

7. Before bringing a case, a Member shall exercise its judgment as to whether action under these procedures would be fruitful. The aim of the dispute settlement mechanism is to secure a positive solution to a dispute. A solution mutually acceptable to the parties to a dispute and consistent with the covered agreements is clearly to be preferred. In the absence of a mutually agreed solution, the first objective of the dispute settlement mechanism is usually to secure the withdrawal of the measures concerned if these are found to be inconsistent with the provisions of any of the covered agreements. The provision of compensation should be resorted to only if the immediate withdrawal of the measure is impracticable and as a temporary measure pending the withdrawal of the measure which is inconsistent with a covered agreement. The last resort which this Understanding provides to the Member invoking the dispute settlement procedures is the possibility of suspending the application of concessions or other obligations under the covered agreements on a discriminatory basis vis-á-vis the other Member, subject to authorization by the DSB of such measures.

8. In cases where there is an infringement of the obligations assumed under a covered agreement, the action is considered *prima facie* to constitute a case of nullification or impairment. This means that there is normally a presumption that a breach of the rules has an adverse impact on other Members parties to that covered agreement, and in such cases, it shall be up to the Member against whom the complaint has been brought to rebut the charge.

9. The provisions of this Understanding are without prejudice to the rights of Members to seek authoritative interpretation of provisions of a covered agreement through decision-making under

the WTO Agreement or a covered agreement which is a Plurilateral Trade Agreement.

10. It is understood that requests for conciliation and the use of the dispute settlement procedures should not be intended or considered as contentious acts and that, if a dispute arises, all Members will engage in these procedures in good faith in an effort to resolve the dispute. It is also understood that complaints and counter-complaints in regard to distinct matters should not be linked.

11. This Understanding shall be applied only with respect to new requests for consultations under the consultation provisions of the covered agreements made on or after the date of entry into force of the WTO Agreement. With respect to disputes for which the request for consultations was made under GATT 1947 or under any other predecessor agreement to the covered agreements before the date of entry into force of the WTO Agreement, the relevant dispute settlement rules and procedures in effect immediately prior to the date of entry into force of the WTO Agreement shall continue to apply.[16]

12. Notwithstanding paragraph 11, if a complaint based on any of the covered agreements is brought by a developing country Member against a developed country Member, the complaining party shall have the right to invoke, as an alternative to the provisions contained in Articles 4, 5, 6 and 12 of this Understanding, the corresponding provisions of the Decision of 5 April 1966 (BISD 14S/18), except that where the Panel considers that the time-frame provided for in paragraph 7 of that Decision is insufficient to provide its report and with the agreement of the complaining party, that time-frame may be extended. To the extent that there is a difference between the rules and procedures of Articles 4, 5, 6 and 12 and the corresponding rules and procedures of the Decision, the latter shall prevail.

Article 4. Consultations

1. Members affirm their resolve to strengthen and improve the effectiveness of the consultation procedures employed by Members.

2. Each Member undertakes to accord sympathetic consideration to and afford adequate opportunity for consultation regarding any representations made by another Member concerning measures affecting the operation of any covered agreement taken within the territory of the former.[17]

---

[16] This paragraph shall also be applied to disputes on which panel reports have not been adopted or fully implemented.

[17] Where the provisions of any other covered agreement concerning measures taken by regional or local governments or authorities within the territory of a Member

3. If a request for consultations is made pursuant to a covered agreement, the Member to which the request is made shall, unless otherwise mutually agreed, reply to the request within 10 days after the date of its receipt and shall enter into consultations in good faith within a period of no more than 30 days after the date of receipt of the request, with a view to reaching a mutually satisfactory solution. If the Member does not respond within 10 days after the date of receipt of the request, or does not enter into consultations within a period of no more than 30 days, or a period otherwise mutually agreed, after the date of receipt of the request, then the Member that requested the holding of consultations may proceed directly to request the establishment of a panel.

4. All such requests for consultations shall be notified to the DSB and the relevant Councils and Committees by the Member which requests consultations. Any request for consultations shall be submitted in writing and shall give the reasons for the request, including identification of the measures at issue and an indication of the legal basis for the complaint.

5. In the course of consultations in accordance with the provisions of a covered agreement, before resorting to further action under this Understanding, Members should attempt to obtain satisfactory adjustment of the matter.

6. Consultations shall be confidential, and without prejudice to the rights of any Member in any further proceedings.

7. If the consultations fail to settle a dispute within 60 days after the date of receipt of the request for consultations, the complaining party may request the establishment of a panel. The complaining party may request a panel during the 60-day period if the consulting parties jointly consider that consultations have failed to settle the dispute.

8. In cases of urgency, including those which concern perishable goods, Members shall enter into consultations within a period of no more than 10 days after the date of receipt of the request. If the consultations have failed to settle the dispute within a period of 20 days after the date of receipt of the request, the complaining party may request the establishment of a panel.

9. In cases of urgency, including those which concern perishable goods, the parties to the dispute, panels and the Appellate Body shall make every effort to accelerate the proceedings to the greatest extent possible.

---

contain provisions different from the provisions of this paragraph, the provisions of such other covered agreement shall prevail.

10. During consultations Members should give special attention to the particular problems and interests of developing country Members.

11. Whenever a Member other than the consulting Members considers that it has a substantial trade interest in consultations being held pursuant to paragraph 1 of Article XXII of GATT 1994, paragraph 1 of Article XXII of GATS, or the corresponding provisions in other covered agreements,[18] such Member may notify the consulting Members and the DSB, within 10 days after the date of the circulation of the request for consultations under said Article, of its desire to be joined in the consultations. Such Member shall be joined in the consultations, provided that the Member to which the request for consultations was addressed agrees that the claim of substantial interest is well-founded. In that event they shall so inform the DSB. If the request to be joined in the consultations is not accepted, the applicant Member shall be free to request consultations under paragraph 1 of Article XXII or paragraph 1 of Article XXIII of GATT 1994, paragraph 1 of Article XXII or paragraph 1 of Article XXIII of GATS, or the corresponding provisions in other covered agreements.

Article 5. Good Offices, Conciliation and Mediation

1. Good offices, conciliation and mediation are procedures that are undertaken voluntarily if the parties to the dispute so agree.

2. Proceedings involving good offices, conciliation and mediation, and in particular positions taken by the parties to the dispute during these proceedings, shall be confidential, and without prejudice to the rights of either party in any further proceedings under these procedures.

3. Good offices, conciliation or mediation may be requested at any time by any party to a dispute. They may begin at any time and be terminated at any time. Once procedures for good offices, conciliation

[18] The corresponding consultation provisions in the covered agreements are listed hereunder: Agreement on Agriculture, Article 19; Agreement on the Application of Sanitary and Phytosanitary Measures, paragraph 1 of Article 11; Agreement on Textiles and Clothing, paragraph 4 of Article 8; Agreement on Technical Barriers to Trade, paragraph 1 of Article 14; Agreement on Trade-Related Investment Measures, Article 8; Agreement on Implementation of Article VI of GATT 1994, paragraph 2 of Article 17; Agreement on Implementation of Article VII of GATT 1994, paragraph 2 of Article 19; Agreement on Preshipment Inspection, Article 7; Agreement on Rules of Origin, Article 7; Agreement on Import Licensing Procedures, Article 6; Agreement on Subsidies and Countervailing Measures, Article 30; Agreement on Safeguards, Article 14; Agreement on Trade-Related Aspects of Intellectual Property Rights, Article 64.1; and any corresponding consultation provisions in Plurilateral Trade Agreements as determined by the competent bodies of each Agreement and as notified to the DSB.

or mediation are terminated, a complaining party may then proceed with a request for the establishment of a panel.

4. When good offices, conciliation or mediation are entered into within 60 days after the date of receipt of a request for consultations, the complaining party must allow a period of 60 days after the date of receipt of the request for consultations before requesting the establishment of a panel. The complaining party may request the establishment of a panel during the 60-day period if the parties to the dispute jointly consider that the good offices, conciliation or mediation process has failed to settle the dispute.

5. If the parties to a dispute agree, procedures for good offices, conciliation or mediation may continue while the panel process proceeds.

6. The Director-General may, acting in an *ex officio* capacity, offer good offices, conciliation or mediation with the view to assisting Members to settle a dispute.

Article 6. Establishment of Panels

1. If the complaining party so requests, a panel shall be established at the latest at the DSB meeting following that at which the request first appears as an item on the DSB's agenda, unless at that meeting the DSB decides by consensus not to establish a panel.[19]

2. The request for the establishment of a panel shall be made in writing. It shall indicate whether consultations were held, identify the specific measures at issue and provide a brief summary of the legal basis of the complaint sufficient to present the problem clearly. In case the applicant requests the establishment of a panel with other than standard terms of reference, the written request shall include the proposed text of special terms of reference.

Article 7. Terms of Reference of Panels

1. Panels shall have the following terms of reference unless the parties to the dispute agree otherwise within 20 days from the establishment of the panel:

> "To examine, in the light of the relevant provisions in (name of the covered agreement(s) cited by the parties to the dispute), the matter referred to the DSB by (name of party) in document . . . and to make such findings as will assist the DSB in making the recommendations or in giving the rulings provided for in that/those agreement(s)."

[19] If the complaining party so requests, a meeting of the DSB shall be convened for this purpose within 15 days of the request, provided that at least 10 days' advance notice of the meeting is given.

2. Panels shall address the relevant provisions in any covered agreement or agreements cited by the parties to the dispute.

3. In establishing a panel, the DSB may authorize its Chairman to draw up the terms of reference of the panel in consultation with the parties to the dispute, subject to the provisions of paragraph 1. The terms of reference thus drawn up shall be circulated to all Members. If other than standard terms of reference are agreed upon, any Member may raise any point relating thereto in the DSB.

Article 8. Composition of Panels

1. Panels shall be composed of well-qualified governmental and/or non-governmental individuals, including persons who have served on or presented a case to a panel, served as a representative of a Member or of a contracting party to GATT 1947 or as a representative to the Council or Committee of any covered agreement or its predecessor agreement, or in the Secretariat, taught or published on international trade law or policy, or served as a senior trade policy official of a Member.

2. Panel members should be selected with a view to ensuring the independence of the members, a sufficiently diverse background and a wide spectrum of experience.

3. Citizens of Members whose governments[20] are parties to the dispute or third parties as defined in paragraph 2 of Article 10 shall not serve on a panel concerned with that dispute, unless the parties to the dispute agree otherwise.

4. To assist in the selection of panelists, the Secretariat shall maintain an indicative list of governmental and non-governmental individuals possessing the qualifications outlined in paragraph 1, from which panelists may be drawn as appropriate. That list shall include the roster of non-governmental panelists established on 30 November 1984 (BISD 31S/9), and other rosters and indicative lists established under any of the covered agreements, and shall retain the names of persons on those rosters and indicative lists at the time of entry into force of the WTO Agreement. Members may periodically suggest names of governmental and non-governmental individuals for inclusion on the indicative list, providing relevant information on their knowledge of international trade and of the sectors or subject matter of the covered agreements, and those names shall be added to the list upon approval by the DSB. For each of the individuals on the list, the list shall indicate specific areas of experience or expertise of

[20] In the case where customs unions or common markets are parties to a dispute, this provision applies to citizens of all member countries of the customs unions or common markets.

the individuals in the sectors or subject matter of the covered agreements.

5. Panels shall be composed of three panelists unless the parties to the dispute agree, within 10 days from the establishment of the panel, to a panel composed of five panelists. Members shall be informed promptly of the composition of the panel.

6. The Secretariat shall propose nominations for the panel to the parties to the dispute. The parties to the dispute shall not oppose nominations except for compelling reasons.

7. If there is no agreement on the panelists within 20 days after the date of the establishment of a panel, at the request of either party, the Director-General, in consultation with the Chairman of the DSB and the Chairman of the relevant Council or Committee, shall determine the composition of the panel by appointing the panelists whom the Director-General considers most appropriate in accordance with any relevant special or additional rules or procedures of the covered agreement or covered agreements which are at issue in the dispute, after consulting with the parties to the dispute. The Chairman of the DSB shall inform the Members of the composition of the panel thus formed no later than 10 days after the date the Chairman receives such a request.

8. Members shall undertake, as a general rule, to permit their officials to serve as panelists.

9. Panelists shall serve in their individual capacities and not as government representatives, nor as representatives of any organization. Members shall therefore not give them instructions nor seek to influence them as individuals with regard to matters before a panel.

10. When a dispute is between a developing country Member and a developed country Member the panel shall, if the developing country Member so requests, include at least one panelist from a developing country Member.

11. Panelists' expenses, including travel and subsistence allowance, shall be met from the WTO budget in accordance with criteria to be adopted by the General Council, based on recommendations of the Committee on Budget, Finance and Administration.

Article 9. Procedures for Multiple Complainants

1. Where more than one Member requests the establishment of a panel related to the same matter, a single panel may be established to examine these complaints taking into account the rights of all Members concerned. A single panel should be established to examine such complaints whenever feasible.

2. The single panel shall organize its examination and present its findings to the DSB in such a manner that the rights which the parties to the dispute would have enjoyed had separate panels examined the complaints are in no way impaired. If one of the parties to the dispute so requests, the panel shall submit separate reports on the dispute concerned. The written submissions by each of the complainants shall be made available to the other complainants, and each complainant shall have the right to be present when any one of the other complainants presents its views to the panel.

3. If more than one panel is established to examine the complaints related to the same manner, to the greatest extent possible the same persons shall serve as panelists on each of the separate panels and the timetable for the panel process in such disputes shall be harmonized.

Article 10. Third Parties

1. The interests of the parties to a dispute and those of other Members under a covered agreement at issue in the dispute shall be fully taken into account during the panel process.

2. Any Member having a substantial interest in a matter before a panel and having notified its interest to the DSB (referred to in this Understanding as a "third party") shall have an opportunity to be heard by the panel and to make written submissions to the panel. These submissions shall also be given to the parties to the dispute and shall be reflected in the panel report.

3. Third parties shall receive the submissions of the parties to the dispute [at] the first meeting of the panel.

4. If a third party considers that a measure already the subject of a panel proceeding nullifies or impairs benefits accruing to it under any covered agreement, that Member may have recourse to normal dispute settlement procedures under this Understanding. Such a dispute shall be referred to the original panel wherever possible.

Article 11. Function of Panels

The function of panels is to assist the DSB in discharging its responsibilities under this Understanding and the covered agreements. Accordingly, a panel should make an objective assessment of the matter before it, including an objective assessment of the facts of the case and the applicability of and conformity with the relevant covered agreements, and make such other findings as will assist the DSB in making the recommendations or in giving the rulings provided for in the covered agreements. Panels should consult regularly with the parties to the dispute and give them adequate opportunity to develop a mutually satisfactory solution.

Article 12. Panel Procedures

1. Panels shall follow the Working Procedures in Appendix 3 unless the panel decides otherwise after consulting the parties to the dispute.

2. Panel procedures should provide sufficient flexibility so as to ensure high-quality panel reports, while not unduly delaying the panel process.

3. After consulting the parties to the dispute, the panelists shall, as soon as practicable and whenever possible within one week after the composition and terms of reference of the panel have been agreed upon, fix the timetable for the panel process, taking into account the provisions of paragraph 9 of Article 4, if relevant.

4. In determining the timetable for the panel process, the panel shall provide sufficient time for the parties to the dispute to prepare their submissions.

5. Panels should set precise deadlines for written submissions by the parties and the parties should respect those deadlines.

6. Each party to the dispute shall deposit its written submissions with the Secretariat for immediate transmission to the panel and to the other party or parties to the dispute. The complaining party shall submit its first submission in advance of the responding party's first submission unless the panel decides, in fixing the timetable referred to in paragraph 3 and after consultations with the parties to the dispute, that the parties should submit their first submissions simultaneously. When there are sequential arrangements for the deposit of first submissions, the panel shall establish a firm time-period for receipt of the responding party's submission. Any subsequent written submissions shall be submitted simultaneously.

7. Where the parties to the dispute have failed to develop a mutually satisfactory solution, the panel shall submit its findings in the form of a written report to the DSB. In such cases, the report of a panel shall set out the findings of fact, the applicability of relevant provisions and the basic rationale behind any findings and recommendations that it makes. Where a settlement of the matter among the parties to the dispute has been found, the report of the panel shall be confined to a brief description of the case and to reporting that a solution has been reached.

8. In order to make the procedures more efficient, the period in which the panel shall conduct its examination, from the date that the composition and terms of reference of the panel have been agreed upon until the date the final report is issued to the parties to the dispute, shall, as a general rule, not exceed six months. In cases of

urgency, including those relating to perishable goods, the panel shall aim to issue its report to the parties to the dispute within three months.

9. When the panel considers that it cannot issue its report within six months, or within three months in cases of urgency, it shall inform the DSB in writing of the reasons for the delay together with an estimate of the period within which it will issue its report. In no case should the period from the establishment of the panel to the circulation of the report to the Members exceed nine months.

10. In the context of consultations involving a measure taken by a developing country Member, the parties may agree to extend the periods established in paragraphs 7 and 8 of Article 4. If, after the relevant period has elapsed, the consulting parties cannot agree that the consultations have concluded, the Chairman of the DSB shall decide, after consultation with the parties, whether to extend the relevant period and, if so, for how long. In addition, in examining a complaint against a developing country Member, the panel shall accord sufficient time for the developing country Member to prepare and present its argumentation. The provisions of paragraph 1 of Article 20 and paragraph 4 of Article 21 are not affected by any action pursuant to this paragraph.

11. Where one or more of the parties is a developing country Member, the panel's report shall explicitly indicate the form in which account has been taken of relevant provisions on differential and more-favourable treatment for developing country Members that form part of the covered agreements which have been raised by the developing country Member in the course of the dispute settlement procedures.

12. The panel may suspend its work at any time at the request of the complaining party for a period not to exceed 12 months. In the event of such a suspension, the time-frames set out in paragraphs 8 and 9 of this Article, paragraph 1 of Article 20, and paragraph 4 of Article 21 shall be extended by the amount of time that the work was suspended. If the work of the panel has been suspended for more than 12 months, the authority for establishment of the panel shall lapse.

Article 13. Right to Seek Information

1. Each panel shall have the right to seek information and technical advice from any individual or body which it deems appropriate. However, before a panel seeks such information or advice from any individual or body within the jurisdiction of a Member it shall inform the authorities of that Member. A Member should respond promptly and fully to any request by a panel for such information as the panel considers necessary and appropriate.

Confidential information which is provided shall not be revealed without formal authorization from the individual, body, or authorities of the Member providing the information.

2. Panels may seek information from any relevant source and may consult experts to obtain their opinion on certain aspects of the matter. With respect to a factual issue concerning a scientific or other technical matter raised by a party to a dispute, a panel may request an advisory report in writing from an expert review group. Rules for the establishment of such a group and its procedures are set forth in Appendix 4.

Article 14. Confidentiality

1. Panel deliberations shall be confidential.

2. The reports of panels shall be drafted without the presence of the parties to the dispute in the light of the information provided and the statements made.

3. Opinions expressed in the panel report by individual panelists shall be anonymous.

Article 15. Interim Review Stage

1. Following the consideration of rebuttal submissions and oral arguments, the panel shall issue the descriptive (factual and argument) sections of its draft report to the parties to the dispute. Within a period of time set by the panel, the parties shall submit their comments in writing.

2. Following the expiration of the set period of time for receipt of comments from the parties to the dispute, the panel shall issue an interim report to the parties, including both the descriptive sections and the panel's findings and conclusions. Within a period of time set by the panel, a party may submit a written request for the panel to review precise aspects of the interim report prior to circulation of the final report to the Members. At the request of a party, the panel shall hold a further meeting with the parties on the issues identified in the written comments. If no comments are received from any party within the comment period, the interim report shall be considered the final panel report and circulated promptly to the Members.

3. The findings of the final panel report shall include a discussion of the arguments made at the interim review stage. The interim review stage shall be conducted within the time-period set out in paragraph 8 of Article 12.

Article 16. Adoption of Panel Reports

1. In order to provide sufficient time for the Members to consider panel reports, the reports shall not be considered for adoption by the

DSB until 20 days after the date they have been circulated to the Members.

2. Members having objections to a panel report shall give written reasons to explain their objections for circulation at least 10 days prior to the DSB meeting at which the panel report will be considered.

3. The parties to a dispute shall have the right to participate fully in the consideration of the panel report by the DSB, and their views shall be fully recorded.

4. Within 60 days after the date of circulation of a panel report to the Members, the report shall be adopted at a DSB meeting[21] nless a party to the dispute formally notifies the DSB of its decision to appeal or the DSB decides by consensus not to adopt the report. If a party has notified its decision to appeal, the report by the panel shall not be considered for adoption by the DSB until after completion of the appeal. This adoption procedure is without prejudice to the right of Members to express their views on a panel report.

Article 17. Appellate Review

Standing Appellate Body

1. A standing Appellate Body shall be established by the DSB. The Appellate Body shall hear appeals from panel cases. It shall be composed of seven persons, three of whom shall serve on any one case. Persons serving on the Appellate Body shall serve in rotation. Such rotation shall be determined in the working procedures of the Appellate Body.

2. The DSB shall appoint persons to serve on the Appellate Body for a four-year term, and each person may be reappointed once. However, the terms of three of the seven persons appointed immediately after the entry into force of the WTO Agreement shall expire at the end of two years, to be determined by lot. Vacancies shall be filled as they arise. A person appointed to replace a person whose term of office has not expired shall hold office for the remainder of the predecessor's term.

3. The Appellate Body shall comprise persons of recognized authority, with demonstrated expertise in law, international trade and the subject matter of the covered agreements generally. They shall be unaffiliated with any government. The Appellate Body membership shall be broadly representative of membership in the WTO. All persons serving on the Appellate Body shall be available at

---

[21] If a meeting of the DSB is not scheduled within this period at a time that enables the requirements of paragraphs 1 and 4 of Article 16 to be met, a meeting of the DSB shall be held for this purpose.

all times and on short notice, and shall stay abreast of dispute settlement activities and other relevant activities of the WTO. They shall not participate in the consideration of any disputes that would create a direct or indirect conflict of interest.

4. Only parties to the dispute, not third parties, may appeal a panel report. Third parties which have notified the DSB of a substantial interest in the matter pursuant to paragraph 2 of Article 10 may make written submissions to, and be given an opportunity to be heard by, the Appellate Body.

5. As a general rule, the proceedings shall not exceed 60 days from the date a party to the dispute formally notifies its decision to appeal to the date the Appellate Body circulates its report. In fixing its timetable the Appellate Body shall take into account the provisions of paragraph 9 of Article 4, if relevant. When the Appellate Body considers that it cannot provide its report within 60 days, it shall inform the DSB in writing of the reasons for the delay together with an estimate of the period within which it will submit its report. In no case shall the proceedings exceed 90 days.

6. An appeal shall be limited to issues of law covered in the panel report and legal interpretations developed by the panel.

7. The Appellate Body shall be provided with appropriate administrative and legal support as it requires.

8. The expenses of persons serving on the Appellate Body, including travel and subsistence allowance, shall be met from the WTO budget in accordance with criteria to be adopted by the General Council, based on recommendations of the Committee on Budget, Finance and Administration.

Procedures for Appellate Review

9. Working procedures shall be drawn up by the Appellate Body in consultation with the Chairman of the DSB and the Director-General, and communicated to the Members for their information.

10. The proceedings of the Appellate Body shall be confidential. The reports of the Appellate Body shall be drafted without the presence of the parties to the dispute and in the light of the information provided and the statements made.

11. Opinions expressed in the Appellate Body report by individuals serving on the Appellate Body shall be anonymous.

12. The Appellate Body shall address each of the issues raised in accordance with paragraph 6 during the appellate proceeding.

13. The Appellate Body may uphold, modify or reverse the legal findings and conclusions of the panel.

Adoption of Appellate Body Reports

14. An Appellate Body report shall be adopted by the DSB and unconditionally accepted by the parties to the dispute unless the DSB decides by consensus not to adopt the Appellate Body report within 30 days following its circulation to the Members.[22] This adoption procedure is without prejudice to the right of Members to express their views on an Appellate Body report.

Article 18. Communications with the Panel or Appellate Body

1. There shall be no *ex parte* communications with the panel or Appellate Body concerning matters under consideration by the panel or Appellate Body.

2. Written submissions to the panel or the Appellate Body shall be treated as confidential, but shall be made available to the parties to the dispute. Nothing in this Understanding shall preclude a party to a dispute from disclosing statements of its own positions to the public. Members shall treat as confidential information submitted by another Member to the panel or the Appellate Body which that Member has designated as confidential. A party to a dispute shall also, upon request of a Member, provide a non-confidential summary of the information contained in its written submissions that could be disclosed to the public.

Article 19. Panel and Appellate Body Recommendations

1. Where a panel or the Appellate Body concludes that a measure is inconsistent with a covered agreement, it shall recommend that the Member concerned[23] bring the measure into conformity with that agreement.[24] In addition to its recommendations, the panel or Appellate Body may suggest ways in which the Member concerned could implement the recommendations.

2. In accordance with paragraph 2 of Article 3, in their findings and recommendations, the panel and Appellate Body cannot add to or diminish the rights and obligations provided in the covered agreements.

Article 20. Time-frame for DSB Decisions

Unless otherwise agreed to by the parties to the dispute, the period from the date of establishment of the panel by the DSB until

---

[22] If a meeting of the DSB is not scheduled during this period, such a meeting of the DSB shall be held for this purpose.

[23] The "Member concerned" is the party to the dispute to which the panel or Appellate Body recommendations are directed.

[24] With respect to recommendations in cases not involving a violation of GATT 1994 or any other covered agreement, see Article 26.

the date the DSB considers the panel or appellate report for adoption shall as a general rule not exceed nine months where the panel report is not appealed or 12 months where the report is appealed. Where either the panel or the Appellate Body has acted, pursuant to paragraph 9 of Article 12 or paragraph 5 of Article 17, to extend the time for providing its report, the additional time taken shall be added to the above periods.

Article 21. Surveillance of Implementation of Recommendations and Rulings

1. Prompt compliance with recommendations or rulings of the DSB is essential in order to ensure effective resolution of disputes to the benefit of all Members.

2. Particular attention should be paid to matters affecting the interests of developing country Members with respect to measures which have been subject to dispute settlement.

3. At a DSB meeting held within 30 days[25] after the date of adoption of the panel or Appellate Body report, the Member concerned shall inform the DSB of its intentions in respect of implementation of the recommendations and rulings of the DSB. If it is impracticable to comply immediately with the recommendations and rulings, the Member concerned shall have a reasonable period of time in which to do so. The reasonable period of time shall be:

(a) the period of time proposed by the Member concerned, provided that such period is approved by the DSB; or, in the absence of such approval,

(b) a period of time mutually agreed by the parties to the dispute within 45 days after the date of adoption of the recommendations and rulings; or, in the absence of such agreement,

(c) a period of time determined through binding arbitration within 90 days after the date of adoption of the recommendations and rulings.[26] In such arbitration, a guideline for the arbitrator[27] should be that the reasonable period of time to implement panel or Appellate Body recommendations should not exceed 15 months from the date of adoption of a panel or

---

[25] If a meeting of the DSB is not scheduled during this period, such a meeting of the DSB shall be held for this purpose.

[26] If the parties cannot agree on an arbitrator within ten days after referring the matter to arbitration, the arbitrator shall be appointed by the Director-General within ten days, after consulting the parties.

[27] The expression "arbitrator" shall be interpreted as referring either to an individual or a group.

Appellate Body report. However, that time may be shorter or longer, depending upon the particular circumstances.

4. Except where the panel or the Appellate Body has extended, pursuant to paragraph 9 of Article 12 or paragraph 5 of Article 17, the time of providing its report, the period from the date of establishment of the panel by the DSB until the date of determination of the reasonable period of time shall not exceed 15 months unless the parties to the dispute agree otherwise. Where either the panel or the Appellate Body has acted to extend the time of providing its report, the additional time taken shall be added to the 15-month period; provided that unless the parties to the dispute agree that there are exceptional circumstances, the total time shall not exceed 18 months.

5. Where there is disagreement as to the existence or consistency with a covered agreement of measures taken to comply with the recommendations and rulings such dispute shall be decided through recourse to these dispute settlement procedures, including wherever possible resort to the original panel. The panel shall circulate its report within 90 days after the date of referral of the matter to it. When the panel considers that it cannot provide its report within this time frame, it shall inform the DSB in writing of the reasons for the delay together with an estimate of the period within which it will submit its report.

6. The DSB shall keep under surveillance the implementation of adopted recommendations or rulings. The issue of implementation of the recommendations or rulings may be raised at the DSB by any Member at any time following their adoption. Unless the DSB decides otherwise, the issue of implementation of the recommendations or rulings shall be placed on the agenda of the DSB meeting after six months following the date of establishment of the reasonable period of time pursuant to paragraph 3 and shall remain on the DSB's agenda until the issue is resolved. At least 10 days prior to each such DSB meeting, the Member concerned shall provide the DSB with a status report in writing of its progress in the implementation of the recommendations or rulings.

7. If the matter is one which has been raised by a developing country Member, the DSB shall consider what further action it might take which would be appropriate to the circumstances.

8. If the case is one brought by a developing country Member, in considering what appropriate action might be taken, the DSB shall take into account not only the trade coverage of measures complained of, but also their impact on the economy of developing country Members concerned.

Article 22. Compensation and the Suspension of Concessions

1. Compensation and the suspension of concessions or other obligations are temporary measures available in the event that the recommendations and rulings are not implemented within a reasonable period of time. However, neither compensation nor the suspension of concessions or other obligations is preferred to full implementation of a recommendation to bring a measure into conformity with the covered agreements. Compensation is voluntary and, if granted, shall be consistent with the covered agreements.

2. If the Member concerned fails to bring the measure found to be inconsistent with a covered agreement into compliance therewith or otherwise comply with the recommendations and rulings within the reasonable period of time determined pursuant to paragraph 3 of Article 21, such Member shall, if so requested, and no later than the expiry of the reasonable period of time, enter into negotiations with any party having invoked the dispute settlement procedures, with a view to developing mutually acceptable compensation. If no satisfactory compensation has been agreed within 20 days after the date of expiry of the reasonable period of time, any party having invoked the dispute settlement procedures may request authorization from the DSB to suspend the application to the Member concerned of concessions or other obligations under the covered agreements.

3. In considering what concessions or other obligations to suspend, the complaining party shall apply the following principles and procedures:

(a) the general principle is that the complaining party should first seek to suspend concessions or other obligations with respect to the same sector(s) as that in which the panel or Appellate Body has found a violation or other nullification or impairment;

(b) if that party considers that it is not practicable or effective to suspend concessions or other obligations with respect to the same sector(s), it may seek to suspend concessions or other obligations in other sectors under the same agreement;

(c) if that party considers that it is not practicable or effective to suspend concessions or other obligations with respect to other sectors under the same agreement, and that the circumstances are serious enough, it may seek to suspend concessions or other obligations under another covered agreement;

(d) in applying the above principles, that party shall take into account:

(i) the trade in the sector or under the agreement under which the panel or Appellate Body has found a violation or other nullification or impairment, and the importance of such trade to that party;

(ii) the broader economic elements related to the nullification or impairment and the broader economic consequences of the suspension of concessions or other obligations;

(e) if that party decides to request authorization to suspend concessions or other obligations pursuant to subparagraphs (b) or (c), it shall state the reasons therefor in its request. At the same time as the request is forwarded to the DSB, it also shall be forwarded to the relevant Councils and also, in the case of a request pursuant to subparagraph (b), the relevant sectoral bodies;

(f) for purposes of this paragraph, "sector" means:

(i) with respect to goods, all goods;

(ii) with respect to services, a principal sector as identified in the current "Services Sectoral Classification List" which identifies such sectors,[28]

(iii) with respect to trade-related intellectual property rights, each of the categories of intellectual property rights covered in Section 1, or Section 2, or Section 3, or Section 4, or Section 5, or Section 6, or Section 7 of Part II, or the obligations under Part III, or Part IV of the Agreement on TRIPS;

(g) for purposes of this paragraph, "agreement" means:

(i) with respect to goods, the agreements listed in Annex 1A of the WTO Agreement, taken as a whole as well as the Plurilateral Trade Agreements in so far as the relevant parties to the dispute are parties to these agreements;

(ii) with respect to services, the GATS;

(iii) with respect to intellectual property rights, the Agreement on TRIPS.

---

28 The list in document MTN.GNS/W/120 identifies eleven sectors.

4. The level of the suspension of concessions or other obligations authorized by the DSB shall be equivalent to the level of the nullification or impairment.

5. The DSB shall not authorize suspension of concessions or other obligations if a covered agreement prohibits such suspension.

6. When the situation described in paragraph 2 occurs, the DSB, upon request, shall grant authorization to suspend concessions or other obligations within 30 days of the expiry of the reasonable period of time unless the DSB decides by consensus to reject the request. However, if the Member concerned objects to the level of suspension proposed, or claims that the principles and procedures set forth in paragraph 3 have not been followed where a complaining party has requested authorization to suspend concessions or other obligations pursuant to paragraph 3(b) or (c), the matter shall be referred to arbitration. Such arbitration shall be carried out by the original panel, if members are available, or by an arbitrator[29] appointed by the Director-General and shall be completed within 60 days after the date of expiry of the reasonable period of time. Concessions or other obligations shall not be suspended during the course of the arbitration.

7. The arbitrator[30] acting pursuant to paragraph 6 shall not examine the nature of the concessions or other obligations to be suspended but shall determine whether the level of such suspension is equivalent to the level of nullification or impairment. The arbitrator may also determine if the proposed suspension of concessions or other obligations is allowed under the covered agreement. However, if the matter referred to arbitration includes a claim that the principles and procedures set forth in paragraph 3 have not been followed, the arbitrator shall examine that claim. In the event the arbitrator determines that those principles and procedures have not been followed, the complaining party shall apply them consistent with paragraph 3. The parties shall accept the arbitrator's decision as final and the parties concerned shall not seek a second arbitration. The DSB shall be informed promptly of the decision of the arbitrator and shall upon request, grant authorization to suspend concessions or other obligations where the request is consistent with the decision of the arbitrator, unless the DSB decides by consensus to reject the request.

---

[29] The expression "arbitrator" shall be interpreted as referring either to an individual or a group.

[30] The expression "arbitrator" shall be interpreted as referring either to an individual or a group or to the members of the original panel when serving in the capacity of arbitrator.

8. The suspension of concessions or other obligations shall be temporary and shall only be applied until such time as the measure found to be inconsistent with a covered agreement has been removed, or the Member that must implement recommendations or rulings provides a solution to the nullification or impairment of benefits, or a mutually satisfactory solution is reached. In accordance with paragraph 6 of Article 21, the DSB shall continue to keep under surveillance the implementation of adopted recommendations or rulings, including those cases where compensation has been provided or concessions or other obligations have been suspended but the recommendations to bring a measure into conformity with the covered agreements have not been implemented.

9. The dispute settlement provisions of the covered agreements may be invoked in respect of measures affecting their observance taken by regional or local governments or authorities within the territory of a Member. When the DSB has ruled that a provision of a covered agreement has not been observed, the responsible Member shall take such reasonable measures as may be available to it to ensure its observance. The provisions of the covered agreements and this Understanding relating to compensation and suspension of concessions or other obligations apply in cases where it has not been possible to secure such observance.[31]

Article 23. Strengthening of the Multilateral System

1. When Members seek the redress of a violation of obligations or other nullification or impairment of benefits under the covered agreements or an impediment to the attainment of any objective of the covered agreements, they shall have recourse to, and abide by, the rules and procedures of this Understanding.

2. In such cases, Members shall:

(a) not make a determination to the effect that a violation has occurred, that benefits have been nullified or impaired or that the attainment of any objective of the covered agreements has been impeded, except through recourse to dispute settlement in accordance with the rules and procedures of this Understanding, and shall make any such determination consistent with the findings contained in the panel or Appellate Body report adopted by the DSB or an arbitration award rendered under this Understanding;

---

[31] Where the provisions of any covered agreement concerning measures taken by regional or local governments or authorities within the territory of a Member contain provisions different from the provisions of this paragraph, the provisions of such covered agreement shall prevail.

(b) follow the procedures set forth in Article 21 to determine the reasonable period of time for the Member concerned to implement the recommendations and rulings; and

(c) follow the procedures set forth in Article 22 to determine the level of suspension of concessions or other obligations and obtain DSB authorization in accordance with those procedures before suspending concessions or other obligations under the covered agreements in response to the failure of the Member concerned to implement the recommendations and rulings within that reasonable period of time.

Article 24. Special Procedures Involving Least-Developed Country Members

1. At all stages of the determination of the causes of a dispute and of dispute settlement procedures involving a least-developed country Member, particular consideration shall be given to the special situation of least-developed country Members. In this regard, Members shall exercise due restraint in raising matters under these procedures involving a least-developed country Member. If nullification or impairment is found to result from a measure taken by a least-developed country Member, complaining parties shall exercise due restraint in asking for compensation or seeking authorization to suspend the application of concessions or other obligations pursuant to these procedures.

2. In dispute settlement cases involving a least-developed country Member, where a satisfactory solution has not been found in the course of consultations the Director-General or the Chairman of the DSB shall, upon request by a least-developed country Member offer their good offices, conciliation and mediation with a view to assisting the parties to settle the dispute, before a request for a panel is made. The Director-General or the Chairman of the DSB, in providing the above assistance, may consult any source which either deems appropriate.

Article 25. Arbitration

1. Expeditious arbitration within the WTO as an alternative means of dispute settlement can facilitate the solution of certain disputes that concern issues that are clearly defined by both parties.

2. Except as otherwise provided in this Understanding, resort to arbitration shall be subject to mutual agreement of the parties which shall agree on the procedures to be followed. Agreements to resort to arbitration shall be notified to all Members sufficiently in advance of the actual commencement of the arbitration process.

3. Other Members may become party to an arbitration proceeding only upon the agreement of the parties which have agreed to have recourse to arbitration. The parties to the proceeding shall agree to abide by the arbitration award. Arbitration awards shall be notified to the DSB and the Council or Committee of any relevant agreement where any Member may raise any point relating thereto.

4. Articles 21 and 22 of this Understanding shall apply *mutatis mutandis* to arbitration awards.

Article 26.

1. *Non-Violation Complaints of the Type Described in Paragraph 1(b) of Article XXIII of GATT 1994*

Where the provisions of paragraph 1(b) of Article XXIII of GATT 1994 are applicable to a covered agreement, a panel or the Appellate Body may only make rulings and recommendations where a party to the dispute considers that any benefit accruing to it directly or indirectly under the relevant covered agreement is being nullified or impaired or the attainment of any objective of that Agreement is being impeded as a result of the application by a Member of any measure, whether or not it conflicts with the provisions of that Agreement. Where and to the extent that such party considers and a panel or the Appellate Body determines that a case concerns a measure that does not conflict with the provisions of a covered agreement to which the provisions of paragraph 1(b) of Article XXIII of GATT 1994 are applicable, the procedures in this Understanding shall apply, subject to the following:

(a) the complaining party shall present a detailed justification in support of any complaint relating to a measure which does not conflict with the relevant covered agreement;

(b) where a measure has been found to nullify or impair benefits under, or impede the attainment of objectives, of the relevant covered agreement without violation thereof, there is no obligation to withdraw the measure. However, in such cases, the panel or the Appellate Body shall recommend that the Member concerned make a mutually satisfactory adjustment;

(c) notwithstanding the provisions of Article 21, the arbitration provided for in paragraph 3 of Article 21, upon request of either party, may include a determination of the level of benefits which have been nullified or impaired, and may also suggest ways and means of reaching a mutually satisfactory adjustment; such suggestions shall not be binding upon the parties to the dispute;

(d) notwithstanding the provisions of paragraph 1 of Article 22, compensation may be part of a mutually satisfactory adjustment as final settlement of the dispute.

2. *Complaints of the Type Described in Paragraph 1(c) of Article XXIII of GATT 1994*

Where the provisions of paragraph 1(c) of Article XXIII of GATT 1994 are applicable to a covered agreement, a panel may only make rulings and recommendations where a party considers that any benefit accruing to it directly or indirectly under the relevant covered agreement is being nullified or impaired or the attainment of any objective of that Agreement is being impeded as a result of the existence of any situation other than those to which the provisions of paragraphs 1(a) and 1(b) of Article XXIII of GATT 1994 are applicable. Where and to the extent that such party considers and a panel determines that the matter is covered by this paragraph, the procedures of this Understanding shall apply only up to and including the point in the proceedings where the panel report has been circulated to the Members. The dispute settlement rules and procedures contained in the Decision of 12 April 1989 (BISD 36S/61–67) shall apply to consideration for adoption, and surveillance and implementation of recommendations and rulings. The following shall also apply:

(a) the complaining party shall present a detailed justification in support of any argument made with respect to issues covered under this paragraph;

(b) in cases involving matters covered by this paragraph, if a panel finds that cases also involve dispute settlement matters other than those covered by this paragraph, the panel shall circulate a report to the DSB addressing any such matters and a separate report on matters falling under this paragraph.

Article 27. Responsibilities of the Secretariat

1. The Secretariat shall have the responsibility of assisting panels, especially on the legal, historical and procedural aspects of the matters dealt with, and of providing secretarial and technical support.

2. While the Secretariat assists Members in respect of dispute settlement at their request, there may also be a need to provide additional legal advice and assistance in respect of dispute settlement to developing country Members. To this end, the Secretariat shall make available a qualified legal expert from the WTO technical cooperation services to any developing country Member which so requests. This expert shall assist the developing

country Member in a manner ensuring the continued impartiality of the Secretariat.

3. The Secretariat shall conduct special training courses for interested Members concerning these dispute settlement procedures and practices so as to enable Members' experts to be better informed in this regard.

APPENDIX 1

AGREEMENTS COVERED BY THE UNDERSTANDING

(A) Agreement Establishing the World Trade Organization

(B) Multilateral Trade Agreements

Annex 1A:	Multilateral Agreements on Trade in Goods
Annex 1B:	General Agreement on Trade in Services
Annex 1C:	Agreement on Trade-Related Aspects of Intellectual Property Rights
Annex 2:	Understanding on Rules and Procedures Governing the Settlement of Disputes

(C) Plurilateral Trade Agreements

Annex 4:	Agreement on Trade in Civil Aircraft
	Agreement on Government Procurement
	International Dairy Agreement
	International Bovine Meat Agreement

The applicability of this Understanding to the Plurilateral Trade Agreements shall be subject to the adoption of a decision by the parties to each agreement setting out the terms for the application of the Understanding to the individual agreement, including any special or additional rules or procedures for inclusion in Appendix 2, as notified to the DSB.

APPENDIX 2

SPECIAL OR ADDITIONAL RULES AND PROCEDURES CONTAINED IN THE COVERED AGREEMENTS

Agreement	*Rules and Procedures*
Agreement on the Application of Sanitary and Phytosanitary Measures	11.2

Agreement on Textiles and Clothing	2.14, 2.21, 4.4, 5.2, 5.4, 5.6, 6.9, 6.10, 6.11, 8.1 through 8.12
Agreement on Technical Barriers to Trade	14.2 through 14.4, Annex 2
Agreement on Implementation of Article VI of GATT 1994	17.4 through 17.7
Agreement on Implementation of Article VII of GATT 1994	19.3 through 19.5, Annex II.2(f), 3, 9, 21
Agreement on Subsidies and Countervailing Measures	4.2 through 4.12, 6.6, 7.2 through 7.10, 8.5, footnote 35, 24.4, 27.7, Annex V
General Agreement on Trade in Services	XXII:3, XXIII:3
Annex on Financial Services	4
Annex on Air Transport Services	4
Decision on Certain Dispute Settlement Procedures for the GATS	1 through 5

The list of rules and procedures in this Appendix includes provisions where only a part of the provision may be relevant in this context.

Any special or additional rules or procedures in the Plurilateral Trade Agreements as determined by the competent bodies of each agreement and as notified to the DSB.

Table of Cases

Index

References are to Sections